$\mathscr{I}$ntegrating Language Arts Through Literature and Thematic Units

Betty D. Roe

Professor Emerita

Tennessee Technological University, Cookeville

Elinor P. Ross

Professor Emerita

Tennessee Technological University, Cookeville

PEARSON

OCM 57168588

Boston • New York • San Francisco
Mexico City • Montreal • Toronto • London • Madrid • Munich • Paris
Hong Kong • Singapore • Tokyo • Cape Town • Sydney

Senior Series Editor: Aurora Martínez-Ramos
Editorial Assistant: Kevin Shannon
Developmental Editor: Alicia Reilly
Senior Marketing Manager: Krista Groshong
Editorial-Production Administrator: Elaine Ober
Editorial-Production Services: Helane M. Prottas
Photo Research: Helane M. Prottas/Posh Pictures

Interior Designer: Schneck-DePippo Graphics
Cover Coordinator: Linda Knowles
Cover Designer: Studio Nine
Composition and Prepress Buyer: Linda Cox
Manufacturing Buyer: Andrew Turso
Electronic Composition: Dayle Silverman/Silver Graphics

For related titles and support materials, visit our online catalog at www.ablongman.com.

Library of Congress Cataloging-in-Publication Data

Roe, Betty D.
    Integrating language arts through literature and thematic units/Betty D. Roe, Elinor P. Ross.
       p. cm.
    Includes bibliographical references and index.
    ISBN 0-205-39510-4.
     1. Language arts.   I. Ross, Elinor P. (Elinor Parry).   II. Title.
    LB1576. R64 2005
    72.6—dc23

                                      2004062707

Printed in the United States of America
10 9 8 7 6 5 4 3 2 1   VHP   09 08 07 06 05

Photo credits begin on page 646 which constitutes a continuation of the copyright page.

Brief Contents

Minilessons

Applications for . . .

Classroom Assessments

Classroom Vignettes

Figures

Contents

CHAPTER *8*

Developing Writing Proficiency   288

CHAPTER *9*

Types of Writing   338

CHAPTER *10*

The Tools of Language   372

CHAPTER *11*

Visual and Media Literacy   416

CHAPTER *12*

Literacy in the Content Areas   450

CHAPTER *13*

Assessment and Intervention   498

Preface

*L*ANGUAGE IS the basis for communication, and communication is essential for acquiring knowledge, expanding horizons, and relating to others. Learning to communicate through language is therefore at the heart of what we know and who we are. We learn language naturally early on by listening to and imitating the language of others, and then by using language as best we can to express our needs. Through modeling and feedback, family members and teachers help children understand how to interpret and construct language for their own purposes.

In this text, we are emphasizing two major aspects of language arts instruction. The first is integrating children's and young adult literature into the teaching of language arts at every level and in all subjects. Literature serves as a model for language use, promotes interest in reading, addresses diversity through a multitude of multicultural selections, expands vocabulary, and increases knowledge and awareness of other people and the world around us. The second aspect is integration through thematic units. We know that children learn best when concepts are connected in meaningful ways, rather than when facts are taught in isolation. Thematic units provide authentic ways to connect content areas and language arts through a variety of activities that are designed to achieve goals and objectives.

The National Council of Teachers of English (NCTE) and the International Reading Association (IRA) have established standards for instruction in the language arts, and many states have identified their own standards derived from those on the national level. These standards are intended to guide teachers in planning and implementing instruction, and relevant standards appear near the beginning of each chapter to show how they are being addressed. NCTE has also identified six language arts: listening, speaking, reading, writing, viewing, and visually representing. Although each of these is addressed separately in this text, they are highly interrelated and can often be taught in an integrated manner.

Over the years many changes have occurred in language arts instruction: increased use of technology, recognition of diversity, belief in the constructive nature of learning language, and emphasis on the importance of viewing and visually representing. In this text, we present a balanced approach by recognizing valid, time-tested ideas and practices and by also including current, research-based techniques that we have observed being used in today's classrooms. We have incorporated many holistic practices that have retained their value over the years, including integration across the curriculum, use of children's literature, a process writing approach, alternative assessments, thematic units, authentic activities, and child-centered approaches. We have also recognized recent research in the areas of phonemic awareness, phonics, fluency, vocabulary, and text comprehension, as well as the current movement to emphasize media and visual literacy instruction.

Because we believe that all students learn differently, we have included a variety of approaches and strategies so that teachers will be able to find a technique that will match each student's strength. We also believe that no scripted text or single procedure is a magic answer to providing effective instruction; instead, we value the teacher's professional judgment as a decision maker in knowing what methods are most appropriate. Therefore, we have advocated a balanced, diversified approach that will enable teachers to make educated choices to meet the needs of their students.

Purpose and Coverage

THIS TEXTBOOK is an introductory language arts text directed toward preservice and inservice teachers. Our purpose is to provide a solid research base for presenting practical, hands-on classroom procedures and strategies. We have made the text easy to read and provided opportunities for students to reflect, apply teaching tips, and learn from classroom vignettes and minilessons. Each chapter contains boxed material on applications for English Language Learners and students with special needs to help teachers modify or adjust instruction for these special students. Much of the content that appears in this text is found on the Praxis test that most students must pass.

Because of increasing interest in providing guidance for literacy learning for young children, the text includes a chapter on three-, four-, and five-year-olds. This chapter includes family literacy and preschool programs, so it can be used with students who are majoring in early childhood education. The text extends through eighth grade, covering a great deal of material related to teaching language in the content areas. A special chapter on visual literacy addresses the two most recent language arts skills identified by NCTE, and it deals extensively with the use of technology. Although a brief section on assessment is included in most chapters, an entire chapter deals with various standardized and alternative assessments, as well as interventions for students who indicate a need for special assistance. The chapter on literature provides methods for using it with young people, which can be particularly helpful if students have had no course in children's literature or if it has been taught as a literature course by the English Department. Appendix B lists award winners for children's and young adult literature. The Grammar Handbook, Appendix A, is a reference for teachers to use when they are uncertain about grammar usage themselves before teaching it to their students. Students no longer need to purchase a separate grammar handbook to accompany their language arts book. It is conveniently designed with a blue tab for easy reference. This text may be easily adapted for field-based courses, with its many practical examples and minilessons and its suggested activities.

Special Features

Graphic Organizers: Each chapter opens with a graphic organizer that shows the topics within that chapter and their relationships to each other. Graphic organizers are also found within chapters, particularly Chapter 12 on content area reading.

Learner Objectives: At the beginning of each chapter is a list of objectives that helps students identify their purposes for reading the chapter. The last objective contains important vocabulary words that are later boldfaced within the text, along with their definitions and/or explanations.

Standards: NCTE/IRA standards relevant to the chapter are listed at the beginning of each chapter to enable students to see how the chapter content relates to one or more of the national standards.

Chapter Introductions: The introduction to each chapter gives an overview or a framework for the contents. It helps the reader create an expectation for what follows.

Classroom Vignette 5.5

Miss Geyer is giving an assignment for reinforcing a lesson on compound words.

MISS GEYER: I want everyone to listen carefully to these directions. Let me see your eyes when you are ready to listen.

After all but one student is quietly looking at her, Miss Geyer begins.

MISS GEYER: Jimmy, please give me your attention.

Jimmy hears his name and looks up.

MISS GEYER: Now that everyone is ready, I'll tell you what I want you to do in the next 30 minutes. This is an assignment to help you work on understanding compound words.

Get out the book that we have just been reading, *Don't You Know There's a War On?* by Avi. Look through the book and find at least six examples of compound words. Write the sentence in which you found each word and underline the compound word. Think about the meaning of the word in the sentence and read the sentences

around it for more information, if you need it. Write the page number on which you found the word beside each sentence. After 30 minutes are up, we will discuss the words you found and their meanings. Does anyone have a question about the assignment? (pause)

MISS GEYER: When you finish your work, you may sit with your language partner and go over your answers together quietly until the 30 minutes time is up. Now are there any questions? (pause)

MISS GEYER: If not, then you may begin.

What's happening here?

Miss Geyer is making sure that she has everyone's attention before she begins to give directions. After she gives directions, she asks if there are any questions so that she can clarify the instructions before the students start to work. She has increased the likelihood that the students will listen carefully to the assignment and understand it through the procedure she uses.

Classroom Vignettes: A vignette appears at the beginning of each chapter, and other vignettes appear throughout the chapter. By examining vignettes, students see how the chapter content becomes classroom reality. "What's happening here?" appears at the end of each vignette to point out how children are benefiting from their interactions.

Classroom Vignette 7.1

Diana enters first grade eager to read and learns to recognize words quickly. She listens to her teacher read expressively, and soon she is reading stories fluently to her classmates. Diana becomes deeply involved with the characters and story situations, so she reads with feeling. One day, near the end of the year, her first-grade teacher lets her select a favorite story, practice reading it to the class, and return to her former kindergarten class where she reads aloud to the children there.

What's happening here?

Diana is modeling fluent reading for her classmates. By doing this, she is showing them how they, too, can be fluent readers. She is gaining confidence in her ability to read aloud. The kindergartners not only enjoy the story, but also are able to see what they may be able to do when they reach first grade. Her example provides motivation for them to learn to read.

Minilesson 9.2

Cooperative Writing in Science

Jennifer Magnusson reads a picture book entitled *Trapdoor Spiders* to her class, section by section. After she reads a section of the book—for example, one called "Shapes"—she asks the students to summarize on a transparency the information that they acquired from the reading, so that everyone can see what is written and can contribute. One student is the scribe for the class, taking dictation, as the others provide information. After the material is summarized on the transparencies, another student becomes the scribe, and the students cooperatively edit their work. Finally, they all write the edited material in their notebooks for future reference. Figure 9.11 shows their first draft, complete with editing marks (which are in a contrasting marker on the transparencies), and a typed copy of the entire edited piece.

What are the students learning?

The students are learning to listen to informational material for important details, cooperatively summarize material learned from informational books, cooperatively edit material, and use class-produced material as supplementary study resources.

Minilessons: Minilessons show step-by-step lesson procedures, including what teachers say and how they interact with students when presenting material. The "What are the students learning?" feature at the end of each lesson helps readers become aware of the many ways that children are learning from the lesson.

Teaching Tips: Interspersed throughout the chapters, teaching tips offer practical, teacher-tested suggestions for implementing ideas in the classroom. They often provide shortcuts, time-saving methods, or cost-cutting procedures for the busy teacher.

Teaching Tip

Help left-handed children write comfortably by following these suggestions. (1) Have students slant their papers to the right. (2) Teach them to use pushing strokes instead of pulling strokes. (3) Seat left-handers in slightly lower desks so that they can see what they have written. (4) Have students place the paper to the left side of the desk. (5) Have them grip the writing instrument about one and a half inches from the point (farther away than for right-handers).

Reflections

Social studies involves many language processes and artistic expressions. From the overview of thematic units given here, what ways did students use language arts to develop their understanding of social studies, including the arts? Can you think of other possibilities for integrating language arts?

Reflections: Reflections ask readers to stop and think about the meaning of what they have read in terms of their own experiences and insights. Reflections can stimulate class discussion if individuals or small groups reflect on the subject and share their thoughts.

Applications for English Language Learners

Use of wordless picture books is especially helpful in working with ELLs. They can analyze the pictures either in English or in their first language as they work on visual literacy skills. In this way, as long as there is a person present to translate their first language contributions, they can offer as much to the learning process as a native English speaker does.

Applications for English Language Learners, Students with Special Needs, and Struggling Learners: In recognition of the special needs of some students, these boxed applications show how skills or strategies can be modified to help students learn in ways that they can best understand.

Applications for Students with Special Needs

Many students with learning disabilities can find misspelled words from their journal entries or other writing and are able to use the Have-a-Go sheet effectively. Routman (1991) reports that a child with special needs was able to find and circle words that looked wrong and then work them out with the help of his tutor, a spelling dictionary, and other resources.

Applications for Struggling Learners

Struggling learners benefit from writing in a pattern that has been heard in a simple patterned book, such as Bill Martin, Jr.'s *Brown Bear, Brown Bear, What Do You See?* The simplicity of the pattern takes some of the pressure for organization off of the children, and they can focus on writing a new story based on the pattern.

Student Work Samples: Appearing throughout the chapters are samples of students' work. They show the capabilities of students at different levels who have chosen or been assigned different tasks.

Classroom Assessments: Near the end of the each chapter is a brief section on assessment that recommends particular types of assessment appropriate for the knowledge and skills addressed within the chapter. Chapter 13 treats assessment more thoroughly, elaborating on the techniques referred to in each chapter.

Writing and Technology: Both of these topics receive concentrated attention in several individual chapters. However, writing and technology pertain to all areas of literacy and, indeed, to each other. Thus, you'll find references to writing and technology topics throughout every chapter in this text. Those of special interest or importance are highlighted with margin icons.

Summaries: Each chapter contains a summary of the content presented within the chapter. It serves as a quick review of the material.

Discussion Questions: Near the end of each chapter is a list of questions for encouraging students to think beyond the text and discuss issues related to the chapter content.

Suggested Activities: The suggested activities provide opportunities for students to become actively engaged in learning.

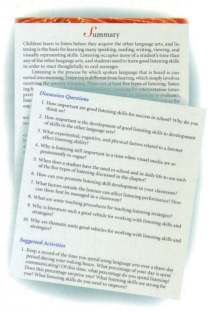

References: A list of books used as references for this text is given in alphabetical order by author.

Books for Children and Adolescents Cited in This Chapter: For convenience in locating sources of books discussed within each chapter, bibliographic information is provided at the end of the chapter.

Appendix A: Grammar Handbook: This handbook covers commonly accepted rules for using grammar, punctuation, and capitalization, as well as correct and incorrect examples of potential problem areas. It is a reference for teachers who may need to know these rules before teaching them to students, and it is marked with a blue tab for easy access.

Appendix B: This appendix contains lists of award-winning books. They include Newbery, Caldecott, and Coretta Scott King book awards.

Chapter Organization

THE FIRST three chapters are the foundation for the remainder of the text. Chapter 1 lays the groundwork for studying language arts instruction, emphasizing its importance. It covers the six major language arts individually and in relation to each other and introduces the concept of literature and thematic units as methods of integrating language arts instruction in the curriculum. Chapter 2 contains information about involving students in literature from preschool through grade 8, and Chapter 3 deals with the importance of teaching vocabulary effectively in order for students to have a solid base for learning language.

Chapter 4 covers early childhood education, an area that is becoming increasingly significant as preschool educators realize the value of developing literacy. Chapters 5 and 6 deal with ways of promoting literacy, with **Chapter 5** focusing on developing listening skills and **Chapter 6** covering speaking skills.

Chapters 7, through 9 deal with literacy. In **Chapter 7** reading is discussed with an emphasis on balance among many approaches. Since writing is such a broad subject, it is addressed in every chapter in this text, as well as in its own two separate chapters. **Chapter 8** deals with procedures for teaching writing: writing instruction, the writing process, instructional applications for writing, and organizing for writing instruction. **Chapter 9** covers a variety of authentic purposes for writing, including (but not limited to) stories, poetry, journals, letters, reports, and writing in the content areas.

The tools of language—spelling, grammar, punctuation, and capitalization—are covered in **Chapter 10**, and **Chapter 11** contains information on visual literacy, particularly viewing and visually representing. **Chapter 12** deals extensively with language arts as they appear within content areas, and **Chapter 13** is an overview of various types of standardized and informal assessments. The text concludes with **Chapter 14**, which presents a variety of thematic units on different topics for different grade levels which are easily identified by a green tab. Two appendixes, already identified, complete the text.

Acknowledgments

WE FIRST want to acknowledge the help we have received from the staff at Allyn and Bacon, particularly Alicia Reilly who worked with us consistently by offering suggestions and providing information. Aurora Martínez was the guiding force behind our work, and we also appreciate support from Erin Beatty and Kevin Shannon. Elaine Ober, Helane Prottas, and Dayle Silverman have been extremely helpful during the production process.

We especially appreciate the teachers who allowed us to visit their classrooms and provided samples of children's work, along with parental permissions. This type of classroom observation and participation is invaluable for creating a book that will be practical and useful for other classroom teachers. We also appreciate the many university students whose lessons we observed during practicum experiences and whose comments guided our instruction in the college classroom.

Thanks also go to those who have allowed us to reprint or cite material from their original works. We also thank our reviewers who offered constructive criticism during revisions.

June Hyndman
Eastern Kentucky University

Kathy Itterly
Westfield State University

Lonnie R. McDonald
Henderson State University

Lillian McEnery
University of Houston–Clear Lake

Bonita L. McKenzie
Ball State University

Sara Rung-Pulte
Northern Kentucky University

Maureen Siera
St. Martin's College

Beth Tope
Louisiana State University

$\mathcal{S}$upplements

Supplements and Learning Aids

To get the most use of *Integrating Language Arts Through Literature and Thematic Units*, a number of useful supplements are available for students and instructors. Speak with your representative about obtaining these supplements for your class.

For the Instructor

- **Instructor's Manual with Test Items** provides a variety of instructional tools, including chapter summaries, student objectives, activities and discussion questions, vocabulary, test questions, and reflections inspired by the text.

- **VideoWorkshop** is a new way to bring video into your course for maximized learning. This total teaching and learning system includes quality video footage on an easy-to-use CD-ROM plus a Student Learning Guide and an Instructor's Teaching Guide. The result? A program that brings textbook concepts to life with ease and that helps your students understand, analyze, and apply the objectives of the course. VideoWorkshop is available for your students as a value-pack option with this textbook. (Special package ISBN required from your representative.)

- **My LabSchool**   Discover where the classroom comes to life! From videoclips of teachers and students interacting to sample lessons, portfolio templates, and standards integration, Allyn & Bacon brings your students the tools they'll need to succeed in the classroom—with content easily integrated into your existing courses. Delivered within CourseCompass, Allyn & Bacon's course management system, this program gives your students powerful insights into how real classrooms work and a rich array of tools that will support them on their journey from their first class to their first classroom. There is an entire module of videoclips that pertain to Language Arts.

- **Allyn & Bacon Digital Media Archive for Literacy**   This CD-ROM offers still images, video clips, audio clips, weblinks, and assorted lecture resources that can be incorporated into multimedia presentations in the classroom.

- **PowerPoint™ Presentation**   This presentation is ideal for lecture presentations or student handouts. You'll find this available for download from the Instructor Resource Center of the Allyn & Bacon catalog. Go to www.ablongman.com/catalog. Find the catalog page for this book and click on "Instructor" in the Resources section on the left. Follow the prompts and you'll be able to download this and other available supplements.

- **Professionals in Action: Literacy Video**   This 90-minute video consists of 10- to 20-minute segments on phonemic awareness, teaching phonics, helping students become strategic readers, organizing for teaching with literature, and discussions of literacy and brain research with experts. The first four segments provide narrative along with actual classroom teaching footage. The final segments present, in a question-and-answer format, discussions by leading experts in the field of literacy.

- **Allyn & Bacon Literacy Video Library**   Featuring renowned reading scholars Richard Allington, Dorothy Strickland, and Evelyn English, this three-video library addresses core topics covered in the literacy classroom: reading strategies, developing literacy in multiple intelligences classrooms, developing phonemic awareness, and much more.

For Students

- A **Companion Website** (www.ablongman.com/roe1e) provides a link to additional study items, special *New York Times* articles, annotated weblinks, and a complete guide to conducting research on the Internet

- **My LabSchool**   Discover where the classroom comes to life. Allyn & Bacon's My LabSchool program provides you with everything you will need to succeed in the classroom, including videoclips of teachers and students interacting, sample lessons, portfolio templates, and standards integration. You'll get powerful insights into how real classrooms work and a rich array of tools to support you on your journey from your first class to your first classroom.

Chapter

1

INTEGRATING THE LANGUAGE ARTS: AN INTRODUCTION

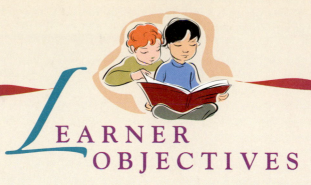

LEARNER OBJECTIVES

At the conclusion of this chapter

YOU SHOULD BE ABLE TO

1. Name and describe the six language arts and their functions.

2. Discuss the interrelationships among the language arts.

3. Explain reasons for integrating language instruction across the curriculum.

4. Discuss reasons that literature is a good vehicle for integration.

5. Describe the advantages of thematic teaching.

6. Discuss standards for the English language arts.

7. Identify the following terms that are defined or explained in this chapter:

communication 13
critical literacy 17
cross-curricular thematic
  units 23

English language learners
  (ELLs) 7

metalinguistic
  awareness 5

NCTE/IRA Standards addressed in this chapter

In this chapter, all twelve of the Standards for the English Language Arts developed by the International Reading Association and the National Council of Teachers of English are introduced in the final section. In subsequent chapters, relevant standards are listed at the beginning of each chapter.

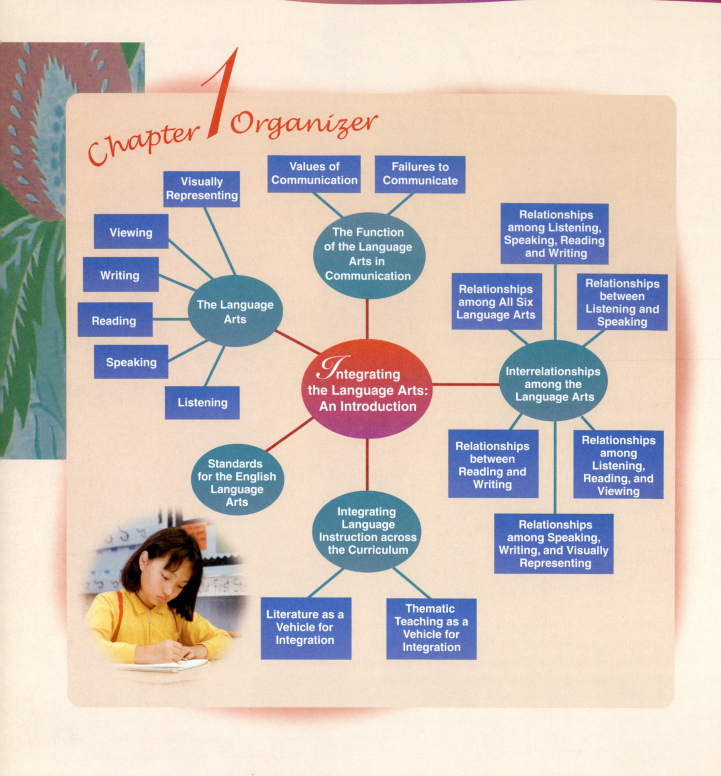

Chapter 1 Organizer

Integrating the Language Arts: An Introduction

The Language Arts
- Visually Representing
- Viewing
- Writing
- Reading
- Speaking
- Listening

The Function of the Language Arts in Communication
- Values of Communication
- Failures to Communicate

Interrelationships among the Language Arts
- Relationships among Listening, Speaking, Reading and Writing
- Relationships among All Six Language Arts
- Relationships between Listening and Speaking
- Relationships between Reading and Writing
- Relationships among Listening, Reading, and Viewing
- Relationships among Speaking, Writing, and Visually Representing

Standards for the English Language Arts

Integrating Language Instruction across the Curriculum
- Literature as a Vehicle for Integration
- Thematic Teaching as a Vehicle for Integration

A GROUP OF sixth graders is sitting in the corner of the room at a table near a computer station, working on a transportation unit. Paul, one of the brightest students in the class, is intently reading an article in an encyclopedia. Kelly, another extremely bright student, is sitting at the computer, with her back to the rest of the group, reading from an Internet site that she has located. Marcia, an average student, is looking through some pamphlets. Andrea and Tony, students who do not perform on a high level scholastically but are talented artistically, are examining pictures in a large illustrated book on transportation.

The teacher has chosen Paul as a group leader and asked him to be sure that the work progresses and that everyone has a useful task. She has suggested some possible tasks most appropriate for each group member. She has asked him to encourage all of the group members as they work.

Suddenly Marcia exclaims, "Here's a good source! This tells all about airplane travel today. We can use it with the information that we have already found in the encyclopedia on airplanes, and we'll probably have enough for that part of our report."

Paul looks up from the encyclopedia article and comments, "That's good. Now see if you can find anything in the pamphlets on the Amtrak system. It seems to be an important thing to put in this part on train transportation."

Andrea picks up the book that she and Tony have been examining. "Here's a picture of an Amtrak train. Do you want Tony and me to draw it for the report?"

Paul replies, "Yes, that would be a good illustration. Have you finished the airplane that you were working on yesterday?"

Tony responds, "I finished it last night. Do you want to see it? It turned out great!"

Paul nods, causing Tony to hurry over to his desk to locate the drawing. In the meantime, Andrea has already started to sketch the Amtrak train. When Tony returns, all eyes turn to his drawing.

"It's a beauty," says Marcia.

"Andrea and I both worked on it," says Tony, "but I put on the finishing touches."

"This picture will really help our report," Paul responds. "Both of you did a good job. We can put it first in the section on air transportation, and the written report Kelly and I are working on can follow it. All we lack is some information that I found in this encyclopedia and the information that Kelly has found on the computer. We'll have to double-check her information before we can use it, because Ms. Markam says that some stuff on the Internet isn't reliable. We can check it out in some of these reference books, or maybe find it on another site that we are more sure is okay."

"I hope you write that report neatly," teases Marcia. "I'm going to be the one that has to read it so that I can tell the class about it."

"Don't worry," replies Paul. "Kelly's handwriting is the best in the class, but I wish we had more computer time, so that she could word process it."

What's happening here?

This group of children is taking part in a research group investigating transportation because the teacher understands the possibilities of the children all bringing their language skills into play to produce a good report. The better readers are given the task of extracting information from more difficult reference sources. The most proficient computer user is assigned to search the Internet for information. An average reader works with less demanding material that still needs some degree of reading expertise. Two poor readers work with books that consist mainly of illustrations pertaining to the topic, although they have to do minimal reading to locate relevant pictures.

Paul is effective in performing his leadership role. He reinforces the positive activities, suggests next steps, and sets a good example by working himself.

In the course of this group activity, group members listen to their leader and to each other. They read related material to include in the report and, in some cases, read or plan to read the material written by their classmates. They double-check information gathered from an Internet site. They speak to each other to convey instructions, ask questions, express appreciation, and make explanations. Some of them are writing the report, and one or more of them are going to give the report orally. The language arts are integrated naturally in this activity.

The language arts are a vital part of every school's curriculum because they are the means through which people communicate. Without oral and written language, people would be reduced to using gestures and pantomime to convey thoughts. Anyone who has ever played charades realizes how incomplete communication can be when it is limited in that way. Although each language art requires special skills and has its own advantages and disadvantages in the communication process, all of the language arts are interrelated. Because of these interrelationships, language arts strategies and skills are often best taught when integrated with one another rather than being treated as separate and independent entities. Language usage is also central to learning in the other content areas, such as science, social studies, mathematics, and the fine arts. Therefore, integrating instruction in language arts into instruction in these curricular areas is particularly effective.

Compare the effectiveness of using the language arts as indicated in the chapter-opening classroom vignette with that of addressing each area individually. How could the experience described in the vignette have been made even more useful?

Research suggests that language is learned more effectively through experiences with complete language units, such as oral or written stories or informational talks and articles, than through activities that do not involve connected discourse, such as worksheet pages that focus on single words or sentences. Authentic communication events (such as reading, telling, and writing stories and reading informational material and presenting it in oral and written forms) involve the use of complete language structures. Literature—both fiction and nonfiction—is a strong vehicle for engaging children in language activities, and thematic units help students to see the purpose for the strategies and skills they are learning.

A wide range of differences exists in the language attainment levels of children in any classroom. These differences result from both the variation in rates of language acquisition among children and language-related factors in the home environment. These factors include the availability of books in the home, a positive family atmosphere, and verbal interaction with adults. Conversations with adults enable children to try out new vocabulary and get feedback, as well as to use words to express thoughts and ideas. Adults also help children learn language by expanding children's telegraphic speech into complete sentences. For instance, a child may say "Train go fast," and the adult may respond by saying, "Yes, the train is going very fast." In homes in which children are to be seen and not heard, they seldom initiate conversations or use language to clarify and extend their experiences.

Reading aloud to children, even when they are very young, is an excellent way for parents to help children become better readers. The verbal interaction that accompanies the reading is also valuable for promoting interest and achievement in reading and advancing children's thinking skills. Reading aloud to children exposes them to a variety of terms and language patterns that may enhance their speaking and writing skills.

Preschoolers who have writing implements available and who are encouraged to scribble or draw stories write with greater ease and confidence than children who have not received these advantages at home.

As children begin to understand and use language, they develop **metalinguistic awareness**. This is the ability to think about language objectively and to analyze consciously its phonetic, syntactic, and semantic elements. In other words, children learn to separate knowledge about language from the meaning of language. They realize that *house* is a noun or the name of something, as well as a place to live. By studying language apart from its message, students learn how to manipulate and control it. Meta-

Students construct sentences with different meanings by varying the adjectives in the sentences.

linguistic awareness increases as children advance to higher linguistic and cognitive levels.

Bewell and Straw (1981) reported H. Francis's findings from a study of children's comprehension of instructional terms and their ability to identify units in spoken and written language (sounds and words). Francis found that learning to read enhanced the development of the children's metalinguistic awareness. Reading appeared to force them to recognize the subdivisions of language. Therefore, it appears that metalinguistic awareness enhances reading performance, and learning to read enhances metalinguistic awareness.

The work of Piaget and Vygotsky stresses the importance of a child's ability to understand the concept of *word* (Bewell & Straw, 1981). Although children may use individual words to form sentences, they are often unable to identify single words within the stream of speech. Most preschoolers regard the utterance "Pat the doggie" as a single unit rather than three words. To succeed in beginning reading, a child needs to develop an awareness of words as entities. Otherwise, sight word recognition and other early reading tasks have little meaning. Early writing attempts are also affected by the inability to segment language into word units (Bewell & Straw, 1981).

Writing

You should evaluate your students' levels of metalinguistic awareness before providing instruction in language arts. Some children need teacher assistance in developing higher levels of awareness before they can perform certain language tasks. Gradually, as the children increase their awareness, you can give less assistance and allow children to use their own increasing skill in learning language. (More on metalinguistic awareness is located in Chapter 4.)

Language is learned best through active use in meaningful situations. A language classroom cannot

Reflections

What are some phrases or short sentences that preschoolers might think of as units? How might you help them realize that these thought units consist of individual words?

Teaching Tip

To help students develop a concept of word, write this sentence on the board and read it to the students as you point to each word: "The boy is going to town." Frame the word *boy* with your hands and tell the children, "This is the word *boy*. See how there is white space on each side of the word." Then frame the word *going* with your hands and say, "This is the word *going*. See the white space on each side of the word *going*." Finally, read the sentence again and ask if any of the students can come to the front and frame the word *The* or another word in the sentence.

be a silent one if oral language is to be learned. Students can work with partners or in small groups to "talk through" their learning tasks in all of their school subjects. They can tell stories to each other, do choral reading, participate in Readers Theatre, and, in general, become directly involved in using language. Their own writing efforts can be a basis for spelling instruction, and their oral and written language can be used to determine curricular offerings in grammar and usage. You can ask students to proofread their own or other students' writing in order to provide critical reading practice. Handwriting practice can be accomplished when final drafts of their writing are being prepared for publication.

Writing

You can use journals, book publishing, literature study, and thematic units to help students learn language strategies and skills. You can provide print-rich environments and give students opportunities for using print in many contexts. You can introduce students to audiovisual presentations and teach them the skills necessary to present ideas visually.

English language learners (ELLs) for whom the home language is not English face particular challenges. They may be learning vocabulary and syntax that their English-proficient classmates have already mastered. Unfortunately, ELLs who are struggling to learn to read English tend not to make enough strategic reading connections between their first and second languages (Rubinstein-Avila, 2003/2004). You can help them to make such connections. Some teachers believe that they are not capable of effectively teaching students who come from cultures other than their own. However, Rubinstein-Avila (2003/2004) agrees with Au and Raphael (2000) that instruction can be culturally responsive even when teachers do not belong to the same cultural or linguistic group as their students.

Even when ELLs have developed some proficiency in English, they are in an unusual situation. "Bilingual students should be recognized as having dual language abilities and viewed in that light rather than compared only to . . . monolingual students" in

Applications **for English Language Learners**

Set up informal role-playing sessions in which an ELL is paired with a student or paraprofessional who is fluent in both English and the ELL's first language (fluent bilingual assistant).

First, give the fluent bilingual assistant a brief oral or written English message to translate into the student's first language, as if the student understood no English. The student responds to the communication in his first language, and the assistant then translates the student's message for you, as the student listens.

Next, give the student either a simple oral message or a simple written message to translate to the assistant as if he does not speak English. If the message is not clearly conveyed due to inaccurate translations, the fluent bilingual assistant can ask questions that are designed to make the ELL aware of the lack of clarity of the translation. The ELL then modifies the message to clarify it or ends the role-playing session and asks the assistant for pointers on translating the difficult parts. If the ELL clearly translates the message, the assistant replies in the ELL's first language, and the student translates this reply for you.

Keep the process very informal and friendly, and do not grade the activity. Activities such as this provide the ELL with a useful life skill that also helps other family members and friends.

using a single language, according to Jimenez (2001, p. 739). They have to expend their effort to contend with both languages. They are often expected to be translators for monolingual relatives or for their caretakers who do not speak English. This places pressure on them to be accurate in comprehending and expressing themselves in both languages. These translations may involve both spoken and written language. You should take the needs of such students into consideration and give them opportunities to practice these practical applications of language.

Concerns about students' proficiency in the language arts have resulted in the development of standards for the English language arts. Both governmental agencies and professional organizations have developed standards.

The Language Arts

THE SIX language arts, as designated by the National Council of Teachers of English (NCTE) and the International Reading Association (IRA) (*Standards for the English Language Arts*, 1996), are listening, speaking, reading, writing, viewing, and visually representing. The first four have traditionally been considered to be the language arts; however, since visual media have become more important in everyday life, viewing and visually representing have become more important as means of communicating. Each language art is examined briefly in this section. They are given further attention later in this text. Figure 1.1 provides an overview of the six language arts, as identified by NCTE/IRA.

All meanings that are attached to the words that we use are obtained through experience. Infants begin experiencing the world as soon as they are born. From the beginning, they experience light and darkness, being held and fed, having their diapers changed, and many other things. These experiences are often accompanied by words spoken by people around them. The language arts are tied to experience through words and the images that words represent. Listening involves making connections between spoken words (abstract oral symbols) and their meanings. Speaking involves taking command of the words by using them orally to communicate with others. Reading involves translating written symbols into the oral symbols that they represent and, finally, into their meanings; and writing involves encoding written symbols so that they will convey information to others. Viewing involves interpreting the images for which words stand and connecting visual images in videos, computer programs, and websites with accompanying printed or spoken words. Visually representing involves presenting information through still or motion pictures, either alone or accompanied by written or spoken words.

Although children come to school with a wide variety of background experiences, their experiences may or

FIGURE 1.1   The Language Arts

Listening:
understanding spoken language

Speaking:
communicating ideas through oral language

Reading:
understanding written language

Writing:
communicating ideas through written language

Viewing:
understanding visual images and connecting them to accompanying spoken or written words

Visually representing:
presenting information through images, either alone or along with spoken or written words

may not be applicable to the focus of the school. Some know the language of street corners and alleys but do not know the language required for school activities. Children from low socioeconomic backgrounds may not have had experiences with computers or even such school supplies as pencils, scissors, and crayons and may not have traveled beyond their immediate neighborhoods. Such children are limited in their exposure to a variety of places, people, animals, and other things. Those children who have had varied experiences related to topics covered in the schools' curricula have enhanced comprehension of material that they listen to, read, and view and more relevant material to draw on when they speak, write, or prepare visual presentations.

Schoolchildren are developing all of their language skills simultaneously. Expanded classroom experiences enhance this development. Language skills also continue to be refined throughout life. Individuals continue to have experiences, to listen, to speak, to view, to read, to write, and to make visual presentations of various types. Their experiences provide them more opportunities to learn through listening and viewing; to use this learning by imitating in their own speech, writing, and visual presentations the things heard or seen; and to understand better the things that they read. The following is an example of the continuing refinement of language knowledge that occurs for people at all ages.

Writing

> Bryan had never gone sailing until he was an adult. In the course of sailing with an experienced friend, Sean, Bryan for the first time used the sheet to raise the sail, placed the centerboard, used the rudder, and experienced running before the wind and tacking to sail upwind back to shore. Sean kept up a commentary on what was happening as it took place. Bryan listened to Sean's conversation, watched his actions, and used the context of the direct experience to give it meaning. Eventually he began to make comments of his own, sprinkling them with the newly learned terminology. Sean's responses clarified Bryan's understanding of the language of sailing even more. The next day Bryan wrote to his brother and described his sailing adventure. He used many terms in his letter that he had never used in writing before, at least not in that context. He even drew a diagram of a sailboat and labeled it to clarify his comments.

Listening

The language art of listening begins developing at birth and provides the basis for development of speaking, reading, and writing skills. Listening can be defined as the interpretation of sounds that are heard. When a baby is first born, he immediately begins to receive sensory impressions, including hearing sounds. However, in this early stage, the sounds are merely received by the ears; they are not interpreted by the brain. As time passes and the child hears a particular sound, such as *milk,* which is accompanied by the presence of a particular substance, the child begins to associate the substance with the sound. This is the place where experience produces meanings for the child. When a mere mention of the word *milk* by another person excites the child, he is probably interpreting the sounds. At that time, listening has taken place.

Young children learn much language by listening to those around them. They listen not only to spoken words but also to the rhythms and intonation patterns

Reflections

Consider a recent new experience that you have had. How did the different language arts play a part in the experience? How did you use the meanings derived from the experience later in interpreting things you listened to, read, or viewed? How did you use the new knowledge in speaking, writing, or visually representing?

of the language that they hear. They take the language they hear and make generalizations based on it. For example, they may generalize about how adjectives are changed to the comparative degree. They may say that something is "gooder" than something else, having applied the generalization to an irregular construction. Because they learn much through their listening and thinking behavior, children enter school when they are five or six years old able to converse with their teachers and their peers in understandable language.

It is possible to hear sounds and not listen to them. You have probably, at some time, been engrossed in an activity and not responded when a friend asked you a question. When the friend persisted by saying something such as "Well, is it?" you may have been able to reconstruct what you heard him say originally, interpret the sounds that you received, and respond to the question appropriately.

Children who are not hearing impaired come to school with a fairly long history of hearing, but their listening skills are not necessarily good. Children learn to "tune out" things around them that they do not choose to hear and, therefore, may need to be taught what things are important to listen to in school.

Listening is a skill that allows a person to receive oral information from others. It is therefore sometimes referred to as a receptive skill and as an oral language skill. Through it, a person can take in new ideas by decoding into meanings the oral symbols (words, phrases, and sentences) that make up the communication.

Listening is often not given adequate attention in the classroom, partially because some people seem to equate listening and hearing. Chapter 5 presents an expanded treatment of listening; other related material appears in Chapter 2 on literature, Chapter 4 on early experiences with language, and Chapter 6 on oral expression.

Speaking

Speaking is making use of vocal sounds to communicate meaning to others. The newborn baby comes into the world making a variety of sounds. These sounds, however, are not produced in an overt effort on the part of the child to convey meaning in his early days. Except in the case of crying and whimpering, the child is simply producing random sounds of which his vocal mechanism is capable. Meaningful speech develops as children learn the effects of particular sounds on the people around them. When a child deliberately uses a word to communicate with others, speech has occurred. The child has attached meaning to the sounds that he makes, based on past experience.

Speaking is often referred to as an expressive skill and an oral language skill. The speaker encodes (represents in oral symbols, or words) a thought into an oral message and transmits this message to a listener, who must decode (translate into meaning) the oral symbols in order to understand the message. Speakers can transmit information about past and present circumstances, as well as about future events and abstract ideas.

Chapter 6 presents an expanded treatment of oral expression. Note that the areas of listening and oral expression are complementary and closely interrelated and that Chapters 5 and 6 of necessity contain material relevant to both areas. Chapter 2 deals with oral presentation of literature, and Chapter 4 has material on oral language, as well. Chapter 10 includes a discussion of usage, which is also relevant.

Reading

Reading is the interpretation of written symbols. It involves visual perception of the symbols, sometimes translation of the visual symbols into auditory ones, and the

Applications for English Language Learners and Students with Special Needs

Scan material that you plan to use for reading or content area classes for vocabulary terms that are not common in everyday conversations or are unfamiliar to the ELLs' cultures. Preteach such terms, using concrete objects and demonstrations, audiovisual aids, and graphic organizers, such as webs that connect new vocabulary words to known ones. See Chapter 3 for techniques to use for teaching vocabulary.

connection of meaning with these symbols. Although in later stages of reading readers may move directly from print to meaning, in the early stages children generally decode to sound and then associate the resulting oral words with their experiences with those words. If the reader has no experience to relate to the words in the text, the reader cannot construct meaning, and reading does not actually occur. For example, if a child sounds out the word *walrus*, the child can attach meaning to the word only if he has had experiences with walruses, through seeing them at a marine exhibit or reading about them and seeing their pictures. Understanding is a necessary part of the reading process.

Initial stages of learning to read generally follow those of learning to listen and learning to speak, and ideas understood in oral language form a basis for the understanding of ideas found in print. Learning to read is often associated with starting school, but many children come to school already reading to some extent. They often recognize common product names and signs found in their environments (although some of this recognition can be attributed to their facility in viewing), and some can read stories and other printed information.

Reading is a way of taking in information that has been recorded in print by another person. Thus, it is classified as a receptive skill and a written language skill. The reader decodes a written message that has been encoded by a writer and interprets that message in light of his or her own experiences. Information that was written today or many years ago may be read now or in the future, allowing readers to learn from the accumulated records of literate humankind.

Reading serves many functions for the reader. It provides information or entertainment. It offers challenges or relaxation. Each reading act may be for a slightly different purpose.

Chapter 7 deals with the area of reading. It is of necessity an abbreviated treatment, since many complete textbooks focus on this area, which is often covered in a separate course in universities. It is included here because it is a language art and should be integrated into language instruction in the classroom. Chapter 2, with its focus on literature, is closely related to Chapter 7.

Writing

Writing involves communicating with others through the printed word or recording ideas for yourself. It is classified as an expressive skill and a written language skill. The writer encodes a message that is decoded and interpreted by the reader.

Learning to read often spurs the desire to learn to write, but reading and writing may be taught simultaneously.

A writer passes along experiences to a prospective reader through inscribed symbols that stand for these experiences. If the reader's experiences encompass the concepts expressed by the symbols or are sufficiently close to help the reader make new connections, communication occurs. If the writer and the reader do not have enough commonality of experience related to the written message, meaning is not likely to be transmitted.

Writing allows a person to communicate with others who are contemporaries or to leave records that may be read by succeeding generations. This ability to span time offers many possibilities to writers with varying purposes—transmission of instructions for performing tasks, preservation of the folklore and customs of a people, entertainment of the reader, and persuasion of a reader to adopt a point of view, among many possibilities.

Writing is a complex topic that has many facets. Chapters 8, 9, and 10 address the process of written composition; types of writing; handwriting; and spelling, grammar, and the conventions for written language.

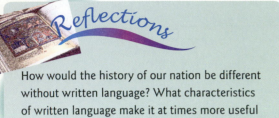

Reflections

How would the history of our nation be different without written language? What characteristics of written language make it at times more useful than spoken language?

Viewing

Technology

Viewing refers to interpreting visual media. These media include photographs, illustrations, graphs, maps, and diagrams found in books, as well as video presentations found on television, Internet sites, CD-ROMs, or DVD-ROMs. It can even include live performances in theaters and classrooms. Students today are inundated with visual media that are attempting to convey information to them, persuade them to do or believe something, or entertain them. The messages received from these media must be comprehended using the same thinking skills needed for comprehending print material that is read. Critical analysis of the material on the Internet is vital, as the Internet is used more and more as an information source for reports in classes and as more and more sites with unreliable information are added to reputable sites that also reside on the Internet. Chapter 11 addresses viewing in more detail.

Visually Representing

Visually representing refers to communicating through visual images. These images include photographs, drawings, graphs, maps, and diagrams, as well as video pre-

Viewing critically is an important skill for students to learn.

sentations, dioramas, models, and dramatizations. This form of communication requires the student to collect and organize information, decide on the best way to convey it to others, and produce a visual product to accomplish this communication, often incorporating print and sound (including speech) with the visual images, if the student is trying to convey information or sway opinion. It requires organizing and representing an event or sequence of events for the pleasure or diversion of an audience, if the purpose of the representation is to entertain. Chapter 11 addresses visually representing in more detail.

The Function of the Language Arts in Communication

COMMUNICATION IS the process of transmitting information from one person to another. The language arts are all important to the communication process. Listening and speaking are basic to oral communication; reading and writing are basic to written communication; and viewing and visually representing are basic to visual communication. Listening, reading, and viewing are ways of receiving information. Speaking, writing, and visually representing are ways of conveying information.

Values of Communication

Communication is an essential element in our lives today. Almost every endeavor depends on some form of communication: oral or written instructions or demonstrations for performing an activity; oral or written information or gestures to coordinate the activities of several people who are participating in an activity; oral or written queries about objects, procedures, or locations; oral or written evaluation of the outcome of an activity. Examples abound: A parent follows a recipe or watches a cooking show to discover how to prepare a special dish for the children's dinner. A teacher tells his class who is assigned to go to the learning center and how many are allowed to be there at one time or posts a diagram of the classroom and lists the names of several students under each of several centers that are currently being used. A child asks an adult where the sun goes at night. A supervisor writes a commendation for an employee, based on her handling of a project.

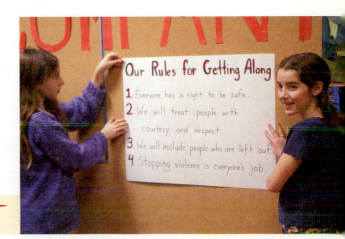

    Some of these uses of communication are based on current actions: A person asks an oral question and is answered orally; someone makes a telephone call for the purpose of transmitting information or ideas; a person

Written lists are used to transmit information.

wishes to share an abstract thought with a friend and expresses it orally; a salesman sends an e-mail to a client to explain a delay in an order; a supervisor writes a note containing instructions for a secretary to use the next day, handing it to the secretary personally before leaving for the day. Other uses for communication involve transmission of information over time. A child leaves a note for her parents, informing them of where she will be that afternoon and how she can be reached; a friend writes a letter telling about the fun he is having on his trip; an associate sends a videotape of a meeting in the mail, so that the information can be shared by those not able to attend; a student reads a reference book describing a subject he is studying or reads the same information from an Internet site; scholars study a book written in the sixteenth century for clues to current happenings.

Children come to school knowing many ways of communicating: They know how to inform, to inquire, to console, to joke, to argue, and to persuade, for example. Children, however, come from diverse backgrounds, culturally and linguistically, and they may not perform these communication functions in the same ways. Most children also come to school with knowledge of a wide range of communication events, such as telephoning, e-mailing, storytelling, sermonizing, questioning, and searching the Internet, but some have had more experience with particular situations than have others because of differences in culture, socioeconomic status, and other background conditions. Some may not have had experiences with computer uses, for example, whereas others may have had little or no exposure to storytelling.

Reflections

What are some other values of communication? How is communication valuable in the lives of elementary-grade students?

Failures to Communicate

Failures to communicate can cause serious consequences to the people involved. If a building is on fire and the person who sees it is unable to convey the problem to emergency personnel, the building inhabitants may be injured. Salespeople who fail to communicate may lose sales. Teachers who fail to communicate may have students who cannot perform at appropriate levels in school. If a child feels sick and cannot explain

Applications **for English Language Learners and Students with Special Needs**

ELLs are often faced with puzzling figurative expressions for which the meanings of individual words do not add up to the meanings of the expressions as whole thoughts. Many students with special needs due to physical, mental, or learning challenges or those who simply have limited experiential backgrounds also have trouble with these expressions because these students attempt to take them literally.

Scan students' reading material for figurative language and plan minilessons to teach the meanings of these expressions when they are essential to learning the content or comprehending the story. Chapter 3 contains information on figurative expressions that can be used for such minilessons.

© Zits Partnership. Reprinted with special permission of King Features Syndicate.

the problem in an understandable way, she may suffer a more severe or prolonged illness because the discovery of the illness was delayed. The inability of infants to tell adults what is causing their discomfort when they cry is a good illustration of the problem that exists.

In the *Zits* comic strip above, Jeremy's mom is trying to communicate with him.

In school, failures to communicate may result from cultural differences. For example, the teacher who asks a child, "Can you find your seat?" does not want the question to be answered with a "yes" or "no." This teacher is asking the student to go to the proper seat. A child who has not been exposed to this type of communication may respond inappropriately, in the teacher's opinion, causing the teacher to think the child is uncooperative.

Students from different cultural backgrounds also may not understand the idioms they encounter in school. If they hear the teacher or a classmate say, "Are you pulling my leg?" they may be completely bewildered, since no physical contact has taken place. They, in turn, use idioms relevant to their own cultures that confuse their teachers and classmates.

Reflections

In the *Zits* comic strip above, does Jeremy's mom succeed in communicating with him? Does she think she was successful? (Examine Jeremy's words and expression in the last frame to decide.) In what two ways does Jeremy's mom try to modify her communication? Are they successful? Is Jeremy's reaction typical of a teenager? Does his mother show understanding of the situation in the final frame?

Reflections

What are some other examples of failures to communicate, and what are their consequences?

Interrelationships among the Language Arts

ALTHOUGH THE language arts have their own individual characteristics, they are highly interrelated. Because of their interrelationships, instruction in one language skill often improves others. For example, learning to identify main ideas when listening to a speaker is likely to improve the individual's ability to identify main ideas when reading or when viewing, since the cognitive activity is essentially the same after the decoding of oral, written, or visual symbols has taken place.

Relationships among All Six Language Arts

The six language arts are not only all interrelated and necessary to communication, as indicated in the previous section, but they also all involve both thinking and construction of meaning. Figure 1.2 shows these interrelationships.

How does instruction in speaking skills benefit the other language arts?

THINKING

Thinking skills are necessary for the proper functioning of all the language skills. Thoughts are expressed through language, and it takes thought to interpret language. Communication requires both literal thinking—getting directly stated or presented information—and higher order thinking—making inferences, generalizing, synthesizing, analyzing, and evaluating material that is presented.

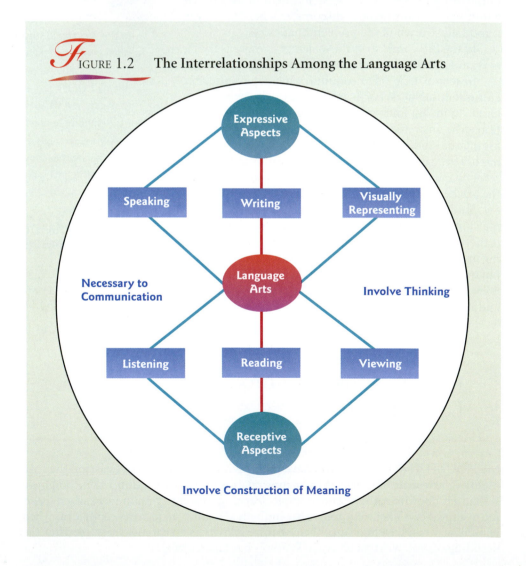

FIGURE 1.2   The Interrelationships Among the Language Arts

Obviously, students will not excel in interpreting communications if they cannot extract directly stated facts in written or spoken form or extract directly conveyed visual information, such as the shape of a diamond in an illustration. On the other hand, if communication ended with just details of this sort, it would be extremely limited.

When listening to or reading a story or viewing a televised or theatrical presentation, many inferences must be made. A character in a written or told story or in a drama may say, "Tamara is getting ready for school." Immediately, the reader, listener, or viewer makes the inferences that Tamara is dressing, grooming herself, and getting her supplies together to go to school. He pictures books, notebooks, pens, pencils, and the like as the supplies. These inferences are formed based on his background experiences. All of the details do not have to be explicitly presented to the audience for the communication, because the communicator expects the audience to draw on this background. Otherwise, all communications would be extremely tedious because of endless details.

Students who are gathering information from multiple sources, visual and auditory, to prepare reports or presentations or solve personal problems, must organize the information, make generalizations about their findings, synthesize their findings into a coherent whole, and decide how to communicate the information to others. In the process, they must analyze each information source and evaluate it for accuracy, completeness, timeliness, and bias. They must create a new whole that is cohesive and coherent from a number of diverse bits of information. They must decide on a form of communication—speech, writing, visual presentation, or a combination of forms—based on their knowledge of their audiences and the materials and equipment at hand. This process requires further thinking at the levels of analysis and evaluation. They must also consider the aesthetic effect that the presentations will have on the audiences to achieve their desired effects.

When students critically consider material that is presented to them, they evaluate it based on their prior knowledge. **Critical literacy** involves analysis and evaluation of texts and media presentations. It is an active process that includes reflection, focusing on complexity of situations, and examining multiple perspectives. It depends heavily on adequate background information (McLaughlin & DeVoogd, 2004). Teachers must provide background information related to critical literacy needs, model critical literacy practices, and offer many opportunities for students to practice critical literacy.

Au (2002, p. 401) points out, "English language learners, like struggling readers, are often subject to instruction oriented toward lower level skills rather than higher level thinking." This is not advisable, as it can cause such students to fall even further behind, and it tends to lead them into boredom and disinterest in school.

CONSTRUCTION OF MEANING

All of the language arts involve the construction of meaning. It may seem obvious that sending information to others involves construction of meaning. Speaking, writing, and visually representing are expressive language arts. They are ways of conveying information. Speaking involves constructing a message for the listener with oral symbols (spoken words). Writing involves constructing a message for the reader with written symbols (printed words). Visually representing involves constructing a message for the viewer with visual symbols (pictures, diagrams, maps, graphs, videos, and so on).

Writing

It may seem less obvious that receiving information involves construction, but it does. Listening, reading, and viewing are receptive language arts. They are ways of taking in information. Listening involves attempting to reconstruct the meaning behind the words of a speaker. In the process, something new may be constructed from the intersection of the background knowledge of the listener that is not shared by the speaker and the new ideas that the speaker presents to the listener. Reading involves attempting to reconstruct the meaning behind the words of a writer. In the process, something new may be constructed from the intersection of the background knowledge of the reader that is not shared by the writer and the new ideas that the writer presents to the reader. Viewing involves attempting to construct the meaning behind visual images that are presented. In the process, something new may be constructed from the intersection of the background knowledge of the viewer that is not shared by the presenter and the new ideas that the presenter presents to the viewer. Whether new information is constructed or conveyed information is reconstructed, thinking skills at every level are of vital importance.

Relationships among Listening, Speaking, Reading, and Writing

Listening, speaking, reading, and writing all require knowledge about and use of vocabulary and grammar.

VOCABULARY

Listening, speaking, reading, and writing all depend on the common building blocks of words for communication. This aspect of their likeness is covered extensively in Chapter 3. Visual representations are often accompanied by oral or written words for enhanced clarity, for without words, communication is greatly limited. Children for whom English is not their home language need more attention and support with vocabulary to function well in language activities.

GRAMMAR AND USAGE

Listening, speaking, reading, and writing also make use of the language's grammar. Regular arrangements of words help both senders and receivers of messages construct meaning. This aspect of language may be problematic for students who are not proficient in English because it is not their first language. Special attention to the needs of these students is necessary if they are to progress at a desirable pace. You must be aware that it takes several years for students to acquire language skills that are needed in everyday and school communication, and they pick up the skills needed for general communication long before they develop the skills needed for academic purposes. Wong Fillmore (1986) points out the research evidence that most children require four to six years of instruction to achieve a level of proficiency in a second language needed for full participation in school. These children, in particular, need to learn language as a part of meaningful communication. Their language usage may be nonstandard for some time, even though they are capable of communicating ideas in English. The topics of grammar and usage are covered in Chapter 10.

Relationships between Listening and Speaking

Listening and speaking are complementary skills; they are somewhat dependent on each other. There is no need to speak if there is no one to listen, and, although it is possible to listen to things other than speech, spoken communications are a prime reason for listening.

Listening and speaking are both oral language skills. They require the decoding and encoding of oral symbols.

As indicated earlier in this chapter, much of the language used in speaking is learned through listening to and imitating speech. Children not only imitate speech that they understand but also try out things that they hear and do not understand. This relationship between speech and listening is a good argument for teachers and parents to act as positive language models for children because children often copy sloppy, as well as embarrassing, speech patterns.

All students need practice in listening and speaking fluently and clearly. Wormeli (2001) has his students periodically paraphrase what they have heard. He participates in the activity as well, providing a model for the students.

Reflections

How does a wink change the meaning of a speaker's message?

Relationships among Listening, Reading, and Viewing

Listening, reading, and viewing are receptive, or input, skills. As such, they involve similar thinking processes for information collection.

Decoding oral symbols (listening) involves only one level of abstraction, going from the sound to the experience on which it is based. Decoding written symbols (reading) involves two levels of abstraction, at least for beginning readers. It requires going from the written symbol to the oral word that it represents and then further back to the experience for which it stands. Therefore, working on listening skills is good for developing readiness for reading skills, since listening requires many of the same mental processes as reading but involves a different level of decoding.

Teaching children to look at visual presentations for main ideas, details, sequence, causes and effects, critical evaluations, and other elements of the message familiarizes them with these processes. Teaching them to listen for these elements favorably affects the children's ability to read for these same things. Adding a word to the children's listening vocabularies increases the chance that they will be able to interpret its meaning when reading and apply it to something that they view.

Listening may require more intense concentration than reading because it is usually not possible to go back and relisten to the exact words again, even if the speaker tries to repeat them. (This, of course, is not the case if the discourse is recorded.) A reader can reread at will. The listener is also not in control of the rate of presentation and may miss information that is presented too rapidly to absorb. The reader can set her own pace, depending on the purpose for the reading.

Listeners often have the advantage of watching the speaker's gestures and facial expressions and hearing the intonation of voice. This adds the aspect of viewing to the listening. Readers must glean much of the same type of information provided by gestures, facial expression, and intonation from punctuation, which may not be sufficient to pass along the complete flavor of the presentation.

Viewing of images is often combined with spoken or written words, and, therefore, the three types of information can enhance one another. Viewing a static image allows reexamination, just as reading does, but viewing images in motion, as in a video, has the same increased difficulty that listening has when compared to reading, unless the video is available for playback.

Technology

Technology

Relationships among Speaking, Writing, and Visually Representing

Speaking, writing, and visually representing are expressive, or output, skills. They are generally used to transfer information to others. They require the encoding of symbols to be transmitted—oral symbols in the case of speaking, written symbols in the case of writing, and visual images in the case of visually representing. There is evidence that related oral discourse is important in the development of writing skills (Thaiss, 1990) and results in students writing with more awareness of their audience and more coherence.

In speaking, writing, and visually representing, organization of thoughts is important. Organization may be easier to work with in writing because information can be rearranged easily after it is written down and before it is given to others to read. After a disorganized message has been spoken, however, it still exists in the listeners' minds, even if it is corrected. For this reason, many speakers plan what they are going to say in writing before they present it orally. In this case, the writing serves as a method of enhancing organization of spoken messages. Speaking activities, however, may also serve as good readiness activities for writing. This is true because oral symbols are generally learned first, and, as a general rule, children do not discuss in their writing things about which they are unable to converse.

Visually representing also has a need for organization. Some visual presentations have the added need for organization in terms of arrangement in space. Visual presentation shares a hazard of speaking when it is a "live" presentation—once a scene is enacted, it cannot be undone. Videotaping of three-dimensional presentations, however, allows for adjustments, just as audiorecording allows for adjustments in speaking situations.

Relationships between Reading and Writing

Reading and writing are complementary skills. There is no point in writing something if there is no one to read it, and there is nothing to read if something has not been written. Both are written language skills, making use of visual symbols that represent both spoken words and the experiences behind the words.

When writing, people are more likely to use words that they recognize and believe that they understand well in their reading materials. However, much material that they feel comfortable reading never appears in their own writing, because using a word in writing requires a more thorough knowledge of its implications than does reading it with a reasonable degree of understanding.

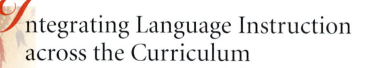

Integrating Language Instruction across the Curriculum

LANGUAGE ARTS are essentially tools for collecting and disseminating information. As shown earlier in this chapter, they are interrelated, and instruction in one

Applications
for English Language Learners

ELLs particularly benefit from integrated language learning. Use of the language experience approach is very effective for these students because they see their own language usage in print. (See Chapter 7 for information about this method.) These students refine their understanding of language (word meanings, syntax, print conventions, and so on) by writing on a regular basis.

tends to enhance acquisition of the others. Although each language art has its own characteristics and needs to be specifically addressed in the overall language program, the commonalities and interrelationships among the language arts make integrating instruction in these areas appropriate. For example, anytime there is spoken language in the classroom, the possibility of teaching and refining listening skills is present. Oral language is needed for work on listening skills. While such instruction is taking place, there are likely to be possibilities for improving speaking skills as well. Integration of reading and speaking activities can take place when students planning oral presentations read about the topic to plan what they are going to say. Integration of writing and speaking may consist of a person making written notes in preparation for the oral report. In this book, the language arts are addressed individually at times, but this approach is intended only to allow more focus on each area to avoid overemphasis on some and too little emphasis on others.

Writing

As a group, the language arts are useful in the study of every content area. Students listen to, read, and view information about science, social studies, mathematics, and other content areas to learn the basic concepts in these areas. They use speaking, writing, and visually representing to share the results of their investigations into these other areas and to provide evidence of learning in these areas.

Literature as a Vehicle for Integration

Literature is a wonderful vehicle for integrating the language arts and for integrating language arts across the entire curriculum. Students listen to stories and nonfiction selections from literature, view video presentations and live performances of literature selections, and read stories and articles for themselves. They then organize the material that they

English language learners refine their understanding of language by regularly writing in class.

have acquired, talk about the literature selections, write about them, and visually present information from them. (See Chapter 2.)

Literature selections touch on every area of the curriculum. (See Chapter 2 and Chapter 12.) Exceptional nonfiction selections elaborate on topics that are taught in subject textbooks, which do not have the space to provide this elaboration. Textbooks sometimes make historical periods, scientific concepts, and other content material

---

*F*IGURE 1.3   Possible Activities for Unit on Mechanical Transportation

1. Holding discussions of the pros and cons of particular modes of transportation for particular people (e.g., children without adult assistance, soldiers, large families) or particular purposes (e.g., getting to an island, going into space, crossing a desert)

2. Making timelines of the introduction of each of several modern types of transportation

3. Constructing graphs to compare the numbers of students in the class who have used various types of transportation

Writing

4. Writing letters to manufacturers and salespeople for information about certain types of transportation

5. Making webs of information about each of the types of transportation and writing reports based on the webs

6. Drawing pictures and making models of various forms of transportation to share with other classes

Technology

7. Singing songs about modes of transportation

8. Studying maps to decide what types of transportation would be appropriate for trips between various locations

9. Writing creative stories that incorporate types of transportation

10. Comparing and contrasting characteristics of types of transportation with semantic feature analysis

11. Locating information about famous people who were involved in innovations in transportation or famous events related to transportation

seem dry and unconnected to everyday life. Both nonfiction and fiction selections offer elaboration and connections to real life that students need to "buy in" to the instruction based on the textbooks. These selections also motivate students to learn by offering lively narratives, extensive visuals, and characters who seem more real because of their richer details.

Thematic Teaching as a Vehicle for Integration

Thematic teaching is an excellent way to integrate instruction. Thematic units can be centered around a topic or theme, a genre of literature, an author, or even a single book. **Cross-curricular thematic units** combine study in all related content areas that are appropriate to the chosen theme.

A thematic unit on types of mechanical transportation could include both informational books and fiction books that center around different types, print and electronic reference books with sections about transportation, related websites for students to visit under supervision, models, related videos or CD-ROMs on the topic, brochures, magazines, newspapers, and other reference sources. There are many possible activities, in addition to reading the fiction and nonfiction selections and viewing the related videos. (See Figure 1.3 for some possible activities.) Such a unit could include social studies, science, mathematics, art, music, literature, listening, speaking, reading, writing, viewing, and representing visually. Each area would be introduced as it naturally enhanced the study of the subject. Through a unit like this one, students would learn skills, concepts, and vocabulary for all of these areas in an integrated fashion. The interrelated presentation of information would enhance retention of the material.

Reflections

What is one activity that you could use with children that would incorporate all of the language arts? Visualize it and describe it in detail.

Technology

Children who come from different cultural backgrounds can explore and experience each other's cultures through group multicultural experiences. They can, for example, study emigration patterns of families, involving map reading and use of other applicable materials, and turn family histories into narratives through class interaction. They can share, discuss, and change culturally and ethnically based perceptions through planned activities. Stories from different cultures can be shared and discussed, different languages can be analyzed, and different cultural backgrounds can be explored (Piper, 1986).

Standards for the English Language Arts

IN RECENT years, people have become concerned that students are not performing as well as they should in school. As a result, they have developed or requested the development of standards that "define what students should learn" (Agnew, 2000, p. 1). Professional organizations and individual states sought to develop standards in various curricular areas. Some states have such extensive lists of standards that meeting them

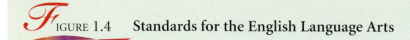

FIGURE 1.4   **Standards for the English Language Arts**

Sponsored by NCTE and IRA

The vision guiding these standards is that all students must have the opportunities and resources to develop the language skills they need to pursue life's goals and to participate fully as informed, productive members of society. These standards assume that literacy growth begins before children enter school as they experience and experiment with literacy activities—reading and writing, and associating spoken words with their graphic representations. Recognizing this fact, these standards encourage the development of curriculum and instruction that make productive use of the emerging literacy abilities that children bring to school. Furthermore, the standards provide ample room for the innovation and creativity essential to teaching and learning. They are not prescriptions for particular curriculum or instruction. Although we present these standards as a list, we want to emphasize that they are not distinct and separable; they are, in fact, interrelated and should be considered as a whole.

1. Students read a wide range of print and non-print texts to build an understanding of texts, of themselves, and of the cultures of the United States and the world; to acquire new information; to respond to the needs and demands of society and the workplace; and for personal fulfillment. Among these texts are fiction and nonfiction, classic and contemporary works.

2. Students read a wide range of literature from many periods in many genres to build an understanding of the many dimensions (e.g., philosophical, ethical, aesthetic) of human experience.

3. Students apply a wide range of strategies to comprehend, interpret, evaluate, and appreciate texts. They draw on their prior experience, their interactions with other readers and writers, their knowledge of word meaning and of other texts, their word identification strategies, and their understanding of textual features (e.g., sound-letter correspondence, sentence structure, context, graphics).

4. Students adjust their use of spoken, written, and visual language (e.g., conventions, style, vocabulary) to communicate effectively with a variety of audiences and for different purposes.

5. Students employ a wide range of strategies as they write and use different writing process elements appropriately to communicate with different audiences for a variety of purposes.

6. Students apply knowledge of language structure, language conventions (e.g., spelling and punctuation), media techniques, figurative language, and genre to create, critique, and discuss print and non-print texts.

7. Students conduct research on issues and interests by generating ideas and questions, and by posing problems. They gather, evaluate, and synthesize data from a variety of sources (e.g., print and non-print texts, artifacts, people) to communicate their discoveries in ways that suit their purpose and audience.

8. Students use a variety of technological and information resources (e.g., libraries, databases, computer networks, video) to gather and synthesize information and to create and communicate knowledge.

9. Students develop an understanding of and respect for diversity in language use, patterns, and dialects across cultures, ethnic groups, geographic regions, and social roles.

10. Students whose first language is not English make use of their first language to develop competency in the English language arts and to develop understanding of content across the curriculum.

11. Students participate as knowledgeable, reflective, creative, and critical members of a variety of literacy communities.

12. Students use spoken, written, and visual language to accomplish their own purposes (e.g., for learning, enjoyment, persuasion, and the exchange of information).

Source: Standards for the English Language Arts, by International Reading Association and the National Council of Teachers of English. Copyright 1996 by the International Reading Association and the National Council of Teachers of English. Reprinted with permission.

in the time available is unrealistic, prompting Schmoker and Marzano (1999, p. 21) to suggest that standards should be "clear, not confusing; essential, not exhaustive." The National Council of Teachers of English and the International Reading Association cooperatively developed a set of standards for the English language arts (see Figure 1.4) that specify a range of areas in the English language arts in which students must be proficient. They do not specify levels of proficiency (Smagorinsky, 1999). Some states have standards that are similar to these.

SUMMARY

The language arts—listening, speaking, reading, writing, viewing, and visually representing—are highly interrelated, although each one has its own individual characteristics. All of the language arts are important to communication. Listening, speaking, reading, and writing use words as basic units and word order for organization. Without words, communication would be very difficult or, in some cases, impossible. Communication among people in the present time and over time makes operating as humans much easier and more effective. When communication fails to occur between individuals, the results can be unpleasant or even disastrous.

As children develop skill in using language, they acquire metalinguistic awareness, or the ability to think about the components of language objectively. Many factors in the home environment affect the way a child learns language, particularly the availability of books in the home and the way that parents interact with their children.

Integration of language arts across the curriculum can result in more connected learning, and the connections make retention of the material more likely. Literature and thematic units are two vehicles for integrating learning across the curriculum.

The recent movement to setting standards in curricular areas has resulted in standards being set by both states and professional organizations. The National Council of Teachers of English and the International Reading Association have collaborated on a set of standards for the English language arts.

Discussion Questions

1. Describe three very different types of reports that students could make about a topic that they have researched. Identify the language art or language arts involved in each type.

2. What way do you receive information best—listening, reading, or viewing? Why do you think this is true for you? Will all students respond as you do?

3. What are some advantages of listening over reading about an unfamiliar topic? What are advantages of reading over listening in the same situation?

4. How does the students' metalinguistic awareness affect your ability to teach language skills?

5. How are parents important to developing language arts skills?

6. Does having written standards improve language instruction and learning? Why do you believe that?

Suggested Activities

1. Work with a group of your classmates to invent a new language with which you can communicate among yourselves. Afterward, discuss the difficulties that you faced and the things you had to accomplish.

2. Write a short paper on a topic related to the language arts class that you are taking. Without reading the paper, present the content orally to the class, recording your presentation on either audiotape or videotape. Play the recording and compare the spoken presentation with the written one. Decide how they differ and why. If you used videotape, consider any gestures or facial expressions that you used. Decide if they enhanced the clarity of your presentation.

3. Read five pages of a section of this text that you have not read previously. Write down everything you learned from the reading. Then have a classmate read to you five additional pages of the text that you have not read previously. Write down everything you learned from listening. Compare the amounts of information that you learned from listening and reading. Decide why one way of receiving information was easier or more difficult for you.

4. With a group of your classmates, brainstorm ways to integrate instruction in the language arts.

5. With a group of your classmates, brainstorm ways to use the language arts for learning across the curriculum. Pick a topic that must be taught in a content area of your choice and come up with ways to use the language arts in teaching about this topic. Don't forget to include literature in your plan.

References

AGNEW, W. J. (Ed.). (2000). *Standards based language arts curriculum.* Boston: Allyn & Bacon.

AU, K. H. (2002). Multicultural factors and the effective instruction of students of diverse backgrounds. In A. E. Farstrup & S. J. Samuels (Eds.), *What research has to say about reading instruction* (pp. 392–413). Newark, DE: International Reading Association.

AU, K. H., & RAPHAEL, T. E. (2000). Equity and literacy in the next millennium. *Reading Research Quarterly, 35,* 170–188.

BEWELL, D. V., & STRAW, S. B. (1981). Metalinguistic awareness, cognitive development, and language learning. In V. Froese & S. Straw (Eds.), *Research in the language arts* (pp. 105–122). Baltimore: University Park Press.

JIMENEZ, R. T. (2001, May). "It's a difference that changes us": An alternative view of the language and literacy learning needs of Latina/o students. *The Reading Teacher, 54,* 736–742.

MCLAUGHLIN, M., & DEVOOGD, G. (2004). Critical literacy as comprehension: Expanding reader response. *Journal of Adolescent & Adult Literacy, 48,* 52–62.

PIPER, D. (1986, January). Language growth in the multi-ethnic classroom. *Language Arts, 63,* 23–36.

RUBINSTEIN-AVILA, E. (2003/2004). Conversing with Miguel: An adolescent English language learner struggling with later literacy development. *Journal of Adolescent & Adult Literacy, 47,* 290–301.

SCHMOKER, M., & MARZANO, R. J. (1999, March). Realizing the promise of standards-based education. *Educational Leadership, 56,* 17–21.

SMAGORINSKY, P. (1999, March). Standards revisited: The importance of being there. *English Journal, 88,* 82–88.

Standards for the English Language Arts. (1996). Urbana, IL: National Council of Teachers of English and the International Reading Association.

THAISS, C. (1990). Language across the curriculum. In R. Graves (Ed.), *Rhetoric and composition: A sourcebook for teachers and writers* (pp. 33–37). Portsmouth, NH: Boynton/Cook.

WONG FILLMORE, L. (1986, September). Research currents: Equity or excellence. *Language Arts, 63,* 474–481.

WORMELI, RICK. (2001). *Meet me in the middle: Becoming an accomplished middle-level teacher.* Portland, ME: Stenhouse.

LITERATURE AND READER RESPONSE

LEARNER OBJECTIVES

At the conclusion of this chapter

YOU SHOULD BE ABLE TO:

1. Appreciate the value of literature in the language arts program.

2. Name and identify the literary elements and genres.

3. Understand how to use multicultural literature.

4. Use a variety of techniques for selecting and presenting literature.

5. Understand reader response theory and its significance.

6. Describe ways to generate thoughtful responses to literature.

7. Identify the following terms that are defined or explained in this chapter:

aesthetic 53	genres 35	sketch-to-stretch 67
book clubs 58	literary elements 34	story map 34
creative drama 62	multicultural literature 45	Sustained Silent Reading
dialogue 59	prompts 56	(SSR) 50
double-entry journal 59	puppetry 66	text sets 37
Drop Everything And	reader response theory 53	Think-Pair-Share 59
Read 50	Readers Theatre 63	trade books 34
efferent 53	sign systems 55	twin texts 42

NCTE/IRA Standards addressed in this chapter

STANDARD 1. Students read a wide range of print and non-print texts to build an understanding of texts, of themselves, and of the cultures of the United States and the world; to acquire new information; to respond to the needs and demands of society and the workplace; and for personal fulfillment. Among these texts are fiction and nonfiction, classic and contemporary works.

STANDARD 2. Students read a wide range of literature from many periods in many genres to build an understanding of the many dimensions (e.g., philosophical, ethical, aesthetic) of human experience.

STANDARD 11. Students participate as knowledgeable, reflective, creative, and critical members of a variety of literacy communities.

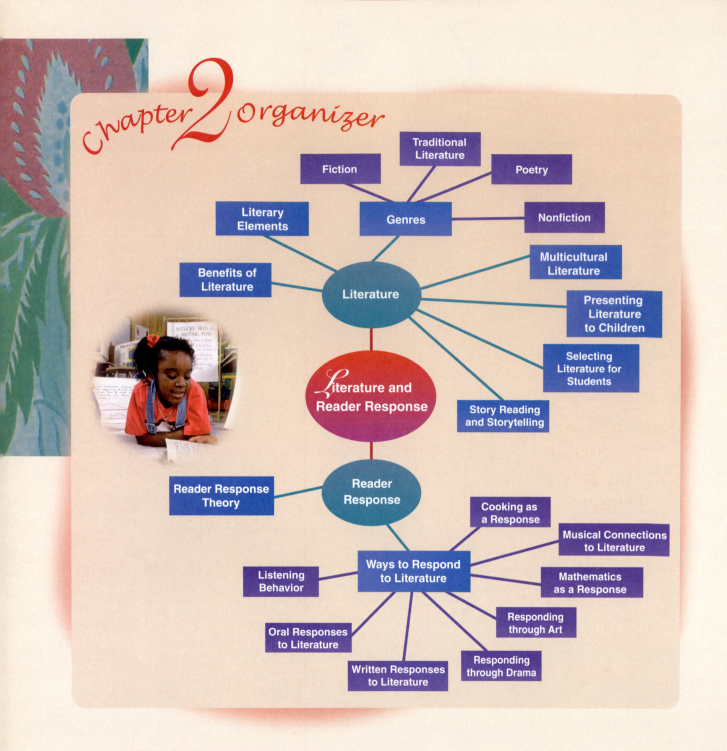

Chapter 2 Organizer

Literature and Reader Response

Literature

- Literary Elements
- Benefits of Literature
- Genres
  - Fiction
  - Traditional Literature
  - Poetry
  - Nonfiction
- Multicultural Literature
- Presenting Literature to Children
- Selecting Literature for Students
- Story Reading and Storytelling

Reader Response

- Reader Response Theory
- Ways to Respond to Literature
  - Listening Behavior
  - Oral Responses to Literature
  - Written Responses to Literature
  - Responding through Drama
  - Responding through Art
  - Mathematics as a Response
  - Musical Connections to Literature
  - Cooking as a Response

*E*ARLIER IN the day, just before lunch, Mrs. Couch sat in a rocking chair in the corner of her classroom, and the children sat on a rug in front of her. All listened raptly as she read Judith Viorst's *Alexander and the Terrible, Horrible, No Good, Very Bad Day.* Halfway through the story, Bob, a student from a local university, arrived to observe the language arts class. He walked into the room, looked at the group briefly, and then turned and walked out.

After school, Bob returns and says to Mrs. Couch, "I guess I came at the wrong time this morning. You were just reading to the children instead of teaching language arts. I'd like to come back another time, if it's okay with you."

Mrs. Couch looks at Bob in surprise. "We are working on listening skills this week," she responds. "Yesterday we talked about the importance of listening carefully and ways that we could improve listening skills. The children made a chart of listening habits that they should try to develop." Mrs. Couch gestures toward a prominently displayed chart that includes such items as "Watch the speaker closely" and "Think about what the speaker is saying." "Today I read them a story and told them to practice the listening skills that they listed yesterday," she continues. "After I finished reading, we discussed the story, giving some work on oral communication. They recalled details of the story and discussed causes and effects: For example, they discussed why the teacher wouldn't appreciate a picture of something that was invisible. Then each of them wrote a story about a bad day that they could recall. This, of course, gave purposeful practice in writing. Today I wasn't 'just reading to them,' although that in itself is important."

Bob is disappointed that he missed such a good lesson. "I'll try not to make such a quick decision next time," he says.

What's happening here?

Mrs. Couch is integrating language skills in her classroom, using literature as a vehicle for doing so. She believes in the value of reading books, holding meaningful discussions, and allowing thoughtful responses.

The world of children's literature is filled with colorful characters, lively dialogue, fascinating facts, and poignant moments. We see individuals struggle: Nory Ryan against poverty in Ireland, Sadako against illness in Japan, and Anne Frank against Nazi persecution in Germany. We discover great engineering feats by examining cross sections and investigating how things work. We find a dejected Alexander who has an absolutely horrible day and a clever gingerbread baby who outwits his pursuers. We gain insights into the lives of famous and not-so-famous personalities, and we learn why it is important to respect our environment. Fresh versions of familiar classic folklore, each version reflecting its own culture, await us. We relate to humorous, contemporary poems that cause us to chuckle, and we reflect on other poems that are rich in imagery and reach into our hearts.

Children's literature is part of our literary heritage. It helps us to become and understand who we are, and it enables us to appreciate the diversity among us. As the chapter-opening classroom opening vignette shows, children's literature relates to different aspects of the language arts as we listen to books and read them, discuss our reactions, and write responses. In fact, it enriches all areas of the curriculum, bringing life to people who shaped history, offering knowledge of nature and the environment, and giving in-depth coverage to topics of special interest.

In this chapter, we look more closely at the many benefits of using children's literature. Then we present the literary elements that most stories have and consider the various genres, or types, of literature available for children. The second part of the chapter focuses on reader response to literature—its importance and the many forms it takes, including music, art, drama, writing, and thoughtful discussions. How do we select appropriate literature from the thousands of children's books available? How can we present it so that children learn to love books? How should we ask children to respond to literature in meaningful ways? By reading this chapter, you should find the answers to these and other questions.

LITERATURE

READING BOOKS to and with children brings joy into the school day for both you and your class. It also offers countless cognitive and social benefits.

Benefits of Literature

Literature is an important component of a total language arts program at all grade levels because of the many benefits it offers. Here are some reasons for integrating literature into your curriculum.

Literature provides pleasure to listeners and readers. It is a relaxing escape from daily problems, and it fills leisure moments. Making time for recreational reading and using high-quality literature help to develop enthusiastic readers and improve achievement (Block & Mangieri, 2002). According to Rosenblatt (1995, p. 175), "The power of literature to offer entertainment and recreation is . . . still its prime reason for survival." Developing a love of literature as a recreational activity is possibly the most important outcome of a literature program.

Literature builds experience. Children expand their horizons through vicarious experiences. They visit new places, gain new experiences, and meet new people. They learn about the past as well as the present and learn about a variety of cultures, including their own. They discover the common goals and similar emotions found in people of all times and places. Two examples of books that provide such experiences are *Nory Ryan's Song* by Patricia Reilly Giff, a harsh survival story set in Ireland during the potato famine of 1845, and Patricia Polacco's *The Butterfly,* dealing with Nazis, resistance, and Jewish persecution during World War II.

Literature provides a language model for those who hear and read it. Good literature exposes children to correct sentence patterns, standard story structures, and varied word usage. Children for whom English is a second language can improve their English with the interesting context, and all children benefit from new vocabulary that is woven into the stories.

Literature develops thinking skills. Discussions of literature bring out reasoning related to sequence; cause and effect; character motivation; predictions; visualization of actions, characters, and settings; critical analysis of the story; and creative responses.

Literature supports all areas of the language arts curriculum. The chapter-opening classroom vignette shows how literature brings together all of the language arts. Listening to stories provides opportunities for honing listening skills, and discussion allows children to express their thoughts, feelings, and reactions. When students read literature, they are practicing their comprehension strategies in meaningful situations. Young writers may use various genres of literature as models for their own writing, and literature can be the basis for creative dramatics. Children can find stories to read and puzzles to solve on the Internet, and the computer can serve as a word processor for creating stories of their own.

Literature helps children deal with their problems. By finding out about the problems of others through books, children receive insights into dealing with their own problems, a process called *bibliotherapy.* Children might identify with Gilly, living resentfully in a foster home in Katherine Paterson's *The Great Gilly Hopkins,* or with Mary Alice, a city girl forced to live with her grandma in a "hick town" in Richard Peck's *A Year Down Yonder.*

Picture books develop visual literacy. The carefully crafted, creative illustrations in picture books develop children's awareness of line, color, space, shape, and design. Some illustrations complement or reinforce the story, whereas others enhance or extend the text. Pictures convey meaning and open new opportunities for interpretation (Giorgis et al., 1999).

Multicultural literature helps readers value people from different races, ethnic groups, and cultures. Excellent, well-illustrated books are available for many cultural groups.

Reflections

Think about your exposure to literature in the elementary grades. How was literature a part of your curriculum? Did some teachers use it more than others? How did they use it? How would you use it?

Children from such populations gain self-esteem by seeing themselves represented in books, and mainstream children begin to appreciate others from culturally diverse backgrounds.

Literature helps establish career concepts. For children who have limited knowledge of occupations, literature expands their ideas for potential careers (Harkins, 2001). Peggy Rathman's *Officer Buckle and Gloria,* about a police officer who shares information, and Alexandra Day's *Frank and Ernest on the Road,* about truck driving, give insights into two career choices.

Literature integrates the curriculum. **Trade books** (books of the trade, or library books) supplement and enrich any part of the curriculum. Instead of relying solely on textbooks, look for recent, brightly illustrated books on specific topics related to your theme or subject area. Remember that textbooks are assigned, but trade books are often chosen.

Literature improves reading ability and attitudes. A study of thirty second-, third-, fourth-, and sixth-grade classrooms by Block, Reed, and deTuncq (2003) indicated that students benefited more from twenty minutes of daily trade book or short story reading instruction. The researchers claim that reading from trade books resulted in increased reading ability, improved attitudes toward reading, and increased reading rate.

Literary Elements

Good teachers provide direct instruction about **literary elements**, which include plot, characterization, setting, theme, style, and point of view. Lessons related to *plot* focus on the order of events and the development of conflict, with special attention to the problem to be resolved. Students examine stories for *characterization* by asking themselves such questions as these: Are the characters realistic? Do they show signs of growth? Can I compare them with people I know or characters in another book? In order for readers to interact with the text and deepen their understanding, they must identify with the characters and realize that the characters may have similar personality traits to their own or to those of people they know (Bluestein, 2002). Using a character map, or graphic organizer, such as the one in Figure 2.1, lets the reader identify outstanding personality traits and give supporting evidence for each trait from information in the book. Figure 2.1 is based on Gloria Houston's *My Great-Aunt Arizona*, the story of a young girl from a rural area who becomes a teacher when she grows up.

The *setting* is the time and place for a story. It may be a unique setting or a familiar one, imagined or real. A story's strong sense of time and place allows readers to identify with a character's situation and relate it to their own circumstances (Giorgis & Johnson, 2001a). Identifying a *theme* (the moral or underlying message) can be a personal endeavor, since each reader may perceive a slightly different message, depending on the reader's attitude and prior experiences. Discussing the various *styles of writing* that authors use and their *points of view* helps expand students' understanding and appreciation of literature. Paying attention to all of these elements also benefits students with their own writing. Minilesson 2.1 illustrates how to help students identify a theme.

A **story map** or framework draws students' attention to literary elements by providing an organizational plan. Staal (2000) cites research showing that some form of visualization, such as a graphic representation of story elements, helps readers remember. In order to provide a visual reminder for your students, you could provide a simple framework for literary elements, such as the one in Figure 2.2.

Genres

Children's literature consists of **genres**, or specific kinds, such as poetry or historical fiction. Each genre has unique characteristics and serves a different purpose. Genres provide a way to organize or classify the thousands of children's books available, and you should become familiar with a variety of genres and understand how and when to

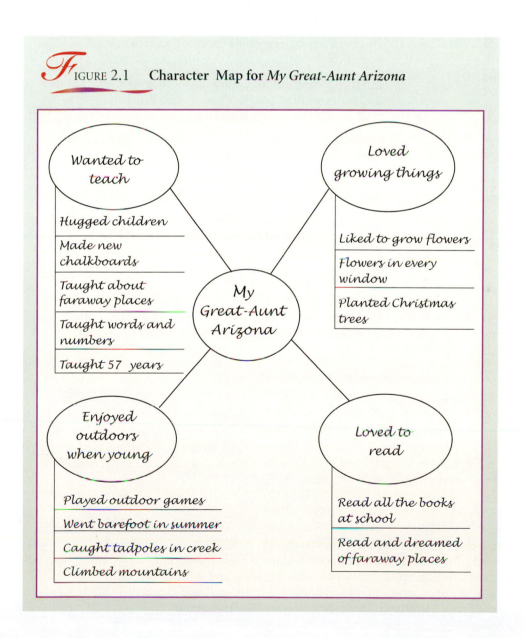

FIGURE 2.1   **Character Map for** *My Great-Aunt Arizona*

Wanted to teach
- Hugged children
- Made new chalkboards
- Taught about faraway places
- Taught words and numbers
- Taught 57 years

Loved growing things
- Liked to grow flowers
- Flowers in every window
- Planted Christmas trees

My Great-Aunt Arizona

Enjoyed outdoors when young
- Played outdoor games
- Went barefoot in summer
- Caught tadpoles in creek
- Climbed mountains

Loved to read
- Read all the books at school
- Read and dreamed of faraway places

Identifying a Theme

Mrs. Reeves has explained to her fifth-graders that the theme of the book is the author's message, but each reader may interpret the theme differently. There is no single correct answer as long as it makes sense. Some books can have many themes. She has just finished reading aloud Vashanti Rahaman's *Read for Me, Mama,* the story of Joseph, a boy who loves to read books, and Mama, who is illiterate. Not realizing his mother cannot read, Joseph begs Mama to read to him until she breaks down and cries, admitting she cannot read. Together they go to a reading class where other parents are also learning to read.

MRS. REEVES: This book has many possible themes. Can someone tell me what you think the author of this book is trying to say?

CLAY: I think it means that there are adults who cannot read, but there are classes for these people. That's a good thing—to help people read, even if they're grown up.

MARVIS: Joseph and Mama seem to be getting closer. Joseph is still learning to read, and now Mama is also learning.

FLORIE: I think how sad it is that Mama has had to get along all her life without knowing how to read. It must have been hard for her to go to the store and to read signs.

BRETT: I wonder if the school didn't teach her right, or if she didn't go to school. Why are there grown-ups who never learned to read?

ELOISE: This story shows us that if we can't do something or don't know something, we can still learn, even when we grow up.

MRS. REEVES: Good ideas! You came up with different answers, but all of them make sense. I like the way you thought about this book.

What are the students learning?

They are learning that it is important to go beyond the literal meaning of a story and think about its underlying message or theme. They are also realizing that it is okay to have different ideas about its theme, that there can be more than one acceptable answer. Each individual is unique and brings certain attitudes and prior experiences to a story that affect the reader's interpretation of the theme.

use them for classroom activities (Hancock, 2000; Harkins, 2001; Popp, 1996; Spillman, 1996). Picture books are available in many genres, and many of these books, especially those with complex and sophisticated themes and with connections to the curriculum, are appropriate for older children (Martinez, Roser, & Strecker, 2000). Genres in children's literature include the following (Norton, 2003).

- *Poetry:* a form of writing characterized by rhyme, rhythm, repetition, and/or imagery
- *Historical fiction:* a fictional story set in the past that brings history alive
- *Contemporary realistic fiction:* a fictional story that could happen in today's world
- *Traditional literature:* folktales that have been handed down orally from generation to generation
- *Modern fantasy:* make-believe tales of unreal worlds, characters, or situations that originated in written form
- *Science fiction:* fiction based on scientific or technological attainments
- *Biography:* true story of all or part of a person's life
- *Informational books:* books that provide accurate information on specific topics

*F*IGURE 2.2   **Story Map for Literary Elements**

Title _____

Author _____

Main characters _____

_____

Setting (time and place) _____

_____

Problem or conflict _____

_____

Event _____

Event _____

Event _____

Solution _____

Theme _____

_____

Children's books fall into three major categories: *fiction*, imaginative, creative books that tell stories and entertain; *nonfiction,* books that provide information about real events, people, or things; and *poetry*, a form characterized by rhythm, rhyme, repetition, and imagery (Popp, 1996).

Text sets are a good way to introduce a variety of genres. They may focus on a theme or topic and may consist of five to ten books of varied reading levels and genres (Giorgis & Johnson, 2002). They can also let students see topics from different perspectives and allow them to investigate a topic thoroughly to get information and generate ideas. Students can brainstorm connections among texts and discuss them, comparing and contrasting information. A text set on the topic of trees or a thematic unit on the environment might consist of the selections in Figure 2.5 that represent different genres and varying reading levels. For upper grades, a text set on the Holocaust offers students insights into a historical period and its effects on people living during that time (see Figure 2.6).

FICTION

Fiction is a *narrative*, or story, intended to entertain. It appears in many forms, including contemporary realistic fiction, fantasy and science fiction, and historical fiction.

A popular genre with children, *contemporary realistic fiction* consists of stories that are realistic, but the stories themselves are not true (Norton, 2003). Plots deal with familiar, everyday situations; characters are realistic in their behaviors; and settings are authentic in our contemporary world. Children can relate to many of the subjects, which include such topics as family life, growing up, survival, and death. Teachers often select realistic chapter books, such as Phyllis Reynolds Naylor's *Shiloh* or Katherine Paterson's *The Great Gilly Hopkins*, to read aloud to their classes.

Classroom Vignette 2.1

Dale Glatthorn has taught his third-graders to identify literary elements in the stories they encounter, and now he wants to give them practice in locating them in the books they are reading. He realizes that many of his students are hands-on learners, so he has made patterns that they can follow to create three-dimensional book reports that focus on the literary elements. He creates a T-shaped pattern with six numbered squares (see Figure 2.3) and asks the students to use the first square for the title, the next for the author, the third for the setting, and the remaining three squares for story events in sequential order. The children may illustrate the story in any remaining space. When they fold the pattern on the lines and glue or staple the tabs, they create a cube. Austin Ashburn, a third-grader, completed the pattern shown in Figure 2.3 for Mary Pope Osborne's *Mummies in the Morning*.

Dale also lets his students make story balls, a more complex activity that involves writing and illus-

FIGURE 2.4   Story Ball

Source: Joseph Stujenske, Sycamore School, Cookeville, TN. Used with permission.

trating literary elements on twelve panels that are stapled together to form a sphere. After reading a book, the child provides the following information on the twelve panels: title, author, illustrator, setting, characters, problem or main idea, two events that occur at the beginning of the story, two that are found in the middle, and two that conclude the story. The child writes a draft before copying the information onto each panel, illustrating it, decorating the edges, and forming the ball. Figure 2.4 shows a beginning event that appears on one panel of a story ball from Kate Duke's *Aunt Isabel Tells a Good One*.

What's happening here?

Children are learning to focus on literary elements in their reading, and they have an opportunity to identify them in an interesting way. Instead of writing book reports, they select the information they need, write it briefly in the correct space, and illustrate it. Since the colorful story balls are often suspended from the ceiling, children take pride in viewing their work and that of others. Such displays motivate them to read books and complete the activities.

FIGURE 2.3   T-Shape for Literary Elements

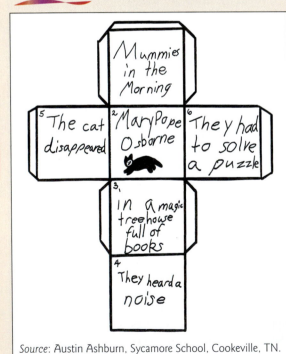

Source: Austin Ashburn, Sycamore School, Cookeville, TN. Used with permission.

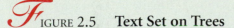

FIGURE 2.5   Text Set on Trees

"Trees," a poem about the loveliness of trees by Joyce Kilmer

Whisper from the Woods, a story that personifies trees by Victoria Wirth

Red Leaf, Yellow Leaf, a blend of fiction and nonfiction by Lois Ehlert

The Giving Tree, a story open to various interpretations by Shel Silverstein

The Great Kapok Tree, an environmental story of the rain forest by Lynne Cherry

Just a Dream, a story about planting a tree and protecting the environment by Chris Van Allsburg

Johnny Appleseed, a legend about planting apple trees, retold and illustrated by Stephen Kellogg

Sky Tree: Seeing Science through Art, paintings of a tree through the seasons by Thomas Locker

A Tree Is Nice, representation of different trees with children playing by Janice Udry

The Tremendous Tree Book, a nonfiction book by Barbara Brenner and May Garelick

FIGURE 2.6   Text Set on the Holocaust

We Are Witnesses: Five Diaries of Teenagers Who Died in the Holocaust, told in diary form by Jacob Boas

I Have Lived a Thousand Years, an autobiography by Livia Bitton-Jackson

Hiding to Survive, first-person accounts of those who resisted the Nazis by Maxine Rosenberg

Memories of Anne Frank, a partial biography by Alison Gold

The Upstairs Room, an autobiography by Johanna Reiss

The Devil's Arithmetic, fictional story of a Jewish girl experiencing the Holocaust by Jane Yolen

We Remember the Holocaust, nonfiction account of the Holocaust by David Adler

Number the Stars, fictional story that takes place during the Nazi occupation of Denmark by Lois Lowry

Modern fantasy often begins with realistic situations and moves into fantasy with the reader scarcely aware that the story is no longer in the realm of reality. According to Norton (2003), one of the greatest requirements of modern fantasy is the author's ability to allow readers to suspend disbelief and consider the possibility that the story could actually have happened. For instance, in Carlo Collodi's *The Adventures of Pinnochio*, Geppetto carves a wooden puppet that comes to life, and in James Barrie's *Peter Pan*, the children fly from their nursery, where their parents have left them, to Never Land with Peter Pan and Tinker Bell.

A form of modern fantasy, *science fiction* is based on current or potential scientific and technological developments. Now a classic in science fiction, Madeleine L'Engle's *A Wrinkle in Time* transports children from their home by means of a wrinkle in time, or a tesseract, to an evil planet in order to seek their missing father. Lois Lowry gives us two examples of science fiction that deal with controlled societies: *The Giver*, the story of Jonas who becomes the Receiver of Memory, and its companion book, *Gathering Blue*, which tells of Kira who possesses a magical talent as a weaver.

Historical fiction brings historical events and people to life. Although the text is essentially fiction, it is authentic in the sense that it usually covers a particular time period or an incident in a famous person's life. Most students find the story lines and in-depth treatments more interesting than brief accounts in textbooks. In Esther Forbes's *Johnny Tremain,* the young hero is an apprentice to Paul Revere, a silversmith, during prerevolutionary days, and Donald Hall's story of *The Ox-Cart Man,* accompanied by Barbara Cooney's beautiful illustrations, shows the cycle of events in the life of a New England farmer during the 1800s.

TRADITIONAL LITERATURE

Traditional tales, often called folklore, represent an interesting genre of fiction for simple enjoyment or in-depth study. Classic stories such as "Cinderella," "Snow White," and "Sleeping Beauty" are favorites with young children, but they also offer middle-grade students a unique way to understand their literary heritage and compare cultures. Some tales appear in nearly every culture (Norton, 2003). Magical objects, names, and settings may differ, but the basic patterns, or motifs, are similar. Many folktale variants passed down by storytellers came into being long ago, and contemporary authors have written modern folktales with new twists.

Comparing and contrasting folktale variants makes an interesting thematic unit. Students must first identify a favorite tale and locate as many versions of it as they can. Then, working in teams, they find the origin of each story, look for cultural features, and compare events, objects, or actions that are relevant to that particular tale. When they have completed their research, they can report their findings to the class in a meaningful way, perhaps as a Microsoft PowerPoint presentation, through art or music, as a video-taped production, or in some other way. The example given in Figure 2.7 shows a way to compare the results of an investigation of the story of "Little Red Riding Hood."

Students can make a similar table for any popular tale that has many versions. Here are some resources for "Cinderella" stories, which have over one thousand versions from around the world (Norton, 2003): Shirley Climo's *The Egyptian Cinderella,* Penny Pollock's *The Turkey Girl* (Zuni), Walt Disney's *Cinderella,* Alan Shroeder's *Smoky Mountain Rose* (Appalachian), Ai-Ling Louie's *Yeh-Shen: A Cinderella Story from China,* Charles Perrault's *Cinderella* (French), Charlotte Huck's *Princess Furball,* and "Aschenputtel" in *Sixty Fairy Tales of the Brothers Grimm* (German).

POETRY

Even though many teachers seem reluctant to teach poetry, this genre offers many benefits and should be part of every teacher's daily repertoire (Hancock, 2000; Perfect, 1999; Tiedt, 2002). Many children come to school already familiar with the rhythm and rhyme of simple poems, so it is natural to expand this fondness for the sounds of language. Tiedt (2002) says that students need the humor and whimsicality of poetry, as well as its serious treatment of feelings and commentaries on life around us. Poetry helps students understand themselves and others, enhances their thinking skills, and develops personal connections to content area subjects (Perfect, 1999). Poetry can be part of the total curriculum by providing perspectives that differ from the typical textbook approach.

Teaching poetry can begin with something as simple as reading poems aloud, for poetry is meant to be heard. Immerse students in all kinds of poems and use them often, perhaps first thing in the morning, when you have a few minutes before the buses

*F*IGURE 2.7   Comparison of Versions of "Little Red Riding Hood"

	Setting	What LRRH* took to Grandma	What happened to LRRH and Grandma (or Mother)	What happens to wolf	Moral**	Interesting features
Red Riding Hood (Marshall)	Deep, dark woods	Custard	Wolf eats them. Hunter cuts wolf open. They jump out.	Hunter kills him.	Yes	Granny says it's too dark inside to read a book.
Red Riding Hood (de Regniers)	Woods	Little cake	Wolf eats them. Hunter cuts wolf open. They jump out.	Hunter kills him. Fills with stones; wolf drops dead.	No	Written as a poem.
Little Red Riding Hood (Ernst)	Prairie, fields with crops	Wheat berry muffins, lemonade	Granny opens muffin store; LRRH delivers muffins.	Granny grabs him, scolds him, takes him home.	Yes	Contemporary Midwestern setting.
Lon Po Po (Young)	Country– side of northern China		Children and Mother safe at home.	Falls from tree, dies	No	Wolf visits three daughters; Caldecott winner.
Little Red Riding Hood (Hyman)	Middle of forest	Bread, butter, wine	Wolf ate them. They come out of wolf.	Hunter cuts wolf open, fills with stones; wolf drops dead.	Yes	Richly illustrated borders; Caldecott runner-up.
Little Red Riding Hood (Rowland)	Forest	Honey cakes, oranges	Wolf ate them. They come out.	Hunter cuts wolf open; fills with stones; wolf drops dead.	Yes	Reverse side of book gives wolf's point of view.

*LRRH stands for "Little Red Riding Hood."
**Moral refers to whether or not LRRH admits to learning a lesson at the end.

come in the afternoon to pick up the children, or during a thematic unit. Keeping a card file of favorite poems or purchasing a children's poetry anthology helps you to have the right poem for any occasion. Children prefer poems that are funny, have a story element, and are contemporary, but are less likely to enjoy poems with extensive imagery (Norton, 2003; Tiedt, 2002). Encourage students to recite poems, sing poems set to music, clap the rhythm, and engage in choral speaking or Readers Theatre (discussed on page 63). Move them gradually into discussing the imagery of poems, encouraging them to visualize what might be happening and how this relates to their lives. Share your own feelings about poems and encourage them to share theirs. Introduce them to writing poetry, beginning with easy forms such as unrhymed listings and free verse, and help them express their thoughts and feelings with language from the heart. Rhyme is not important, but emotion is. In response to the Mexican folktale *Mediopollito Half-Chicken,* written in Spanish and English by Alma Flor Ada, fourth-grader Adrienne wrote a poem about fire (see Figure 2.8). The folktale tells of the power of wind, fire, and water. (See Chapter 9 for more discussion of poetry writing and more examples of poetry written by children.)

Reflections

How do you feel about poetry? When you were in school, how did teachers share poetry with you? What positive experiences have you had with poetry? How would you like to share poetry with your class?

NONFICTION

Nonfiction, consisting of biography and other informational books, is another form of literature that is often neglected. **Twin texts,** sometimes referred to as paired books, lead children from fiction into nonfiction by pairing related books, one of fiction and one of fact. An authentic way to introduce content material, twin texts form a bridge from reading stories to understanding subjects in all areas of the curriculum (Camp, 2000). The fiction book gives lived-through experiences in a familiar format, and the informational book provides background knowledge to deepen understanding. You can often entice children who think they prefer fiction to read nonfiction by putting these books together. Create your own pairs of books or purchase them from various publishers, including Steck-Vaughn (Pair-It Books, P.O. Box 26015, Austin, TX 78755) and The Wright Group (19201 120th Avenue NE, Bothell, WA 98011-9512). Figure 2.9 gives some examples of twin texts, with the first book being fiction and the second one nonfiction.

Biography appeals to many students because it deals with the lives of real people, including famous historical persons, athletes, and heroes. Taylor (2002/2003) points out

FIGURE 2.8   Poem about Fire

Fire Fire
Wonderful Fire
lighting the dusky sky at night
You dazzel in the dark
Your hot and you hurt
But your beneficial
Fire woderful Fire

Source: Adrienne Ballard, Northeast Elementary School, Cookeville, TN. Used with permission.

Applications *for English Language Learners*

Poetry is particularly effective with ELLs because of its unique qualities, such as brevity, strong rhythm, powerful imagery, focused content, and strong emotional connection (Hadaway, Vardell, & Young, 2001). Choral reading and other ways of sharing poetry orally provide language practice in a setting that is pleasurable and relaxed so that all students can participate equally while enjoying the playfulness and power of language.

that investigating the lives of other people enables students to expand their knowledge about themselves, other people, and the surrounding world while refining their literacy skills. She also finds that biography study supports the Standards for the English Language Arts by encouraging exploration of a wide range of materials in a variety of genres and covering many time periods. Taylor uses two activities that cause students to think about the characters they are investigating. One strategy requires students to prepare Literary Expense Accounts by studying a character's personality traits and

 IGURE 2.9   **Twin Texts**

Mary Hoffman, *Amazing Grace*, and Ruby Bridges, *Through My Eyes*, both with African American heroines. Grace convinces people that she should be Peter Pan in the school play, and Ruby gives the true story of how she braved angry mobs to enter an all-white school.

Mary-Louise Gay, *Angel and the Polar Bear*, and Carolyn Lesser, *Great Crystal Bear*, both about polar bears. The first book is the humorous relationship between a girl named Angel and a polar bear, and the second is the life story of a great polar bear.

Patricia McKissack, *Flossie and the Fox*, and Elizabeth Russell-Arnot, *Foxes*. Feisty Flossie outwits the fox as she carries a basket of eggs. Through colorful photos and text, *Foxes* presents information about foxes.

Lois Lowry, *Number the Stars*, and Anne Frank, *The Diary of a Young Girl*, both about the Nazis in World War II. Annemarie emerges as a heroine during the Nazi occupation of Denmark in a historical fiction book, and Anne Frank writes about her real-life experiences while being concealed during the war.

Karen Hesse, *Out of the Dust*, and Jerry Stanley, *Children of the Dust Bowl*, both about the Depression-era life for children from Oklahoma. Hesse's fictional account was a Newbery Medal winner. Stanley tells his story largely through actual words of migrants and period photographs.

Students are selecting biographical and informational books as resources for their unit.

priorities. They then make pie graphs that show how they think each individual would likely spend money. In Link-up, the other activity, students list traits for their selected individuals from the biographies they read, and then they read newspapers and magazines to try to match each individual with a contemporary who has similar traits.

Excellent biographies are available for all ages, and they can be used for recreational reading, for instructional purposes, and as resources for thematic units. In *Lincoln: A Photobiography,* Russell Freedman carefully documents Abraham Lincoln's life, using photographs and excerpts of his actual writings to supplement the text. Jean Fritz humanizes the characters she addresses, such as Sam Houston and Theodore Roosevelt, by including humorous anecdotes and relating their faults as well as their strengths. Peter Sis's beautifully illustrated *Starry Messenger* is the story of Galileo Galilei, revolutionary astronomer who lived 350 years ago, and Marie Bradby's *More Than Anything Else* shows us how desperately Booker T. Washington wanted to learn to read during his early years spent slaving in the saltworks. Through his richly illustrated biography *Coming Home,* Floyd Cooper tells us how Langston Hughes dreamed of having a real home, and in *Emily,* Michael Bedard gives us a glimpse into the reclusive life of Emily Dickinson. In her autobiography *Through My Eyes,* Ruby Bridges shares her scary experience of being the first African American child to enter an all-white school in Louisiana in 1960. *Ten Queens: Portraits of Women in Power* by Milton Meltzer presents brief biographies of ten of the most powerful women in history, including Eleanor of Aquitaine.

Researchers are finding that nonfiction often does not get the attention it deserves in elementary classrooms. Duke's study of informational texts in first grade found a scarcity of these materials, and she discovered that an average of only 3.6 minutes daily was spent with informational texts (2000). She believes, however, that using informational texts in the early grades may improve later performance in language arts and content area work. Dreher (1998/1999) reports that students perform better with narratives than with informational texts, and she finds that they encounter nonfiction less often than fiction in the elementary grades. She concludes that children need more exposure to nonfiction. Likewise, Moss and Hendershot (2002) find that nonfiction seldom appears in intermediate classrooms, even though many middle-graders may prefer reading informational texts. In a study of elementary students, Block, Reed, and deTuncq (2003) found that the reading of two nonfiction books on the same topic back to back increased students' immediate identification and recall of main ideas and details and also improved their higher level thinking skills.

Teaching Tip

Instead of adhering closely to textbooks, use a variety of nonfiction trade books, which are more likely to capture students' interest. Children absorb and retain information more easily when they are intrigued by the text.

 *Applications* **for English Language Learners and Students with Special Needs**

Multimedia technology may facilitate English language acquisition among ELLs and help students with special needs. Many electronic, interactive books allow students to listen to stories in Spanish or Japanese (Labbo, Reinking, & McKenna, 1999). Discis Books produces interactive storybooks that appear on screen as pages with illustrations, music, sound effects, animation, and voices. These electronic books also encourage discussions and social interactions among students (Morrow & Gambrell, 2001).

Technology

Nonfiction offers many benefits for young students (Dreher, 1998/1999; Harvey, 1998; Harvey, 2002; Moss & Hendershot, 2002). Books are more appealing than ever before with attractive illustrations, a wide range of topics, and a variety of reading levels that meet the interests and abilities of nearly every student. Biographies and informational books complement textbooks, which students often find dull. Nonfiction can satisfy curiosity, expand vocabulary, help readers grasp new concepts, provide information, enhance understanding, and serve as a model for student writing.

Encourage children to read nonfiction by reading it aloud, giving book talks, and forming book clubs or study groups around a common interest. Encourage children to choose nonfiction for their free reading time, and make sure you have a wide selection of informational material readily accessible. Many excellent children's informational magazines are also available (see Figure 2.10), and their format may be more appealing than books for some readers.

To find out if students could enjoy nonfiction as much as fiction, Ross (2001) conducted a study with second-, fourth-, and sixth-graders. Lessons varied from simply reading and discussing books to extending information across the curriculum. Teachers found that all eighty-four of the students studied liked listening to nonfiction books, but few preferred nonfiction over fiction. Benefits of using nonfiction included expanding students' interests, integrating the curriculum, learning through inquiry, and collaborating with the media specialist. The teachers recommended alternating genres instead of focusing on just nonfiction, using recent and appealing books, reading selectively instead of from cover to cover, ordering class sets of nonfiction, and correlating nonfiction with thematic units.

Multicultural Literature

Available in all genres, **multicultural literature** represents the beliefs, customs, and experiences of people from different nationalities and races (Harris & Hodges, 1995). Ann Morris has written a series of multicultural books illustrated with photographs, with each book focusing on a different topic, such as hats, bread, or transportation around the world, and Mary Lankford authored *Hopscotch*, which shows nineteen ways to play hopscotch in different countries. Children need to see themselves in books; when they do not see themselves represented, they are likely to become frustrated (Hefflin &

FIGURE 2.10   Children's Nonfiction Magazines

Calliope World History for Kids, Cobblestone Publishing, 7 School Road, Peterborough, NH 03458. www.cobblestonepub.com. World history. (Ages 9-14)

Chickadee, 49 Front Street East, #200, Toronto, ON, Canada M5E 1B3. www.owlkids.com. Science and nature, hands-on activities. (Ages 6-9)

Cobblestone, Cobblestone Publishing, 7 School Street, Peterborough, NH 03458. www.cobblestonepub.com. American history. (Ages 9-15)

Faces: People, Places, and Culture, Cobblestone Publishing, 7 School Street, Peterborough, NH 03458. www.cobblestonepub.com. World cultures. (Ages 9-14)

National Geographic for Kids, PO Box 63002, Tampa, FL 33663-3002. www.nationalgeographic.com/education. Geography, science. (Ages 8 and up)

Owl, 49 Front Street East, #200, Toronto, ON, Canada M5E 1B3. www.owlkids.com. Science, nature, environment, and how things work. (Ages 9-13)

Ranger Rick, National Wildlife Federation, PO Box 2038, Harlan, IA 51593. www.nwf.org/kids. Nature, environment, outdoors, animal photos. (Ages 7-12)

Scholastic News, Scholastic Magazines (several options), PO Box 3710, Jefferson City, MO 65102-3710. http://teacher.scholastic.com/products/classmags/index.htm. Math, news, current events, home economics, social studies. (Separate editions for different grade levels)

Sports Illustrated for Kids, PO Box 60001, Tampa, FL 33660. www.sikids.com. Sports news, articles, and photos. (Ages 8-15)

Time for Kids, PO Box 60001, Tampa, FL 33660. www.timeforkids.com. Current events, sports, entertainment, and games. (Separate editions for grades K-1, 2-3, and 4-7)

Weekly Reader, 200 Stamford Place, PO Box 120023, Stamford, CT 06912-0023. www.weeklyreader.com. World and national news and current events. (Separate editions for grades K-12)

Your Big Backyard, National Wildlife Federation, PO Box 2038, Harlan, IA 51593. www.nwf.org/kids. Nature and conservation, animal photos. (Ages 3-7)

Zoobooks, Wildlife Education Ltd.,12233 Thatcher Court, Poway, CA 92064. www.zoobooks.com. Facts and photos about animals. (Ages 4-11)

Source: Based on information from Kletzien, S., & Dreher, M. (2004), *Informational text in K–3 classrooms* (Newark, DE: International Reading Association); and Kristo, J., & Bamford, R. (2004), *Nonfiction in focus* (New York: Scholastic).

Barksdale-Ladd, 2001). Multicultural literature offers opportunities for all children to do the following (Norton, 2001; Opitz, 1999):

- Identify with characters
- Consider different points of view
- Recognize similarities and differences among people
- Become part of an interracial community
- Respect the contributions of individuals from different cultural and ethnic groups
- Identify cultural heritages

When selecting multicultural literature, choose books with well-developed characters who are portrayed in authentic, realistic settings (Hefflin & Barksdale-Ladd, 2001). Avoid stereotypes that tend to generalize characteristics of certain groups, and instead look for authenticity of values, beliefs, and cultural backgrounds. We briefly consider four major ethnic groups here: African American, Native American, Latino, and Asian American.

AFRICAN AMERICAN The number of African American children's books has steadily increased in recent years (Hefflin & Barksdale-Ladd, 2001; Norton, 2001), and a number of outstanding authors and illustrators have emerged. Themes in picture storybooks include reliving the past through stories, realizing that black is powerful and wonderful, knowing that changes are part of living, and learning that life is precious (Norton, 2001). Patricia Polacco's *Pink and Say* is a touching fictionalized historical account of how an African American boy befriended a Caucasian boy during the Civil War. Virginia Hamilton's fine novels about African Americans include *The House of Dies Drear*, a suspenseful story related to slavery and the Underground Railroad, and *Zeely*, a novel that leads to the realization that who a person is inside is most important.

Another book with African American characters, Valerie Flournoy's *The Patchwork Quilt*, tells the contemporary realistic story of how Tanya helped finish a special quilt when Grandma got sick. Third-grade teacher Linda Lee developed a thematic unit centered around this book and taught her students about quilts—how they are made, their uses, the designs, and so forth. Linda's students created their own patches as part of an art project and wrote personal responses to the story. Daron responded by using the new word *masterpiece*, identifying with the character's illness, and giving his recommendation (see Figure 2.11). For another activity, Linda asked the children to compare *The Patchwork Quilt* with Barbara Smucker's *Selina and the Bear Paw Quilt*, using semantic feature analysis. Figure 2.12 shows how children compared the two books (+ means same; – means different).

NATIVE AMERICAN Traditional literature is vitally important to Native Americans because it reflects their values and heritage. These values include living in harmony with nature, viewing religion as closely related to nature, and respecting elders (Norton, 2001). Examples of Native American traditional literature include Jamake Highwater's *Anpao: An American Indian Odyssey* and Barbara Esbensen's *The Star Maiden*. Stephen Krensky's *Children of the Wind and Water*, an example of historical fiction, tells five stories of Native American children living almost two hundred years ago who shared some activities in common, such as hunting and carving, even though they came from different tribes. *Dancing Teepees: Poems of American Indian Youth* by Virginia Driving Hawk Sneve is a collection of traditional, authentic poems in the form of chants, songs, and prayers from various tribes.

F IGURE 2.11   **Response to *The Patchwork Quilt***

The Patchwork Quilt
Author-Valerie Flourpay
Illustrator-Jerry Pinkney

This story is about a masterpiece quilt
that Grandma and Tanya wants to make.
All the family helps make the quilt and
they get put into the quilt. I think I would
love the quilt. One day Grandma
became ill, and I felt sad because I don't
like it when I'm ill. I like this story, I think
other people should read it.

Source: Daron Bushy, Jere Whitson School, Cookeville, TN. Used with permission.

L ATINO   Latino literature comes from the people of Latin America and South America, but, despite the rapidly growing number of Latinos, there are fewer books about them than about African Americans and Native Americans. Many contemporary books portray themes that deal with overcoming problems (Norton, 2001). Gary Soto, a favorite

Applications

for English Language Learners

ELLs benefit from listening to stories, particularly those that enable them to relate to their own cultures in terms of characters and settings. These students often become aware of the structure and cadences of language by listening to good literature read by proficient readers. Familiarity with the culture is likely to make the stories more comprehensible to the students, and sharing responses during the group discussion that follows helps them develop their English (Searfoss, Readence, & Mallette, 2001).

FIGURE 2.12   Semantic Feature Analysis for Comparing Two Books

Name of book	Main character is a girl	Past setting	Present setting	Main character helps make the quilt	Main character is given the quilt	The Grandmother is the quilt designer	Family lives in the city	Has a special design pattern quilt	Has random design style quilt
Selina and the Bear Paw Quilt	+	+	−	−	+	+	−	+	−
The Patchwork Quilt	+	−	+	+	+	+	+	−	+

Source: Linda Lee's class, Jere Whitson School, Cookeville, TN. Used with permission.

Latino author, wrote *Too Many Tamales,* which tells about losing and then attempting to find a ring on Christmas Eve. Soto also authored *Baseball in April and Other Stories,* a collection of short stories portraying Latino children and adolescents in their daily lives. The illustrations in Carmen Garza's *Family Pictures,* written in Spanish and English, reveal activities on various family and neighborhood occasions. For older students, James Watson's *Talking in Whispers,* a survival story, tells how the main character is pursued by the inhumane security forces of a South American government.

ASIAN AMERICAN Asian American literature covers the diverse cultural heritage of such countries as Japan, Korea, China, Vietnam, and India. It also shows how Asian immigrants try to preserve their previous culture while adapting to a new land (Norton, 2001). Yin's *Coolies,* based on actual events in the history of the American railroad, depicts the harsh truth about the lives of Chinese laborers who came to the United States hoping for a better life. Edna Coe Bercaw's *Halmoni's Day* is the realistic fictional story of a Korean grandmother who at first embarrasses Jennifer but later earns her love and respect. Older students who read Laurence Yep's *Dragonwings* learn the true story of a Chinese American who built and flew an airplane in 1903 in San Francisco.

Presenting Literature to Children

Nothing rivals sharing good books with children for relieving stressful situations, building a class community, and simply bonding. You and your class will discover that you share common emotions by laughing at a ridiculous situation, weeping over a loss, or eagerly anticipating the next event in a story. Whether you are empathizing with poor Alexander during his very bad day (in Judith Viorst's *Alexander and the Terrible, Horrible, No Good, Very Bad Day*), chuckling with Brer Rabbit as he tricks Brer Fox in the Uncle

Remus tales, or laughing hysterically at some of the situations in Richard Peck's *A Year Down Yonder*, you are creating memories and instilling a love for literature.

Selecting Literature for Students

Of the thousands of books available for students, how do you select the ones that are right for your class? Browsing through books at a bookstore or library gives you some ideas, but other guides are available as well. You may want to look at award-winning books. The Caldecott Award is given to the illustrator of the best picture book for children, and the Newbery Award is given for the most distinguished contribution to children's literature. Both awards are given annually to an illustrator (Caldecott) or author (Newbery) within the United States, and both awards have runners-up, which are also excellent possibilities. The Coretta Scott King Award is given to one black author and one black illustrator for inspirational contributions to children's literature. Children's Choices is a list of favorite books for beginning, young, and intermediate readers that has been compiled from the votes of ten thousand schoolchildren from different regions of the United States (IRA/CBC, 2002). Teachers' Choices is a list of books that teachers have identified as exceptional for curriculum use and reading aloud (IRA, 2002). Both lists are published annually in *The Reading Teacher*. In addition, you might want to select classics that you consider part of a child's literary heritage or books that represent different cultures or promote certain social values. *The Horn Book Magazine, Language Arts, Book Links, Childhood Education, The Reading Teacher*, and the *Journal of Adolescent & Adult Literacy* are periodicals that keep teachers informed about new books through reviews and articles. Commercial book clubs, such as Scholastic (1-800-SCH-2222 or http://www.scholastic.com) or Troll (1-800-454-8765 or http://www.troll.com), offer selections monthly for you and your students. Many of these selections include award-winning and high-quality books at discounted prices, and you can accumulate bonus points to redeem for additional selections. In choosing material to use in your classes, ask yourself the questions that appear in Figure 2.13.

Build your class library with quality books from many sources, perhaps discount stores or garage sales, if your funds are limited. You may want to borrow books from the school library or from other teachers so that the selection is constantly changing. Make your library an attractive place where children can browse and read in comfortable surroundings. Colorful rugs or carpet squares, displays, posters, floor cushions, and elevated "reading roosts" entice children to sit or lie down and read.

Children need more than a wide selection of books and a comfortable place to read; they also need time to read. **SSR (Sustained Silent Reading)** or **DEAR (Drop Everything And Read)** is a period of time set aside when both you and the children read without interruption (Anderson, 2000; Tre-

Reflections

What books do you want to include most of all in your class library? Why are these selections important to you? How will you get them? What do you remember about your class libraries in elementary school?

Teaching Tip

Get to know the media specialist in your school and ask for help in finding twin texts, checking out sets of books related to a theme, and selecting good books to read aloud. The media specialist is usually eager to help if you ask.

 IGURE 2.13   **Questions about Book Selection**

1. Do the books represent people from a variety of racial and ethnic backgrounds without stereotyping them?

2. Do the books show people of both sexes in a variety of roles?

3. Are the elderly and people with disabilities represented in the materials?

4. Is the collection balanced, with both old favorites and new material included?

5. Does the collection include poetry, fiction, and nonfiction on topics covering a wide range of interests?

6. Are there high-quality books by respected authors and illustrators?

7. Is there a range of reading levels appropriate for my class?

8. Is a variety of media represented (e.g., magazines and interactive electronic books)?

Technology

lease, 1995). You may start with only a few minutes at first and gradually build up to longer periods of time, such as fifteen to twenty minutes. Seeing you silently reading something of interest and obviously enjoying it helps children realize that reading is for everyone, not just children. Readers may select magazines, newspapers, or any type of book that they prefer and read at their own speed. Some inquisitive students may be fascinated by David Macaulay's *The Way Things Work* or Richard Platt's *Stephen Biesty's Incredible Cross-Sections,* whereas others are happily immersed in the Babysitters Club series. Children may volunteer to share what they have read during this time but are not required to do so. Do not question them, test them, or assign any follow-up activities. As a result of this opportunity to read purely for pleasure, students are likely to improve their reading and learn to love to read.

Teaching Tip

Advise students who have trouble selecting books at an appropriate reading level to apply the "rule of the thumb" (Veatch, 1968). Say to the students: Choose an interesting book, select a page in the middle that has a lot of words on it, read the page, and hunt for unknown words. Put your thumb down on the table for the first word you don't know and a finger down for each other word you don't know on that page. If you put all of your fingers down, the book is probably too hard and you should select another book.

Story Reading and Storytelling

No single activity appears to be more productive for developing language than reading aloud to children. In *Becoming a Nation of Readers*, Anderson and colleagues (1985, p. 23) state, "The single most important activity for building the knowledge required for eventual success in reading is reading aloud to children." Although story reading and storytelling may be viewed as entertainment, they may be the most important part of the school day. Listening to stories draws children to quality literature that they might never discover on their own. After hearing a spellbinding tale or a poem filled with strong rhythms and powerful images, children often choose to read similar materials for themselves.

Read stories to children that they either cannot or will not read for themselves. Many picture books are too difficult for young children to read independently, and older students may think old classics are dull choices. By choosing books such as these to read aloud in whole or part, you are introducing them to books they may later select for themselves.

To enrich the curriculum, you may choose to read *The King Who Rained* by Fred Gwynne as an introduction to a lesson on multiple-meaning words or homonyms, the poem "Sick" by Shel Silverstein in *Where the Sidewalk Ends* to develop critical thinking, one of many stories about Davy Crockett to create interest in studying the people who defended the Alamo, or Jonathan London's *The Eyes of Gray Wolf* to understand the habits of wolves running free in Alaska. These books can make content lessons meaningful or simply provide enjoyment. (More on using literature to enhance the curriculum is found in Chapter 12.)

You may prefer to tell stories, and children enjoy listening to stories that are told. As one first-grader said, "I like it when you tell stories straight from your face." Similarly, even active middle schoolers will settle down to listen to an interesting story. Storytelling requires preparation. Select a story that you like and read it over several times until you have learned it well. Do not memorize it, except for a few phrases or rhymes that are essential to the story. Visualize the setting, action, and characters. Then relax, tell the story directly to the children, and enjoy it along with them.

Reading aloud is an enjoyable experience for both the reader and the listener, and it offers rich rewards in terms of developing positive attitudes toward learning to read. The reader should always choose a favorite selection, even an older book fondly remembered from childhood, because the children will sense the

Reflections

Why do you think reading aloud to children could be the most important activity for building the knowledge required for eventual success in reading? Was it important for you?

Students listen intently as their teacher shares a favorite story.

reader's enthusiasm when it is read aloud. They will often want to examine the illustrations or read it for themselves if the book is made available. Few activities can surpass reading aloud in terms of ease of preparation and presentation, developing language skills, creating an awareness of story structure, building a classroom community, and creating interest in learning to read and write.

Reflections

Think of some books that you loved as a child. Why were they so special for you? Who read them to you, or did you read them yourself? What do you remember about them?

Reader Response

WHATEVER WE read, it is the response that matters, whether it is silent or shared, written or spoken. Without response, reading is flat, but with response it is rich and brimming with life. Printed words mean little to us until we reflect on them, connect them to our experiences, and construct meaning from them. In recent years, educators have had much to say about reader response.

Reader Response Theory

Louise Rosenblatt, a leader in **reader response theory**, believes that reading is a transaction between the reader and the text (1978, 1995). Meaning results from what the author says and how the reader interprets it. According to Rosenblatt (1978, p. 18), "The transactional phrasing of the reading process underlines the essential importance of both elements, reader and text, in any reading event." She also states (1995, p. 26), "The relation between reader and signs on the page proceeds in a to-and-fro spiral, in which each is continually being affected by what the other has contributed." The transaction occurs as a result of the life experiences that the reader brings to the text and the truly personal response that the literature evokes (Hancock, 2000). This means that each of us constructs meaning slightly differently because of who we have become and what the text means to us personally.

According to Rosenblatt (1978, 1995), readers respond to a text along a continuum marked by **efferent**, or informational, responses at one end and by **aesthetic**, or emotional, responses at the other. A reader assumes an efferent stance when focusing on facts, analyzing material, and obtaining information, but takes an aesthetic stance when dealing with feelings, attitudes, and lived-through experiences. It is not uncommon to shift from one position along the continuum to another while reading. Although emotional or aesthetic involvement is usually associated with fiction, Moss and Hendershot (2002) point out that children may also read high-quality nonfiction aesthetically.

Carolyn Lesser's *Storm on the Desert* is a good example of a book that can be appreciated from both an efferent and an aesthetic stance. The poetic language quickly moves us into feeling the dry, cracked, parched earth of the desert and the thirst of the plants and animals that inhabit it. Then, as clouds gather and distant lightning flashes, we feel the excitement of the approaching storm. Winds blow, whipping the plants, and sheets of rain pelt the earth. Soon rivulets become cascades, then torrents. Suddenly, the storm is gone and the earth is refreshed. Plants soak up the water and animals refresh themselves from the puddles that remain. From this book we learn a great deal about the desert—the creatures that live in it and the cycle of a rain storm—but we also experience the feelings generated by a gathering storm, the powerful force of rain, and the calm that follows.

Another example of a book that can be read from both an efferent and aesthetic stance is Christopher Paul Curtis's *Bud, Not Buddy.* Readers learn about the conditions in which some people lived during the Great Depression of the 1930s. At the same time, the author explores Bud's feelings as he waits in line for food at missions and later as he discovers the world of jazz bands in his search for his father.

Typically, teachers ask efferent questions to check comprehension. These are usually quick, objective questions—the *who, what, where,* and *when* questions that are essential for literal understanding. Aesthetic questions are more difficult to phrase and to assess because they address the reader's thoughts and feelings. Figure 2.14 gives some examples of aesthetic questions.

Rosenblatt's work has inspired educators to develop reading approaches that examine the relationship between the reader and the text. Jewell & Pratt (1999) began using an approach with their second- and third-graders that focused on allowing students to choose their own books and engage in discussions based on their individual responses

*F*IGURE 2.14   **Examples of Aesthetic Questions**

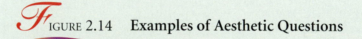

1. Which character do you identify with most?

2. What thoughts occur to you as you are reading?

3. How does the author make you feel the way you do?

4. What part seems especially real to you?

5. How could you enter into this story?

6. What part causes you to react strongly (to be happy, disappointed, angry, upset, or something else)?

7. Did you ever live through a similar experience? What was it like?

8. What words do you find especially unusual or interesting?

9. How might you illustrate this story?

10. How would you share it with others?

11. Does this selection remind you of anything else, perhaps a television show, a video, an experience, or another book?

12. What new insights or ideas did you gain from reading this selection?

Source: Based on Ross, E. (1998). *Pathways to Thinking.* Norwood, MA: Christopher-Gordon.

to their selections. At the beginning of the year, teachers talked with children about the kinds of thinking that occur during reading. After reading aloud, teachers encouraged children to ask questions about the story, share thoughts about a character's actions, tell how they were able to make predictions, and discuss personal connections. This whole-class literature study included reading, writing responses, and discussing. Later in the year, teachers divided their classes into halves, then into small groups, where children responded to the text and to each other's responses. Children's responses reflected the transaction between the reader and the text, as well as between each child's response and the responses of her or his peers. Overall, the teachers observed the following outcomes: quality student-led discussions; more inferential thinking, opinion statements, and connections with the interpretations of their peers; greater use of supporting evidence; and increased motivation.

Also basing their work on Rosenblatt and other researchers of reader response, Lehr and Thompson (2000) analyzed the responses of two ethnically diverse fifth-grade classes. They asked children to read and respond to *The Friendship* by Mildred Taylor and *Maniac Magee* by Jerry Spinelli, two books that explore racial prejudice, discrimination, and segregation. They classified the responses into three major categories: literal, consisting of concrete statements about the text; inferential, involving making inferences about characters' acts through personal perceptions; and moral response, a means for examining moral issues. The researchers found that children could interpret problems that the characters faced, and that their interpretations reflected their own life experiences and personal understanding of the world.

One widely used commercial program offers an extensive selection of books; provides short, factual tests over the books; awards points for correct answers; and rewards children with incentives, such as prizes and recognition. This program motivates children to read, but, as used in many classrooms, fails to provide opportunities for thoughtful responses. Obviously, children need to get the facts as they read, but they also need time to reflect on what they read to receive the full benefit from literature. You should supplement such programs with in-depth study of selected literature.

Ways to Respond to Literature

Children learn in different ways and have different strengths, so you should provide a variety of ways for them to show their understanding and appreciation of literature, including drawing pictures, acting out parts of a story, discussing books, or writing responses in journals. Whatever the form of response, it should be reflective, thoughtful, or personally meaningful in some way.

Children need a variety of ways of thinking about and responding to literature across multiple **sign systems,** or different ways of knowing (Short, Kauffman, & Kahn, 2000). These systems are ways people share and make meaning (Short, Harste, & Burke, 1996). Students read and discuss literature, glean understandings from it, and express their ideas through art, music, drama, or math, as well as through speech and writing. As they transfer understandings from one sign system to another,

Teaching Tip

Sometimes extensive projects consume valuable time that is better used reading, reflecting, and discussing. Be sure that the activity advances the appreciation of the literary selection enough to warrant the time and effort. Also, don't plan an activity as a response for every book that is read. Sometimes children want to listen or read simply for personal enjoyment.

they see additional possibilities and generate new ideas so that their understandings of the literature selection become more complex. They are using these sign systems as tools for thinking instead of simply giving book presentations or doing activities.

LISTENING BEHAVIOR

The earliest and most natural form of response is listening, which may generate physical, spontaneous, and participatory reactions (Hancock, 2000). Young children may crowd closer to examine the illustrations, clap in delight, join in on repetitive phrases, move like a story character, or giggle at silly talk. Older students lose themselves while listening to books that cause them to shed a tear, sigh in relief, chuckle at ridiculous situations, empathize with a character, or marvel at amazing facts or feats. Active listening is the foundation for a variety of other responses.

ORAL RESPONSES TO LITERATURE

For most children, oral responses to literature come naturally. During class discussions they are eager to share their views. From such social interactions they gain insights into other points of view that enhance their own interpretations. They become aware of nuances that they may have missed. As the teacher, you can facilitate discussion by helping readers visualize the story, think critically about it, and respond aesthetically and/or efferently. In addition, you can encourage readers to think about the themes, as in Minilesson 2.1 earlier in this chapter, consider the growth and realism of characters, analyze the effects of the setting on the story, identify the problem, and reflect on events leading to its solution. Johnson and Giorgis (2001) endorse literature-based discussions because they give readers opportunities to identify with characters and situations. They suggest choosing books that invite readers to "dip beyond the surface"—those that have compelling characters, reflect childhood concerns, and deal with tough choices to encourage such discussions.

To move past spontaneous comments about literature, you may want to use prompts to facilitate a more structured oral response (Hancock, 2000). These **prompts** are open-ended questions that call for unique, individual responses. Students are not limited to right or wrong answers, but are encouraged to interpret literature from their own perspectives. Figure 2.15 is a list of books that stimulate thinking, along with brief annotations and prompts for each selection. Although these selections are picture books, students of any age can explore their themes and issues.

Student-led discussions are based on the ideas and thoughts of other participants and provide opportunities for deep thinking and free, unique expression (Hancock, 2000). Based on Rosenblatt's theory that reading is a transaction, Bond (2001) implemented student-led book groups in which students could interpret books differently and help each other deepen understandings. She established five roles designed to invite different interpretations of texts and provide some structure for discussion. She facilitated the experience by modeling these roles and brainstorming guidelines for reading and discussion with the students. The roles are as follows:

1. *Discussion director:* asks thinking questions that require the group to explore different feelings and perspectives

2. *Passage master:* identifies passages that might be funny, interesting, confusing, or important to reread to the group

 IGURE 2.15   **Thinking about Literature**

Ackerman, Karen. *Song and Dance Man.* (Scholastic, 1988). Children discover that their grandfather is a talented and entertaining person. *What older people do you know who are active and interesting company? Why do you enjoy being with them?*

Bradby, Marie. *More Than Anything Else.* (Orchard, 1995). Booker T. Washington works in the saltworks but is determined to learn to read. *Are determination and ambition good qualities? Can you be or do anything you set your mind to?*

Bunting, Eve. *Swan in Love.* (Atheneum, 2000). Despite the ridicule of the other animals, Swan persists in his adoration of a swan-shaped boat named Dora. *What does it mean to love someone? How can we show our love? Who loves you?*

Cherry, Lynne. *The Great Kapok Tree.* (Harcourt Brace Jovanovich, 1990). The various animals that live in a great kapok tree convince a man not to cut down their home. *How can we protect our environment? Why is it important for our survival?*

Johnston, Tony. *Amber on the Mountain.* (Dial, 1994). Isolated on her mountain, Amber befriends a girl from the city who helps her learn to read and write. *How could a book make Amber feel less lonely? Why is it important to have friends? How can we make and keep friends? What is a good friend?*

Lucado, Max. *You Are Special.* (Scholastic, 1997). The Wemmicks gave dots to underachievers like Punchinello, but Eli tells him that what others think doesn't matter. *Do we label underachievers in some way? Is this fair? How does it make them feel?*

MacLachlan, Patricia. *All the Places to Love.* (HarperCollins, 1994). A young boy describes the favorite places on his grandparents' farm. *What are some of your favorite places? Why do they mean so much to you?*

McCully, Emily. *Mirette on the High Wire.* (Scholastic, 1992). Mirette gives Bellini, a retired high-wire walker, courage to walk the wire again. *What is courage? Do you have it? How can we help other people by offering encouragement and support?*

McKee, David. *Tusk, Tusk.* (Kane/Miller, 1979). At one time, all elephants were black or white. Black elephants hated white elephants, and vice versa. *How can we appreciate the differences in others instead of finding fault? How would our world change if all people were the same? Would we like it that way?*

Pfister, Marcus. *The Rainbow Fish.* (North-South Books, 1992). A fish with silvery scales discovers the real value of beauty and friendship. *Is it more important to keep all of our good things for ourselves or to share them with others? Why?*

Polacco, Patricia. *Thank You, Mr. Falker.* (Philomel, 1998). Trisha has difficulty learning to read until a teacher helps her. *How can teachers help us? What teacher has helped you? Can you help someone else?*

Rathman, Peggy. *Officer Buckle and Gloria.* (Putnam, 1995). The children in an elementary school ignore Officer Buckle's safety tips until his police dog Gloria goes with him. *How can it be helpful to work with a partner or as a team member? What character traits do you need to work with others?*

Ryan, Pam. *The Flag We Love.* (Charlesbridge, 1996). Patriotic verse and dazzling illustrations present the history of our flag. *What are our country's ideals? How can we show our patriotism?*

Stevens, Janet. *Tops and Bottoms.* (Harcourt Brace, 1995). Hare turns his bad luck around by arranging a deal with the lazy bear. *Is it important for all of us to do our share of the work? Why?*

Stewart, Sarah. *The Gardener.* (Farrar Straus Giroux, 1997). Cheerful Lydia Grace moves to the city to live with her cantankerous Uncle Jim and tries to make him smile with her secret garden. *How can we make unhappy people feel happy? What helps you feel happy when you are sad?*

Taback, Simms. *Joseph Had a Little Overcoat.* (Viking, 1999). A very old overcoat is recycled many times into a variety of clothing. *How can we make something of nothing? What can we recycle?*

Yolen, Jane. *Owl Moon.* (Scholastic, 1987). A child and a father go out one wintry night in search of an owl. *What special things do you do with your family? Why is family important?*

Yorinks, Arthur. *Hey, Al.* (Farrar Straus Giroux, 1986). Al and his dog Eddie lived in small quarters and yearned for something better, but found their former home was best after all. *How can we learn to appreciate our present situations? What can we find that is good about how we live?*

Applications for English Language Learners and Students with Special Needs

Conversations offer a chance for ELLs to become collaborators and meaning makers, and they enable children who have been referred for special education to participate successfully (Roser, Strecker, & Martinez, 2000). In a culturally and linguistically diverse fourth- and fifth-grade class, one teacher created a book club that was a year-long, literature-based instructional program (Kong & Fitch, 2002/2003).

The program consisted of small-group discussions, whole-class discussions, reading, and individual writing. Discussion was at the heart of the program, and the emphasis was on responding to quality literature and sharing responses. Standardized tests showed considerable growth in both vocabulary and use or awareness of reading comprehension strategies.

3. *Illuminator:* draws a favorite scene from the story and writes about the significance of the scene

4. *Word wizard:* locates words for the group to discuss that are new, strange, different, funny, important, interesting, or hard

5. *Connector:* finds connections between the story and life experiences in the outside world

Bond concluded that fifth-graders could lead book groups successfully because they were able to stay on task and demonstrate critical thinking during their discussions.

Student-led **book clubs**, or informal meetings among students for the purpose of sharing books, offer another opportunity for holding conversations about books in group settings. The kind of book talk that occurs in book clubs and literature circles needs a good book, agreed-upon goals, a chance for each participant to think and talk, and a conversational setting (Roser, Strecker, & Martinez, 2000). In a second-grade class, children selected their own books, met in groups of four or five once every other week, and read their letters about books, showing illustrations and discussing favorite parts with other club members (Frank, Dixon, & Brandts, 2001). The teacher guided students in discussing themes, main ideas, and characters and helped them make inferences and interpret meanings. Researchers focused attention on how children's conversations about books helped them build understandings. The letters that children wrote answered questions about the main idea of the book, the problem and solution, the characters and how they change, and why someone else might like to read this book. As children became accustomed to the routine, the teacher gave them time to talk without direct supervision and eventually turned the direction of the book club

Students become actively engaged in book discussions during groups that they lead themselves.

over to them. Through their experiences in book club, they learned to construct understandings, relate situations to their lives, acquire information about the world, remember events, and make connections to other texts.

In their book *Grand Conversations*, Peterson and Eeds (1990) use the term **dialogue** instead of *discussion* to convey a greater degree of intensity and involvement during book group interactions. They suggest following two rules: (1) respect the interpretations of others and support their development when possible, and (2) value spontaneous responses. Dialogue requires initiative, critical thinking, inquiry, intelligence, and imagination, but it offers the likelihood of a dynamic exchange of ideas and fresh, original perspectives.

Think-Pair-Share is an activity in which students find partners with whom they share their thoughts (Rasinski & Padak, 1996). The teacher identifies stopping points before the children start reading. As they come to a stopping point, the students pause to reflect on what they've read, take notes about their ideas, talk with partners about their thoughts, and share interesting ideas with the entire group. They continue this procedure, pausing to think and discuss at each stopping point, until they finish. This activity is especially helpful for students with reading disabilities who may need support as they read.

A study of first- and second-graders focused entirely on their oral responses to picture storybook read-alouds (Sipe, 2000). This study indicated that young children are capable of impressive critical literary thought. They were able to understand and interpret stories, respond to a story as a lived-through experience, use the story as a basis for creative expression, and connect the story to themselves and their personal experiences. Researchers observed that children made two-thirds of their comments during the reading of the story and only one-third at the end. Thus, teachers should allow relevant discussion *during* the story so that children won't forget their ideas before the story is over.

Teaching Tip

Whenever possible, let students choose the book to read, the place to read, and the type of response to give.

WRITTEN RESPONSES TO LITERATURE

As we have seen, children participating in discussions learn to think about literature in different ways and come to realize that a wide range of valid interpretations are possible. They can engage in the same types of thinking with written responses, which capture their thoughts, feelings, and reactions in print for later reference. (See Chapter 9 for more about writing.) For some children, this private expression of thoughts is less inhibiting than sharing their innermost thoughts aloud (Hancock, 2000). Typically, children write in literature journals or logs, which can take various forms, such as the following (Hancock, 2000).

Writing

- *Literature response journal*: an unstructured written account of events and reactions that is done *during* the reading
- *Dialogue journal:* continuous written dialogue between the reader and a respondent, who may be a peer, the classroom teacher, or someone else
- *Character journal:* a first-person interaction with a book, with the reader taking on the role of one of the book's characters

Another way to respond to literature in writing is by using a **double-entry journal**. The format consists of a sheet of paper divided into two columns. In the left column, the reader enters direct quotes from the text that generate thoughtful responses and

Writing

$\mathcal{F}$IGURE 2.16   **Double-Entry Journal for *The Door in the Wall***

Quotation from Book	Student Response
I trust you are improving in health, my son.	I love to see a message from my father showing he cares.
I know not which road to take.	It is a hard decision to make when it may alter the future.
Ever since he could remember, Robin had been told what was expected of him as son of his father.	I felt that Robin was used by people. I believe it is up to Robin to decide what he wants to be, not anyone else.
Robin promised that he would not forget the door in the wall.	That means reaching your goals. And don't stop trying, which is hard.
He told of Roman legions who had come to Britain centuries before, and of Saxon and Danish kings who in turn had ruled their land.	Wow! What I would give to hear stories like that. Imagine the words fill your ears. You can almost see the men flying into battle, smell and taste the smoke.
"By night, or under cover of mist," said Adam, "a whole army could creep over hill and through forest without being seen."	I wondered how severe the mist/fog would have had to be for an entire army to sneak through open land and attack.
"But I cannot walk," said Robin.	I think Robin can't walk because he has polio. Polio and the plague were spreading.

Source: Karen Fesler's Sixth Grade, Prescott Central Middle School, Cookeville, TN. Used with permisison.

writes a response for each quotation in the right column. Figure 2.16 shows how several of Karen Fesler's sixth-graders used the double-entry format to respond to quotations from Marguerite de Angeli's *The Door in the Wall*, a story set in fourteenth-century England that is about a crippled boy who wished to serve his king.

In their study of first-graders, Wollman-Bonilla and Werchadlo (1999) found that children could write thoughtful, personal responses to books if they had been provided with teacher support. The teacher in this case modeled her personal responses to a chapter and then encouraged children to write something about another chapter that she had just read to them. She occasionally taught a brief minilesson before they began writing, and she provided one-on-one feedback. She allowed them to share their responses with the whole class immediately after they wrote and enthusiastically reinforced what they said. As a result of learning to value their personal responses to texts, the children became more engaged and eager readers.

Anna Faye Burgess introduced a thematic unit on tall tales to her fourth-graders. The children listened to and read stories about super-heroic deeds and talked about the traits of tall-tale characters. Mrs. Burgess read them Julius Lester's *John Henry* and then asked the children to create a tall-tale character and write about the character's exaggerated feats. In his story of Recycle Man, Jamin created a contemporary hero who uses technology to clean up the earth (see Figure 2.17).

RESPONDING THROUGH DRAMA

Wagner (1998) finds drama to be powerful because its balance of thought and feeling make learning challenging, exciting, enjoyable, and relevant to real-life concerns.

Writing

FIGURE 2.17   Recycle Man

Recycle Man

My favorite hero is Recycle Man. He lives in the town of Green peace. His job is to recycle trash. He can make almost anything out of trash and clean the whole earth in a month. He's really tall, strong, and has a recycling logo on him.

He can make remote control cars, robots, computers, and much more. He has his own toy business, and he has almost every toy that exists. His computers talk to you, his remote control cars have a real engine, and his robots obey your every comand. Help him to recycle by picking up trash all over the world.

I'm glad that Recycle Man is here because now the earth is clean. Thats why he's my favorite hero!

By: Jamin Thornsberry

Source: Jamin Thornsberry, Northeast Elementary School, Cookeville, TN. Used with permission.

Responding to literature through various forms of drama helps children understand, interpret, and internalize literature. We look here at three forms of dramatization: creative drama, Readers Theatre, and puppetry.

CREATIVE DRAMA One of the most effective responses to literature is **creative drama**, which enables students to develop literacy skills in a purposeful manner. By establishing cognitive, emotional, and physical connections between prior knowledge and new ideas as they dramatize stories, students engage in problem solving and higher order thinking (Douville & Finke, 2000).

Creative drama is the spontaneous, unrehearsed enactment of situations, concepts, or stories and poems. Children experience literature on a very personal level when they participate in acting out scenes from the stories that they hear or read. They develop a sense of sequence, a feel for the importance of detail, an understanding of characters and their feelings, and an appreciation of setting that is seldom acquired from just reading the material. There are no scripts to memorize and few, if any, props.

The value of creative drama lies partly in developing language skills. In an informal situation such as this, children act and speak spontaneously, experimenting with language that is appropriate for the occasion. They learn how to use language to communicate in order to extend the story. Because they have fun acting out stories, they also develop better attitudes toward learning.

Some poems are particularly well suited to dramatization. Shel Silverstein's poems are good choices because of their humor and realistic characterization. Children may try to convince others of their dreadful illnesses as did Peggy Ann McKay in "Sick," or they may share Hector's pleasure with his accumulated treasures in "Hector the Collector" (from *Where the Sidewalk Ends*). Narrative poems with plenty of action, clearly identifiable scenes, and strong visual images are especially good to dramatize. Robert Browning's "The Pied Piper of Hamelin" has these qualities, as well as a good story line. Any number of actors can play the parts of the concerned townspeople, the merry children, and the troublesome rats. Ernest Thayer's "Casey at the Bat" focuses on a central character who demonstrates a wide range of emotions. Other players can be his teammates and fans, who react with great feeling to the mighty Casey's swaggering attempt, but ultimate failure, to win the game.

Young children enjoy acting out Esphyr Slobodkina's *Caps for Sale* where they can be the discouraged peddler, the tricky monkeys, or the busy townspeople. In Maurice Sendak's *Where the Wild Things Are*, one child plays Max and the other children become the monsters. They join in a wild rumpus, but Max takes charge as he bids farewell to his new friends and returns to the security of his own bedroom. This story offers many opportunities for movement and characterization.

Most folktales are excellent sources of dramatic material because they contain elements of fantasy, quick-moving plots, and strong characters. The humorous escapades of the animal characters in Joel Chandler Harris's Brer Rabbit tales are fun for children to act. "Snow White and the Seven Dwarfs" lets children develop the characters of the different dwarfs whose names give clues to their

In creative dramatics, children enjoy acting out a story without any need for costumes, sets, or props.

behavior. Other stories and excerpts from chapter books appropriate for dramatization are given in Figure 2.18.

Preparing the children for acting out a story is an important step. Let them know in advance that they will be acting out a story or poem if they enjoy it so that they will listen closely to the sequence, the dialogue, and the feelings of the characters. Let the whole class move as they think the characters would move, recall the sequence, and repeat any special phrases. Set your scene by marking off certain areas of the classroom, and ask for volunteers to play different parts. You may sometimes want to choose the players to give shy children a chance to perform. Minilesson 2.2 shows how a teacher prepares the children for dramatizing Marcia Brown's *Stone Soup,* a folktale about three weary soldiers who arrive at a village seeking food and a good night's sleep.

READERS THEATRE Another way to dramatize literature is through **Readers Theatre,** a performance of scripted literature read expressively by two or more readers for an audience. A narrator usually conveys information not revealed through dialogue. Reading a script requires students to visualize the setting and the action and to use their voices according to their understanding of the characters' emotions and thoughts. Although each participant is reading from a script, individual interpretation of the story and expressiveness of oral reading constitute a personal response (Hancock, 2000). Pitch, tone, volume, and delivery are the means by which the reader shares the emotion of the text with the audience.

Two second-grade classes participated in a study that focused on increasing meaningful and fluent reading through Readers Theatre (Martinez, Roser, & Strecker, 1998/1999). Teachers conducted daily thirty-minute sessions for ten weeks, with the teacher reading three stories on Monday, the children rehearsing through the week, and the children performing on Friday. The teachers found that Readers Theatre enabled children to go "inside" the story to experience the thoughts and feelings of the characters. They believed that Readers Theatre benefited their children in two ways: improved comprehension as a result of becoming the characters and understanding their feelings, and improved fluency from repetition and practice.

FIGURE 2.18   Stories to Dramatize

Miss Nelson Is Missing! by Harry Allard

Tuck Everlasting by Natalie Babbitt

Gingerbread Baby by Jan Brett

Stone Soup by Marcia Brown

The Watsons Go to Birmingham–1963 by Christopher Paul Curtis

There Was an Old Lady Who Swallowed a Fly by Simms Taback

Click, Clack, Moo: Cows That Type by Doreen Cronin

James and the Giant Peach by Roald Dahl

The View from Saturday by E. L. Konigsburg

A Wrinkle in Time by Madeleine L'Engle

Frederick by Leo Lionni

Number the Stars by Lois Lowry

Sarah, Plain and Tall by Patricia MacLachlan

Shiloh by Phyllis Reynolds Naylor

Piggy Pie! by Margie Palatini

The Great Gilly Hopkins by Katherine Paterson

The Rainbow Fish by Marcus Pfister

Holes by Louis Sachar

Caps for Sale by Esphyr Slobodkina

Maniac Magee by Jerry Spinelli

Teaching Tip

When there is a limited number of characters in a story, such as "The Three Billy Goats Gruff," involve other children by letting them be plants, small creatures, or inanimate objects as part of the setting. For example, they could be frogs, butterflies, sunflowers, or huge rocks.

Minilesson 2.2

Preparing to Dramatize *Stone Soup*

MR. ORTEGA: Now that you are familiar with the story of *Stone Soup*, we are ready to act it out. What characters will we need?

CHILDREN: We need three soldiers and some villagers.

MR. ORTEGA: Yes. Do you remember how the soldiers felt? How should we play them?

CHILDREN: They were so tired from walking so far. It was late and they were hungry. They wanted the villagers to feed them because they couldn't walk any farther.

MR. ORTEGA: Can you show me how you could be tired, hungry soldiers? Each of you stand up and walk a few steps without bumping into anyone. Remember how tired and hungry you are.
(Children walk as weary soldiers.)

MR. ORTEGA: I saw some very fine soldiers who really looked exhausted. Now, let's think who else we need.

CHILDREN: We need some villagers.

MR. ORTEGA: Right . . . What should we use for a pot and where should we put it?

CHILDREN: Let's use the trash can and put it in the middle of that open space.

MR. ORTEGA: Good idea. Maria, will you please move the can for us? Thank you. Where should the soldiers be coming from?

CHILDREN: They should be coming in the door as if they are entering our village.

MR. ORTEGA: That makes sense. Now, where will the villagers live?

CHILDREN: We can let each table be someone's home.

MR. ORTEGA: That'll work. Let's identify the villagers and where they live. Eduardo, maybe you can write their names on these cards and put them on each table so we'll know who lives where. Let's look back at the book to be sure we have the names right.
(Eduardo begins writing as other children tell him the names.)

MR. ORTEGA: Can we remember what each couple brought?
(Children try to recall, with help from the book.)

MR. ORTEGA: Okay. We have the setting and we know the characters. Do you remember how the peasants acted? How did they feel about having soldiers coming to their village? What did they do with their food?

CHILDREN: They were selfish and didn't want to share. They hid their food. They gave excuses to the soldiers so they wouldn't have to share their food and homes.

MR. ORTEGA: Remember to show their selfishness when you play their parts. Who wants to volunteer to be villagers?
(Children eagerly volunteer and Mr. Ortega chooses some.)

MR. ORTEGA: Remember, if you don't get a part to play this time, you'll have a part next time. If I don't choose you, you'll be part of the audience and you'll need to be attentive listeners. Now I need three soldiers. (He picks the soldiers.)

MR. ORTEGA: Let's go over the story one more time before we play it so that you'll be sure to know what to do and say. Your words don't have to be exactly like those in the book, but make sure you understand the order of the story and have a general idea of what your character says. Be sure you show the feelings of the tired, hungry soldiers and the feelings of the selfish peasants. Villagers, make sure you know what your excuse is at first and then what you contribute to the pot later. You may want to check the book. (Children look over their parts and get ready to play.)

MR. ORTEGA: All right, actors take your places. Audience, find seats that are out of our play area. I think we're ready to begin.

Follow-up lessons

Children may play this story several times with different children acting the parts. Discussion of this story might center around its theme, the cleverness of the soldiers, and the selfishness of the peasants. Children might compare this story to other stories or situations. Once they understand the procedure, they can perform other poems or stories that are particularly enjoyable for them and amenable to dramatization. No props other than the trash can were used in this performance, but children might want to bring in food or use drawings or clay reproductions for future performances.

What are the students learning?

Children are learning to be attentive listeners now that they have a special purpose for listening. They are recalling events in order and portraying the feelings of the characters. As they play their parts, they are improving their oral communication by improvising speech and actions based on their understanding of the play. By dramatizing the story, they are extending their appreciation of this piece of literature.

They concluded that encouraging oral interpretation helps students become expressive readers and also gives them keen insights into the literature for both themselves and their audience.

Commercially prepared scripts for Readers Theatre are available, but you can create your own scripts by converting stories into dialogue with a role for a narrator. Older children may be able to write their own scripts from favorite literature selections. When choosing stories for Readers Theatre, Hancock (2000) suggests looking for books that are short, follow a simple story line, have three or four main characters, and contain ample dialogue. A good choice is *A House for Hermit Crab* by Eric Carle. Hermit Crab is the main character, but he interacts respectfully with all sorts of sea creatures who respond to his wishes to decorate his shell. Scenes from E. B. White's *Charlotte's Web* are also appropriate for converting into scripts. For example, Chapter 4 tells of Wilbur's loneliness and attempts to make friends when he first goes to the barnyard. We feel his sense of abandonment as he asks the rat, the goose, and the lamb to play with him, and each animal rejects him in its characteristic manner. Other good choices for Readers Theatre include P. D. Eastman's *Are You My Mother?* (easy), Janet Stevens's *Tops and Bottoms,* (average), and James Marshall's *Hansel and Gretel* (challenging) (Martinez, Roser, & Strecker, 1998/1999).

PUPPETRY   Children can also respond to literature using **puppetry**. You can construct a puppet theater from a large appliance carton with a rectangle cut out for viewing and a piece of cloth covering it for a curtain. Children can make their own puppets from paper bags or socks, or you can purchase commercially made puppets. With their imaginations, children can envision a single puppet representing different creatures, such as a furry green head with trimmings being a worm, an alligator, or even a dragon. A hand puppet that changes from a caterpillar to a butterfly by turning inside out is available for use with Eric Carle's *The Very Hungry Caterpillar.*

Shy children often build confidence when they use puppets because they feel safer speaking as puppet characters than as themselves. By listening carefully to the other puppeteers to know when to move their puppets and what to have them say, children are developing listening skills. By using their voices and hand movements, they are able to portray the moods, feelings, and actions of their characters. Selections mentioned previously for dramatic interpretations are also appropriate for puppetry.

RESPONDING THROUGH ART

Dioramas, clay sculptures, mobiles, soap carvings, drawings, murals, and computer designs are all art forms that can grow out of literature presentations. Some illustrated books lend themselves to certain forms of artistic representation, such as those by Eric Carle, whose cutouts from brightly painted tissue paper may inspire children to create their own collages. Eleanor Coerr's *Sadako,* which tells of folding paper to make a thousand cranes, is a natural springboard for making origami, and the detailed description of an old country house in Mary Norton's *The Borrowers* could motivate children to make a diorama. Another way children can respond is by drawing maps of story lines. For instance, in "Little Red Riding Hood" they might draw the heroine's path from her cottage, through the woods (showing encounters with the wolf), to Grandma's house. *Homecoming* by Cynthia Voigt provides a story line that can be mapped on an outline map of the United States. Sometimes books inspire the construction of special places to read, such as cardboard castles based on fairy tales, train cars from the Thomas the Train series, or an elevated reading platform in the form of an artificial tree from "Jack and the Beanstalk."

The **sketch-to-stretch** strategy enables students to show what a story means to them by using color and by sketching lines, shapes, symbols, or pictures (Short, Harste, & Burke, 1996; Whitin, 2002). This process is not merely drawing a favorite part, but it is a means for expressing children's thinking about the story's ideas. For some children, drawing is a better avenue for expression than speaking or writing, and the sketches that children share offer opportunities for opening literary discussions. The procedure goes as follows.

- The teacher reads a story, and the class discusses the feelings it evokes.
- The teacher asks what colors, shapes, or symbols might represent those feelings.
- The children contribute ideas, giving reasons for each idea.
- Working collaboratively with partners or in small groups, the children talk about their ideas as they make their sketches.
- The teacher and children reassemble as a large group to share their sketches and extend their thinking about the story. The teacher welcomes new ideas.

MATHEMATICS AS A RESPONSE

Although responses through mathematics may seem less obvious than those through the arts, teachers have found that children do use math to understand literature (Short, Kauffman, & Kahn, 2000). Students refer to such concepts as money, directionality, time, distance, and probability, and they use logical thinking to pose and solve problems. Judith Viorst's *Alexander, Who Used to Be Rich Last Sunday* causes children to think about the value of money; Rod Clement's *Counting on Frank* demonstrates the usefulness of finding and solving problems; and Jon Scieszka's *Math Curse* shows how everything can be thought of as a math problem. Moyer (2000) observed a fourth-grade class in which children were responding to Pat Hutchins's *The Doorbell Rang*, a story in which Grandma brings a dozen cookies that must be divided among increasing numbers of children. Among other activities, the children acted out sharing cookies while the teacher wrote the corresponding equation on the board. For example, when there were four children, the teacher wrote $12 \div 4 = 3$ to show that each child would receive three cookies.

MUSICAL CONNECTIONS TO LITERATURE

For children with a natural sense of rhythm and an ear for music, a musical response is natural. Beginning in their very early years, children can sing nursery rhymes, such as "Three Blind Mice" and "Twinkle, Twinkle Little Star." Background music sets the mood for some stories and poems; for example, square dance music is an appropriate accompaniment for *Barn Dance!* by Bill Martin, Jr., and John Archambault. Moving to music during or following such books as Ann Jonas's *Color Dance* with its flowing, colorful scarves enables children to experience stories in a different way. Children can learn about instruments of the orchestra in Lloyd Moss's *Zin! Zin! Zin! a Violin*, and Gene Baer's *Thump, Thump, Rat-a-Tat-Tat* is a stimulus for forming a rhythm band. Along with expressing the beauty and harmony of our world, *What a Wonderful World* by George David Weiss and Bob Thiele tempts readers to sing the words to the familiar song made famous by Louis Armstrong.

From Sea to Shining Sea, compiled by Amy Cohn, is a treasury of American folklore and folk songs, including such favorites as "Oh, Susannah" and "Shenandoah." *Lift Every Voice and Sing* by black poet James Weldon Johnson is often referred to as the African American national anthem (Norton, 2003). Graeme Base's *The Worst Band in the Universe* is a fantasy of a young performer seeking musical freedom, and it includes a CD featuring live performances from the annual Worst Band in the Universe Com-

Classroom Vignette 2.2

Mrs. Burgess has been reading Mildred Walter's *Justin and the Best Biscuits in the World* to her fourth-graders. This chapter book leads them to think about their favorite foods and family recipes. Mrs. Burgess brings in some cookbooks for the children to peruse and then challenges them to make their own cookbook. She asks them to go home and interview some of the good cooks in their extended families and come back with recipes. The children seek out recipes, compile them, assemble them into a classroom cookbook called *Family Recipes*, and make multiple copies for distribution. Homestyle favorites include Mom's World Famous Fried Chicken, Nana's Cranberry Relish, Big Momma's Chess Pie, and Granny Thomas's Chocolate Pie.

What's happening here?

While savoring memories of food delights, the children are learning to interview family members and appreciate their contributions during meal times. They encounter cookbooks as another type of informational book, and they recognize the need for exact instructions in sequential order in this form of reading and writing. They learn new vocabulary, such as *dissolve, ingredients,* and *congeal,* as they write their recipes and read other recipes, and they take pride in producing a cookbook to share with others.

petition. Students can experiment with matching poetry to classical compositions that call for similar responses, and literature can provide inspiration for students to compose their own music (Huck, Hepler, Hickman, & Kiefer, 2001).

COOKING AS A RESPONSE

Munching on food during or following a story heightens and extends the experience for many of us, and books often lend themselves to enjoying food (Hancock, 2000). The series by Numeroff about giving a mouse a cookie, a moose a muffin, or a pig a pancake offers opportunities for sharing food, as does Paddington Bear's love of orange marmalade in books by Michael Bond. Jan Brett's *Gingerbread Baby* and other gingerbread tales lend themselves to gingerbread treats, and Grandma's muffins in Lisa Campbell Ernst's *Little Red Riding Hood: A Newfangled Prairie Tale* offer an opportunity for baking and eating tasty muffins. Some books provide actual recipes, such as the one for baking thundercake in Patricia Polacco's *Thundercake.* Tomie De Paola gives the recipe for making pancakes in his book *Pancakes for Breakfast* and provides directions for popping corn in *The Popcorn Book.* The taste experiences children gain from eating as a response will cause them to recall fond memories of these books for years to come.

Classroom Assessment for Literature

Since appreciation and enjoyment are primary goals for literature, the most useful assessment tools are observation of reading behaviors and informal interest and attitude surveys to determine students' preferences and feelings about literature. Short tests over facts are also sometimes given to measure comprehension.

$\mathcal{S}$UMMARY

Children's literature offers many benefits, including providing pleasure, building experiences, developing thinking skills, and enhancing all areas of the language arts. Literature consists of six literary elements: plot, characterization, setting, theme, style, and point of view. Genres of literature include contemporary realistic fiction, science fiction, historical fiction, traditional literature, modern fantasy, poetry, biography, and informational books. Children need exposure to all genres to appreciate the variety and versatility of literature.

As a teacher, you not only need to know the elements and genres of literature, but also how to select it for children and present it to them. Award books, classics, and books with social merit are all worthy choices, but children also need to be able to select reading material for themselves. No activity is more important for a student's eventual success in reading than listening to stories, and story reading and storytelling are both effective ways to present literature.

Rosenblatt's reader response theory tells us that reading is a transaction between the reader and the text and that both contribute to making meaning. She explains that there are basically two ways to respond to text: efferently by recalling information, and aesthetically by responding emotionally. There are many ways that readers can respond to literature, beginning with the earliest form of simply listening and reacting spontaneously. Children can also respond through discussions and in writing. Three types of dramatic responses are creative dramatics, an informal enacting of stories; Readers Theatre, the expressive reading of a script; and puppetry. Art and music also offer various ways to respond, as do mathematics and cooking. What matters most is not the type of response, but the depth or intensity of the personal response for each individual.

Discussion Questions

1. Why is it important to include children's literature in the curriculum?

2. How would you motivate reluctant readers to begin reading for pleasure?

3. Giving honest responses to literature causes children to take risks by revealing their thoughts and feelings. How will you encourage children to do this?

4. What books and authors do you know that are good to use for stimulating thinking? Why are they good choices? Consider both primary and intermediate levels.

5. How will you find time to *think* about literature during a busy school day? What priority will you give to thinking about and responding to literature?

6. What criteria will you consider when selecting books to read aloud to your class?

7. How can you design a literature program that appeals to learners of different ethnic groups, including those with limited knowledge of the English language?

8. How will you avoid giving or expecting the "one correct answer" and allow for different interpretations of literature?

9. How can you evaluate the effectiveness of the literature program in your class?

Suggested Activities

1. Choose one piece of literature appropriate for presenting to students in a grade level of your choice. Show how you could use this piece of literature to enhance learning in all of the language arts.

2. Compile a bibliography of books on a particular topic or theme for primary or middle grades. Choose a topic that you would actually like to teach.

3. Using a children's book that you have read recently, complete the story map for literary elements in Figure 2.2.

4. Develop a grid for "Cinderella" similar to the one given in Figure 2.7 for "Little Red Riding Hood." You may use the books listed in the text or find other versions.

5. Sign up for membership in Scholastic, Troll, or another commercial book club so that you can order books at reduced prices.

6. Design and/or construct a library center for your classroom. It may be a reading loft, a nook, a set of shelves, an enclosure, or something else.

7. Identify three children's books that are particularly well suited to a certain type of response. Tell how you would encourage children to respond.

8. Identify sources of inexpensive but good-quality books. Begin or add to your classroom library.

9. Form a book club in your classroom with a group of students who are interested in sharing books. Consider the following: When and how often will it meet? Who will be members? How will you conduct it? What student involvement will there be in the planning and operation? What books will you include?

10. Set up a reading-for-pleasure program, such as SSR, for your class. How will you operate it?

11. Develop a thematic unit based on literature that focuses on a particular topic, book, genre, or author.

Writing

12. Make a double-entry journal. Copy a sentence from this chapter that you find interesting and write a personal response.

References

Anderson, C. (2000). Sustained silent reading: Try it, you'll like it! *The Reading Teacher, 54,* 258–259.

Anderson, R., Hiebert, E., Scott, J., & Wilkinson, I. (1985). *Becoming a nation of readers: The report of the Commission on Reading.* Washington, DC: National Institute of Education.

Block, C., & Mangieri, J. (2002). Recreational reading: 20 years later. *The Reading Teacher, 55,* 572–580.

Block, C., Reed, K. M., & deTuncq, J. K. (2003). *All time-on-task is not equal: Effects of trade books, short story workbooks, and basal reading instruction on students' reading achievement.* Executive Summary. Research Report 476. Charlotte, NC: Institute for Literacy Enhancement.

Bluestein, N. A. (2002). Comprehension through characterization: Enabling readers to make personal connections with literature. *The Reading Teacher, 55,* 431–434.

Bond, T. (2001). Giving them free rein: Connections in student-led book groups. *The Reading Teacher, 54,* 574–584.

Camp, D. (2000). It takes two: Teaching with twin texts of fact and fiction. *The Reading Teacher, 53,* 400–408.

Douville, P., & Finke, J. (2000). Literacy as performance: The power of creative drama in the classroom. In K. Woods & Dickinson, T. (Eds.), *Promoting literacy in grades 4–9* (pp. 370–381). Boston: Allyn & Bacon.

Dreher, M. (1998/1999). Motivating children to read more nonfiction. *The Reading Teacher, 52,* 414–417.

Duke, N. (2000). 3–6 minutes per day: The scarcity of informational texts in first grade. *Reading Research Quarterly, 35,* 202–224.

Frank, C., Dixon, C., & Brandts, L. (2001). Bears, trolls, and pagemasters: Learning about learners in book clubs. *The Reading Teacher, 54,* 448–462.

Giorgis, C., & Johnson, N. (2001a). Finding a place. *The Reading Teacher, 55,* 304–311.

Giorgis, C., & Johnson, N. (2001b). The language of story. *The Reading Teacher, 54,* 824–834.

Giorgis, C., & Johnson, N. (2002). Text sets. *The Reading Teacher, 56,* 200–208.

Giorgis, C., Johnson, N., Bonomo, A., Colbert, C., Conner, A., Kauffman, G., & Kulesza, D. (1999). Visual literacy. *The Reading Teacher, 53,* 146–153.

Hadaway, N., Vardell, S., & Young, T. (2001). Scaffolding oral language development through poetry for students learning English. *The Reading Teacher, 54,* 796–806.

Hancock, M. (2000). *A celebration of literature and response.* Upper Saddle River, NJ: Merrill/Prentice Hall.

Harkins, M. (2001). Using literature to establish career concepts in early childhood. *The Reading Teacher, 55,* 29–32.

Harris, T. L., & Hodges, R. E. (Eds.). (1995). *The literacy dictionary.* Newark, DE: International Reading Association.

Harvey, S. (1998). *Nonfiction matters: Reading, writing, and research in grades 3–8.* York, ME: Stenhouse.

Harvey, S. (2002). Nonfiction inquiry: Using real reading and writing to explore the world. *Language Arts, 80,* 12–22.

Hefflin, B., & Barksdale-Ladd, M. (2001). African American children's literature that helps students find themselves: Selection guidelines for grades K–3. *The Reading Teacher, 54,* 810–819.

Huck, C., Hepler, S., Hickman, J., & Kiefer, B. (2001). *Children's literature in the elementary school* (7th ed.). New York: McGraw-Hill.

International Reading Association. (2002). Teachers' Choices for 2002. *The Reading Teacher, 46,* 255–262.

International Reading Association and The Children's Book Council. (2002). Children's Choices for 2002. *The Reading Teacher, 56,* 139–153.

Jewell, T., & Pratt, D. (1999). Literature discussions in the primary grades: Children's thoughtful discourse about books and what teachers can do to make it happen. *The Reading Teacher, 52,* 842–850.

Johnson, N., & Giorgis, C. (2001). Cultural voices. *The Reading Teacher, 54,* 720–728.

Kletzden, S., & Dreher, M. (2004). *Informational text in K–3 classrooms.* Newark, DE: International Reading Association.

Kong, A., & Fitch, E. (2002/2003). Using book clubs to engage culturally and linguistically diverse learners in reading, writing, and talking about books. *The Reading Teacher, 56,* 352–362.

Kristo, J., & Bamford, R. (2004). *Nonfiction in focus.* New York: Scholastic.

Labbo, L., Reinking, D., & McKenna, M. (1999). The use of technology in literacy programs. In L. Gambrell, L.

Morrow, S. Neuman, & M. Pressley (Eds.), *Best practices in literacy instruction* (pp. 311–327). New York: Guilford.

Lehr, S., & Thompson, D. (2000). The dynamic nature of response: Children reading and responding to *Maniac Magee* and *The Friendship. The Reading Teacher, 53,* 480–492.

Martinez, M., Roser, N., & Strecker, S. (1998/1999). "I never thought I could be a star": A readers theatre ticket to fluency. *The Reading Teacher, 52,* 326–324.

Martinez, M., Roser, N., & Strecker, S. (2000). Using picture books with older students. In K. Woods & T. Dickinson (Eds.), *Promoting literacy in grades 4–9* (pp. 250–262). Boston: Allyn & Bacon.

Morrow, L. & Gambrell, L. (2001). Literature-based instruction in the early years. In S. Neuman & D. Dickinson (Eds.), *Handbook of early literacy research* (pp. 348–360). New York: Guilford.

Moss, B. (2002). Motivating middle grade reading through nonfiction trade books. Presentation at International Reading Association.

Moss, B., & Hendershot, J. (2002). Exploring sixth graders' selection of nonfiction trade books. *The Reading Teacher, 56,* 6–17.

Moyer, P. (2000). Communicating mathematically: Children's literature as a natural connection. *The Reading Teacher, 54,* 246–255.

Norton, D. (2001). *Multicultural children's literature: Through the eyes of many children.* Upper Saddle River, NJ: Merrill/Prentice Hall.

Norton, D. (2003). *Through the eyes of a child* (6th ed.). Upper Saddle River, NJ: Merrill/Prentice Hall.

Opitz, M. (1999). Cultural diversity + supportive text = perfect books for beginning readers. *The Reading Teacher, 52,* 888–890.

Perfect, K. (1999). Rhyme and reason: Poetry for the heart and head. *The Reading Teacher, 52,* 728–737.

Peterson, R., & Eeds, M. (1990). *Grand conversations.* New York: Scholastic.

Popp, M. (1996). *Teaching language and literature in elementary classrooms.* Mahwah, NJ: Lawrence Erlbaum.

Rasinski, T., & Padak, N. (1996). *Holistic reading strategies.* Englewood Cliffs, NJ: Merrill/Prentice Hall.

Rosenblatt, L. (1978). *The reader, the text, the poem.* Carbondale: Southern Illinois University Press.

Rosenblatt, L. (1995). *Literature as exploration* (5th ed.). New York: Modern Language Association of America.

Roser, N., Strecker, S., & Martinez, M. (2000). Literature circles, book clubs, and literature discussion groups. In K. Wood and T. Dickinson (Eds.), *Promoting literacy in grades 4–9* (pp. 295–305). Boston: Allyn & Bacon.

Ross, E. (1998). *Pathways to thinking.* Norwood, MA: Christopher-Gordon.

Ross, E. (2001). "They are cool and sometimes amazing": Using nonfiction trade books with elementary students. *Tennessee English Journal, 12,* 16–19.

Searfoss, L., Readence, J., & Mallette, M. (2001). *Helping children learn to read* (4th ed.). Boston: Allyn & Bacon.

Short, K., Harste, J., & Burke, C. (1996). *Creating classrooms for authors and inquirers.* Portsmouth, NH: Heinemann.

Short, K., Kauffman, G., & Kahn, L. (2000). "I just *need* to draw": Responding to literature across multiple sign systems. *The Reading Teacher, 54,* 160–171.

Sipe, L. (2000). The construction of literary understanding by first and second graders in oral response to picture storybook read-alouds. *Reading Research Quarterly, 35,* 252–275.

Spillman, C. (1996). *Integrating language arts through literature in elementary classrooms.* Phoenix: Oryx.

Staal, L. (2000). The Story Face: An adaptation of story mapping that incorporates visualization and discovery learning to enhance reading and writing. *The Reading Teacher, 54,* 26–31.

Taylor, G. (2002/2003). Who's who? Engaging biography study. *The Reading Teacher, 56,* 342–344.

Tiedt, I. (2002). *Tiger lilies, toadstools, and thunderbolts: Engaging K–8 students with poetry.* Newark, DE: International Reading Association.

Trelease, J. (1995). *The read-aloud handbook* (4th ed.). New York: Penguin.

Veatch, J. (1968). *How to teach reading with children's books.* New York: Citation.

Wagner, B. (1998). *Educational drama and language arts.* Portsmouth, NH: Heinemann.

Whitin, P. (2002). Leading into literature circles through the sketch-to-stretch strategy. *The Reading Teacher, 55,* 444–450.

Wollman-Bonilla, J., & Werchadlo, B. (1999). Teacher and peer roles in scaffolding first graders' responses to literature. *The Reading Teacher, 52,* 598–607.

Books for Children and Adolescents Cited in This Chapter

ACKERMAN, K. (1988). *Song and dance man.* New York: Scholastic.

ADA, A. F. (1995). *Mediopollito half-chicken.* New York: Dell.

ADLER, D. (1989). *We remember the Holocaust.* New York: Trumpet.

ALLARD, H. (1977). *Miss Nelson is missing!* Boston: Houghton Mifflin.

BABBITT, N. (1975). *Tuck everlasting.* New York: Farrar Straus Giroux.

BAER, G. (1989). *Thump, thump, rat-a-tat-tat.* New York: Harper & Row.

BARRIE, J. (1911). *Peter Pan.* New York: Scribner's.

BASE, G. (1999). *The worst band in the universe.* New York: Abrams.

BEDARD, M. (1992). *Emily.* New York: Doubleday.

BERCAW, E. (2000). *Halmoni's day.* New York: Dial.

BITTON-JACKSON, L. (1997). *I have lived a thousand years.* New York: Scholastic.

BOAS, J. (1995). *We are witnesses: Five diaries of teenagers who died in the Holocaust.* New York: Scholastic.

BOND, M. (1960). *A bear called Paddington.* Boston: Houghton Mifflin.

BRADBY, M. (1995). *More than anything else.* New York: Orchard.

BRENNER, B., & GARELICK, M. (1979). *The tremendous tree book.* Honesdale, PA: Caroline House.

BRETT, J. (1999). *Gingerbread baby.* New York: Putnam.

BRIDGES, R. (1999). *Through my eyes.* New York: Scholastic.

BROWN, M. (1975). *Stone soup.* New York: Scribner.

BUNTING, E. (2000). *Swan in love.* New York: Atheneum.

CARLE, E. (1987). *A house for Hermit Crab.* New York: Scholastic.

CARLE, E. (1971). *The very hungry caterpillar.* New York: Crowell.

CHERRY, L. (1990). *The great kapok tree.* San Diego: Harcourt Brace Jovanovich.

CLEMENT, R. (1990). *Counting on Frank.* Auckland, NZ: William Collins.

CLIMO, S. (1989). *The Egyptian Cinderella.* New York: HarperCollins.

COERR, E. (1993). *Sadako.* New York: Putnam.

COHN, A. (1993). *From sea to shining sea.* New York: Scholastic.

COLLODI, C. (1892). *The adventures of Pinnochio.* New York: Macmillan.

COOPER, F. (1994). *Coming home.* New York: Philomel.

CRONIN, D. (2001). *Click, clack, moo: Cows that type.* Boston: Houghton Mifflin.

CURTIS, C. (1999). *Bud, not Buddy.* New York: Delacorte.

CURTIS, C. (1995). *The Watsons go to Birmingham—1963.* New York: Delacorte.

DAHL, R. (1961). *James and the giant peach.* New York: Knopf.

DAY, A. (1994). *Frank and Ernest on the road.* New York: Scholastic.

DE ANGELI, M. (1949). *The door in the wall.* New York: Doubleday.

DE PAOLA, T. (1978). *Pancakes for breakfast.* Orlando: Harcourt Brace Jovanovich.

DE PAOLA, T. (1978). *The popcorn book.* New York: Holiday House.

DE REGNIERS, B. (1972). *Red Riding Hood.* New York: Atheneum.

DISNEY, W. (1950). *Cinderella.* New York: Golden Press.

DUKE, K. (1992). *Aunt Isabel tells a good one.* New York: Penguin.

EASTMAN, P. D. (1998). *Are you my mother?* New York: Random House.

EHLERT, L. (1991). *Red leaf, yellow leaf.* New York: Scholastic.

ERNST, L. (1995). *Little Red Riding Hood: A newfangled prairie tale.* New York: Simon & Schuster.

ESBENSEN, B. (Ed.). (1988). *The star maiden.* Boston: Little, Brown.

FLOURNOY, V. (1985). *The patchwork quilt.* New York: Dial.

FORBES, E. (1943). *Johnny Tremain.* Boston: Houghton Mifflin.

FRANK, A. (1995). *The diary of a young girl: The definitive edition.* New York: Doubleday.

FREEDMAN, R. (1987). *Lincoln: A photobiography.* New York: Clarion.

FRITZ, J. (1991). *Bully for you, Teddy Roosevelt.* New York: Putnam.

FRITZ, J. (1986). *Make way for Sam Houston.* New York: Putnam.

GARZA, C. (1990). *Family pictures.* San Francisco: Children's Book Press.

GAY, M. (1993). *Angel and the polar bear.* Toronto: Stoddart.

GIFF, P. (2000). *Nory Ryan's song.* New York: Delacorte.

GOLD, A. (1997). *Memories of Anne Frank.* New York: Scholastic.

GRIMM, BROTHERS. (1979). Aschenputtel. In Mrs. E. Lucas, (Trans.), *Sixty fairy tales of the Brothers Grimm.* New York: Weathervane.

GWYNNE, F. (1970). *The king who rained.* New York: Windmill Wander Books.

HALL, D. (1979). *The ox-cart man.* New York: Viking.

HAMILTON, V. (1968). *The house of Dies Drear.* New York: Macmillan.

HAMILTON, V. (1967). *Zeely.* New York: Macmillan.

HESSE, K. (1997). *Out of the dust.* New York: Scholastic.

HIGHWATER, J. (1977). *Anpao: An American Indian Odyssey.* New York: Lippincott.

HOFFMAN, M. (1991). *Amazing Grace.* New York: Scholastic.

HOUSTON, G. (1992). *My Great-Aunt Arizona.* New York: HarperCollins.

HUCK, C. (1989). *Princess Furball.* New York: Greenwillow.

HUTCHINS, P. (1986). *The doorbell rang.* New York: Morrow.

HYMAN, T. (1983). *Little Red Riding Hood.* New York: Holiday House.

JOHNSON, J. W. (1993). *Lift every voice and sing.* New York: Walker.

JOHNSTON, T. (1994). *Amber on the mountain.* New York: Dial.

JONAS, A. (1989). *Color dance.* New York: Greenwillow.

KELLOGG, S. (1988). *Johnny Appleseed.* New York: Morrow.

KONIGSBURG, E. L. (1996). *The view from Saturday.* New York: Atheneum.

KRENSKY, S. (1994). *Children of the wind and water.* New York: Scholastic.

LANKFORD, M. (1992). *Hopscotch.* New York: Beech Tree.

L'ENGLE, M. (1962). *A wrinkle in time.* New York: Farrar Straus Giroux.

LESSER, C. (1996). *Great crystal bear.* San Diego: Harcourt Brace.

LESSER, C. (1997). *Storm on the desert.* New York: Harcourt Brace.

LESTER, J. (1994). *John Henry.* New York: Dial.

LESTER, J. (1994). *The last tales of Uncle Remus.* New York: Dial.

LIONNI, L. (1973). *Frederick.* New York: Random House.

LOCKER, T. (1995). *Sky tree: Seeing science through art.* New York: HarperCollins.

LONDON, J. (1993). *The eyes of gray wolf.* San Francisco: Chronicle.

LOUIE, A. (1982). *Yeh-Shen: A Cinderella story from China.* New York: Philomel.

LOWRY, L. (2000). *Gathering blue.* Boston: Houghton Mifflin.

LOWRY, L. (1993). *The giver.* Boston: Houghton Mifflin.

LOWRY, L. (1989). *Number the stars.* Boston: Houghton Mifflin.

LUCADO, M. (1997). *You are special.* New York: Scholastic.

MACAULAY, D. (1988). *The way things work.* Boston: Houghton Mifflin.

MACLACHLAN, P. (1994). *All the places to love.* New York: HarperCollins.

MACLACHLAN, P. (1985). *Sarah, plain and tall.* New York: Harper & Row.

MARSHALL, J. (1990). *Hansel and Gretel.* New York: Dial.

MARSHALL, J. (1987). *Red Riding Hood.* New York: Scholastic.

MARTIN, B., JR., & ARCHAMBAULT, J. (1986). *Barn dance!* New York: Holt.

MCCULLY, E. (1992). *Mirette on the high wire.* New York: Scholastic.

MCKEE, D. (1979). *Tusk, tusk.* Brooklyn: Kane/Miller.

MCKISSACK, P. (1986). *Flossie and the fox.* New York: Scholastic.

MELTZER, M. (1998). *Ten queens: Portraits of women in power.* New York: Penguin Putnam.

MORRIS, A. (1989). *Bread, bread, bread.* New York: Mulberry.

MOSS, L. (1995). *Zin! zin! zin! A violin.* New York: Simon & Schuster.

NAYLOR, P. (1991). *Shiloh.* New York: Atheneum.

NORTON, M. (1952). *The borrowers.* San Diego: Harcourt Brace Jovanovich.

NUMEROFF, L. (1991). *If you give a moose a muffin.* New York: HarperCollins.

NUMEROFF, L. (1985). *If you give a mouse a cookie.* New York: Harper & Row.

NUMEROFF, L. (1998). *If you give a pig a pancake.* New York: HarperCollins.

OSBORNE, M. P. (1993). *Mummies in the morning.* New York: Random House.

PALATINI, M. (1995). *Piggie pie!* New York: Clarion.

PATERSON, K. (1978). *The great Gilly Hopkins.* New York: HarperCollins.

PECK, R. (2000). *A year down yonder.* New York: Scholastic.

PERRAULT, C. (1954). *Cinderella.* New York: Scribner.

PFISTER, M. (1992). *The rainbow fish.* New York: North-South Books.

PLATT, R. (1992). *Stephen Biesty's incredible cross-sections.* New York: Knopf.

POLACCO, P. (2000). *The butterfly.* New York: Philomel.

POLACCO, P. (1994). *Pink and Say.* New York: Philomel.

POLACCO, P. (1998). *Thank you, Mr. Falker.* New York: Philomel.

POLACCO, P. (1990). *Thundercake.* New York: Philomel.

POLLOCK, P. (1996). *The turkey girl.* Boston: Little, Brown.

RAHAMAN, V. (1997). *Read for me, Mama.* Honesdale, PA: Boyds Mills.

RATHMAN, P. (1995). *Officer Buckle and Gloria.* New York: Putnam.

REISS, J. (1972). *The upstairs room.* New York: HarperCollins.

ROSENBERG, M. (1994). *Hiding to survive.* New York: Clarion.

ROWLAND, D. (1991). *Little Red Riding Hood.* New York: Carol.

RUSSELL-ARNOT, E. (1999). *Foxes.* Crystal Lake, IL: Rigby.

RYAN, P. (1996). *The flag we love.* Watertown, MA: Charlesbridge.

SACHAR, L. (1998). *Holes.* New York: Delacorte.

SCHROEDER, A. (1997). *Smoky Mountain Rose.* New York: Dial.

SCIESZKA, J. (1995). *Math curse.* New York: Viking.

SENDAK, M. (1963). *Where the wild things are.* New York: Harper & Row.

SILVERSTEIN, S. (1964). *The giving tree.* New York: Harper & Row.

SILVERSTEIN, S. (1974). *Where the sidewalk ends.* New York: Harper & Row.

SIS, P. (1996). *Starry messenger.* New York: Farrar Straus Giroux.

SLOBODKINA, E. (1947). *Caps for sale.* New York: Scott.

SMUCKER, B. (1999). *Selina and the bear paw quilt.* New York: Crown.

SNEVE, V. (1989). *Dancing teepees: Poems of American Indian youth.* New York: Holiday House.

SOTO, G. (1990). *Baseball in April and other stories.* San Diego: Harcourt Brace.

SOTO, G. (1993). *Too many tamales.* New York: Putnam.

SPINELLI, J. (1990). *Maniac Magee.* Boston: Little, Brown.

STANLEY, J. (1992). *Children of the dust bowl.* New York: Crown.

STEVENS, J. (1995). *Tops and bottoms.* San Diego: Harcourt Brace.

STEWART, S. (1997). *The gardener.* New York: Farrar Straus Giroux.

TABACK, S. (1999). *Joseph had a little overcoat.* New York: Viking.

TABACK, S. (1997). *There was an old lady who swallowed a fly.* New York: Viking.

TAYLOR, M. (1986). *The friendship.* New York: Dial.

UDRY, J. (1957). *A tree is nice.* New York: Harper.

VAN ALLSBURG, C. (1990). *Just a dream.* Boston: Houghton Mifflin.

VIORST, J. (1973). *Alexander and the terrible, horrible, no good, very bad day.* New York: Atheneum.

VIORST, J. (1978). *Alexander, who used to be rich last Sunday.* New York: Scholastic.

VOIGT, C. (1981). *Homecoming.* New York: Atheneum.

WALTER, M. (1986). *Justin and the best biscuits in the world.* New York: Lothrop, Lee & Shepard.

WATSON, J. (1983). *Talking in whispers.* London: Victor Gollancz.

WEISS, G., & THIELE, B. (1995). *What a wonderful world.* New York: Atheneum.

WHITE, E. B. (1952). *Charlotte's web.* New York: Harper & Row.

WIRTH, V. (1991). *Whisper from the woods.* New York: Simon & Schuster.

YEP, L. (1975). *Dragonwings.* New York: Harper & Row.

YIN. (2001). *Coolies.* New York: Philomel.

YOLEN, J. (1988). *The devil's arithmetic.* New York: Puffin.

YOLEN, J. (1987). *Owl moon.* New York: Scholastic.

YORINKS, A. (1986). *Hey, Al.* New York: Farrar Straus Giroux.

YOUNG, E. (1989). *Lon Po Po.* New York: Philomel.

Chapter 3

VOCABULARY

LEARNER OBJECTIVES

At the conclusion of this chapter

YOU SHOULD BE ABLE TO

1. Understand the importance of vocabulary instruction to the overall language arts program.

2. Describe the relationship between concept development and word meanings.

3. Identify the four vocabularies that children have.

4. Discuss a variety of vocabulary instructional techniques that make possible diverse and creative approaches to vocabulary development.

5. Discuss special types of words and phrases that can cause difficulties for children and ways to teach these different types.

6. Identify the following terms that are defined or explained in this chapter:

NCTE/IRA Standards addressed in this chapter

STANDARD 3. Students apply a wide range of strategies to comprehend, interpret, evaluate, and appreciate texts. They draw on their prior experience, their interactions with other readers and writers, their knowledge of word meaning and of other texts, their word identification strategies, and their understanding of textual features (e.g., sound-letter correspondence, sentence structure, context, graphics).

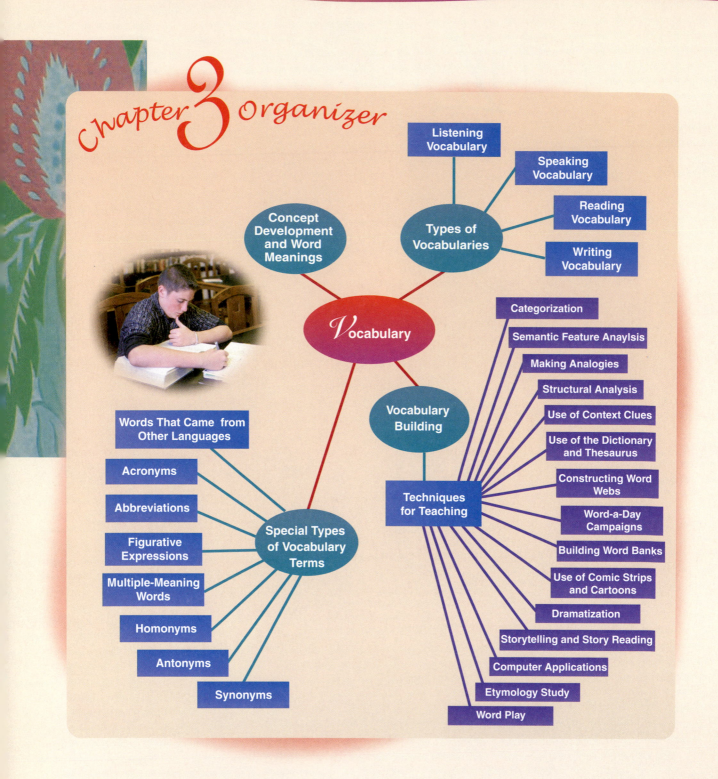

Chapter 3 Organizer

Vocabulary

Concept Development and Word Meanings

Types of Vocabularies
- Listening Vocabulary
- Speaking Vocabulary
- Reading Vocabulary
- Writing Vocabulary

Special Types of Vocabulary Terms
- Words That Came from Other Languages
- Acronyms
- Abbreviations
- Figurative Expressions
- Multiple-Meaning Words
- Homonyms
- Antonyms
- Synonyms

Vocabulary Building

Techniques for Teaching
- Categorization
- Semantic Feature Anaylsis
- Making Analogies
- Structural Analysis
- Use of Context Clues
- Use of the Dictionary and Thesaurus
- Constructing Word Webs
- Word-a-Day Campaigns
- Building Word Banks
- Use of Comic Strips and Cartoons
- Dramatization
- Storytelling and Story Reading
- Computer Applications
- Etymology Study
- Word Play

*I*N A second-grade class, Mark, a gifted student, and David are both painting on a large piece of newsprint. David is leaning on the paper, engrossed in his painting. "Rotate the paper so I can finish," Mark directs curtly. David is puzzled. From Mark's tone of voice, David picks up clues that Mark is irritated, but he does not understand the demand. He thinks Mark is asking him to give up his painting, and, since he is not finished, he keeps his elbow planted on the paper. Impatiently Mark tugs at the paper, tearing it at the point where David's elbow rests. David howls with anger, "Now look what you've done. It's ruined."

The teacher comes over to check on the disturbance. Mark is quick to explain, "I asked him to turn the paper around, and he wouldn't, so I tried to turn it myself."

"You didn't say to turn it around," David complains. "You said to rotate it."

"David, do you remember how to locate words in the dictionary?" asks the teacher quickly, before Mark can respond. She remembers that David had done well with that lesson last week.

"Yeah, I think so," replies David.

"Here is the spelling of *rotate*," the teacher says, writing the word on a piece of paper and handing it to David. "Look it up in your dictionary and see what it means."

David goes to his desk and looks up the word. He comes hurrying back to the teacher in a few minutes. "It does mean 'turn around,'" he admits. "I'll know that next time!"

David is using the context of the situation to attempt to make sense of a word he does not know. The verbal context is not complete enough to provide him with the meaning. He uses nonverbal clues to detect Mark's irritation but does not come to a correct conclusion when he tries to put the clues together. The teacher sees an opportunity to encourage David to use his dictionary skills when he is confused about a word's meaning. She knows that he has the skills and wants him to see their application. Children need to realize that context clues are not always explicit enough to clarify a word's meaning. They need to go to the dictionary to find a precise meaning that the context cannot provide.

Reflections

What do you think about the teacher's approach to Mark's situation in the opening vignette? What would you have done if you had been the teacher?

Writing

Vocabulary is central to communication through language. When students acquire new vocabulary, they are acquiring building blocks of language. Words are abstract symbols that we are able to manipulate without actually having present the things that they represent. This situation makes possible communication with others on countless topics, both familiar to and far removed from our existence. Without vocabulary, most oral and written communication would be impossible. Try to tell someone something without using words. You will be reduced to making imitative sounds (for example, making animal sounds when you are trying to pass along an idea about an animal), pantomiming actions, or drawing pictures. None of these procedures offers as explicit a message as is conveyed by using words.

Knowledge of word meanings is important to comprehension. Therefore, teaching word meanings is a vital part of language instruction. Stahl (1986) found that both definitions and context have to be provided for a word in order for vocabulary instruction to improve comprehension, that methods requiring students to think deeply about words are more likely to be effective, and that multiple exposures to a word and its meaning in different contexts are important.

In the comic strip shown at the top of page 81, Jeremy evidently does not know the meaning of the word *depress* in the context in which he has found it. Most seventh- and eighth-graders, asked why this comic strip is funny, would either reveal their knowledge of the multiple meaning or go to the dictionary to find out the meaning of this word. Some might also need to discover the meaning of *harsh*.

A person's vocabulary has a strong relationship to general intelligence and to reading comprehension. As children get older, their vocabularies grow and become more diverse. Gray reported the results of a review of the literature concerning vocabulary by Gray and Holmes which showed "that growth in meaning vocabulary is correlated more or less closely with intelligence, the

Reflections

How would you tell someone that your house was on fire without using words? Try it.

© Zits Partnership. Reprinted with special permission of King Features Syndicate.

nature of the instruction given, the experience and cultural influences of the pupils and interest in the meanings of words" (Guthrie, 1984, p. 35). Gray was most encouraged by the fact that instruction appeared to be an important determinant of the development of meaning vocabulary (Guthrie, 1984).

Vocabulary instruction should take place in every class throughout the day. In general, teachers should choose terms for vocabulary instruction from classroom reading materials that are central to those materials (Blachowicz & Lee, 1991; Dixon-Krauss, 2001/2002; Rupley, Logan, & Nichols, 1998/1999). Teaching content area vocabulary when the students need it to understand their textbooks is much more effective than teaching it in isolation. Thematic units should always have a vocabulary instruction component.

Concept Development and Word Meanings

WORDS ARE just oral or written symbols for concepts that we have developed through various avenues of experience. The relationship of the words that stand for the concepts to the concepts themselves is arbitrary. A word means what a group of people agree that it means. That is why words are easily added to our language through coinage of new terms and why words that have been a part of our language for years change in meaning over time or add new meanings.

The idea that words are not inherent in their objects must be developed by young children. Five-and six-year-olds gradually make this discovery. Children who know more than one language learn this more readily because they know more than one word that stands for an object or idea. Learning the different meanings of multiple-meaning words in English, such as *bear* meaning "to carry" or "an animal," helps native English speakers acquire this concept. Students in the intermediate grades may develop this concept more firmly by reading and discussing the book *Frindle* by Andrew Clements.

Many words are learned by children through listening to their parents, other adults, and siblings talk about the things around them. Children experiment with using words

Teaching Tip

If there are ELLs or even students from other English-speaking countries in your class, make connections for them between the vocabulary in their culture and the vocabulary in the reading material. Sometimes only the vocabulary terms, but not the concepts behind them, are confusing. For instance, a speaker of American English may understand the sentence: "He raised the hood of the car." Speakers of British English could be confused by the sentence because they call that part of the car a *bonnet*, not a *hood*. Discussing the fact that these are two terms for the same thing may clear up the misunderstanding without further instruction. In this case, the students are just learning a new label for a known concept (Armbruster & Nagy, 1992).

and with seeing what effect the words have on those around them. Most people have encountered a small child repeating an unacceptable word or phrase for its obvious shock value. Although their understanding of the words that they use may be incomplete when they first attempt to use them, their trial-and-error method of usage eventually leads to a degree of mastery over the terms.

Children do not just randomly imitate the sounds they hear. They "select from the flow of language those words and sound patterns which have meaning to them: *mama, milk, daddy*" (Forester & Mickelson, 1979, p. 76). The first words are largely connected to concrete objects and events, but gradually the vocabularies will expand from a base of mainly nouns and verbs to include other word types. Chomsky (1979) points out that the most important part of the language learning that children do is not imitative; it is constructive, taking language rules that have been internalized by exposure to language usage in their environment and applying the rule system that they have inferred to produce new results. For example, when something comes apart, a child may say it is "untogether" because of the understanding she has of the function of the prefix *un-* in other words. Even though adults view such a usage as an error, it shows the child's evolving knowledge of language structure and is a very reasonable deduction in the early stages of language learning.

Children learn much vocabulary from listening to the speech around them. You can promote vocabulary growth by not "talking down" to your students. You should use precise terminology as you discuss things in class. You should encourage curiosity about words and their meanings to develop word consciousness (Graves & Watts-Taffe, 2002). Calling attention to excellent word choices in literature selections is a good method of fos-

Using manipulatives is one good way to work on teaching vocabulary and concepts.

tering word consciousness. The book *Miss Alaineus: A Vocabulary Disaster* by Debra Frasier offers an excellent vehicle for talking about word meanings and possibilities for misunderstanding words and their meanings.

Read-aloud sessions by both parents and teachers help students to build vocabulary knowledge. As parents read stories aloud to their children, they may casually define unfamiliar words or help the child make connections with the unfamiliar words and events and their everyday experiences. Teachers may have more structured plans for teaching vocabulary through read-alouds.

Generally, more **concrete (direct) experiences** with objects and ideas result in development of deeper understanding of the words associated with that object or idea. Eating fresh pineapple develops a sensory base for understanding the concept of *pineapple* that showing pictures of the pineapple cannot equal. Even describing the taste, appearance, and other characteristics of the pineapple for someone does not add enough sensory input to equal letting that person taste, touch, smell, and see the pineapple. Using manipulatives in class to work on vocabulary and concepts is a way to provide concrete experiences. For example, students can measure *feet, inches,* and *yards* with tape measures and rulers to develop concepts of length and measure *cups, pints,* and *quarts* with measuring cups for measures of volume. They can pour water on cotton balls to show *absorption* or stretch rubber bands to demonstrate *elasticity* (Petrick, 1992). Experiences that are not concrete are called **vicarious experiences**. Vicarious experiences do not involve all of the senses—perhaps sight alone is involved (as with still pictures) or sight and hearing (as with a videotape).

Words are of little use to people if they do not represent known concepts, for under these circumstances they

Reflections

What other instances of logical vocabulary errors that young children make can you name? What grammatical rules are they trying to follow?

Reflections

What other types of experiences qualify as vicarious experiences? Are they helpful to concept development? If so, how?

Applications for English Language Learners and Students with Special Needs

A technique suggested by Hickman, Pollard-Durodola, and Vaughn (2004) for use with ELLs is also helpful to struggling readers who speak English but have limited vocabularies. Hickman and colleagues recommend daily story read-aloud sessions from both narrative and informational trade books. They choose material that is one or two grade levels higher than the grade placement of the students. If several books are chosen with the same theme, vocabulary can be reinforced across texts. The texts are divided into short passages (200-250 words long), and three vocabulary words are introduced for each section. The story is read sequentially over several days so that the students are exposed to the entire story. Review of the words takes place daily, and at the end of the reading there is a final review and activities to reinforce the word meanings. It is best if such activities require active responses on the part of the students.

Words that evoke mental images are easier to learn than words that do not.

are just meaningless sounds. Therefore, if we are to add words to children's vocabularies, we must ascertain if the related concepts are known by the children, and, if they are not known, we must attempt to develop them.

The concepts that people have are based on their backgrounds of experiences. Children with limited experiences have fewer concepts to which they can attach vocabulary terms. For these children, concept development becomes a natural part of vocabulary instruction. A lesson for teaching the concept of "eraser" is presented in Minilesson 3.1.

Concepts develop in interrelated clusters. If you are trying to teach the concept of *fishing*, you have to relate such concepts as *rod, reel, bait, hook, cast, line,* and so on.

Words that have concrete referents *(treadmill)* are easier to learn than are abstract words *(fitness)*. Words that evoke mental images *(rhinoceros)* are easier to learn than words that do not *(jealous)*. Words that relate to students' experiences *(thoroughbred* for Kentucky students) are easier than ones that do not *(tundra* for Kentucky students). Structure words, such as *what* or *though,* are generally harder to learn than are nouns and verbs. Children

Reflections

How do you develop understanding of an abstract concept, such as justice?

Minilesson 3.1

Concept Development

Begin to teach the concept of eraser by showing the children many different kinds of erasers: pencil, ink, dry erase board, and so on. Show different sizes and shapes of these erasers as you repeat the label *eraser.* Demonstrate the function of each eraser *and,* for maximum effectiveness, allow the students to use the erasers, which gives them the opportunity to see, touch, and even smell the erasers. Next, let students identify examples and non-examples of erasers. If you write with your finger in a sand tray and then wipe the letters away with your hand, and the children recognize that your hand is being used as an eraser, they probably have the concept, since the concept of *eraser* implies a function, not a shape or size or color.

What are the students learning?

Through direct experiences, the students are learning to extract the essential features that fit the concept and to discard the irrelevant details.

Applications *for English Language Learners and Students with Special Needs*

Focus on teaching several word meanings each week to students who lack the vocabulary and concepts that will help them be successful with school work. Consider individual needs in planning such lessons. Teach words that are meaningful to and immediately useful for these students. Include planned repetition throughout the week for each word that receives instructional attention.

---

in first grade generally have structure words in their listening and speaking vocabularies already, but may not yet have them in their reading and writing vocabularies. If all other things are equal, it is probably wise to teach first the words that are needed earliest or most frequently for completing school assignments or for activities in daily life.

Children may have less differentiated meanings for words than do adults. They may respond to the word *take* in the same way they respond to the word *buy*. They have the correct direction for the transaction, but do not include the necessary exchange of money. As time passes, they add more of the adult distinctions to the word meanings (Anderson & Freebody, 1981).

Teaching Tip

To teach word meanings, provide links with the students' experiences, examples of several contexts in which each word may be used, and much review. Point out the ways that function words establish relationships between other words in sentences.

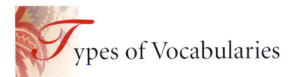

Types of Vocabularies

EVERYONE HAS four different vocabularies: listening, speaking, reading, and writing. Each of these vocabularies may be developed to different levels in an individual.

Listening Vocabulary

The listening vocabulary is composed of those words a person understands when he hears them spoken. It is possible for a word to be in a person's listening vocabulary and not in his speaking, reading, or writing vocabulary. For many children, the listening vocabulary exceeds each of the other vocabularies by a large margin. Listening develops in a child before speaking, reading, and writing and may serve as a readiness agent for the other areas.

When a child begins to recognize that the word *cookie* refers to the sweet treat that she enjoys, the child at first probably responds positively only when hearing the word.

Later the child feels confident enough of the word to use it to communicate with others orally. Still later, reading and writing of the word are likely to develop.

Speaking Vocabulary

The speaking vocabulary is composed of those words a person can use orally to communicate information to others. The child who exclaims "Cookie!" while reaching toward the cookie jar is effectively transmitting the desire for a cookie to another person. Since speaking vocabularies are usually based on listening vocabularies, they are generally smaller than the listening vocabularies. Most people understand many words that they never feel confident enough to use orally.

Much vocabulary is learned by children listening to the conversations of others in their environment and gradually beginning to participate, using words that they have heard. Acquisition of vocabulary is enhanced by a language-rich environment, so having good language models is important (Anderson & Nagy, 1991; Brabham & Villaume, 2002).

Reading Vocabulary

The reading vocabulary is composed of the words that a person recognizes and understands when they are seen in print. A word may be in a person's listening and speaking vocabularies and still not be in his reading vocabulary for at least two reasons. First, the person may not yet have learned the sound-symbol relationships that are needed to read that word, even though there is a regular sound-symbol association involved. For example, a young child may understand the word *brick* when he hears it and may be able to use the word when speaking, but, because the child has not learned the *br* blend (or some other part of the word), he may not be able to read the word *brick* yet. Another reason a word may not be in a person's reading vocabulary is that the word does not fit a regular sound-symbol association pattern. For example, a person may have used a chamois before, may understand the word when it is spoken, and may be able to use the word orally, and still not be able to recognize it in print because the sound-symbol associations are not regular in English.

Especially for older children and adults, words may be in reading vocabularies, but not in listening and speaking vocabularies. This may be true of any word whose meaning is gained from reading context or from a dictionary or glossary, but which has never been encountered in oral situations.

Research shows increases in students' vocabularies when they read material that has numerous new words (Pressley, 2002). The vicarious experiences gained through reading provide them with words and concepts that are not present in daily language interactions (Brabham & Villaume, 2002). Therefore, increasing the reading that students do can result in a substantial increase in the words they learn (Graves & Watts-Taffe, 2002).

Writing Vocabulary

The writing vocabulary is composed of words that a person can use accurately in written communications. Most people have fewer words in their writing vocabularies than in their listening, speaking, and reading vocabularies. Using a word in writing requires more than just understanding it when it is heard (listening vocabulary) or read (reading vocabulary). Just as speaking the word does, writing the word requires the ability to recall the word and its meaning and to place it in meaningful relationships to other words, but writing requires one additional step—encoding the word into printed symbols. Writing vocabulary therefore takes somewhat longer to acquire. In addition, the permanence of the written word, as opposed to the spoken word, and its openness to close scrutiny make many people unwilling to use in writing any words that they are not sure they have under complete control. Students writing themes often have excellent descriptive words in mind to use, but opt for easier words because they are more sure of either their spellings or meanings.

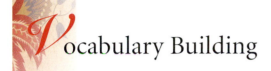

Vocabulary Building

VOCABULARY INSTRUCTION is a complex area. You must choose effective techniques for teaching word meanings.

Techniques for Teaching

Although the content of reading materials for primary-grade children generally is not filled with complex concepts that need development for all children, some children may need concept development for some of these stories. In one school situation, Betty Roe found several children who had never used scissors and crayons prior to their school experience. Their home environments lacked the stimulation of extensive possessions, reading materials, and conversation. Before they could be successful with class activities, these children needed concept development that the rest of the children did not require.

Because older students encounter many abstract concepts in their reading materials, they often need extensive concept development and vocabulary instruction. In addition, children with special needs, such as ELLs, may require even more attention to vocabulary development. In one case, rural fourth-graders were brought to the nearest town to ride the only elevator in the county so that they could understand a basal reader story about an elevator.

Concept development is a necessary part of vocabulary instruction in content area studies. Many of the terms that are presented are not a part of the students' everyday language and need to be developed separately.

Students may be more receptive to vocabulary instruction when they have had input into the content. Ainslie (2000/2001) turns her students into "word detectives" who look for unknown words that they refer to as "suspects." The students take notes on their words, and each week two students make graphic organizers based on words they have found. These organizers include the words, their definitions, their parts of speech, the sentences in which they were found, other contextual clues for the words, and student-created sentence examples to show to their classmates. Other students put information about these words in their own notebooks, sometimes questioning the detective about her word. The words are put on a word wall and reviewed during the week. Brabham and Villaume (2002) also believe that students should select their own words for vocabulary instruction.

Rosenbaum (2001) also developed a word map for her students to use with words they located during independent reading. On the maps, students included "synonyms, brief descriptions, examples and nonexamples, rephrasing, repetition, associations, and unique expression" (Rosenbaum, 2001, p. 45).

Ruddell and Shearer (2002) believe that students learn new words not through verbal explanations that also involve new words, but from ongoing transactions with the words, in social interactions in the classroom, and in general life experiences. These ongoing transactions with a word increase word awareness and word learning strategies. Ruddell and Shearer had at-risk middle school students choose words both from their content area classes and from nonschool sources. During the week the words were discussed, and semantic mapping and semantic feature analysis were employed. Ruddell and Shearer felt that the words the students chose were important and challenging words. These middle school students learned the words and retained them.

Vocabulary development techniques should actively involve the learner as much as possible. Students understand and retain better those things that they have experienced most directly and have been involved in analyzing and discussing. Encouraging use in spoken and written language of the vocabulary terms that are receiving attention is therefore a good idea. One active method of learning word meanings is through conversations with the teacher and other students about a topic related to the words.

Students need instruction that provides them with strategies for independent vocabulary development outside of the classroom. Learning the use of reference sources related to vocabulary is one way to accomplish this. Learning to use structural analysis and context clues are two other ways.

Vocabulary that receives attention should be reviewed periodically, because repetition helps retention and, in varying contexts, broadens understanding. Give students positive reinforcement when they use previously studied vocabulary terms in their oral and written assignments.

Some specific techniques for teaching vocabulary are described next. They are not meant to be used in isolation, but in combinations that allow the students to manipulate the words being studied in a variety of ways. These techniques may be used in conjunction with development of basal reader vocabulary, general vocabulary knowledge, or content area vocabulary.

Reflections

What terms related to the study of different climates and different terrains require special vocabulary development for children in your geographic area? How would you handle this instruction?

Teaching Tip

Realize that children many not have learned some words that were previously presented. Be alert for this possibility and be ready to work with words other than "new" words that require attention. Make it standard procedure to pay attention to difficult words from previous lessons that require reteaching or elaboration in new contexts.

CATEGORIZATION

One of the most effective ways to work with word meanings is to place the words into categories. By seeing the relationships among many familiar words and the new words, children build connections between new information and prior knowledge. **Categorization** of words is also one way to develop the thinking skill of classifying.

A popular children's game is the classification activity "Animal, Vegetable, Mineral," in which one person thinks of an item and the others try to identify it by first determining the general category and then asking questions about it that can be answered by "yes" or "no." If the item is not identified in a specified number of questions, the questioner has lost, the other player identifies the item and then thinks of another item, and the game begins again. This game might be played in the classroom with new vocabulary terms being interspersed with familiar words.

Plastic miniatures of people, animals, vehicles, and buildings can also be used as the basis for classification activities. The teacher may place the items on a table in an arrangement such that all of the items except one could fit into a common category, such as *people*. The children are asked to find and remove the item that does not fit and to tell why they chose that item. The items may also be grouped into classifications such as living and nonliving, movable and stationary, and so on. The movable items may be further classified into those with wheels, those with runners, those with legs, and so on, and the animals may be further classified into families, for example. The teacher should lead the children to discuss reasons for groupings that they develop, pointing out common characteristics.

At first the teacher may designate the categories, but eventually the children need to come up with the categories independently. This same sequence can be used with word lists in reading. When students are asked to put terms into categories, they are performing **word sorts**. When they are asked to place the words into predetermined categories, they are performing closed sorts. When they are asked to place items in categories that they discover themselves, they are performing open sorts. Both types of sorts are good learning activities. Figure 3.1 shows an open word sort.

*F*IGURE 3.1   **Open Word Sort**

Place the following words into categories of things that are related. Be ready to explain your categorization in class.

kayak	jet liner	sedan
canoe	pick-up truck	ocean liner
convertible	bicycle	rowboat
hot-air balloon	glider	eighteen wheeler
motorcycle	submarine	space shuttle

The teacher may also provide a category, without providing items to place within the category, and let the children suggest appropriate items. We asked first-graders to name things that grow and got the following list of suggestions:

grass	trees	flowers	hair
animals	your education	your vocabulary	children

Johnson and Pearson (1978) suggest an activity with word categories that is enjoyable for children and promotes vocabulary development at the same time. A word is written vertically on the left side of the paper as shown in Figure 3.2. (A child's name may be used, as is the case in this example.) Categories are placed in a row across the top of the page. The children are challenged to use reference books to help them fill in the resulting grid with words for each category that start with each letter on the left.

SEMANTIC FEATURE ANALYSIS

Semantic feature analysis is another good way to conduct word study (Johnson & Pearson, 1978). In it, a number of words are categorized in relationship to several characteristics. For example, musical instruments are located under such classifications as string, woodwind, brass, percussion, mouthpiece, bow, and others, as shown in Figure 3.3.

The more features that are considered, the more knowledge the children have to display about the target words to complete the chart. If enough features are included along the top of the chart, no two items will have exactly the same pattern of pluses and minuses. In Figure 3.3, for example, timpani and snare drum have the same pattern, but the addition of *snare* to the list of features would differentiate the two items. Similarly, trumpet and trombone have the same pattern, but the addition of *slide* to the list of features would change the pattern. Johnson and Pearson (1978) suggest either the use of the plus to show the presence of a feature and the minus to show its absence or the use of a scale of numbers to show the varying degrees to which the features exist.

Ranking words on one feature is one activity related to semantic feature analysis. For example, words such as *none, some, many,* and *all* could be ranked on the basis of

FIGURE 3.2   Categorization Activity

	Games	Birds	Foods	Clothes	Actions
B	badminton	bluebird	banana	blouse	bounce
A	Aggravation	albatross	apricots	apron	arise
B	baseball	blackbird	beef	bonnet	burst
S	softball	sandpiper	sandwich	suit	sit

FIGURE 3.3   **Semantic Feature Analysis**

	String	Woodwind	Brass	Percussion	Mouthpiece	Bow
Trumpet	–	–	+	–	+	–
Clarinet	–	+	–	–	+	–
Trombone	–	–	+	–	+	–
Timpani	–	–	–	+	–	–
Guitar	+	–	–	–	–	–
Violin	+	–	–	–	–	+
Snare Drum	–	–	–	+	–	–
Oboe	–	+	–	–	+	–

amount. Ranking synonyms on one feature is another helpful activity. For instance, the words *smell, odor,* and *stench* might be rated according to intensity.

MAKING ANALOGIES

Making **analogies** is a good way to learn about words, as well as to develop thinking skills related to classifying, comparing, and contrasting. Young children start learning the skills necessary for making analogies when they engage in categorization activities, since successful analogy construction requires the recognition of the relationships among words. With young children, the teacher may say, "A sock goes on your foot like what goes on your hand?" The children are led to see that both relationships are the same type. Gradually the analogies come to be stated as "Sock is to foot as _____ is to hand." Analogies can be developed on the basis of a multitude of possible relationships: part-whole, synonym, antonym, homonym, member-organization, and function-object, to name a few. Older students can be introduced to the symbols related to analogies, as the analogies become "Sock : foot :: _____ : hand." Children enjoy completing such analogies and also creating analogies of their own. Such activities require the use of higher order thinking skills.

STRUCTURAL ANALYSIS

Structural analysis involves learning to recognize common word parts, such as prefixes, suffixes, inflectional endings, parts of compound words, and parts of contractions, and associating meaning with these word parts. Knowledge of structural analysis gives students a powerful tool in learning the meanings of new words. It also enables them to develop skill in analytical thinking as they learn how to understand and use parts of words.

   Prefixes and **suffixes** are common word parts that influence the meanings of the words of which they are a part. Prefixes are groups of letters attached to the beginnings of words that modify the meanings of the words (e.g., *tie—untie).* Suffixes are groups of letters added to the endings of words that may change their meanings or parts of speech (e.g., *act—action).* Remy Charlip's *Fortunately* is an excellent book to use with teaching the prefix *un-*.

Inflectional endings are letters or groups of letters added to the endings of words that may change the tense (e.g., *hop—hopped*) or person (e.g., *go—goes*) of a verb; the number (e.g., *girl—girls*), case (e.g., *girl—girl's*), or gender (e.g., *host—hostess*) of a noun; or the degree (e.g., *big—bigger*) of an adjective. Students are exposed to these endings from their earliest language experiences and benefit from learning to recognize them and the effects that they have on root words.

In working with inflectional endings, emphasize the effects that the endings have on root words. First-graders may benefit from a practice activity such as the one in Figure 3.4. After the children have completed the written activity, lead a discussion about the endings of the words in the second column and ask children to produce the singular forms of these words for comparison.

During class instruction, show the children a piece of rope that is three feet long and say, "This is a short rope." Show another piece of rope that is two feet long and say, "This is a shorter rope than the other one." Finally, show a one-foot length of rope and say, "This rope is the shortest of the three ropes." Choosing two children of different heights, ask, "Which one is shorter?" After a correct decision is made, add another child to the group and ask, "Who is shortest?" Using the ropes again, ask, "Which rope is longest?" Then ask, "Of the remaining two ropes, which is longer?" Such questioning guides the children's thinking processes.

Another inflectional ending practice activity is found in Figure 3.5. Also consider using the book *Pig, Pigger, Piggest* by Rick Walton when teaching the comparative and superlative forms of adjectives. The children will be laughing as they learn. They will soon be chiming in with enthusiasm on the words that are intended to show degree.

Compound words are words made up of two or more smaller words that combine to produce a new meaning (e.g., *houseboat.*) Sometimes compound nouns are written as two separate nouns, as is true in the term *police officer*. This is not just an instance of an adjective modifying a noun, because *police* is not an adjective. The term *new officer* has an adjective modifying a noun. It can be restated as "the officer who is new." Our original example cannot be restated as "the officer who is police."

$\mathcal{F}$IGURE 3.4 **Inflectional Ending Activity for Plurals**

Directions: Put each word under the correct heading.

Words	One Thing	More Than One Thing
tree		
toys		
birds		
hat		
bees		

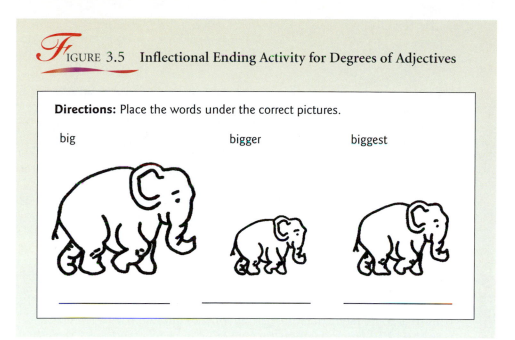

FIGURE 3.5   **Inflectional Ending Activity for Degrees of Adjectives**

Directions: Place the words under the correct pictures.

big   bigger   biggest

Not all compound words can be defined by linking the definitions of the component parts, for example, *butterfly*. When a compound word that cannot be defined using its component words' meanings together is encountered, students should be encouraged to apply context clues to help in defining the word. Sometimes, as in the word *butterfly*, one component word may be helpful. If other means fail, students can use the dictionary to determine the meanings of compound words.

Contractions are formed by joining two words, leaving out one or more letters, and replacing them with an apostrophe (e.g., *he would—he'd.*) Some children have trouble differentiating between contractions and possessives, which are also formed with apostrophes. Have them substitute the two words from which the contraction would have been formed for the word in the sentence. The result is nonsense when the word is possessive. (For example: "Tom's hat is here." "Tom is hat is here" makes no sense. "Tom's going to town." "Tom is going to town" makes sense.)

Teaching prefixes and suffixes by presenting lists of the word parts and their meanings is not a good practice. The word parts are learned best if they are taught in the context of words for which the children can see some use in their school activities. A good technique for teaching prefixes is found in Minilesson 3.2.

Children have fun drawing the parts of compound words and letting their classmates guess the words. They also enjoy computer activities in which they match parts of compound words, contractions with meanings, prefixes or suffixes with roots, and so on. The correct choices may result in spoken reinforcement, such as, "Great job, Johnny," or in a rewarding visual display, such as fireworks.

More information on structural analysis is presented in Chapter 7. You may want to refer to both chapters as you work on this area of reading.

Teaching Tip

Choose words from content area textbooks that have prefixes and suffixes that are found in that subject area; for example, in math, *tri-* is found in *triangle*.

Minilesson 3.2

Prefixes

List several words containing the prefix in question on the board (e.g., *un-afraid, unaware, unconcerned, unhappy*). Ask the children what word part is common to all the words. They will readily identify the *un-*. Have them define each of the words ("not afraid," "not aware," "not concerned," "not happy"). Ask them what is common to all the definitions. They will be likely to identify the *not.* Then ask them what part of the words they think has the meaning of *not.* By this time, they should be ready to respond with *un-*. Ask them to suggest some other words that have this common part. Write them on the board, define them, and check to see if they fit the pattern. Also ask them to be on the alert for new words with this common part as they go about their regular reading activities and use the meaning of the word part to help them understand the meaning of the new words. (Basically the same process can be used to teach word parts orally. Children would name the words, listen for the common parts, define the words, find the commonalties, generate other examples, and check them for applicability to the pattern.)

What are the students learning?

They are learning to attend to common word parts and their meanings, which will help them figure out the meanings of new words that they encounter.

USE OF CONTEXT CLUES

Teaching students to use **context clues** to determine word meanings is a valuable practice. At times, context clues are helpful enough to directly define words. At other times, they may offer comparisons or contrasts or examples related to the term. *Pictures* are the most common context clues used by primary-grade children in reading, but older children make much use of print clues, and all children use other types of context clues in their attempts to understand spoken language.

In both spoken and written language, there are often semantic and syntactic clues to word meanings. *Semantic clues* are clues found in the meanings of the surrounding words and sentences. *Syntactic clues* are clues found in the grammar of the language. In our language, certain types of words usually appear in certain positions in sentences. For example, adjectives generally appear before nouns. Syntactic clues also allow us to expect singular or plural forms in certain positions in sentences. The nonsense poem "Jabberwocky" begins as follows:

Twas brillig, and the slithy toves

Did gyre and gimble in the wabe:

All mimsy were the borogoves,

And the mome raths outgrabe.

—Lewis Carroll, *Through the Looking Glass*

In this poem we know that "slithy toves" is a phrase made up of an adjective and a plural noun, because the *-y* is a common ending for an adjective and *toves* appears to be the subject of the verb "did gyre and gimble." The *-s* ending on *toves* indicates the plural, and the *did* is a verb marker for us. Even though there is no meaning to be gained from this particular poem, the use of English syntax allows speakers of English to make many decisions about the functions of the nonsense words in it.

A story that said a man was paid 10 denarii for his work could be expected to cause no problem for the typical child in understanding of the passage. Most children will recognize the position in the sentence to indicate a noun and from the meanings of the surrounding words will decide that *denarii* refers to a type of money. Even though the exact amount may be unknown, the ability to equate the unfamiliar word with money allows the children to understand the general activity being described and, therefore, allows them to proceed to listen to or read the story without losing the meaning, in spite of the unfamiliar word.

A word may actually be *defined* in the context, especially in nonfiction books. *Mummies & Their Mysteries* by Charlotte Wilcox contains the following definition in context: "A mummy is the body of a human or animal in which some of the soft tissues (skin, muscles, or organs) did not decay after death" (p. 7). In the book *The Bone Wars* by Kathryn Lasky, Thaddeus asks, "What's extinct?" (p. 30) and is told, "More dead than dead. . . . Gone forever as a species." (p. 31). In *The Phantom Tollbooth* by Norton Juster, Milo is told, "The Doldrums, my young friend, are where nothing ever happens and nothing ever changes" (p. 23). Sometimes a number of sentences are used to define or explain the word completely, as in this excerpt from *Dragonwings* by Laurence Yep:

> Over tea he told us about some crazy demon, *Baldwin*, who put air into a big canvas bag and then floated up into the sky, where he was under the control of the winds. He had a special, sausage-shaped canvas bag built for him, maybe about thirty feet long. It was covered with a giant net which went down to its belly, from which a wooden frame was suspended. There were *propellers* and a motor in the frame, and they sent the bag lumbering through the air, so he could guide his own flight.
>
> It was one of the pioneer *dirigibles,* but at that time we thought of it as almost a miracle (pp. 60-61).

A similar definition/explanation is found in Yep's *Hiroshima*:

> Everything is made up of tiny particles called atoms. They are so small they are invisible to the eye. The atoms are also made up of even smaller parts. Energy holds these parts together like glue (pp. 18-19).

This piece of historical fiction would enrich a unit study of World War II, clarifying a number of concepts with clear context clues. Many selections for children and adolescents define words in context to ensure understanding and thus promote vocabulary development.

Books such as *A Gaggle of Geese* by Philippa-Alys Browne, *A Gaggle of Geese* by Eve Merriam, and *A Cache of Jewels and Other Collective Nouns* by Ruth Heller present collective terminology for groups in an interesting context. These are all picture books, but they can be used in all grade levels for the purpose of teaching collective nouns.

Sometimes the context provides a *restatement* of the word's meaning, as it does in this excerpt from *My Daniel* by Pam Conrad: "And the year before the drought began, my father's whole crop was eaten by locusts. Bugs that flew in one afternoon and ate everything" (p. 21). Sometimes there is a description followed by a word that the description fits, as in this sentence in *Dragonwings:* "His hair was brown, and his face was covered with brown spots—*freckles*, Robin told me later" (p. 112).

Books may offer glimpses of the meanings of words from other languages in their restatements. *Farewell to Manzanar* by Jeanne Wakatsuki Houston and James D. Houston, which might be used in a unit on World War II and the Japanese internment camps in the United States, offers some Japanese, as in the following excerpt: "Happily, gratefully, Mama bowed again and said, '*Arigato*' (Thank you). '*Arigato gozaimas*' (Thank you very much)" (p. 32).

Children need to realize that context clues may be in the sentence in which an unfamiliar word is found, in adjacent sentences, or even in sentences far removed from the unfamiliar word. Being alert for clues whenever unfamiliar words appear in speech or writing helps them figure out likely word meanings, although context is not always sufficient, as is evident in the classroom vignette at the beginning of the chapter and in many literature selections.

In *One More River* by Lynne Reid Banks, the context clues are not always found in the sentence or in adjacent sentences. In this book, Lesley's father says, "We're going to emigrate," and then two paragraphs down are the sentences "Because emigrating meant leaving Canada. Permanently" (p. 6). Later, on page 51, Banks uses almost a paragraph to have Lesley describe a kibbutz to her parents, letting readers in on the information at the same time. This book also has a number of places where Lesley is given Hebrew words for English ones that she knows, helping her to learn the language and exposing readers to a bit of Hebrew.

In a unit study of Israel, *One More River* would provide students with a wealth of information about Jewish culture and the Hebrew language while entertaining the students with an engaging story that entices them to learn the material. This is also true of Banks's sequel, *Broken Bridge*. In it, vocabulary is naturally incorporated, as in this excerpt:

A strange bird with barred wings, and a crest that nodded forward and then sank back, landed on the path in front of them.

"Look! What's that?"

"It's a hoopoe," said her father dully (p. 118).

The book continues to expose students to a different culture and the accompanying language.

Sometimes context clues are helpful, even when they are much less explicit. In *One More River*, it says, "There were to be no allies. She would have to fight on her own" (p. 17). The context offers a *contrast* clue to the meaning of *allies*, but the reader must make an inference to decide on a meaning.

There may be several context clues available to help in figuring out a particular word's meaning. Consider the following passage, which has a *comparison* clue for the word *daunted*:

Marty was a devoted fan of pro football. No matter what the weather, he was never daunted. Others would be dismayed by rain or snow. Not Marty. He hurried to the games and cheered enthusiastically through sunshine or blizzard. Nothing discouraged him from being there to support his team.

In this passage the word *daunted* may be an unfamiliar word to listeners or readers. It is compared first with *dismayed* and later with *discouraged,* since these are things that others may be, but not Marty; he was said not to be *daunted* by the weather. Inference is necessary for the listener or reader to decide that all three of the words refer to a similar concept, a trait that Marty does not have. Therefore, the listener or reader can decide that *daunted* has a meaning close to that of *dismayed* or *discouraged*.

Vocabulary instruction and word study in the context of a literature selection have been found effective in vocabulary building. Teachers can work on the unfamiliar vocabulary words by defining them through word structure or meaning clues or connecting them with word origin information. Students can then provide synonyms for these words or use them in sentences. Finally, students can examine the use of the words within the literature selection. Teachers can model use of unfamiliar words in class discussions of literature, and students can begin to use these words in literature response journals that provide material for their class contributions (Dixon-Krauss, 2001/2002). Because of the beneficial effect of using context clues to build meaning vocabulary, wide reading in a variety of literary genres of literature written by a variety of authors is likely to result in increased reading vocabulary, which in turn may be added to writing, listening, and speaking vocabularies as time passes.

More information on use of context clues is presented in Chapter 7. You may want to refer to both of these chapters when dealing with instruction in use of context clues.

USE OF THE DICTIONARY AND THESAURUS

Use of the dictionary and thesaurus is another approach to vocabulary development that should not be overlooked. Dictionary skills need to be deliberately taught so that students can use them independently when the need arises. The thesaurus should be introduced also, because it offers a special type of reference function that is particularly useful to writers. Dictionaries are available on a wide range of difficulty levels. Choose dictionaries to use in class that are on or below the reading level of your students so that the definitions offered are understandable to them. Junior thesauruses are also available. Teachers and students may prefer to use electronic dictionaries or thesauruses that are available on CDs for computers or on various Internet sites.

When students look up words in the dictionary, they often do not need all of the information that is found. If they need help only on pronunciation of the word, the phonetic respelling and the pronunciation key hold the information sought. If they are seeking information about word meaning, however, they need to be led to use some information that they may have been ignoring. In addition to the lists of meanings that the students expect to find in the dictionary, there are part-of-speech labels, sometimes represented by abbreviations that have to be looked up in lists of abbreviations located elsewhere in the dictionary. There may also be special forms of words with varying endings; indications of languages of origin, along with the meanings of the words in those languages; pictures that represent the words; or sentences that show the words in context. All of these features can be helpful in the exploration of word meaning.

Checking the part of speech listed before a particular set of meanings may help the dictionary user avoid

Dictionaries help students discover different meanings for familiar words.

reading meanings not directly related to the word in the particular context in question. Many words can be used as different parts of speech and, as such, have very different meanings. For example, in the sentence "He tried to block the passage of the bill," the word *block* is a verb and has a very different meaning from the one it has in the sentence "I will run around the block five times for exercise," in which the word is a noun. Checking the meanings of *block* only in the places where it is defined as a verb will reduce the amount of time spent searching for the intended meaning.

The listings of special forms of the word with varying endings are helpful to the writer who may be using variant forms of the word and may need to check the appropriate spelling of the word with particular endings. Discovering the language of origin may give the children clues to why the word is not spelled as they would have expected it to be, and seeing the meaning of the word and its component parts in the original language will give some background for appreciation of the meaning that it has taken on in our language. Pictures that show the word's meaning are very helpful to children who have difficulty visualizing the meanings of printed terms, and sample sentences with the word in context often help them to apply the dictionary definition more accurately.

Discuss the definitions with the children, making sure that they realize that a word may have many different meanings, only one of which will make sense in the context in which they have heard or seen it. Each definition, or at least each definition of the word that is listed under the appropriate part of speech, must be read carefully and tested to see if it makes sense in the context under consideration. When children find a word whose meaning they do not know, they too often try to force the first definition listed in the dictionary to fit the context, ignoring others that fit more exactly.

One problem that arises with dictionary use is that the definitions are frequently brief and abstract, and, except in some children's dictionaries, concrete examples generally are not provided (Rhoder & Huerster, 2002). Sometimes the words in the definitions are more difficult than the entry word. Despite these potential problems, the dictionary is helpful when used appropriately, along with other ways of determining word meanings.

Frindle by Andrew Clements is a good literature selection for sharing when dictionary use is being taught. This book helps students understand how words come to be included in dictionaries.

The thesaurus offers another avenue to vocabulary expansion. This useful source of synonyms and antonyms allows word meaning to be considered in the context of many things that mean "something like" the words the children are trying to learn or clarify and a few that mean the opposite of the words.

The thesaurus is probably most useful to a writer who is trying to express a thought and cannot think of exactly the right word to convey the needed meaning. By examining many possibilities of words to use in the situation, the choice of a precise term is made easier. Writers may use the thesaurus to find words to replace overused or uninteresting words in their writing. A caution about such use is in order, however. Encouraging students to always use synonyms instead of a familiar word, such as *say*, may result in the use of an excess of "fifty-cent words" in their writing and may also result in less exact expression of thought than would have occurred if the common word had been used. Many elementary-level students may not know the meanings or nuances of many of the synonyms offered and therefore may be unable to pick appropriate ones from the choices offered. Using a junior thesaurus can help with the problem of words being too difficult, but, if the children are not clear about what they want to say before they consult the thesaurus, they will still have difficulty choosing reasonable alternatives.

Some activities that involve students in vocabulary building through use of the dictionary and thesaurus follow.

1. Write a list of questions that must be answered by looking up the key word in the dictionary. Some examples follow.

   a. Can you drink out of a bluebottle? Why, or why not?

   b. Can you eat a damson? Why, or why not?

   c. Is excelsior good for a stomachache? Why, or why not?

2. Have the students look up a word in the dictionary and write the meaning that fits each of several contexts provided. Examples of some contexts that could be used for the word *act* follow.

   a. They left the theater before the first act was over.

   b. Don't act like you have never been taught any manners.

   c. I wish I could act that part the way Syl did.

   d. Taking them in was an act of mercy.

3. Let students search their dictionaries for words that they do not know but want to learn. Let each one read one definition of a chosen word to the class, and let the class members (and the teacher, too) guess the word from the meaning. If the word is not guessed on the basis of the first meaning read, let the student continue to read meanings until the word is guessed or the definitions are exhausted. Then hold a class discussion of the word, its various definitions, and possible uses of the word in context. (In a variation of this activity, you choose the words to be guessed, and the students take turns guessing the words.)

4. Set situations, such as the following one, and have the students use the thesaurus to answer the question.

   I want to write that I am angry about what happened, but I want a word that is stronger than *angry*. It doesn't show just how upset I am. What word could I use?

   More information on dictionary use is presented in Chapter 7. You may want to refer to both chapters when dealing with dictionary skills.

CONSTRUCTING WORD WEBS

The construction of **word webs** is a good way to examine many characteristics of words and their meanings and relationships with other words. A group of students was preparing to read a selection about a theater. Some of the children had been to a theater, some had seen theaters on television or in the movies, and still others had heard some things about theaters. Exploring the term *theater* before the reading began brought out the things the children already knew about a theater and meaningfully related things that they knew with things that other children knew. The discussion that accompanied building the web was good preparation for reading the story. Words related to theaters were suggested in rather random order, but the teacher wrote them on the board with related ideas close together and later asked the students for a category name for each group of ideas. For example, the teacher asked, "What is a word that includes concession stand, waiting area, and restrooms?" Figure 3.6 is the partial web that was developed before the reading. After reading, the web was expanded, based on added information.

WORD-A-DAY CAMPAIGNS

Word-a-day campaigns interest the students in building vocabulary. Students can bring in words that they want to learn, or you can choose the words, keeping partic-

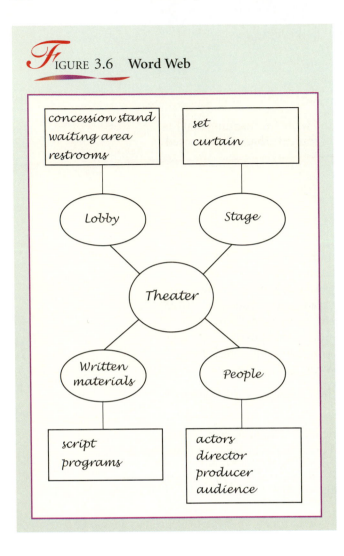

*F*IGURE 3.6   **Word Web**

concession stand
waiting area
restrooms

set
curtain

Lobby

Stage

Theater

Written
materials

People

script
programs

actors
director
producer
audience

ular curricular objectives in mind. A combination of the two methods of choosing words can also be used. Regardless of how the words are chosen, the campaign focuses attention on the word for the day, using a number of devices. There may, for instance, be a "Today's Word" bulletin board. You write the word in the middle of the bulletin board in large letters and around the word place definitions, sentences using the word in context, pictures illustrating the word, and clippings from newspapers and magazines in which the word is used. If the word is chosen the day before it is stressed in class, the students can begin to look and listen for instances of its use the night before it is the focus in class. You and your class may cooperate to construct the bulletin board, with different people contributing definitions, sentences, pictures, and clippings.

You can start by pronouncing the word, having the students pronounce the word, and discussing the meanings of the word with the students. Students will be encouraged to relate the word to their personal experiences. A word web may be constructed around the word. The word may be placed in categories and used in analogy exercises, and synonyms and antonyms for the word may be discussed.

Students may be given extra credit for using the word orally or in writing in a meaningful context related to the class activities. You will evaluate the contexts in which the words are used. This aspect of the campaign will tend to keep the words chosen from being too exotic to be beneficial to the students. Students will also be alerted to listen for the word throughout the day. Anytime it is heard, the students who hear it can raise their hands, and the use

Writing

of the word in that particular context can be discussed. In some cases, you may accumulate the week's words and allow the students to continue to earn credit at any time during the week that they use a word that has been chosen for emphasis. This repetition of the word orally and visually throughout the day or week will help to make the word a part of their permanent vocabularies. The focus on meaning will increase the chances of the students' being able to use the word in the future.

BUILDING WORD BANKS

Building a word bank is a good individual vocabulary development activity. In this activity, students write words that they want to add to their meaning vocabularies on 3" x 5" index cards, often called **word bank cards** for primary-grade students and **concept cards** for older ones. These word cards have the word, possibly its phonetic respelling if pronunciation is difficult, a definition or synonym, possibly a picture illustrating the word or a sentence using it in context, and a personal example related to the word. (First-graders may have only the word, the word and a picture, or the word and a sentence containing the word on their cards, depending on their level of development.) A word card for the word *humiliating* might look something like the one in Figure 3.7.

After a number of word cards have been accumulated in a student's word bank, you may use the word bank cards in classroom activities. For example, you may ask each student to locate in his word bank all of the words that describe things, all of the words that name things, all of the words that show action, and so on, essentially using the word banks for word sort activities. The words may also be alphabetized when alphabetical order is being studied. They may be used as story starters for creative writing or stimulators for extemporaneous speaking.

USE OF COMIC STRIPS AND CARTOONS

A great deal of vocabulary learning results from reading and studying comic strips and cartoons. The vocabulary in many of these materials is very sophisticated. Read *Spiderman* comic strips and notice the "web-spinner's" use of words. Learning vocabulary terms from comic strips is highly motivational. Much of the humor of comic strips comes from use of multiple-meaning words in unexpected ways, use of figurative expressions, and use of obscure terms. Puns, or plays on words, are also frequently found. Students can explain how the word plays make the strips funny; reword the strips, using synonyms or more literal language; or turn them into narrative paragraphs to encourage practice with the vocabulary. One example of the use of comic strips for vocabulary learning is found near the beginning of this chapter.

DRAMATIZATION

Dramatization is a good way to set word meanings firmly in mind. A game called Magic Modifiers starts by having the children choose a noun or verb to modify. Then you call out adjectives or adverbs to modify the noun or verb, and the children act out the new meaning. The children might be asked to act out first a sleepy giant, then an angry giant,

FIGURE 3.7   **Concept Card**

humiliating - disgracing, embarrassing

It was humiliating to have my mistake pointed out in front of everyone.

(The time I spilled my spaghetti on my clothes was a humiliating experience.)

Applications for English Language Learners and Students with Special Needs

Dramatization activities are especially good in helping ELLs, struggling students, gifted students, and kinesthetic learners. They help make the word meanings more concrete for ELLs and struggling students.

They challenge the creativity of gifted students as the students work on the best interpretations for particular words. They fit the preferred mode for learning for kinesthetic learners, who learn best through movement.

and finally a friendly giant. Similarly, they might act out eating daintily and eating hungrily. If you wish to turn this activity into a reading activity, the nouns, verbs, adjectives, and adverbs could be written on word cards that the children draw from stacks and read before they act out the meanings. The Varied Verbs and Opposites games mentioned later in this chapter are also examples of using dramatization.

STORYTELLING AND STORY READING

Storytelling and story reading are activities that any classroom teacher can use to help children build vocabulary. Roe (1985) studied the effects of hour-long storytelling and story-reading sessions that included follow-up language activities over a seven-week period in a first-grade classroom. The children in the experimental group scored significantly better than those in a control group on total number of words used in telling a story, number of different words used, number of multisyllabic words used, and number of standard story elements included. In addition, the children in the program spontaneously called attention to words learned from previous stories when the words appeared in new stories. Roe's study was replicated in another school, using kindergarten through second-grade classes, and significant differences in favor of the experimental group were found for all three levels of students on all four measures (Pigg, 1986; Roe, 1986).

Reading stories that explain concepts and word meanings related to content areas definitely enhances vocabulary learning. For example, there are many good examples in the area of math that make good additions to math units. The book *The Fly on the Ceiling: A Math Myth* by Julie Glass has an engaging story and explains *coordinates* and their use in locating points on a grid through words and illustrations. Both *The Phantom Tollbooth* by Norton Juster and *On Beyond a Million: An Amazing Math Journey* by David M. Schwartz have explanations of *infinity* embedded in narratives. *Sir Cumference and the First Round Table: A Math Adventure* by Cindy Neuschwander is a delightful story that leads students to understand the meanings of the terms *diameter, radius,* and *circumference,* and *Sir Cumference and the Dragon of Pi: A Math Adventure,* by the same author, helps students understand the meaning of *pi.*

Technology

COMPUTER APPLICATIONS

Computer applications also lend themselves to vocabulary development. Many vocabulary programs of both drill-and-practice and tutorial types are available from a variety of sources. Drill-and-practice programs simply offer practice on skills that have previously been taught, while tutorial programs offer actual instruction. Especially numerous are programs concerning synonyms, antonyms, and homonyms, but there are also programs on prefixes and suffixes, on categorization of words, and on making analogies. Some programs construct crossword puzzles and hidden-word puzzles quickly and easily; however, the use of the hidden-word puzzles as generated is questionable because some words appear backward or upside down and meanings are generally not emphasized.

The quality of the available programs varies widely, but the computer itself has the capabilities necessary to present vocabulary instruction very effectively. Graphics show how prefixes and suffixes change word meanings when added to the words. Animated graphics show the movement necessary for understanding the meanings of verbs. Use of synthesized speech makes possible the clarification of pronunciation of words. Words can be moved around on the screen and put into juxtaposition with their synonyms, antonyms, or homonyms or with words that some people confuse with the target words.

Computer use motivates students and has much potential for vocabulary instruction. Simply be aware of the need to evaluate each program separately to be sure that it is accurate in its contents and is pedagogically sound. Because many programs are developed by programmers rather than educators, good pedagogy is not always present in available programs. More and more, educators and programmers are working as teams to produce quality materials.

ETYMOLOGY STUDY

Etymology study is a powerful vocabulary-building tool. It leads students to much enriching information about our language, including where words originated and how they have changed in meaning over time. Charles Earle Funk's *Heavens to Betsy!* and *A Hog on Ice* are two sources of word and phrase origins that will fascinate children. *Eat Your Words: A Fascinating Look at the Language of Food* by Charlotte Foltz Jones explains how many food names originated. It also includes the origins of figurative expressions.

WORD PLAY

Word play is an enjoyable way to promote vocabulary growth. Word play may include use of puns, hinky-pinkies, rhymes and silly songs, riddles, Tom Swifties, crossword puzzles, hidden-word puzzles, scrambled-word puzzles, word shapes, games based on traditional games, and commercial games.

Puns are plays on words that have the same sound but different meanings or plays on different uses of the same word to create a humorous effect. An example is, "Clarinet music is printed for people who can reed."

Hinky-pinkies are definitions that lead to the use of rhyming words as responses. Actually, some people divide them into hink-pinks, for one-syllable rhymes; hinky-pinkies, for two-syllable rhymes; and hinkety-pinketies, for three-syllable rhymes. Following are some examples.

Hink-pink: an overly warm small child—hot tot

Hinky-pinky: an excellent sweet treat—dandy candy

Hinkety-pinkety: a yearly handbook—annual manual

Children enjoy both guessing hinky-pinkies and creating them for others to guess.

A love of words is promoted by using rhymes and silly songs in class (Brabham & Villaume, 2002). Riddles also promote thought about word meanings: "What is black and white and read all over?" a child will ask. "A newspaper," cry students who have just learned the effect of using homonyms orally. Older students may have fun with Tom Swifties, quotations followed by an adverb or verb that plays on the meaning of the quotation. Examples include 'Don't play with that knife,' his mother said sharply, and 'Look out, it's a lion!' he roared." Students enjoy making up their own Tom Swifties.

Crossword puzzles are enjoyable activities, and you can construct crossword puzzles to fit any set of words that is being studied. The easiest way to construct crossword puzzles is to take paper that has a grid printed on it and start by printing the longest word under consideration on the paper, one letter to a square. Then begin overlapping other words with the long word and with each other until a complete puzzle is formed. Consecutively number the first letter of each word made, regardless of whether it runs across or down. Then make up clues for the "Across" and "Down" words, and write them below the puzzle. You may want to darken in unused squares.

Children also enjoy hidden-word puzzles. To make the puzzle emphasize meaning, give only the definitions of or synonyms for the words that the children are seeking, rather than telling them the words themselves. When they find a word, they circle the word and put the number of the definition or synonym in the circle. Grid paper aids in construction of these puzzles. Write the target words in the squares running left-to-right horizontally, down vertically, or on a left-to-right diagonal. Do not enter words backward or bottom-to-top, because those are unnatural ways to view words and may deter recognition. Place random letters in all remaining squares, after your words have been entered. Children can also construct hidden-word puzzles to share with classmates. A hidden-word puzzle is shown in Figure 3.8.

$\mathcal{F}$IGURE 3.8 **Hidden-Word Puzzle**

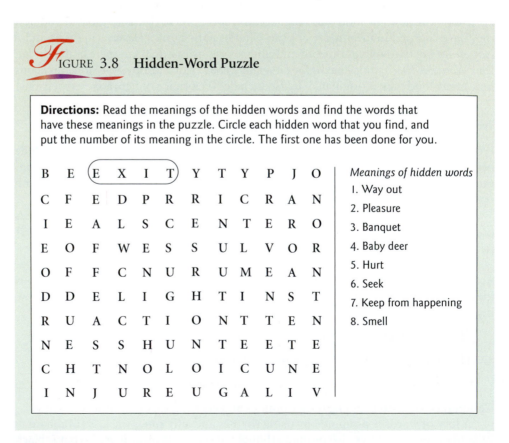

Directions: Read the meanings of the hidden words and find the words that have these meanings in the puzzle. Circle each hidden word that you find, and put the number of its meaning in the circle. The first one has been done for you.

B	E	E	X	I	T	Y	T	Y	P	J	O
C	F	E	D	P	R	R	I	C	R	A	N
I	E	A	L	S	C	E	N	T	E	R	O
E	O	F	W	E	S	S	U	L	V	O	R
O	F	F	C	N	U	R	U	M	E	A	N
D	D	E	L	I	G	H	T	I	N	S	T
R	U	A	C	T	I	O	N	T	T	E	N
N	E	S	S	H	U	N	T	E	E	T	E
C	H	T	N	O	L	O	I	C	U	N	E
I	N	J	U	R	E	U	G	A	L	I	V

Meanings of hidden words

1. Way out
2. Pleasure
3. Banquet
4. Baby deer
5. Hurt
6. Seek
7. Keep from happening
8. Smell

FIGURE 3.9   **Scrambled-Word Puzzle**

Directions: Read the definitions beside the scrambled letters, and unscramble the letters to make words having those meanings. Write each unscrambled word in the blanks provided by the number of the scrambled letters. When you have unscrambled all of the letters, the first letters of the scrambled words will form a word meaning "one who belongs."

1. d l m e o y   ___ tune   1. __ __ __ __ __ __

2. e e d t u a c ___ teach   2. __ __ __ __ __ __ __

3. e m i k a s t ___ an error   3. __ __ __ __ __ __ __

4. r b s i l t e ___ a coarse, stiff hair   4. __ __ __ __ __ __ __

5. p e e n e x s ___ cost   5. __ __ __ __ __ __ __

6. g o r u h   ___ not smooth   6. __ __ __ __ __

Writing

When you prepare a hidden-word puzzle, you will probably include words that have been studied in one or more classes. There may be other words in the grid for which there are no meanings in the clues. When the children find these, they can write clues for them and add them to the puzzle for future users. In the puzzle in Figure 3.8, the children can find the words *action, mean,* and *ten,* as well as several others that do not have clues provided.

Scrambled-word puzzles are also motivational devices. Once again, after scrambling the words, provide definitions of the words to be unscrambled to reinforce the importance of meaning in the activity. Figure 3.9 shows a scrambled-word puzzle.

Playing with word shapes helps children clarify word meanings. They try to write the words so that the meaning of the words are shown in the way they are written. Examples are found in Figure 3.10.

Games based on traditional games are good motivators for learning vocabulary. Words can be written on the squares of a checkerboard, and the children can be required to pronounce the word and tell its meaning before they can make the move to a particular square. If the words are attached with spots of Velcro, the words can be changed regularly to provide more varied practice. Bingo can be played by writing vocabulary words on the squares under the letters *B, I, N, G,* and *O* and calling out definitions for the words, rather than the words themselves, when playing the game—for example, saying "Under the *B,* a word that means 'freedom.'"

Commercial games can also be used for vocabulary development. For example, games like Scrabble,

FIGURE 3.10   **Word Shapes**

balloons   crooked

small   large   down

Probe, and Boggle involve word construction. You probably will want to add the requirement that the students tell the meanings of the words that they make. Password is a commercial game that emphasizes word meaning.

Word play abounds in the book *The Phantom Tollbooth* by Norton Juster. There is a Whether Man, Lethargarians who live in the Doldrums, a Watchdog named Tock who ticks like a clock and sees that people don't waste time, a town named Dictionapolis where everything centers around words and where Milo meets the Spelling Bee and the Humbug, among others. The word play is both fun and informational, and fifth- through seventh-graders especially should enjoy it.

Special Types of Vocabulary Terms

SOME WORDS and phrases have special attributes that make them particularly interesting to study. Synonyms, antonyms, homonyms, multiple-meaning words, words borrowed from other languages, figurative expressions, abbreviations, and acronyms can all be the basis for meaningful lessons. Knowledge of these special types of words and phrases makes understanding spoken and written language easier and enhances usage in personal speaking and writing activities.

Synonyms

Knowledge of **synonyms** increases a person's range of understanding when listening and reading and makes her spoken and written language more varied, interesting, and exact. Although synonyms may have almost identical meanings, in most cases there are fine distinctions among the exact meanings of synonyms. A person may be pleased to be called "slender," but may take offense at being called "thin," which is one synonym. Both *thin* and *slender* mean "not thick," but *thin* implies a lack of fullness, whereas *slender* implies a graceful leanness. Carefully choosing synonyms may make it possible to flatter, rather than insult, people, or to give a positive, rather than a negative, slant to what you are saying.

Playing a game called Varied Verbs helps children work on the fine distinctions in meaning among verbs that are listed as synonyms. For example, *Webster's New World Thesaurus* lists *march, amble,* and *saunter* as synonyms for *walk.* Children can act out the meanings of these verbs, and the class can discuss the differences among the ways of walking. Students can clarify the meanings of the separate words while they are adding to the repertoires of words that they can use to express themselves more exactly in speaking and writing.

Writing

Using the dictionary and thesaurus to promote understanding of synonyms is an effective strategy. Children can look up words in these sources and discuss in class the information presented by them, calling attention to fine differences in word meanings, even when the words are very close in meaning. They can construct sample sentences to highlight the differences. For example, *fried* is listed as a synonym for *heated* in *Webster's New World Thesaurus*. A sentence such as the following shows how the meanings differ somewhat: "Since the potatoes had been fried earlier, I did not feel that they needed to be fried again, so I just heated them in the oven." You do indeed heat something that you fry, since heat is necessary for frying, but not everything that is heated is fried. You should think through some of these small differentiations and first explain them to the children as a model for the activity, and then let the children try to come up with similar differentiations for other words.

The Phantom Tollbooth has an extensive section with examples of synonyms, which are spouted by the king's advisors. Students enjoy role-playing the parts of the advisors and producing other sets of synonyms after reading or listening to this section of the book. For primary-level students, *Alexander and the Terrible, Horrible, No Good, Very Bad Day* by Judith Viorst is a good choice for finding synonyms.

Antonyms

Antonyms are word pairs that have opposite meanings, such as *up* and *down*. Knowledge of antonyms makes speech and written communications clearer and more exact. This knowledge can also help an individual use context clues involving contrast to best effect when listening to oral communications or when reading. Students sometimes have some difficulty in differentiating between a word that has a meaning that is opposite from that of another word and a word that simply has a meaning that is different from that of the other word. For example, when asked for an antonym for *hot*, they may say *warm* rather than *cold*. Quite a bit of instructional attention may be necessary to develop the idea that *hot* and *cold* represent extremes on the scale of temperature, whereas *warm* lies somewhere in between and is commonly thought to be the opposite of *cool*, another term that does not designate an extreme.

Knowledge of the limits of meaning of words is valuable in vocabulary development, and study of antonyms brings these limits into focus for students. In addition, the study of antonyms enhances the study of synonyms. Powell (1986) reported research results that indicated that synonym production was facilitated by antonym production, but the converse was not true.

Although there are several kinds of opposition that could be considered, Powell (1986) suggests that two forms be dealt with in instruction—polar antonyms and scalar antonyms. According to Powell (1986, p. 618), "[T]he first type is categorical and allows no intermediate terms (*husband/wife*). Polar terms are dichotomous; the assertion of one implies the denial of the other. . . . Scalar terms, i.e., contraries, allow mediation by gradation and are often linked to the process of comparison (*hot, warm, tepid, cool, cold*). Middle terms are permitted and often possible with a neutral zone at midpoint in the dimension of meaning."

Playing a game called Opposites is good for developing meanings of antonyms. You can write pairs of antonyms on word cards and give one card to each of a pair of students. The students act out the words on their cards simultaneously, while the children in the class try to identify the antonym pair involved. The pairs can be as simple as *high* and *low* or as hard as *rude* and *polite*. The difficulty level can be varied to fit the specific class.

As is true with synonyms, using the thesaurus and the dictionary is helpful in teaching antonyms. Students can rewrite sentences, producing opposite meanings by changing single words. Debates on the accuracy of the outcomes can be arbitrated through use of the dictionary or thesaurus.

Writing

Exactly the Opposite by Tana Hoban is a concept book for helping young children develop a concept of antonyms. *Fortunately,* mentioned earlier as a good book to use for the prefix *un-,* and *That's Good! That's Bad!* by Margery Cuyler each illustrate one antonym pair for young students.

Homonyms

Writing

Homonyms are sets of words that sound alike but have different spellings and different meanings, for example, *pear, pair,* and *pare.* Homonyms may cause special decoding problems for some children in reading, since they have to learn that two or three different spellings result in the same pronunciation; however, these different spellings may actually have an overall positive effect on the reading act because the different spellings cue different meanings for the children. Homonyms cause many problems for students in writing, however. Recalling the correct spelling for the particular usage appears to be very difficult for many students, and incorrect choices abound in writing samples.

Encourage students to use the dictionary to decide on the spelling for the particular homonym that they wish to use. Activities in which the students replace incorrect homonyms in passages encourage them to be aware of the need to check their own writing. The following passage could be used for practice and as a focus for class discussion.

> Leon has a *knew pear* of shoes. They are *blew* and *read* and have rubber *souls.* That *weigh,* when he goes hunting with his dad, he can sneak up on his *pray* more easily.

The King Who Rained and *A Chocolate Moose for Dinner* by Fred Gwynne present homonyms in humorous contexts that will entice young readers. These books can be shared orally with the youngest students, who later will want to read them for themselves. Delightful pictures add to the effectiveness of both texts.

Multiple-Meaning Words

Multiple-meaning words can cause difficulties in understanding to both listeners and readers. Very common words are often the ones that have the most different meanings associated with them. For example, *run* has a different meaning in each of the following sentences.

1. I will run around the track for fifteen minutes every day.

2. Mom was mad because she had a run in her knee highs.

3. Let the water run until it gets hot.

4. We are about to run out of milk.

5. There was a run on the bank when people heard about the arrest of the employee.

6. Will you run an errand for me?

7. Mark had a run of bad luck.

8. Christine plans to run for mayor.

9. They sold out the entire print run of the booklet.

These are only a few of the possibilities for using *run* in different contexts. Children may have one or two of the most common meanings of a word like this one in their vocabularies, but fail to have many others that may appear in school-related or outside reading materials.

Mason and others (1979/1980) found that elementary school children have difficulty using the context when less familiar meanings of multiple-meaning words are found in sentences. This could be either because they do not know the particular meanings involved or because they fail to attend to important context clues. Students need to be exposed to different meanings associated with the same word, *and* they need to be helped to use context clues effectively.

Brainstorming about multiple-meaning words is a worthwhile activity, especially among gifted learners, who tend to have more meanings collected for the words in their vocabularies. In one brainstorming activity, you put a word on the board and have the children give as many different meanings as they can for it. Then you write the different meanings on the board, surrounding the word, as in Figure 3.11. The children discuss each meaning and make up sentences fitting each one.

Writing

Another good technique to use when brainstorming about multiple-meaning words is to have the children come to the chalkboard and illustrate the different meanings of the chosen word. They could even illustrate the meanings on large sheets of paper that become murals in the classroom.

Students need to learn to use the dictionary to decide on the meanings for multiple-meaning words that fit the particular situations in which the words are found. To do this, the children must look up the word, read each definition, and decide if that meaning fits the context in which the word is found. They need help in seeing that some of the definitions do not make sense in the given context and that a search for an appropriate definition, not just any definition, is necessary. They can take a list of dictionary definitions for a given word and a number of occurrences of that word in context and match each context example to a definition that makes sense.

One multiple-meaning word that has a specialized meaning in mathematics is the word *power*. *On Beyond a Million: An Amazing Math Journey* by David Schwartz has an example of counting by powers of 10 and also has sidebars that show the mathematical notation and explain related words, such as *exponents*.

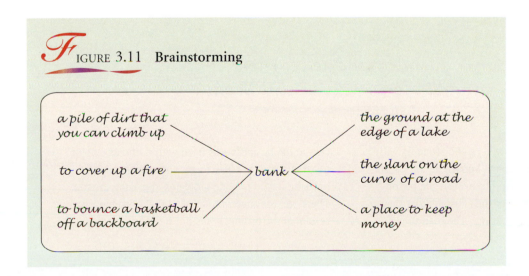

*F*IGURE 3.11   **Brainstorming**

a pile of dirt that you can climb up

to cover up a fire

to bounce a basketball off a backboard

bank

the ground at the edge of a lake

the slant on the curve of a road

a place to keep money

Figurative Expressions

Many children are confused by the **figurative expressions** that they encounter in their reading materials because they try to interpret them literally. Figurative expressions are found in everyday conversation, in stories that are heard and read, and even in school textbooks. Children need systematic instruction to help them with the meanings of such expressions. Common types of figurative expressions that should receive attention are similes, metaphors, personification, hyperbole, euphemisms, allusions, and idioms. Many of these expressions involve children in thinking about comparisons and relationships. Literature is filled with figurative expressions that can enhance understanding of the material, if they are correctly interpreted, or undermine understanding of the material, if they are not. Even textbooks contain quite a bit of figurative language.

Interpreting figurative expressions involves use of background knowledge that many ELLs and at-risk students do not possess. Different cultural backgrounds often cause confusion with figurative expressions even among university students. These students need much help in developing the needed schemata for interpreting figurative expressions (Palmer & Brooks, 2004).

Palmer and Brooks (2004) suggest having fluent, bilingual speakers come to your classroom to discuss figurative expressions in other languages. This should help ELLs to understand better the nature of figurative language in English.

Similes are comparisons that contain either the word *like* or *as.* Because of the presence of these cue words, similes are relatively easy to teach. Lead the children to see that only one characteristic of the two items is being compared and that the comparison is not implied for all characteristics. For example, when a person says, "He was as red as a beet," only the color of the person and the beet are being compared. It is helpful to provide lists of commonly used similes and have the children pick out the characteristics being compared. Then encourage them to compose some similes of their own. Try giving the children a list of items for comparison and having them say or write the similes that come to mind. One second-grader, when responding to the word *snow,* said, "Snow is as cold as ice cream."

Writing

When introducing similes to primary-level students, you may want to read *Quick as a Cricket* by Audrey Wood. This appealing picture book provides numerous examples that can be the basis for class discussion.

Applications **for English Language Learners and Students with Special Needs**

Use "think-alouds" to show ELLs and students with special needs the connections implied in comparisons in figurative expressions and to explain the historical connections for many of the allusions that they encounter. For example, if using "The road to success in the business was filled with potholes," point out that a road is a way to get somewhere and potholes on a road provide problems in making the trip. Therefore, the sentence is saying that becoming successful in the business was not free of problems.

In Mildred D. Taylor's *Roll of Thunder, Hear My Cry,* one sentence, describing Little Man's reaction to the book he is issued, says that he "sprang from his chair like a wounded animal, flinging the book onto the floor and stomping madly upon it" (p. 17). Here students who have seen wounded animals will understand the comparison of the physical reaction to the pain they felt and visualize Little Man's reaction more accurately.

In Bette Bao Lord's *In the Year of the Boar and Jackie Robinson,* there is a reference to "bombs falling like hailstones" (p. 22). Since many children have experienced hailstorms, the comparison can help them to visualize the bombs falling out of the sky. This expression also is an example of hyperbole, a type of figurative expression discussed below.

Metaphors are direct comparisons that do not use the words *like* or *as,* but make statements that sound as if two things are being equated. Still, only one characteristic of the items is the basis for the comparison. In the metaphor "Jody is a thorn in my side," for example, the comparison refers to the mental pain that Jody causes the speaker, just as a thorn causes physical pain. Once again, as in the case of similes, it is usually helpful to list some metaphors and let the children pick out the characteristics being compared. Illustrating the literal meanings of metaphors is an enjoyable activity for children and sometimes leads them to picking out the comparison more easily. For example, when a child draws a person in the position of a "pillar of the church," he sees that the person is helping to support the church and thereby is led toward the correct interpretation.

In *Roll of Thunder, Hear My Cry,* Miss Crocker says, "And to all our little first grade friends only today starting on the road to knowledge and education, may your tiny feet find the pathways of learning steady and forever before you" (p. 13). Two metaphors are presented in this one sentence, comparing schooling to a road and to pathways.

Personification is giving the characteristics of a person to an inanimate object or abstract idea. Saying, "The water held him in its icy grasp," implies that the water has hands for grasping, just as a person does. One activity to teach personification is to show children examples of personification and tell them which characteristics of people are given to the objects or ideas in the expressions. Then have the children identify the characteristics in other examples of personification.

Hyperbole is an extreme exaggeration used for emphasis. For example, a person might say that a skirt is "miles too long" when it is really only a few inches too long but looks so bad that it is definitely not acceptable at that length. A common hyperbole is "I've told you that a million times." You might have students in the intermediate grades say something one hundred times while timing themselves and then have them multiply to see how much time it would have taken to say the thing a million times. This brings out the extremeness of the exaggeration very clearly.

In *Roll of Thunder, Hear My Cry,* Uncle Hammer tells Stacy, "If you ain't got the brains of a flea to see that this T. J. fellow made a fool of you, then you'll never get anywhere in this world" (p. 108). Uncle Hammer compares Stacy's brains unfavorably to those of a flea, and the exaggeration that we see makes more emphatic the point that Stacy's move was not smart.

Euphemisms are less offensive expressions used in the place of expressions that people do not like to hear. There are more euphemisms used to refer to death than to most things, since many people find death an unpleasant subject. Therefore, death is referred to as "passing away," "going home," or "going to eternal rest." Such expressions are often extremely confusing to children. "Passing away," for example, does not seem to have the sense of finality that death does, and they may not make the connection. Euphemisms are best handled as they arise in class discussions, story materials, or even textbooks, with the literal meanings being clarified by the teacher and the reasons for the euphemisms being discussed by the children. They may come to the conclusion, for example, that "sanitation engineer" sounds more high-class than "garbage collector" and that garbage collectors who want to be called sanitation engineers may be looking for more respect from the people around them.

Allusions are indirect references to well-known events, people, places, or literary works. Listeners or readers must use their backgrounds of experiences in combination with inferential and critical thinking skills to interpret allusions. Unfortunately, if the background experience is missing, the interpretation is not possible. People who have had limited experiences with literary classics may not understand references to someone being a "Prince Charming" or a "Scrooge," or recognize the meaning of "sour grapes," "crocodile tears," or a "Pandora's box." Those who have never been exposed to biblical stories may miss allusions to people being "as old as Methuselah," being "as wise as Solomon," or having "the patience of Job." Those who know little of history may miss allusions in which people are compared to Ghengis Khan or Florence Nightingale or are said to have met their "Waterloo." Exposure to many types of literature through storytelling and story reading and teaching of significant historical events helps children develop the background needed to understand allusions. When allusions are used in your classroom material, you may need to have an on-the-spot story time or history lesson to fill in the missing information. It is desirable, however, for the students to fill in the information from their own backgrounds whenever possible, with you filling in the gaps that remain.

Idioms have meanings other than their literal ones, and sometimes they actually have no literal meanings, but simply are a collection of words with a special meaning attached. In addition, they are often specific to a particular language (Palmer & Brooks, 2004). An example of an idiom is "Harry was just *pulling my leg*," which means that he was telling me something that wasn't true. It has nothing to do with legs or pulling something. One reference source for idioms is the *Scholastic Dictionary of Idioms, Phrases, Sayings, and Expressions.*

Reflections

What are some other euphemisms that may cause problems for children? How could you help them understand each one better?

Abbreviations

Abbreviations are shortened forms of words, generally ending with a period. You need to lead children to see that some of the original letters are left out of words to form abbreviations. Have the children discuss why it is often convenient to abbreviate a word instead of writing it out completely. Introduce and discuss common abbreviations, such as *Mr., Mrs., Dr., in., mm, A.M.,* and *P.M.* The children can practice using these abbreviations in writing assignments requiring the use of such specific terms. You may also construct activities in which you ask the students to match the words with their abbreviations.

Writing

Acronyms

Acronyms are words that are formed from the first letters or initial syllables of a series of words in a term. For example, *NATO* stands for "North Atlantic Treaty Organization," and *radar* stands for "radio detecting and ranging." *Radar* has been in use for so long that most people think of it as just a regular word and do not realize its origin. Students may understand acronyms better if they construct pronounceable acronyms for fictitious organizations in which the acronyms say something about the organization, just as is true of many actual organizations (for example, *MADD* is "Mothers Against Drunk Driving"). This activity is a good one to stimulate creative thinking.

Words That Came from Other Languages

Our language has borrowed many terms from other languages. Because many of these words are not pronounced the way that they look, they often cause reading difficulties for students. They are, however, a fertile ground for study of the different cultures that have influenced our country, and they provide a high interest area of language study for many students. Try giving the children a sheet such as the one in Figure 3.12 to complete, and then follow this assignment with class discussion of the results.

*F*IGURE 3.12   **Word Origins**

Word	Borrowed from
chocolate	Spanish
moccasin	
croissant	
weiner	
mosquito	
patio	
opera	
bungalow	
pajamas	
alphabet	

Classroom Assessment for Vocabulary

Observation of a student's use of vocabulary is the best way to assess proficiency in vocabulary use. Teachers can observe the appropriateness of responses when the student hears certain words spoken, to assess listening vocabulary; observe the correct or incorrect use of words in conversations, discussions, or oral presentations to assess speaking vocabulary; observe oral and written responses to passages that the student has read to assess reading vocabulary; and observe written products for correct or incorrect use of vocabulary to assess writing vocabulary.

Teachers also often assess vocabulary knowledge through informal multiple-choice, matching, and constructed answer (essay or short answer) tests. Of these choices, constructed answer tests probably provide the best picture of the student's vocabulary proficiency.

A comprehensive treatment of assessment measures is in Chapter 13.

Writing

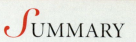

Writing

Technology

SUMMARY

The words that people use are symbols for concepts that they possess. The process of vocabulary development, therefore, often involves concept development as well. Concepts are based on concrete and vicarious experiences, which indicates that many varied experiences in the classroom will enhance vocabulary development.

Everyone has four vocabularies that develop both simultaneously and independently. They are listening, speaking, reading, and writing vocabularies. These vocabularies are not equal in size for most people.

The best techniques for teaching words actively involve the learners and provide them with strategies for independent vocabulary development outside of the classroom. Some useful techniques include categorization activities, semantic feature analysis, making analogies, structural analysis activities, use of context clues, use of the dictionary and thesaurus, construction of word webs, word-a-day campaigns, word bank building, use of comic strips and cartoons, dramatization, storytelling, computer applications, etymology study, and word play activities.

There are a number of special types of vocabulary terms that are of particular interest in vocabulary study. These include synonyms, antonyms, homonyms, multiple-meaning words, figurative expressions, abbreviations, acronyms, and words that come from other languages.

Discussion Questions

1. How is concept development related to vocabulary instruction? What are the most effective ways to develop new concepts? What types of concepts are hardest to develop?

2. What different types of vocabularies do students have? What are some ways that you can help them to develop each type?

3. What techniques for vocabulary instruction have you found to be most effective in your teaching experiences or classroom observations?

4. What are advantages to activities such as use of cartoons and dramatization?

5. What special types of words need to receive special attention in vocabulary instruction? What evidence have you seen for this in classroom observation, as well as in newspaper items and signs in the community?

6. Why do figurative expressions cause children problems? Why are they especially problematic for ELLs?

Suggested Activities

1. Without using words, tell the class about something that happened to you recently. Analyze the way that you tried to express yourself.

2. Tape-record a conversation that you have with a preschool-aged child. Analyze the child's word usage for nonstandard usage that appears to be related to learning how words are constructed.

3. Plan a technique for teaching the concept of *liberty* to a child. Share your plan with your classmates.

4. Think about the characteristics of the students in your hometown or the town in which you are presently living. With these students in mind, examine a chapter in a science textbook for a grade level of your choice. Decide which terms in the chapter should be taught before the students are asked to read the chapter. Record these decisions. Explain your choices to your classmates.

5. Make a list of words with multiple meanings that occur frequently in children's reading materials. Choose four or five of the words and explain how you would help children learn both the different meanings and how to recognize which meaning is appropriate in a particular context.

6. Develop a board game that focuses on vocabulary knowledge. Write a complete set of directions for the game, construct the game, and demonstrate it in class.

7. Examine a book for children or adolescents to find some of the special vocabulary described in this chapter. You may want to look for figurative expressions, synonyms, antonyms, or something else. Record your source, list examples from it, and share it with your classmates.

References

Ainslie, D. (2000/2001). Word detectives. *The Reading Teacher, 54,* 360–362.

Anderson, R. C., & Freebody, P. (1981). Vocabulary knowledge. In J. T. Guthrie (Ed.), *Comprehension and teaching: Research reviews* (pp. 77–117). Newark, DE: International Reading Association.

Anderson, R. C., & Nagy, W. E. (1991). Word meanings. In R. Barr, M. L. Kamil, P. Mosenthal, & P. D. Pearson (Eds.), *Handbook of reading research, Vol. II* (pp. 690–724). New York: Longman.

Armbruster, B. B., & Nagy, W. E. (1992). Vocabulary in content area lessons. *The Reading Teacher, 45,* 550–551.

Blachowicz, C. L. Z., & Lee, J. J. (1991). Vocabulary development in the whole literacy classroom. *The Reading Teacher, 45,* 188–195.

Brabham, E. G., & Villaume, S. K. (2002). Vocabulary instruction: Concerns and visions. *The Reading Teacher, 56,* 264–268.

Chomsky, C. (1979). Language and reading. In R. E. Sharer (Ed.), *Applied linguistics and reading* (pp. 112–128). Newark, DE: International Reading Association.

Dixon-Krauss, L. (2001/2002). Using literature as a context for teaching vocabulary. *Journal of Adolescent & Adult Literacy, 45,* 310–318.

Forester, A. D., & Mickelson, N. I. (1979). Language acquisition and learning to read. In R. E. Sharer (Ed.), *Applied linguistics and reading* (pp. 74–88). Newark, DE: International Reading Association.

Graves, M. F., & Watts-Taffe, S. M. (2002). The place of word consciousness in a research-based vocabulary program. In A. E. Farstrup & S. J. Samuels (Eds.), *What research has to say about reading instruction.* (Newark, DE: International Reading Association.

Guthrie, J. T. (Ed.). (1984). *Reading: A research retrospective (1881–1941)* by William S. Gray. Newark, DE: International Reading Association.

HICKMAN, P., POLLARD-DURODOLA, S., & VAUGHN, S. (2004). Storybook reading: Improving vocabulary and comprehension for English-language learners. *The Reading Teacher, 57,* 720–730.

JOHNSON, D. D., & PEARSON, P. D. (1978). *Teaching reading vocabulary.* New York: Holt, Rinehart & Winston.

MASON, J. M., KNISELEY, E., & KENDALL, J. (1979/1980). Effects of polysemous words on sentence comprehension. *Reading Research Quarterly, 15,* 49–65.

PALMER, B. C., & BROOKS, M. A. (2004). Reading until the cows come home: Figurative language and reading comprehension. *Journal of Adolescent & Adult Literacy, 47,* 370–378.

PETRICK, P. B. (1992). Creative vocabulary instruction in the content area. *Journal of Reading, 35,* 481–482.

PIGG, J. R. (1986). The effects of a storytelling/storyreading program on the language skills of rural primary students. Unpublished problems paper. Cookeville: Tennessee Technological University.

POWELL, W. R. (1986). Teaching vocabulary through opposition. *Journal of Reading, 29,* 617–621.

PRESSLEY, M. (2002). Metacognition and self-regulated comprehension. In A. Farstrup & S. J. Samuels (Eds.), *What research has to say about reading instruction,* (pp. 291–309). Newark, DE: International Reading Association.

RHODER, C., & HUERSTER, P. (2002). Use dictionaries for word learning with caution. *Journal of Adolescent & Adult Literacy, 45,* 730–735.

ROE, B. D. (1985). *Use of storytelling/storyreading in conjunction with follow-up language activities to improve oral communication of rural first grade students: Phase I.* Cookeville, TN: Rural Education Consortium.

ROE, B. D. (1986) *Use of storytelling/storyreading in conjunction with follow-up language activities to improve oral communication of rural primary grade students: Phase II.* Cookeville, TN: Rural Education Consortium.

ROSENBAUM, C. (2001). A word map for middle school: A tool for effective vocabulary instruction. *Journal of Adolescent & Adult Literacy, 45,* 44–49.

RUDDELL, M. R., & SHEARER, B. A. (2002). "Extraordinary," "tremendous," "exhilarating," "magnificent": Middle school at-risk students become avid word learners with the Vocabulary Self-collection Strategy (VSS). *Journal of Adolescent & Adult Literacy, 45,* 352–363.

RUPLEY, W. H., LOGAN, J. W., & NICHOLS, W. D. (1998/1999). Vocabulary instruction in a balanced reading program. *The Reading Teacher, 52,* 336–356.

STAHL, S. A. (1986). Three principles of effective vocabulary instruction. *Journal of Reading, 29,* 662–668.

Books for Children and Adolescents Cited in This Chapter

BANKS, L. R. (1994). *Broken bridge.* New York: Avon Flare.

BANKS, L. R. (1992). *One more river.* New York: Avon Camelot.

BROWNE, P. (1996). *A gaggle of geese.* New York: Atheneum.

CARROLL, L. (1999). *Through the looking glass.* Mineola, NY: Dover.

CHARLIP, R. (1964). *Fortunately.* New York: Scholastic.

CLEMENTS, A. (1996). *Frindle.* New York: Aladdin .

CONRAD, P. (1989). *My Daniel.* New York: HarperTrophy.

CUYLER, M. (1991). *That's good! That's bad!* New York: Scholastic.

FRASIER, D. (2000). *Miss Alaineus: A vocabulary disaster.* New York: Harcourt.

FUNK, C. E. (2002). *Heavens to Betsy!* New York: HarperResource.

FUNK, C. E. (2002). *A hog on ice.* New York: HarperResource.

GLASS, J. (1998). *The fly on the ceiling: A math myth.* New York: Scholastic.

GWYNNE, F. (1976). *A chocolate moose for dinner.* New York: Prentice Hall.

GWYNNE, F. (1970). *The king who rained.* New York: Prentice Hall.

HELLER, R. (1987). *A cache of jewels and other collective nouns.* New York: Sandcastle.

HOBAN, T. (1990). *Exactly the opposite.* New York: Scholastic.

HOUSTON, J. W., & HOUSTON, J. D. (1973). *Farewell to Manzanar.* New York: Bantam.

JONES, C. F. (1999). *Eat your words: A fascinating look at the language of food.* New York: Delacorte.

JUSTER, N. (1989). *The phantom tollbooth.* New York: Knopf.

LASKY, K. (1988). *The bone wars.* New York: Morrow.

LORD, B. B. (1984). *In the year of the boar and Jackie Robinson.* New York: Harper Trophy.

MERRIAM, E. (1960). *A gaggle of geese.* New York: Knopf.

NEUSCHWANDER, C. (2000). *Sir Cumference and the dragon of pi: A math adventure.* New York: Scholastic.

NEUSCHWANDER, C. (1997). *Sir Cumference and the first round table: A math adventure.* New York: Scholastic.

SCHWARTZ, D. M. (1999). *On beyond a million: An amazing math journey.* New York: Scholastic.

TAYLOR, M. D. (1976). *Roll of thunder, hear my cry.* New York: Scholastic.

TERBAN, M. (1998). *Scholastic dictionary of idioms, phrases, sayings, and expressions.* New York: Scholastic.

VIORST, J. (1972). *Alexander and the terrible, horrible, no good, very bad day.* New York: Atheneum.

WALTON, R. (1997). *Pig, pigger, piggest.* New York: Scholastic.

WILCOX, C. (1993). *Mummies & their mysteries.* New York: Scholastic.

WOOD, A. (1982). *Quick as a cricket.* Singapore: Child's Play.

YEP, L. (1975). *Dragonwings.* New York: HarperCollins.

YEP, L. (1995). *Hiroshima.* New York: Scholastic.

EARLY EXPERIENCES WITH LANGUAGE

LEARNER OBJECTIVES

At the conclusion of this chapter

YOU SHOULD BE ABLE TO

1. Describe how language develops in three-, four-, and five-year olds.
2. Recognize the value of reading aloud to children.
3. Discuss the importance of the home and family in a child's development.
4. Explain how preschool and kindergarten programs promote literacy.
5. Appreciate the importance of developmentally appropriate practices.
6. Explain why play is important and how to set up centers that promote literacy.
7. Describe how to establish a supportive classroom environment.
8. Explain ways that literacy (reading and writing) emerges in young children.
9. Identify the following terms that are defined or explained in this chapter:

alphabetic principle 145
big books 145
developmentally
    appropriate practice
    (DAP) 135
directionality 144
dramatic play 137
Drop Everything And Read
    (DEAR) 146

emergent literacy 142
environmental print 140
family literacy 130
invented spelling 151
metalinguistic
    awareness 124
phonemic awareness 142
print awareness 144
print conventions 130

print-rich environment 140
scaffolding 123
shared reading 145
shared writing 153
word walls 141
Zone of Proximal
    Development 123

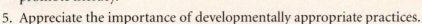

NCTE/IRA Standards addressed in this chapter

STANDARD 9. Students develop an understanding of and respect for diversity in language use, patterns, and dialects across cultures, ethnic groups, geographic regions, and social roles.

STANDARD 10. Students whose first language is not English make use of their first language to develop competency in the English language arts and to develop understanding of content across the curriculum.

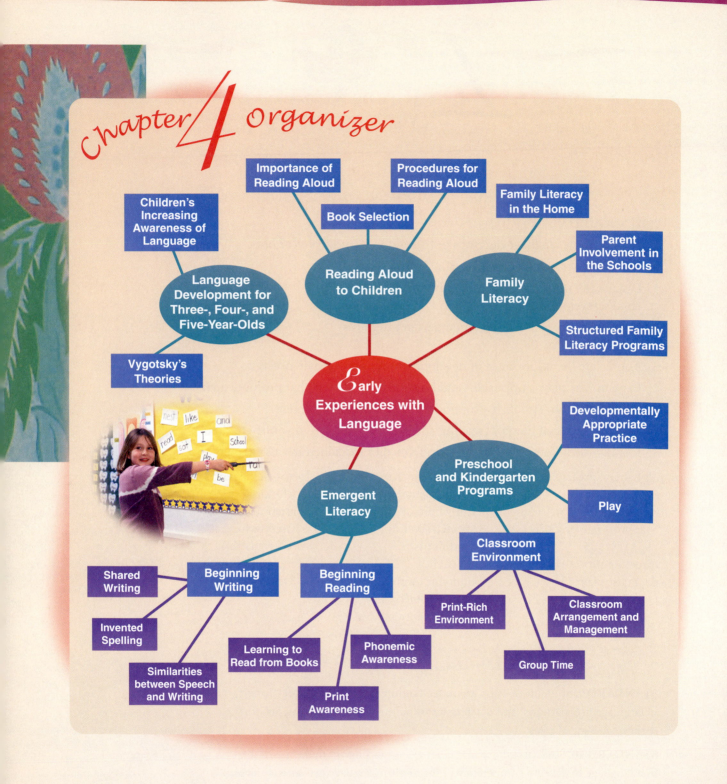

Chapter 4 Organizer

Early Experiences with Language

Reading Aloud to Children
- Importance of Reading Aloud
- Procedures for Reading Aloud
- Book Selection

Language Development for Three-, Four-, and Five-Year-Olds
- Children's Increasing Awareness of Language
- Vygotsky's Theories

Family Literacy
- Family Literacy in the Home
- Parent Involvement in the Schools
- Structured Family Literacy Programs

Preschool and Kindergarten Programs
- Developmentally Appropriate Practice
- Play
- Classroom Environment
  - Print-Rich Environment
  - Classroom Arrangement and Management
  - Group Time

Emergent Literacy
- Beginning Writing
  - Shared Writing
  - Invented Spelling
  - Similarities between Speech and Writing
- Beginning Reading
  - Learning to Read from Books
  - Print Awareness
  - Phonemic Awareness

*T*HE CHILDREN are participating in a theme study about their feelings. They sing songs about feelings, role-play different feelings, and listen to stories about feelings, including Jamie Lee Curtis's *Today I Feel Silly and Other Moods That Make My Day* and Molly Bang's *When Sophie Gets Angry—Really, Really Angry.* . . . At group time, Miss Angela calls on them to make "feelings faces" and then to tell what kinds of feelings their faces show. She records the experiences that they dictate to her on a large chart with the child's name by each entry. The chart looks like this:

Preschool/Gold Room Identifies Our Feelings

I have feelings!

I feel angry when . . . Mommy and Daddy stay home and I'm in school. Aislyn

I feel happy when . . . I share with my sister Sophie. Jessie

I feel surprised when . . . my birthday is here and I get presents. Rachel

I feel silly when . . . my little kitty plays with me. Caylee

I feel worried when . . . Sugar goes under the fence. Levi

What's happening here?

Children are learning that it is all right to have different feelings and to be able to express them. They learn words to tell how they feel and build self-esteem by realizing that what they say is important enough to write on the chart. They see that what they say can be written down; they reinforce their awareness of top-down (top of the page to the bottom) and left-to-right directionality; and they begin to learn some sight words, particularly their own names.

No time is more critical for the development of language and literacy than a child's early years. This is the time when children form concepts about their world, rapidly acquire vocabulary, and learn the functions of language. Recent brain research confirms that parents and preschools can exert crucial influence during these years by providing stimulation (Hendrick, 2001). The International Reading Association (IRA) and the National Association for the Education of Young Children (NAEYC) issued a joint statement in 1998 on developmentally appropriate practices for young children. It emphasized the importance of providing rich language and literacy experiences. An extensive study of three-, four-, and five-year-olds revealed that homes and preschool classrooms that support literacy in kindergarten contribute substantially to later success in reading (Snow, Tabors, & Dickinson, 2001). This research shows that the foundation of kindergarten abilities is built in home and preschool language and literacy environments.

In this chapter, we look at the contributions Lev Vygotsky has made to our understanding of how children learn and consider ways that three-, four-, and five-year-olds benefit from language experiences in the home and early school settings. We present information about oral language development, family literacy, home-school connections, and ways that children begin to read and write. A strong foundation in language arts is likely to lead to lifelong proficiency with communication and literacy skills.

Language Development for Three-, Four-, and Five-Year-Olds

YOUNG CHILDREN have an amazing ability to learn language by observing how others use it and by experimenting with using it themselves

Vygotsky's Theories

Learning language is a social activity, according to Lev Vygotsky (1986), a Russian psychologist. As children interact with others, they receive feedback that reinforces or modifies their use of language. Vygotsky emphasized the social aspect of language and cognitive growth and believed that all learning takes place in social contexts (Dixon-Krauss, 1996; McGee & Richgels, 2000). Many opportunities for social interactions occur with families or at school. Children can help bake cookies or place fast-food orders when they are with their families, and they might play such roles as mail sorter in a post office center or check-out clerk at a grocery store center in their classroom. Oral language develops in social contexts when children listen to bedtime stories and comment on them at home, as well as during conversations in preschool settings. For example, a small group of preschoolers observed during snack time were discussing sign language, teaching each other signs, correcting one another, and signing familiar

Applications for English Language Learners and Students with Special Needs

To help children acquire language, talk to them and encourage them to talk to each other. Use the correct words for objects and actions, interact with children in their play, engage them in talk about what they are do- ing, and make sure they understand what you are saying (Morrison, 2000). Provide ELLs with time to talk during show-and-tell and group activities (Barone, 1998).

words. In the give-and-take of conversation, they were learning to use language purposefully while exploring a different language.

One of Vygotsky's best-known contributions to understanding how learning occurs is his theory of the **Zone of Proximal Development (ZPD**). The ZPD is the distance between a child's actual level of development and potential level of development when assistance is given. For example, a child who is adequately coordinated wants to learn to tie a shoe. An adult models the process by providing multiple one-on-one demonstrations and guided practice sessions over time until the child can do it independently. In another case, a teacher realizes the students do not know how to make a five-pointed star. The teacher takes a few minutes to demonstrate and explain how to make five slanted, connected strokes; the children practice several times; and soon everyone is making five-pointed stars.

Children are able to move through the ZPD from their present level to a higher level when someone more knowledgeable, either child or adult, offers support, as in the previous examples. This support is sometimes referred to as **scaffolding**, and a great deal of help is given initially. By repeated modeling, the teacher enables the child to grasp the concept or procedure. The teacher then gradually withdraws support as the learner becomes increasingly competent at the higher level (Griffin, 2001). The teacher's role is to understand a child's current stage of development and then collaborate by asking questions, offering suggestions, and assisting in other ways to extend the child's ability beyond the current level (Hendrick, 2001). In other words, a child who is unable to do a task alone may be able to do it with help and then learn to do it independently.

Vygotsky also connects language and thought, believing that language provides the means for developing the ability to think. Hendrick (2001, p. 475) explains Vygotsky's theory this way: "[O]f particular importance to preschool teachers is his emphasis on the significance of spoken language as the mediator between the world, the child's mind, and his ability to express, understand, and explain to other people what he knows." Vygotsky reasons that children use language to understand themselves, become independent, and control their thoughts and behaviors.

Reflections

What do you think about Vygotsky's belief that learning language is a social activity? How do social interactions promote language development in young children? How might limited exposure to such interactions hinder a child's emerging sense of language?

Children's Increasing Awareness of Language

In addition to helping children think about themselves and their world, oral language serves a number of other purposes. Children use language to express ideas, ask questions, interact with others at playtime, and make their desires known. Growth in language occurs as children acquire new concepts and vocabulary through their experiences and as a result of expressing their curiosity. For instance, four-year-old Veronica said, "Oooo, look at that bug with all the legs on it," and an adult responded, "Yes, we call that a centipede." The next time Veronica saw a centipede, she recognized it and called it by name. On another occasion, Veronica saw a water tower and asked, "What's that? What's it for?" The answers provided her with a new term and a new concept. Through such verbal interactions, Veronica not only is learning new words, but also is acquiring a sense of the form and structure of language that is the foundation for reading and writing.

As four- and five-year-olds approach readiness for reading, they need to develop **metalinguistic awareness,** or the language user's awareness of language as an object in itself (Harris & Hodges, 1995). This means that children can distinguish among the letters, words, and sounds of language in order to use and discuss them meaningfully. Teachers may introduce linguistic terminology by modeling the use of letters and words in a variety of ways. They might talk about words, letters, and sounds in big books and ask children to show which letter is at the beginning or end of a word. They might also invite children to dictate a chart story and ask them to suggest the letters needed to spell some of the words. As kindergartners write in their journals, they might help each other spell words, figure out what letters make certain sounds, or see how to shape certain letters. As they talk, they reinforce their understanding of how language works. Metalinguistic awareness is also discussed in Chapter 1.

Teaching Tip

When writing charts from children's dictation, always use proper terminology when recording their words. For example, say, "I'm starting this *first word* with a *capital letter*" and "I'll remember to put a *period* at the *end* of this *sentence*." Soon most children will learn these terms and be able to use them in their reading and writing.

Writing

Applications

for English Language Learners

Parents of children whose home language is not English should continue reading and speaking to their children in their primary language because a child's ability to acquire a second language is related to proficiency in his home language. Ideally, someone familiar with the child's primary language should also interact with the child in the classroom during the day. *Code switching,* changing from one language or dialect to the other, should be accepted without comment (Kostelnik, Soderman, & Whiren, 1999).

Reading Aloud to Children

READING ALOUD is an experience that both you and your children can savor. It is a time to relax, share, learn, think, appreciate, respond, and enjoy being together.

Importance of Reading Aloud

Most children enjoy listening to stories, and the benefits of reading aloud to them are numerous. The joint position statement of IRA and NAEYC (1998) recommends that adults read high-quality books daily to children, especially those that reflect a child's identity, culture, and home language. In their review of literature, Snow, Tabors, and Dickinson (2001) found a consensus among researchers that reading books to young children is linked to early literacy and later success in school, and Paratore (2002) claims that the importance of storybook reading for success in beginning literacy is undisputed. In his *Read-Aloud Handbook,* Trelease (1995) acknowledges that language is the basic ingredient of success in school and community, and that reading aloud is the best way to nurture language skills. Why does reading aloud make such a difference? Many educators have addressed this question, and Figure 4.1 gives some answers.

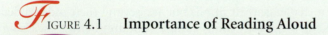

FIGURE 4.1   **Importance of Reading Aloud**

- Children learn new vocabulary in meaningful contexts.

- They discover new concepts and develop them through book discussions.

- They learn to make predictions by examining pictures and listening for clues.

- Well-selected, high-interest books motivate children to learn to read.

- These books cause children to think deeply about the content and encourage them to explore related situations and topics in depth.

- They introduce children to different experiences and world cultures.

- They help children develop a sense of book language and story structure that prepares them for reading and writing independently.

- Children use their imaginations to explore new ideas as they listen to books.

Writing

Book Selection

Book selection is an important issue. Choose books that are appropriate for the age level of the children and that appeal to their interests. Keep in mind their limited attention span and find books of a length that will not exceed it. Try to select books that stimulate discussion, and encourage it by asking students to anticipate plot development, analyze a character's behavior, or relate to personal experiences.

Children themselves may want to make book selections. Read books that are popular with children and know when to stop reading a book if they are bored. Children have their favorite authors and characters, such as H. A. Rey's Curious George, the monkey who gets into mischief; Norman Bridwell's Clifford, the big red dog that forgot to stop growing; and Marc Brown's Arthur, the aardvark who has a somewhat normal human-style family life. Eric Carle is another favorite with his colorful collages, stories about nature's creatures, and special features (for example, *The Very Quiet Cricket* that actually chirps).

Predictability, repetition, and rhyme are features that preschoolers enjoy during read-alouds. Dr. Seuss Beginner Books nearly always have these features, as in *Green Eggs and Ham* and *The Cat in the Hat.* Many of Bill Martin's books, such as *Brown Bear, Brown Bear, What Do You See?,* are also repetitive and predictable, thus allowing children to join in the reading when they recognize the pattern. In Gene Baer's *Thump, Thump, Rat-a-Tat-Tat*, children not only can recite the refrain, but also can simulate instruments in a band that get louder, then softer, as the story progresses. Children love repeating "but peanut butter and jelly is my favorite thing to eat" that appears throughout Joanne Nelson's *Peanut Butter and Jelly* book, and they pick up the cumulative pattern in *There Was an Old Lady Who Swallowed a Fly* by Simms Taback.

Because young children are lacking or limited in their ability to decode words, they are unable to read challenging books for themselves. Nevertheless, their young minds can grapple with ideas and concepts that promote reasoning and thinking. Select books, therefore, that challenge their minds but are beyond their independent reading levels (Beck & McKeown, 2001). A good example is Audrey Penn's *The Kissing Hand*, which tells of Chester, a raccoon, going off to kindergarten for the first time. His mother kisses the palm of his hand as a secret way to remind him of her love for him. Here are some discussion questions that might be used with the story:

- What special ways does your family show their love for you?
- How can you show your love?
- How do you feel when you leave home to go to school?
- Why do you think Chester went to school at night?

As you choose books to read aloud, consider those that represent diverse cultures so that children can see their own cultures represented and appreciate the existence of others (Opitz, 1999). Classrooms have increasingly diverse populations, and each child should be able to identify with storybook characters at least some of the time. By reading multiethnic books, you help children become aware of similarities and differences among people and enable them to consider different points of view. *Whoever You Are* by Mem Fox and *All the Colors of the Earth* by Sheila Hamanaka are well-illustrated books that show similarities and differences among people in a positive light. In recent years, authors and illustrators have created many enticing books that represent diverse cultures and ethnic groups.

Many informational trade books are appropriate to read to preschoolers and kindergartners, some simply to show and discuss the colorful illustrations and others to share both pictures and content. In some cases, you may paraphrase or skip over some of the material if it is too complex. In Seymour Simon's books *Sharks* and *Whales*, the text may be too detailed for little ones, but the full-page colored pictures and amazing facts appeal to any age. At age five, Veronica listened to excerpts from *Whales* and on her own initiative wrote a full page of information about "the bigsd anml" (biggest animal) and its "blo hol" (blow hole). Eric Carle's books with their unique illustra-

$\mathcal{F}$IGURE 4.2   **Informational Books for Young Children**

- *The Science Book of Weather*, Neil Ardley. Simple experiments.
- *Where the Forest Meets the Sea*, Jeannie Baker. Features of an Australian rain forest.
- *Airport*, Byron Barton. Airline travel and airports.
- *A House for Hermit Crab*, Eric Carle. Special features of various sea creatures.
- *I Took a Walk*, Henry Cole. Beauty of the natural world.
- *Turtles*, The Cousteau Society. Life cycle of the green sea turtle.
- *Tiger with Wings: The Great Horned Owl*, Barbara Esbensen & Mary Brown. Habitat and life of horned owls.
- *In the Small Small Pond*, Denise Fleming. Life in a small pond.
- *Out of the Ocean*, Debra Frasier. Sea treasures to be found on the beach.
- *Dinosaurs and Their Young*, Russell Freedman. Information on duck-billed dinosaurs.
- *Dinosaurs*, Gail Gibbons. Highly illustrated book on dinosaurs.
- *A Look at Spiders*, Jerald Halpern. Information with photographs about spiders.
- *Assateague: Island of the Wild Ponies*, Andrea Jauck & Larry Points. Life and natural environment of wild ponies.
- *The Seashore*, Gallimard Jeunesse & Elizabeth Cohat. Sea animals on the beach, with overlays.
- *Bunnies*, Norbert Landa & Ona Pons. Information and crafts about bunnies.
- *The Eyes of Gray Wolf*, Jonathan London. Life of a gray wolf in the arctic cold.
- *Polar Bear Cubs*, Downs Matthews. Typical polar bear cubs exploring their arctic home.
- *The Icky Bug Alphabet Book*, Jerry Pallotta. Amazing facts about bugs.
- *First Comes Spring*, Anne Rockwell. Seasonal changes, appropriate activities and clothing.
- *Insects and Crawly Creatures*, Angela Royston. Identification of insects and information about each of them.
- *A First Look at Caterpillars*, Millicent Selsam. Habits and life cycle of caterpillars.
- *Seymour Simon's Book of Trucks*, Seymour Simon. Kinds and functions of trucks.
- *Hidden by Darkness*, Kim Taylor. Creatures of the night; night noises.

tions contain information about science along with the stories, for example as in *The Very Busy Spider* and *The Very Lonely Firefly*. Lois Ehlert's *Red Leaf, Yellow Leaf* is a combination storybook and informational book about a boy and his maple tree, and *Creepy, Crawly Baby Bugs* by Sandra Markle tells fascinating facts about bugs, accompanied by enlarged, colorful photographs. Figure 4.2 (see page 127) shows additional informational books suitable for young children.

Another genre appropriate for reading aloud, or simply reciting, is poetry, particularly nursery rhymes. Children delight in the repetition, rhyme, alliteration, and rhythm of such classics as "A tisket, a tasket, a pretty yellow basket," "Simple Simon met a pieman," and "Twinkle, twinkle, little star; how I wonder what you are!" They laugh at the silliness of a cow jumping over the moon or the dish running away with the spoon. They wonder about poor Humpty Dumpty who fell off a wall and couldn't be put back together again, even with all the king's horses and all the king's men, and they have fun acting out simple rhymes such as "Jack be nimble, Jack be quick, Jack jump over the candlestick." Children will readily join in as the rhymes become more and more familiar with repeated readings, and they will complete a verse with the correct rhyming word if the reader omits it. An added benefit of sharing these rhymes is the development of phonemic awareness that occurs as children hear and repeat similar and contrasting sounds of language. (Phonemic awareness is addressed later in this chapter.)

Procedures for Reading Aloud

Technology

Varying your approach to reading aloud makes storytime a special treat. To heighten interest, use props, such as a flannel board with felt figures or an object that is featured in the book. Choose a child to hold a puppet, perhaps one of Clifford, while the class listens to a story about him. Read books into a tape recorder and let children use headphones to follow along at a listening station. Show a video of a children's story

---

Classroom Vignette 4.1

Miss Christy gathers her preschoolers on the carpet in front of her, tells them she will be reading them a story about families, and reminds them that they have been learning about different kinds of families all week. She shows them the cover of Cynthia Rylant's *The Relatives Came* and explains that *relatives* means all your family members, including aunts and uncles, grandparents, and cousins. She asks them to predict what might happen from the funny picture on the cover and then tell them that all the packed bags on top of the car are called *luggage*. Miss Christy encourages the children to talk about how they feel when relatives come to visit and then begins reading the story. The children listen attentively, continue making predictions, and respond to Miss Christy's occasional comments or questions as she reads. When the story is over, they enthusiastically share their own experiences about family visits.

What's happening here?

As a result of listening to this story, the children are learning two new vocabulary words, expanding their concept of *family*, connecting to their own experiences with family members, and making predictions from the cover and as the story unfolds. Their delight in the story and their eagerness to share strengthens the bond among members of this small classroom community.

or on a subject related to one, such as one about owls after reading Jane Yolen's *Owl Moon*, or simply gather your children together to share a story as Miss Christy does in Classroom Vignette 4.1.

Although young children love to listen to picture storybooks, they also enjoy hearing a variety of other styles and genres, including informational books (Richgels, 2002). Kindergartners are capable of responding to informational books, often building on what they already know. Nonfiction trade books can enrich all areas of the curriculum and support theme studies that are related to the environment, the seasons, the community, or other such topics. Three principles apply to using informational books in kindergarten. First, integrate informational books with other informational text (for example, labels, posters, recipes) and storybooks on the same topic. Teacher-led discussions can help children sort out the differences between fact and fiction. Second, help children use informational text purposefully to find answers to questions that arise during discussions, and third, engage the students in writing their own informational texts by recording what they find on signs, posters, and labels.

Teaching Tip

Set up a corner of your room for reading aloud with you in the corner and the children facing you so that they are not distracted by anything that might be going on in the room. The children are on a rug or carpet squares, and you are in a rocking chair. Set the mood by turning on a lamp, ringing a chime, or playing soft music.

Writing

Beck and McKeown (2001) point out certain procedures that are likely to support young children's use of language and comprehension ability through thought-provoking experiences while listening to and talking about stories. Their project, *Text Talk,* is based on extensive observations and reviews of research, and it includes the procedures shown in Figure 4.3. Effective story reading can be a complex and challenging proce-

FIGURE 4.3   Procedures for Text Talk

- Select stories that contain some complexities and cause children to construct meaning.

- Intersperse open-ended questions that encourage children to explain ideas instead of recall facts, as suggested with *The Kissing Hand.*

- Ask follow-up questions that build on children's responses and cause them to develop their thoughts more fully.

- Show pictures *after* reading the story so that children focus on the linguistic content and visualize the story for themselves.

- Relate stories to background knowledge judiciously for the purpose of building meaning. Avoid extended discussions of minimally related experiences.

- Select a few key vocabulary words for study after reading the story.

dure; getting the maximum benefit from reading aloud is not always easy. Remember to focus on important ideas while monitoring children's responses and helping them to construct meaning.

Family Literacy

FAMILIES OFFER children their first experiences with language. By interacting with family members, children learn to speak and to become familiar with the nature and functions of language. These early years are the foundation for literacy and are critically important for later success in reading and writing (IRA & NAEYC, 1998; Smith & Elley, 1997a; Snow, Burns, & Griffin, 1998; Tabors, Snow, & Dickinson, 2001).

Writing

Family Literacy in the Home

Family literacy may simply involve informal, everyday interactions consisting of language among family members, or it may take on the formality of a structured program that attempts to increase the literacy level of both parent and child. We first look at the home, where abundant opportunities exist for children to discover how language and literacy work. Children learn to use language to get what they want, ask questions about what they don't understand, and demand attention. They observe as parents write checks, read catalogs, receive and read mail, fill out applications, and select items at the grocery store. Parents perform valuable support when they take children to the library, encourage and respond to questions, take time to explain how things work, and, of course, read aloud. They should provide books for children to handle and paper with an assortment of markers for writing. Family members should not "skill and drill" preschoolers, but allow language and literacy to develop in natural, authentic situations. Preschoolers may experiment with writing by designing greeting cards or writing notes, which might consist of only a few marks on paper with an initial added. Such shared, purposeful activities help create a bond between the child and other family members.

A grandfather and grandson delight in sharing a favorite story.

In Figure 4.4, we see how family support, combined with natural ability and preschool experiences, can facilitate literacy development. Victoria wrote this story just before entering kindergarten. She used many **print conventions**, or rules about the use of print, and showed a sense of story structure. At home, her parents read to her regularly and made storytime a happy experience. They pointed out words in the stories, taught her the alphabet song, and encouraged her to read words on signs. She began writing her name before her fourth birthday and was soon reading and writing. All family members are avid readers, and her home is filled with books of all kinds.

Writing

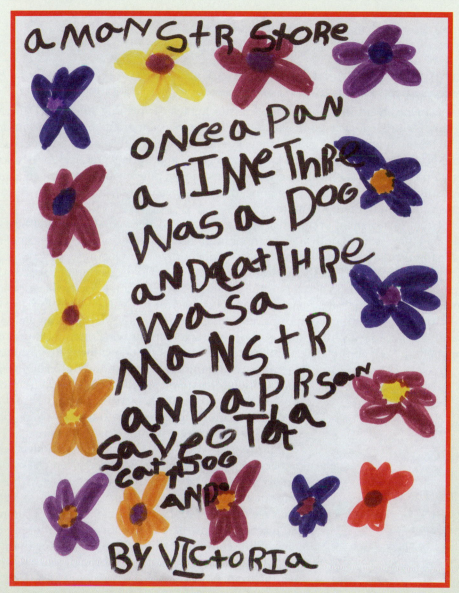

$\mathcal{F}$IGURE 4.4   **Monster Story**

The story reads as follows: A Monster Story   Once upon a time there was a dog and a cat. There was a monster and a person saving the cat and dog. By Victoria

Source: Victoria Idem, Child Development Laboratory, Cookeville, TN. Used with permission.

Most parents want their children to succeed in school (Nistler & Maiers, 2000; Paratore, 2002; Thomas, Fazio, & Stiefelmeyer, 1999). Unfortunately, many parents lack the literacy skills and knowledge that would enable them to support their children's early attempts with language. They may be unaware of the benefits of such ordinary tasks as those just mentioned, or they may lack the resources to supply children's books and writing materials in the home. Different cultures and home languages, although valid in themselves, may not be consistent with school expectations. Some children, therefore, enter school without an optimal foundation for language development. Teachers can help to alleviate the language difficulties by communicating with parents and involving them in school activities.

Parent Involvement in the Schools

Parent involvement in schools often leads to higher performing students (Delgado-Gaitan, 1990; Hendrick, 2001; Porche, 2001). Involving parents helps them understand how to support their child's language and literacy growth at home and in school. Parents observe and participate as you demonstrate appropriate practices for developing literacy skills. Not only do parents learn from you, but you also learn much about your students' backgrounds by listening to parents' perceptions of what they consider to be important in literacy (Paratore, 2002).

Parent involvement occurs in a variety of ways. Nistler and Maiers (2000) established a home/school family literacy program in the first grade of an urban school so that parents could see ways to contribute to their children's developing literacy skills. In a truly collaborative effort, the classroom teacher listened to the parents and welcomed them as equal partners in developing the program. The teacher modeled behaviors that would support literacy at home and encouraged parents to use literacy in a variety of ways, including reading, composing letters, keeping journals, and cooking. Parents eventually became aware of the value of their interactions with their children and confident in their ability to help children with school activities. Cline (2001) involved parents by arranging reading parties that freely distributed books, information, and educational supplies. Host families invited other families to their homes where they were able to acquire the knowledge and resources needed for creating a literate environment in the home.

Morningstar (1999) used home response journals to connect home and school in a kindergarten classroom. Parents recorded their children's interactions with language in a journal, thus enabling Morningstar to learn about each child's literacy development at home; parents and teacher became partners in assessing children's literacy. While communicating with parents, Morningstar also interacted with her students through journals and literature centers.

Reflections

How might you involve parents in language and literacy activities in your classroom? Can you recall some ways parents participated in your classrooms, other than hosting parties? What types of programs or activities could parents do that would enable them to help their own children develop literacy at home and school?

Structured Family Literacy Programs

Family literacy intervention programs are increasing, and most of them focus on teaching parents and children to participate in family storybook reading, the practice most likely to help children achieve success in school (Paratore, 2002). Even Start, the largest federally funded family literacy program in the United States, enables low-income families to participate in parenting education and adult basic education. While learning how to help their young children develop language and literacy skills, many parents increase their own proficiency. Ninety percent or more of the sites offer reading, storytelling, prereading activities, language development activities, and work with letters and numbers (Paratore, 2002).

Not only is it important for parents to read to their children, but it is important for them to know *how* to read most effectively (Tabors, Snow, & Dickinson, 2001). Many parents are uncertain about what they should do or say when reading aloud. At one Even Start site, researchers videotaped parents as they read one-on-one with their own children. This tape was copied and distributed widely to other centers in the region that worked with family literacy. The set of guidelines for reading with children that accompanied each tape is shown in Figure 4.5 (Ross, Elkins, & Petty, 1999).

A variety of formal family literacy programs exist to help parents support their children's growth in language and literacy. Project FLAME (Shanahan, Mulhern, & Rodriguez-Brown, cited in Paratore, 2002) offers literacy training to parents with limited English proficiency to enable them to help their children's literacy learning. The project focuses on

FIGURE 4.5   Guidelines to Parents for Reading with Children

▶ Encourage your child to join in on familiar words.

▶ Direct your child's attention to certain pictures.

▶ Make comments that link the story to your child's life.

▶ Sit close together.

▶ Make sure both of you have a good view of the book.

▶ Make your voice interesting and playful.

▶ Allow your child to tell a favorite part of the story.

▶ Pause to ask questions, make comments, and enjoy the humorous parts.

teaching school-based literacy behaviors, but also considers the cultural knowledge that each family brings. The Home-School Study of Language and Literacy Development (Snow, Tabors, & Dickinson, 2001) investigated the preschool and home literacy environments of preschool and kindergarten children from low-income families. Researchers found that the home environment contributes significantly to positive outcomes for young learners, that preschool factors lead to even greater positive outcomes, and that home and school interact in producing outcomes (Tabors, Snow, & Dickinson, 2001). The U.S. National Center for Family Literacy brings children and parents together to play and learn. It emphasizes literacy activities for both home and school (Thomas, Fazio, & Stiefelmeyer, 1999). Regardless of the type of family literacy program, whether it be informal or structured, families play an important role in developing a young child's language and literacy skills.

Preschool and Kindergarten Programs

EXCELLENT PRESCHOOLS advance all children's literacy skills and help compensate for homes that give little access to language and literacy (Tabors, Snow, & Dickinson, 2001). In the past few decades, the number of children enrolled in preschools has increased tremendously, and programs for three- and four-year-olds play an important

Communicate with parents early in the year and frequently, ideally every week, throughout the school year. Send letters home that contain information about what you are teaching, your theme for each week, and how parents can help at home (see Figure 4.6). Most parents will cooperate when they understand what you are trying to do. Occasionally, send a note home that tells when a child does something good.

FIGURE 4.6 **Sample Letter to Parents**

WEEKLY UPDATE FROM MRS. ROSS

 Week of October 6-10

Next week we will be working on:

Language Arts:

The letter *e* including Elf and Elephant activities and poem "Eeny Meeny Miney Mo"

High-frequency words to recognize by sight: *the, a, my, that, and*

Story details from shared reading (*The Elves and the Shoemaker, An Extraordinary Egg*)

Daily writing activities, including journals, class books, and "My Alphabet Book"

Handwriting practice with tracing and writing *e* on lined paper

Math and Science:

Shape and size patterns

Daily calendar and graph activities

Animals that hatch from eggs

Homework:

Today I will be sending home a plastic egg with each child. Please help your child either draw a picture or cut out a picture of an animal that hatches from an egg. Put the picture in the plastic egg and send it back Monday. Thank you for your participation!

Report Cards:

A report card is being sent home today in your child's take-home folder. This reflects beginning-of-the-year evaluation. Please sign and return it in the folder. If you feel we need a conference, let me know. If I feel we need a conference, I'll let you know.

Applications for English Language Learners

Working with Spanish-speaking four-year-olds at a high-poverty, inner-city child care facility, researchers studied the effectiveness of literacy intervention through a variety of reading and writing activities at school, at home, and in the community (Yaden et al., 2000). Both preschool teachers and parents regularly involved children in shared book reading and provided ways for them to write and display their work. Children showed gains in knowledge of letter and word concepts, understandings of print, directionality, and awareness of handling books. Researchers found that participating preschoolers were above grade level in understanding concepts about print when they entered kindergarten and that children were able to transfer early language awareness in Spanish to English. This study provides support for involving young children in literacy events in their home language to prepare them for school.

role in preparing children for later school achievement (Porche, 2001). These programs may operate in private child care centers, through federally funded programs such as Head Start, or in public preschools. Research findings indicate that the most effective preschools for enhancing literacy development significantly increase children's experiences with print by immersing them in books, stories, and opportunities to write (Allington, 2002).

Developmentally Appropriate Practice

To make sure that preschools and kindergartens provide each child with the right kind of support, teachers employ **developmentally appropriate practice (DAP).** DAP refers to those learning activities that are at the right level for the children's ages and are appropriate for their individual tastes, abilities, and cultures. Children are usually eager to engage in activities that are at the appropriate developmental level, but they are likely to become uncomfortable and frustrated if they are forced to work beyond their abilities (Hendrick, 2001). Developmental appropriateness consists of three principles (Bredekamp, 1987; Jackman, 1997):

- *Activities should be age appropriate.* There are widely recognized, predictable patterns of growth and change in children in all areas of development—social, emotional, physical, and intellectual—that can guide choice of activities.
- *Activities should be individually appropriate.* Individual timing and sequence of growth, including personality, family background, and learning style, can guide choice of activities.
- *Activities should fit the social, linguistic, and cultural contexts in which children live.* Social interactions, home environment, language spoken in the home, and family expectations can guide choice of activities.

Writing

> ## FIGURE 4.7   Features of a DAP Classroom
>
> An integrated curriculum that enables children to learn primarily through projects and learning centers
>
> Opportunities for working alone or in small groups on self-selected activities
>
> Activities that promote active involvement and socialization
>
> Learning centers that contain many literacy artifacts, such as paper, pencils, and books
>
> Learning activities that are concrete, real, and meaningful
>
> Materials that are varied and appropriate for the children's developmental levels
>
> Play as an important part of learning

Good teachers consider these principles when planning programs for young children. What does a DAP classroom look like? Based on these principles, most DAP classrooms would consist of the features shown in Figure 4.7 (Rog, 2001).

Teachers circulate in the DAP classroom, providing guidance and support as needed and encouraging social interactions. They are aware of general developmental characteristics, as well as each child's interests, needs, and capabilities. They realize that children progress at different rates and that no single instructional strategy or set of materials will suffice for all children; instead, they are flexible and able to use a wide range of instructional methods and materials.

Play

Play is a child's primary learning tool (Owocki, 2002) and the most important learning activity in the preschool classroom (McGee & Richgels, 2000). Children naturally and spontaneously engage in many forms of play. Katz (2001) says that play consists of activities that children find enjoyable and participate in voluntarily to have fun. Such activities include building with blocks, playing with water, digging in mud or sand, molding clay, and pretending. Although some play may be solitary, much play is socially interactive and requires such skills as negotiating, problem solving, and decision making, along with using language purposefully. When two children decide to construct a tower of blocks, for example, they may use lan-

Children appreciate the need for literacy as they pretend to read and write at dramatic play centers.

guage to decide which blocks to use, where to place them, and how high to build the tower before it might collapse.

In this section, we focus on dramatic play and its potential for developing language and literacy. **Dramatic play** occurs when children pretend to be something or someone else (Birckmayer, 2002). A child can engage in dramatic play alone (for example, when a child pretends to be a truck driver), but it often occurs through social interactions. By simulating real-life experiences, dramatic play enables children to imitate grown-up behaviors and to try out alternative courses of action. Your role is to allow children to take the initiative and develop their own situations, but to enter subtly into the play on occasion to facilitate the continuation of the scenario and promote language interactions.

Much dramatic play occurs at centers, which may be any setting familiar to the child, such as the kitchen, a fast-food restaurant, a bank, or a beauty shop. To promote literacy development, each center should contain print materials that are often found in such places. Before children use each center, you should explain and model the different materials so that children will know what they are and how to use them. Of course, materials must be safe (for example, no sharp edges on cans) and authentic but perhaps not valid (for example, only canceled checks with account numbers obliterated). You may keep prop boxes that hold center materials (Jackman, 1997) and introduce them when the time is appropriate, such as when the center is related to a field trip or a theme. Figure 4.8 provides examples of dramatic play centers and related literacy materials.

Teaching Tip

Most grocery stores, fast-food restaurants, and community service organizations will give you free materials if you tell them you plan to use them with your class.

*F*IGURE 4.8 **Dramatic Play Centers and Related Literacy Materials**

Fast-Food Restaurant
Menus, place mats, signs, cash register, posters, bags, cups, containers

Kitchen
Cereal boxes, grocery lists, recipes, calendar, cookbook, empty cans

Library
Library card, books, stamp pad, index cards, bookmarks, pencils

Travel Agency
Posters, brochures, tickets, schedules, maps, calendar

Doctor's Office
Prescription pads, pens, appointment cards, charts, check-in sheet

Bank
Checks, bank books, deposit slips, stamp pad, signs (e.g., Cashier, Teller)

Beauty or Barber Shop
Hair spray, posters, shampoo and conditioner, appointment book

Grocery Store
Empty food containers, coupons, labels (e.g., Dairy, Bakery), register tapes

Post Office
Stamps, air mail stickers, special delivery, Express Mail, and other envelopes

Classroom Environment

The classroom environment consists of both the physical surroundings and the emotional climate established by the teacher. The physical environment should be safe, comfortable, and flexible, and the emotional climate should be one in which children feel secure and appreciated.

Reflections

Many children enter school feeling afraid and inadequate. How would you create an environment in which they feel secure and appreciated? What could you do to convince them that they are safe with you and that you care about them? How do you develop trust?

Writing

Technology

CLASSROOM ARRANGEMENT AND MANAGEMENT

Many early childhood classrooms are divided into small areas designed for special purposes. Bookshelves, portable white boards, easels, and other large objects can serve as partitions. Such divisions tend to reduce disruptive behavior and create a calmer, more pleasant tone. One area might be a rug in front of a rocking chair where students gather to listen to stories, and dramatic play centers would be located elsewhere. Additional centers might include areas for blocks, water play, puppets, art, writing, and carpentry. All of these centers would not be available at the same time, of course, because few classrooms would be big enough for so many. You need to eliminate some, combine others, and change them according to seasons, holidays, and themes. Centers might be marked by rugs, tables, cozy book nooks, or "castles" constructed from large appliance cartons. Literacy materials, such as signs, labels, and magazines, could be used in any of these areas.

A computer center is now part of many early childhood classrooms. The center should display a pictorial chart showing basic computer operating procedures, as well as some computer-generated products that are likely to motivate children to explore a variety of graphics and text. As children experiment on the computer, they observe how it reacts to certain commands and share ideas with each other. Some computer programs resemble talking books and enable children to view pictures and text while listening to a story; others let them create text and graphics on the monitor and print them. Early exposure to computers prepares children for using more complex technology skills later, helps them gain insights into literacy, and enhances purposeful language communication. (See Chapter 11 for more information about technology.)

Managing so many areas and activities can be a challenge unless you patiently and consistently help children control their behavior. When children understand why a rule is necessary, they are likely to follow it and develop inner control. Classroom Vignette 4.2 shows how one kindergarten teacher manages her centers.

GROUP TIME

Gathering children together, especially at the beginning of the day, is a good way to welcome them and make them feel that they belong. Having children sit on lines or carpet squares with space between them reduces confusion and disturbances. This is a time for children to share and for you to review what they have been doing and introduce new ideas. Many teachers use this time to discuss the weather, move numbers on a calendar, or go over words on the word wall. If the class is following a theme, this is a good time to elaborate on it.

Classroom Vignette 4.2

Mrs. Ramsey believes her kindergartners can learn to be responsible for their behavior. She begins the year by carefully introducing them to one center, then adding others gradually until the children are able to manage their activities with little intervention.

Seated on the rug in front of Mrs. Ramsey, the children listen to her explanation of the centers they will visit this morning. She carefully explains what they will find at each of the centers and what they are to do with the materials. She reminds them that they are responsible for their behavior, for completing work at each center, and for putting finished work with their names on it in their cubbies.

MRS. RAMSEY: Who is responsible for your behavior?

CHILDREN: We are!

MRS. RAMSEY: At one center I'll give you a cup of cookie letters. You may sort them and find the letters in your name. We'll put these letters in a baggie for you to take home, and you may eat three other letters. Does that sound fair?

CHILDREN: Yes!

MRS. RAMSEY: If I am busy, who can help you?

CHILDREN: A friend.

MRS. RAMSEY: You may go quietly to your centers now.

The children move to centers of their own choice, work on tasks, and rotate to different centers as they complete their work. Mrs. Ramsey directs the center with the cookies, but lets the children work independently at other centers. At one center, children are drawing pictures of their family members and labeling them with proper names or relationships. They are quick to help each other spell words by listening for sounds. At another center, they are circling each lowercase *h* and capital *H* that they find on a magazine page. After a few weeks of participating in center activities, the children know what they are expected to do and work eagerly and cooperatively.

What's happening here?

Children are assuming responsibility for their own behaviors, practicing writing their names on each paper they complete, and cooperating by sharing materials and helping each other spell. They are learning to take turns and to avoid disturbing others as they progress toward becoming mature, independent workers.

Group time provides opportunities for children to engage in finger plays, games with rhyming words, stories, poems, and songs, all of which contribute to language development. When planning these activities, be sure to include those that are developmentally appropriate and appealing to a culturally diverse class. Finger plays involve finger movements along with verse, and songs combine music, rhythm, and rhyme. Children can guess the rhyming word in a familiar verse, such as a nursery rhyme, or complete a couplet such as the following:

This old cat   See the boy

Is very (*fat*).   Play with a (*toy*).

Anthologies often include poems appropriate for young children, and some of these may be done with movements or as choral reading (for example, you read the verse and the children repeat the refrain). The class can use group time to discuss real-life problems and how to solve them, as well as make decisions about issues that

A child points to a designated word on a word wall.

concern them. Such discussions not only develop speaking and listening skills, but also promote reasoning.

PRINT-RICH ENVIRONMENT

As children enter preschool or kindergarten, many are already aware that print carries meaning. They have seen caregivers read mail, signs, newspapers, and store advertisements to get and share information, and the lucky ones have had stories read to them by caring adults. An extension of the real-world print environment should be found in the classroom, along with additional purposeful displays of print. In a **print-rich environment,** there would likely be dozens of books, labels on furniture and equipment at children's eye level, names taped on cubbies and table tops, magazines, a bulletin board with captioned drawings, color and number charts, posters featuring favorite books, big books resting on easels, computers, dictated experience charts, and, of course, literacy materials at play centers. A writing center might offer a variety of writing tools (for example, pens, markers, colored pencils, crayons) and different colors and textures of paper, and a listening station would have headphones for children who want to hear a taped story and follow along in a book that someone has read to them. In the library corner, children would find inviting displays, comfortable furnishings, and books for looking at pictures, pretend reading, and sharing with others.

Technology

Writing

Environmental print refers to print and other symbols that occur in the environment, such as street signs, names of stores and fast-food franchises, billboards, and television commercials. Many children already recognize many of these logos and words, so this print can be used to show them the purpose of reading and as a start for learning letter-sound correspondences. For example, the word *EXIT* could be taped by the door, the word *STOP* might be placed by a street corner in a play area, and *Cheerios* might be on a box in a center. In one classroom, the pre-first-grade teacher placed the side of a corrugated refrigerator carton under the marker tray of the white board. Children brought in environmental words that they could read, such as product names and familiar neighborhood words, and read the words to the class. They then tacked their words onto the corrugated board, and in their free time children sat in front of it, eagerly reading the words they recognized to each other.

Teaching Tip

Children often depend on shape and color to identify environmental print. To help them recognize the words in other contexts, change the color, shape, and size of the print and help the children to see that the letters still match the word in its familiar form.

Hamner (2002) created a theme about traffic safety using environmental words that focused on traffic signs. He also encouraged children to bring in examples of other environmental print and asked them to sort items into categories. Children made class books from the words they collected on such topics as traffic safety, cereals and foods, and fast-food restaurants. Hamner laminated the books,

Applications for English Language Learners

Strategies that support the first language of students in the regular classroom include displaying environmental print written in the first language; writing and posting messages in the students' first language; making available books, magazines, and newspapers written in languages other than English; sending home some of these materials for parents to read; reading aloud to children from books written in their primary language; and allowing students to publish books and share stories in their home language. Although a teacher may not be proficient in each child's first language, a family member or volunteer may be able to translate (Freeman & Freeman, 1993).

bound them, and placed them in the class library, where they quickly became favorite, much-used selections.

Many kindergarten and first-grade teachers use **word walls**, collections of words mounted on the wall, for a variety of purposes, including the following (Brabham & Villaume, 2001).

- Alphabetical list of student names, with a name being added each day, until the whole class has been listed
- High-frequency words, especially those with common endings to use for recognizing and spelling other words
- Theme words, which change as themes are completed and new ones are introduced.

Except for theme or holiday words, words on word walls are cumulative with former words being reviewed as new ones are added. To get the most benefit from word walls, teachers need to involve the children in word-wall

Reflection

Think about your early experiences with reading and writing. What do you remember about how you began learning to read and write? What was helpful? Was there anything you disliked? How can these experiences help you as a teacher?

Applications for Students with Special Needs

Both the physical and social environments are important for learning, so adjust both environments so that all children feel involved in each activity. Establish routines that offer comfort, security, and predictability, and use play as a primary method for teaching and learning (Morrison, 2000). Children with special needs can learn in a literate environment that includes wall charts, access to multimedia materials, an in-class library, and displays of student work (Pressley & Rankin, 1994).

activities, such as counting letters, clapping syllables, chanting letters, comparing word lengths, and matching beginning sounds. As children identify and play with the words, they develop phonemic awareness and knowledge of letter names and letter-sound relationships.

Emergent Literacy

THE CONCEPT of **emergent literacy** refers to a child's developing awareness of the association between print and meaning that begins early in life and continues until the child is able to read and write conventionally (Harris & Hodges, 1995). Educators realize that a child doesn't suddenly begin to read and write upon entering kindergarten or first grade, but that language experiences in the home and early school settings contribute substantially to what a child knows and is able to learn about reading and writing.

Such experiences as family literacy activities, listening to stories, and participating in conversations enable children to develop proficiency in oral language, the foundation for literacy. With exposure to environmental print and exploration of literacy materials at centers in the classroom, most children are already beginning to read and write, whether they realize it or not. Calling their attention to words they know enhances their self-esteem and builds confidence for later reading and writing.

Writing

Most children learn to read and write at about the same time. In fact, it is hard to separate beginning reading from writing because each supports the other. We look first at reading and then at writing, but it is important to keep in mind that they emerge concurrently.

Beginning Reading

We have seen that children have gradually been acquiring the knowledge they need for beginning to read. They have listened to stories and nursery rhymes, and they have played with the sounds of language in songs, chants, and word games. This section deals with activities specifically geared toward preparing children to read.

PHONEMIC AWARENESS

An essential component for learning to read is **phonemic awareness**, the awareness of the sounds in spoken words. It is the foundation for phonics, discussed in Chapter 7. The term comes from *phoneme*, the smallest unit of sound, and is part of the larger concept of *phonological awareness*, the awareness of the sound structure of language that includes larger spoken units. *Auditory discrimination*, also based on sounds, is simply the ability to hear likenesses and differences in phonemes and words. Phonemic awareness is a powerful determinant in learning to read (Adams, 1990) and one of the most important foundations of success in reading (IRA/NAEYC, 1998; National Reading Panel, 2000; Yopp & Yopp, 2000). Enhancing children's awareness of the sounds of language should be a priority in kindergarten, so that by the end of the year children will have some basic phonemic awareness (Snow, Burns, & Griffin, 1998).

Until children are ready to read and write, they have no need to attend to the individual sounds of language; making sense of speech is all that is necessary (Adams, 1990; Richgels, 2001). As children move into reading, however, teachers should intentionally guide them toward phonemic awareness, being sure to engage them in activities that are playful and developmentally appropriate. Teachers can continue using word play and rhyming activities, but should draw attention to specific sounds of language and ways to manipulate these sounds. Figure 4.9 shows some of the skills and activities associated with facilitating phonemic awareness. These are arranged in approximate order of difficulty with rhyming as the easiest task and phonemic manipulation as the most complex task, but any activity may be presented as an opportunity arises. (When a letter or letters are placed between slashes, as /s/, pronounce the sound of the letter or letters, not the letter names.)

Phonemic awareness for young children should be a natural part of daily activities. Opportunities can occur anytime, such as noticing during group

Teaching Tip

When emphasizing the sounds of consonant letters and letter combinations, begin with *continuants*, speech sounds that can be held without distorting the sounds (*m, n, f, v, s, z, th, sh, l, r*). *Stops* are speech sounds that are hard to pronounce without adding *uh* (*p, b, t, d, k, g, ch, j*) (Ehri & Nunes, 2002).

$\mathcal{F}$IGURE 4.9   **Phonemic Awareness Skills and Activities**

Skill	What It Means	Activity
Rhyming	Listening for and creating rhymes	Find rhyming sounds in nursery rhymes. What are some words that rhyme with *cat*?
Comparing and contrasting	Identifying like and unlike phonemes	Do these start alike? *top, time* (yes) Which word doesn't begin like the others? *pet, party, happy* (happy)
Blending	Combining phonemes	What word is /s/ /n/ /ā/ /l/? (snail)
Segmentation	Breaking a syllable into its phonemes	What sounds do you hear in *fan*? (/f/ /ă/ /n/)
Manipulation: deletion and substitution	Removing or changing a phoneme	Say *small* without the /s/. What word do we have now? (mall) If we take /sh/ off *ship* and put on /z/, what word do we hear? (zip)

time that the sounds at the ends of the days of the week are alike or that the words *milk money* sound alike at the beginning. No scripted lesson is necessary, because teachers can simply point out interesting phonemes during such ordinary events as the following.

TEACHER: With all those clouds out there, I'd call today a *gray day*. Hmmm—*gray day*. What do you notice about these two words? Yes, they rhyme. Can you think of other words that rhyme with *gray day*?

TEACHER: Sam, will you please stand up? Let's think of how Sam's name begins—/s/. If your name starts with the same sound we hear at the beginning of Sam's name, will you stand up too? Say your names and we'll listen for the beginning sound. What other words can you think of that begin the same way?

Children's books offer many opportunities for playing with the sounds of language. Dr. Seuss's *Green Eggs and Ham* and *Hop on Pop* contain a multitude of rhyming combinations, and many other Dr. Seuss books offer phonemic experimentations. *Thump, Thump, Rat-a-Tat-Tat* by Gene Baer involves children in rhythm, repetition, and rhyme as the instruments toot and the drums beat, and Helen Lester's *Hooway for Wodney Wat*, a story based on Rodney's inability to pronounce his *r*'s, presents an opportunity to focus on phonemic substitution. *Chicka Chicka Boom Boom* by Bill Martin Jr. and John Archambault lets children chime in with the catchy title words, become familiar with the letters of the alphabet, and attend to the rhyme in the story line. Bruce Degan's *Jamberry* toys with rhymes, alliteration, and make-believe words, as in the following portion of the text (unpaged):

Rumble and ramble

In blackberry bramble

Billions of berries

For blackberry jamble

Most children naturally acquire phonemic awareness as they learn to read, but about 20 percent require additional training (IRA/NAEYC, 1998). For children who do not seem to grasp the concept, teachers should use letter sounds that can be stretched (continuants), select words with only two or three phonemes, and work with familiar letters (Yopp & Yopp, 2000). Children seem to benefit more when phonemic awareness activities are combined with letter-sound instruction so that they can apply what they learn in meaningful contexts (IRA/NAEYC, 1998; Yopp & Yopp, 2000). Although an important component of learning to read, phonemic awareness is only one aspect of a total literacy program.

PRINT AWARENESS

Print awareness, consisting of a number of factors regarding the characteristics and functions of written language, helps determine a child's readiness for reading. Children need to know that pictures are different from print and that print carries a message. They discover that drawing and writing are different, and that letters are different from numerals. They realize that words are combinations of letters with spaces on either side and become aware of the role of punctuation in written material. They begin to acquire a sense of **directionality,** the awareness that words on a page are read from left to right and top to bottom, and that books are read from front to back. Of particular significance for beginning reading and writing is the **alphabetic principle**, the understanding that letters represent the sounds heard in spoken words. These print conventions, or concepts about print, are essential for literacy.

Clay (1985) identifies four categories of concepts about print as follows.

- Concepts about books, including awareness of format, directionality, and the role of print
- Concepts about sentences, including recognition of sentences and awareness of their beginnings (capitalization) and endings (punctuation)
- Concepts about words, particularly awareness that a word consists of a letter or letters with a space on both sides
- Concepts about letters, including the order of letters in the alphabet and recognition of capital and lowercase letters

Through a variety of early experiences, children begin to understand the functions of print. They see print everywhere, both in the home and in the world around them. They realize that print conveys messages, as in mail or newspapers, and that it offers information in such ways as providing directions or giving the television schedule. They learn that stories entertain, and they acquire concepts about story, such as the knowledge that characters may be animals or people and that characters have problems that they try to solve in various ways (McGee & Richgels, 2000). Awareness of the purposes and value of written language can motivate children to become readers and writers themselves.

Reflections

Can you think of other reasons why young children should value reading? How could you demonstrate the usefulness of the printed word to them? What are some ways reading is important to you?

LEARNING TO READ FROM BOOKS

Children pretend to read books long before they actually match spoken words to words in print. Four-year-old Veronica has heard Cinderella so many times that she now retells it herself, using the illustrations to remind her of events in the story. She uses her story-reading voice, which reflects the intonations of expressive adult readers. Children frequently hear a story so often that they memorize repetitive parts. They may role-play as teacher by repeating familiar words in big books, or they may follow along in smaller versions of the big books as they listen to cassette tapes of recorded stories. All of these experiences create motivation and readiness for reading.

Technology

Shared reading is reading books with children and actively engaging them in the text while helping them learn basic print conventions and comprehension strategies. Good **big books** for shared reading are oversized books that use repetition, rhyme, and predictability so that children can follow them easily. Shared reading originated in the belief that children begin to enjoy reading through the warm, intimate sharing of bedtime stories with family members (Holdaway, 1979). The big books may be storybooks, informational books, or poetry

Teaching Tip

Instead of purchasing cassette tapes of books, read stories into a tape recorder, using a signal such as a bell to let the children know when to turn the pages.

During shared reading, the teacher points to words and pictures in a big book while encouraging children to read repetitive parts with him.

and are best shared when placed on an easel so that all children can see them easily.

The first priority in shared reading is enjoyment—the pleasure and delight that comes from sharing a good book. You can create anticipation by talking about the cover illustration, reading the title, pointing out the author and illustrator, relating the topic to the children's experiences, and encouraging them to make predictions. The children listen as you read, responding to an occasional comment or question about the book and chiming in on repetitive phrases. You may move a pointer under each line of print as it is read, thus reinforcing the concept of directionality. If the children are enjoying the book, they will want to hear it again and again. On successive readings, you may point out certain features that are unique to that book. Minilesson 4.1 on Eric Carle's *The Very Hungry Caterpillar* shows how you might use this big book with a group of youngsters.

Introducing children to reading through shared big books has a number of advantages. Children can develop print awareness quite naturally by the enjoyable experience of listening to a story and watching what the teacher does. The teacher can point out print conventions while reading the story. All the children can delight in the colorful illustrations and see the large-print words at the same time. Shared reading provides developmentally appropriate practice for children who are at different levels, that is, for those who are already able to recognize words as well as for others who are simply acquiring basic understandings of how print works. The teacher can systematically introduce various skills within the context of an increasingly familiar text during subsequent readings instead of teaching skills in isolation. When teachers introduce letter-sound correspondences in this way, they are providing whole-to-parts (story-to-skills) phonics instruction that is explicit, systematic, and meaningful (Moustafa & Maldonado-Colon, 1999). Research studies conducted in countries around the world support the practice of shared reading for promoting reading comprehension, word recognition, oral language, vocabulary acquisition, and positive attitudes toward reading (Smith & Elley, 1997a).

Bryan (1999) took another approach to reading books with his kindergartners. He introduced them to **Drop Everything And Read (DEAR)** early in the year. In this activity, the children selected books and found comfortable spots to read them, and Bryan read along with them. The children read in groups, with Bryan sometimes reading to an individual or small group. Later in the year, Bryan turned DEAR time into a reading workshop by spending the first few minutes working with the whole class. He read predictable and repetitive books aloud and involved children in different types of related literary activities. They predicted outcomes, related events and characters to their own lives, and engaged in higher level thinking. During most of the workshop, the children read their own books, selecting one that Bryan had shared and one of their own choice.

Beginning Writing

Beginning reading and writing occur together with one reinforcing the other. This section shows how writing emerges from early experiences with language.

SIMILARITIES BETWEEN SPEECH AND WRITING

Speech and writing are both expressive ways to communicate, and most preschoolers have learned to talk well enough to express their thoughts. In many cases, they learn to talk by interacting with others around them and imitating their speech. They also experiment with constructing their own speech by approximating standard English or the language that is spoken in the home. The feedback from their attempts to use language meaningfully guides them toward standard speech patterns. For example, a child who uses knowledge of speech about something that happened in the past might say, "I finded a penny." An adult providing feedback might respond, "You *found* a penny? Good for you." The child then tucks away this bit of information and knows to use *found* instead of *finded* another time. Of course, it will probably take many such encounters before standard language is used consistently. In the classroom, the teacher should provide similar feedback during informal conversations with the children and by modeling standard usage.

Writing is more challenging than speech but parallels it in many ways (Smith & Elley, 1997b). Most of a child's native language is learned incidentally in real-life situations, and likewise the child's early writing begins as needs arise in authentic contexts, such as in a dramatic play center where a grocery list is needed. The child makes approximations in speech and also in writing through the use of scribbling, randomly placed letters, and invented (or temporary) spellings. Adults provide models for speaking through verbal interactions with children, and they do the same for writing through shared and interactive writing. Thus, the general process for learning to write resembles that for learning to speak, but writing also requires an awareness of print conventions and a knowledge of spelling that is initially based on the alphabetic principle.

Early experiences with writing occur both at home and school. Teachers should communicate with parents and build on literacy skills that children have already acquired. Through experiences at home, children come to recognize the connection between speech and print by realizing that they can represent spoken words with pretend writing. For example, a child writes a holiday list of desired toys by scribbling a row of lines on a piece of paper and then telling what each line means. Children recognize their names on gift cards and begin signing their names on thank you notes and greeting cards. At school they send notes to friends, place orders at a fast-food center, and write in journals long before they can use standard print conventions and conventional spelling. Many early childhood classrooms have writing centers where children can use a variety of writing tools, such as pens, crayons, markers, and colored pencils, on different materials including labels, sticky notes, old envelopes, and paper of different colors and textures. Children are likely to need help with letter formation, and teachers can provide models of upper- and lowercase letters of the alphabet, preferably on strips of paper taped to table tops so that children can see and copy them easily. Children also learn to form letters by finger painting, tracing letters in sand, and writing them in shaving cream sprayed on a smooth surface. Classroom Vignette 4.3 shows how one preschool teacher helps a child with his writing.

Minilesson 4.1

Shared Reading

TEACHER: Today we have a new book by an author we all know. The title of our book is *The Very Hungry Caterpillar.* Who do you think wrote and illustrated it?

CHILDREN: Eric Carle!

TEACHER: How could you tell?

CHILDREN: It has bright colors. It's the kind of eyes he makes. It looks funny.

TEACHER: You're all right. We've seen other books by Eric Carle, so it is easy to recognize his style. What do you think this book will be about?

CHILDREN: A fat caterpillar. He's hungry.

TEACHER: Have any of you ever seen a caterpillar?

CHILDREN: (They respond with kinds and colors of caterpillars they've seen.)

TEACHER: See if you can read the title and the author with me. (The teacher points to the title and author, and the children read with the teacher.)

TEACHER: Let's look at the title page. What do you see here? (The children read the title and author again as the teacher points.) I see it's published by Scholastic. This is where it says *Scholastic.* Now we'll turn to the first page and I'll begin reading. You can follow the words as I point to them. (The teacher reads the story, occasionally commenting on the illustrations, asking for predictions about what the children expect to see next, letting them count how many fruits the caterpillar eats each day, and inviting them to say the repeated words "But he was still hungry.")

TEACHER: Did you enjoy the story? Would you like to hear it again?

CHILDREN: Yes! Read it again!

TEACHER: We'll read it one more time now, and we may read it some other days, too. This time when I read the story I want you to think about all the words that begin with the same sound as the first sound in *caterpillar.* When I read one of these words, raise your hand and tell me what the word is. Then I'll write the word on this chart. (The children identify the words that start with the beginning sound of *caterpillar* on the first few pages of the book, and the teacher helps them notice that they all start with the letter *c.*)

TEACHER: Here is another word that starts with *c, chocolate,* but does it sound like the *c* at the beginning of *caterpillar*? No, it has a different sound, and I'll tell you why. In this word, the *h* after the *c* makes it sound different. Let's see if there are any other words that begin with *ch* as we read the rest of the story. (The teacher reads on and the children find other *ch* words, as well as words beginning with *c*. The teacher is now making a list of words from the story that begin with *c* (for example, *cupcake, cocoon, Carle*) and another list of words beginning with *ch* (for example, *cherry, cheese*).

TEACHER: Now we've finished our story, and we have two lists of words. Let's read the words that begin with *c* first and see if these words sound alike at the beginning. (The teacher points to the words and pronounces them, emphasizing the beginning sound. The children read along with the teacher and agree that these words all begin with the same sound. The teacher repeats this procedure with the words beginning with *ch*.)

Follow-up lessons

During repeated readings, the teacher may focus on days of the week, counting and counting words, the life cycle of a caterpillar, and various aspects of print. For example, the exclamation mark that follows "That night he had a stomachache!" presents an opportunity to talk about end punctuation and what it means. Because the caterpillar eats through one or more food items, children can begin thinking about singular and plural forms of nouns. Responses through art include making decorated sock puppets of caterpillars, constructing caterpillars from egg cartons, and fashioning tissue paper butterflies (Hancock, 1989).

What are the children learning?

The children are learning to enjoy literature by sharing the story. They know about the author, illustrator, and publisher and begin to recognize styles of writing and illustrating. They are finding that print determines what words are spoken and are becoming aware of such print conventions as directionality, alphabetic principle, punctuation, and terminology (for example, first page, exclamation mark, word). In this story, they are learning initial sounds of words beginning with the letters *c* and *ch*. They are beginning to relate stories to their own experiences, make predictions, and become aware of sequence. They are connecting the content to other areas of the curriculum, such as science (metamorphosis), math (counting), and days of the week.

Classroom Vignette 4.3

Miss Angela calls Nathaniel over during center time and places a large sheet of white paper on the table in front of him. She asks him what he would like to be when he grows up, and he replies, "a cowboy." She asks him to make a sentence with these words that she could write on the paper. Guiding him by asking questions, she gets him to say, "I want to be a cowboy." She asks him to watch her carefully while she writes his words and repeats them aloud. She asks him to read the sentence back with her and then dots the letters of his name for him to trace. He then draws a picture of a cowboy on a horse and adds several lines radiating from the cowboy's head. He explains that the cowboy didn't comb his hair that morning so he has spiky hair. Miss Angela praises him for his idea and adds his words to his story. Proud of his picture and story, Nathaniel goes over to show Miss Martha.

What's happening here?

Nathaniel gets one-on-one attention while his teacher encourages him to think about a career choice, helps him understand the concept of sentence, and shows him that what he says can be written down and read back. He also gains confidence in his ability to create a worthwhile story, an important step on the road to literacy.

INVENTED SPELLING

Children progress through developmental stages when they learn to write, but not necessarily at the same rate (see Chapter 10). Learning may be recursive rather than linear; that is, children may revert to earlier stages or function at different levels for different purposes (Rog, 2001). Writing usually begins as scribbles and then proceeds to randomly placed letter-like forms, upper- and lowercase letters mixed together, and letters that are reversed. When children realize that letters represent sounds, they often

FIGURE 4.10   **Titanic Story**

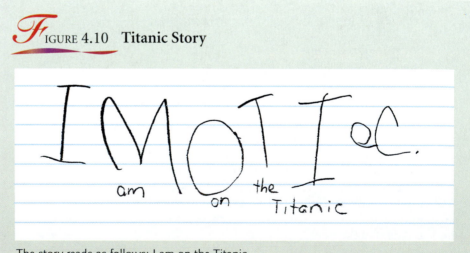

The story reads as follows: I am on the Titanic.

Source: Robert McCade Wynne, Kingston Elementary School, Kingston, TN. Used with permission.

write the first consonant to represent a word, then add additional consonants that they hear, and finally add vowels. Mac's story about the Titanic (see Figure 4.10) shows an early stage of development and so is limited to mostly initial consonants to represent words, whereas Sarah's story about her camping trip (see Figure 4.11) reveals a later stage in both invented spelling and story composition. The teacher asked the children to draw a picture and then write a story about it. Notice that the teacher has transcribed what they wrote so that the meaning will not be lost if they want to read their stories back later.

Invented spelling consists of the approximations a child makes in an attempt to match letter sounds with letter names. Encouraging invented spelling is considered good teaching practice for helping developing writers and receives wide support (Adams, 1990; Gentry, 2000; IRA/NAEYC, 1998; Sipe, 2001). When children are not concerned about accurate spelling, they are free to express their thoughts and use a wide vocabulary to create stories or send messages. They gain confidence in their ability to write and think of themselves as writers. Spelling *piano* obviously did not deter Kelsey from what she wanted to write (see Figure 4.12). She simply listened to the sounds and matched them as well as she could to the letters. She also demonstrated attention to detail in her drawing, a characteristic that is likely to help with letter and word identification.

𝓕IGURE 4.11   **Camping Trip Story**

The story reads as follows: Me and my family are camping and we are having fun. We built a fire.

Source: Sarah Woody, Kingston Elementary School, Kingston, TN. Used with permission.

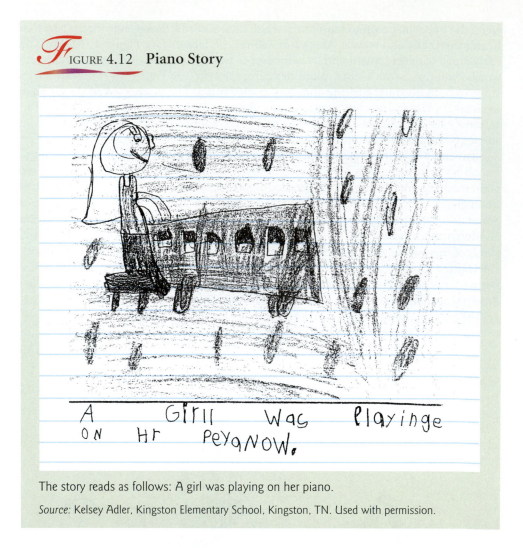

$\mathcal{F}$IGURE 4.12   **Piano Story**

A   GIrll   WAs   PlayiNge
ON   Hr   PeYaNOW.

The story reads as follows: A girl was playing on her piano.

Source: Kelsey Adler, Kingston Elementary School, Kingston, TN. Used with permission.

When children match letters to sounds, or *encode,* they are applying the same skills they need for decoding words in reading. By observing children's invented spelling, teachers can assess their ability to make sense of sound-letter relationships and plan instruction accordingly (Gentry, 2000; Sipe, 2001). They need to realize, however, that children should use invented spelling only on a temporary basis and should move gradually toward correct spelling. They should also encourage children to use

Teaching Tip

Let children sit in small groups when they are writing so that they can help each other with spelling. You can't help everyone at once, and children can be very effective teachers. In fact, they are likely to use your very own words, such as "What letter makes the sound you hear at the beginning of . . . ?"

correct spelling whenever they can, particularly when it is visible on charts, books, or labels in the room.

SHARED WRITING

One way that children learn how to write occurs through **shared writing** when the teacher models the procedure and actively engages them in the process. This procedure is similar to the language experience approach, discussed in Chapter 7. The teacher demonstrates left-right and top-bottom directionality, reminds the children of letter-sound correspondences, points out the use of capital letters and punctuation, and invites the children to participate. In shared writing, the children dictate their ideas and the teacher records what they say while talking through the process. In interactive writing, children write many of the words on the chart themselves (Rog, 2001; Sipe, 2001). Mrs. Bell, a kindergarten teacher, writes *Morning News* at the top of a page on a chart tablet each day, gathers the children around her in front of the chart, and asks them to contribute items. Her lesson might proceed like Minilesson 4.2 on shared writing.

Kindergarten children should write every day to develop an understanding of sound-letter relationships and an appreciation of the functions of print (Rog, 2001). Many kindergarten teachers expect children to begin writing on the first day of school and to keep journals. The journals may consist simply of scribbles at first, but are likely to show children's movement through developmental stages as the year progresses. One K-1 teacher motivated her children to create interesting stories by reading aloud expressively (for example, changing her voice to reflect the characters) and giving her children plenty of time to write, usually first thing in the morning. Children's writings covered the walls of her classroom and children were busily writing or conferring. One first-grader who had started his second year in this class confided that he was writing a ten-chapter book about Frisky, the squirrel. He was already into the eighth chapter.

Storybooks often motivate children to write similar stories with the same pattern. Mrs. Ross read *The Mitten* by Jan Brett about all of the animals that crawl into a mitten. She asked the children to brainstorm animals that might be able to crawl into a mitten and then suggested that each child draw a picture and write a version of the story. Figure 4.13 shows Cara's illustration and story.

On another occasion, Mrs. Ross centered a theme on a favorite book. She read *Chicka Chicka Boom Boom*, an alphabet story about letters that climb a coconut tree. After sharing the book with her kindergartners, she developed activities that spanned the curriculum. Figure 4.14 outlines the activities she used and the curriculum areas covered.

Even in kindergarten, children are able to engage in a simple form of *writer's workshop*, a procedure that begins with a minilesson, continues with time for children to

When children first begin to write, teach them to spell some common words or word parts, such as *the* and *-ing* for adding to action words, as in *baking* and *playing*. Knowing frequently used letter combinations prevents the children from having to sound them out each time they need to write them.

Shared Writing

MRS. BELL: It's time for our morning news. Who can read what it says at the top of this chart?

CHILDREN: Morning news!

MRS. BELL: That's right. Who has something to share with us this morning?

DAKOTA: I lost my tooth last night.

MRS. BELL: My goodness! That's pretty exciting. Let's write about Dakota's lost tooth. I think the first thing we need to write is Dakota's name. Dakota, can you tell me what letters I need to spell your name?

DAKOTA: *D-a-k-o-t-a*

MRS. BELL: That's right, and what kind of *d* do we need at the beginning of a name?

CHILDREN: Capital *D*

MRS. BELL: Right. I'll begin with a capital *D* and make the other letters lower-case. Would you please spell it again for me, Dakota?

DAKOTA: *D-a-k-o-t-a*

MRS. BELL: (prints *Dakota*) What do we want to say about Dakota?

CHILDREN: She lost her tooth.

MRS. BELL: So the next word we need is *lost*. Can you help me spell *lost*? Let's listen to how it begins. (Teacher says word and stretches the beginning sound.)

CHILDREN: (guess different letters but most say *l*)

MRS. BELL: That's right. *L* is the letter we need. How did you know that?

CHILDREN: (various answers, with some saying because it begins like *little* and *Lucy*)

MRS. BELL: Good for you! It does sound like *little* and *Lucy* at the beginning. I'll write the next letter because you can't hear it very well. It's *o*. But I think you can tell me the next two letters. Listen. (Teacher says *lost* and stretches the pronunciation of the last two letters.)

CHILDREN: (various responses, but most say they hear an *s* and then a *t*)

MRS. BELL: I hear you saying *s* and *t*, so we'll put those letters at the end of the word and spell *lost*. Now let's remember the sentence: *Dakota lost her tooth*. What is our next word?

CHILDREN: *her*

MRS. BELL: That's right. The first letter is a little hard. It makes sort of a breathy sound. Listen carefully. (Teacher pronounces *her,* slightly exaggerating the sound that *h* makes.)

CHILDREN: (several letters mentioned, with only a few children correctly saying *h*)

MRS. BELL: I heard someone say *h* and that's correct. I'll begin *her* with an *h* and I'll write the next letter. It's an *e*, but I think you'll know the last letter. Listen: *her*. What is it? You can almost hear this letter say its name on the end of the word.

CHILDREN: It's an *r*! (most agreeing on this letter)

MRS. BELL: You've got it. Now here is our sentence so far. *Dakota lost her...* What is the last word in our sentence?

CHILDREN: *tooth*

MRS. BELL: That's right. Only one more word. Can you tell me how it starts?

CHILDREN: (chorus of voices with many saying *t* and volunteering that it starts like *two* and *today*, words they already know by sight)

MRS. BELL: Right. I'll start with *t* and I'll put in the next two letters—*oo*—but I want to see if anyone knows what letters go at the end of this word. *Tooth.*

CHILDREN: (most just guessing randomly, but a few saying *th* because they relate it to the *th* in *thin, three,* or *thumb*)

MRS. BELL: Some of you are very clever. The last two letters are *th*, so now we have the word *tooth*. This is the end of our first sentence, so what do we need to put here?

CHILDREN: (some saying to put a period, but many do not know)

MRS. BELL: I'll put a period at the end because this sentence *tells* something about Dakota. Now let's read our sentence together.

MRS. BELL AND CHILDREN:
Dakota lost her tooth.

MRS. BELL: Very good. Who else would like to give us a sentence? (Mrs. Bell proceeds in the same way for one or two additional sentences and asks the children to read the entire chart when they complete the dictation.)

What are the children learning?

The children are learning directionality and terminology for such concepts as *word, sentence, period, next, end, letters,* and *spell*. The teacher is demonstrating how speech can be written down and is letting the children know that what they say is important. She is reinforcing their knowledge of letter-sound correspondences by asking them to help her spell and questioning them about other words that begin the same way. This is a risk-free situation because the children can call out letters without being embarrassed if they are wrong, and each child participates in writing the chart. Shared writing reaches children at different levels, so that the more advanced are helping with the spelling whereas some of the others are simply learning directionality and some terminology.

Writing

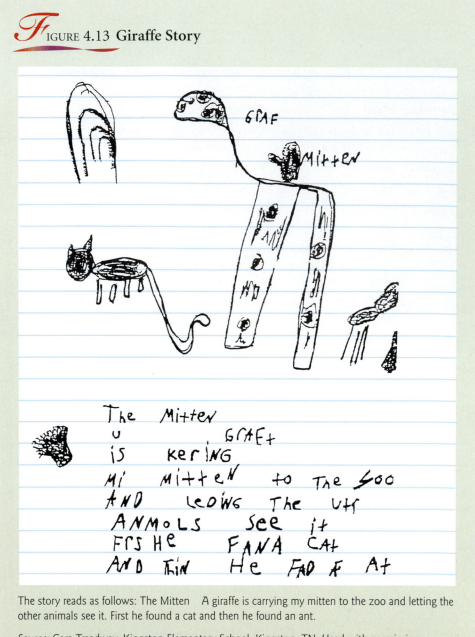

$\mathcal{F}$IGURE 4.13 **Giraffe Story**

The story reads as follows: The Mitten   A giraffe is carrying my mitten to the zoo and letting the other animals see it. First he found a cat and then he found an ant.

Source: Cara Treadway, Kingston Elementary School, Kingston, TN. Used with permission.

write, and concludes with sharing (Cecil, 1999; Rog, 2001). The teacher may begin by modeling writing or reading aloud and inviting comments, and then giving children a chance to share ideas for the writing that follows. Children have time to write, using the shared writing or reading as a stimulus or coming up with ideas of their own. As they write, they help each other with spelling words and constructing stories, and when they finish writing, they share what they have written. This procedure involves all children in writing and places value on their work.

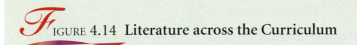

IGURE 4.14 **Literature across the Curriculum**

Source: Chicka Chicka Boom Boom by Bill Martin Jr. and John Archambault

Language

Read the story and let children chime in on repetitive parts.

Make sentence strips or picture cards of events and let children arrange them in sequence.

Have children cut out puzzle pieces of letters and put them together to spell words from the story.

Make cards mounted on cutouts of palm trees for children to complete. The cards read:

(*child's name*)

climbed to the top of

the coconut tree to see

(*what child saw*)

Ask children to listen for rhyming words in the story.

Let them find new words that begin with /ch/ as in *Chicka*. (This activity reinforces the lesson on the sound of /ch/ from *The Very Hungry Caterpillar*.)

Have children make a human alphabet by using their bodies to form letter shapes.

Ask each child to be a letter and tell what happened when climbing the coconut tree.

Science

Bring in a coconut, cut it open, and let children see the milk and meat inside. Then let them taste the coconut and also taste shredded coconut from a package.

Discuss characteristics of palm trees; compare them with other trees.

Geography

Discuss where palm trees grow and their need for a warm, tropical climate.

Mathematics

Go through the alphabet and count how many children's names begin with each letter.

Make a graph to compare frequencies of beginning letters.

Make two felt palm trees and several coconuts. Place a few coconuts on each tree and create addition and subtraction problems by comparing and totaling the coconuts on the trees.

Creative drama

Ask the children to stand in alphabetical order and hold letter cards that represent letters with special features, for example, skinned-knee D and loose-tooth T. Children act their letter characters as you read the story.

Classroom Assessment for Emergent Literacy

Of course, teacher observation is the most effective way to assess literacy development in young children. They reveal much about their levels as they play, respond to stories, and interact socially with others. In addition, there are tests available to measure their understanding of concepts about print and phonemic awareness.

Summary

Vygotsky's theories have influenced early childhood programs, particularly his beliefs about the social aspects of language and cognitive growth. A wide variety of early experiences with language at home and during early schooling enable children to acquire basic concepts about literacy.

A number of factors affect children's growth in literacy, and no activity appears to be more significant than reading aloud to them. Predictable and repetitive books are particularly appealing, and selections should include books representing different ethnic groups and books from different genres. Family literacy also plays an important role by encouraging language development through conversations and purposeful literacy activities. Some families provide rich home environments with many books and writing materials available and time for shared reading, and various agencies have established more structured family literacy programs.

Preschool and kindergarten programs provide many opportunities for children to become literate. Most programs employ developmentally appropriate practice (DAP) so that activities are geared to the ages and interest levels of the children. Play is a primary way of learning for many children, particularly in dramatic play centers that offer authentic purposes for reading and writing. Children also learn during group time by sharing information, discussing ideas, and listening to stories. Early childhood classrooms should have a print-rich environment that includes charts, books, labels, writing centers, word walls, and environmental print.

Without doubt, early childhood is a crucial period for a child's emerging literacy. Children learn to read and write concurrently, with one process reinforcing the other. Phonemic awareness, the awareness of sounds in spoken words, is important for learning to read, and children must become aware of the functions of print and its many purposes. Shared reading, usually with big books, is a viable way for children to enjoy reading and learn about the reading process. Early writing is similar to speech, but involves knowledge of print conventions and spelling. Writing activities should be meaningful, and teachers should encourage children to use invented spelling to express their ideas until they are able to use conventional spelling.

Writing

Writing

Discussion Questions

1. How might you scaffold a child who wants to write but has not yet discovered the alphabetic principle?

2. Since children develop at different rates, how will you know if the activities you plan are developmentally appropriate?

3. If you have a child from a home where there are no books, and this child has had few experiences outside the home, what would you do?

4. Whole-to-parts phonics begins with the teacher reading a story and selecting skills to teach from the story. Some educators believe teachers should begin reading instruction by teaching the skills first before children begin reading stories. What do you think?

5. What are your goals and objectives for children in preschool or kindergarten? What priorities would you set for what you want them to learn?

6. What additional resources would you investigate before attempting to develop emergent literacy with three-, four-, and five-year-olds? What do you believe you need to know most, and how would you find it out?

7. Express in your own words what you think emergent literacy means. How can you promote it as a teacher?

Suggested Activities

1. Apply Vygotsky's theory of the Zone of Proximal Development by helping a child accomplish a task she is unable to do without assistance. Provide scaffolding until this child is able to perform the task independently.

2. Make a list of your favorite books to read aloud. Include bibliographic information and a brief annotation for each book. Select one of these to read to a child or a small group of children.

3. Think of a dramatic play center not described in Figure 4.8 and list all the literacy materials and events that could relate to that center.

4. Visit a preschool or kindergarten classroom and look for evidence of a print-rich environment. What do you find?

5. If you had your own early childhood classroom, what arrangement would you use? How would you accommodate centers, group time, and other areas? Draw a layout.

6. Begin a collection of phonemic awareness tasks, such as rhyming couplets or phonemic manipulations, that will help young children attend to the sounds of language.

7. Design a program for parent involvement. What is your purpose, and how will you achieve it? What types of language and literacy activities will you include, and how can you encourage parents to participate?

8. Direct an activity or a lesson for preschoolers. From your observations and reflections, answer the question, "What's happening here?"

9. Observe a young child's print awareness and write a summary of your observations. Consider the child's understanding of both the conventions and functions of print.

Writing

10. Look at the examples of stories written by children with invented spelling and tell what each child knows about spelling, the conventions of print, and story structure. What can you say about what each of these children knows about writing and has yet to learn?

11. Create a prop box for a literacy center. Select a theme, either one given in this chapter or another of your choice (perhaps a bakery or toy store), and place literacy materials in your box.

References

ADAMS, M. J. (1990). *Beginning to read: Thinking and learning about print.* Cambridge, MA: MIT Press.

ALLINGTON, R. (2002). Research on reading/learning disability interventions. In A. Farstrup and S. J. Samuels (Eds.), *What research has to say about reading instruction* (3rd ed., pp. 261–290). Newark, DE: International Reading Association.

BARONE, D. (1998). How do we teach literacy to children who are learning English as a second language? In S. Neuman & K. Roskos (Eds.), *Children achieving* (pp. 56–76). Newark, DE: International Reading Association.

BECK, I., & McKEOWN, M. (2001). Text talk: Capturing the benefits of read-aloud experiences for young children. *The Reading Teacher, 55,* 10–20.

BIRCKMAYER, J. (2002). Web-based learning units: Dramatic play. State College, PA: Better Kid Care Program. Retrieved September 23, 2002, and November 11, 2004, from http://www.betterkidcare.psu.edu/UnitsWeb/DramaticPlay/DramaPlay2.html

BRABHAM, E., & VILLAUME, S. (2001). Building walls of words. *The Reading Teacher, 54,* 700–702.

BREDEKAMP, S. (Ed.). (1987). *Developmentally appropriate practice in early childhood programs serving children from birth through age 8* (expanded ed.). Washington, DC: National Association for the Education of Young Children.

BRYAN, J. (1999). Reader's workshop in a kindergarten classroom. *The Reading Teacher, 52,* 538–540.

CECIL, N. (1999). *Striking a balance—Positive practices for early literacy.* Scottsdale, AZ: Holcomb Hathaway.

CLAY, M. (1985). *The early detection of reading difficulties* (3rd ed.). Auckland, NZ: Heinemann.

CLINE, Z. (2001). Reading parties: Helping families share the joy of literacy. *The Reading Teacher, 55,* 236–237.

DELGADO-GAITAN, C. (1990). *Literacy for empowerment: The role of parents in children's education.* New York: Falmer.

DIXON-KRAUSS, L. (1996). *Vygotsky in the classroom.* White Plains, NY: Longman.

EHRI, L., & NUNES, S. (2002). The role of phonemic awareness in learning to read. In A. Farstrup & S. J. Samuels (Eds.), *What research has to say about reading instruction* (3rd ed., pp. 110–139). Newark, DE: International Reading Association.

FREEMAN, D., & FREEMAN, Y. (1993). Strategies for promoting the primary languages of all students. *The Reading Teacher, 46,* 18–25.

GENTRY, J. R. (2000). A retrospective on invented spelling and a look forward. *The Reading Teacher, 54,* 318–332.

GRIFFIN, M. L. (2001). Social contexts of beginning reading. *Language Arts, 78,* 371–378.

HAMNER, D. (2002). From stop signs to the golden arches: Environmental print. *NCTE read-write-think.* Retrieved October 29, 2002, and November 11, 2004, from http://www.readwritethink.org/lessons/lesson_view.asp?id=27

HANCOCK, P. (1989). Big book teaching guide for *The very hungry caterpillar.* New York: Scholastic.

HARRIS, T. L., & HODGES, R. E. (Eds.). (1995). *The literacy dictionary.* Newark, DE: International Reading Association.

HENDRICK, J. (2001). *The whole child* (7th ed.). Upper Saddle River, NJ: Merrill.

HOLDAWAY, D. (1979). *The foundations of literacy.* Portsmouth, NH: Heinemann.

INTERNATIONAL READING ASSOCIATION AND NATIONAL ASSOCIATION FOR THE EDUCATION OF YOUNG CHILDREN. (1998). Learning to read and write: Developmentally appropriate practices for young children. *The Reading Teacher, 52,* 193–216.

JACKMAN, H. (1997). *Early education curriculum: A child's connection to the world.* Albany, NY: Delmar.

KATZ, J. (2001). Playing at home: The talk of pretend play. In D. Dickinson & P. Tabors (Eds.), *Beginning literacy with language* (pp. 53–73). Baltimore: Paul H. Brookes.

KOSTELNIK, M., SODERMAN, A., & WHIREN, A. (1999). *Developmentally appropriate curriculum* (2nd ed.). Upper Saddle River, NJ: Merrill.

MCGEE, L., & RICHGELS, D. (2000). *Literacy's beginnings: Supporting young readers and writers* (3rd ed.). Boston, MA: Allyn & Bacon.

MORNINGSTAR, J. W. (1999). Home response journals: Parents as informed contributors in the understanding of their child's literacy development. *The Reading Teacher, 52,* 690–706.

MORRISON, G. (2000). *Fundamentals of early childhood education* (2nd ed.). Upper Saddle River, NJ: Merrill.

MOUSTAFA, M., & MALDONADO-COLON, E. (1999). Whole-to-parts phonics instruction: Building on what children know to help them know more. *The Reading Teacher, 52,* 448–458.

NATIONAL READING PANEL. (2000). *Teaching children to read: An evidence-based assessment of the scientific research literature on reading and its implications for reading instruction.* Washington, DC: National Institute of Child Health and Human Development.

NISTLER, R., & MAIERS, A. (2000). Stopping the silence: Hearing parents' voices in an urban first-grade family literacy program. *The Reading Teacher, 53,* 670–680.

OPITZ, M. (1999). Cultural diversity + supportive text = Perfect books for beginning readers. *The Reading Teacher, 52,* 888–890.

OWOCKI, G. (2002). Literacy through play. Paper presented at the World Congress of the International Reading Association, Edinburgh, Scotland.

PARATORE, J. (2002). Home and school together: Helping beginning readers succeed. In A. Farstrup & S. J. Samuels (Eds.), *What research has to say about reading instruction* (3rd ed., pp. 48–68). Newark, DE: International Reading Association.

PORCHE, M. (2001). Parent involvement as a link between home and school. In D. Dickinson & P. Tabors (Eds.), *Beginning literacy with language* (pp. 291–312). Baltimore: Paul H. Brookes.

PRESSLEY, M., & RANKIN, J. (1994). More about whole language methods of reading instruction for students at risk for early reading failure. *Learning disabilities: Research & practice, 9*(3), 157–168.

RICHGELS, D. (2001). Phonemic awareness. *The Reading Teacher, 55,* 274–275.

RICHGELS, D. (2002). Informational texts in kindergarten. *The Reading Teacher, 55,* 586–595.

ROG, L. (2001). *Early literacy instruction in kindergarten.* Newark, DE: International Reading Association.

ROSS, E., ELKINS, S., & PETTY, P. (1999). *Promoting family literacy in the Upper Cumberlands.* Cookeville, TN: Phi Delta Kappa Grant.

SEARFOSS, L., READENCE, J., & MALLETTE, M. (2001). *Helping children learn to read* (4th ed.). Boston: Allyn & Bacon.

SIPE, L. (2000). The construction of literary understanding by first and second graders in oral response to picture storybook read-alouds. *Reading Research Quarterly, 35,* 252–275.

SIPE, L. (2001). Invention, convention, and intervention: Invented spelling and the teacher's role. *The Reading Teacher, 55,* 264–273.

SMITH, J., & ELLEY, W. (1997a). *How children learn to read.* Katonah, NY: Richard C. Owen.

SMITH, J., & ELLEY, W. (1997b). *How children learn to write.* Katonah, NY: Richard C. Owen.

SNOW, C. E., BURNS, M. S., & GRIFFIN, P. (1998). *Preventing reading difficulties in young children.* Washington, DC: National Academy.

SNOW, C., TABORS, P., & DICKINSON, D. (2001). Language development in the preschool years. In D. Dickinson & P. Tabors (Eds.), *Beginning literacy with language* (pp. 1–25). Baltimore: Paul H. Brookes.

TABORS, P., SNOW, C., & DICKINSON, D. (2001). Homes and schools together. In D. Dickinson & P. Tabors (Eds.), *Beginning literacy with language* (pp. 313–334). Baltimore: Paul H. Brookes.

THOMAS, A., FAZIO, L., & STIEFELMEYER, B. (1999). *Families at school: A handbook for parents.* Newark, DE: International Reading Association.

TRELEASE, J. (1995). *The read-aloud handbook* (4th ed.). New York: Penguin.

VYGOTSKY, L. (1986). *Thought and language* (rev. ed.), Kozulin, A., (Ed.). Cambridge, MA: MIT Press.

YADEN, D., TAM, A., MADRIGAL, P., BRASSELL, D., MASSA, J., ALTAMIRANO, L. S., & ARMENDARIZ, J. (2000). Early literacy for inner-city children: The effects of reading and writing interventions in English and Spanish during the preschool years. *The Reading Teacher, 54,* 186–189.

YOPP, H., & YOPP, R. (2000). Supporting phonemic awareness development in the classroom. *The Reading Teacher, 54,* 130–143.

*B*ooks for Children Cited in This Chapter

ARDLEY, N. (1992). *The science book of weather.* San Diego: Gulliver/Harcourt Brace.

BAER, G. (1989). *Thump, thump, rat-a-tat-tat.* New York: Harper & Row.

BAKER, J. (1988). *Where the forest meets the sea.* New York: Greenwillow.

BANG, M. (1999). *When Sophie gets angry—really, really angry . . . .* New York: Scholastic.

BARTON, B. (1982). *Airport.* New York: Crowell.

BRETT, J. (1989). *The mitten.* New York: Putnam.

BRIDWELL, N. (1985). *Clifford and the grouchy neighbors.* New York: Scholastic.

BROWN, M. (1994). *Arthur's first sleepover.* Boston: Little, Brown.

CARLE, E. (1987). *A house for Hermit Crab.* New York: Scholastic.

CARLE, E. (1985). *The very busy spider.* New York: Putnam.

CARLE, E. (1987). *The very hungry caterpillar.* New York: Scholastic.

CARLE, E. (1995). *The very lonely firefly.* New York: Philomel.

CARLE, E. (1997). *The very quiet cricket.* New York: Philomel.

COLE, H. (1998). *I took a walk.* New York: Greenwillow.

COUSTEAU SOCIETY, THE. *Turtles.* New York: Little Simon.

CURTIS, J. (1998). *Today I feel silly and other moods that make my day.* New York: HarperCollins.

DEGEN, B. (1983). *Jamberry.* New York: Scholastic.

EHLERT, L. (1991). *Red leaf, yellow leaf.* San Diego: Harcourt Brace Jovanovich.

ESBENSEN, B., & BROWN, M. (1991). *Tiger with wings: The great horned owl.* Danbury, CT: Orchard.

FLEMING, D. (1993). *In the small, small pond.* New York: Holt.

FOX, M. (1997). *Whoever you are.* San Diego: Harcourt Brace.

FRASIER, D. (1998). *Out of the ocean.* San Diego: Harcourt Brace.

FREEDMAN, R. (1983). *Dinosaurs and their young.* New York: Holiday House.

GIBBONS, G. (1987). *Dinosaurs.* New York: Holiday House.

HALPERN, J. (1998). *A look at spiders.* Austin, TX: Steck-Vaughn.

HAMANAKA, S. (1994). *All the colors of the earth.* New York: Morrow.

JAUCK, A., & POINTS, L. (1993). *Assateague: Island of the wild ponies.* New York: Macmillan.

JEUNESSE, G., & COHAT, E. (1990). *The seashore.* New York: Scholastic.

LANDA, N., & PONS, O. (2001). *Bunnies.* Hauppauge, NY: Barron's.

LESTER, H. (1999). *Hooway for Wodney Wat.* Boston: Houghton Mifflin.

LONDON, J. (1993). *The eyes of Gray Wolf.* San Francisco: Chronicle.

MARKLE, S. (1996). *Creepy, crawly baby bugs.* New York: Scholastic.

MARTIN, B. (1982). *Brown bear, brown bear, what do you see?* Toronto: Holt, Rinehart & Winston.

MARTIN, B., & ARCHAMBAULT, J. (1989). *Chicka chicka boom boom.* New York: Scholastic.

MATTHEWS, D. (1989). *Polar bear cubs.* New York: Simon & Schuster.

NELSON, J. (1989). *Peanut butter and jelly.* Cleveland: Modern Curriculum.

PALLOTTA, J. (1986). *The icky bug alphabet book.* Watertown, MA: Charlesbridge.

PENN, A. (1993). *The kissing hand.* Washington, DC: Child Welfare League of America.

REY, H. A. (1966). *Curious George goes to the hospital.* New York: Scholastic.

ROCKWELL, A. (1985). *First comes spring.* New York: Crowell.

ROYSTON, A. (1992). *Insects and crawly creatures.* London: Dorling Kindersley.

RYLANT, C. (1985) *The relatives came.* New York: Simon & Schuster.

SELSAM, M. (1987). *A first look at caterpillars.* New York: Walker.

SEUSS, DR. (1957). *The cat in the hat.* New York: Random House.

SEUSS, DR. (1960). *Green eggs and ham.* New York: Random House.

SEUSS, DR. (1991). *Hop on pop.* New York: Random House.

SIMON, S. (2000) *Seymour Simon's book of trucks.* New York: HarperCollins.

SIMON, S. (1995). *Sharks.* New York: Scholastic.

SIMON, S. (1989). *Whales.* New York: Scholastic.

TABACK, S. (1997). *There was an old lady who swallowed a fly.* New York: Penguin.

TAYLOR, K. (1990). *Hidden by darkness.* New York: Delacorte.

YOLEN, J. (1987). *Owl moon.* New York: Scholastic.

Chapter

5

DEVELOPING
LISTENING
PROFICIENCY

LEARNER OBJECTIVES

At the conclusion of this chapter

YOU SHOULD BE ABLE TO

1. Discuss the importance of listening as a form of communication.

2. Define listening and discuss the process.

3. Explain the relationship of listening to viewing.

4. Discuss the various types of listening.

5. Describe conditions for enhancing listening in the classroom.

6. Explain specific strategies for teaching listening skills.

7. Identify the following terms that are defined or explained in this chapter:

NCTE/IRA Standards addressed in this chapter

STANDARD 6. Students apply knowledge of language structure, language conventions (e.g., spelling and punctuation), media techniques, figurative language, and genre to create, critique, and discuss print and non-print texts.

STANDARD 8. Students use a variety of technological and information resources (e.g., libraries, databases, computer networks, video) to gather and synthesize information and to create and communicate knowledge.

STANDARD 10. Students whose first language is not English make use of their first language to develop competency in the English language arts and to develop understanding of content across the curriculum.

Chapter 5 Organizer

Developing Listening Proficiency

- The Listening Process
- Importance of Listening
- The Relationship of Listening to Viewing

Strategies for Teaching Listening
- Reconstructing the Text
- Listening Centers
- Say Something
- Other Activities
- Listening-Reading Transfer Strategy
- InQuest
- Structured Listening Activity
- Directed Listening-Thinking Activity

Types of Listening
- Listening for Information
- Listening for Interpretation
- Listening for Critical Analysis
- Listening for Creative Applications
- Listening for Enjoyment

The Role of the Teacher
- Modeling Good Listening Behaviors
- Preparing Students to Listen
- Providing Appropriate Listening Material
- Considering the Students
- Reinforcing Good Listening Practices
- Providing Opportunities for Practice

Instruction in Listening
- Materials for Teaching Listening
- The Classroom Environment

*M*S. HARRIS has just taught a lesson on compound words, and now she wants the students to do an assignment on finding compound words in sentences. Several children are moving about the room or talking quietly with their friends.

MS. HARRIS: Now that you know about compound words, I want you to look through the book we just finished, *Don't You Know There's a War On?* by Avi, and find the compound words in the book. Everyone get to work.

MICKEY: Do you want us to find all of them?

MS. HARRIS: As many as you can.

PATRICIA: Do we have to write the sentences or can we just write the compound words?

MS. HARRIS (hesitating):

Let's see—ummm.

SEVERAL STUDENTS:

Don't make us write the whole sentence. That takes too long. Just let us write the words.

MS. HARRIS: Well, O.K. I guess that will do.

RANDY: Do we have to turn in our papers?

MS. HARRIS: Yes, turn in your papers.

SUSAN: I don't understand what we're supposed to do.

MS. HARRIS: All right, everybody listen. Find compound words in *Don't You Know There's a War On?* Just write the compound words and then turn in your papers.

FRANK: How many words do we have to find?

MS. HARRIS: As many as you can.

FRANK: What if we don't find any? When do we turn in our papers?

MS. HARRIS: Find at least six. You have 30 minutes to finish and turn in your papers.

What's happening here?

Ms. Harris fails to observe some principles for encouraging children to become good listeners. She does not get everyone's attention before giving directions, so the students are not prepared to listen carefully. Ms. Harris also repeats the assignment instead of expecting the students to listen the first time. (Of course, since she is at fault in not getting their attention, in this case it is only fair.) She does not really know what she wants the students to do before making the assignment, so her directions are unclear and incomplete. A similar scenario is described later in this chapter, with a teacher who promotes good listening behaviors.

Writing

Reflections

What are some mistakes that teachers sometimes make when giving directions, which cause students not to listen well? What are some procedures you might follow for facilitating good listening skills in the classroom?

Listening, speaking, reading, writing, viewing, and visually representing are interrelated, and thinking is an important part of each. Although the language arts overlap in many areas, each has its own specific characteristics and is addressed separately in this book. Because listening is not only the first of the language arts that children acquire, but also the basis for learning the other language arts, it is a logical place to begin. Despite its importance in communication, it has been neglected in many classrooms (Brent & Anderson, 1993; Jalongo, 1991; Lerner, 2003).

Listening skill instruction can quite naturally be incorporated into study of literature selections and into unit studies. Oral presentations of literature can be made by both the teacher and the students. In unit studies, students must listen to informational presentations, to one another in group discussions, and to directions given by the teacher. Reading aloud is a common way for teachers to provide content for thematic units (Moss, 1995). Use of thematic units has been shown to be especially effective with linguistically and culturally diverse children (Garcia, 2002). Thematic units, with the varied, small-group activities, offer these students a chance to learn more about English while hearing it in meaningful contexts.

Listening skills can be taught, if teachers are willing to do so. The classroom environment is an important factor in the success of listening activities. Many strategies for teaching listening have been successful.

The Listening Process

LISTENING IS the main way of acquiring linguistic skill and knowledge (Strickland & Feeley, 2003). It is the process by which spoken language that is heard is converted into meaning. The term *listening* is actually much more complex than indicated by this simple definition, and the implications for teaching listening skills are better understood by considering the listening process and the relationship of listening to other language arts (discussed in Chapter 1 of this book).

A distinction should be made between hearing and listening. **Hearing** is the physiological act of receiving sound stimuli; listening is the ability to interpret the meanings of the sounds. For example, people who do not speak German can *hear* German words but be unable to *listen* to them, because they cannot interpret the words (Lerner, 2003). **Auding** is another term for listening comprehension (Harris & Hodges, 1995), but for the purposes of this discussion, we simply refer to listening comprehension.

Reflections

Regarding the spoken statement "Coal is our best source of energy," what is the difference between hearing the statement and listening to it?

© Bill Keane, Inc. Reprinted with special permission of King Features Syndicate.

Reflections

What might be some competing sounds in the environment that make it difficult to concentrate on a speaker's message?

In the *Family Circus* comic strip, does Billy have something wrong with his hearing? If not, what is the problem?

When a person listens, sound is received or heard, is attended to (focusing on the specific stimulus, an action that requires effort on the listener's part), is assigned meaning (depending upon the listener's background of experiences and attitudes), and finally is stored in the mind so it can be recalled later (Wolvin & Coakley, 1979).

Importance of Listening

EARLY RESEARCH indicates the prevalence of listening as a means of communication. Over the years, research findings have repeatedly shown that large amounts of time have been devoted to listening by both adults and children (Chaney & Burk, 1998; Goodlad, 1984; Pinnell & Jaggar, 2003; Rankin, 1928; Strickland & Feeley, 2003; Wilt, 1950). Hunsaker (1990) found that most adults have a 25 percent listening efficiency level or less. Today printed materials appear to be rapidly losing ground to media such as television, videotapes, and movies, and students may be spending increasingly greater proportions of their time listening, for listening accompanies these activities. With listening as a dominant form of communication, it is essential for students to learn to listen well.

Technology

Many young people have become passive listeners from watching television, which in most cases requires no active response. As a result, they lack the ability to listen carefully and critically in situations that call for thoughtful responses. Some television programs, however, demand close attention and careful listening—quiz shows and how-to shows, for example. Connecting discussion of the importance of listening attentively to television shows that the students enjoy watching can help to encourage students to work on listening skills. Pinnell and Jaggar (2003) point out that following listening activities with active responses is likely to be more effective than using passive activities.

To perform well in daily life, students need to develop their listening abilities. They need to listen to directions from parents, teachers, doctors, employers, and acquaintances in order to perform tasks correctly, get to places that they want to go, and be on time for events. They need to listen to product descriptions to decide if a product is one that they need. They need to listen to the conditions of agreements so that they will meet their responsibilities and know what to expect from others.

To become responsible citizens, students need to be able to listen critically to make intelligent decisions, analyze a speaker's message, react against false claims, and support just causes. Many educators therefore advocate instruction in listening skills, a much-neglected area of the curriculum, to promote effective listening. Listening has been shown to improve with instruction that helps students learn to "tune in" sounds that they need to listen to (Lerner, 2003).

Reflections

Why do you think listening is a "much-neglected area of the curriculum"? If it is so much a part of our daily lives, why is it not taught?

Check television listings for game shows that are appropriate for the students in your class, such as the *Jeopardy* episodes that involve adolescents. Have the students view a game show and try to answer the questions that are asked before the show's participants do. Have them keep a record of their successes.

Follow the viewing with a variation of the *Jeopardy* show in your classroom, using questions in categories of study that are taking place or have taken place in your classroom. Offer small prizes, such as paperback books, pencils, or erasers, for the winners (or winning teams). Impress upon the students that careful listening is a key to answering the questions correctly and winning the game.

The Relationship of Listening to Viewing

STUDENTS TODAY are inundated with television programs, videotapes, DVDs, and movies that involve both visual and auditory input. In some cases, the auditory input is crucial to understanding the action on the screen. Depending upon the type of program or feature that is being viewed, the students have to decide upon the amount of attention that the dialogue requires and the type of listening that is needed for the particular situation. Sometimes they are viewing programs for study purposes and sometimes strictly for pleasure. Material viewed for study purposes needs to be attended to more closely for detecting factual information, for making interpretations, for critical analysis, or for creative response. Material viewed for pleasure (perhaps cartoons, in which the animation carries most of the information) may be enjoyed with only cursory listening. Regardless, there is very little viewing that does not involve listening.

Many books with television program tie-ins have been written to interest young people. You may want to use one of these as a read-aloud and ask the students to compare and contrast the book with an episode of the television show.

Listening is usually an important factor in watching television programs.

One example is the series that features Dora the Explorer. You may want to read one or more of these books, such as *Dora's Backpack* by Sarah Willson, aloud to kindergarten or beginning first-graders. You may make them available for browsing or reading by the first-graders. A bonus is that Dora is Latina and uses some Spanish words. The books ask questions and ask for help in solving problems. This is a very effective way to encourage listening skills. These books are probably best used with small groups of students so that everyone can see the illustrations and become more actively involved in listening and responding.

Types of Listening

ORAL COMMUNICATION involves a speaker and a listener. In some cases, a listener who is engrossed in another activity may block out the message and ignore it. In other cases, the listener may be only marginally involved because attention is divided between two or more competing activities (for example, watching television while someone is talking). In other situations, the listener pays close attention to the message in order to understand it and respond to it in some way. In this section, we consider five types of listening: listening for information, interpretation, critical analysis, creative applications, and enjoyment.

Listening for Information

In listening for information (efferent listening), the listener simply receives directly stated information in a noncritical manner. The speaker must first get the attention of the listeners, and the listeners must focus their attention on the message to absorb and retain it. Examples of opportunities to listen for information that occur regularly in school include the following.

1. Agreed-upon topics for unit study

2. Options available for projects related to a unit

3. Homework assignments

4. Directions for completing work or taking tests

5. Announcements over the public address system

6. Procedures for fire drills

7. Plans for organizing into groups

8. Directions for playing a new game or using a new center

9. Informational books or articles that are read to students (for facts about a topic of study)

Applications for English Language Learners

In a classroom in which there are ELLs, introduce books from their cultures of origin that have some words from their languages in them. Expose the other students to the cultures and languages of their classmates by reading these books during read-aloud sessions. If there are Arabic-speaking students in a primary-level classroom, *Sitti's Secrets* by Naomi Shibab Nye is a good book to share in a read-aloud. A good purpose for the listeners is to listen for the Arabic words in the book and their meanings. On a second reading, the students could listen to compare and contrast the way Mona's grandmother and her other Palestinian relatives lived and the way the students live here in the United States.

For students in middle school, you might read the first two or three chapters of Suzanne Fisher Staples's *Shabanu*, a novel for young people. The purposes could be the same as above, but the task is more difficult, because the context clues are more subtle in this book. This situation would very likely give the Arabic speakers in the class a chance to excel and provide valued information.

An excellent book to use in a class that includes young children who have Spanish as a first language is Arthur Dorros's *Abuela*, which has Spanish words and sentences embedded in context that defines them and has a glossary with a pronunciation key (Meier, 2003). The pronunciation key is helpful to teachers who don't speak Spanish.

Listening for Interpretation

Just as people "read between the lines" to interpret what writers mean, they listen to speakers to interpret what they mean when they imply, but do not directly state, their message. This is **interpretive listening**. An interpretive listener responds not only to the words that are said, but also to the inflections of the voice and the body language of the speaker. Research indicates that nonverbal cues carry a great deal of meaning (Wolvin & Coakley, 1979). If a co-worker who is working on a project with you sud-

Applications for English Language Learners and Students with Special Needs

Choose books for read-alouds that have characters who represent your students' cultures or have similar needs or challenges to ones that your students face. Choosing books that connect to the children's lives is extremely important (Meier, 2003). Students make inferences based upon their backgrounds of experiences, and they are more likely to make needed inferences if they perceive a connection with the book.

denly stops what she is doing, stands up and stretches, and says, "I'm tired. Do you want to call it a day?," she is implying that she wants to quit for the day, even though she does not directly say it.

Students have many opportunities to work on reading for interpretation during class read-alouds of books and stories. They can listen to make inferences about characteristics of characters, times in which the stories are set, places in which stories are set, how characters feel about themselves, how characters feel about one another, and so on.

Interactive read-alouds can enhance the construction of meaning by listeners and help them to see how to make sense of text. They help students to monitor their own comprehension and to know what to focus attention on as the story is read. Since facility with listening comprehension processes and strategies generally is not learned through single exposures, multiple read-alouds with similar focuses are needed to help students become proficient (Barrentine, 1996). Read-alouds should include nonfiction as well as fiction (Harvey, 2002). Interactive read-alouds by parents to their children create motivation to read, as well (Fisher, Flood, Lapp, & Frey, 2004; Sulzby & Teale, 2003).

When you use an interactive read-aloud like the one modeled in Minlesson 5.1, choose materials that are developmentally appropriate and fit the interests of your chil-

Minilesson 5.1

Interpretive Listening

Before you begin a read-aloud of Kate DiCamillo's *Because of Winn-Dixie*, tell the students that you are going to ask them to make some interpretations about the story as you read. Tell them to listen carefully to the details in the story so that they can put the details together to form their interpretations. Then read the first four pages of the book to them. This part ends when Opal tells the store owner the dog's name is Winn-Dixie.

Ask the students, "Does the dog belong to Opal? If not, why does she claim that he does? What kind of person does this make you believe Opal is?"

Let the students answer the questions and give their reasons. Encourage them to listen to one another and not just repeat what another person has said. Instead have a student say something like, "I think John is right that Opal is a kind person because . . ," adding her own reasons.

Ask additional interpretive questions and have oral discussions about them as you continue to read the book, even if you read only a few chapters a day for a week or so.

What are the students learning?

The students are learning to listen to put together information that they hear to make inferences about situations and people. They are learning to back up their interpretations with reasons. They are also learning to listen to one another as well as to the teacher and to respond appropriately after another person has spoken.

Read-aloud or storytelling time offers an opportunity for the students to listen for critical analysis.

dren. Preview and practice the materials before reading with children so that you will read fluently with good expression and provide a good model for the students. You should always establish a purpose for the reading. Purposes may range from listening for enjoyment and appreciation to listening for specific information, to make inferences or predictions, to detect author bias, or to make connections with personal experiences. Periodic stops for thoughtful questions about the material for the children to answer enhance the read-aloud sessions. These pauses can also be used to discuss the vocabulary of the selection. A mixture of efferent and aesthetic questions helps students understand what they are hearing and also engage with the text and appreciate the feelings evoked and the language used (Fisher et al., 2004). Questions may be answered to the teacher, to the whole group, or to a partner or small group. The act of answering the questions encourages engagement with the text, and discussing it with others enhances this engagement. You may want to follow the interactive read-aloud with journal writing or related independent reading, tying in more of the language arts. Minilesson 5.1 demonstrates how you might use an interactive read-aloud.

Writing

Listening for Critical Analysis

In addition to understanding the literal meaning of a spoken message, listeners may need to analyze and evaluate the message. This is listening for **critical analysis**. In the case of a teacher assigning homework, a student who observes a stern expression on the part of the teacher might evaluate the message as "You'd better do this assignment or you will probably fail the test." On the other hand, if the teacher smiles and winks as

Teaching Tip

Use a brief but issue-laden book, such as Joy Cowley's *Drumbeat*, as a read-aloud in a primary-grade class. Ask students to listen to evaluate the actions of the characters. Some questions to discuss are: Why did the Union soldiers take the cow and hogs from a woman and her two children? Was their reason acceptable, in your opinion? Why did the mother lie to the children about the noise of the guns? Was she justified? Should the two children have gone to the barn without their mother? Why, or why not? Why might the Union soldier have resisted being taken into the house? Why did the mother decide to take care of him? Was it reasonable for her to do so? Why, or why not?

he says, "I know all of you will work hard on these problems rather than wasting your time at the ball game tonight," the student might evaluate the message as "I know you probably won't get around to this."

Often, listening for critical analysis is done in order to provide a rebuttal to the material that has been heard. It involves winnowing out the implausible or false statements and the statements of opinion in order to dispute the assertions. In doing this, the listener needs to take in the information, make inferences about it, and analyze and evaluate the situation. Critical listening can also be done to detect bias in material that is presented. Minilesson 5.2 offers a model of listening for critical analysis.

A person can think at four to five times the rate that speech occurs (Wolvin & Coakley, 1979), so the listener has a great deal of time to process information. While someone is speaking, the listener may tune the speaker in and out. When tuned out,

Minilesson 5.2

Technology

Critical Listening

Gather the students around a large-screen television. Tell them that they are about to see four videotaped commercials for products that are marketed to young people. Ask them to listen to and watch each commercial and jot down statements that they believe to be statements of fact. Give them time to write their ideas after each commercial ends. Play each commercial again and ask the students to jot down statements that they believe to be opinions, false information, or misleading information. Once again, give them time to write. Play the commercials a third time for the students to fill in any information that they missed before. Give them some more time to add ideas to their papers.

Divide the class into groups of four students each. Let the groups meet. Each student in each group should orally share her lists of facts and other information about each commercial and give her reasoning. (A different student should share first for each different commercial.)

Tell the group members to continue to discuss the commercials until they reach agreement about the facts and the opinions, false information, or misleading information. Then let a spokesperson for each group share the conclusions with the class as a whole. If there is not general agreement in the class, whole-class discussion should be held to resolve any disagreement.

What are the students learning?

They are learning to listen for details that agree with information that they already know and for details that either disagree or are not facts, but opinions. They are learning that they need to have reasons for saying that particular statements are facts or opinions and that they must put together ideas in such a way that people listening to them will understand and be persuaded. Therefore, this lesson is a good one for developing both listening and speaking skills.

the listener's mind may wander to other interests or may summarize or evaluate what the speaker is saying. Effective listeners use this extra time to think about the speaker's message in order to respond appropriately.

Read-aloud or storytelling time is a great time to have students listen for critical analysis. Have them listen to decide if the main character made a wise choice in responding to a crisis or if a writer or storyteller has developed believable characters and plot.

Listening for Creative Applications

Listening for **creative applications** is listening for something that prompts you to go beyond the material presented in some way and create something new. It could be listening to a story to create a sequel, listening to a story or poem to develop a sound track to play behind the reading or to make an illustration of the content, listening to a story or poem to turn it into a play format, or listening to a person express a need for a gadget that you might be able to invent. In these cases, the content of the message must be absorbed and transformed for use in a new situation. It involves imagination, **mental imagery** (making pictures in your mind), and creative thinking. Minilesson 5.3 illustrates how you can encourage children to visualize or create mental images as they listen and respond to a poem.

Listening for Enjoyment

Listening for enjoyment or appreciation (aesthetic listening) requires less attention and is more relaxing and pleasurable than other forms of listening. The listener calls on his imagination and feelings to create a very personal response, which might take the form of vivid sensory impressions, humor, **visualization** (forming a mental picture) of a scene, or sensitivity to mood. Listening for enjoyment may include elements of all the other types of listening, but generally there is no urgency to perform any of the specific tasks required of the other types.

By reading aloud to students, you facilitate appreciation of language and literature, especially for those children who read with difficulty. Listening to a story or poem allows students to

1. Make visual images (visualize).

2. Appreciate the rhythm and sounds of speech.

3. Reflect on the sense of mood.

4. Share laughter at ridiculous situations or humorous lines.

5. Appreciate dialect that is well read.

If in Minilesson 5.3 the children had not been asked specifically to listen in order to draw a picture, some of them would not have noticed all of the details or had complete mental images that they could draw, but they probably would have either enjoyed the creepy mood that the poet evoked or disliked it. The ones who enjoyed it would have focused more attention on the poem and probably would have expressed the desire

Minilesson 5.3

Listening for Creative Application: Imagery

Tell the children that you will be reading them a poem about a very strange creature. You want them to listen carefully so that they will be able to draw a picture of the creature they see in their minds as they listen. Ask them to think about what the creature looks like and how it makes them feel. Tell them that the poem is "What's That?" by Florence Parry Heide (in Prelutsky, 1983). Then read the poem expressively.

Discuss what tentacles are. Ask the students to close their eyes and listen while you read the poem again. Then ask them to think about and to draw what they see most vividly in their minds. Remind them that what they see may be completely different from what someone else sees. Ask if anyone would like to hear the poem again.

Writing

When the children are satisfied with their illustrations, ask them each to write a new name for the poem or a sentence about it that tells what they saw in the poem. Then place the children in small groups and let them show their pictures and discuss their responses to the poem with one another.

Figure 5.1 is the result of an activity based on Minilesson 5.3. Eight-year-old Wayles, who drew the picture shown, was imagining so vividly that about halfway through the rereading her eyes flew open and she called out, "Ooooo—I can't watch it anymore." From the poem, Wayles got the "creepy crawly hair," "the seven slimy eyes," and the "flabby grabby tentacles." Notice that she had to use details from the poem to form her picture, but the creature in the poem could have been drawn in many different ways. She has aptly transferred her own image to the page.

What are the students learning?

The students are learning to listen for details that they can apply with their imaginations to produce a creative product, in this case a picture. They are also learning that creative applications are divergent in nature, and everyone's product is likely to be different, even if they all started with the same details.

Teaching Tip

At least every week, read a literature selection to the class that is chosen simply for enjoyment. For example, you might read *The Cousins' Club: I'll Pulverize You, William* by Patricia Hermes. Always be sure to tell the students who the author of the book is, and the ones who particularly enjoy the book can look for other books by that author.

𝓕IGURE 5.1   **Student Response to Listening for Creative Application**

Source: Wayles Stapor, Sycamore Elementary, Cookeville, TN. Used with permission.

to listen to more poetry of that type or by that poet. The ones who did not may have "tuned out" before the poem ended, not attending to the rest of it at all. When listening for enjoyment, the listeners have this luxury of focusing their listening on things that appeal to them.

Listening for enjoyment is a perfectly acceptable purpose for listening (Roe, Alfred, & Smith, 1998). Many students become eager readers because they discover during read-alouds that books have enjoyable material in them.

Reflections

What are some listening situations in which several of the five types of listening might be appropriate to use simultaneously?

𝓘nstruction in Listening

EDUCATORS HAVE found that listening does not automatically improve as students become more mature, but that, for some students, it does improve with training (Brent & Anderson, 1993; Funk & Funk, 1989; Jalongo, 1991; Leverentz & Garman, 1987). Students benefit from direct instruction in listening, as well as from the integration of listening skills in all areas of the curriculum (Devine, 1978; Rubin, 1985). Many school systems have developed curricula in listening and speaking, but instruction in oral communication is often poorly implemented (Rubin, 1985).

Based on a review of research, Pearson and Fielding (1982) observed that listening comprehension is improved by listening training in the same skills generally taught for reading comprehension (for example, finding the main idea, sequencing, recalling details, and summarizing). They also noted that oral responses by students during and after listening enhance listening comprehension and that listening to literature seems to aid listening comprehension. Direct teaching of listening skills makes children more aware of their listening habits than does incidental instruction. Finally, some types of instruction intended primarily for other forms of language arts, such as writing or reading comprehension, also improve listening comprehension.

Goodman and his colleagues (1987) point out that listening deserves better treatment than it generally receives in most school programs. Training in listening should consist of authentic oral-communication events rather than series of exercises. (See Figure 5.2 for examples of authentic listening activities.) Students should have opportunities to discuss what they understand from spoken messages, and they should be aware that effective listening is a valuable skill.

Reflections

Why do you think listening comprehension is so closely related to reading comprehension? (You may want to review Chapter 1 before answering this question.)

The Role of the Teacher

Even though listening has often taken a back seat to other language arts in terms of instructional time, there are many things that you can do to enhance the listening skills of your students.

MODELING GOOD LISTENING BEHAVIORS

One of the most effective ways that you can help students become good listeners is to model good listening yourself. You should ask yourself how well you listen in the classroom. Do you do all the talking, or do you listen to what the students say? Do you pay more attention to what the more capable students say than what the less capable students say, or do you listen attentively to all of your students? Do you interrupt students who are in the midst of stories, or do you let them complete their stories when it is appropriate? Do you listen to what students tell you about their successes and problems to add to your knowledge about their strengths and weaknesses?

Hansen and Graves (1986) described a study of a K-5 reading and writing program in which the teachers were the listeners. As the children read their stories, teachers listened and then asked informed questions, a procedure that the children quickly adopted. By listening to the children talk about their reading and writing, teachers found that they learned more about these children and their needs than they had known about their former students.

Good listeners are attentive and courteous, think about what the speaker is saying,

FIGURE 5.2   Examples of Authentic Listening Activities

1. Acting out a story from one that is read aloud

2. Making or doing something by following oral directions

3. Participating in class or group discussions

4. Getting information by listening to an announcement

5. Working on group projects

6. Critiquing a peer's draft of a story after listening to it

7. Enjoying good literature that is well presented orally

8. Evaluating an issue that is being debated

9. Evaluating products advertised in commercials

10. Evaluating candidates from their campaign speeches

and respond appropriately (Roe, Alfred, & Smith, 1998). Although students cannot observe the teacher's thought processes, they can observe attentive and courteous behavior and appropriate responses.

PREPARING STUDENTS TO LISTEN

Students can listen with better comprehension if they have the correct mental set for listening. Students focus their listening better if they have well-defined purposes for doing so. You should help students establish authentic purposes for listening or set purposes for the listening yourself and make sure that students understand what these purposes are. Then offer the students opportunities to respond appropriately to the oral material in order to complete the purpose.

Sometimes students do not have the background information necessary to understand the information that is being provided orally. Consider the children's prior knowledge and help them relate new material to what they already know. If they lack essential background knowledge, work on building it before presenting new material.

Get the students' attention before beginning to speak. If students don't "tune in" to your words until the middle of something, they may never be able to orient themselves to the topic and make proper associations.

At times, students are not prepared to listen when you tell them something because they don't expect to be held accountable for the information. They often plan to ask you to repeat what you said when they are ready to use the information, rather than to listen when the material is first presented. As a teacher, you should tell the students that you will give information only once, and keep your word. When you give the information, be sure you allow the students to ask any questions that they may have about the material at that time, not penalizing good listeners just because your explanation was unclear or incomplete for some reason. After all of the students have had a chance to ask questions, however, do not repeat the information to students who just "forgot."

Reflections

In what ways does a teacher who models good listening behaviors encourage children to become good listeners?

Teaching Tip

Tape spelling tests and have students take the tests knowing that they can't ask for a word to be repeated, so they must listen and get the word the first time. When making the tape, pronounce each word clearly and use it in a meaningful sentence to distinguish it from other words that sound something like it or that are pronounced the same but spelled differently (homonyms). Pause for the students to write the word. Then repeat the word again. Pause briefly again and go to the next word. Always begin by telling the number of the word that you are about to pronounce so that students do not get lost on their test pages.

Never use taped tests with equipment and tapes that do not have good sound quality or sufficient volume for the task. Check them out in an area the size of your classroom before you use them in class.

Technology

Applications *for Students with Special Needs*

Young gifted students are often capable of listening with comprehension to material well beyond their current reading levels. To be absorbed by these students, the material may need to be broken down into shorter segments than older students would need. Classroom Vignette 5.1 gives an example of this type of application.

You may want to encourage them to make notes about directions you give, if they are important and detailed. That way, they have to attend to what you say to write the notes. In order to complete assignments or other activities appropriately, they will either have to listen to your initial presentation or ask another student to repeat the instructions.

PROVIDING APPROPRIATE LISTENING MATERIAL

Speakers, whether they are teachers, students, or other participants, should speak expressively and maintain eye contact. Students have difficulty focusing on a presentation that is given in a monotone, and their attention may wander. Maintaining eye contact is one way to hold their attention, but it is not sufficient if expression and enthusiasm are lacking in the oral delivery.

Classroom Vignette 5.1

After listening to the teacher read about making weather observations, six-year-old Dryden follows directions and observes the weather outside.

"There are clouds all over," he says. "There's not a bit of blue sky. I guess it will rain a lot because there are so many clouds."

Then the teacher shows pictures of the different types of clouds, and Dryden is able to identify the clouds he has seen as either altostratus or nimbostratus clouds. The teacher reads the detailed information about altostratus clouds and nimbostratus clouds, and then asks Dryden if his earlier guess about the clouds he saw was correct. Dryden points out that it says it *may rain* with altostratus clouds, but the material about nimbostratus clouds says that rain or snow is falling. He also says that altostratus clouds are lighter than nimbostratus clouds. Dryden concludes that, since it isn't raining and the clouds are fairly light, he has seen altostratus clouds.

What's happening here?

A child who is reading on first-grade level but is capable of understanding material far above grade level, is given an opportunity to hear information from a text well beyond his reading ability. He uses his listening skills and his analytic picture-reading skills to make a reasonable inference from the first portion that has been read and the pictures. Then he modifies his inference when he has additional input through listening to the detailed description read to him. He is allowed to expand his information base through the auditory mode, so that he can use his advanced reasoning abilities, rather than being held back to material that he is capable of reading on his own at this time.

Students must be able to *hear* what teachers say in order to *listen* with comprehension.

Oral readers also have a responsibility to read expressively, in well-modulated voices, and with appropriate facial expressions. They should choose stories to read that are interesting to them and are well written, in order to maintain their own interest and enthusiasm and that of the students. There is some advantage to reading aloud stories that the students cannot read for themselves (Roe, Smith, & Burns, 2005). Readers should practice reading the story ahead of time, so that it is read fluently, without hesitations or pauses due to surprises at word use or statements that are in the material. Jim Trelease's *The Read-Aloud Handbook* (1995) offers suggestions for good oral reading practices.

New information should be presented in a simple, direct, and organized manner so that students can comprehend it easily. Following complex organizational patterns in oral presentations is more difficult than following them in written presentations, because you can't "listen back" to check statements that you hear, but you can "look back" at statements that you read.

Adults who are making oral presentations to children should keep in mind that young children have limited attention spans. The length of presentation should be adjusted to fit these attention spans. Children's attention spans improve as they get older, so although primary-level children have short attention spans for sustained listening, older students can listen for relatively longer periods of time.

Technology

Sometimes you will want students to listen to taped presentations. If you do this, be sure to provide appropriate content, adequate volume, and good sound quality. Classroom Vignette 5.2 shows what could happen with a taped presentation.

Classroom Vignette 5.2

Don Radley tells his group of sixth-graders that they are going to listen to a tape of a well-known poet reading his own poetry. Mr. Radley has made the decision to use the tape because he doesn't think he can read the free-verse poetry to them effectively. As the tape begins, it becomes obvious that the poet does not read his own work well either. He mumbles and has poor oral expression. The students are soon squirming in their seats, whispering to one another, and doodling.

Mr. Radley, dismayed by the activity, stops the tape, to everyone's relief. Then he hesitantly begins to read the poems to the students himself. He discovers that he can indeed read the poems better than the author does, and the students settle down and listen as he reads.

What's happening here?

Mr. Radley's lack of self-confidence led him to look for a technological solution to his perceived problem of not being able to read the poems well. He found what he believed was an answer to his problem, but he failed to take his preparation far enough. He could have avoided this problem by previewing the tape, discovering that the tape was not good for use with his students, and then practicing reading the poems himself ahead of time.

Applications for Students with Special Needs

Make sure that students who are supposed to be using hearing aids have them turned on before you give oral directions. If these students come to school without their hearing aids, contact their parents and discuss a strategy for ensuring that the hearing aids arrive at school with the children.

CONSIDERING THE STUDENTS

Sometimes students do not listen as well as they are able, and sometimes they are considered to be not *listening* when they are actually just not *hearing*. Students will not attend as well, and therefore not listen as well, as they can if they are feeling restless because of pent-up energy, are extremely tired, are hungry, or are uncomfortably warm or cold. Teachers need to adjust their speaking to the physical conditions under which the students are working. Students who have known hearing impairments may have hearing aids, but may not always use them. Classroom Vignettes 5.3 and 5.4 point out such possibilities.

Classroom Vignette 5.3

Betty Roe is leading a discussion in a sixth-grade social studies class near the beginning of a school year. Noticing that Kenny has not been active in the discussion, she asks him a question to encourage him to participate. Kenny doesn't respond to her question. He doesn't even look up from his book. Betty has read in Kenny's cumulative file that he has a history of not paying attention in class and not completing assignments. He so far has been a well-behaved student, and Betty wants to change his pattern of attention this year. She steps in front of Kenny's desk. He looks up at her. She repeats her question, and he answers it appropriately.

"Why didn't you answer me when I asked you the first time?" she queries.

"I'm sorry," he says. "I didn't hear you."

Not convinced of his statement in view of his school history, Betty replies, "Try to concentrate on what we are saying, and I'll call on you again later."

Then the class continues the discussion. Instead of looking at his book, Kenny starts following Betty with his eyes as she circulates around the room. When she looks at him to ask another question, he turns his head to the right side, so that his left ear is toward her. He responds to the question that she asks, but his answer is not correct. When she gives him feedback, he turns his head to the right once again.

What's happening here?

Betty decides that Kenny might be having trouble hearing with his right ear. She contacts his parents and suggests that they might want to have a physician check his hearing. The result? Kenny has impacted ear wax in both ears, with a 60 percent hearing loss in his right ear. The physician removes the ear wax, and Kenny is no longer an inattentive student.

Classroom Vignette 5.4

Hal is a student in the same sixth-grade class as Kenny (Classroom Vignette 5.3). Hal is absent quite a bit because of repeated ear infections. He often asks for directions to be repeated and fails to respond to people when they talk to him in a normal tone of voice. The experience with Kenny has alerted Betty to the devastating effects on classroom performance of hearing loss, and she decides to speak to Hal while standing behind him at various distances. He cannot hear her until she speaks quite loudly very near his ear.

What's happening here?

Betty detects a hearing problem and alerts the parents to the need for Hal to see a physician. Hal has fused bones in his inner ears and, as a result, a considerable hearing loss. Surgery results in great improvement in Hal's hearing and in his classroom work.

From the cautions given, you can see that before and after recess are both challenging times for listening to take place. Before recess students are often restless, and after active games on the playground they are often tired. Before lunch is also not a good time, because many of the students are hungry. (Of course, teachers know that there are some students who come to school hungry and do not take advantage of free breakfast programs, so those students may be challenged listeners for much of the day.) The temperature problem is sometimes unavoidable, but adjusting it for student comfort can result in better student listening performance.

Applications for English Language Learners

Especially when students come from homes in which English is a second language, encourage parents to tell or read stories to their children, either in the home language or English. You may ask a parent to come to your class and read a book to the children in the parent's home language (Schwarzer, Haywood, & Lorenzen, 2003).

Riojas-Cortez, Flores, Smith, and Clark (2003) held a parent institute for parents of students in the school's preschool program to identify family literacy traditions and make connections with school literacy practices. One part of the institute focused on storytelling by the parents. The parents worked in groups to develop stories to tell their children. Many of the parents had Spanish as their first language, and the stories they developed generally had a moral, as is the custom with stories from their culture. The parents were surprised that they could be contributing to their children's school success by telling stories to them in their home languages. Some translated the stories into English, but Riojas-Cortez and colleagues found that the stories did not have to be in English to be learning experiences for the children (Meier, 2003).

REINFORCING GOOD LISTENING PRACTICES

Students who practice good listening habits should be rewarded by recognition for this accomplishment. Routinely praise students for following oral directions correctly, responding appropriately to comments and questions in discussions, questioning oral assertions for which they believe there is insufficient evidence, and so on. Emphasize the benefits of good listening, such as more complete art projects, correctly worked problems, and more accurate reports and discussion comments.

PROVIDING OPPORTUNITIES FOR PRACTICE

Students cannot learn to listen in a totally silent environment. Learning listening skills requires having something to listen to. Provide opportunities for whole-class and small-group discussion, partner activities, and time for sharing of information with large and small groups of classmates, such as oral reports, story dramatizations, or role-playing activities. Provide material for listening through storytelling and story reading, giving oral directions, holding conferences, and doing oral testing. Throughout each day, offer

---

Classroom Vignette 5.5

Miss Geyer is giving an assignment for reinforcing a lesson on compound words.

MISS GEYER: I want everyone to listen carefully to these directions. Let me see your eyes when you are ready to listen.

After all but one student is quietly looking at her, Miss Geyer begins.

MISS GEYER: Jimmy, please give me your attention.

Jimmy hears his name and looks up.

MISS GEYER: Now that everyone is ready, I'll tell you what I want you to do in the next 30 minutes. This is an assignment to help you work on understanding compound words.

Get out the book that we have just been reading, *Don't You Know There's a War On?* by Avi. Look through the book and find at least six examples of compound words. Write the sentence in which you found each word and underline the compound word. Think about the meaning of the word in the sentence and read the sentences around it for more information, if you need it. Write the page number on which you found the word beside each sentence. After 30 minutes are up, we will discuss the words you found and their meanings. Does anyone have a question about the assignment? (pause)

MISS GEYER: When you finish your work, you may sit with your language partner and go over your answers together quietly until the 30 minutes time is up. Now are there any questions? (pause)

MISS GEYER: If not, then you may begin.

What's happening here?

Miss Geyer is making sure that she has everyone's attention before she begins to give directions. After she gives directions, she asks if there are any questions so that she can clarify the instructions before the students start to work. She has increased the likelihood that the students will listen carefully to the assignment and understand it through the procedure she uses.

opportunities for students to develop listening skills in every area of the curriculum.

In Classroom Vignette 5.5, Miss Geyer is presenting the same assignment that Ms. Harris presented in the classroom vignette at the beginning of this chapter. Miss Geyer is observing many of the guidelines for facilitating good listening.

In the course of learning through thematic units, there are many opportunities for listening activities. Figure 5.3 shows some of the many possibilities.

Reflections

Compare the ways that Ms. Harris and Miss Geyer presented the same assignment. Then consider suggestions for facilitating good listening and identify those that these teachers either followed or disregarded.

FIGURE 5.3   Listening Opportunities in a Thematic Literature Unit on Cinderella

1. During the introduction to the unit, the teacher asks the students if they know the story of Cinderella. Students who say that they do are given a chance to tell the story as they know it. The other students *listen* to decide if they remember the story the same way. Students are given the opportunity to tell the group details they remember differently from classmates' telling or to tell other versions of the story, such as a version from a different culture. Classmates must *listen* to respond to these comments as well.

2. The teacher introduces to the class a number of picture books and one novel with versions of the Cinderella story. Students must *listen* and take notes in order to choose the books that they will read individually and present to the class. These books include *Ella Enchanted* by Gail Carson Levine; *The Egyptian Cinderella*, retold by Shirley Climo; *Yeh-Shen: A Cinderella Story from China*, retold by Ai-Ling Louie; *Cinderella*, translated by Marcia Brown; *The Irish Cinderlad*, retold by Shirley Climo; *Mufaro's Beautiful Daughters: An African Tale*, by John Steptoe; *The Turkey Girl: A Zuni Cinderella Story*, retold by Penny Pollock; and *Cinderella* by Charles Perrault, retold by Amy Ehrlich.

3. The teacher uses the book *Just Ella* by Margaret Peterson Haddix as a daily read-aloud throughout the unit. The children *listen* to the read-aloud in order to discuss the story and its relationship to

the more familiar Cinderella story. They must *listen* to one another during the discussion.

4. The students read *Ella Enchanted* by Gail Carson Levine as a whole class and have class discussions about it. First, they predict what it will be about by looking at the cover and the title. They *listen* to one another's predictions so that they can agree or disagree and tell why. They read the book in manageable segments of five chapters at a time, writing comments in their literature logs. During class discussion of each segment, students share entries from their literature logs orally while their classmates *listen* in preparation for responding. They may also compare the book *Ella Enchanted* with the movie.

5. Each student reads one of the Cinderella picture-book versions independently and chooses a way to present the story or some aspect of it to the class. The class *listens* to the presentation and responds with questions and comments. The presenter must *listen* to her classmates to answer questions and respond to comments.

6. In a final whole-class discussion, the teacher and the students discuss the elements that the stories have in common and the ones in which they differ. They also discuss possible reasons for the differences. They must *listen* to one another's comments during the discussion.

The Classroom Environment

The classroom environment can either enhance listening instruction or deter it. Many classrooms contain distractions that detract from good listening. Extraneous noise makes focusing on oral presentations or discussions more difficult. Although expecting to create a completely silent classroom is unrealistic, when asking students to focus on oral input that is important to class activity, try to eliminate the noise of computer beeps; television sounds; nonwork-oriented talking; loud talking, even if it is work-oriented; and hall and outside noises.

Computer sounds can be turned off, or headphones can be used by students who are working on computers instead of listening to the presentation or participating in the discussion. In some cases, headphones can be used with televisions; if this is not an option, the television should not be in use during important oral presentations.

Students should be asked not to talk to one another during an oral presentation, but to save discussion for the designated discussion period. Students who are working on another project (as may be the case in split-grade classrooms, for example) and not expected to focus on the presentation should be asked to keep their talk to a minimum and to use very soft voices; some teachers refer to these as "one-inch voices."

Hall and outside sounds may be unavoidable at times, but sometimes they can be diminished by closing doors and windows. Scheduling oral language activities when the grass is not being cut and the hall is not being polished can make a difference in the effectiveness of your students' listening.

The classroom temperature should be adjusted so that the students are not too hot or too cold. Sometimes you must contact a custodian to accomplish this task.

You should locate sources of such possible distractions as animals in cages or tanks behind the students, so that the animals' activities are not distracting. Some students focus their listening better if you have them clear their desks before the activity starts. However, some students listen quite well when doodling, so adjust your requests for clear desks to fit your students.

If there is more than one activity going on in the room, students who are expected to listen to a speaker or participate in a small-group discussion can be arranged in a semicircle or series of semicircles around the speaker or discussion leader, or they may

Applications for Students with Special Needs

Seat students close to the speaker (or television or audio player), especially students who have hearing impairments or are easily distracted. If there is a live speaker, be sure the students can see his face, particularly his lips, to facilitate lip reading. Avoid having the speaker stand in front of a window or light source that would put his face in shadow.

be in a circle for a discussion. They should be located as far away from other activities in the class as possible.

Materials for Teaching Listening

You can offer students authentic listening experiences by selecting appropriate materials. These may be provided at learning centers.

Audio media on nearly any topic are available in the form of tapes and compact discs (CDs). Sometimes recorded stories and songs are accompanied by written text, so children can follow along. Students can listen to recordings of classics from literature, sometimes read by the author or a professional actor. Sound effects often enhance the performance and add to the children's enjoyment. For children who are accustomed to viewing video performances, experiences with listening allow them the freedom to imagine and interpret scenes as they choose. Media that focus on listening include the following commercial or teacher-made products.

1. Audiotapes, CDs, and videos of children's literature selections (some are for listening only, and some come accompanied by books for read-alongs)

2. Audiotapes, CDs, and videos of storytelling

3. Audiotapes, CDs, and videos of information about topics of study

4. Audiotaped spelling and math-facts tests

5. Audiotapes or videotapes of students' group meetings

6. Audiotapes or videotapes of students' oral reading, either individually, chorally, or in Readers Theatre

7. Computer programs with sound components

8. Television programs

Audio-media offer the most basic listening activities, but much listening skill is needed in comprehending the information presented in video-media as well.

Strategies for Teaching Listening

Whereas general policies that promote good listening are important, educators have also developed a number of structured techniques for teaching listening (Choate & Rakes, 1987; Cunningham, 1975; Shoop, 1986; Stauffer, 1980). Because both listening and reading are ways of receiving and comprehending information, many of the plans are useful for improving both listening and reading skills. For instance, you can follow the same procedure for helping both the listener and the reader learn to arrange a sequence of events in the correct order. A discussion of some of these teaching techniques follows.

DIRECTED LISTENING-THINKING ACTIVITY

Stauffer's **Directed Listening-Thinking Activity (DL-TA)** (Stauffer, 1980) corresponds to his Directed Reading-Thinking Activity (DR-TA) (Stauffer, 1975), discussed in Chapter 7. The DL-TA technique focuses on thinking and predicting while listening. It is used with stories that are read aloud. The DL-TA follows the sequence shown in Figure 5.4.

STRUCTURED LISTENING ACTIVITY

Based on concepts supported from research about comprehension, the **Structured Listening Activity (SLA)** provides a sequence of five steps you can apply to most listening situations (Choate & Rakes, 1987). Field testing has indicated that use of this technique produces gains in listening comprehension for children in kindergarten through third grade. The sequence of activities appears in Figure 5.5.

INQUEST

Another technique, called **InQuest** (from Investigative Questioning Procedure), combines spontaneous drama with student questioning to advance reading and listening comprehension for children in third grade and above (Shoop, 1986). This strategy offers opportunities for self-monitoring of comprehension and thoughtful analysis of story events. Figure 5.6 shows the steps in this procedure.

LISTENING-READING TRANSFER STRATEGY

For those children who can decode words but have difficulty understanding what they read, the **listening-reading transfer strategy** may be helpful (Cunningham, 1975). Since listening ability is generally superior to reading ability during the elementary grades, children comprehend material better by listening to it than by reading it. Therefore, you can plan parallel lessons so that students realize that they can respond to listening and reading lessons in the same way. See Figure 5.7 for an outline of the listening-reading transfer strategy.

SAY SOMETHING

In the **Say Something** technique, you read a story and stop periodically, giving students opportunities to respond by summarizing

FIGURE 5.4   The Directed Listening-Thinking Activity (DL-TA)

Step 1: Before Listening
Introduce the story by showing the title and opening illustration. Let students discuss what they think the book is about, make predictions about what will happen, and set purposes for listening.

Step 2: Listening during the Story
Read the story aloud, stopping at key points to ask the students to confirm, modify, or reject their predictions. Encourage them to make further predictions based on new information.

Step 3: After Listening
Review the story, letting students summarize what happened and explain reasons for making and modifying their predictions. Expand new vocabulary and concepts derived.

Figure 5.5 The Structured Listening Activity (SLA)

Step 1: Concept Building
Relate content to the students' prior experiences. Build background for unfamiliar concepts and vocabulary.

Step 2: Listening Purpose
Set purposes for listening in order to provide a mental set for understanding the material.

Step 3: Reading Aloud
Use visual aids, such as pictures and flannelboard figures, to supplement the material while presenting a passage.
Ask prediction questions (such as "What do you think they will do next?") to guide thinking and keep students actively involved.

Step 4: Questioning
Ask three types of questions — important literal, interpretive, and critical ones. Intersperse questions with the reading, and let students explain their answers.

Step 5: Recitation
Use guided questioning to help listeners retell, summarize, or elaborate on the passage.

or telling what they found interesting. After the students respond, you pose prediction questions and then continue reading, repeating the process at breaks in the story. Then the students are placed in pairs and told to follow the same procedure, with students taking turns reading and responding (Stice, 1987). This activity promotes both listening and reading comprehension. It also provides purposeful speaking practice.

The Say Something strategy requires students to attend to what they are reading.

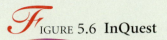

FIGURE 5.6 **InQuest**

Step 1: Reading the Story
Choose a story that builds to a critical point and has interesting plot and character development. As students listen, tell them to think of questions to ask particular story characters. Continue reading the story up to the critical incident and then stop.

Step 2: Role-Playing a News Conference
Have one student role-play a significant story character, and let other students role-play reporters at a news conference. The reporters ask investigative questions, and the character answers from information available up to the critical point in the story. When there are additional critical points, the same procedure may be repeated, perhaps with different characters being interviewed. If students seem uncertain about their roles, you may model the role of either a reporter or the character being questioned.

Step 3: Evaluating the Interview
At the end of the story, help students evaluate their question-and-answer procedures used during the news conference.

RECONSTRUCTING THE TEXT

You can read a complete, well-structured story aloud, preferably more than once. Then you can cut the story apart in natural divisions and ask groups of students to decide how it should be put back together. Old basal readers or typed copies of stories are useful for this activity, and group discussion is valuable for understanding story structure (Stice, 1987). This activity is good for both listening and reading comprehension.

LISTENING CENTERS

You can also create learning centers with sets of headphones for listening activities. Students may use commercially prepared tapes of children's literature for listening appreciation or for understanding story structure. You may also prepare series of tasks for students to perform at the centers. The tasks should have clear directions, and all materials needed for the tasks should be readily available at the centers.

OTHER ACTIVITIES

Although listening skills should be developed primarily with authentic purposes, some warm-up activities to promote alert listening can be both useful and fun. The games and activities that follow are examples of possible listening activities.

FIGURE 5.7 Listening-Reading Transfer Strategy

Step 1: Establishing Purposes
Set specific purposes for developing comprehension (such as identifying sequence of events, inferences, or main idea).

Step 2: Reading the Selection
Read the selection straight through or stop at critical points to permit interaction with the children. For instance, stop reading to let students predict how they think the story will end. Encourage them to support their predictions with incidents from the story.

Step 3: Developing the Skill
Teach the skill by using a combination of listening and reading experiences. For example, after the children have listened to a story for the purpose of learning sequence, have them read sentence strips of key events in the story and arrange them in order.

Step 4: Letting Students Read
Let the students read for themselves and perform the same skill that they learned by listening. Students must understand that they can transfer skills from listening to reading.

Step 5: Group Sharing
Have students share their answers and discuss reasons for them.

1. Play Simon Says. Children follow only those oral directions preceded by "Simon says."

2. Play Gossip. The teacher whispers a message to one child, who repeats it to another child. The message is whispered from one to another until the final child repeats the message she received, which is usually quite different from the original.

3. Play memory games. Each participant repeats a series of items introduced previously by other players and adds another item to the series.

4. Dramatize a literature selection that the class has read. Students must listen to the other actors when they take a part in a dramatization.

5. Have the students participate in Readers Theatre. The students have to listen to the other readers to perform the selection.

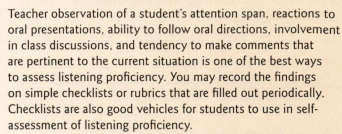

Classroom Assessment for Listening Proficiency

Teacher observation of a student's attention span, reactions to oral presentations, ability to follow oral directions, involvement in class discussions, and tendency to make comments that are pertinent to the current situation is one of the best ways to assess listening proficiency. You may record the findings on simple checklists or rubrics that are filled out periodically. Checklists are also good vehicles for students to use in self-assessment of listening proficiency.

Two other ways to assess listening proficiency are through retelling and through the use of an informal reading inventory. The capacity level of an informal reading inventory is a listening comprehension level.

Chapter 13 addresses the topic of assessment in detail.

Summary

Technology

Children learn to listen before they acquire the other language arts, and listening is the basis for learning many speaking, reading, writing, viewing, and visually representing skills. Listening occupies more of a student's time than any of the other language arts, and students need to learn good listening skills in order to react thoughtfully to oral messages.

Listening is the process by which spoken language that is heard is converted into meaning. Listening is different from hearing, which simply involves receiving the sensory stimulus. There are at least five types of listening: listening for information (literal comprehension), listening for interpretation (interpretive comprehension), listening for critical analysis (listening to evaluate), listening for creative applications (creative comprehension), and listening for enjoyment (relaxed listening).

Listening is closely related to viewing, and students today are inundated with material in the form of television programs, videotapes, and CDs that involve listening along with viewing.

Children learn to listen when listening activities are integrated into the curriculum and also through direct instruction in listening. Children should be taught listening skills through authentic listening activities as much as possible. Teachers should be good listeners, and they should set conditions that enhance listening abilities.

The classroom environment can either enhance listening activities or detract from them. Sound, temperature, and other distractions in the classroom must be carefully managed.

Many materials are available that are useful in teaching listening skills. Among the specific techniques that are good for teaching listening are the Directed Listening-Thinking Activity, the Structured Listening Activity,

InQuest, the listening-reading transfer strategy, Say Something, reconstructing the text, and listening centers.

Discussion Questions

1. How important are good listening skills for success in school? Why do you think so?

2. How important is the development of good listening skills to development of skills in the other language arts?

3. What experiential, cognitive, and physical factors related to a listener affect listening ability?

4. Why is listening still important in a time when visual media are so prominently in vogue?

5. When does a student have the need in school and in daily life to use each of the five types of listening discussed in the chapter?

6. How can you promote listening skill development in your classroom?

7. What factors outside the listener can affect listening performance? How can these best be managed in a classroom?

8. What are some teaching procedures for teaching listening strategies?

9. Why is literature such a good vehicle for working with listening skills and strategies?

10. Why are thematic units good vehicles for working with listening skills and strategies?

Technology

Suggested Activities

1. Keep a record of the time you spend using language arts over a three-day period during your waking hours. What percentage of your day is spent communicating? Of this time, what percentage do you spend listening? Does this percentage surprise you? What listening skills are strong for you? What listening skills do you need to improve?

2. Find some tapes or CDs of children's literature. Then:

   a. Make an annotated bibliography of some sources you might want to use.

   b. Listen to five stories, songs, or poems and critique them in relation to their appeal for the listener.

3. Visit a classroom that has a listening center. Find out the purposes, materials, and activities used.

4. In your classes, observe teachers as they speak. Does their nonverbal communication affect the meaning of what they say? Write up three incidents in which body language or voice inflection appears to change the meaning of the words.

5. What do you do with your extra "think time" while you are listening? Observe your behavior regarding the use of this time for letting your mind wander, concentrating on the speaker's message, or thinking about applications of the material. Keep a journal of your observations for one week.

6. Read a story to a class and have someone videotape the children as you read. Watch the videotape later to see how attentive the children were. Write your conclusions about their attentiveness and give reasons to explain why you think they were or were not attentive.

7. Work with a group of children who are writing and reading informally. Practice being a good listener by asking questions, listening to the children's answers, and making appropriate comments.

8. Choose one of the teaching techniques suggested in this chapter and use it as a basis for teaching a listening lesson to a group of students.

9. Visit a classroom and observe the teacher to see what techniques for enhancing listening abilities suggested in this chapter are being used.

References

BARRENTINE, S. J. (1996). Engaging with reading through interactive read-alouds. *The Reading Teacher, 50,* 36–43.

BRENT, R., & ANDERSON, P. (1993). Developing children's classroom listening strategies. *The Reading Teacher, 47,* 122–126.

CHANEY, A. L., & BURK, T. L. (1998). *Teaching oral communication in grades K–8.* Boston: Allyn & Bacon.

CHOATE, J. S., & RAKES, T. A. (1987). The structured listening activity: A model for improving listening comprehension. *The Reading Teacher, 41,* 194–200.

CUNNINGHAM, P. (1975). Transferring comprehension from listening to reading. *The Reading Teacher, 29,* 169–172.

DEVINE, T. C. (1978). Listening: What do we know after fifty years of research and theorizing? *Journal of Reading, 21,* 296–304.

FISHER, D., FLOOD, J., LAPP, D., & FREY, N. (2004). Interactive read-alouds: Is there a common set of implementation practices? *The Reading Teacher, 58,* 8–17.

FUNK, H. D., & FUNK, G. D. (1989). Guidelines for developing listening skills. *The Reading Teacher, 42,* 660–663.

GARCIA, E. (2000). *Student cultural diversity: Understanding and meeting the challenge* (3rd ed.). Boston: Houghton Mifflin.

GOODLAD, J. I. (1984). *A place called school.* New York: McGraw-Hill.

GOODMAN, K. S., SMITH, E. B., MEREDITH, R., & GOODMAN, Y. M. (1987). *Language and thinking in school* (3rd ed.). New York: Richard C. Owen.

HANSEN, J., & GRAVES, D. (1986). Do you know what backstrung means? *The Reading Teacher, 39,* 807–812.

HARRIS, T. L., & HODGES, R. E. (Eds.). (1995). *The literacy dictionary: The vocabulary of reading and writing.* Newark, DE: International Reading Association.

HARVEY, S. (2002). Nonfiction inquiry: Using real reading and writing to explore the world. *Language Arts, 80,* 12–22.

HUNSAKER, R. R. (1990). *Understanding and developing the skills of oral communication: Speaking and listening.* Englewood, CO: Morton.

JALONGO, M. R. (1991). *Strategies for developing children's listening skills.* Bloomington, IN: Phi Delta Kappa Educational Foundation.

LERNER, J. W. (2003). *Learning disabilities: Theories, diagnosis, and teaching strategies* (9th ed.). Boston: Houghton Mifflin.

LEVERENTZ, F., & GARMAN, D. (1987). What was that you said? *Instructor, 96,* 66–68.

MEIER, T. (2003). "Why can't she remember that?": The importance of storybook reading in multilingual multicultural classrooms. *The Reading Teacher, 57,* 242–252.

Moss, J. F. (1995). Talking about books. In N. L. Roser & M. G. Martinez (Eds.), *Book talk and beyond: Children and teachers respond to literature* (pp. 53–65). Newark, DE: International Reading Association.

Pearson, P. D., & Fielding, L. (1982). Research update: Listening comprehension. *Language Arts, 59,* 617–619.

Pinnell, G. S., & Jaggar, A. M. (2003). Oral language: Speaking and listening in elementary classrooms. In J. Flood, D. Lapp, J. R. Squire, & J. M. Jensen (Eds.), *Handbook of research on teaching the English language arts* (2nd ed., pp. 881–913). Mahwah, NJ: Erlbaum.

Rankin, P. T. (1928). The importance of listening ability. *The English Journal, 17,* 623–630.

Riojas-Cortez, M., Flores, B. B., Smith, H. L., & Clark, E. R. (2003). Cuentame un cuento [Tell me a story]: Bridging family literacy traditions with school literacy. *Language Arts, 81,* 62–71

Roe, B. D., Alfred, S., & Smith, S. (1998). *Teaching through stories: Yours, mine, and theirs.* Norwood, MA: Christopher-Gordon.

Roe, B. D., Smith, S. H., & Burns, P. C. (2005). *Teaching reading in today's elementary schools* (9th ed.). Boston: Houghton Mifflin.

Rubin, D. L. (1985). Instruction in speaking and listening: Battles and options. *Educational Leadership, 42,* 31–36.

Schwarzer, D., Haywood, A., & Lorenzen, C. (2003). Fostering multiliteracy in a linguistically diverse classroom. *Language Arts, 80,* 453–460.

Shoop, M. (1986). InQuest: A listening and reading comprehension strategy. *The Reading Teacher, 39,* 670–674.

Stauffer, R. G. (1975). *Directing the reading-thinking process.* New York: Harper & Row.

Stauffer, R. G. (1980). *The language experience approach to the teaching of reading* (2nd ed.), New York: Harper & Row.

Stice, C. F. (1987). *Reading and writing strategy lesson ideas (K–6): A whole language perspective.* Nashville: Center of Excellence Basic Skills for the Disadvantaged, Tennessee State University.

Strickland, D. S., & Feeley, J. T. (2003). Development in the elementary school years. In J. Flood, D. Lapp, J. R. Squire, & J. M. Jensen (Eds.), *Handbook of research on teaching the English language arts* (2nd ed., pp. 339–356). Mahwah, NJ: Erlbaum.

Sulzby, E., & Teale, W. H. (2003). The development of the young child and the emergence of literacy. In J. Flood, D. Lapp, J. R. Squire, & J. M. Jensen (Eds.), *Handbook of research on teaching the English language arts* (2nd ed., pp. 300–313). Mahwah, NJ: Erlbaum.

Trelease, J. (1995). *The read-aloud handbook* (4th ed.).New York: Penguin.

Wilt, M. E. (1950). A study of teacher awareness of listening as a factor in elementary education. *Journal of Educational Research, 43,* 626–636.

Wolvin, A. D., & Coakley, C. G. (1979). *Listening instruction.* Annandale, VA: Speech Communication Association.

*B*ooks for Children and Adolescents Cited in This Chapter

Avi. (2001). *Don't you know there's a war on?* New York: HarperCollins.

Brown, M. (1954). *Cinderella.* New York: Aladdin.

Climo, S. (1989). *The Egyptian Cinderella.* New York: HarperTrophy.

Climo, S. (1996). *The Irish Cinderlad.* New York: HarperCollins.

Cowley, J. (2002). *Drumbeat.* Carlsbad, CA: Dominie.

DiCamillo, K. (2000). *Because of Winn-Dixie.* New York: Scholastic.

Dorros, A. (1991). *Abuela.* New York: Puffin.

Haddix, M. P. (1999). *Just Ella.* New York: Scholastic.

Hermes, P. (1994). *The cousins' club: I'll pulverize you, William.* New York: Minstrel.

Levine, G. C. (1997). *Ella enchanted.* New York: Scholastic.

Louie, Ai-Ling. (1982). *Yeh-Shen: A Cinderella story from China.* New York: Sandcastle.

Nye, N. S. (1994). *Sitti's secrets.* New York: Aladdin.

Perrault, C., & Ehrlich, A. (1985). *Cinderella.* New York: Dial.

Pollock, P. (1996). *The turkey girl: A Zuni Cinderella story.* Boston: Little, Brown.

Prelutsky, J. (Ed.). (1983). *The Random House book of poetry for children.* New York: Random House.

Staples, S. F. (1989). *Shabanu.* New York: Random House.

Steptoe, J. (1987). *Mufaro's beautiful daughters: An African tale.* New York: Lothrop, Lee, & Shepard.

Willson, S. (2002). *Dora's backpack.* New York: Simon & Schuster.

DEVELOPING SPEAKING PROFICIENCY

LEARNER OBJECTIVES

At the conclusion of this chapter

YOU SHOULD BE ABLE TO

1. Explain the functions of oral language.
2. Discuss speaking skills that students need to acquire.
3. Describe the teacher's role in oral language instruction.
4. Describe how the classroom environment is important in developing skill in oral expression.
5. Use a variety of purposeful speech activities in the classroom.
6. Identify the following terms that are defined or explained in this chapter:

brainstorming 223
choral reading 226
choral speaking 226
codeswitching 208
conversations 217
creative dramatics 226
debate 222
demonstrations 216
discussions 219

interviews 216
intonation 204
juncture 207
miniperformances 229
oral reports 213
panel discussions 222
pitch 207
puppetry 227
Readers Theatre 224

recitations 218
register 208
show-and-tell 212
story reading 224
storytelling 224
stress 207
tempo 207
vertical construction
   strategy 210

NCTE/IRA Standards addressed in this chapter

STANDARD 4. Students adjust their use of spoken, written, and visual language (e.g., conventions, style, vocabulary) to communicate effectively with a variety of audiences and for different purposes.

STANDARD 6. Students apply knowledge of language structure, language conventions (e.g., spelling and punctuation), media techniques, figurative language, and genre to create, critique, and discuss print and non-print texts.

STANDARD 7. Students conduct research on issues and interests by generating ideas and questions, and by posing problems. They gather, evaluate, and synthesize data from a variety of sources (e.g., print and non-print texts, artifacts, people) to communicate their discoveries in ways that suit their purpose and audience.

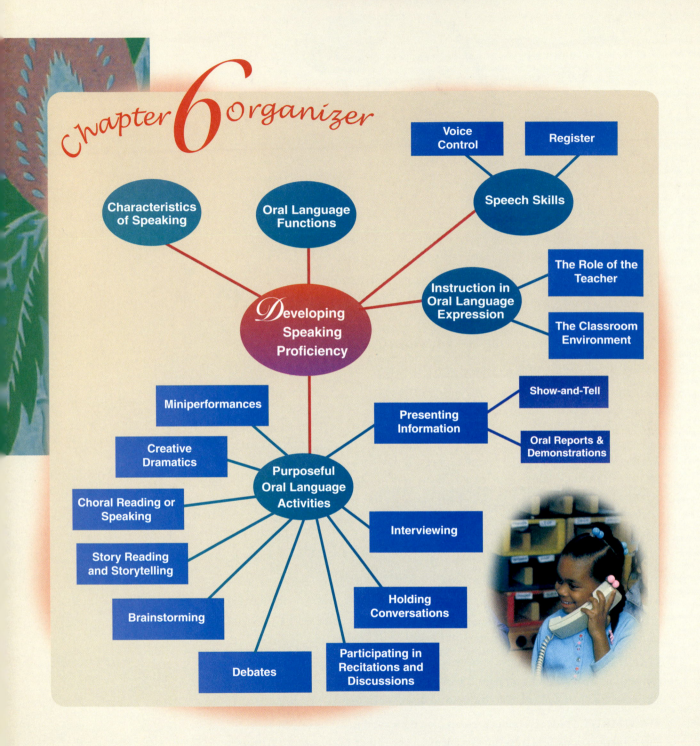

Chapter 6 Organizer

Voice Control

Register

Speech Skills

Characteristics of Speaking

Oral Language Functions

Instruction in Oral Language Expression

The Role of the Teacher

The Classroom Environment

Developing Speaking Proficiency

Miniperformances

Creative Dramatics

Choral Reading or Speaking

Story Reading and Storytelling

Brainstorming

Debates

Purposeful Oral Language Activities

Participating in Recitations and Discussions

Holding Conversations

Interviewing

Presenting Information

Show-and-Tell

Oral Reports & Demonstrations

STANDARD 8. Students use a variety of technological and information resources (e.g., libraries, databases, computer networks, video) to gather and synthesize information and to create and communicate knowledge.

STANDARD 10. Students whose first language is not English make use of their first language to develop competency in the English language arts and to develop understanding of content across the curriculum.

STANDARD 12. Students use spoken, written, and visual language to accomplish their own purposes (e.g., for learning, enjoyment, persuasion, and the exchange of information).

M
R. LEWIS'S class is involved in a thematic unit on how people work together to improve their living conditions. They have been discussing the actions of labor unions, special interest groups' political activities, group processes in general, and individual contributions.

As he introduces his class to brainstorming, Mr. Lewis has two goals in mind other than seeing group process in action: to stimulate thinking skills and to develop effective oral communication in group situations. He begins his lesson by introducing the topic and explaining the procedures, which include generating as many ideas as possible, combining or modifying others' suggestions, and not criticizing anyone's ideas. He then demonstrates how to brainstorm with the whole class before dividing the class into groups. He asks each group to choose a recorder and then gives a different topic to each group. At this point in the lesson, Mr. Lewis is listening in on different groups to make sure they understand what to do.

CAROL: Here's our topic: "How can we make the hallways in our school more attractive?"

BETH: I know. We can paint them bright colors.

STEVE: Bright colors would help. Maybe we could get real painters to come in and do it with school money.

TAD: We might get parent volunteers to paint the halls on weekends and save some money.

ERICA: My uncle's an artist; maybe he could paint some murals or something.

CAROL: Why don't we paint the halls ourselves? Then we could choose our own colors.

STEVE: No way! We'd make an awful mess. That's a dumb idea.

ERICA: I have a better idea. Let's get rid of the walls and have open classes. We could get someone to knock out the walls.

TAD: That's a great idea. Then we wouldn't have to worry about the drab hallways.

STEVE: That's stupid. They'd never do that. The building would probably fall down if the walls didn't hold it up.

CAROL: Here's an idea. Let's have a contest with all the classes to decide what to do and we'll vote on the best idea.

BETH: We could get each class to decorate the hall outside their room with pictures the kids draw.

ERICA: That's good. We might have one idea that everyone would use—like holidays or a fair. And that way we could change the decorations lots of times.

STEVE: The art teacher might help us plan what to put up so it would really look good. He lets us do lots of neat stuff.

TAD: I think it would really be cool to paint a long train on a track that would go all around inside the building.

ERICA: What a good idea! It could have one train car for each class with pictures of all the kids in that room looking out the windows of the train.

What's happening here?

Mr. Lewis's goals are met as students react to the question by thinking divergently and by listening and responding to group members. They generate many ideas in a short period of time. On several occasions, students add to suggestions that others make, a useful strategy for expanding ideas. On two occasions, Steve criticizes suggestions and thus violates brainstorming procedures. Mr. Lewis should remind Steve of this rule.

Speaking is an expressive language art; the speaker composes or constructs meaning in his mind and then communicates the meaning orally to an audience. Children learn speech before they learn written language, and speech is the most frequently used method for communicating with others. People are often judged by their speech—their use of standard or nonstandard English, accompanying nonverbal language, voice control, and effectiveness in conveying ideas.

Reflections

How could brainstorming be used for stimulating thinking and language skills in social studies and science unit activities? Think of specific topics that you might use.

Children learn to speak as part of growing up. They listen, imitate, produce their own speech, and use it to communicate. Although children learn to speak without direct instruction, speech needs to be stimulated and nurtured to develop fully. Such stimulation can occur as children listen to and speak with family members, caregivers, and others in their environments. Figure 6.1 presents an example of the language usage of a child who has learned a new concept and a vocabulary word to express it and has taken an opportunity to try out the new expression on his family.

The effective speaker must reflect on what someone else has said, weigh evidence, organize ideas, choose the right words, and express thoughts logically. In the vignette at the beginning of this chapter, Mr. Lewis's students had to think of ideas before saying them, and the interaction of speaking and listening to group members further stimulated their thinking. Clear thinking enables the speaker to convey messages so that the listener can understand and respond. Another example of reflecting on what someone else has said, choosing the right words, and expressing thoughts logically is shown in Figure 6.2.

*F*IGURE 6.1   **Experimenting with Use of New Concepts and Terminology**

Ray, a first-grader, was trying to get his parents to take him to the carnival. They had expressed several reservations about going that night, including the fact that it was getting late already. Ray told them, "If you would just *cooperate,* we could be there in a few minutes. If you keep talking, it will get to be too late." His parents were so surprised at his argument that they took him to the carnival that night.

Ray's mother found out later from his first-grade teacher that they had been studying the importance of cooperation in class, and she had been modeling the word for them all week, pointing out the advantages in getting things done more quickly when they cooperate. Ray had absorbed the explanation and examples provided by the teacher and had added the concept and word to his speaking vocabulary. The fact that his use of the word was reinforced by actions that he had hoped to achieve was reinforcement for continuing his oral use of the concept and terminology.

$\mathcal{F}$IGURE 6.2   **Constructing Logical Oral Responses**

Dryden Young was dining at a Chinese restaurant at his grandmother's birthday party. One of the guests had not been to the restaurant before and expressed concern about choosing food from the buffet because she couldn't eat spicy-hot food. Dryden, at four years old a regular at the restaurant, heard her state her concern. He tugged on her sleeve and told her, "If the letters [on the labels for the food] are red, the food is hot. If they are black, it isn't hot." Dryden had listened to her concern, analyzed the situation, thought about the solution, and organized his oral response in an "if . . . then" format that was logical and easy to follow. At the time, Dryden could not read any of the words, but he already had and could use the concept of *letters*, knew his colors, and understood the symbolic meanings of both letters and colors in this situation.

Study of literature and learning through thematic units offer many opportunities to work on speaking skills. Oral reading requires many of the same skills that storytelling, oral reports, and dramatization require, and all of them fit well into literature and thematic unit studies.

$\mathcal{C}$haracteristics of Speaking

SPEAKING DIFFERS from written communication in several ways. Speech is more immediate, being produced and received in the present (with the exception of recorded speech, which has the characteristic of written communication in that it can be reviewed in its exact form to fill in memory gaps or clarify exact words). It is multidimensional in that speakers combine gestures, facial expressions, and tones of voice with the words that are spoken (Lipman, 1995). Oral expression that is produced "on the spot" and is not being recorded is sometimes less carefully worded and more prone to misunderstanding. The spoken words are not permanent in the way that writing is, and if the speaker is asked to restate or repeat information, she may not repeat it in exactly the same way. The speaker, not the listener, controls the rate of communication during oral exchanges, whereas the reader controls the rate of communication during written exchanges.

A speaker relies on sound and nonverbal symbols for communication. Voice quality, rate, and **intonation** (the melody of the language produced by the elements of stress, pitch, and pauses), along with such nonverbal aspects as gestures, facial expressions, and body language, are used to communicate messages in speech. The writer, on the other hand, uses written symbols to convey meaning. Written messages rely on the use of punctuation, capitalization, spelling, and such print features as letter size, boldface type, italics, and underlining.

The relationship between the speaker and listener also differs from that of the writer and reader. A speaker's use of language tends to be more informal, concrete, and personal, with simpler vocabulary. The speaker is likely to use more self-references (first-person pronouns) and show more awareness of the time, place, and occasion. The language of the writer, on the other hand, is frequently more formal and abstract.

Reflections

Given the differences between oral and written language, which do you think is more effective for such purposes as (a) providing information, (b) entertaining, and (c) giving directions? Why do you think so?

Writing

Oral Language Functions

OF COURSE, the first and primary purpose of oral expression is communication. Oral language is used to communicate wants, commands, needs, questions, and ideas. Students need to learn how to communicate with different audiences for different purposes.

Children gradually acquire language and thinking skills during their preschool years. After studying children's early language development and related theories, Halliday (1977) devised a list of functions that would be useful for describing the oral language of young children. These functions and the order in which they are likely to occur are given in Figure 6.3 on page 206. Teachers need to be aware of the various functions of oral language so that they can help children maintain and expand them. Too often school requires students to focus on the representational or informative function at the expense of the imaginative, heuristic, and personal functions (Pinnell, 1975).

Sharon Creech, author of the Newbery Medal winner *Walk Two Moons* and the Newbery Honor book *The Wanderer,* told a group of prospective writers at a *Highlights for Children* sponsored writing conference about the language skill that she observed in her granddaughter Pearl when Pearl was about two years old. In a phone call to Sharon, after just returning from an ocean visit with her parents, Pearl said to Sharon, "Nonna! Ocean! Splash! Moon!" Sharon thought these four words sounded like a perfect poem from a child in early language development. On another occasion, when Pearl was with Sharon at the lake, Pearl looked up at the moon and said, "Come on, Moon! Come on down to me." Pearl raised her arm and open hand up toward the moon and said, "I'm feeding the moon." Sharon was impressed by her creative expression of the beauty in the world. On still another day, Sharon was reading a picture book about the ocean to Pearl, who was totally involved in the book. Pearl said, "Step in the ocean? Step in the ocean?" Sharon didn't understand what she meant. Pearl removed her shoe and stepped with her bare foot on the page of the book with a picture of the ocean. She was completely into the story, the way we hope readers will be when they discover the joys of the printed page.

Linda Sue Park, author of the Newbery Medal winner *A Single Shard,* at the same conference told Betty Roe about the way her two-year-old son, Sean, had absorbed

> ℱIGURE 6.3　**Halliday's Language Functions**
>
> 1. *Instrumental function* refers to language that satisfies material needs, such as obtaining food or toys. Speech sample: "I want . . . "
>
> 2. *Regulatory function* refers to ways that the speaker tries to influence the behavior of others. Speech samples: "Do it" or "Let's turn on the TV."
>
> 3. *Interactional function* is based on social interactions between the child and others. Speech sample: "Glad you came."
>
> 4. *Personal function* is used to express the child's unique personality and awareness of self. Speech sample: "I can run fast."
>
> 5. *Heuristic function* refers to asking questions and seeking information. Speech sample: "Tell me why. . . ."
>
> 6. *Imaginative function* is the child's use of language to create a make-believe world. Speech sample: "Let's pretend."
>
> 7. *Representational function* is used to communicate information. Speech sample: "I want to tell you something."

the story that had been read to him from a Disney version of *Winnie the Pooh*. Everyone is tired of Tigger being too bouncy. They decide to teach him a lesson. They take him into the forest and hide from him. When Tigger says, "Hallo. Hallo," they ignore Tigger. When Linda called, "Sean, come to lunch! . . . Sean, come to lunch! . . . Sean, I called you twice." Sean replied, "No one answered." As Linda pointed out, "He was doing the book." On another occasion, her four-year-old daughter, Anna, expressed herself in beautifully poetic language as she described a sunset by saying, "Mommy, the sky looks like pink lemonade."

Award-winning children's author Eileen Spinelli and husband Jerry Spinelli, author of the Newbery Medal winner *Maniac Magee* and the Newbery Honor book *Wringer*, have no lack of inspiration for children's language. They have six children and sixteen grandchildren to draw upon. In an e-mail exchange, Eileen told Betty Roe, "I gave a talk once on the topic of children and poetry . . . children don't need to be taught poetry. They talk in poetry . . . their language is so creative. We just need to nurture that creativity of speech." The Spinellis' grandaughter Rachel once said about a child who died: "She is an angel now. She is playing Frisbee with a star." Eileen used that phrase, "Frisbee with a star," in her book *What Do Angels Wear?* When their son Sean was a little boy, he came clumping down the stairs in his yellow T-shirt saying: "Look Mommy, I'm a thumpy yellow banana." This is what gave Eileen the idea for her book *In My New Yellow Shirt*. When Ashley was five, she described what "being in love" was like. She said, "I think it's like butterflies in your heart."

Like Sharon Creech's granddaughter and Linda Sue Park's daughter, the Spinellis' grandchildren are inspired by looking at the sky. Eileen was out looking at stars with her grandson Ryan one night, and he said: "When I grow up, I'm going to get you that necklace in the sky," and on another occasion her grandson Billy asked Eileen, "What does the moon taste like, Grandmom?"

Speech Skills

SPEECH SKILLS include, in addition to correct pronunciation of words, voice control and register—the use of appropriate speech for different social situations. Each of these skills contributes to effective oral communication.

Voice Control

As children begin to talk, they learn to use pitch, tempo, volume, and pauses in their speech to help convey their meaning. By learning to control their vocalizations, children can also make their speech rhythmic and pleasing to the listener. Variations in **pitch**, the highness or lowness of sound, result in a rise and fall of the voice that help the listener understand the meaning. Speakers may offer emphasis by varying the **tempo**, or rate of speech, and they may use **stress** (breath force) for various purposes, such as emphasizing a point (heavy stress) or confiding a secret (light stress). **Juncture** (pauses between utterances) is also a natural part of speech and is used for signaling the end of a thought, emphasizing the meaning of the previously spoken words, or selecting the exact word to convey the right meaning.

Emotions are likely to affect voice control and quality of speech. A very excited child speaks more rapidly, more loudly, and at a higher pitch than normally. An angry child is likely to speak in a loud voice and a harsh tone, whereas a shy child may speak softly and haltingly.

It is natural for some children to have problems with voice control through first grade, but older students with such difficulties may need speech therapy. Problems with voice control occur when children speak in a monotonous pitch, with a great deal of hesitation, at too rapid a rate, or in too soft a voice to be heard.

Voice control is important to effective communication. Speakers who speak too rapidly or too softly or run their words together are not as likely to be understood as ones who speak at a more moderate pace, with adequate volume, and with appropriate use of juncture.

Voice control is very important to oral reading and storytelling sessions. In such situations, the speakers use voice control to help listeners follow the presentations. They may vary pitch, tempo, and volume of different characters' speech to assist listeners in differentiating among them. These speech elements are also helpful in indicating the pace of the story's action and setting the mood for the story (Roe, Alfred, & Smith, 1998). Modeling by the teacher is one of the best ways to help students learn to control speech elements.

Reflections

How could you vary the pitch, tempo, pauses, and volume of the following sentence to change the meaning? "David is an honest man."

Register

Children's sensitivity to **register** comes as a result of using oral language in a variety of social situations. Register is a style or level of speech, ranging from extremely formal to extremely informal and personal, that varies according to particular speech situations. Register involves both syntactic (sentence structure) and word choice variables. For example, formal texts tend to have more compound, complex, and compound-complex sentences than very informal speech; formal speech is more likely to use the word *canine* when referring to a dog, whereas informal speech might use the word *pooch*. Selecting or changing to the style of language that is appropriate to the context is called **codeswitching** (Wheeler & Swords, 2004).

Children may come to school speaking mostly informal language. In an effort to help them learn to do codeswitching to another register, teachers may differentiate between "home language" and "school language," without implying that either one is superior. Children become aware of the need to vary the style of their language according to the topic, the size and type of audience, the occasion, the location where the discourse takes place, and the purpose of their speech. In other words, children speak differently when they address the whole class, carry on a conversation with a friend, or interview an adult. They speak differently when they are justifying their actions to their friends, their parents, and their teachers. Storytelling, discussed later in this chapter, offers many opportunities to learn codeswitching as the students portray different characters in different situations.

Martin Joos (1967) classified speech registers according to their degree of formality as shown in Figure 6.4. Middle school students can begin to learn some of these finer distinctions.

FIGURE 6.4   **Speech Styles (Registers)**

1. *Oratorical* or *frozen* speech is very formal, carefully rehearsed, and presented to a large audience.

2. *Deliberative* or *formal* speech is also formal and intended for an audience, but the presentation is not as polished as in the oratorical style.

3. *Consultative* speech generally occurs between two people on a somewhat formal basis.

4. A *casual* style is used during informal conversations between acquaintances.

5. An *intimate style* is common with close friends and family members who use informal speech to share thoughts openly.

Reflections

How would your speech differ if you wanted to describe a recent skiing trip to (a) your father, (b) your class for a grade in a speech course, (c) a young child whom you know well, and (d) a friend who may go with you on your next trip?

Instruction in Oral Language Expression

BECAUSE OF differences in language experiences provided at home, speech proficiency among children may vary considerably when they enter school. Most first-graders, however, can speak thousands of words and can use speech effectively for expressing meanings. The teacher should use each child's oral language capabilities as a basis for advancing language skills.

Despite curriculum guides that recommend systematic instruction in oral language, speaking and listening are the most neglected of all the basic skills taught in schools. Fortunately, standards for the English language arts that have been set by states and professional organizations have brought recognition to the importance of including these essential areas in classroom instruction on a regular, planned basis.

The Role of the Teacher

Klein (1979) urged teachers to structure opportunities for talk into the curriculum. Students should be encouraged to use oral communication in many contexts for a variety of purposes. The opportunities are enhanced by a supportive classroom environment (discussed in the next section). For example, you as a teacher must avoid giving fewer speaking opportunities in the classroom to students you think have poor communication skills. This reaction is counterproductive, because students need to practice expressing ideas orally in order to become good speakers (Strickland & Feeley, 2003).

Good teachers set standards for language use by modeling acceptable speech, particularly in their use of appropriate vocabulary and standard English. You should introduce new vocabulary carefully, in context and with examples, so that children can learn the words and try them out for themselves. Make children aware that specialized words enable the speaker to be more precise and caution them to avoid using jargon or using long words just for effect. Reading nonfiction texts to the students to introduce them to new vocabulary in context and then asking them to discuss the texts, using the appropriate vocabulary, is a way to begin adding precise terms to their speaking vocabularies.

You should integrate oral language instruction with instruction in the other language arts and with other subjects across the curriculum. Literature study and thematic unit studies facilitate such integration. You should offer much of the instruction in authentic situations in which the students can see the immediate need for the skills and strategies. The instruction should include your modeling of the skills and strategies and should prepare students for a variety of different oral language situations that they will encounter. All students should be included in the oral language activities, even shy

Teaching Tip

Read aloud a nonfiction selection such as "Run, Marla, Run" by Janice Marriott from the book *Overcoming Obstacles: Against the Odds* to primary-level students who are studying dealing with physical challenges. Encourage them to listen for vocabulary that relates to Marla's physical challenge and her need to overcome it. Afterward, lead them in a discussion of her physical challenge and how she deals with it. If they do not incorporate the key terms *legally blind*, *retina*, and *hurdles*, ask questions that prompt the use of these terms. Some students may actually use the term *Stargardt's disease*. Give those students special acknowledgment for learning such a difficult term, and give all students who use key terms properly in the discussion/recitation appropriate positive reinforcement.

Children learn about effective oral communication from conversing with teachers.

students, speakers of nonstandard dialects, and English language learners. Few skills and strategies are learned without active practice by the learners.

Not all students benefit from the same types of instruction, so you need to assess students' needs in order to help each one learn to speak more effectively. Some students need help in choosing appropriate vocabulary, organizing content, and staying focused on the subject, while others benefit from guidance in use of voice, nonverbal communication, or techniques of delivery. You may need to help some students to build confidence in facing an audience.

Students tend to talk with teachers only about school-related matters, such as doing an assignment or getting help in reading, whereas they talk with other students about many different things. If you also hold conversations with children on a more personal level, children can learn a great deal about effective oral communication (Pinnell, 1975).

Michaels (1984) suggests a strategy called **vertical construction** that uses teacher-student collaboration for developing a topic orally. The student makes a statement; the teacher questions the student about the statement; and the student elaborates on the statement by providing new information. This interaction is helpful because the student learns to produce an expanded message with more precise vocabu-

Classroom Vignette 6.1

This teacher is making use of the vertical construction strategy.

STUDENT: See my pretty rock.

TEACHER: That is a very beautiful rock! It's called a geode, and I can see shiny crystals inside it. How did you get this rock?

STUDENT: At the lake.

TEACHER: How did you find this geode at the lake?

STUDENT: My dad and I found it. It was in a pile of big old dirty rocks. My dad picked it up and took it home, but it was all round and gray looking.

TEACHER: How did you find the crystals inside?

STUDENT: My dad hit it hard with a big old hammer. It broke open and it was pretty inside.

TEACHER: The geode was hollow inside. When your dad cracked it open, you could see the crystals.

STUDENT: That's right. I could see the crystals in the geode.

What's happening here?

A topic is being developed orally through a teacher-student collaboration. The teacher helps the student elaborate on his statement through questioning.

Applications
for English Language Learners

Although students for whom English is a second language often develop conversational skills in around two years, they generally take as long as five to seven years to develop academic proficiency in English. This means that they may do well at interacting with their friends and the teacher in casual conversations, but may not be able to perform adequately in using English for reading, writing, and acquiring information in content area classes (Collier & Thomas, 1999). You can help them to perform better on academic tasks by previewing reading selections and helping the students to focus on the important material by directing them to read to find specific information (Drucker, 2003).

lary and better use of sentence structure. A teacher-student discussion might proceed as shown in Classroom Vignette 6.1 on page 210.

The Classroom Environment

In some classrooms, teachers do nearly all of the talking and students speak only to ask questions or answer them. Students are expected to do their own work and to speak only when they raise their hands and are called on. In such classes, students have few opportunities to develop and practice speaking skills. Some teachers also impede oral language development by criticizing students' use of nonstandard English or slang, imperfect voice control or articulation, or ineffectiveness of communication. Such criticism causes some children to avoid speaking.

In other classrooms, however, teachers establish a relaxed and supportive atmosphere that allows children to speak without fear of criticism. Teachers are tolerant of children's nonstandard speech while they are learning, and they listen primarily for ideas that they express. By their acceptance, teachers encourage students to become risk takers, willing to experiment with new vocabulary and imaginative forms of language. Throughout the day, teachers model standard English themselves, while providing purposeful activities in which students speak in pairs, in small groups, during class discussions, and occasionally to the entire class. Designated assignments may work specifically on use of standard English, and feedback may be given to students privately to avoid embarrassment. Teachers also help students understand that working in pairs or small groups requires them to center their talk on the activity and to avoid disturbing others.

Room arrangement can also contribute to a positive environment for purposeful speech. Learning centers,

Flexible furniture groupings facilitate student interaction.

conversation corners, reading areas, computer centers, and writing tables provide natural opportunities for students to talk to each other. Flexible furniture groupings that can be rearranged for various activities are more conducive to student interaction than straight rows of desks.

Talk in the classroom is essential for language arts instruction. If students are going to learn speaking skills, they must practice speaking (Pinnell & Jaggar, 2003). Some educators have found that peer talk increases motivation to read (Griffin, 2001; Kasten, 1997). Therefore, teachers should work to create situations that foster talk of different kinds (Pinnell & Jaggar, 2003).

Reflections

How would you encourage students in your class to speak by your attitude and your actions?

*P*urposeful Oral Language Activities

LANGUAGE IS best learned when students have opportunities and purposes for communicating with others in natural, informal settings. During the school day, teachers can create a variety of experiences that enable students to develop proficiency in speaking. In this section, purposes for speaking are organized into categories, but in many cases activities could fit into more than one category.

Presenting Information

SHOW-AND-TELL

One of the first public speaking experiences for many children is **show-and-tell**, or sharing time. Children volunteer to report informally on something of interest, such as objects, experiences, or self-made products. Show-and-tell serves many worthwhile purposes if it is well conducted. It allows students to practice speaking before groups in a meaningful way, because the topic is familiar to them and they are the "experts." It gives them practice in selecting a topic for speaking in which their classmates are likely to have some interest. Of course, members of the audience have a chance to practice good listening behaviors while a classmate is speaking.

You may participate by expressing interest, offering encouragement, and making comments, both to model appropriate audience responses and to help the speaker clarify or expand the sharing. As much as possible, however, students should be encouraged to lead and contribute to the discussions.

Effective show-and-tell sessions do not happen without careful planning and good management. Rules

Show-and-tell, or sharing time, allows students to practice speaking to a group for a valid purpose.

Applications

for English Language Learners

If you have ELLs in your class who feel intimidated by participating in show-and-tell because of their limited English proficiency, let them speak in their home language, and use an interpreter for the children who speak only English. The interpreter can be you, a bilingual student, a bilingual parent, or a special bilingual guest to your class. In this way, all of the students have the opportunity to choose topics, plan presentations, share their topics with the class, and answer questions. Students who speak only English are exposed to another language spoken fluently by a classmate who may struggle in English. They may learn something about the other language and feel respect for the classmate's fluency in his own language. This technique can also be applied to storytelling and to oral reports in higher grades.

of behavior should be understood and observed by the speaker and the audience. Rules should include items such as the following.

1. Choose a topic of interest to share when it is your turn.

2. Plan what you are going to say ahead of time.

3. Share your topic briefly and ask for questions or comments.

4. Answer questions and let the next person have a turn.

5. Don't interrupt when another student is speaking. Wait until the classmate pauses or asks for questions and comments to speak.

6. Listen carefully to the speaker so you will be able to make good comments or ask good questions.

7. Talk about the *good* parts of the presentation when you make comments.

After the children have had some experiences with show-and-tell, they may be allowed to add to or modify the rules for participation to clarify the behavior needed for a good experience. The teacher should schedule a regular time for the activity, preferably on a daily basis, and should encourage all children to share their interests sometime during the week.

Reflections

How would you handle a situation in which some children volunteer to participate in show-and-tell nearly every day and other children rarely do?

ORAL REPORTS AND DEMONSTRATIONS

Whereas show-and-tell is most likely to occur in the primary grades, more formal oral reports and demonstrations generally take place in the intermediate grades. These presentations have two focuses: accurate, well-organized content and good oral presentation skills. Minilesson 6.1 shows how one teacher helped to reinforce oral presentation skills with her students.

Oral reports are generally based on research that the students have done on a topic, although sometimes they are based on personal experience. The students need to have well-defined topics, logical development of ideas, and logical conclusions. Use

Writing

of appropriate terminology is important. Students may be encouraged to take notes on their topic and web or outline the report that they plan to give in order to practice it before presenting it to the class. In some cases, the students may write out the entire report, but they should not be allowed to just read it to the class. They should speak it in their own words. They may be allowed some note cards or their webs to keep them on track as they speak, but they should know their topics well enough to make eye contact with the audience as they speak and to answer questions when they are finished. Two questions that they should all be ready to answer are "What are the sources for your information? How did you find them?" (See Chapter 13, Figure 13.15, for a rubric for assessing oral presentations.)

Book reports are special types of oral reports. They are generally done to entice other students to read the book. Book reports may sometimes be summaries of part of

Minilesson 6.1

Presenting Oral Reports

Students are preparing to give oral reports on pioneer life. To remind them of ways to make effective presentations, the teacher asks them to tell some of the things they like speakers to do or not to do. She writes their points on the board as they make them.

MARCIA: I like it when they look at us instead of at the ceiling or the floor.

JEREMY: I don't like it when they say "um" and "ah" all the time. And I like it when they sound natural, not fakey.

LISA: It's better when they make it interesting, like showing us things that go along with the talk.

BART: I like it when they don't talk too long.

RANDY: You always tell us to stand up straight and keep our hands out of our pockets. I guess that does look better.

ANGELA: Sometimes I can't hear because they mumble. I like to be able to hear what they say.

The teacher tells the class that all these comments are good guidelines for speaking that she hopes they will remember when they give their talks. Then she says that they forgot to mention the audience and asks them what the responsibilities of the audience are.

LARRY: Oh, I know. We're supposed to be good listeners and pay attention so we can ask questions later.

The teacher congratulates the students on their good ideas and makes a poster for the room that includes their list in the following format.

Class Guidelines for Speaking

1. Look at the audience.

2. Avoid saying "Um," "Uh," and "Ah" between words and sentences.

Teaching Tip

Let students choose a way to give their book reports from a variety of suggested formats. Encourage them to choose a format that best fits the book about which they are giving the report. For example, a child reporting on Jim Haskins's *I Have a Dream: The Life and Words of Martin Luther King, Jr.,* might pretend to be Martin Luther King, Jr., and tell in first person about his life and beliefs.

3. Speak in a natural voice.

4. Make the presentation interesting. (Use props, if appropriate.)

5. Be brief.

6. Stand up straight.

7. Keep your hands out of your pockets.

Class Guidelines for the Audience

1. Pay close attention.

2. Use all of your good listening skills.

3. Be ready to ask questions of the speaker.

The teacher tells the students that the poster will remain on the wall for the rest of the grading period to remind them of the things that they decided.

What are the students learning?

The teacher is allowing the students to develop the guidelines to follow for speaking during an oral report and for performing as an audience member. They are likely to take these guidelines seriously because they or their classmates thought of them. The guidelines were not just imposed by the teacher.

the plot (generally not giving away the ending), but there are many other formats that they may take. Two students who have read the same book can report on it by having a focused discussion about the book or holding a mock interview, with one student playing the interviewer and the other one playing the author of the book or a character in the book. Several students who have read the same book may draw a series of pictures depicting scenes from the book, and each one may tell about the scene she has drawn. They might even act out a particularly interesting scene from the book. Obviously, this type of reporting calls on skills different from the reporting of research done on a topic. Two of the procedures suggested here for use with book reports—interviewing and creative dramatics—are discussed later in this chapter.

Demonstrations require research and planning, but also generally involve gathering materials necessary to show the audience how to do something. Students may demonstrate a science experiment and explain what happens and why it is happening or give directions for building something. Sequence is generally crucial in demonstrations. Speakers must also be sure that they are speaking to the audience rather than turning away from them as they explain the process that is taking place. Minilesson 6.1 shows how a teacher prepares the class for presenting oral reports on content area subjects.

Several organizations for young people, including the 4-H Club and scouts, and many public libraries involve students in public speaking presentations and contests. Speaking contests rate students on such factors as topic and organization of material, purpose, content, clarity of central thought, use of language, delivery (eye contact, fluency, voice control, pronunciation, articulation, wording, movement, and gesture), and interaction with audience. They are encouraged to plan, organize, and practice before delivering the speech. Students may benefit from joining organizations that encourage development of speaking skills.

Writing

Technology

Interviewing

Students can use **interviews** to obtain information related to a specific project. For example, during the study of a unit on the ways that contagious diseases spread, students might interview doctors and nurses.

Interviewing requires the use of speaking and listening skills, and it is more effective if students proceed according to a plan. The first step should be to have the students consider the purpose for interviewing someone, such as getting information for a class newspaper, collecting material on how people lived many years ago, or learning about the responsibilities of different jobs in order to choose a career. With the specific purpose in mind, they can choose people who are likely to be able to provide appropriate information. The next steps are to arrange an appointment and to plan a series of open-ended questions (ones that cannot be answered with "yes" or "no"). The interviewer may then want to rehearse the interview with another student.

During the interview, the student should refer to the prepared questions, but may also want to pursue an unexpected line of thought that arises. The student should take notes or make an audio or video recording of information for later reference, and, at the conclusion of the interview, should express appreciation to the person who has granted the interview. After reviewing the information gathered, the student should use it to achieve the original purpose of the interview. Classroom Vignette 6.2 shows one teacher's use of interviewing.

Reflections

Interviewing enables students to learn outside their classrooms. What are some other speech-related activities that extend students' experiences beyond the classroom?

Classroom Vignette 6.2

A sixth-grade teacher pairs each of her students with a different second-grader. The sixth-graders prepare questions to use when interviewing the younger children, and then they write and illustrate books about their second-grade partners based on information from the interviews. When the books are complete, the sixth-graders proudly present them to their young partners. Figure 6.5 shows examples of some of the questions that the sixth-graders chose for their interviews.

What's happening here?

The sixth-grade students are given the task of writing and illustrating books for their second-grade partners. To personalize the books for the intended recipients, the students need to know about their partners. With this real-world need existing, the sixth-graders put together a set of interview questions that will help them to write their books. They use oral skills during the interview and also take notes, improving writing skills as well.

Holding Conversations

Conversations are perhaps the most casual and natural form of oral expression, but children have little opportunity for holding conversations during the school day. Especially in the primary grades, teachers may set up conversation centers with comfortable furnishings in which small groups or pairs of students are allowed to carry on conversations for designated periods of time. To stimulate conversation, teachers can place special materials and objects in the corner and change them periodically. The students can pick anything in the center as a topic of conversation; they may even pick more than one thing during their designated time. Some appropriate materials and items are

1. Wordless picture books.
2. Books that have been shared in class read-alouds.
3. Art posters.
4. Travel posters.
5. The children's own artwork from a recent activity.
6. Items related to a unit of study, such as sea shells, starfish, sand dollars, and other things related to a study of the ocean.
7. Toy telephones.
8. Class pets, such as turtles, hamsters, or fish.

Conversations are related to discussions, but they are more loosely focused. Participants in a conversation may choose to change the subject or go off on tangents when they are inspired to do so.

Moran and Carson (2003) call the comments that are made during pauses in reading in the Say Something technique (discussed in Chapter 5) "conversation sparks."

$\mathcal{F}$IGURE 6.5   **Interview Questions**

1. What is your name?
2. How old are you?
3. Whom do you live with?
4. Do you have any brothers and sisters, and what are their names?
5. If you have pets, what kinds do you have?
6. What do you like to do for fun?
7. If you play a sport, what do you play?
8. What is your favorite kind of music?
9. What is your favorite food?
10. What kinds of stories do you like to read or listen to?

Applications

for English Language Learners

Perez (1996) tells about instructional conversations in which ELLs practice their speaking skills while planning a field trip. The second- and third-grade students were deciding who would be guides for a walking field trip to favorite places near the school and how to give directions to the favorite places. The children in this class participated in daily instructional conversations to practice English in authentic situations. They expressed feelings, argued, and negotiated with one another in order to make decisions. These conversations developed more than just social conversational skills because they focused on academic language and content concepts.

Writing

Teachers model these sparks and then encourage students to make comments that include text-to-self connections, text-to-text connections, text-to-world connections, predictions, questions, clarifications, and opinions. They sometimes ask students to write down their sparks before sharing orally, thus making a connection between different language arts in a meaningful manner.

In holding conversations, children should observe courtesies appropriate for different situations. They should express interest in what someone else is saying and should remain attentive. They should not interrupt the speaker, nor should they monopolize the conversation. On occasion, they should observe such social amenities as asking permission, expressing gratitude, giving and accepting compliments, and making special requests. The teacher can model many of these types of social interactions, and children can also practice them through role-playing scenarios in whole-class or small-group instructional settings.

Because many children have had experiences with using telephones, they can relate easily to the need for observing telephone courtesies. Some common courtesies and types of behavior are listed in Figure 6.6. Minilesson 6.2 on page 220 provides ideas for role-playing telephone conversations.

Participating in Recitations and Discussions

Recitation and discussion are both processes in which students give oral responses. During **recitations**, the teacher expects students to give brief answers to questions that primarily test their knowledge of factual material. They are rather like interrogations. The teacher generally asks known-answer questions. Children from some cultures, particularly African American children, do not see the sense of the teacher asking

Phone courtesy needs to receive attention in the oral language program.

$\mathscr{F}$IGURE 6.6   **Telephone Manners**

1. Answer the telephone with a pleasant expression in your voice.

2. Use a polite greeting, such as "Hello. This is the Potter residence."

3. Be courteous to the caller.

4. Speak at a rate that is not too fast or too slow to be understood easily.

5. Speak loudly enough to be heard clearly, but don't speak too loudly.

6. Speak clearly and distinctly. Be precise when saying numbers.

7. Offer to take a message if the call is for someone who is not present.

8. Take messages accurately. Ask how to spell the caller's name correctly if you are not sure. If you are given a telephone number, record it carefully. Repeat the message to the caller to be sure that you have recorded it accurately.

9. Don't try to carry on a conversation with someone in the room with you at the same time you are talking to someone on the telephone. This is rude and confusing to the person on the other end of the line.

10. If you have call waiting and receive another call while you are on the telephone, ask politely if you may see who the other caller is so that you may return that call later. Then speak to the other caller briefly. Don't keep the first caller waiting while you have a long talk with someone else.

11. When you make a call, politely ask to speak to the person whom you are calling. Do not ask, "Who is this?' when someone answers.

12. When you call someone, identify yourself immediately. The person answering may not recognize your voice.

13. If your call may be a long one, ask if the person called has time to talk before beginning your conversation.

14. Let the person making the call end the conversation in most cases.

15. When you hang up the telephone, do so gently, without a bang.

16. If you have a cell phone, turn off the ringer when you are in a public gathering, such as a concert, a play, a church service, a meeting, or a lecture.

questions for which he already knows the answer. The questions are considered silly, and often the children will not respond, even though they know the answers (Meier, 2003).

Discussions, on the other hand, require students to interact with the teacher and/or other students, with all participants expressing their own ideas and listening to the ideas of others. In discussions, students should stay on the topic, express complete

Minilesson 6.2

Telephone Conversations

Remind students that they have discussed some rules for using the telephone. Then explain that you want them to practice using these rules by working with partners and role-playing people who are having telephone conversations. The partners are to take turns being the caller and the one who is being called. Give each pair a slip of paper that briefly describes a situation, and explain that each of them must think of the best way to hold the conversation. Then tell each pair that, as soon as they get their paper, they should think about what to say and how to say it. They must choose who will be the caller first. When they have finished their conversations, they should trade papers with another pair of partners.

Some possible topics follow.

1. Make an appointment for an interview.

2. Give a message for someone else.

3. Invite someone to a party.

4. Ask an adult to speak to the class on a special topic.

5. Give a homework assignment to a sick friend.

6. Ask a parent to accompany the class on a field trip.

7. Place a mail order.

After the students practice making telephone conversations, let them evaluate their own performances. Let them check the list of telephone courtesies that they have constructed, that has been provided by the teacher, or that is in their language textbook. Have them decide what telephone courtesies they remembered and talk about ways to improve their conversations.

What are the students learning?

The students are learning to put telephone courtesies to work, to consider how to communicate ideas orally over the telephone, and to respond appropriately to telephone conversations initiated by others. They are also learning to critique their oral performances in an attempt to improve them.

thoughts, share information, offer reasons for their positions, and consider changing their minds when faced with convincing evidence from other participants. Research indicates that discussion is a more viable instructional strategy than recitation (Alvermann, Dillon, & O'Brien, 1987). Discussions are similar to conversations, but they are more tightly focused.

Group discussion requires students to generalize and reason about topics or issues. Based on their knowledge and experiences, students explore ideas and share information by explaining, describing, forming conclusions, using logic, making decisions,

Applications for English Language Learners and Students with Special Needs

Teachers of young children can teach instructional questioning as a game that teachers play at school. They want the children to give the answers to the "silly" questions, even though the answers are obvious. The children will then be more likely to participate in book discussions and other discussions in which this type of questioning is used (Meier, 2003).

and proposing solutions to problems. As they participate in discussions, they depend less on teachers' "right" answers and look instead to their own ideas and those of their peers (Pinnell, 1975). Classroom Vignette 6.3 shows how one student makes valuable use of a discussion.

Teachers' purposes for holding class discussions vary, but may be related to having students master lessons, consider issues, or solve problems. Subject mastery discussions permit "probing" into related thought-provoking ideas, and discussions of issues allow students to investigate controversial topics from different perspectives. Problem-solving discussions are most effective when the teacher and students identify problems and seek solutions together. Many teachers believe that discussions increase student motivation because of the students' eagerness to share ideas with their peers (Alvermann, Dillon, & O'Brien, 1987).

Teachers or student leaders can guide discussions by directing questions to students who are not actively participating or by refocusing the participants' attention on the topic when their comments wander into unrelated areas. They may clarify points that have been made by restating them in other words or by asking the participant, "Why do you believe that? Where did you find out about that?" They may encourage synthesis of ideas by asking questions such as "How does what you just said relate to Trent's

Classroom Vignette 6.3

During a discussion, Dillon, a beginning seventh-grader, asks if an *organic compound* is a "natural compound." His instructor explains that an organic compound is carbon-based, but that the word *organic*, as it is used in phrases like *organically grown vegetables*, means something like natural, because it refers to being grown without use of chemical fertilizers and pesticides.

Dillon then makes the insightful statement that since any plant is carbon-based, advertisers might not be lying when they refer to their products as organic, but they might be misleading readers into thinking the products were grown without chemical fertilizers and pesticides.

What's happening here?

Dillon is using reasoning about the topic of a discussion to draw a conclusion that results in significant learning about language and its use. He is learning more vocabulary from his instructor's explanation and is putting his new knowledge to use in analyzing a practical situation.

comment?" Teachers encourage more effective discussion with open-ended questions than they do with questions that have single correct answers (Lehman & Scharer, 1996). Commeyras (1994) believes that good discussion questions are ones the students want to discuss.

Literature circles are special groups of students who are reading the same book and come together to discuss it. Students lead the discussion in literature circles. The formation and procedures for literature circles are discussed in detail in Chapter 7. Evans (2002) has found that the fifth-graders she studied doing literature discussions understood the conditions that result in effective discussions, that mixed-gender groups sometimes resulted in some students withdrawing from the discussions, that the students preferred same-gender groups, and that bossy group members affected participation of some students. Evans (2002) believes that teachers should intervene when students exhibit behaviors that marginalize some other group members.

Writing

Writing conferences involving both peers and teachers are another form of discussion. They are good ways to expand language development (Strickland & Feeley, 2003). These conferences are discussed in Chapter 8.

Inquiry teaching, which is often used in social studies and science units, involves generating questions and discussing them with students and teachers. With inquiry teaching, students are involved in deciding upon topics for study and directing discussion. This technique and hands-on activities in these content areas can encourage growth of language skills (Strickland & Feeley, 2003).

As a result of studying an important event or issue, students may participate in **panel discussions**. A panel usually consists of the panelists—students who are prepared to speak on issues related to a certain topic—and a moderator, who opens the discussion with an introductory statement and calls on panelists to speak. At the conclusion of the formal discussion, members of the audience (usually classmates) can pose questions to the panelists.

Panel discussions are important learning activities that integrate the use of reference skills, knowledge of content, and the ability to speak effectively. Before the presentation, each panelist needs to study and organize relevant material. Such discussions are useful for the following purposes.

1. Summarizing material at the end of a unit

2. Informing classmates about a school or community issue

3. Relating information investigated by a special-projects group

Discussions are useful at a number of points during thematic units. Students can have initial discussions about the information they want to discover during the unit, who will be responsible for finding information on each topic chosen, and the resources they might use to find the information. Later they can have discussions about material that they have located, and still later they can discuss ways that they can present the information that they found to their classmates.

Debates

A **debate** consists of two teams of students that present opposing sides of a proposition. Members of the affirmative team present arguments in support of the proposition, whereas members of the negative team offer reasons to reject the proposition. Later, each team member presents a rebuttal to the other team. At the end, a representative

from each team summarizes that team's position. If members of the audience are to judge the debate, they must first establish criteria for judging.

Suitable topics include issues related to students' experiences and interests. Students could take stands for or against such propositions as the following.

1. Some children's books should be censored.

2. Parents should pay children to do household chores.

3. All children should participate in physical fitness programs.

4. The age for obtaining a driver's license should be fourteen.

5. Students should be allowed five unexcused absences a year.

6. Student representatives should help make school policy decisions.

Other debates could center around issues in books the class is reading. They might include the following.

1. Should Japanese Americans have been placed in internment camps during World War II (*Farewell to Manzanar* by Jeanne Wakatsuki Houston & James D. Houston)?

2. Should countries make atomic bombs for defense (*Hiroshima* by Laurence Yep and *The Bomb* by Theodore Taylor)?

3. Should people be allowed to be conscientious objectors or nonparticipants when a war is going on (*Shades of Gray* by Carolyn Reeder)?

> ## Reflections
>
> In what ways can discussion stimulate thinking more than lecture or recitation? What kinds of thinking skills can be promoted through discussion?

In the *Hi and Lois* comic strip above, the children have an argument. How is this like and different from a debate?

Brainstorming

In the classroom vignette at the beginning of the chapter, Mr. Lewis uses **brainstorming** as a means of stimulating thinking and oral expression. Brainstorming also helps to develop verbal fluency. In many ways, brainstorming is a very focused type of discussion. Students are usually enthusiastic about participating in brainstorming sessions because such sessions encourage the use of imagination and creative thinking, and you can use this technique by setting a few simple rules. You first explain the procedures for students as follows.

1. Think of as many ideas as you can related to your topic.

2. Listen to what others say and build on their ideas.

3. Think of original and unusual ideas.

4. Speak one at a time.

5. Do not criticize anyone's ideas.

Then you divide the class into groups, with each group having a recorder who quickly jots down ideas as they are presented. You set a time limit (perhaps 10 minutes) for each group to generate ideas, and then assign specific topics to each group. Topics may be real (such as making the school grounds more attractive) or imaginary (such as entertaining a creature from another planet).

Brainstorming allows students to see that they can learn from and build on what others say and that their ideas are worth sharing with others. It is also a tool that is used in working on problem-solving skills. Often ideas that are jotted down in brainstorming are elaborated on later in discussions by groups. Group members decide which of the ideas is most likely to achieve the goal that was set and think about how to convince the other groups that their choice is the right one.

Story Reading and Storytelling

Story reading and **storytelling** are discussed earlier in this chapter as good vehicles for working on voice control. Readers and tellers of stories can vary the pitch, tempo, and volume of each different character's speech to help distinguish the characters and to add interest to the story. Eye contact is also important in both storytelling and story reading. It is somewhat easier to establish with storytelling because a book is not between the speaker and the listener, but an oral reader should look up periodically and make eye contact with audience members. That requires the reader to scoop up a number of words with her eyes and look up at the audience to deliver them. This eye contact helps to keep the listeners engaged in the story.

A special form of oral interpretation of literature is **Readers Theatre**, in which students read a script for an audience. A narrator, who reads descriptive passages, and enough readers for all of the character parts are used in the production (Huck, Hepler, Hickman, & Kiefer, 1997). In choosing material for Readers Theatre, the teacher should find selections with much dialogue and strong characterization. The material should be relatively easy for the participants to read so that they can concentrate on interpreting the characters vocally. Sandy Smith uses Readers Theatre with a group of gifted students in Classroom Vignette 6.4.

Play reading helps children recognize the connection between oral and written language. Reading a script requires students to visualize the setting and the action and to use their voices according to their understanding of the characters' emotions and thoughts. Students show their ability to translate print into expressive oral language as they read their parts.

Students may make a transition from reading stories to telling them by interpreting wordless picture books orally. The pictures in wordless picture books stimulate

Classroom Vignette 6.4

Sandy Smith has her group of gifted students working with oral presentation skills. She wants them to see how different types of presentations work (Roe, Alfred, & Smith, 1998).

Sandy divides her class into three groups to work with Robert Service's narrative poem, "The Shooting of Dan McGrew." One group reads the narrative poem just as it is written. The second group internalizes the story within the poem and develops it into a story to tell as an eyewitness to the events might have told it. The third group performs a Readers Theatre script as found in *Cowboy*, a collection of Readers Theatre scripts (Adams, 1988).

Then the different presentations are compared and contrasted.

What's happening here?

The students are learning the subtle differences among readings or recitations of poetry, storytelling, and dialogue exchanges. In Readers Theatre, there is a heavy emphasis on conveying the story through dialogue, although there may also be a narrator who makes transitions. When reading dialogue, the students have to use their oral interpretation skills to convey mood and emotion.

---

children to produce stories that make sense with the pictures. One book to consider is Eric Rohmann's *Time Flies*, a wordless picture book that is good to use during a thematic unit on dinosaurs. Other choices for wordless picture books include Jeanne Baker's *Window*, a book that works well with a unit on how humans affect the environment; Emily Arnold McCully's *First Snow*, a book that fits into a unit on winter; Keith Pigdon and Marilyn Woolley's *A Summer Storm*, a book that is appropriate for a unit on weather; and Paula Winter's *The Bear & the Fly*, a book that is perfect for practicing storytelling with expressive language.

Students learn to be good storytellers by being exposed to good teacher modeling of storytelling, picking out relatively simple stories that they like to start telling, mapping the stories or outlining them, practicing telling the stories from the mapped clues, and practicing telling them without notes. They may tape practice sessions and play the tapes back to help them correct problems with voice control, flow, and completeness. They should practice with a friend or family member, if possible, before presenting their stories to a group. This helps them to work on eye contact; body control, including use of appropriate, but not superfluous, gestures; and other presentation factors.

Cumulative tales such as "The House That Jack Built" are good for beginning tellers because their sequence is repetitive and easy to learn. Students may use flannelboards to retell stories. The flannelboards offer visual reinforcement of the story and also provide prompts for the teller; however, they make it harder to maintain eye contact. Students may also use props and puppets with their retellings. Sometimes the children can take turns retelling parts of the story in sequence, using vivid facial and vocal expression (Brand & Donato, 2001). Morrow (1997) suggests that stories to retell should have clear plots. Predictable sequences and repetitive phrases are also helpful. When students retell a novel, they must summarize it or tell only one episode.

Students should have an opportunity to tell their stories in a risk-free environment. Discussion following the presentation should focus on what they did well. You should offer them specific praise rather than a generalized "Good job." For example, you could say, "I like the way you gave your characters different voices, so that we could tell them apart." Classmates should also be encouraged to point out the specific good points of the telling (Roe, Alfred, & Smith, 1998). More information on story reading and storytelling is presented in Chapter 2.

Writing

Technology

Choral Reading or Speaking

Choral reading or **choral speaking** is the oral interpretation of literature that occurs when two or more voices speak as one. A major purpose of choral speaking is enjoyment, so children should be allowed to experiment with choral reading in an atmosphere of enjoyment. It is an excellent way to allow shy students to participate without undue pressure. Norton and colleagues (2003) identify five forms for choral speaking, as shown in Figure 6.7.

Through choral speaking, children can learn to appreciate the sounds of literature—the rhythm, rhyme, alliteration, and mood. Poetry is generally the easiest and most effective type of literature for this activity.

When engaging students in choral speaking, select literature that interests the students, that is appropriate for oral interpretation, and, in many instances, is simple enough to memorize. The earliest experiences might be with Mother Goose rhymes, such as "Sing a Song of Sixpence" or "Simple Simon."

Students who can read may either present choral readings or choral speaking, and choral reading relieves the students of the need to memorize. You may want to read a selection to the children several times, with different interpretations, before asking them to try interpreting it themselves. They should consider the mood of the selection—perhaps humorous, sad, or mysterious—and know where to pause and what words to emphasize. They should avoid reciting it in a sing-song fashion. Teacher modeling is extremely important to help the students see that chanting in a sing-song manner is not as interesting and effective as reading to convey meaning. More information on choral reading and speaking is presented in Chapter 2.

Reflections

How might positive experiences with choral reading or speaking lead to a love of literature?

Creative Dramatics

Creative dramatics is the spontaneous acting out of situations and stories without scripts or prompts with no audience except the others in the class who are not acting at the moment. It is an excellent way to encourage speaking skills. The main focus is on the process of the dramatization rather than on the product. Acting out situations that they may encounter in real life can help students to think through ways to solve problems, as well as help them to hone their speaking skills. Situations that a student might act out include the following.

1. Trying to convince his mother to let him go to a party at a friend's house on a school night

2. Trying to sell a CD she doesn't want to a friend who has never heard it

3. Trying to decide with three friends what kind of pizza to order when they all like different kinds

In a study that Betty Roe did of storytelling and story reading for primary-grade students with language follow-up activities, story dramatization was a favorite follow-up activity. Betty went into kindergarten, first-grade, and second-grade classes in four school systems and shared stories, songs, and poems with the students. One creative drama follow-up activity is described in Classroom Vignette 6.5 on page 228.

Older children may act out chapters from books that they are reading, or they may act out historical events that they are learning about in thematic units. For example, they could act out the scene in Cynthia Voigt's *Dicey's Song* when Mr. Lingerle pays a visit to ask if he can give Maybeth two lessons a week, or they could act out the Boston Tea Party when they are studying the American Revolution.

Sometimes a creative dramatic performance is done with **puppetry**. Shy children are especially freed to speak in public when they can hide behind a puppet stage and speak for the puppet. They can act out simple stories (few characters and settings, much dialogue, simple plots) with commercially made puppets or with puppets that they make themselves.

Whereas talking through a puppet makes many children less self-conscious, it adds one complexity—hand movements. The children have to learn to manipulate the puppets as they speak. Therefore, they need to practice both the dialogue for their puppets and the hand movements. Voice projection becomes particularly important with the speaker behind a puppet stage, and the same voice control factors needed in other creative dramatics are important in order to communicate with the audience.

If children make their own puppets, they can make sock puppets with socks, buttons, cloth scraps, yarn and thread; stick puppets with posterboard and rulers or even popsicle sticks; paper bag puppets from grocery bags and drawing materials, such as felt-tipped markers; and hand puppets, that are generally cut out from a pattern and sewn together, with a head and arms for the child's fingers to go into. Children might even draw faces on wooden spoons and use the spoons as puppets, make fist puppets by drawing faces on their closed fists, or draw faces on their fingernails to act as puppets. Some ideas for making finger puppets are the following.

1. Draw features on small objects that can fit over the fingers, such as thimbles. Use other materials that can be hollowed out to fit over fingers, such as erasers or styrofoam balls.

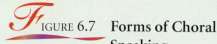 

FIGURE 6.7 Forms of Choral Speaking

Refrain: An adult or competent student presents the major portion of a poem or a story, and the class repeats the chorus or refrain together. Example: Jack Prelutsky's "The Yak."

Line-a-Child or *Line-a-Group:* One child or group begins by reciting the first line; another child or group recites the next line; and this arrangement continues throughout the poem or story. Example: "One, Two, Buckle My Shoe."

Antiphonal or *Dialogue:* Alternate parts are recited by different groups such as boys and girls, high and low voices, or locations of students within the classroom. Example: "Pussy-Cat, Pussy-Cat."

Cumulative: One group recites the first verse, and another group joins in on the second verse. With each succeeding verse, an additional group recites until all participate. Example: "This Is the House That Jack Built."

Unison: The entire class says the selection together. Example: Lillian Morrison's "On the Skateboard."

Talking for a puppet may make shy children less self-conscious.

Classroom Vignette 6.5

Betty Roe shared the story of "The Three Little Pigs" with Barbara Couch's first-grade class a number of times. Each time, the sharing of the story was followed by discussion of the story, including vocabulary used in the story, characters and their characteristics, the settings in the story, and story sequence. As time passed, the students internalized the story by listening to presentations and talking about them.

Then they "tried on" the different characters' parts by practicing how they would speak for the different characters. Every child tried on every part. They did this simultaneously, with everyone first acting and speaking as the first little pig would, then as the second little pig, and so on. Each child was absorbed in his own choices of dialogue and expression and decisions about how the character used his voice and body, so nobody was self-conscious about the process.

Next the group as a whole talked about the settings in the story and cooperatively decided upon the locations for different events in the story. Following this, the students reviewed the sequence, referring to the locations for the actions they were describing. Students were asked to volunteer for the parts, and Betty cast the story first with two strong students as the first little pig and the wolf and other students in less demanding roles. The rest of the students acted as the audience, but they knew that their turns to act would come.

The majority of the students in this class had not only never acted out a story before, but they were also extremely shy about speaking out in front of others. Betty provided stick masks of the characters that the students could hold in front of their faces as they spoke their parts. These masks seemed to relieve the inhibitions that many had for speaking in public. The students played the story without props, pantomiming and using spontaneous dialogue. To do this well, they had to listen to one another to know when to speak, and they had to remember and deliver the appropriate responses with expression, while also pantomiming the action.

After the first performance, audience members told the cast members what they thought was good about the performance, and the performers told how they would play their parts differently if they played them again. J. J., the boy playing the wolf, was universally praised for his vocal interpretation and especially for his pantomiming of the wolf splashing into the pot of boiling water. The girl who played the first little pig received accolades for her rendition of the incident in the apple orchard and of rolling down the hill in the churn.

The parts were then recast, and another group of students interpreted the story dramatically. Some of the children tried out ideas that had been expressed during the evaluation phase of the first playing. This procedure continued until every child had played at least one part in a performance. Each performance also had at least two strong students to help this initial try at creative dramatics work.

(In later creative dramatics presentations in this class, the masks were dispensed with because the children had become comfortable with the activity.)

What's happening here?

The children are learning to follow the sequence of a story, to listen to one another in order to respond appropriately, to speak expressively, to pantomime actions accurately, and to work together. They discovered that some of them perceived the characters differently and played them with different voice inflections and word choices. They learned to look for and compliment positive performances with specific comments and not to be critical. They sometimes tried something that they had seen a classmate do, and sometimes they experimented with new ways of doing things.

2. Glue tiny faces cut from paper or fabric on fingernails. (Rubber cement works well for this.)

3. Use an old glove to fit over all five fingers or cut the fingers out of a glove and use the fingers individually. Decorate the fingers with felt-tipped markers or cloth scraps to represent characters.

4. Place a facial tissue or a square of cloth over the index finger and secure it with a rubber band at the first knuckle. If fingers on both hands are used, the two puppets can carry on a dialogue.

5. Seam a piece of gray felt or fur-like fabric on the wrong side and turn it inside out so that it fits over the finger. Trim it with thread for whiskers, black felt circles for eyes, bits of pink felt for ears and nose, and gray yarn for a tail, and you have a mouse puppet.

Puppets can also be used with improvised conversations and discussions among the puppets. Students can make puppets and act out dramas that they have created.

In a kindergarten class, Maria Gomez takes part in improvising dialogue while acting out stories from predictable children's literature, such as Jan Brett's *Annie and the Wild Animals* and P. D. Eastman's *Are You My Mother?* She provides puppets to aid the improvisation. As she participates in the improvisation, she models language patterns for her students (Ferguson & Young, 1996).

Creative dramatics and puppetry are also discussed in Chapter 2.

Miniperformances

Morado, Koenig, and Wilson (1999) have developed a program for developing language skills of at-risk students that incorporates literature, drama, music, and movement. They call it **miniperformances**. Their program is closely related to creative dramatics, in that familiar stories are reenacted. However, miniperformances use a written script and some minimal props and costumes, although some are left to the imagination; and a practiced performance is given for an audience.

The students adapt a story to make it fit the needs of the group. They may change the gender of a character, have two students play the same character, change animal characters into other animals, and so on. Children decide on elements of the performance such as how to show that time has passed, and they suggest where music should be incorporated. Sometimes they write a song for the story or adjust a familiar song to fit. Special movements may be planned to go along with songs or dialogue. Although the main story line is kept, the students develop the dialogue in their own words, and the adaptations that were mentioned above are incorporated. An adult is the narrator who fills in the part of the story that is not dialogue. The teacher, as scribe, writes the script as it is developed.

The students take copies of the script home to read with members of their families or to have the script read to them if they can't read it for themselves (which would be true for most of the kindergarteners). The first-grade and second-grade participants have another copy of the script in their desks to read at school. The scripts are read

Writing

Reflections

How might early experiences with speaking in front of an audience enable students to talk more easily before audiences in later years?

during rehearsal for the miniperformance. Some memorize their parts, but they know that the wording can vary a bit and still work.

The language skills that the children use in this process are numerous. For example, dramatization helps students understand enacted words and details and facilitates comprehension of main idea and character motivation (Wagner, 2003). Miniperformances, as well as creative story dramatization, are activities that we encourage you to try with all children, not just at-risk students.

Technology

Classroom Assessment for Speaking Proficiency

Observation is an obvious choice for assessing speaking proficiency. You may want to use checklists or rubrics, along with observation, to help you make decisions about strengths and weaknesses in this area. Audiotapes and videotapes of speaking performance are useful for assessment purposes because they can be viewed repeatedly for different purposes, but students may not perform as naturally when they are being taped as they do when they are not. Assessment techniques are covered in detail in Chapter 13.

SUMMARY

Speech is an expressive language art that people use for communicating meaning to others orally. It develops during preschool years as children listen to and imitate the speech of others. Halliday's seven language functions are a way of interpreting children's oral language development.

Speech is closely related to thinking skills and to the other language arts. Voice control relates to the use of pitch, tempo, volume, and pauses, and register refers to the ability to vary speech according to different occasions.

Teachers need to provide purposes for oral communication throughout the day. They should model good speech by choosing vocabulary carefully and using standard English. Teachers also need to establish a supportive environment for children to develop speaking abilities.

Students can participate in such purposeful speech activities as show-and-tell sessions, presentation of oral reports and demonstrations, interviewing resource people, and holding discussions and debates. Students can also develop speech skills by participating in conversations, and they can entertain others with storytelling and story reading, Readers Theatre, choral reading and choral speaking, and creative dramatics, including puppetry, while they hone their speaking skills.

Discussion Questions

1. In what ways does intonation affect an oral message? Can you deliver exactly the same words and convey different ideas by changing vocal inflections? How can you help children see the value in using inflections well?

2. How can you help students see the value of codeswitching, or changing speech registers, depending upon the situation?

3. How quiet should a classroom be when students are trying to learn oral language skills? Do different speaking activities require different amounts of noise and quiet? How can you keep order if the students are all involved in oral activities?

4. What skills do oral reports and written reports share?

5. What are ways to get shy children to participate in speech activities?

6. What skills do storytelling and story reading share? What are the different skills needed for each one?

7. What skills do choral reading and choral speaking share? What are the different skills needed for each one?

8. What are good reasons to use creative drama in the classroom?

Suggested Activities

1. Make an audio recording of the conversation of a three-year-old child. Analyze the recording to determine which of Halliday's language functions the child exhibits. Write your findings and list each language function with the related speech sample.

2. Evaluate three individuals in terms of their voice control, as described in this chapter. Summarize your findings for each individual. Conclude by choosing the most effective speaker and giving reasons for your choice.

3. With a small group of other students, examine several curriculum guides to find what provisions are made for the development of oral expression from kindergarten through grade 8. Categorize your findings according to the types of purposeful speech activities presented in this chapter.

4. Observe a class as it has show-and-tell. Write one paragraph that describes the behavior of the participants, and write a second paragraph to critique the program.

5. Work with a teacher in arranging a panel discussion or debate. What plans must you make and what problems might you encounter? Write a review of the event after it has occurred.

6. Observe critically one of your college teachers who leads good discussions. Make a list of the techniques used to promote and guide the discussions. How could these techniques be adapted for elementary school children?

7. Choose one type of handmade puppet, obtain materials necessary for making it, and help a small group of children make puppets for a puppet show.

8. Work with a small group of children to select a favorite poem to use for choral speaking. Decide what form of choral speaking is most appropriate for this poem; then teach the children to present the poem according to the selected form.

9. Arrange a brainstorming session with a small group of students. Select a topic that interests the students, inform them of the rules, and observe their behavior. Evaluate this activity in terms of both speech and thinking skills.

10. With some other students, brainstorm a list of purposes for having children interview someone. Decide which ideas might be interesting and practical to use when you are teaching, and keep these ideas for future reference.

References

ADAMS, W. (1988). *Cowboy*. San Diego, CA: Reader's Theatre Script Service.

ALVERMANN, D. E., DILLON, D. R,. & O'BRIEN, D. G. (1987). *Using discussion to promote reading comprehension*. Newark, DE: International Reading Association.

BRAND, S. T., & DONATO, J. M. (2001). *Storytelling in emergent literacy*. Albany, NY: Delmar/Thomson Learning.

COLLIER, V. P., & THOMAS, W. P. (1999). Making U.S. schools effective for English language learners, Part 1. *TESOL Matters, 9*(4), 1–6.

COMMEYRAS, M. (1994). Were Janell and Neesie in the same classroom? Children's questions as the first order of reality in storybook discussions. *Language Arts, 71,* 517–523.

DRUCKER, M. J. (2003). What reading teachers should know about ESL learners. *The Reading Teacher, 57,* 22–29.

EVANS, K. S. (2002). Fifth-grade students' perceptions of how they experience literature discussion groups. *Reading Research Quarterly, 37,* 46–69.

FERGUSON, P. M., & YOUNG, T. A. (1996). Literature talk: Dialogue improvisation and patterned conversations with second language learners. *Language Arts, 73,* 597–600.

GRIFFIN, M. L. (2001). Social contexts of beginning reading. *Language Arts, 78,* 371–378.

HALLIDAY, M. A. K. (1977). *Learning how to mean: Explorations in the development of language*. New York: Elsevier.

HUCK, C. S., HEPLER, S., HICKMAN, J., & KIEFER, B. Z. (1997). *Children's literature in the elementary school*. (6th ed.). Madison, WI: Brown & Benchmark.

JOOS, M. (1967). *The five clocks: A linguistic excursion into the five styles of English usage*. New York: Harcourt Brace & World.

KASTEN, W. C. (1997). Learning is noisy: The myth of silence in the reading-writing classroom. In J. R. Paratore & R. L. McCormack (Eds.), *Peer talk in the classroom: Learning from research* (pp. 147–170). Newark, DE: International Reading Association.

KLEIN, M. L. (1979). Designing a talk environment for the classroom. *Language Arts, 56,* 647–656.

LEHMAN, B. A., & SCHARER, P. L. (1996). Reading alone, talking together: The role of discussion in developing literary awareness. *The Reading Teacher, 50,* 26–35.

LIPMAN, D. (1995). *Storytelling games*. Phoenix: Oryx.

MEIER, T. (2003). "Why can't she remember that?": The importance of storybook reading in multilingual multicultural classrooms. *The Reading Teacher, 57,* 242–252.

MICHAELS, S. (1984). Listening and responding: Hearing the logic in children's classroom narratives. *Theory into Practice, 23,* 218–224.

MORADO, C., KOENIG, R., & WILSON, A. (1999). Miniperformances, many stars! Playing with stories. *The Reading Teacher, 53,* 116–123.

Moran, K., & Carson, J. E. (2003). Conversation sparks: How to jumpstart comprehension. *Voices from the Middle, 11*, 29–30.

Morrow, L. M. (1997). *The literacy center: Contexts for reading and writing.* York, ME: Stenhouse.

Norton, D. E., Norton, S. E., & McClure, A. (2003). *Through the eyes of a child.* (6th ed.). Upper Saddle River, NJ: Merrill/Prentice Hall.

Perez, B. (1996). Instructional conversations as opportunities for English language acquisition for culturally and linguistically diverse students. *Language Arts, 73,* 173–181.

Pinnell, G. S. (1975). Language in primary classrooms. *Theory into Practice, 14,* 318–327.

Pinnell, G. S., & Jaggar, A. M. (2003). Oral language: Speaking and listening in elementary classrooms. In J. Flood, D. Lapp, J. R. Squire, & J. M. Jensen (Eds.),

Handbook of research on teaching the English language arts (2nd ed., pp. 881–913). Mahwah, NJ: Erlbaum.

Roe, B. D., Alfred, S., & Smith, S. (1998). *Teaching through stories: Yours, mine, and theirs.* Norwood, MA: Christopher-Gordon.

Strickland, D. S., & Feeley, J. T. (2003). Development in the elementary school years. In J. Flood, D. Lapp, J. R. Squire, & J. M. Jensen (Eds.), *Handbook of research on teaching the English language arts* (2nd ed., pp. 339–356). Mahwah, NJ: Erlbaum.

Wagner, B. J. (2003). Imaginative expression. In J. Flood, D. Lapp, J. R. Squire, & J. M. Jensen (Eds.), *Handbook of research on teaching the English language arts* (2nd ed., pp. 1008–1025). Mahwah, NJ: Erlbaum.

Wheeler, R. S., & Swords, R. (2004). Codeswitching: Tools of language and culture transform the dialectally diverse classroom. *Language Arts, 81,* 470–480.

Books for Children and Adolescents Cited in This Chapter

Baker, J. (1991). *Window.* New York: Puffin.

Brett, J. (1985). *Annie and the wild animals.* Boston: Houghton Mifflin.

Creech, S. (1994). *Walk two moons.* New York: HarperCollins.

Creech, S. (2000). *The wanderer.* New York: HarperCollins.

Eastman, P. D. (1993). *Are you my mother?* New York: HarperCollins.

Haskins, J. (1993). *I have a dream: The life and words of Martin Luther King, Jr.* New York: Milbrook.

Houston, J. W., & Houston, J. D. (1973). *Farewell to Manzanar.* New York: Bantam.

Marriott, J. (2001). Run, Marla, run. In *Overcoming obstacles: Against the odds* (pp. 8–13). Huntington Beach, CA: Pacific Learning.

McCully, E. A. (1985). *First snow.* New York: HarperTrophy.

Milne, A. A. (1989). *Pooh's library: Winnie-The-Pooh, The house at Pooh Corner, When we were very young, Now we are six.* New York: Dutton.

Park, L. S. (2001). *A single shard.* New York: Clarion.

Pigdon, K., & Woolley, M. (1987). *A summer storm.* Cleveland: Modern Curriculum.

Reeder, C. (1989). *Shades of gray.* New York: Avon Camelot.

Rohmann, E. (1994). *Time flies.* New York: Crown.

Spinelli, E. (2001). *In my new yellow shirt.* New York: Holt.

Spinelli, E. (2003). *What do angels wear?* New York: HarperCollins.

Spinelli, J. (1990). *Maniac Magee.* New York: Little, Brown.

Spinelli, J. (1997). *Wringer.* New York: Joanna Cotler Books.

Taylor, T. (1995). *The bomb.* San Diego, CA: Harcourt Brace.

Voigt, C. (1982). *Dicey's song.* New York: Fawcett Juniper.

Winter, P. (1976). *The bear & the fly.* New York: Crown.

Yep, L. (1995). *Hiroshima.* New York: Scholastic.

Developing Reading Proficiency

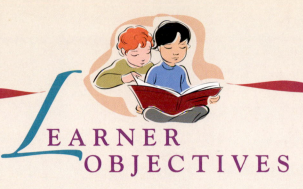

LEARNER OBJECTIVES

At the conclusion of this chapter

YOU SHOULD BE ABLE TO

1. Discuss concepts about balanced reading and teacher effectiveness.

2. Describe some word identification strategies.

3. Explain some comprehension strategies for developing proficient readers.

4. Use the language experience, guided reading, and basal reader approaches to reading instruction.

5. Describe ways to use literature as the core of a reading program.

6. Identify the following terms that are defined or explained in this chapter:

alphabetic principle 242
analytic phonics 242
balanced literacy
   instruction 238
basal reader approach 268
context 245
Directed Reading
   Activity 269
Directed Reading-Thinking
   Activity 259
fluency 260
Four Blocks 239

graphophonic cues 246
guided reading 271
language experience
   approach 264
leveled texts 271
literature-based thematic
   units 277
literature circles 274
metacognition 249
onset/rime 244
phonics 242
pragmatic cues 246

Question-Answer
   Relationships 255
reading workshop 279
reciprocal teaching 255
schema 248
semantic cues 246
semantic mapping 259
sight words 242
structural analysis 244
syntactic cues 246
synthetic phonics 242
think-alouds 254

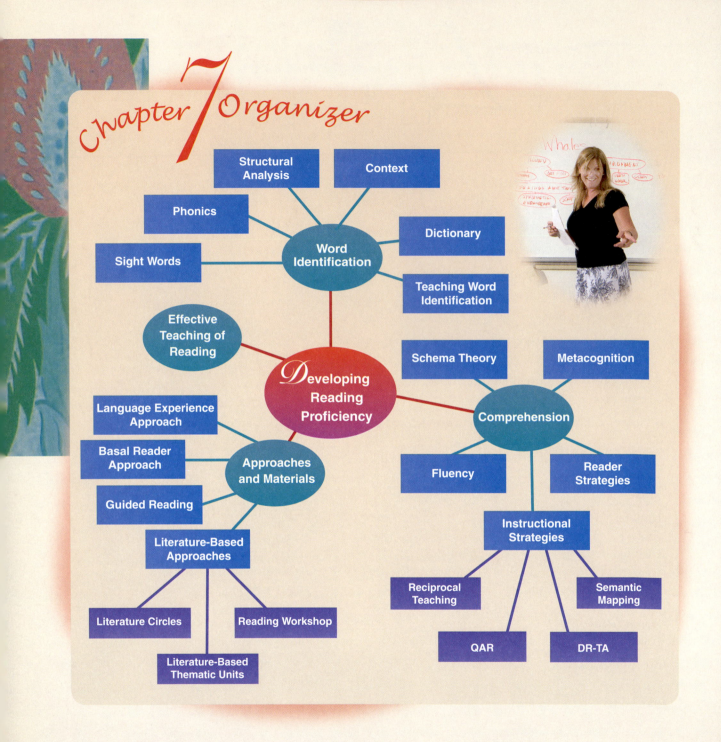

Chapter 7 Organizer

Structural Analysis

Context

Phonics

Dictionary

Sight Words

Word Identification

Teaching Word Identification

Effective Teaching of Reading

Developing Reading Proficiency

Schema Theory

Metacognition

Comprehension

Language Experience Approach

Basal Reader Approach

Approaches and Materials

Fluency

Reader Strategies

Guided Reading

Instructional Strategies

Literature-Based Approaches

Reciprocal Teaching

Semantic Mapping

Literature Circles

Reading Workshop

QAR

DR-TA

Literature-Based Thematic Units

STANDARD 1. Students read a wide range of print and non-print texts to build an understanding of texts, of themselves, and of the cultures of the United States and the world; to acquire new information; to respond to the needs and demands of society and the workplace; and for personal fulfillment. Among these texts are fiction and nonfiction, classic and contemporary works.

STANDARD 3. Students apply a wide range of strategies to comprehend, interpret, evaluate, and appreciate texts. They draw on their prior experiences, their interactions with other readers and writers, their knowledge of word meaning of other texts, their word identification strategies, and their understanding of textual features (e.g., sound-letter correspondence, sentence structure, context, graphics).

K AYLA STRUGGLES to read the sentence, "The locomotive steamed ahead, crossing the bridge high above the river." She thinks to herself, "By looking at the picture I know this story is about a train. 'The,' hmmm, that next word is a long one beginning with *l*, and I know it isn't train, but I don't know what it is. I'll read to the end of the sentence and see if I can figure it out. 'The something something ahead, crossing the something high above the river.' Three words I don't know, but it sounds like it's about a train crossing over a river. I'll try looking at the first word I don't know in parts to see if that helps: 'lo-co-mo-tive.' Oh, I think I know it now. A locomotive is a kind of train. That makes sense. The next word must be about what the locomotive is doing—screamed, streaked? Maybe, but I'd better sound it out to make sure. It's *st-eam-ed* ahead. Does that make sense? Maybe it's a steam locomotive so it's steaming ahead. Yes, I guess that's okay. I'll start from the beginning. 'The locomotive steamed ahead, crossing the something high above the water.' Oh, that word must be *bridge*. That would make sense and it begins with the letters that make the sound at the beginning of *bridge*. Now I can read the whole sentence."

Kayla is using a variety of word recognition and comprehension strategies as she attempts to get meaning from the sentence she is reading. She is carefully monitoring her reading and using "fix-up" strategies when she has problems. She first reads to the end of the sentence to see if she can figure out the words she doesn't recognize. She uses semantic context clues by looking at the picture and knowing that *locomotive* probably refers to a train, and she applies structural analysis to figure out the pronunciation. She uses syntactic context clues to figure out that *steamed* must be something the locomotive did, and she uses phonics (actually onset and rime) to pronounce *steam*, then adds the inflectional ending *-ed.* When she comes to *bridge,* she thinks about what word would make sense and then confirms it by matching the sounds of the first two letters with the beginning sounds of *bridge.* Kayla is using metacognition, or thinking about her reading and making changes as needed in order to make sense. (Metacognition is discussed later in this chapter.)

Reading begins with listening and speaking. Youngsters learn to identify speech sounds and imitate them to communicate their needs. They expand their vocabularies and concepts by listening to adult speech and to stories that are read to them. Their early experiences with listening and speaking prepare them for learning to read and write. They begin pretend reading by imitating the story lines and voice intonations that they have heard, and they begin to write by scribbling or drawing. Most children understand that reading and writing are ways of communicating long before they receive formal instruction in either. Chapter 4, Early Experiences with Language, covers many aspects of beginning reading—language development, preschool and kindergarten programs, emergent literacy, phonemic awareness, print awareness, and beginning reading and writing—so this chapter continues from there. Because reading instruction cannot exist in isolation, this chapter focuses on theories and practices that relate reading instruction to literature and other language arts.

Effective Teaching of Reading

FOR DECADES, teachers have tried to find the best way to teach reading. Is it phonics, literature-based, holistic, or skills/strategy instruction? In recent years, a movement toward **balanced literacy** instruction has developed. Balanced reading instruction means different things to different teachers, depending on their perspectives about effective reading instruction. Educators need to look closely at past practices while searching for balanced literacy instruction (Reutzel, 1998/1999). Some people define balanced literacy instruction as a combination or blend of phonics and holistic practices.

Fitzgerald (1999) suggests that balance is a philosophical view of what kinds of reading knowledge children should acquire and how teachers should develop these kinds of knowledge. She identifies three categories of children's knowledge, each equally important. The first is local knowledge, consisting of decoding and word identification skills; the second is global knowledge, including strategies for comprehending and responding to reading; and the third is love of reading, referring to attitudes toward reading and motivation to read. In order to impart these kinds of knowledge, teachers need to supply students with a wide range of reading materials and find instructional approaches that meet students' needs, although these needs might be quite different.

Duffy and Hoffman (1999) contend that there is no perfect method for teaching reading and that effective teachers realize that different students need a variety of good methods and materials used in various ways. According to Spiegel (1998), research shows that most literacy approaches work for some children, but no approach works for all children. She looks at balanced literacy instruction as a way that the teacher thoughtfully decides each day on the best way to help each child become a better reader or writer. She states that balanced literacy instruction must be based on research and a comprehensive view of literacy and must recognize the teacher as an informed decision maker.

An example of an attempt to balance instructional methods and reach diverse learners is the **Four Blocks** approach (Cunningham, Hall, & Sigmon, 1999). Described as a multimethod, multilevel framework for grades 1 through 3, it often correlates with thematic units and consists of four daily 30-minute blocks as follows.

- *Guided reading:* The teacher guides the children in the reading of the same text, perhaps a big book or multiple copies of a book. Students are involved in comprehension instruction, discussions, or response activities.
- *Working with words:* The teacher introduces new words that are placed on the word wall and engages children with word identification strategies, often focusing on spelling patterns in words. (See Minilesson 10.2 in Chapter 10 for a lesson on making words that focuses on spelling patterns.)
- *Writing:* This block begins with a minilesson as the teacher thinks aloud while writing. Minilessons cover a variety of topics in different formats. Children then write themselves, using the writing process.
- *Self-selected reading:* The teacher reads aloud, and then children choose what they want to read. The teacher holds conferences with the students, and some children may share their reading.

Writing

More information about Four Blocks is available in *The Teacher's Guide to the Four Blocks* (Cunningham, Hall, & Sigmon, 1999).

Allington (2002) reviewed a series of studies that confirmed that effective teachers matter much more than curriculum materials, approaches, or programs. In a study on the expertise of literacy teachers in the elementary grades, Block, Oakar, and Hurt (2002) also found that effective teaching affected the rate and depth of students' literacy growth significantly more than materials and philosophies. They identified the six domains related to effective teaching shown in Figure 7.1.

Taylor and her colleagues (2002) investigated eight schools to determine the relationship between teachers' practices and students' growth in reading. A major finding was that children grew less in reading achievement when the teacher told them information instead of coached them to come up with their own answers. In other words, a

$\mathcal{F}$IGURE 7.1   **Domains of Effective Teaching**

Teacher's role: encourager, demonstrator, manager, coach, or guide

Motivational strategies: authentic explorations, integration with the arts, varied lesson plans

Reteaching strategies: variations in lesson pace, methods, time, contexts, degree of personalization, and levels of challenge

Relationships with students: use of humor, listening, and conversations to establish rapport

Expertise in individual lessons: differentiated, creative, rapid-paced lessons; student selection of goals and strategies

Classroom environments: print-rich, many resources

teacher-directed stance was not as effective as a student-support stance that included coaching, modeling, and other forms of scaffolding. Along the same line, the researchers found that first-graders showed more growth in reading fluency when they were actively, instead of passively, responding to reading activities. Word work (for example, phonemic awareness and sight word activities) seemed most important for kindergartners, whereas higher order questioning appeared to be a significant predictor of reading success in grades 4 through 6. Figure 7.2 shows some characteristics of effective teachers (International Reading Association, 2000).

The Center for the Improvement of Early Reading Achievement (CIERA) conducted an investigation of effective schools and accomplished teachers that involved seventy first- through third-grade teachers from fourteen schools in four states (Taylor, Pearson, Clark, & Walpole, 1999). Researchers found that the most distinguishing feature of effective schools was the time spent in small-group instruction for reading. Instruction included teacher-led reading of both expository and narrative text, literature circles, and instruction in vocabulary, phonics, and comprehension. Teacher scaffolding of word identification while children were reading stories and teacher communication with parents also characterized effective schools. Teachers in these schools offered children more time for reading independently and asked more higher level questions than they did in less effective schools.

Children in many classrooms come from a wide range of racial, ethnic, language, and cultural backgrounds. Effective teachers try to enable each child to be successful, despite these variations. Miller (2001/2002) suggests several ways that teachers can help children succeed and feel part of the classroom community. One way is for teachers to involve students in culturally relevant assignments and activities, such as discus-

𝓕IGURE 7.2 **Characteristics of Effective Reading Teachers**

Writing

Effective reading teachers:

1. Understand reading and writing development and know how children learn.

2. Believe all children can learn to read and write.

3. Offer a variety of materials, literature, and texts for children to read.

4. Serve as coaches by providing help strategically.

5. Create a community of learners in their classrooms.

6. Implement a balanced approach to literacy instruction.

7. Use flexible grouping arrangements to meet students' needs.

8. Use a variety of assessment techniques to record student learning.

9. Relate reading instruction to children's previous experiences.

10. View themselves as lifelong learners and continually strive to improve their practices.

sions of current issues relating to discrimination. Other possibilities are to seek out and use materials that reflect the students' backgrounds and to develop a curriculum that incorporates and respects their perspectives. When designing lessons, teachers should consider differences in learning styles, ways to implement cooperative learning for the benefit of all students, and authentic ways to assess student progress.

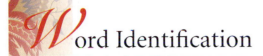

Reflections

From your point of view, who was an effective reading teacher during your early school years? Why was that teacher effective? Would you like to teach the same way? Why, or why not?

𝓦ord Identification

READERS IDENTIFY words by using a combination of skills: sight words, phonics, context clues, structural analysis, and the dictionary. Because many words are not recognized by sight and are not readily decodable, children need to be flexible in their approaches to word identification.

Sight Words

Words that children recognize immediately without analysis are **sight words**. Most children already know many sight words before entering first grade. These include environmental words (those seen on road signs, billboards, fast-food restaurants, and so forth), family-oriented words (names of family members and their addresses), book-related words (titles of favorite books and repetitive words in some stories), and words of special significance (holidays and words associated with meaningful experiences).

Phonics

Phonics is the relationship between the symbols (*graphemes*) in our writing system and the sounds (*phonemes*) in our speech. Phonemic awareness, discussed in Chapter 4, occurs during early childhood as children develop an ear for the sounds of language. Villaume and Brabham (2003) stress the importance of having children gain control of the **alphabetic principle**, the understanding that certain letters represent certain speech sounds, in order to develop word recognition and fluency. They point out that multiple approaches to phonics instruction can help children master the alphabetic principle and can even arouse children's curiosities about words and promote a love of reading. They remind us, however, that phonics instruction should not crowd out instruction based on literature and the rich use of language. Although there are many exceptions to most phonics rules, Figure 7.3 is a list of some of the most useful phonics generalizations (Burns, Roe, & Ross, 1999b).

The **analytic phonics** approach is based on knowledge of sight words, whereas the **synthetic phonics** method starts with word parts (that is, letters or syllables) and combines them into words. The following is an example of applying the analytic method. When Maria notices that her name and Maggie's name begin with the same letter and start with the same sound, Maria becomes aware of certain consistencies in letter-sound relationships. She applies this insight to other words that begin with *m,* and later she is able to make other letter-sound connections by observing the sounds that letters make in familiar words. Although Maria is able to figure out many relationships between letters and sounds for herself, the teacher needs to help most children make these connections by following procedures similar to those that Maria used.

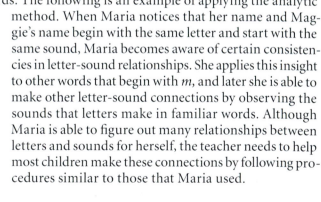

During an analytic phonics lesson, the teacher points to words beginning with *m* as a young child looks on.

$\mathcal{F}$IGURE 7.3   **Useful Phonics Generalizations**

1. When a word has only one vowel and it occurs at the end of the word, the vowel generally has its long sound. (Examples: *go, be.*)

2. When a consonant and the letter *e* follow a vowel in a one-syllable word, the vowel usually has its long sound and the e is not sounded. (Examples: *made, like.*)

3. When a word has only one vowel that is not at the end of the word, the vowel usually has its short sound. (Examples: *at, bus.*)

4. Two vowels that are blended together are called *diphthongs*. These include *oi, oy, ou,* and sometimes *ow.* (Examples: *noise, toy, out, flower.*)

5. In the vowel combinations *ai, ay, oa,* and *ee,* the first vowel is usually long and the second vowel is not sounded. (Examples: *pain, day, coat, beet.*)

6. When a vowel precedes *r* in the same syllable, the vowel usually has neither its short nor its long sound. (Examples: *her, fur, party.*)

7. When the consonants *c* and *g* are followed by *e, i,* or *y,* they usually have soft sounds; that is, the sound of *s* for the letter *c* and the sound of *j* for the letter *g.* (Examples: *cedar, cider, cyclone, gem, giant, gym.*) When *c* and *g* are followed by *a, o,* or *u,* they usually have their hard sounds: *c* sounds like *k* and *g* has its own special sound. (Examples: *can, come, cut, gate, go, gum.*)

8. If two like consonants are beside each other in the same syllable, only one is sounded. (Examples: *call, class.*)

9. *Ch* usually has the sound heard in *church,* but it can also sound like *sh* or *k.* (Examples: usual sound: *cheer, chase;* k sound: *chemistry, chord;* sh sound: *chef.*)

10. Some consonants in certain positions make no sound, particularly *k* in *kn, w* in *wr,* and *c* in *ck.* (Examples: *knee, knit, wrap, write, neck, thick.*)

In the synthetic method, a child isolates each sound and attempts to combine the sounds into words, such as /r/ /u/ /n/ for *run.* Although this method works in some cases, trying to isolate the sounds of consonants can result in distorting the sounds, as in pronouncing /d/ as *duh.*

Many beginning writers use invented spellings, which are unconventional spellings based on their knowledge of letter-sound associations. For instance, a child might write the word *hungry* as *hungre* when attempting to represent each identifiable sound.

(See Chapter 4 for more on invented spelling.) Such use of invented spellings supports phonics development because the child is associating letters with sounds.

Teachers have long used word families, or words sharing common phonograms (word endings), to help children hear, see, and use the ends of rhyming words as reliable clues for reading and spelling new words that sound alike (Johnston, 1999). Reading teachers are now referring to the beginning of a word (the part that precedes the vowel) as the **onset** and the ending part (beginning with the vowel) as the **rime**. For example, in *hen*, *h* is the onset and *en* is the rime, and in *start*, *st* is the onset and *art* is the rime. Working with familiar words, children find the rime and then use it to read and spell other words by blending different onsets with it.

Structural Analysis

Structural analysis is a helpful word identification skill for analyzing words that consist of recognizable units or elements, such as prefixes, suffixes, inflectional endings,

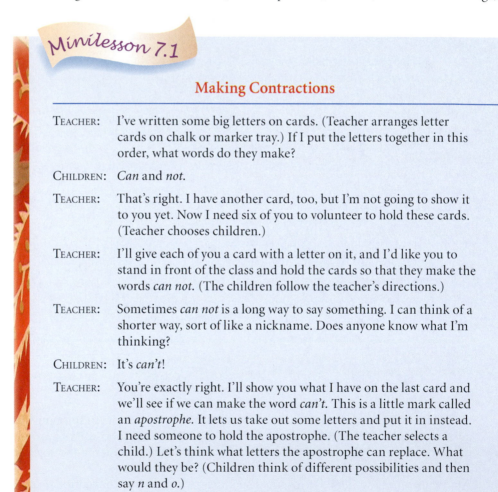

Minilesson 7.1

Making Contractions

TEACHER:	I've written some big letters on cards. (Teacher arranges letter cards on chalk or marker tray.) If I put the letters together in this order, what words do they make?
CHILDREN:	*Can* and *not*.
TEACHER:	That's right. I have another card, too, but I'm not going to show it to you yet. Now I need six of you to volunteer to hold these cards. (Teacher chooses children.)
TEACHER:	I'll give each of you a card with a letter on it, and I'd like you to stand in front of the class and hold the cards so that they make the words *can not*. (The children follow the teacher's directions.)
TEACHER:	Sometimes *can not* is a long way to say something. I can think of a shorter way, sort of like a nickname. Does anyone know what I'm thinking?
CHILDREN:	It's *can't*!
TEACHER:	You're exactly right. I'll show you what I have on the last card and we'll see if we can make the word *can't*. This is a little mark called an *apostrophe*. It lets us take out some letters and put it in instead. I need someone to hold the apostrophe. (The teacher selects a child.) Let's think what letters the apostrophe can replace. What would they be? (Children think of different possibilities and then say *n* and *o*.)
TEACHER:	Let's try that and see if it works. I need the *n* and *o* from the word *not* to go back to their seats. Let's put the apostrophe between the

and root words. Instead of sounding out words phonetically, students can look for familiar units within words and combine them. For instance, the noun *previews* can be broken down into *pre* (prefix), *view* (root word), and *s* (inflectional ending). The meanings of these word units also give clues to word meanings. In the example, *pre* means "before," *view* means "something that is seen," and *s* means "more than one." Therefore, *previews* means "things that can be seen in advance." Other aspects of structural analysis are combining root words to form compound words, making contractions by replacing a letter or letters with an apostrophe, separating words into syllables, and placing accents on stressed syllables. Minilesson 7.1 shows a way to teach contractions through children's active participation.

Context

Word identification should rarely, if ever, be separated from meaning. When words are viewed in **context** (with surrounding words), children often recognize them by know-

n in *can* and the *t* that's all by itself. I think we have a new word. Can you read it for me?

CHILDREN: *Can't.*

TEACHER: Right again. Our new word *can't* is called a *contraction*. What can you tell me about how to make a contraction?

CHILDREN: Take two words and take out some letters. Put an apostrophe where the letters used to be.

TEACHER: Very good! Can you think of other contractions? I'll write them on a chart and then we'll think what two words are replaced each time. (Children name words and the teacher writes them on the chart, along with the two words they represent.)

TEACHER: I think you have the idea. You may want to use some words with apostrophes when you write in your journals today.

What are the students learning?

The children are learning two new terms, *apostrophe* and *contraction*, related to a skill they need to know. They are using their bodies to move the cards (kinesthetic learning), instead of completing a page in a workbook, to help them remember this concept. They will have an opportunity to apply this new skill when they write in their journals, and they will be able to refer to the chart with the list of contractions that they generated.

ing what word makes sense in that position. They use both semantic (meaning) clues and syntactic (grammar) clues to identify the words they do not recognize immediately. See the examples below to understand how children use context clues.

Semantic context clue:

"Carol had the *privilege*, or honor, of being the class leader." The appositive (*or honor*) set off by commas provides a meaning clue (synonym) for the word that the reader may not recognize.

Syntactic context clue:

"Bob spent the *profits* from his summer job on a new DVD." The position of the unidentified word (*profits*) in the sentence lets the reader know that the word is a noun, or a "naming word."

Context clues used without other word identification skills are only educated guesses. When readers use these clues along with other word recognition skills, such as phonics clues (particularly the initial sound), however, they increase their likelihood of identifying the word correctly.

Dictionary

When other methods of word attack fail, students may need to turn to the dictionary for the pronunciations and meanings of words they do not recognize. To find what they need in the dictionary, they should be able to apply their knowledge of alphabetical order, phonetic respellings, and accent. The context of the unknown word is important for identifying the appropriate definition and for selecting the correct pronunciation, if there is more than one way to pronounce a word. For example, the accent shifts in such words as *project, record,* and *desert* from the first syllable for nouns to the second syllable for verbs.

Teaching Word Identification

Children should be able to use all cueing systems, or sources of information for identifying unrecognized words, interactively and in a balanced way (Fielding, 1998/1999). The four cueing systems are **graphophonic**, **semantic**, **syntactic,** and **pragmatic** (Searfoss, Readence, & Mallette, 2001). Graphophonic cues refer to letter-sound relationships, and semantic and syntactic cues relate to context. Pragmatic cues deal with the social and cultural aspects of speech and vary according to social classes, geographic regions, and ethnic groups. In school, we model formal Standard English; but in other situations, children may speak nonstandard English or a dialect. Less formal language is not inferior and communicates effectively among people within the same cultural group, but children should learn Standard English in addition to the speech they use at home in order to communicate effectively in more formal situations. Figure 7.4 summarizes these four cueing systems.

Educators differ in their views about how to teach word identification. The National Reading Panel (2000) stresses the importance of explicit, systematic phonics instruction, but admits that phonics skills "must be integrated with the development of phonemic awareness, fluency, and text reading comprehension skills" (p. 11). Many educators

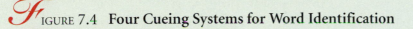

$\mathcal{F}$IGURE 7.4   **Four Cueing Systems for Word Identification**

Writing

Type	Definition	Application
Graphophonic	Relationship of spoken sounds (phonemes) to printed symbols (graphemes)	Sounding out words Using invented spelling Finding rhyming words
Semantic	Meanings of words	Learning new vocabulary Discovering multiple-meaning words
Syntactic	Grammar and arrangement of words in sentences	Writing sentences
Pragmatic	Variations of language for social and cultural reasons	Varying language for specific purposes Comparing Standard and nonstandard English

agree that word identification should be taught within a meaningful context (Dahl & Scharer, 2000; Fielding, 1998/1999; Kane, 1999; Moustafa & Maldonado-Colon, 1999). Juel and Minden-Cupp (1999/2000) found that entering first-graders who were weak in literacy skills needed structured phonics until they learned many letter-sound relationships. Then the children benefited from instruction in combining known letter-sounds with what makes sense when identifying words in text. As a result of her work

Applications for *Students with Special Needs*

Although many children learn to read without direct teaching of skills, those with special needs appear to benefit from explicit instruction. These children need close, personalized teaching with many guided reading opportunities and books at appropriate levels of difficulty (Allington & Baker, 1999). They need a highly structured phonics program and direct in-struction about comprehension strategies to help them become active, involved readers (Searfoss, Readence, & Mallette, 2001). Some highly structured drill-and-practice computer programs, including computerized worksheets that evaluate answers and give feedback, may be useful for these students.

with struggling readers, Fielding (1998/1999) is using less direct, systematic teaching of sound-symbol relationships out of context and more generalizable strategies in context. She believes these young people need to see the whole reading process as it appears in books. Teachers can supply meaningful contexts in which word identification strategies make sense to beginning readers (Kane, 1999).

Moustafa and Maldonado-Colon (1999) argue in favor of teaching reading from whole-to-parts (text to skills) by building on emergent readers' ability to recognize a number of whole words through shared reading with predictable text. Children are taught systematically and explicitly letter-sound correspondences from the words they already know and then shown how to use these correspondences to pronounce unfamiliar words in other stories. Children are likely to recognize words more easily in familiar context than in isolation.

Comprehension

THE ESSENCE of reading is comprehension. Word identification is essential, of course, but reading does not occur until the reader interacts with the text and makes meaning. Even though some readers acquire comprehension strategies informally, the National Reading Panel (2000) recommends teaching comprehension skills explicitly through teacher demonstrations in order to enhance understanding.

Schema Theory

Background experience has a powerful effect on comprehension. Individuals use their experiences to acquire clusters of concepts that they then store in memory. Each of these stored structures is called a **schema**. Readers call on pertinent schemata (plural for *schema*) and relate them to the text in order to comprehend what they are reading. As they acquire additional information from the text, they modify and expand their schemata. In other words, comprehension occurs through the interaction of prior knowledge with new information from the text (Anderson & Pearson, 1984). The National Reading Panel (2000) also found that when readers actively relate their own knowledge and experiences to ideas in the text, their comprehension improves.

If a child's schemata are limited due to lack of experiences, the child will have more difficulty understand-

This fifth-grader is using her existing schemata as she seeks new information in the school library.

ing written information than will one who has had a rich variety of experiences. For example, when reading a story about air travel, the child who has a well-developed schema on this subject from having flown on a commercial airline can use stored knowledge about flight attendants, seat belts, security checks, and so forth. On the other hand, a child who has never been on such a flight may lack a sufficient schema for fully comprehending a story about air travel. The implication, therefore, is that teachers need to build students' experiences directly or vicariously to enhance their comprehension of text.

Metacognition

The ability to understand and control one's own thought processes is **metacognition**. Metacognitive readers realize what they know and what they don't know, set purposes, select appropriate reading and learning strategies, monitor (check) their understanding, and evaluate their performance. Pressley (2002) describes metacognitive readers by saying they are able to use a variety of comprehension strategies effectively, such as relating text to prior knowledge, making predictions, asking questions while reading, constructing images or visualizing, and summarizing what they have read. They are aware that some text can be confusing and know how to use fix-up strategies, such as rereading. Older students and those who perform well academically use more metacognitive skills than younger students and those who are less able. A comparison of these two types of learners is given in Figure 7.5.

Instruction in metacognition begins with direct teacher explanations and modeling strategies, but develops best when students practice using comprehension strategies while they read (Pressley, 2002). At first, you assume nearly all of the responsibility by thinking through an assignment aloud. Prior to doing a specific task, you model the questioning procedure by asking questions such as the following.

- What am I supposed to do?
- What am I looking for?
- What should I find out before I finish?
- How hard will this assignment be?
- What do I already know about it?
- Can I relate it to something else I know?
- How should I start?
- Is there another way to do it?

You continue asking questions while moving through the learning task, as well as after the completion of the assignment. As they listen to you, students observe the types of

$\mathcal{F}$IGURE 7.5   **Metacognitive Characteristics**

Older and Better Students	Younger and Poorer Students
Monitor performance carefully.	Monitor performance very little or with much laborious verbalizing.
Know own capabilities and limitations.	Are often unaware of limitations.
Verbalize difficulties.	Cannot identify sources of confusion and difficulty.
Use variety of strategies to cope with problems.	Cannot choose appropriate strategies for handling problems.
Plan effectively.	Use little planning.
Focus on getting meaning from text.	Focus on decoding words without concern for meaning.
Skim by seeking informative words.	Skim by seeking easy words.
Use "automatic pilot" for word recognition.	Have few skills at automatic level.
Seek ways to fill in gaps of knowledge.	Allow gaps of knowledge to exist.

questions to ask and then practice asking themselves the same kinds of questions. You provide feedback and encouragement until the students are able to formulate appropriate questions for themselves. Eventually, they should be able to establish their own goals, plan strategies for reaching the goals, monitor their progress, and evaluate what they have learned in terms of their goals.

Reader Strategies

You can help children comprehend well by teaching them to read strategically. Reader strategies are flexible plans that readers adapt to specific situations, as opposed to skills, which can be simply automatic responses to drill-and-practice activities. Such strategies involve conscious and thoughtful reasoning about using skills to solve problems that occur during reading. Students who read strategically use their knowledge about how reading works to understand what they read.

Children's trade books are an effective medium for teaching reading comprehension strategies (Baumann, Hooten, & White, 1999; Bluestein, 2002; Headley & Dunston, 2000). Students often find literature more interesting and more relevant to their lives than basal readers or textbooks, so their motivation to read increases along with their ability to read strategically. Bluestein (2002) contends that a characterization strategy enhances comprehension and supports interaction with the text by having readers analyze aspects of a character's life, situations, feelings, problems, and actions. In a study of fifth-graders, Baumann and colleagues (1999) taught three types of comprehension strategy lessons, using a variety of trade books that students read, discussed, and enjoyed. The first type, teacher-directed *elaborated strategy lessons,* introduced a comprehension strategy through explanation, modeling, and guided practice. Planned *brief strategy lessons* reviewed or expanded previous lessons, and *impromptu strategy lessons* allowed teachers to respond to teachable moments that evolved from book discussions. Students learned the comprehension strategies and were able to retain and transfer their strategic learning to other reading situations. In addition, the researchers found that spending one-fifth of the class time on direct strategy instruction was all that students needed to enable them to apply comprehension strategies to their reading during the remainder of the period.

Duke and Pearson (2002, pp. 208-210) offer a research-based model of comprehension strategy instruction that connects and integrates reading, writing, and discussion. It consists of the following components.

1. An explicit description of the strategy and how and when to use it

2. Modeling of the strategy in action by the teacher and/or student

3. Collaboration between teacher and students on using the strategy in action

4. Guided practice of the strategy and a gradual turning over of the responsibility for its application to the students

5. Independent use of the strategy by the students

Minilesson 7.2 shows how you might implement these steps, focusing on one strategy, visualization. Most students need time to practice and internalize a strategy before moving on to another, but they also need to be aware that good readers use multiple strategies. They should learn to select those that help to make sense of the text and reject others. Minilesson 7.3 (see page 254) shows how you might model strategic reading by trying out different strategies.

Some strategies are particularly appropriate for before reading, during reading, or after reading (Cunningham, Moore, Cunningham, & Moore, 2000). Before they begin reading, students make predictions based on their knowledge of the topic, the type of text, and their purposes for reading the text. As they read, they adjust their strategies to solve problems that occur when meaning is blocked or when predictions are incorrect. When they finish reading, they respond by recalling information (efferently) or by reflecting on the meaning in some way (aesthetically). In her comprehension strategy framework, Dowhower (1999) refers to the interactive phases of prereading, active reading, and postreading. The prereading phase consists of such strategies as building background, relating to prior knowledge, and focusing on the specific strategy to be taught; the active phase establishes purpose and involves reading, self-monitoring, and discussing when, where, and how to use the strategy; and the postreading phase deals with recalling content, responding, extending the text, and using self-assessment of the

Minilesson 7.2

Teaching Visualization

Explicit description of the strategy

Boys and girls, sometimes when I read I can see pictures in my mind. The description is so vivid and detailed that it is easy to visualize what the author is saying. I can almost smell the smells, see the colors, and hear the sounds. This is called visualization, and it helps us understand what we read better than the words themselves.

Teacher modeling of the strategy

I'm reading from Richard Peck's *A Year Down Yonder* and I'm trying to visualize what Grandma looks like. The author is describing her like this (p. 5):

> My goodness, she was a big woman. I'd forgotten. And taller still with her spidery old umbrella held up to keep off the sun of high noon. A fan of white hair escaped the big bun on the back of her head. She drew nearer till she blotted out the day.
>
> You couldn't call her a welcoming woman, and there wasn't a hug in her. She didn't put out her arms, so I had nothing to run into. . . . Her skirttails brushed her shoes.

Now, I can see this woman. I visualize her as sort of old fashioned with that long skirt, and I think that skirt must be full and somewhat faded. She must be stern—"no welcome in her." She has to be old because she's a grandmother and she has white hair, so I visualize her face as old and wrinkled. She's a big woman, nearly blotting out the sun. I think I might be a little afraid of her.

Collaborative use of the strategy

I've told you how I visualize this woman so far. Now I want you to tell me how you think she looks. Can you think of someone you know who looks

ability to apply the strategy. Figure 7.6 (see page 256) gives an overview of strategies students can use before, during, and after reading (Ross, 1999, p. 25).

When teaching students to use strategies, model how and when to use them in actual reading situations. If a strategy does not work for a specific situation, show the students how to use alternative strategies until the problem is solved. Cooper (1997) suggests some guidelines for modeling strategies effectively, such as introducing only one or two strategies at a time, modeling the strategy during an actual reading experience, applying the strategy across the curriculum, and making sure that modeling and practicing are collaborative activities. Figure 7.7 (see page 257) shows an example of how you might use a variety of strategies with which the children are familiar while

like her? Can you visualize anything else about her appearance, or perhaps her character? As we read through this book, your image of her may become clearer.

Guided practice using the strategy

During Sustained Silent Reading time today, I want you to visualize as you read. You may read about a scene or a person that you can picture in your mind. Write down the words that help you visualize on one side of a piece of paper, and write what your mind sees on the other side. It may help if you close your eyes. Later, we'll talk about what you were able to visualize.

Independent use of the strategy

Whenever you read, you should try to visualize what the author is saying. It will make the story come alive for you and help you to appreciate it more.

What are the students learning?

The students are learning how to visualize as you guide them through the procedure. Closing their eyes while thinking about a descriptive passage helps them see pictures in their minds and may enable them to call forth similar images from personal experiences. Comprehension is not limited to just the facts, but also involves the senses in meaningful and memorable ways. Students can use this strategy along with many others for improving their understanding.

modeling the reading of a selection. The text for modeling the use of strategies during reading is based on Shelly Gill's *Alaska's Three Bears* and appears below.

Alaska's Three Bears

Once upon a time there were three bears—a big white bear called a polar bear, a medium-sized bear called a grizzly bear, and a small black bear. When spring comes, the bears begin to wander across the great land of Alaska. All three bears live in a wilderness called bear country. The people of Alaska respect the bear because of its wild nature, its strength, and its intelligence. All bears have

Minilesson 7.3

Modeling Strategic Reading

Tell the students that you will model how to use different strategies when there is an unknown word in a sentence. The sentence is "Ruth ate some of her grandmother's *elderberry* jam."

TEACHER: Hmm, I wonder what *elderberry* means. It must be some flavor of jam from the way it is used in the sentence. *Elder* means old, and of course a *berry* is a berry. Does it mean old berries? Maybe the berries are old and rotten. That doesn't seem right to make jam with old berries. I'd better check this word in the dictionary just to make sure. Oh, now I see. Elderberry is the name of a kind of tree and elderberries come from the tree, so the jam is made from this tree's berries. That makes sense.

Point out to the students that you first used context to figure out the word, but that didn't give you enough information. Then you divided the word into parts and looked at the meaning for each part. This strategy also helped, but you weren't satisfied that you were right. You then used a third strategy, the dictionary, to check the meaning. Tell the students that they need to be flexible in their use of strategies and to keep searching until the word makes sense.

What are the students learning?

The students are learning how to think about what they should do when they come to a word they do not recognize. As they listen to you think aloud about ways to approach a new vocabulary word, the children realize that they can apply similar strategies instead of guessing at or skipping over unrecognized words.

a keen sense of smell. They can also see and hear well. When winter comes, the black and grizzly bears hibernate, or sleep all winter.

The **think-aloud** strategy, closely related to metacognition and teacher modeling, enables the reader to verbalize the strategies being used to understand the text (Duke & Pearson, 2002; Oster, 2001). The thoughts that are vocalized might refer to using prior knowledge, making inferences, or predicting. Research studies have confirmed the usefulness of this technique for improving comprehension both when teachers think aloud while reading to students to model the process, and when students think aloud during their reading (Duke & Pearson, 2002). When readers use the think-aloud strategy, they become aware of how they are making meaning and realize when their strategies are or are not working.

When Oster (2001) used the think-aloud strategy with her students, she asked them to write down their questions and comments while they were reading. By reading the responses of her students, Oster was able to assess their reading abilities and plan the instruction they needed. She found think-alouds to be effective for helping students initiate and participate in class discussions, improve reading skills, and appreciate literature.

Wilhelm (2001) recommended using think-alouds with struggling readers who are likely to just give up or else move right through a passage without comprehending it. Think-alouds require readers to slow down and reflect on how they are comprehending the text and also provide them with strategies to try in lieu of giving up.

As we have seen, there are dozens of comprehension skills and strategies. Figure 7.8 summarizes five of the most useful ones.

Reflections

What prior knowledge did you have about this section (Reader Strategies) that was helpful as you read it? What purposes did you set for reading it? Did you achieve them?

Instructional Strategies

We have considered how a reader can use strategies, singly or in combination, to read proficiently. Now we will look at instructional strategies, or integrated sets of practices, that readers can apply to different texts. Notice the emphasis on having students generate their own questions to increase their comprehension in the first two, reciprocal teaching and Question-Answer Relationships.

RECIPROCAL TEACHING

The purpose of **reciprocal teaching** is to increase comprehension and comprehension monitoring. It consists of four major strategies: predicting, generating questions, clarifying, and summarizing (Palincsar & Brown, 1984). Predicting is anticipating what will happen next; generating questions is asking questions from information in the text and background knowledge; clarifying is identifying confusing parts of the text and attempting to clear up the confusion; and summarizing is selecting the most important ideas in the text.

In this instructional strategy, you and the students take turns playing the role of teacher, with you explaining and modeling the process at first and then gradually turning the responsibility over to the students for carrying out each part of the strategy. The students read the beginning of a story or portion of informational text, and you ask a prediction question. Questions should represent different levels of thinking and should activate children's prior knowledge (Ruddell, 2002). Next, you help the children become aware of potential difficulties and how to apply fix-up strategies (clarification). You then model a summary of the important points and suggest predictions for the next part. When the children have seen you modeling and understand the process, they begin to ask questions themselves, with you continuing to guide them.

QUESTION-ANSWER RELATIONSHIPS (QAR)

The **Question-Answer Relationships** (QAR) instructional strategy (Raphael, 1982, 1986) allows children to use information stored in their heads along with information from the text when answering questions. You explain and model the process, provide practice for the students, and give immediate feedback. QAR consists of four types of questions divided into two categories as shown at the top of page 259.

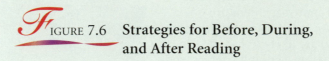

FIGURE 7.6   **Strategies for Before, During, and After Reading**

Before Reading

Previewing
Looking at pictures, examining title and subheadings, skimming or surveying, relating to experience and prior knowledge, generating predictions, setting purposes

During Reading

Identifying Words
Using context clues (semantic and syntactic), reading to the end of the sentence to see what makes sense, using graphophonics (applying knowledge of letter-sound relationships), looking for familiar word parts, skipping the word if not needed for meaning

Identifying Main Ideas

Narrative: finding the story line

Expository: locating the most important information, using format clues (headings and subheadings, italicized words), observing pedagogical features (overviews, introductions, objectives), distinguishing between relevant and irrelevant information, generating topic sentences for paragraphs or sections

Making Inferences
Interpreting, concluding, reasoning, constructing meaning, applying prior knowledge and experience, making sense, observing signal words (for example, *because, however, but*), visualizing (making mental pictures)

Monitoring
Clarifying, knowing when text is making sense, knowing strategies for correcting problems, anticipating and overcoming difficulties, fixing-up, rereading (backtracking), skimming ahead, self-questioning, evaluating, modifying predictions and making new ones, knowing when and how to seek help from outside sources, paraphrasing, focusing thinking, visualizing, adjusting rate, seeing relationships (for example, cause-effect, comparison-contrast), thinking aloud

After Reading

Summarizing
Identifying important parts, finding main ideas, identifying essential information, distinguishing between relevant and irrelevant information, paraphrasing, retelling

Reflecting
Making sense of what was read, reviewing predictions, meeting purposes, assimilating new information into schemata, assessing the significance of the material, looking back for clarification, making connections to life outside school

Recalling
Reading aloud to oneself or writing down important points, paraphrasing main ideas, relating to prior knowledge, remembering important points

𝓕IGURE 7.7   **Modeling Strategies for *Alaska's Three Bears***

Word or Phrase	Think-Aloud	Strategy
Alaska's Three Bears	I wonder if this will be another version of the Goldilocks story.	Predict. Use prior knowledge.
Once upon a time	I guess I'm right. It starts like other folktales.	Confirm prediction.
A big white bear called a polar bear, a grizzly bear, a black bear	Uh-oh. Now it sounds like a factual story. I wonder if it's about three real kinds of bears that live in Alaska.	Modify prediction in light of new evidence.
Great land known as Alaska	Not sure if Alaska is another country or a state. It must be a cold place if polar bears live there.	Seek help from outside source. Make inference about Alaska's climate.
Wilderness	That's a long word. I'll try breaking it apart. *Wild-er-ness.* That doesn't sound right. I'll try something else—*wil-der-ness.* That makes sense.	Use structural analysis. Abandon strategy that doesn't work. Try again.
Respect the bear	I wonder what *respect* means here. It's not the same as showing respect to other people. Maybe I'll read on and see if I can figure it out.	Monitor to make sense. Read on to see if new information helps.
Because	That's a signal word that tells why. It will help me know what *respect* means.	Use signal words as clues to meaning.
Wild nature, strength, intelligence	I think *respect* must mean "don't interfere with" here. The bears are to be respected because of their wild nature, strength, and intelligence.	Make inference, draw conclusion, construct meaning.
Keen sense of smell	I don't know what *keen* is. I'll read ahead to see if it explains what it is. It says they can also see and hear well, so I guess it means good.	Monitor to make sense. Clarify. Read on.
Hibernate	Not sure what this word is. Oh, I see. The next part says *or sleep all winter,* so that's what hibernate is.	Use context clues.

$\mathscr{F}$IGURE 7.8 **Five Comprehension Strategies**

1. ***Making predictions:*** Readers predict from the book's cover illustration, from the title and sometimes the author (if familiar), by flipping through the pages to view graphics or read headings, and by activating prior knowledge about the subject. Such activities cause anticipation, an eagerness to see if predictions are correct (a purpose for reading), and thus increased focus, which results in better comprehension. Readers may need to modify or adjust their predictions during reading if unexpected events occur.

2. ***Observing relationships:*** Once readers get the literal information that is directly stated in the text, they should go beyond that and become aware of relationships. Some types of relationships are cause-effect (reasons for global warming [causes] and the expected results [effects]), time order or sequence (a chronological record of events), comparison-contrast (similarities and differences between the white shark and the hammer-head shark), and problem-solution (identifying the problem in a story and the way(s) it was resolved).

3. ***Drawing inferences:*** Authors are unable to tell every detail, so they expect readers to fill in the gaps by "reading between the lines." Readers rely on prior experiences and their imaginations to make inferences. Young children get many clues from illustrations, but older readers find most clues in words or phrases that help them draw conclusions and gain insight into the author's meaning.

4. ***Reading critically:*** When students read critically, they evaluate the text in terms of its timeliness, accuracy, and appropriateness (Burns, Roe, & Ross, 1999a). They should judge the reliability of the source by considering the credentials of the author, the copyright date, and the adequacy of the material for their purposes. They must learn to distinguish fact from opinion, recognize propaganda, and make informed decisions about such issues as which product to buy and what movie to attend.

5. ***Summarizing:*** By summarizing what they have read, students improve their overall comprehension of text (Duke & Pearson, 2002). A somewhat difficult task that requires instruction and practice, summarizing consists of sifting through information, deleting what is unnecessary or redundant, selecting the most important ideas, and arranging them in a coherent form.

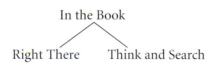

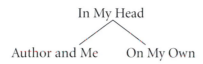

A further explanation of these question types, along with examples of questions based on the previous text about Alaska's bears, follows.

The answers to *Right There* questions are directly stated in the text. Example: What is a big white bear called? (Answer: polar bear.)

The answers to *Think and Search* questions must be put together from the information in different parts of the text. Example: What do bears do in different seasons? (Answer: wander across Alaska in the spring and hibernate in the winter.)

The answers to *Author and Me* questions are not given in the text. Readers use their background knowledge and what the author says to find the answer. Example: What do polar bears do in the winter? (Possible answer: The text says that grizzly bears and black bears hibernate, but doesn't mention polar bears. I might infer that polar bears do not hibernate, possibly because they can tolerate the cold winter weather.)

The answers to *On My Own* questions come from the reader's head without the need to read the selection. Example: What else do I know about bears? (Answer: anything that I can recall about bears from my experience, visits to the zoo, books, or sources other than the current text.)

DIRECTED READING-THINKING ACTIVITY (DR-TA)

The **Directed Reading-Thinking Activity** (DR-TA), developed by Stauffer (1975), has wide application to basal reader stories, trade books, and expository materials. Its purpose is to encourage children to think about their reading by having them make predictions, confirm or reject them as they read, and revise their predictions as the story or information unfolds. Readers make predictions by putting together their background knowledge and information in the text. By doing so, they are setting purposes for reading because they are looking to see if their predictions are correct. In a DR-TA lesson, you might follow the procedure shown in Minilesson 7.4 to help children make predictions. Each child should have a copy of the book.

SEMANTIC MAPPING

Semantic mapping is a graphic display of words organized by meaningful relationships. You can provide instruction in

Students contribute words from their knowledge and experiences as the teacher creates a semantic map.

Minilesson 7.4

Directed Reading-Thinking Activity

- Ask students to open their books to a new story and talk about the picture, title, and author. Ask: What do you think this story will be about? Why do you think that? Encourage children to discuss their predictions and to tell why they think as they do.
- Let the children start reading, but identify a point where they should stop reading and consider the predictions they made. Ask: Are you satisfied with your predictions so far, or would you like to change something? Who can read me the part that verifies your prediction? Who can make a further prediction now that you have more information? How many of you agree with this prediction?
- Continue with this procedure until the children finish the selection. Ask: Did this story turn out according to your predictions? What clues did you have about how the story might end? How did the author lead you to make your predictions?

What are the students learning?

The children are learning to anticipate what they will be reading and to set purposes for comprehending. They focus on the meaning of the words to see if their predictions are correct, and they find that sometimes they must change their predictions if the selection changes direction. They are learning to be alert, flexible, responsive readers who know how to adapt to changes in the text.

Teaching Tip

To make sure students understand how to read semantic maps, let them work in small groups, with partners, or individually to construct their own maps.

creating semantic maps by modeling them on the board, chart paper, or transparencies. Young children can help you construct maps by dictating words for you to record. The children suggest the placement of these words into appropriate categories, which then become the main ideas for the supporting details that surround each category.

Anita Odle's second-graders created a semantic map from their theme study on polar bears. As the children gave ideas about what they had learned, Anita recorded them on chart paper (see Figure 7.9).

Fluency

Most of us enjoy listening to fluent readers who read easily, naturally, with appropriate expression, and without making errors. Richards (2000, p. 534) defines **fluency** as the "ability to project the natural pitch, stress, and juncture of the spoken word

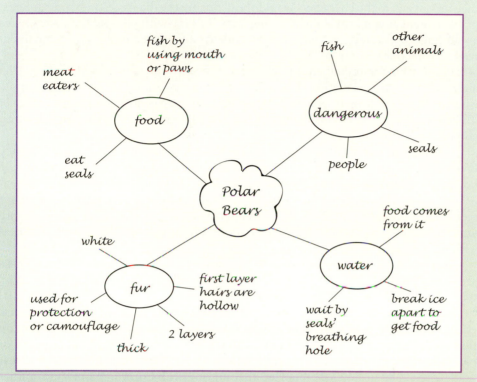

FIGURE 7.9 Semantic Map of Thematic Unit on Polar Bears

Source: Anita Odle's second grade, Jere Whitson School, Cookeville, TN. Used with permission.

on written text, automatically and at a natural rate." Along with rate, accuracy, and automaticity, Worthy and Broaddus (2001/2002) suggest that phrasing, smoothness, and expressiveness are also part of fluency. Fluency, they continue, gives language its rhythm and flow and makes reading seem effortless.

Once believed to be simply a matter of calling words efficiently, researchers now believe that fluency is closely tied to comprehension (Samuels, 2002). Fluency requires readers to identify words quickly and easily and to be able to make inferences automatically when the text omits information. When the reader can decode and make inferences without effort, the reader is free to focus on comprehending the material.

Fluent reading is difficult, particularly for the beginning reader, because it requires the coordination of many of the components of the reading process, including word recognition, word meaning, phrasing into grammatical units, generating inferences, and applying background knowledge (Samuels, 2002). By increasing the amount of time children actually spend reading, they improve their word recognition, ease of reading, speed, and comprehension. Sustained Silent Reading (SSR), which allows children to read self-selected materials, is one method for letting children spend time reading materials of interest to them. (See Chapter 2 for more about SSR.)

Fluency develops over time through modeling, instruction, and guided and independent practice with a variety of reading materials (Worthy & Broaddus, 2001/2002). You can model fluency simply by reading aloud to children, with expression. They learn to appreciate fluency when they hear you modulate your voice to match the mood of the story, speak as the characters would speak during the dialogue, or express interest or excitement as you read about amazing facts. Talking with you and their classmates about how good readers sound can help students know what to do to become fluent readers (Martinez, Roser, & Strecker, 1998/1999).

Performing for an audience is a powerful incentive for fluent oral reading. The audience may simply be other classmates, or it could be more extensive, for example, when a choral reading or Readers Theatre performance is done for parents or other invited guests. In Classroom Vignette 7.1, a first-grader models fluent reading for an audience of kindergartners.

Selection of materials plays an important role in guiding readers toward fluency. Predictable texts with rhyming patterns, cumulative episodes, or repeated refrains help beginning readers feel the rhythm of language. Books should be at students' recreational or independent levels, so that they can focus on fluency instead of struggling with word recognition (Samuels, 2002). For children to read with expression, appropriate rate, and proper phrasing, books should be written in natural language patterns and deal with familiar and interesting topics.

Teachers have tried various ways to help students achieve fluency. Some of these are presented in Figure 7.10 (Martinez, Roser, & Strecker, 1998/1999; Richards, 2000; Worthy & Broaddus, 2001/2002).

Researchers have found that many of the procedures for promoting fluency are effective for improving reading in general. The National Reading Panel (2000) found that guided repeated oral reading procedures, when supported by teachers, peers, or parents, had a positive effect on word recognition, comprehension, and fluency across grade levels. Samuels (2002) reported that findings from over one hundred studies show that the practice of repeated readings produces improvement in reading speed, word recognition, and oral reading expression on passages that students have practiced. Being able to read fluently builds a sense of accomplishment and confidence for students who are often embarrassed by their poor reading skills. In a classroom where Readers Theatre was used to improve fluency, the teacher found that it helped students'

Classroom Vignette 7.1

Diana enters first grade eager to read and learns to recognize words quickly. She listens to her teacher read expressively, and soon she is reading stories fluently to her classmates. Diana becomes deeply involved with the characters and story situations, so she reads with feeling. One day, near the end of the year, her first-grade teacher lets her select a favorite story, practice reading it to the class, and return to her former kindergarten class where she reads aloud to the children there.

What's happening here?

Diana is modeling fluent reading for her classmates. By doing this, she is showing them how they, too, can be fluent readers. She is gaining confidence in her ability to read aloud. The kindergartners not only enjoy the story, but also are able to see what they may be able to do when they reach first grade. Her example provides motivation for them to learn to read.

$\mathcal{F}$IGURE 7.10   **Methods for Promoting Fluency**

Method	Procedure
Modeling	Implicit modeling occurs when a fluent reader reads aloud. With explicit modeling, students follow the print as an expert reads, and they either repeat the text or read along with the expert reader.
Repeated readings	Students read and reread a text many times. The teacher may provide direct instruction with practice, allow students to practice independently, or let students read along with a tape of the book.
Paired oral readings	Each student reads the same passage silently. Then the students take turns reading the passage three times orally in succession to partners, who give suggestions and positive feedback.
Oral recitation lesson	The teacher selects a text, models fluent oral reading, and discusses a comprehension strategy. Students practice reading the text as a group and individually. They then read a portion of the text for an audience as a performance.
Choral reading	Poetry is often used for choral reading. It can be read in unison, one line per child, cumulatively, or in groups.
Readers Theatre	Students practice reading aloud expressively from a script and then perform for an audience.

Applications for English Language Learners

Repeated readings, particularly of predictable books, help ELLs learn new vocabulary. Big books or enlarged texts enable you to direct children's attention to certain text features as books are read and reread (Searfoss, Readence, & Mallette, 2001). After hearing the story you read, the children may listen to the story on tape and follow along, and then take the books or tapes home for additional rereadings (Strickland, Ganske, & Monroe, 2002).

expressiveness and comprehension because they were experiencing the thoughts and feelings of the characters (Martinez, Roser, & Strecker, 1998/1999).

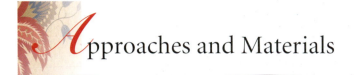

Approaches and Materials

ALTHOUGH DOZENS of sets of reading materials and approaches to reading instruction exist, we consider just a few of the major approaches. We begin with the language experience approach because it integrates the language arts and is a natural transition for children who are beginning to learn to read. The basal reader approach and guided reading are next because of their widespread use. We conclude with literature-based programs that use the rich language of literature as a basis for reading instruction. Many teachers prefer an eclectic approach, which combines desirable elements from a variety of approaches.

Language Experience Approach

The **language experience approach** (LEA) to reading is based on children's own language patterns and personal experiences. By dictating experiences in their own words, children are using familiar vocabulary and sentence structures. They are also using story content that is interesting and meaningful. Many beginning readers find it easier to read their own dialect than Standard English and easier to read about their own experiences than to read about something for which they have little or no prior knowledge.

The LEA is a bridge from oral language to written language. Children speak and listen to one another as they discuss an experience, and then watch you record their dictation and read it back. Through this language cycle, children become aware that writing is recorded thought and that reading is converting printed symbols into meaning. Allen (1999, p. 41) explains the rationale for the LEA in the following words.

What I can think about, I can talk about.

What I can say, I can write (or someone can write for me).

What I can write, I can read.

I can read what others write for me to read.

The procedures for teachers to follow in writing experience charts are as follows.

1. Provide a stimulus or activity, such as a field trip, a resource person, a science experiment, a cooking activity, or an unusual object.

2. Discuss the stimulus or activity in detail.

3. Ask the students to dictate sentences about the stimulus as you record their exact words, usually on a large, lined chart tablet or on a computer with a projection device.

4. Read the chart to the students, asking them to read it with you if they are able.

5. Allow the students to edit the chart for accuracy of information, flow, and grammatical correctness. You may ask questions to focus their attention on possible areas for revision.

6. Teach reading concepts and skills based on the chart.

Minilesson 7.5 shows the procedure for implementing the LEA.

For beginning readers, this approach offers many opportunities to learn about reading and writing. They see that writing occurs from left to right and top to bottom, that words have spaces between them, that titles are names for the stories, that many words that begin with the same letter also begin with the same sound, and that they can already recognize some of the words in their stories.

Emergent readers easily recall many of the words on a chart because of their involvement in creating the story. You can write the words that each child recognizes by sight on cards to make individual sets of cards called *word banks*. Children can use their word bank cards with word sorts of sight words, categorizing the words according to naming or action words and finding words that begin or end alike. In an open word sort, children categorize the cards any way they choose; in a closed word sort, you direct the activity, focusing on a skill such as

Teaching Tip

Put sets of cards for the children in sealable plastic sandwich bags. Ask the children to write their initials on the back of each of their cards in case the cards become mixed up. Let the children keep their word banks with their other school supplies, or keep them yourself and pass them out when you are ready to work with them.

Applications for English Language Learners

The LEA's emphasis on shared oral language provides a strong base for successful literacy development for ELLs of any age, and teachers have used this approach successfully for many years (Mohr, 1999). Second language acquisition theory appears to corroborate the basic principles of the LEA, such as the integration of the language arts, the social nature of language learning, and the value of authentic communication. Integrating language experience activities within a thematic framework, rather than teaching isolated skills, is effective for providing meaningful interactions in English for ELLs (Mohr, 1999).

Duling (1999) implemented a variation of the LEA by applying technology for a class of ELLs. Using a theme on immigration, she asked her students to interview their parents or other relatives about immigration experiences and then report in writing to the class. Students then created a slide show by using Broderbund's Kid Pix software (1992) with voice overlay. Duling found that their spoken English fluency improved noticeably in a very brief time.

Minilesson 7.5

Language Experience Approach

Step 1: *Stimulus*. Bring a turtle to school and let the children observe it.

Step 2: *Discussion*. Lead the children in a discussion about their observations of the turtle, encouraging them to comment on its appearance and behavior.

Step 3: *Story dictation*. Ask the children to make sentences about the turtle while you write them on a chart. They dictate a story, such as the one in Figure 7.11.

Step 4: *Story reading*. Ask the children to listen while you read the story to them, and then ask them to read it with you. Have them find and read individual words and sentences from the chart. Ask them to find words they already know and help them discover that each sentence begins with a capital letter and ends with a period.

FIGURE 7.11   **Our Turtle Story**

Our Turtle

Our turtle has sharp toenails. It has a long neck. Sometimes turtles snap at you. Our turtle likes to crawl and creep around. He carries his house on his back.

arranging words in alphabetical order (Gillett, 1999). Students can also make sentences with their word bank words.

Although the LEA is often used for providing early reading experiences for an entire class of children, it can be used in other ways as well. You can use the approach with groups of children and with individual students. You can extend the LEA into upper grades, as long as it continues to focus on the students' experiences and ways of using language. It works well for writing about direct experiences with content area concepts.

Teachers have found natural computer applications for the LEA. You can enter stories dictated by the children and modify the text as the children embellish or modify

Step 5: *Follow-up lesson.* Run your hand or a pointer under the first sentence and ask the children if they can find two words that begin with the same letter. They find *turtle* and *toenails*. Write these words on cards and tell them that the first letter in each word is *t*. Then ask the children to say these words and think about the sound they hear at the beginning of each word. Ask if the sounds are alike or different, and see if they can think of other words that begin with the same sound. As they think of other words, write these words on cards also, asking the children to observe the beginning letter of each new word. Then ask the children what they can tell you about the sound that the letter *t* makes at the beginning of many words.

You could have selected other skills to teach from this story, but it is important to choose a skill at the children's developmental level. Other possibilities for skill development from this story include the following.

Consonant blends (*crawl, creep, snap*)

Compound words (*toenails, sometimes*)

Short *a* (sn*a*p, *a*t, h*a*s)

r-controlled vowels (t*ur*tle, sh*ar*p)

ou diphthong (ar*ou*nd, h*ou*se)

What are the students learning?

They are learning that their experiences and observations are valued. They see that writing represents speech and that they can read what you have written. They learn basic concepts about print, such as directionality (top to bottom and left to right) and spacing between words. They also learn skills that are needed to read the text, so they can see why it is important to know these skills. They can also practice reading the words that you printed on cards until they become sight words.

Technology

the stories. The class can view the composition of the story on a projection screen or large monitor. By using the printer to make copies, you can provide the children with individual copies of their stories.

Curriculum developers and literacy scholars have found the LEA to be an important and viable approach to reading instruction at all levels (Padak & Rasinski, 1999). A major drawback to its use today, however, is that it lacks the sequence, structure, and correlation with standardized tests that many school systems are seeking through commercial programs (Hall, 1999). Instead, the LEA offers flexibility, responsiveness to students' developmental needs, and relevance to their language and experiences—conditions that may be more important for learning language in the long run.

Applications

for Students with Special Needs

Children with special needs benefit from the LEA because the written material is within their experiences and appropriate for their comprehension abilities. It offers a viable way to enhance the literacy competencies and communication abilities of students with special needs (Robertson, 1999), and it allows you a wide range of choices for adapting instruction to individual learners (Hall, 1999). Figure 7.12 shows an experience story written by a group of Title I students who were given the opportunity to write and read about a meaningful topic.

Basal Reader Approach

The **basal reader approach** is a structured, teacher-directed approach that involves having students read selections from a series of graded readers and learn sequences of skills. In recent years, basal readers have included greater diversity among characters, wider representation of genres, and more good literature, such as award-winning children's books or excerpts from chapter books, than in the past. Books are colorful and attractively illustrated, and the inclusion of more multiethnic characters and settings widens their appeal.

Publishers offer a wide array of materials in basal reader packages. These include readers or literature anthologies for the students, teachers' manuals, practice books, kits, black-line masters, transparencies, trade books, big books, assessment materials,

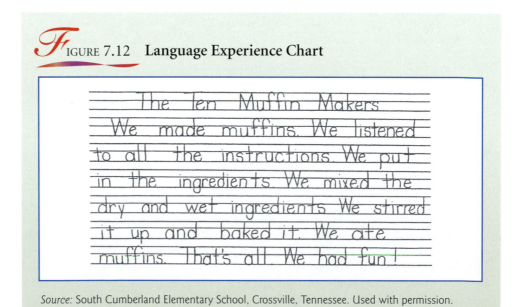

*F*IGURE 7.12 **Language Experience Chart**

The Ten Muffin Makers
We made muffins. We listened to all the instructions. We put in the ingredients. We mixed the dry and wet ingredients. We stirred it up and baked it. We ate muffins. That's all. We had fun!

Source: South Cumberland Elementary School, Crossville, Tennessee. Used with permission.

and multimedia. The teacher's manual is particularly helpful, especially for beginning teachers, because it provides detailed information on ways to introduce the selection, questions to ask, follow-up activities, skills and strategies to develop, suggestions for related trade books, ways to integrate with other language arts, and assessment materials. The readers, manual, and workbooks or skill sheets are generally considered core components, and supplementary materials are added according to the needs of the students and the budget of the school system.

The focus of the basal reader approach is more likely to be on reading skills than on the interrelationships of the language arts, even though many lessons include listening, oral expression, and writing. The **Directed Reading Activity** (DRA), a lesson plan for using the basal reader, usually follows a sequence of five steps.

1. You introduce children to the story by presenting new vocabulary, relating the selection to their experiences, and providing a purpose or purposes for reading.

2. Children first read silently, either the entire selection or a reasonable part of it, seeking the answers to the purpose questions.

3. After they have read the selection silently, there is no point in having them take turns rereading all of it orally. Instead, they should read selected portions orally to answer specific questions, such as those in Figure 7.13. Such questions engage children in thoughtful, reflective, analytic interpretation of the selection. (Note: Questions need to be adapted to specific texts.)

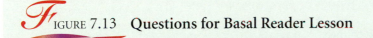

FIGURE 7.13   **Questions for Basal Reader Lesson**

 1. Who can read us the part that gives the answer to our purpose question?

 2. What part led you to confirm or reject our prediction?

 3. Who can find the part that tells (how, when, where, what, or why) something happened?

 4. What paragraph helped you figure out how this story might end?

 5. Find a sentence that tells us something about how the main character feels.

 6. Did any part surprise you? Who can read that part for us?

 7. This author uses good descriptive words. Read a sentence with a descriptive word or phrase and tell us how it made you feel.

 8. What new information did you learn? Read us the part that is new to you.

 9. Why do you think the author said . . . ?

4. You review or teach a strategy, and the children practice the strategy in their practice books or on skill sheets. (In some series, this step occurs before the reading of the story.)

5. During the final phase of a typical basal reader lesson, children participate in a variety of follow-up activities, such as creative drama, writing, artwork, and additional related reading.

An option for silent and oral reading is partner reading, which can operate in different ways (Cunningham & Allington, 1999). One possibility is for children to take turns reading the pages, with one partner supporting the other as needed. Another procedure is for partners to read silently, one page at a time, and then ask each other questions about the page before continuing. A third method requires children to mark interesting, confusing, or important parts with sticky notes for later discussion. You monitor the children as they work together, and each child becomes an active reader. Figure 7.14 shows variations for involving students in reading and responding to basal reader lessons.

When presenting a new basal reader selection to ELLs or students with special needs, let them listen to an audiotape of the story first. They can familiarize them-

FIGURE 7.14 Reading and Responding during Basal Reader Lessons

- Reading with partners

- Sharing answers to purpose-setting questions

- Periodically making predictions, and then revising them in light of new evidence

- Dramatizing by reading a script as found in the basal reader

- Seeking and jotting down difficult or confusing words or concepts for later discussion

- Explaining strategies used to help comprehend difficult or confusing parts

- Taking turns being the teacher and leading the discussion

- Using reciprocal teaching by taking turns with the teacher while predicting, questioning, clarifying, and summarizing

- Completing graphic organizers, such as story frameworks and character maps (explained in Chapter 2)

- Using echo reading (following the teacher's expressive voice to develop fluency)

- Using selective oral reading, such as reading aloud the funniest, scariest, or most exciting parts

Applications *for English Language Learners and Students with Special Needs*

Partner, or buddy, reading is particularly helpful for students who want to contribute their ideas but may not have the language skills to do so. When ELLs or struggling readers partner with proficient English speakers, they are supported in their efforts and encouraged to develop their abilities (Bromley, 1999). Bilingual students can act as translators and as cultural mediators when paired with ELLs (Au, 2002). Also, a proficient reader can read a book to the ELL and then let the ELL try to translate the book into his first language. This student could then read the translated story independently and compare it to the book written in English.

selves with the characters, the basic content, and vocabulary before attempting to read it for themselves.

Although publishers of basal readers often claim that their programs are complete, no single commercial program can meet the reading levels, special needs, or interests of all students. Many teachers use the basal reader as the core of their reading instruction, but they often add supplemental activities and materials, particularly trade books, to round out their programs.

Guided Reading

With **guided reading,** you show children how to read and offer them support as they read. You help each reader develop effective strategies for processing texts at increasing levels of difficulty (Fountas & Pinnell, 1996).

Guided reading can be used with basal readers, children's literature, decodable texts, informational articles, or textbooks (Villaume & Brabham, 2001), but it is intended to be used with **leveled texts**, those that have been evaluated as to level of difficulty (Fountas & Pinnell, 1996). Rog and Burton (2001/2002) use vocabulary, size and layout of print, predictability, illustration support, and complexity of concepts as criteria for leveling books. In many cases, however, teachers lack a sufficient number of leveled texts, so they use whatever books are available to match the children's reading levels as closely as they can. Most teachers have multiple copies of graded basal readers, so basals are a viable option, even though selections within the basals vary as to difficulty (Fawson & Reutzel, 2000). Also, children like to choose their own books and will often stretch their capabilities to read books that interest them.

The goal of guided reading is to help children use reading strategies effectively to become independent readers (Fawson & Reutzel, 2000; Fountas & Pinnell, 1996). The practice is flexible, provides critical scaffolding and support, and addresses students' instructional needs. You match students with books appropriate for their levels and place them in small groups for instruction. Lessons progress through three steps (Fawson & Reutzel, 2000).

1. You introduce a story or a meaningful part of it by focusing on major concepts to be presented and help children build background information.

2. The children read aloud quietly or read silently while you observe each child's use of reading strategies and give support as indicated.

3. Children may participate in follow-up activities or use a strategy introduced during the reading.

Janet Ross followed these procedures when teaching a small group of second-graders who were reading at a high first-grade level. Notice how in Minilesson 7.6 she lets the children read first from familiar, leveled books before introducing them to a new, unfamiliar text.

Small groups enable you to provide strategic coaching that is so important for guided reading instruction, but what should you do with the rest of the class while you are meeting with groups? Ford and Opitz (2002, pp. 714-716) suggest setting up learning centers where students can work individually or together on literacy activities. Six possible centers are summarized in Figure 7.15 (see page 274).

Guided reading instruction is similar to the Directed Reading Activity (DRA), but differs in some ways (Fawson & Reutzel, 2000). Instead of preparing students to

Minilesson 7.6

Guided Reading Lesson

Janet called the children together and let them read aloud at the same time from different, familiar leveled books that she had placed on the table. The children read softly while she did a running record (marked correct responses and miscues) on one of the children. When the child she was assessing finished reading, Janet went back over some of the words the child had missed, reminding her how to apply known strategies to decode the words. In this case, Janet focused on chunking by asking the child to look for familiar word parts such as *-tion* in *perfection* and *-ing* in *drifting*.

Janet then presented the children with multiple copies of a new, unfamiliar book. Together, they read the title and discussed what it meant, observed the author's and illustrator's names, and took a picture walk through the book. During the picture walk, Janet and the children covered the words and focused on what they thought was happening in the pictures. The children then read orally while Janet listened for any difficulties. When a child was uncertain about a word, Janet asked the child to "frame that word," which meant that the child should use both hands to enclose the word in order to focus on its parts. She kept a large pad and marker available for writing parts of particularly difficult words, with the expectation that children might recognize the parts and be able to combine them into meaningful words. She helped children with ambiguous sounds by telling them when a vowel said its name or reminding them that *c* could make different sounds, and sometimes the children helped each other. After the children finished the story, Janet discussed it with them, talking about the surprise ending and clarifying word meanings. Children next read with partners, alternating pages.

read a specific selection as in DRA, guided reading helps students develop strategies for using multiple cueing systems in order to become fluent, independent readers. In the guided reading procedure, teachers offer support throughout the lesson on ways to integrate effective reading strategies.

Literature-Based Approaches

Literature is an integral part of instructional programs. In addition to being a source of pleasure, it is often found in basal readers, adapted for Readers Theatre, and used to supplement content area studies. In this section, we show how literature can actually be the core of reading instruction by investigating three literature-based programs: literature circles, thematic units, and reading workshop.

Teaching Tip

When introducing a story to beginning readers, take them on a *picture walk* by having them look at the illustrations and comment on them together (Cunningham & Allington, 1999).

This lesson concluded with having each child identify and print "your hardest word" on a white board three times. Children said the letters as they wrote them, underlined their words, and pronounced them. They looked for these words in their books and then read them again from the white board. They spelled their words without looking, and Janet playfully planted the words in their brains by clapping her hands on both sides of each child's head. Janet explained that this had been a rather challenging book, so they would be working with it again tomorrow.

What are the students learning?

The children are learning to apply various strategies in the context of the story they are reading, as they need to use them. They are focusing on a particular skill, that of "chunking," as their teacher calls their attention to word parts. They are becoming aware of such book features as title, author, and illustrator, and they are learning to make predictions about the story as they preview it by taking a picture walk. They are learning to focus on a particular word and its parts by framing the word, and they are using relevant phonics skills as their teacher reminds them. Through discussion, they are clarifying their understanding of some vocabulary words, and they are using different ways to remember difficult words (writing the words three times, saying the letters, underlining the words, pronouncing them, and finding the words again in their books).

FIGURE 7.15 Learning Centers during Guided Reading

Listening post: The listening post consists of a recorded story with multiple copies of the text so that children can warm up prior to the lesson, review after it, or extend beyond the lesson.

Readers Theatre: Readers Theatre encourages children to build fluency and oral performance skills. The center has a practice space, multiple copies of a script, guidelines for practicing, and perhaps a few masks or puppets.

Writing: This center supplies students with a variety of writing tools and resources. Students have opportunities to generate their own text or respond to a text while using their knowledge of writing conventions.

Responding through art: One art center could contain varieties of pasta and sheets of colored construction paper for children to design projects. They could label pictures, add talking bubbles, and write descriptive sentences.

Reading: Creative reading centers invite children to select books, find comfortable spots, and read individually or with a buddy or a coach.

Poems/story packs: These packs of words, phrases, or sentences are created from former large-group practice situations and placed in transparent envelopes. Students use them for reconstructing the original text or for various classifying and sorting activities.

LITERATURE CIRCLES

Literature circles are groups formed for the purpose of reading and discussing the same books or books that share an author, genre, or theme (Harris & Hodges, 1995; Spiegel, 1998). They are sometimes referred to as *grand conversations* (Peterson & Eeds, 1990), *literature conversations* (Routman, 2000), or *literature response groups* (Spiegel, 1998). Good book discussion groups motivate readers to think deeply about the texts that they have read and to respond both individually and collaboratively.

Book selection is an important consideration for literature circles. Good choices provoke thinking and reflection, cause readers to examine their values and beliefs, and allow them to contemplate views that may differ from their own. Selections should deal with strong themes, such as survival, multicultural issues, moral choices, death, and dysfunctional families. Readers need sufficient background knowledge to understand the text and relate to it in some way, and books should be at levels that enable most students to read them successfully. Figure 2.15 in Chapter 2 gives a list of thought-provoking books suitable for readers at various levels, and Figure 7.16 is an annotated list of additional recommended books for literature circles.

Literature circles should be flexible and adaptable for different class situations, so their management and operation may differ. Groups are of mixed ability levels, usually consist of four to six students, and meet for about 20 minutes. Students often assume

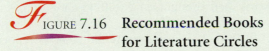 

FIGURE 7.16 **Recommended Books for Literature Circles**

Babbitt, N. *Tuck Everlasting*. Winnie Foster discovers the Tuck family, whose members have drunk from a magic spring that gives them eternal life.

George, J. *Julie of the Wolves*. Miyax, an Alaskan Eskimo girl, runs away from home and becomes lost, but she survives when a pack of Arctic wolves adopt her.

L'Engle, M. *A Wrinkle in Time*. This science fiction selection is a search through time and space for Meg's missing father.

Lowry, L. *The Giver*. Jonas is charged with the responsibility of handing down the rules and regulations of a controlled society.

Lowry, L. *Number the Stars*. Brave Annemarie helps save her Jewish friends from the Nazis during their occupation of Denmark.

Naylor, P. *Shiloh*. Marty faces a moral dilemma when he tries to save an abused dog.

O'Dell, S. *Island of the Blue Dolphins*. Karana, an Indian girl, survives the hardships of living alone for eighteen years on an island off the coast of California.

Park, L. *A Single Shard*. Thirteen-year-old Tree-ear living in medieval Korea overcomes many obstacles to deliver a single shard of his master's pottery.

Paterson, K. *Bridge to Terabithia*. Despite their differences, Jess and Leslie bond and create the magical kingdom of Terabithia, and then tragedy strikes.

Paterson, K. *The Great Gilly Hopkins*. A gutsy child rejects the kindness of her foster family while seeking her birth mother.

Paulsen, G. *Hatchet*. Brian's plane crashes in Canada and leaves him as the sole survivor in a wilderness.

Peck, R. *A Year Down Yonder*. A young girl encounters a different environment and lifestyle when she stays with her feisty grandmother.

Sachar, L. *Holes*. Unjustly accused, Stanley Yelnats is sent to a reform school where he must dig holes in the hard, sunbaked earth.

Spinelli, J. *Maniac Magee*. Maniac performs superhuman feats and makes friends in the black East End and the white West End of town.

Spinelli, J. *Wringer*. A young boy challenges a town tradition by refusing to be a part of violence.

Taylor, M. *Roll of Thunder, Hear My Cry*. Living in Mississippi during the Depression, the Logans struggle to save their land and their independence.

Voigt, C. *Dicey's Song*. Abandoned by their mother, the four Tillerman children went to live with their grandmother. Dicey watches over her younger siblings.

roles similar to those mentioned in Chapter 2 for student-led discussion groups. Multiple copies (usually about four to six) of several books must be available. Generally, you give a short book talk about each available book, and children write their first and second choices on slips of paper. You then place children in groups according to their preferences. Students meet in literature circles for the first time to share their reasons for choosing a particular book, predict what will happen, and decide how far to read for the next time. After their first meeting, children should read the assigned

Teaching Tip

Ask children to place a sticky tab on the page of the book where it first "hooks" them. Let them share their results and tell why they chose that part.

pages before coming to group and be prepared to discuss their thoughts and feelings about it and to raise questions.

Instead of assigning conventional book reports, many teachers ask students to respond to literature in more meaningful and authentic ways. One way is the literature log, in which students record their responses as they read or immediately after reading the selected pages. Written responses help them recall their "wonderings" so that they won't forget when groups meet for discussion, and they are also helpful as springboards for discussions. In addition to writing in literature logs, readers may jot down thoughts on sticky notes that they attach to relevant pages, or map their ideas on large sheets of paper (Brabham & Villaume, 2000). Responses may refer to parts that were especially puzzling or intriguing, where they had trouble making meaning, or that contained ideas that caused them to stop and reflect (Peterson & Eeds, 1990). Here are some tips about conducting literature circles that worked for Trena Farmer, a fifth-grade teacher in Alaska, who introduced literature circles to her students.

- Give children one minute to come to group because otherwise they tend to dawdle.
- Guide children in dividing books into reasonable chunks for future meetings.
- Let children decide in the first two minutes how far to read, to avoid wasting time.
- At first, give children generic prompts to get them started with their logs, such as asking them to make predictions, describe the setting, identify a favorite character, find the problem, and critique the story.
- Ask children to enter the page number of each comment in case they need to refer to the source during the discussion.

Applications **for English Language Learners and Students with Special Needs**

Literature circles are effective for all types of learners, including ELLs, struggling readers, and those in special education classes (Wood & Dickinson, 2000). In a collaborative study of a bilingual first grade, teachers selected quality books that positively represented the children's cultures, as well as other cultures. They read each book to the class in both Spanish and English and gave the children time to think about the books so that they would be prepared to discuss them. Children began to feel comfortable sharing their thoughts and

experiences about books, so their second-grade teacher continued with literature circles. In second grade, children took their books home for parents to read to them several times in preparation for class discussions. Because book talk during literature circles was bilingual, children were learning language and how to use it to express their ideas (Martinez-Roldan & Lopez-Robertson, 1999/2000). Many trade books are available in both English and Spanish, and sometimes both languages are presented in the same book.

During literature circles students read from copies of the same book, record thoughts and responses in literature logs, and share ideas in groups.

Readers come together to talk about books in personal and thoughtful ways while gaining insights about reading, writing, and learning. Through literature circles, skillful readers make predictions, construct visual images, monitor their reading for making sense, argue with the author, solve word- and text-problems flexibly, and evaluate content and writing style (Brabham & Villaume, 2000). As they share their views and listen to the views of others, readers must be able to interpret, analyze, and search for evidence to support their positions (Peterson & Eeds, 1990). You should rotate from one group to another, observing and occasionally interjecting comments or questions, while students take the lead in conducting the conversations according to what interests them.

Although literature circles were originally designed for middle school students, they can be easily adapted for younger children. One scenario is for you to select a few books worthy of discussion, talk about each book, let children vote on their preferred books, and place children in groups according to their preferences. Read the chosen book to each group while children follow along as best they can in their own copies. They mark places that interest them with sticky notes and draw or write responses in preparation for the group discussion that is to follow. Another scenario begins the same way with you talking about the books and forming groups, but in this case you send books home for parents to read to and discuss with the children over the weekend. When the children return to school, they meet in groups and talk about their books with you. When you are with a group, other children may be reading independently or working at centers.

LITERATURE-BASED THEMATIC UNITS

A thematic unit, discussed more fully in Chapter 14, is a framework for integrating learning experiences and content across the curriculum over a period of time. When it is literature-based, it may focus on an author, a topic, a genre, an illustrator, or a book. **Literature-based thematic units** enable students to examine particular aspects of literature in depth, study them from different perspectives, and acquire insights and understandings not possible from single encounters with books and authors.

Topics can deal with almost any subject, such as oceans, space travel, communities, immigrants, patriotism, and reptiles. The topic should be worthy of study, and a sufficient number of books at appropriate levels should be available. Chapter 2 suggests using text sets that span several genres about given topics, and it also presents variations of "Little Red Riding Hood" as a text set for comparing and contrasting versions of the story.

A theme can be centered around a genre, or classification of literature. It might deal with informational books on various topics, or it might include biographies of famous people such as Abraham Lincoln, George Washington Carver, or Eleanor Roosevelt. The many versions of biographies about Abraham Lincoln present opportunities for readers to view him in different ways. Russell Freedman's *Lincoln: A Photobiography* reveals the human side of Lincoln, and the text is supported with photographs of authentic artifacts. Carl Sandburg tells about Lincoln's early years in *Abe Lincoln Grows Up*, and Cheryl Harness includes interesting details in her well-illustrated *Abe Lincoln Goes to Washington: 1837-1865*.

Other genres that could be the focus for a theme include historical fiction, folklore, modern fantasy, multiethnic literature, or poetry. If you were to choose poetry, you would probably need to select just one form, such as ballads or free verse, so that children would be able to investigate it thoroughly. Two popular contemporary poets are Jack Prelutsky (*A Pizza the Size of the Sun* and *The Random House Book of Poetry for Children*) and Shel Silverstein (*Where the Sidewalk Ends* and *A Light in the Attic*). Children relate well to both of these poets because they enjoy the humor and ridiculous situations. Related activities for developing the theme could include dramatizing or illustrating some of the poems, reading them as choral readings, and using them as models for children's own poetry creations.

Many children's authors and illustrators are worthy of study, particularly those who have produced a large number of quality books. Eric Carle is an example of an author-illustrator known for his science-oriented story text and his unique collage illustrations. As part of a thematic unit on Eric Carle, one first-grade class learned to make tissue paper paintings, cut shapes from them, glue the shapes onto sheets of paper to form illustrations, and create big books, which they displayed at a literature conference. Jan Brett is another author-illustrator respected for her clever stories and her beautifully detailed art found in both the central pictures and the borders of her pages. You can find information about Jan Brett at her website (http://www.janbrett.com), and she may even send you some posters, cards, and masks to use for an author-illustrator study. For upper grade students, some recommended authors for thematic units are Katherine Paterson, Lois Lowry, Richard Peck, Jerry Spinelli, Laurence Yep, Virginia Hamilton, Phyllis Reynolds Naylor, and Christopher Paul Curtis.

When a book is the focus of your thematic unit, you must choose carefully. Look for one that has a worthy theme (or themes), connects to different areas of the curriculum, is of high interest to the students, and offers opportunities for learning and discovery. An example is Yin's *Coolies*, illustrated by Chris Soentpiet. It is a picture book that tells the story of two brothers, Shek and Little Wong, who arrived in America in 1865 to help build a railroad across the West. Along with thousands of other Chinese laborers, they worked hard and encountered great hardships. This book gives insights into Chinese culture, a slice of U.S. history, the building of a great railroad, and the loyalty between two brothers who survived the experience.

Anna Faye Burgess chose Beverly Cleary's *Dear Mr. Henshaw* as the focus of her fourth-grade thematic unit. Drawing on episodes from the book, she was able to promote reading and writing, integrate vocabulary lessons, support critical thinking and reflection, and connect the curriculum. Children learned geography from the places Leigh Botts's father traveled in California and science from the migration of Monarch butterflies to a local park. They considered the career of a trucker (Leigh's father) and found out about foods through the catering service run by Leigh's mother. They did an author study of Beverly Cleary and constructed a Venn diagram to compare Leigh with his best friend. Based on Leigh's letters and diary entries, these fourth-graders learned

Writing

the format for business letters and wrote responses in their journals. In the story, Leigh was bothered by a number of things, so Mrs. Burgess asked the students to write what bothered them in their journals. Here are some excerpts from their entries.

- When I get a bad grade because I was in a hurry and not doing my best—David
- My mom and dad smoking because I know they might get lung cancer—Nathaniel
- When someone blames me for something I didn't do—Trey
- When my pet died and I felt empty in my heart—Josiah
- It bothers me that there are so many illegal drugs out there—Jeff
- When people break promises and I lose my trust in them—Sonia
- And the thing that bothers me most is what happened on September 11, 2001—Julie

READING WORKSHOP

Introduced by Atwell (1998), the **reading workshop** is a framework for organizing reading activities around children's book selections. It usually begins or ends with you reading aloud from excellent books that children might not choose or be able to read themselves (Cooper, 1997). During the reading of the book and the ensuing discussion, you and the students share your enthusiasm for reading good literature.

The actual reading workshop consists of four components: minilesson, status of the class, individualized reading, and group sharing (see Figure 7.17). The minilesson is brief and geared to the needs and reading levels of the children so that they can apply the lesson to their current reading. Minilesson 7.7 (see page 280) is a sample minilesson on identifying the problem and solution in stories (Ross, 1996).

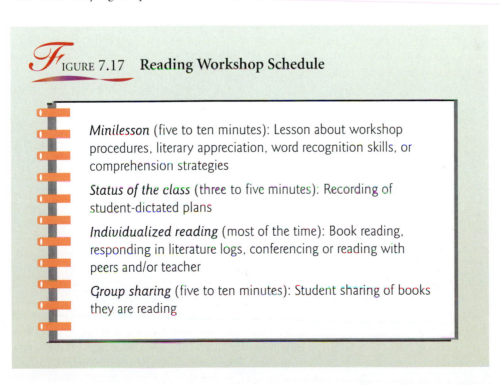

FIGURE 7.17   Reading Workshop Schedule

Minilesson (five to ten minutes): Lesson about workshop procedures, literary appreciation, word recognition skills, or comprehension strategies

Status of the class (three to five minutes): Recording of student-dictated plans

Individualized reading (most of the time): Book reading, responding in literature logs, conferencing or reading with peers and/or teacher

Group sharing (five to ten minutes): Student sharing of books they are reading

Minilesson 7.7

Minilesson for Reading Workshop

TEACHER: Do you remember that I read *Mirette on the High Wire* by Emily Arnold McCully to you earlier in the week? This story had a problem and a solution. Can someone tell me what the problem was?

DEREK: The high-wire walker lost his courage and was afraid to try again. I think his name was Bellini.

TEACHER: You're right. Who can tell me what helped him regain his courage?

JOSH: He saw Mirette walking on the high wire. He thought she had a lot of courage so maybe he could do it too.

TEACHER: You will find that many story structures have a problem and a solution. Can you think of other stories that have a problem and a solution? (The children hesitate and then tentatively begin thinking of possibilities.)

KENT: I'm thinking of *King Bidgood's in the Bathtub*. King Bidgood wouldn't get out of the tub. Then the Page pulled the plug to make him get out.

TEACHER: Very good. There certainly was a problem and a solution in that book!

CELIA: In *Sarah, Plain and Tall,* the father needed a mother for his children after their mother died.

TEACHER: That's the problem, all right. How did he solve it?

CELIA: He advertised for one and Sarah came.

TEACHER: We have three examples of stories that have problems and solutions. While you're reading today, I want you to look for problems and solutions in your books. See if you can find some other good examples.

What are the students learning?

The children are learning about the problem-solution feature that is common to many stories. After their teacher has pointed out this feature to them in one book, they are able to find other examples. This lesson will heighten their awareness of problem-solution structures in other books that they read.

During status of the class, you quickly call on students to say what they plan to do during their reading time and record what they say, usually in a two- or three-letter code such as SSR for Sustained Silent Reading, SB for select book, or LL for write responses in literature log. By stating their objectives, children set purposes for their

$\mathcal{F}$IGURE 7.18   **Guidelines for Reading Workshop**

1. Read books, not magazines, newspapers, or comic books.

2. Give a book serious consideration before abandoning it.

3. You can reread a book you love.

4. Keep records of books you finish or abandon and look for patterns about yourself as a reader.

5. Reading is thinking, so don't distract others.

6. Use a soft voice or whisper during conferences.

7. Reflect periodically on a book as you read it.

activities, and you have a record of what they are doing during each workshop session. The first two components take little time so that students can spend most of their time actually reading self-selected books. At the conclusion of the workshop, a brief time is allotted for students to share and comment on what they have read. For this minilesson, they might mention problems and solutions that they found while they were reading.

Operation of workshops differs according to grade level, students' interests and responses, and time available. The most important consideration is that children have time for reading and responding to books. Procedural minilessons are necessary in the beginning so that students learn how to select, locate, and check out books; understand how conferences are scheduled; know how to use logs or other types of responses; understand general rules and procedures; and know when they have opportunities to share. Atwell (1998) suggests following the guidelines shown in Figure 7.18.

Reflections

What are some ways that you could be sure that children are learning the skills and strategies they need in a literature-based reading program?

Classroom Assessment for Reading

Daily observation is probably the most effective assessment technique. Assessment tools include checklists, rubrics, performance sampling for portfolio inclusions, running records, and informal reading inventories. Basal reader series often include periodic assessments also.

Summary

Reading builds on listening and speaking and has a reciprocal relationship with writing. Balanced reading instruction is based on a view of what children need to know and learn about reading and the best ways to help a child become a proficient reader. It often includes a balance among literature-based skills, whole language, and phonics instruction. The Four Block approach offers one concept of a balanced program. Effective teachers are more important than materials, programs, or approaches in determining how well children learn to read.

Word identification techniques include sight word recognition, phonics, structural analysis, semantic and syntactic context clues, and dictionary skills. Children need a combination of these skills to decode words.

Comprehension is essentially reading with understanding. Schema theory says that readers draw on clusters of concepts acquired through their experiences to get meaning from text. Metacognition is the reader's ability to understand and control thought processes, and it can be taught through teacher modeling. Good readers use a variety of strategies to understand what they read, and they apply these strategies before, during, and after reading. Although there are dozens of strategies, the five that are emphasized here are making predictions, observing relationships, drawing inferences, reading critically, and summarizing. Instructional strategies, or integrated procedures that can be applied to strategic reading of texts, include reciprocal teaching, Question-Answer Relationships (QAR), the Directed Reading-Thinking Activity (DR-TA), and semantic mapping. Fluency, also related to comprehension, is the ability to read easily, naturally, with expression, and without errors.

You can use many approaches and sets of materials for reading instruction. The language experience approach uses a child's own language and experiences as the basis for constructing text. From the stories they create, children learn about concepts of print and acquire skills derived from these stories. The basal reader approach is widely used and consists of a specific set of materials, including a reader, materials for skills practice, and a manual. The five-step Directed Reading Activity (DRA) is a plan for using the basal reader. Guided reading is an approach that focuses on teaching small groups of children to apply strategies during their reading in order to become independent readers.

Three major literature-based approaches are discussed. Literature circles meet so that students can read and discuss the same books or books of a common author, genre, or theme. Children usually respond in literature logs. Literature-based thematic units integrate learning across the curriculum and focus on a topic, author, illustrator, genre, or book. The reading workshop is a framework for organizing reading activities and consists of a minilesson, a status-of-the-class report, reading and responding (most of the allotted time), and group sharing.

Discussion Questions

1. What is your concept of an effective reading teacher? How does an effective teacher help struggling readers and children with special needs?

2. As a first-grade teacher, how would you prepare children for reading a story? How would you introduce the story so that they would eagerly anticipate reading it?

3. How would you prepare sixth-graders for reading a story? Why would you use different approaches for different age groups?

4. What do you think is the most important thing you can do for young children who are beginning to read?

5. How can you entice middle school students to choose reading over television or computer games?

6. Why do children need a variety of word identification skills? Isn't phonics skill enough?

7. What components would you put into a balanced reading program?

8. Which literature-based reading program would you prefer to implement in your classroom? Why? What are its advantages?

9. How will you accommodate learners with special needs in your reading instruction?

10. Suppose your children speak nonstandard English and dictate sentences that are grammatically incorrect during a language experience lesson. According to LEA practice, the teacher should use the children's own language. How can you justify writing and reading sentences that do not conform to Standard English? Are there any alternatives?

Writing

Suggested Activities

1. Ask a student to read a paragraph in which some of the words may be difficult. When the child comes to an unknown word, find out what word identification strategies she uses to decode the word. Write a paragraph critiquing this child's ability to apply reading strategies to the selection.

2. Figure 7.15 describes learning centers where children can work independently while you are with a small group. What are some additional worthwhile activities that you could plan for children to do while you are busy elsewhere?

3. Make a semantic map with a group of children on a topic they are studying. If you are not working in a classroom, choose a topic and construct a map about it.

4. List your favorite books from elementary school. Which would you like to read to your class? Why?

5. Choose a story from a basal reader or from a trade book that involves concepts or settings that may be unfamiliar to the children. Develop plans for relating children's prior experiences to these unfamiliar concepts or settings so that they can read with understanding.

Writing

6. Do a language experience lesson with a group of children. Provide the experience, discuss it, ask them to dictate sentences, write them on a chart, read them back, and plan a follow-up activity.

7. With two or three other students, brainstorm ideas for obtaining books to establish a classroom library. Record your ideas and put them in your portfolio.

8. Review an article from a professional journal on reading comprehension strategies. Write a summary of it and record your personal reactions.

9. Interview a teacher from your school system to find out what reading approaches teachers are using. Learn as much as you can about how teachers integrate the language arts with reading and how they use literature in their reading programs.

10. Outline or make a semantic map of a literature-based thematic unit that focuses on a genre, topic, author, illustrator, or book.

11. Choose a topic you are likely to teach. Create a text set for this topic of at least ten books that represent different genres. List the books with their bibliographic information and brief annotations.

*R*eferences

ALLEN, R. V. (1999). Using language experiences in beginning reading: How a language experience program works. In O. Nelson & W. Linek (Eds.), *Practical classroom applications of language experience* (pp. 41–47). Boston: Allyn & Bacon.

ALLINGTON, R. (2002). What I've learned about effective reading instruction. *Phi Delta Kappan, 83,* 740–747.

ALLINGTON, R., & BAKER, K. (1999). Best practices in literacy instruction for children with special needs. In L. Gambrell, L. M. Morrow, S. Neuman, & M. Pressley (Eds.), *Best practices in literacy instruction* (pp. 292–310). New York: Guilford.

ANDERSON, R., & PEARSON, P. D. (1984). A schema-theoretic view of basic processes in reading comprehension. In P. D. Pearson (Ed.), *Handbook of reading research* (pp. 255–291). New York: Longman.

ATWELL, N. (1998). *In the middle* (2nd ed.). Portsmouth, NH: Heinemann.

AU, K. (2002). Multicultural factors and the effective instruction of students of diverse backgrounds. In A. Farstrup & S. J. Samuels (Eds.), *What research has to say about reading instruction* (3rd ed., pp. 392–413). Newark, DE: International Reading Association.

BAUMANN, J., HOOTEN, H., & WHITE, P. (1999). Teaching comprehension through literature: A teacher-research project to develop fifth graders' reading strategies and motivation. *The Reading Teacher, 53,* 38–51.

BLOCK, C., OAKAR, M., & HURT, N. (2002). The expertise of literacy teachers: A continuum from preschool to grade 5. *Reading Research Quarterly, 37,* 178–206.

BLUESTEIN, N. A. (2002). Comprehension through characterization: Enabling readers to make personal connections with literature. *The Reading Teacher, 55,* 431–434.

BRABHAM, E., & VILLAUME, S. (2000). Continuing conversations about literature circles. *The Reading Teacher, 54,* 278–280.

BROMLEY, K. (1999). Key components of sound writing instruction. In L. Gambrell, L. M. Morrow, S. Neuman, & M. Pressley (Eds.), *Best practices in literacy instruction* (pp. 152–174). New York: Guilford.

BURNS, P. C., ROE, B. D., & ROSS, E. P. (1999a). *Teaching reading in today's elementary schools* (7th ed.). Boston: Houghton Mifflin.

BURNS, P. C., ROE, B. D., & ROSS, E. P. (1999b). *Word recognition and meaning vocabulary.* Boston: Houghton Mifflin.

CAMBOURNE, B. (2002). Holistic, integrated approaches to reading and language arts instruction: The constructivist framework of an instructional theory. In A. Farstrup & S. J. Samuels (Eds.), *What research has to say about reading instruction* (3rd ed., pp. 25–47). Newark, DE: International Reading Association.

COOPER, J. D. (1997). *Literacy: Helping children construct meaning* (3rd ed.). Boston: Houghton Mifflin.

CUNNINGHAM, P., & ALLINGTON, R. (1999). *Classrooms that work* (2nd ed.). New York: Longman.

CUNNINGHAM, P., HALL, D., & SIGMON, C. (1999). *The teacher's guide to the Four Blocks.* Greensboro, NC: Carson-Dellosa.

CUNNINGHAM, P., MOORE, S., CUNNINGHAM, J., & MOORE, D. (2000). *Reading and writing in elementary classrooms* (4th ed.). New York: Longman.

DAHL, K., & SCHARER, P. (2000). Phonics teaching and learning in whole language classrooms: New evidence from research. *The Reading Teacher, 53,* 584–594.

DOWHOWER, S. (1999). Supporting a strategic stance in the classroom: A comprehension framework for helping teachers help students to be strategic. *The Reading Teacher, 52,* 672–683.

DUFFY, G., & HOFFMAN, J. (1999). In pursuit of an illusion: The flawed search for a perfect method. *The Reading Teacher, 53,* 10–16.

DUKE, N., & PEARSON, P. D. (2002). Effective practices for developing reading comprehension. In A. Farstrup & S. J. Samuels (Eds.), *What research has to say about reading instruction* (3rd ed., pp. 205–242). Newark, DE: International Reading Association.

DULING, V. (1999). Literacy development of second language learners with technology and LEA. In O. Nelson & W. Linek (Eds.), *Practical classroom applications of language experience* (pp. 248–256). Boston: Allyn & Bacon.

FAWSON, P., & REUTZEL, D. R. (2000). But I only have a basal: Implementing guided reading in the early grades. *The Reading Teacher, 54,* 84–97.

FIELDING, L. (1998/1999). Making balanced use of cues when reading. *The Reading Teacher, 52,* 392–393.

FITZGERALD, J. (1999). What is this thing called "balance"? *The Reading Teacher, 53,* 100–107.

FORD, M., & OPITZ, M. (2002). Using centers to engage children during guided reading times: Intensifying learning experiences away from the teacher. *The Reading Teacher, 55,* 710–717.

FOUNTAS, I. C., & PINNELL, G. S. (1996). *Guided reading: Good first teaching for all children.* Portsmouth, NH: Heinemann.

GILLETT, J. (1999). Sorting: A word study alternative. In O. Nelson & W. Linek (Eds.), *Practical classroom applications of language experience* (pp. 156–160). Boston: Allyn & Bacon.

HALL, M. (1999). Focus on language experience learning and teaching. In O. Nelson & W. Linek (Eds.), *Practical classroom applications of language experience* (pp. 12–18). Boston: Allyn & Bacon.

HARRIS, T. L., & HODGES, R. E., (EDS.). (1995). *The literacy dictionary.* Newark, DE: International Reading Association.

HEADLEY, K., & DUNSTON, P. (2000). Teachers' choices books and comprehension strategies as transaction tools. *The Reading Teacher, 54,* 260–268.

INTERNATIONAL READING ASSOCIATION. (2002). Excellent reading teachers. *The Reading Teacher, 54,* 235–240.

JOHNSTON, F. (1999). The timing and teaching of word families. *The Reading Teacher, 53,* 64–75.

JUEL, C., & MINDEN-CUPP, C. (1999/2000). One down and 80,000 to go: Word recognition instruction in the primary grades. *The Reading Teacher, 53,* 332–334.

KANE, S. (1999). Teaching decoding strategies without destroying story. *The Reading Teacher, 52,* 770–772.

MARTINEZ, M., ROSER, N., & STRECKER, S. (1998/1999). "I never thought I could be a star": A Readers Theatre ticket to fluency. *The Reading Teacher, 52,* 326–334.

MARTINEZ-ROLDAN, C., & LOPEZ-ROBERTSON, J. (1999/2000). Initiating literature circles in a first-grade bilingual classroom. *The Reading Teacher, 53,* 270–281.

MILLER, H. (2001/2002). Teaching and learning about cultural diversity. *The Reading Teacher, 55,* 346–347.

MOHR, K. (1999). Variations on a theme: Using thematically framed language experience activities for English as a Second Language (ESL). In O. Nelson & W. Linek (Eds.), *Practical classroom applications of language experience* (pp. 237–247). Boston: Allyn & Bacon.

MOUSTAFA, M., & MALDONADO-COLON, E. (1999). Whole-to-parts phonics instruction: Building on what children know to help them know more. *The Reading Teacher, 52,* 448–458.

NATIONAL READING PANEL (2000). *Teaching children to read: An evidence-based assessment of the scientific research literature on reading and its implications for reading instruction.* National Institute of Health Pub. No. 00–4769. Washington, DC: National Institute of Child Health and Human Development.

OSTER, L. (2001). Using the think-aloud for reading instruction. *The Reading Teacher, 55,* 64–69.

PADAK, N. & RASINSKI, T. (1999). The language experience approach: A framework for learning. In O. Nelson & W.

Linek (Eds.), *Practical classroom applications of language experience* (pp. 1–11). Boston: Allyn & Bacon.

PALINCSAR, A. S., & BROWN, A. L. (1984). Reciprocal teaching of comprehension fostering and monitoring activities. *Cognition and Instruction, 1,* 117–175.

PETERSON, R., & EEDS, M. (1990). *Grand conversations: Literature groups in action.* New York: Scholastic.

PRESSLEY, M. (2002). Metacognition and self-regulated comprehension. In A. Farstrup & S. J. Samuels (Eds.), *What research has to say about reading instruction* (3rd ed., pp. 291–309). Newark, DE: International Reading Association.

RAPHAEL, T. E. (1982). Question-answering strategies for children. *The Reading Teacher, 36,* 186–190.

RAPHAEL, T. E. (1986). Teaching question-answer relationships, revisited. *The Reading Teacher, 39,* 516–522.

REUTZEL, D. R. (1998/1999). On balanced reading. *The Reading Teacher, 52,* 322–324.

RICHARDS, M. (2000). Be a good detective: Solve the case of oral reading fluency. *The Reading Teacher, 53,* 534–539.

ROBERTSON, H. (1999). LEA and students with special needs. In O. Nelson & W. Linek (Eds.), *Practical classroom applications of language experience* (pp. 221–223). Boston: Allyn & Bacon.

ROG, L., & BURTON, W. (2001/2002). Matching texts and readers: Leveling early reading materials for assessment and instruction. *The Reading Teacher, 55,* 348–356.

ROSS, E. (1996). *The workshop approach: A framework for literacy.* Norwood, MA: Christopher-Gordon.

ROSS, E. (1999). Teaching strategic reading. *Journal of Reading Education, 24,* 20–25.

ROUTMAN, R. (2000). *Conversations.* Portsmouth, NH: Heinemann.

RUDDELL, R. (2002). *Teaching children to read and write* (3rd ed.). Boston: Allyn & Bacon.

SAMUELS, S. J. (2002). Reading fluency: Its development and assessment. In A. Farstrup & S. J. Samuels (Eds.), *What research has to say about reading instruction* (3rd ed., pp. 166–183). Newark, DE: International Reading Association.

SEARFOSS, L., READENCE, J., & MALLETTE, M. (2001). *Helping children learn to read* (4th ed.). Boston: Allyn & Bacon.

SPIEGEL, D. (1998). Silver bullets, babies, and bath water: Literature response groups in a balanced literacy program. *The Reading Teacher, 52,* 114–124.

STAUFFER, R. (1975). *Directing the reading-thinking process.* New York: Harper & Row.

STRICKLAND, D., GANSKE, K., & MONROE, J. (2002). *Supporting struggling readers.* Portland, ME: Stenhouse; Newark, DE: International Reading Association.

TAYLOR, B., PEARSON, P. D., CLARK, K., & WALPOLE, S. (1999). Effective schools/accomplished teachers. *The Reading Teacher, 53,* 156–159.

TAYLOR, B., PETERSON, D., PEARSON, P. D., & RODRIGUEZ, M. (2002). Looking inside classrooms: Reflecting on the "how" as well as the "what" in effective reading instruction. *The Reading Teacher, 56,* 270–279.

VILLAUME, S., & BRABHAM, E. (2001). Guided reading: Who is in the driver's seat? *The Reading Teacher, 55,* 260–263.

VILLAUME, S., & BRABHAM, E. (2003). Phonics instruction: Beyond the debate. *The Reading Teacher, 56,* 478–482.

WILHELM, J. (2001). *Improving comprehension with think-aloud strategies.* New York: Scholastic.

WOOD, K., & DICKINSON, T. (Eds.). (2000). *Promoting literacy in grades 4–9.* Boston: Allyn & Bacon.

WORTHY, J., & BROADDUS, K. (2001/2002). Fluency beyond the primary grades: From group performance to silent, independent reading. *The Reading Teacher, 55,* 334–343.

Books for Children and Adolescents Cited in This Chapter

BABBITT, N. (1975). *Tuck everlasting.* New York: Farrar Straus & Giroux.

CLEARY, B. (1983). *Dear Mr. Henshaw.* New York: Morrow.

DEEDY, C. (2000). *The yellow star.* Atlanta: Peachtree.

FREEDMAN, R. (1987). *Lincoln: A photobiography.* New York: Clarion.

GEORGE, J. (1972). *Julie of the wolves.* New York: Harper & Row.

GILL, S. (1990). *Alaska's three bears.* Homer, AK: Paws IV.

HARNESS, C. (1997). *Abe Lincoln goes to Washington: 1837–1865.* Washington, DC: National Geographic.

L'ENGLE, M. (1962). *A wrinkle in time.* New York: Farrar Straus & Giroux.

LOWRY, L. (1993). *The giver.* Boston: Houghton Mifflin.

LOWRY, L. (1989). *Number the stars.* Boston: Houghton Mifflin.

MACLACHLAN, P. (1985). *Sarah, plain and tall.* New York: Harper & Row.

McCULLY, E. (1992). *Mirette on the high wire.* New York: Putnam.

NAYLOR, P. (1991). *Shiloh.* New York: Atheneum.

O'DELL, S. (1960). *Island of the blue dolphins.* Boston: Houghton Mifflin.

PARK, L. (2001). *A single shard.* New York: Clarion.

PATERSON, K. (1977). *Bridge to Terabithia.* New York: HarperCollins.

PATERSON, K. (1978). *The great Gilly Hopkins.* New York: HarperCollins.

PAULSEN, G. (1987). *Hatchet.* New York: Bradbury.

PECK, R. (2000). *A year down yonder.* New York: Scholastic.

PRELUTSKY, J. (1996). *A pizza the size of the sun.* New York: Greenwillow.

PRELUTSKY, J. (1983). *The Random House book of poetry for children.* New York: Random House.

SACHAR, L. (1998). *Holes.* New York: Farrar Straus & Giroux.

SANDBURG, C. (1954). *Abe Lincoln grows up.* San Diego: Harcourt Brace Jovanovich.

SILVERSTEIN, S. (1981). *A light in the attic.* New York: Harper & Row.

SILVERSTEIN, S. (1974). *Where the sidewalk ends.* New York: Harper & Row.

SPINELLI, J. (1990). *Maniac Magee.* New York: Scholastic.

SPINELLI, J. (1997). *Wringer.* New York: HarperCollins.

TAYLOR, M. (1976). *Roll of thunder, hear my cry.* New York: Dial.

VOIGT, C. (1982). *Dicey's song.* New York: Atheneum.

WOOD, A. (1985). *King Bidgood's in the bathtub.* San Diego: Harcourt Brace Jovanovich.

YIN. (2001). *Coolies.* New York: Philomel.

DEVELOPING WRITING PROFICIENCY

LEARNER OBJECTIVES

At the conclusion of this chapter

YOU SHOULD BE ABLE TO

1. Discuss instructional focuses for teaching the process of written composition.

2. Describe the stages in the writing process, and offer assistance to children during each stage of writing.

3. Describe a method of organization for writing instruction.

4. Describe general approaches to use with instruction in all kinds of writing.

5. Identify the following terms that are defined or explained in this chapter:

audience 314	functional writing 297	Sustained Spontaneous Writing (SSW) 332
Author's Chair 325	prewriting 309	voice 309
creative writing 297	publishing 325	word processing software 323
draft 315	revising 321	
editing 322		

NCTE/IRA Standards addressed in this chapter

STANDARD 4. Students adjust their use of spoken, written, and visual language (e.g., conventions, style, vocabulary) to communicate effectively with a variety of audiences and for different purposes.

STANDARD 5. Students employ a wide range of strategies as they write and use different writing process elements appropriately to communicate with different audiences for a variety of purposes.

STANDARD 6. Students apply knowledge of language structure, language conventions (e.g., spelling and punctuation), media techniques, figurative language, and genre to create, critique, and discuss print and non-print texts.

STANDARD 7. Students conduct research on issues and interests by generating ideas and questions, and by posing problems. They gather, evaluate, and synthesize data from a variety of sources (e.g., print and non-print texts, artifacts, people) to communicate their discoveries in ways that suit their purpose and audience.

Chapter 8 Organizer

Emphasis on Communication

Purposeful Assignments

Stimuli for Writing

Time for Writing

Encouragement of Risk-Taking in Writing

Successful Experiences

Exposure to Good Literature

Teacher Modeling

Focuses for Writing Instruction

Prewriting

Writing a Draft

Revising

Editing

Publishing and Sharing

The Stages of the Writing Process

*D*eveloping Writing Proficiency

Sustained Spontanous Writing

Use of Computers

General Approaches to Writing Instruction

Organizing for Instruction

STANDARD 11. Students participate as knowledgeable, reflective, creative, and critical members of a variety of literacy communities.

STANDARD 12. Students use spoken, written, and visual language to accomplish their own purposes (e.g., for learning, enjoyment, persuasion, and the exchange of information).

LANGUAGE INSTRUCTION in Mr. Drake's fourth-grade classroom is from 10:00 A.M. to 10:45 A.M. This time period is intended for work on all language skills except spelling, which has its own 15-minute block of time.

At 10:00 on this Monday morning, Mr. Drake announces to his class, "Today I want you to write a story about what you did over the weekend. Use cursive handwriting and remember to be careful with punctuation. Be neat."

"Should we tell everything that happened?" asks Jeff.

"Not necessarily," replies Mr. Drake.

"How long does it have to be?" asks Tina.

"At least two pages," Mr. Drake says.

"What if we didn't do anything?" Donavon complains.

"Everybody did something," Mr. Drake says. "Now get busy writing."

Some students start immediately. Others sit and stare at their blank papers. Donavon leans over and whispers to Chad, "Do you think I could tell about my dog chasing the skunk?"

Surveying the class, Mr. Drake says, "Some of you are not writing. You need to get started right away. Donavon, stop talking and do your work."

After he collects and reads the products of this class, Mr. Drake complains, "This is so discouraging. Nobody said anything interesting. Some of them just listed activities, one after the other. Not one of them picked an incident and developed it. And look at these simple sentences. We worked on compound and complex sentences last week. You would think they would use them."

What's happening here?

Mr. Drake gives an assignment that has little chance for success. He does nothing to activate the background information that the children have that could be applied to the assignment. He gives them no opportunity for thinking and rehearsal of ideas prior to writing, and he actively discourages attempts of the students to accomplish prewriting tasks. The idea of drafting a piece and then revising it does not appear to occur to him. His admonitions seem to be aimed toward a perfect first draft. Additionally, he gives no purpose for the writing and specifies no audience or format. There seems to be no reason to do it except for an exercise. The only audience is the teacher, who obviously is interested in neatly written, well-punctuated sentences—in cursive handwriting, of course.

Missing from this situation are prewriting activities, drafting with feedback opportunities, time for revision, and a means of publishing or sharing the work. There is little wonder that Mr. Drake receives sterile papers with minimal content.

Observers would also do well to question whether or not Mr. Drake gives preliminary instruction even in the mechanical aspects of writing that he emphasizes. Students do not automatically use correct punctuation or correct handwriting forms without direct attention in the classroom on how to do it.

Reflections

How could Mr. Drake have given this assignment purpose and a sense of audience for the work? What prewriting activities would have improved the quality of the products? Why is it not a good idea to expect a perfect first draft?

Written communication is vitally important in everyday life, yet many students today are unable to communicate clearly in writing. One possible reason is that the techniques used to teach them to write have not been effective. They may have been taught to form letters of the alphabet correctly (handwriting), use Standard English constructions (usage), and capitalize words and punctuate sentences correctly (written language conventions or mechanics). Still, they may not be able to compose a sensible story, letter, report, or other work. All of the instruction may have focused on the small components of writing that are most evident to a casual observer of a product. None of it may have focused on the *process* of composition, or how the product is developed. There seems to be an assumption that, if the students are proficient in mechanical aspects of writing, they will automatically be able to write coherent material. This is unfortunately untrue, as Mr. Drake in the opening classroom vignette discovers. Attention must be given to the

Classroom Vignette 8.1

Mr. Ryder's fourth-grade class, across the hall from Mr. Drake's class, is also scheduled to have language arts from 10:00 A.M. to 10:45 A.M. He also plans to have the students write stories in class. He told the students on Friday that he would be asking them to write about things that happened to them, their family members, or their friends this week. He suggested that they make notes about funny, exciting, interesting, or irritating things that happened over the weekend and that they choose one of these events to write about in class. He told them that they would read their stories to their classmates, so they should choose topics that would be of interest to their classmates.

On this Monday, Mr. Ryder asks his class, "Did all of you pick out topics to write about today?"

Most of the students reply, "Yes," but he sees several students shaking their heads, "No."

"Those of you who have chosen topics, please start by making a list of good descriptive words to use that will help us to see, hear, smell, taste, and feel the experiences that you had," Mr. Ryder says. As he says this, he lists the five senses on the board. "Using words that fit into these categories can make the experience more real for your readers. Remember the book we read last week, *In the Year of the Boar and Jackie Robinson*?"

There are nods all around the room. Mr. Ryder picks up the book from his desk, opens it to a marked page, and says, "When Shirley and her father went into the basement, Bette Bao Lord, the author, used sensory words to help you picture and feel what was happening. Remember these descriptions?" He looks down at the book and reads, "The door creaked open. Father disappeared into the darkness. . . . The walls were stone, dirty, and damp. The ceiling was cluttered with pipes that dripped, dripped, dripped and enough spider webs to keep Irvie content for a year."

Mr. Ryder looks up. "What sensory words did you hear?" he asks.

Tyler says, "*Creaked* and *dripped* helped us to hear the sounds."

Rachel says, "*Disappeared into the darkness* made me see what happened."

"So did *stone* and *dirty* and *cluttered with pipes* . . . and *spider webs*," Tracy says.

"*Stone* and *damp* both made me feel what it was like," Madison adds.

"Very good," Mr. Ryder says. "Those of you who have a story picked out, think about the stories you want to write and make lists of words that let your senses know what is happening. If you are trying to decide between two stories, make two lists and see which one will be more interesting to write. You can start writing the story when you have your list of descriptive words. Remember the parts of a story that we have been talking about, and be sure to include all of the parts in your story. The rest of you join me in the reading corner, and we will brainstorm some types of things that you may decide to write about."

As soon as the smaller group joins Mr. Ryder, Dewayne complains, "I didn't do anything this weekend."

"Everybody did something," Mr. Ryder says. "Did you eat anything? Did you see any of your friends? Did you have company?"

Dewayne grins. "My granddaddy came and gave me a pennywhistle. I about drove my family crazy."

"Do you see how you could make a story about that?" Mr. Ryder asks. "What are some good sensory words for your story?"

"*Screeched, yelled, played a tune*," he replies. "My playing *screeched*; Mom and Dad *yelled*; and Granddaddy *played a tune*."

"Did you have fun with the whistle?" Mr. Ryder asks.

"Yeah," Dewayne says.

"Then tell in your story how you had fun, and work in your sensory words. Go back to your seat and get started. Did that give anyone else an idea?"

"Yeah. I can tell about accidentally stepping on my brother's truck and having to give him one of mine," Sean says. "He *bawled, screamed,* and

(continued)

Classroom Vignette 8.1 *(continued)*

stomped. The *truck crunched when I stepped on it. Its top caved in, and it made a deep scratch on Mom's shiny, hardwood floor.* It hurt when Bobby *stomped* on my foot, and I *yelped.*"

"You are really on a roll. You can go back and write this down before you forget," Mr. Ryder says.

He helps two others find topics by questioning them, and three more think of their own topics as they listen. Twenty minutes pass before he rejoins the whole class.

Some students are writing diligently. Others are quietly conferring with one another about their stories. Mr. Ryder begins to circulate and confer briefly with students who seem to be having problems. Generally he asks them questions that help them to think through their blocks and begin to write again.

When the period for language ends, most of the students are either still writing first drafts or are making revisions in their drafts, based on the discussions they have held with peers or the teacher. "Put your work in your writing folders for now," Mr. Ryder tells them. "Tomorrow you can finish writing, and some of you will have time to share your work in the author's chair."

What's happening here?

Mr. Ryder had spent quite a bit of time in class previously, helping the students with writing techniques. He warned them ahead of time that he would be asking them to write about a personal experience, so that they could have some think-time. He told them who the audience for the stories would be and suggested categories of experiences that would work for the assignment. On the day that they begin writing, he provides a minilesson on use of sensory descriptive words, using literature. For students who still do not have a topic, he does some questioning to activate their background knowledge.

Mr. Ryder is accepting of the decisions of some students to confer with their classmates about their writing, as he had suggested that they do for earlier assignments, and he also offers his assistance as he circulates while they work.

Mr. Ryder realizes that the 45-minute period is not sufficient for writing and revising a story for most of the students. He assures them that he will provide additional time for them to finish the assignment in another class. He also lets them know how the work will be shared with their classmates.

Mr. Ryder includes prewriting activities, drafting with feedback opportunities, time for revision, and a means of publishing or sharing the work.

Reflections

How does Mr. Ryder's lesson in Classroom Vignette 8.1 differ from Mr. Drake's lesson in the chapter's opening classroom vignette? Have you ever experienced a lesson or lessons like either of these? If so, how effective was the instruction in engaging you actively in the writing activity?

organizational stage of prewriting, as well as to drafting the material, revising it, and sharing the finished product with a genuine audience.

In addition, students need to see a purpose for writing. Writing about the books they are reading, writing in the same genres as books they are reading, and writing related to thematic units in the classroom are ways to provide genuine purposes for writing. Thematic units allow the integration of writing instruction into the learning of concepts in various curricular areas, making the time expended on instruction more efficient. Purposes for writing can be both functional and creative.

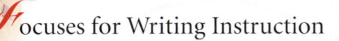ocuses for Writing Instruction

TEACHERS CAN develop a classroom environment that is conducive to writing instruction. Over the years, we have learned that effective instruction in written composition has eight focuses:

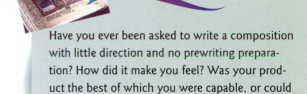

1. Emphasizing writing for communication

2. Making purposeful writing assignments

3. Providing children with stimuli for writing

4. Providing adequate time for writing on a daily basis

5. Encouraging risk taking in learning to write

6. Using writing activities that are likely to provide successful experiences

7. Exposing students to good literature as a part of the background development for writing

8. Modeling appropriate writing behavior for the students

Have you ever been asked to write a composition with little direction and no prewriting preparation? How did it make you feel? Was your product the best of which you were capable, or could it have been improved? How does this knowledge affect the way you intend to teach composition?

Emphasis on Communication

A basic purpose of writing is communication. The concept of communication assumes a sender and a receiver. Writers as senders seek to communicate with audiences who act as receivers of the communication. Writers must include sufficient information in their products to convey the desired information to their chosen audiences. Generally, written products are designed to transmit information from one person to another, but sometimes they are just for the use of the writers. For example, they may serve as the writers' memory prompts, or they may be produced simply to clarify the writers' thoughts for themselves.

Written communication sometimes incorporates symbols that are not words, but that convey meaning. In the *Family Circus* cartoon on page 296, Billy has modified his Olympics shirt to convey meaning through the use of a symbol with which he is familiar. He expects his audience to also understand the meaning of the symbol.

Sometimes writing is done simply for jogging the writer's memory.

"I was just trying to make my Olympics shirt look happier."

© Bill Keane, Inc. Reprinted with special permission of King Features Syndicate.

Purposeful Assignments

School writing assignments often tend to have little purpose other than skill building. By having students write for purposes that are important to them, you can help them understand the usefulness of the skills and see the communicative function of writing more clearly. Instead of writing "a paragraph that describes the way something looks," each student could write a paragraph describing the class's culminating experience for a thematic unit (a cultural food fair, for example) to a classmate who is in the hos-

Applications

for English Language Learners

ELLs may find it easier to write their material initially in their first language and then translate it into English with the help of a bilingual classmate, a classroom assistant, or a bilingual dictionary.

pital. Instead of writing "a paragraph that will persuade someone to do something," each student could write to his parents, guardians, or close friends to persuade them to attend a performance of a play for which the class members had written the script, based upon a book that they had read or on a historical event they had studied in a thematic unit. Instead of filling in workbook pages on sentence completion, students could write notes to their classmates about the book that they are reading or about a project related to a thematic unit. The classmates would then respond in writing. The need for clarity in such assignments is much more obvious than it is in many traditional writing assignments.

FUNCTIONAL AND CREATIVE WRITING

Sometimes writing instruction is separated into functional writing and creative writing. This is a somewhat false dichotomy, since most functional writing exhibits creativity in the manner of presentation and choice of terminology, and most creative writing serves some function, such as entertainment. **Functional writing** is also called practical writing, since it is writing that serves a practical purpose. Because it is often used to convey information of importance to others, correct form is given much attention in functional writing instruction. Some functional writing, however, such as the writing of a diary or journal, is personal in nature. **Creative writing** is sometimes referred to as *imaginative writing*. It is a very personal type of writing because it results from the desire to share inner feelings through a written product. In it, children express their own unique perceptions of their world and their experiences. Emotions and attitudes may be expressed in creative writing.

Opportunities for functional writing occur in every classroom every day. Such activities as journal writing, labeling, listing, filling out forms, keeping records and logs, writing explanations, making reports, and letter writing are examples of functional writing activities.

You can provide opportunities for creative writing by encouraging your students to use their imaginations to create stories or to use their originality in putting together reports. Some teachers view creative writing as a "frill," not realizing how much it contributes to the students' facility in communicating ideas to others in a clear, palatable manner.

Children of any age can do both creative and functional writing. Kindergarteners may begin by dictating to you, while you write or type the material for them, or the children may write for themselves, using invented spellings.

Stimuli for Writing

Students must be encouraged to produce writing that expresses their feelings, engages their imaginations, utilizes their thinking skills, and performs useful functions. Functional writing may be done for self-satisfaction, including clarification of the writer's own thoughts or feelings; sharing information with others; communicating with friends or for business purposes; or learning in the content areas.

Some children are internally motivated to write. Others need your assistance to become engaged in a topic. Stimuli for writing can take a variety of forms. You can provide assignments that stir the students' interest and imaginations. You can also help them to see how certain functional writing activities benefit them in both school and home settings. Some ideas appear in the following sections.

Give students the opportunity for choice in their writing whenever it is appropriate. However, do not allow students to avoid functional writing completely in favor of creative writing. After all, in real life people often have to write things that they would not choose to write in order to meet requirements of organizations or jobs. Some students who lack previous experience choosing topics and formats for creative writing may feel relieved to have several suggestions for focus when they begin the process, and some students need to be asked to try new forms of writing in class in order to expand their options. Many are initially hesitant to try a new form or a new technique, but, after trying it in a risk-free environment, they find that it is useful for their own purposes. This seems to be true of students at all levels—even in graduate school. Unfortunately, many high-stakes tests require students to write to restrictive prompts, without taking into consideration any aspects of individual students. The students are likely to fare better in such situations and be less stressed if they have had the opportunity to write to prompts in a less pressured classroom setting.

RELATING WRITING TO PERSONAL EXPERIENCES AND REAL EVENTS

Encourage students to write personal narratives or stories based on direct personal experiences. Ask them to relate experiences that they have had to concepts being studied in a thematic unit or to a book that the class has been reading. For example, when reading *Shiloh* by Phyllis Naylor, you might ask them, "Have you ever seen someone mistreat an animal? What kind of animal? What did the person do? How did it make you feel?" Then you might suggest that they write either a factual account of their personal experience or a creative story based on the situation that they knew firsthand.

Memoirs are one form of writing based on personal experience. Memoirs are memories from an author's life formed into a piece of narrative writing (Arnberg, 1999). Writers sift through past experiences and produce a cohesive storyline (Sluys, 2003).

Try providing experiences that can serve as the basis for writing. Have the children taste foods, follow recipes to prepare food, follow directions to make things, visit special places, and so on. The story in Figure 8.1 resulted when a teacher brought popcorn to school for the children to examine and eat. Although some of the children chose to describe the way the popcorn looked, tasted, smelled, felt, and sounded when they ate it, Amanda chose to take the viewpoint of the popcorn and tell a story about its experience. Notice that Amanda has word processed her story. Children are often very motivated to write on the computer, and their written products are easy to read compared to some of the handwritten products.

Applications *for English Language Learners and Struggling Learners*

ELLs and struggling learners benefit from teacher-provided experiences followed by group discussion before the writing takes place. Listing important words on the board and encouraging students to jot down key ideas and number them in sequence before they begin to write is helpful to these students.

Students can be encouraged to emphasize sensory aspects as they write about their experiences—for example, what they saw, heard, smelled, tasted, and felt during the experiences. Students may find this hard at first. Therefore, some lessons may focus on each single sense before all senses are combined. For example, for sight, the students could choose objects and describe them, including color, shape, size, and so on; for hearing, they could write about a bird's song, a dog's bark, the rustling of the wind in the trees, or a power mower's roar, describing the characteristics of the sound and telling its effect on them; for smell, they could describe a skunk's odor, a flower's aroma, or that of freshly baked bread; for taste, they might describe that of a lemon, a chocolate pie, or cough syrup; and for touch, they might describe a rock, an ironed sheet, an ice cube, or a velvet jacket. Encourage the use of similes in these descriptions: "The smell of _____ is like . . ." Using similes engages the mind in making comparisons, an important thinking skill.

Children do not live in vacuums. They know much about the events that are going on around them and the characteristics of their environments. This knowledge can and should be used in their writing. To use real events for motivation, you could have the children write a story about someone who has been in the news, including their opinions about the person; write a factual or fictional story about a festival or fair that is taking place or has taken place in your town; write a story about your school's football, baseball, or basketball team or a member of one of the teams; or write about the weather and what people can do in that type of weather.

Students can record experiences in different formats. They may write personal diaries or journals; record happenings, feelings, and thoughts over a period of weeks; or keep logs of observations related to a science experiment. They may write letters to friends or notes to classmates at school.

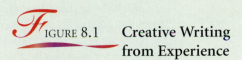

FIGURE 8.1   **Creative Writing from Experience**

```
Popcorn
Hi I am a little   corn .
Some one is picking me up!
I am swimming, I said
I am oily.
POP, I am jumping.
I look like fireworks.
There is snow .
I am not snow! I am not snow! I am
popcorn.
Popcorn, I am growing up.
Oh now some one is picking me up again.
They  are putting salt on me.
It feels good.
I am with a lot of popcorns.
I am big .
Some one is picking me up again.
Crunch crunch by by!
```

Source: Amanda Wyatt, Second Grade, Crossville Elementary School, Crossville, TN. Used with permission.

ENCOURAGING IMAGINATION

Anyone who has talked to young children knows that they are blessed with active imaginations. Some motivators may be designed particularly to tap active imaginations. You could give the students a list of unusual situations and let each child choose one and write a story about what she would do in that situation; for example, "What if a person gives you a million dollars?" "What if you are accidentally sent backward (or forward) in time?" "What would things be like if everybody told the truth all of the time?" "What would you do if you were a spy (or firefighter, or astronaut, and so on)?"

Another good imagination stretcher is displaying a group of common objects and having each child choose one and write about it as if it had a special property—for example, a window that provides a view into the future. Children could also use the displayed objects in another way. They could write about the objects' lives; for example, they could write about days in the lives of their pencils, desks, jackets, or other objects. They may tell what happens to the objects and how they feel. They may want to write in first person from the viewpoint of an object or in third person from their own viewpoints. They may decide to write conversations that two inanimate objects (for example, a cup and saucer) might hold, or conversations between inanimate objects and themselves. The children may also enjoy writing stories or poems about holidays from unusual viewpoints, such as a Thanksgiving story from the viewpoint of a turkey, or they might want to write conversations between two animals.

Children can be encouraged to think about what it would be like to have magic hands, feet, eyes, noses, or ears. They could consider what the magic would allow them to do and how it might help them or get them into trouble.

Children can also be asked to think of an invention that they would like to create. Then they can write about it as if it existed, telling what it does and how it affects their lives.

An enjoyable motivational activity is going outside and watching the clouds for about 15 minutes, looking for images of people, animals, or objects in them. Then the children can return to the classroom and write about the things they saw.

A particularly interesting focus for imaginative writing could be writing about current wishes or dreams. Brainstorming, either individually or collectively, could help activate ideas for this writing.

PROVIDING AUDIOVISUAL PROMPTS

Audiovisual prompts, such as pictures, recordings, videos, and unfinished stories, may activate background knowledge or imaginations to stimulate written endeavors.

SHOWING PICTURES You may show the students a picture and give them a list of questions, such as the following, to ponder: What caused this situation? What might happen next? Who are these people? What are these people thinking? What would you do in this situation?

The answers to the questions may be discussed by the whole class or by small groups, or the individual children may formulate their answers without sharing. The questions encourage the students to make inferences and predictions and to think about causes and effects. The discussion will also activate the children's background knowledge about the situation pictured. Then the children may be encouraged to write a poem or story, individually or cooperatively, about the picture or about a topic that the picture calls to mind. Once again, the children need to understand that there is no one way that the picture must be used in the story formulation. For example, if the picture shown is of a picnic, a child might wish to write about a picnic in which he participated or about the picnic actually shown in the picture. Either response would be acceptable. A similar activity could also be done using a series of related pictures.

PLAYING RECORDINGS You can play a recording of music without words for the children and encourage them to listen to the recording and picture what the music seems to be saying. Then they can write stories or poems about what the music said or descriptions of how the music made them feel. Classical music works particularly well for this purpose.

SHOWING VIDEOS You can show videos (particularly ones that have little or no dialogue) as a stimulus for discussion and subsequent writing. Even students who have trouble connecting ideas will be able to describe the actions in the videos.

PRESENTING UNFINISHED STORIES The children can listen to you read the beginning of a story, and then each of them can finish it in her own way. The part that is read should introduce the characters, set the scene, and begin the action.

RELATING WRITING TO LITERATURE

One of the best stimulators for writing is literature. Stories that have been read to or by the children act as springboards to their own creative products. You may wish to use some of the following motivators.

1. Write another episode to a story you have read. Base the story on the same characters and setting, but invent a new plot. For example, write another adventure for Maniac after reading Jerry Spinelli's *Maniac Magee*.

2. Write about why you would or wouldn't want a character from a story for your friend. For example, write about whether or not you would want James, Dicey's brother in Cynthia Voigt's *Dicey's Song,* for a friend and why you answered this way.

3. Write about what you would have done if you had faced the problem that the main character of a story faced. For example, write what you would have done if you had been Brian in *Hatchet* by Gary Paulsen.

4. Write a letter that one character in a story might have written to another character in that story or in another story. For example, write what Mary Alice from *A Year Down Yonder* by Richard Peck might have written to Dicey from *Dicey's Song* about her grandmother.

5. Write a diary for a character from a story, covering at least a week. Tell about the character's feelings and reactions to events.

6. Write a story from the point of view of an inanimate object or animal in a story you have read or heard. For example, write a story from the point of view of the school that the Herdmans attended in *The Best Christmas Pageant Ever* by Barbara Robinson.

7. Write a letter to one of the characters in a story, telling him or her how his or her actions make you feel or are affecting others in the story.

8. Write a story of the same type as one you have just read, for instance, a myth or a tall tale.

9. Write a patterned story with the same organizational pattern as a story you have just read or heard, for example, "The House That Jack Built." Judith Viorst's *Alexander and the Terrible, Horrible, No Good, Very Bad Day* has a pattern that children can discern and subject matter that sparks their imaginations.

Applications

for Struggling Learners

Struggling learners benefit from writing in a pattern that has been heard in a simple patterned book, such as Bill Martin, Jr.'s *Brown Bear, Brown Bear, What Do*

You See? The simplicity of the pattern takes some of the pressure for organization off of the children, and they can focus on writing a new story based on the pattern.

Some educators think that much use of patterned writing (writing that follows an organizational pattern of another story or other stories that the children have read or heard) may restrict students' thought processes and limit creativity. While this may be true when patterns are reduced to story frames to be filled in, Betty Roe did not find this to be true when she asked first-grade students to write a story together with the same pattern as the one in "The House That Jack Built," and second-grade students to write stories with the same pattern as the one in *Alexander and the Terrible, Horrible, No Good, Very Bad Day*. The children personalized their stories extensively, and their interest levels did not appear to be diminished when they worked on these stories. Sometimes patterned writing (and other assigned writing), rather than restricting children, challenges them to discover new things within their capabilities.

10. Write a story based on a poem or a poem based on a story.

11. Write a narrative for a wordless picture book.

CREATING NEEDS TO SHARE INFORMATION

Information may be shared with others in a variety of forms. You can make assignments that require the sharing of information to stimulate writing activities. Dialogue journals (journals in which you and a student or two students correspond with one another, alternating entries), labels, forms, explanations, and written reports are all ways in which children share information. The need to be exact and precise in order to communicate clearly the information to be shared provides motivation to learn these writing forms. You can impress upon the students that, if a form is not correctly filled out, you may not have enough information to let someone participate in a special event or sport. Similarly, you can tell them that, if a written report is not well worded, classmates may be confused, rather than enlightened, by it.

Bloem (2004) had her preservice teachers correspond with fifth-grade students in dialogue journals. She found these written exchanges to be tools for risk-taking and reflection on the part of the participants. The university students first read polished stories written by their fifth-grade correspondents. Then they began corresponding with their partners in journals that the fifth-grade partners had made. They shared personal information, discussed writing issues, recommended books to their partners, and discussed two polished papers that their partners had written. They even scored one of the papers with the classroom teacher's rubric. Each partner wrote seven letters over a period of eight weeks. The letters caused the fifth-graders to reflect on possible answers to questions that were raised. They also provided role models for the children's writing.

ENCOURAGING COMMUNICATION WITH FRIENDS

Children are highly motivated to communicate with their friends. They voluntarily write notes to each other about personal plans, likes and dislikes, and other matters, generally without your knowledge or approval. They readily can be led to see the advantages of being able to write good friendly letters to friends when they are on trips, when the friends are in the hospital, or when they or their friends move away.

ENCOURAGING COMMUNICATION FOR BUSINESS PURPOSES

Even children have times when a business letter is the appropriate written form. They may wish to write to someone in the government or in business to obtain information for a report in science, health, or social studies. They may wish to write to the editor of a newspaper about something that appeared in the paper or to an elected official about an issue that is important to them. You can lead students to understand that communications are taken more seriously if they are done in the correct form and are easily understandable.

SHOWING STUDENTS HOW TO WRITE TO LEARN IN THE CONTENT AREAS

Writing has always been done in content areas for the purposes of reporting, recording, and testing. It should also be used as a method to help students learn to think and learn the concepts of the subjects that they are studying. The nature of writing demands the application of such thinking skills as recall, organization, classification, generalization, and evaluation. Students should be led to realize how the use of techniques such as keeping learning logs (journals in which written responses to and questions and concerns about content area reading assignments are kept) can help them to learn the content area material more thoroughly, while helping them clarify their thoughts about the content. One sixth-grader wrote in his journal, "The German leader Adolf Hitler (who was a very evil person) believed that Jews should be killed. . . . He also believed that the perfect race had blue eyes and blond hair" (Young, 2004). He used his journal to state something that he had learned and gave a value judgment about the information. Journal entries like this one allow the teacher a glimpse of the thought processes of the student.

Writing before discussion when content has been presented through a demonstration, field trip, or other method is a valuable task. It activates the students' background knowledge about the topic. The students can share their writing with partners or in small-group dis-

Communicating with sick friends is a purposeful form of writing.

cussions, and later some students or representatives from each small group can share in a whole-class discussion. Misconceptions that some children have about the learning experiences can be cleared up as the writing samples are shared.

The students can produce creative writing that is based on characters presented in social studies class, inventions studied in science class, diseases studied in health class, and so on. You could let them write newspaper articles that might have appeared one hundred years ago or that might appear one hundred years from now; choose familiar characters from history and write about what they would do if they came back to life in the present time; write imaginary letters from one historical character to another; or write about the result if a television, tape player, or personal computer had been found back in 1800.

Chapter 12 on literacy in the content areas contains various suggestions for and descriptions of writing to learn. That chapter's Figure 12.26 presents a list of alternatives to traditional research reports that incorporates a number of genres for writing. In addition, there are many examples of children's writing to learn in the content areas, including the following: three examples of fourth-grade science journals that cover different types of information; a third-grader's K-W-L chart; an attribute map drawn by a fourth-grader; a pyramid organizer created by a class of first-graders; a semantic map created by a class of third-graders; a flow chart developed by a fourth-grader; a data chart developed by a sixth-grader; and a third-grader's flip booklet on polar bears.

Reflections

What are some other good stimuli for writing? Why is it important to offer stimuli for writing and then allow students to make choices about how they use the ideas that are activated?

Time for Writing

In a very real sense, children learn to write by writing. They do not develop much writing skill from lectures, grammar exercises, and workbook pages that isolate aspects of writing. For this reason, they need to write every day of the school year. This includes kindergarteners or first-graders who are attending their first day of school. They can use invented spellings and picture writing at first (see Chapter 4) and pretend to read

Teaching Tip

Start each school day with a period of time for students to write in their journals. You may wish to provide writing prompts for the entries or let the students choose their content freely. You may provide prompts for the use of students who don't have an idea of their own for a particular day. Possible prompts include: "The best book I have read this year (or month or week) is . . . . The most interesting thing I have learned in school this year (or month or week) is . . . . The biggest event in my life this year was . . . . The best trip that I have ever taken was . . . . When I grow up, I want to . . . ."

their material to you. You may want to transcribe it in standard form or just respond to the children orally about the content of the messages.

Daily writing may include many functional types of writing, such as writing in journals, brainstorming about a project, and making lists of things to do. Time that is provided for writing should include time for the children to think about what they want to write, to converse with you or other students about possible subjects, to draft the message, and to revise the message, if desired. Not all writing that children do will need to be polished into a draft suitable for others to read, but material that is to be read by others should be revised and edited for completeness, clarity, and quality of expression.

Encouragement of Risk-Taking in Writing

If students know that whatever they write will be graded on the basis of correct spelling, usage, and punctuation, they will be likely to write only those things that they are sure they can produce without error. This situation is unfortunate, because they are generally capable of composing ideas that are beyond their current levels of mechanical skill in writing. Allowing experimentation with spelling, sentence structure, and punctuation during the drafting process is likely to bring out some excellent ideas that would never have been expressed by students looking for mechanical perfection. Nonstandard forms (for example, grammatical errors, dialects other than Standard English, or slang) can be checked during the editing phase, if the child decides that the piece of writing under consideration is to be published for others to read. Otherwise, some of the forms may be discussed during a teacher-student conference about the writing. The student can be praised for correct generalizations about language use and questioned about reasons for other choices. You may find that there is logic behind these choices that you can praise also, even though you will want to show the child the way to express the idea in Standard English.

Successful Experiences

The statement that success breeds success is certainly true. Therefore, writing experiences that have a high likelihood of success should be used in the language arts curriculum. After children have a taste of success with their writing, they are more willing

Applications for English Language Learners and Struggling Learners

You may want to have ELLs and struggling learners begin their writing experiences with making lists and labeling objects and pictures. These activities are less demanding and are more likely to result in success for students who do not have facility with the language.

to apply themselves to subsequent writing tasks, because they have reason to believe that they can perform acceptably. The writing tasks will not engender fear if they are couched firmly in a context of success.

Exposure to Good Literature

To develop a good background for writing, you should expose your students to much good literature through telling and reading stories and informational selections to them. Hearing the structures of a variety of narrative and expository types familiarizes students with these structures, which they can then use in their own productions. (See Chapter 2 for an explanation of narrative and expository writing.) Hearing the sentence patterns used by skilled authors acquaints the students with patterns that they may seldom hear. Hearing the words chosen by these authors adds to the children's listening, speaking, reading, and writing vocabularies. Any activity that nurtures writing in so many ways should surely be a part of writing instruction that occurs daily.

Teaching Tip

Set aside a period every day to read high-quality literature to your students. Choose books that are useful models for sentence structure, vocabulary usage, and organization.

READING LIKE A WRITER

As children develop proficiency in reading, they can read some literature selections for themselves and thereby add to their background and their models for their own writing. Smith (1983) believes that people learn to be writers by learning to read like writers. They must see themselves as writers in order to analyze writing for techniques to use in their own stories. An analogy to this situation may help to clarify this idea. Suppose two people are sitting in the front row of a concert, watching a guitar player performing. One of these people plays the guitar at home for his personal pleasure. The other one

Applications

for English Language Learners

Lance Jasitt, a doctoral student at Tennessee Technological University, begins each tutoring session with his elementary-level Hispanic ELLs by reading aloud from a colorfully illustrated bilingual children's book. This legitimizes writing stories in their first language as well as in English. As an extension to experiences with the bilingual trade books, he has led bilingual language experience activities and creative writing activities with these students. The students dictate stories to him in Spanish, and then he and the students jointly translate the stories into English. See Classroom Vignette 8.2 for a description of this activity and its results.

Classroom Vignette 8.2

Lance Jasitt tutors elementary Hispanic ELLs. His middle Tennessee students have recently arrived in the United States from Mexico and Central America. Their primary language is a regional dialect of Spanish, and they have had limited academic experiences and have little reading or writing proficiency in any language. Lance routinely begins instructional sessions with reading aloud from a bilingual children's trade book.

The bilingual picture books are colorfully illustrated and reflect an appreciation for the cultural uniqueness of the region about which the story is written or of the community of which the main character is a member. The illustrations are captioned in both English and Spanish. Though initially surprised to hear children's stories read at school in their native language, Lance's students have been routinely delighted by these warm-up reading activities. Lance has used these shared book experiences to model reading aloud, emphasize letter-sound correspondences, make word-to-word connections,

emphasize concepts of print, and introduce story structures. These children are moving toward applying basic decoding and expressive strategies as they begin to read and write independently. Lance also has let the children borrow these books to take home and share with their families.

As an extension to their experiences with bilingual trade books, Lance introduced bilingual language experience approach (LEA) activities after a couple of months working with his students. Initially one-page stories are dictated by the students in Spanish and then jointly translated into English. These abbreviated stories frequently are associated with a story recently read in class or involve topics associated with popular culture. These single-page projects can evolve into mini-books created by the students. An example of one story that was developed is shown below.

Tutoring sessions with two young Guatemalan brothers incorporated the LEA and progressed to the development of an eight-page bilingual narrative

Un día en la selva un lion salió afuera del hospital. Se corrió porque no le gustaba el hospital. El lion fue feliz en la selva.

One day in the jungle a lion left the hospital He ran because he did not like the hospital. The lion was happy in the jungle.

Classroom Vignette 8.2 (continued)

entitled *The Boat Titanic (El Barco Titanic)* that was dictated in Spanish, jointly translated into English with the tutor's assistance, and wonderfully illustrated by the children. Copies were made for the students, and these were bound in notebooks, using sheet protectors to preserve the illustrations and text. Everyone involved in the project was proud of the final product, especially the child authors.

What's happening here?

Through the use of a student's primary language, many critical emergent literacy skills are reinforced.

Simultaneously, lessons are taught and respect for the children's culture is demonstrated. By lending the children these bilingual trade books to take home and by encouraging the students to share them and their LEA stories with their Spanish-speaking family members, Lance reinforces the critical home-school connection and gains family support for his tutoring program, helps the students improve their reading and writing skills, and helps these students build self-esteem.

Reflections

Consider the eight instructional focuses discussed in this section. How will you include each of these focuses in your writing instruction?

does not play the guitar and does not think he could ever learn. The first person watches the guitar player's fingers intently, attempting to pick up new chording and strumming techniques. The other person pays little attention to the fingers. Later on, the first person may pick up a guitar and attempt a strum that he saw the entertainer use. The other person would not even consider such an attempt.

Teacher Modeling

Teachers of writing should also model writing behaviors. During part of the time in the classroom when the students are writing, you should be writing. Seeing you model the writing process motivates students to write. You should go through prewriting activities and then construct a first draft, making use of conferences with students concerning the written piece. The draft should be revised and edited and shared with the class orally or in written form. When students see you going through the same steps that they are expected to follow to produce a workable piece of writing, they are more amenable to following this procedure. They begin to see that the revision process is not just something that teachers make students do, but something that all good writers use.

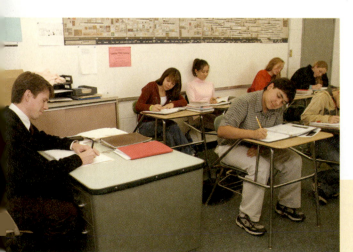

During part of the time when students are writing, the teacher should be writing to model good writing behaviors.

The Stages of the Writing Process

ALTHOUGH IT is possible to segment the writing process in a number of different ways, in this text it has been divided into five distinct, although overlapping and recursive, stages. These stages are prewriting, writing a draft, revising, editing, and publishing and sharing. The stages are recursive because students move back and forth among the stages as they develop a piece of writing, repeating activities that occurred in earlier stages in order to improve the piece by rethinking the material, gathering more data, reorganizing, and filling in gaps.

Underlying all of the stages of the writing process is writing with **voice.** Graves (1994, p. 81) points out, "Voice is the imprint of ourselves on our writing. . . . Voiceless writing is addressed 'to whom it may concern.'" When a person writes with voice, you can hear her speaking to you as you read. The writing is stronger and makes more impact.

One commercial language series that focuses on the process writing approach is *Write Source* (Great Source, 1997). It has *Write One* for first grade, *Write Away* for second grade, *Write on Track* for third grade, *Writers Express* for grades 4 and 5, and *Write Source 2000* for grades 6 through 8. As an example of the series, the third-grade materials, *Write on Track*, have three components: a student handbook, a program guide that is a teacher's planning resource, and a sourcebook for students for practice in editing and proofreading skills that are explained in the handbook. The student handbook contains guidelines for various forms of writing, student models, strategies for improving writing, publishing opportunities, and a proofreader's guide for help with mechanics, usage, and grammar. The stages of the writing process are emphasized; and many forms—personal writing, subject writing, research writing, story and play writing, and poetry writing—are presented. Other language arts are given attention in sections on the tools of learning, proofreading, and the student almanac. The teacher's program guide has suggestions for linking literature and writing activities, suggestions for student activities to go along with the student handbook, and guidelines for assessment, among the many planning tools. Other commercial programs have similar offerings. However, you can implement a process writing approach without the aid of a commercial program, if you desire.

An overview of the five stages in a process writing approach is presented in Figure 8.2 on page 310. Each stage is considered in turn.

Stage One: Prewriting

During the **prewriting** phase of the writing process, much thinking takes place. In this phase, students select and delimit a topic for their writing; rehearse ideas for organizing information; decide on the audience for the piece; and choose the organizational pattern, format, and point of view for the writing. They activate ideas about the topic from prior knowledge and collect information from new sources. Then they organize these ideas in some manner.

SELECTING AND DELIMITING A TOPIC

When children are initially learning the writing process, they should be allowed to choose their own topics for writing. Although there is a place for assigned topics in

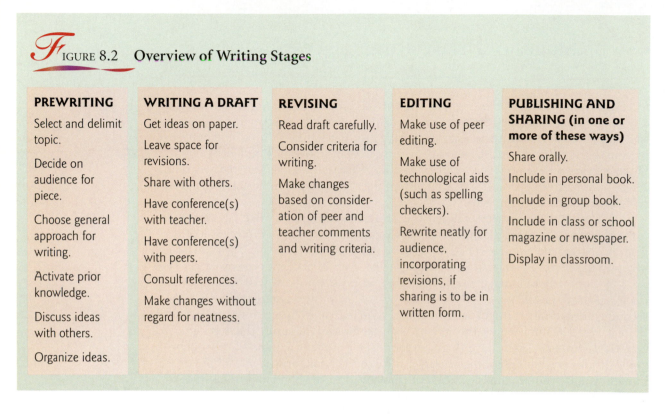

FIGURE 8.2   Overview of Writing Stages

PREWRITING	**WRITING A DRAFT**	**REVISING**	**EDITING**	**PUBLISHING AND SHARING (in one or more of these ways)**
Select and delimit topic.	Get ideas on paper.	Read draft carefully.	Make use of peer editing.	Share orally.
Decide on audience for piece.	Leave space for revisions.	Consider criteria for writing.	Make use of technological aids (such as spelling checkers).	Include in personal book.
Choose general approach for writing.	Share with others.	Make changes based on consideration of peer and teacher comments and writing criteria.	Rewrite neatly for audience, incorporating revisions, if sharing is to be in written form.	Include in group book.
Activate prior knowledge.	Have conference(s) with teacher.			Include in class or school magazine or newspaper.
Discuss ideas with others.	Have conference(s) with peers.			Display in classroom.
Organize ideas.	Consult references.			
	Make changes without regard for neatness.			

school settings, such as for content area report writing, children need at first to have control of topic selection, so that they will be able to write about things that are important to them and that they know about. This approach gives the children an opportunity to focus on the manner of expression, rather than worrying a great deal about content for the writing. Writing about personal experiences is often a good starting place, because the children have the background knowledge necessary for the writing.

Some teachers, however, start by giving students topics to write about. Your students, especially if they are older ones who have been given all of their writing topics in the past, may need help in learning how to choose topics.

Delimiting a topic refers to focusing the topic narrowly enough that it can reasonably be handled in the time allowed for the assigned writing and the length of paper that has been requested. Students often pick such broad topics that it would be impossible to do them justice in anything less than a book-length manuscript.

A good way to help children in topic selection is through modeling. Minilesson 8.1 shows one example of how you might start the first writing session with a particular group of students. There are many other ways that you may help students choose topics.

REHEARSING IDEAS FOR ORGANIZATION OF MATERIAL

List making, semantic webbing, drawing, and discussion with the teacher and other students are all forms of rehearsing to organize ideas before writing. They help to keep the children from beginning to write aimlessly and getting bogged down in disorganized ideas. Although they do not ensure good organization after the writing has begun, they make it more likely.

Minilesson 8.1

Initiating Writing Sessions and Modeling Topic Selection

Before beginning the initial writing session with a group of intermediate-grade students, distribute folders to the students, explaining that the writing they will be doing during the year will be kept in these folders. Pocket folders are particularly useful for this purpose. Tell the students that they should write their names on the front covers of their folders, and that they may decorate these covers in any way that they desire. Take a folder for your personal use and write your name on it. Give the students time for folder decoration at this time, or tell them that they may do this at any free time that they have during the day.

Next, have the students open their folders to the inside of the front covers, instructing them to write "Possible Topic Choices" at the tops of these pages, while you write the words on your personal folder. Explain that this is the place that good ideas for things to write about should be listed at any time that they occur to the students. A topic that is listed may not be used immediately, but it will always be there for possible later use.

Further explain that all of the writing that the children do during the year will be kept in their folders—even writing that they start and decide not to finish or writing that they do and then leave out of their final drafts. This material will give the children ideas to polish or expand later, and it will serve as a reminder of the progress that they are making in their writing throughout the year. Urge the children to date each piece of writing that goes into the folder. This procedure makes progress over time more obvious to the children as they browse through earlier writing attempts.

Now you are ready for the first writing session to begin. The students must choose topics for writing, but you may know that they have never been asked to choose their own topics before, so modeling of the process of topic selection is in order.

Say, "Before we begin to write, we need to think about some topics that we may want to write about. Let's try to list three or four topics that we could write about and then choose just one to write about today."

At this point, begin to list topics in your personal folder, allowing the students to try to list some topics themselves. Very quickly, before the students have a chance to become frustrated, say, "I have thought of two topics that I might use—'My Cat's New Kittens' and 'My Trip to the Museum of Natural History.' I have things that I could say about both of these topics. I wonder what else I could write about?"

A pause can follow for students to consider the possibilities that the two topics mentioned open up for them. They may think about many pet-related topics and trip-related topics. After a minute or two, say, "Oh! I have two other ideas for topics—'My Visit to the Dentist' and 'The Thanksgiving Day Parade in the Snow.' I wonder which one I should choose? The kittens are pretty and fun to play with. I enjoyed my visit to the museum, and I learned

(continued)

Minilesson 8.1

Initiating Writing Sessions and Modeling Topic Selection
(continued)

new things from it, too. My visit to the dentist was uncomfortable for me, but it worked out well in the end. I nearly froze trying to march with the band in the Thanksgiving Day Parade. Maybe the most interesting topic would be the new things that I learned at the museum. I can't tell about everything that I saw; it would be too much. I think I will write about the new things I learned about dinosaurs. That was fascinating to me! I guess my topic for today will be 'Learning About Dinosaurs at the Museum.' Some other day I may write about other things that I saw there. I'll always have the museum on my list of possible topics."

Next you may ask children who have chosen topics to share some of them with the class. These topics will serve as memory prompts to other children who have had similar experiences. You may even make the links more explicit by responding to the topic "The Day I Spilled Spaghetti on Myself in the Restaurant" with "I'll bet you were embarrassed. Have any of the rest of you done something embarrassing that you could write about?"

Then say, "Now I want you to take another minute to finish listing some topics and choosing one. You may discuss possibilities with each other if you speak quietly." Circulate about the room and ask questions designed to elicit topics from some of the students who have not yet listed anything. A comment might be "Do you have a pet? Has it done anything interesting lately?" or "Have you ever been to a museum? What did you like best about it?" or "You told about your new sister in class yesterday. Is there something about her that you would like to write?"

Other students may have a list of topics, but they may be struggling with which one to choose. You may say, "These topics sound wonderful! Tell me about each one of them. I usually find that talking about a topic helps me to decide whether I want to write about it or not."

After a couple of minutes for topic selection, encourage the children to start writing. You may suggest that, if they begin to write about certain topics, the topics may become more clear to them. After they start to write, they may realize that they want to modify their topics. They need to realize that this is acceptable and that writers often do this.

What are the students learning?

They are learning to keep their writing attempts together in order to observe progress over time. They are also learning to choose topics to write about from their background experiences.

Technology

Modeling by the teacher is a good way to introduce all parts of the writing process, not just the selection and delimitation of topics. Therefore, you might continue the modeling experience by brainstorming about the trip to the museum while jotting down the ideas on the board or a transparency. A list might include things such as the following.

Reconstructed dinosaur skeletons

How dinosaurs walked and ran (for example, the position of the tail)

How dinosaurs ate

What dinosaurs ate

Why dinosaurs died out

You might even expand this list from brainstorming into a semantic web (or word web) of information about the dinosaur before starting to write. The semantic web would have dinosaurs as the center and the brainstormed categories connected to it with lines, with more specific details from the trip connected to each category. Figure 8.3 shows a fifth-grader's organizational web for a piece of writing.

Children may find that drawing a picture related to their topic is a good way to bring ideas about it to the forefront of their consciousness. You could encourage them

𝓕IGURE 8.3 **Web for Organization**

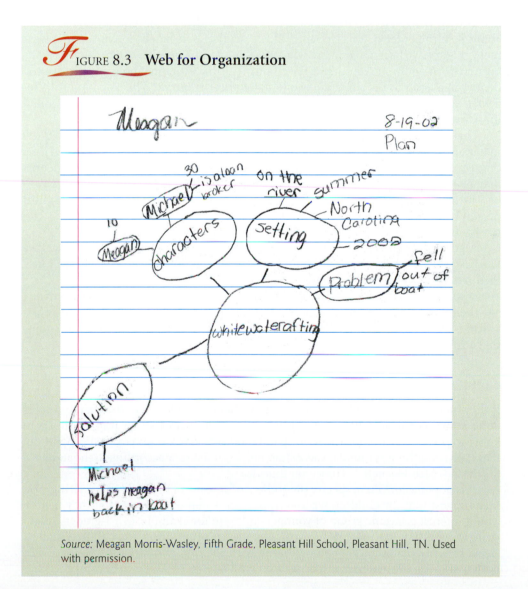

Source: Meagan Morris-Wasley, Fifth Grade, Pleasant Hill School, Pleasant Hill, TN. Used with permission.

to draw pictures related to their topics, even before they are adept at private brain-storming and semantic webbing.

Another good technique is for you to ask the children questions to help them make decisions about what should be included in the writing. In the minilesson on topic selection, you might ask, "Should I tell how I felt about the dinosaurs or just give information?" When the children respond, you could question them about why they believe the feelings should or should not be included. In an attempt to introduce the concept of audience for a piece of writing, you might say, "I want to write this for you to read, so that you can see what I learned about the museum. What will I need to include to help you understand better?" On the other hand, you might say, "I want to write this to share with Mrs. Beckett's first-grade class, so that they will know what I learned in the museum. What will I need to remember as I write this material for their teacher to read to them?"

In the prewriting phase, it is also important to consider the organizational pattern that is to be taken in the writing. In Minilesson 8.1, you might have modeled this for the students by deciding out loud to discuss three categories of information about the dinosaurs—their appearance, their eating habits, and the reason that they died. If you had chosen the Thanksgiving Day Parade topic, the decision might have been to tell about it in the order that it happened. If the dentist topic had been chosen, the treatment might have been to compare what was expected before the visit to what actually occurred. In addition, you might have said, "I think I'll write about my visit to the dentist in a letter to my aunt. She would like to hear about it." This situation calls for a writing form very different from the one needed for presenting information about dinosaurs to first-graders.

Part of the approach to writing is deciding on the point of view from which the material is to be written. You may model different points of view in personal writing that you share with the students. For example, the story about the visit to the dentist may be written from your viewpoint in first person, whereas the story about the cat's new kittens may be written in first person from the point of view of the cat or in third person from your point of view. The students can discuss what they would need to do to take the point of view of other people or animals.

A good book to use in the class to focus discussion on point of view is *The True Story of the 3 Little Pigs* by Jon Scieszka. This is the old folktale of "The Three Little Pigs" retold from the point of view of the wolf.

If students want to write about a content topic, such as tropical fish, you can encourage them to visit the library to collect information about the topic to include in their writing. Occasionally you may model the checking of reference sources about a topic that a student has chosen.

CONSIDERING THE AUDIENCE FOR THE WRITING

If the students cannot see how a particular **audience** should affect the writing that is done, some specific instruction will be needed to help them see how important it is to know who the audience for the writing is. Goodman and Goodman (1983) point out that even something as mundane as a shopping list must vary according to the audience for the list. Minilesson 8.2 is based on this idea.

It is possible for you to specify the audience for some of the children's writing. You may suggest that the children write stories or informational pieces that they believe would interest a specific group of younger children; for example, third-graders might write for children in kindergarten or first grade. At other times, the children may be asked to write material that can be shared with the other children in their class. In both instances, the material will be written with a sense of audience beyond a teacher,

Importance of Audience

Ask the children to write grocery lists with four to six items on them. One such list might look like this:

bread	milk	cheese
margarine	mayonnaise	steak

Ask the students to exchange lists with partners. Each student then reads his partner's list and decides what knowledge is needed before the shopping can be done. The students ask each other questions and expand the lists to make them more explicit. After the students have worked on this task for a while, write a list such as the one above on the board or on a transparency and ask if the children would know what to buy if they had to use the list to shop for you. A chorus of "No" should result. The list can then be expanded in response to the students' questions. The questions concerning the item "milk" might be: What brand? How much? What kind? What kind of container? The expanded list might say, "A gallon of Brand Z skim milk in a plastic jug."

Follow up with a discussion of why they needed more information for others than they needed for themselves. Then expand the discussion to include why personal-experience stories written for other people to read need to include more detail than ones written only for the author's personal use. Some students have trouble realizing that not every audience will know everything that the students know about what they have written, making it necessary for them to be very specific in the information that they provide.

What are the students learning?

They are learning that writing is done for particular audiences and that they must provide more detail when they are writing for other people than they need to provide if the writing is for themselves.

who may be perceived as someone who knows all about the information anyway or someone who will not be interested in "made up" stories.

The teacher in the classroom vignette at the beginning of this chapter, Mr. Drake, ignored the entire prewriting phase. He even discouraged the discussion between two students that could have been a helpful rehearsal technique. Such methods are not likely to encourage the best writing that students can do.

Stage Two: Writing a Draft

When the children are ready to begin writing, it is important for them to realize that the first **draft** is not final and does not have to be perfect. They need to understand that writers first get their ideas down on paper and then make the changes necessary to polish the writing. Teachers like Mr. Drake give the students the impression that they must write flawless first drafts. This causes excessive attention to mechanical considerations and leaves less of the writers' attention for the content of the writing.

This composing phase consists of recording ideas on paper as they are formed. You may want to encourage the children to skip every other line, if they are writing on lined paper, so that after the draft is completed there will be room for changes that they wish to make. You may also suggest that the children keep writing if there are words that they do not know how to spell or punctuation marks about which they are unsure. The children can underline or circle potential problems and come back to them after the flow of ideas has been recorded.

You need to help the students understand that drafts are generally messy—some call them sloppy copy—and that there is nothing wrong with crossing out words and phrases, writing ideas in between the lines, and drawing arrows to material that is to be inserted. Cutting a draft page apart and pasting the paragraphs on another page in a different order is another procedure that can be used when children realize that they have things "mixed up." One of the best ways for you to make the point that first (and other early) drafts of writing are usually messy is to show them your own messy drafts, complete with insertions, deletions, and rearrangements. If the students have been told for years that their papers *must* be neat, they need to see evidence that lack of neatness is not bad in writing drafts, other than final ones that are designed for others to read. Figure 8.4 shows a page from the rough draft that was written based on the web in Figure 8.3.

Technology

ENCOURAGING STUDENT CONVERSATIONS ABOUT THEIR WRITING

Piazza and Tomlinson (1985) suggest that allowing spontaneous conversation among children who are writing their drafts is beneficial. The children are essentially continuing rehearsal of their ideas as they talk to their peers about their drafts. The peer reactions help them to shape their writing and to keep the process of composing from seeming to be such a lonesome task. Student interactions occur naturally when children are seated together at tables for their writing. The learning that takes place in such a setting parallels the language learning that takes place in the home, in which children are allowed, without reprimand, to ask for information when they feel a need. The social situation makes the learning more pleasant and less threatening than it might be otherwise, and, when the children act as resource persons for each other, the teacher has more freedom to circulate and attend to problem areas. This peer interaction also tends to make a sense of audience for the writing easier to attain. Such a writing atmosphere was even successful with students in a resource classroom, when their writing efforts had a well-defined purpose (Church, 1985).

You may want to assign reading-writing partners to provide students with readily available, meaningful audiences (and helpful critics) for their writing attempts. In all of these social interactions, the writer of the material being discussed is the decision maker. That person considers the input from the others and then does whatever seems right to her.

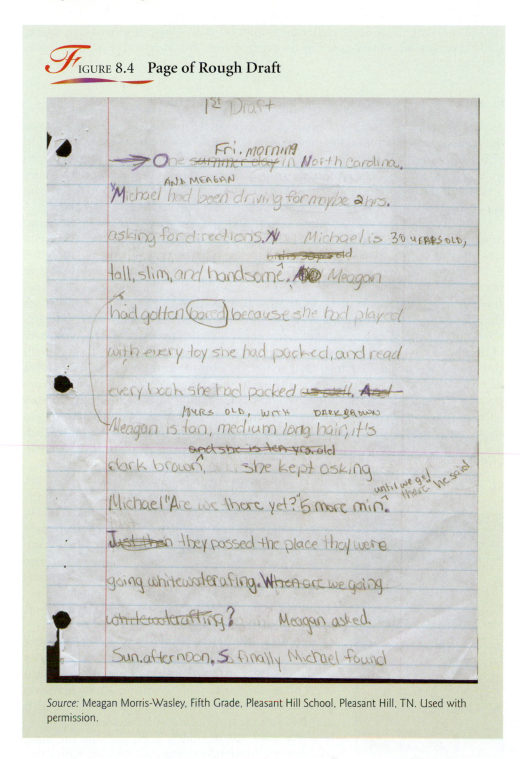

FIGURE 8.4   **Page of Rough Draft**

Source: Meagan Morris-Wasley, Fifth Grade, Pleasant Hill School, Pleasant Hill, TN. Used with permission.

Long and Bulgarella (1985) found that first-grade children who are allowed to write stories cooperatively do much thinking as they write, exchanging ideas continuously and discussing the content of stories, as well as mechanics. The clashes of opinion that are inevitable when people work jointly on a piece of writing encourage children to use critical thinking skills. Since consensus is important on cooperative writing projects, skills of persuasion must be used by the participants, thus sharpening oral, as well as written, skills.

HOLDING BRIEF TEACHER CONFERENCES DURING DRAFTING

As the children work on their drafts, you may circulate among them, conferring with them about any difficulties that they may be having. These conferences probably will be brief, but they help the writers both to clarify what they are doing and to continue to write productively. Nickel (2001) suggests that conferences may be more effective if they are done at the children's request, because the children may not be ready to talk to you about their work when you call them for conferences on a predetermined schedule.

Conducting these quick conferences effectively depends on skillful questioning. A good opening question to use is "How is your writing going?" or "What are you writing about?" As the children respond to one of these questions, you can listen for clues that will suggest further questions. For example, if a little girl responds to the first question with "Awful. I want to write about losing my tooth, but I can't get started," you could say, "Tell me about what happened when you lost your tooth." As the girl describes the experience orally, she is rehearsing the information that she has about her topic. You could respond, "You had quite an experience. You told me a lot of things that you could put into your story. Work on it for a while, and I'll check with you again later." On the other hand, if you found a boy writing busily and asked what he was writing about, the child would be likely to respond with details from his story, such as "I'm writing about going to the moon. I'm telling what I would have to take with me, like food in tubes." You could receive his information and ask something to show comprehension of his topic and perhaps lead him to think about it more, such as "How did you know that you would need food in tubes? Did you hear that on television or read it in a book? Can just anybody go to the moon?"

A good question sequence for a child such as the boy mentioned above, who has written some material and seems to be flagging in the process is, "What else do you think your readers will want to know about your trip to the moon? Where could you find out more things to tell?" Often children begin to write about a topic with limited information and "run dry" without additional input. This situation provides a good opportunity to lead them to consider the use of reference materials or resource people who are available to provide information.

Sometimes you may want to read the child's work aloud as the child listens. This technique often causes the child to realize that there are gaps, points of confusion, or inconsistencies in the writing. It also may alert the child to missing words or punctuation marks, without you actually mentioning such problems.

If a child has obviously been revising the material as the writing takes place, you can recognize this in the conference and encourage the child to explain the reason. For example, you might say, "I see that you changed your opening sentence to say 'The boy was

The teacher must question students skillfully during student-teacher conferences.

standing on the dock,' instead of saying 'I was standing on the dock.' That helped your story. What caused you to decide to do that?"

Gaskins (1982) points out the need for the teacher to encourage some children to reread what they are writing as they write, particularly when they are unsure what they should write next. Reviewing what they have already written may give them clues for continuing. Although some children seem to do this rereading spontaneously, many do not and, therefore, need to have this possibility suggested to them.

If a child reads a portion of his writing to you and there is a problem in the writing that needs to be resolved, you may ask a leading question, such as "How did Jamie get the $20? At the beginning he didn't have it, but later on he does." The child may answer the question orally, and you may want to ask, "Where should you put that information?" If the child doesn't know, you can leave him to work out the problem or ask, "If you don't know how he could have gotten the money, what can you do to your story?" The child may answer, "Not let him have it," and proceed to mark out the references to the money late in the story. This action may need to be followed by another question from you: "If you take that part out, how will the ending change?" Eventually the child will be able to work out the conflicts within the writing. The decisions will be those of the child, however. You should not supply ideas for the child, no matter how tempting it is to do so.

Focusing on the content of the selections in early conferences lets the children see that meaning is important. Mechanical problems generally are not discussed in these conferences unless the children bring them into the discussion themselves. Even then, you should try to shift the focus to content until the draft is completed, suggesting that the mechanics can be taken care of during editing.

Sometimes children are helped with resolving questions about style of writing by being referred to literature that they have read or had read to them recently. For example, if a child says, "This just doesn't sound like the beginning of a story to me," you may suggest that the child look in several books that he or she knows well to see how these stories begin. The same technique can be used for writing endings, humorous passages, dialogue, and many other types of text.

In addition to these brief conferences held as the children work on their drafts, there should be regularly scheduled, slightly more formal conferences with each of the children. The children should know what day of the week that they are scheduled for a formal conference and should be prepared to discuss what they are currently writing with you in some depth. You may ask some of the same questions indicated for the brief conferences described above, but you may ask for more elaboration and ask about more aspects of the writing. Generally, you should begin by making a statement that shows understanding of what has been written. A typical statement to a child who is writing about ice skating might be "I'm glad you decided to write about your ice-skating party. I didn't know you were a skater. I like to ice skate, too." This kind of statement may be followed by questions that will cause the writer to recall more information that may be useful to the piece being developed, such as "When did you learn to skate? Who taught you?"

Some ideas about teacher conferences gleaned from Graves (1983), Russell (1983), and Temple and colleagues (1988) are summarized in Figure 8.5.

ARRANGING FOR PEER CONFERENCES

There may also be times when children ask peers to confer with them about their work in much the same way that you have done. Some teachers assign students to peer-conferencing groups of four or five students each. As each member of the group experi-

$\mathcal{F}$IGURE 8.5 **Teacher Conferences**

Tips for Teacher Conferences

1. Listen to children read their drafts to you.

2. Concentrate on the writers' information. Respond to it and ask questions about it.

3. Let the students talk first during the conferences.

4. Listen to the children's perceived problems with the drafts.

5. Choose only one thing to teach during a conference, if you are trying to work on specific skills. Retention is usually better when you don't dilute your teaching effort.

6. If the children do not want to change their pieces, find out *why* they think the pieces are good as they are.

7. Confer with every child at least once a week.

8. Have the other children in the class writing on their own pieces while you are conferring.

9. Ask questions, such as the following, that cause the children to reflect on their writing.

   a. What are you writing about?

   b. How do you feel about the piece you are writing?

   c. Why did you choose this topic?

   d. What problems are you having with your writing?

   e. Do you have more than one story in this piece?

   f. Do you have a good opening sentence?

   g. Do you have a satisfying ending?

   h. Is there any part that is not clear?

   i. Are your ideas presented in the right order?

   j. Have you been repetitious?

   k. Can you combine some sentences to make the piece sound better?

   l. Have you used words that say *exactly* what you want to say?

   m. What are you going to do next with this piece?

   (Uses of some of these questions and others are demonstrated in context in earlier portions of this section.)

ences difficulty with a composition or has written something to which she would like an audience reaction, that person arranges for a peer-group conference. Certain areas of the room may be set aside for such conferences. In them, the child reads the piece of writing to the rest of the group and tells the group what kind of help she needs. The group members, based on teacher modeling, first make statements that indicate that

Teaching Tip

Before any peer conferences are held, role-play in front of the class the types of comments and questions that should be included, using an assistant or some student volunteers who have been briefed on proper responses. For example, after a student shares his composition with a peer or a group of peers, you might prompt a response that includes the words, "I liked the _____, because _____." A response to a student who has written an account of a fire might be, "I liked the descriptive words that you used to describe the fire, because they helped me to see it, smell it, hear it, and feel the heat. It made me feel as if I were there." Indicating what is good about a piece of writing and adding the reason that it is good is more helpful than a comment such as "Good story!"

they have received the content and give positive feedback. Then they give suggestions for improving the area with which the writer is concerned and ask questions about parts that they find unclear. If you have peer-conferencing groups, attend the peer conferences at first and model appropriate interactions. Later these conferences can go on while you are having conferences with other children.

Most peer conferences are held to talk about what to change in the writing, to tell what was good about the writing, and to get ideas and suggestions about the writing. Other purposes include getting help with titles, sharing, getting help on informational gaps in the material, and editing the writing.

Stage Three: Revising

Revising includes reorganizing and clarifying ideas, adding information, and deleting unneeded or confusing material. You and your students must realize that revision is not just a "last step" in writing. It is recursive; that is, it can occur at any stage of the writing process. It can even occur during prewriting activities, as the students delimit their topics, but it most often occurs when students review their own drafts or consider peer or teacher comments. To revise effectively, writers need to be aware of the characteristics of good writing so that they can match these characteristics in their own work.

Children should understand that revision may not be necessary for everything that they write. If the writing is personal and not intended to be shared with others and if it meets its goals without revision, it need not be revised. Few people revise notes to themselves, personal journal entries, and other similar writing. However, if writing is to be shared with others, revision becomes important.

Depending on the level of development of the children involved, various lists of criteria on which to judge their work may be constructed. Primary-grade students might ask the following questions about their writing to guide revision.

1. *Beginning:* Does it start with something that will catch the reader's interest?

2. *Middle:* Is the action or information presented in an appropriate order?

3. *Ending:* Does it have a good ending?

4. Do all of the sentences make sense?

A list for writers in intermediate and upper grades might include additional such items as the following.

1. *Vocabulary:* Do the words used say exactly what you wanted to say?

2. *Point of view:* Is the whole story written from one point of view?

3. *Focus:* Are there parts of the story that are not closely related to the main theme?

4. *Audience:* Is the story written with a particular audience in mind? Is it right for this audience?

Many other lists of criteria may be developed to fit the needs of different classes at different times. The author should read the story several times, each time checking for one or more of the criteria for which the class is responsible. Any problems that the author finds should be immediately corrected by using carets and arrows to insert information between lines or in the margins, striking out unwanted material, or moving sections of writing around. These changes do not need to be neat, but they do need to be clear.

At this point, students may turn to peer partners for input. Peer partners exchange papers and read each other's material carefully. They write positive comments about the piece, and then they make specific suggestions for changes or ask questions about parts that are unclear. After they have done this, the partners read the piece together and discuss the comments. The author takes these comments into consideration and makes the changes that appear to be needed. For the author to feel ownership of the writing, it is necessary to let her make the final decision on each point of revision. Peer partners can work similarly to the peer-conference groups described earlier. A difference is that the peer partners focus on all aspects of the piece that are included in the criteria for judging work, instead of simply focusing on an area that the author designates.

If peer partners help with revision, you should explain and model the process before the children attempt to implement it. Sometimes you will have revision conferences with individual children, and each of these conferences will serve as a model for future peer conferences also.

Direct instruction about the revision process can be helpful. You can introduce the topic of revision and present an overview of the topic; model the revision process for the students, pointing out key aspects; provide guided practice for the students as they revise their own pieces or a piece that they have been given to analyze, as you circulate to offer assistance; and, finally, provide independent practice for them. When modeling, you can present text on an overhead projector or computer projection device or write the text on the board. You can locate each point of needed revision, discuss the needed changes, and make the changes. The students see the entire process take place. The guided practice may be done individually or in pairs, with the students following steps for revision presented on a handout or displayed on the board or on a poster.

Stage Four: Editing

Editing for spelling, grammar, and punctuation is important in writing material that is easily understood by others. The first step toward editing is a careful reading of the draft by the author. An author may ask questions such as the following about the writing.

1. Is it written in complete sentences?

2. Are capital letters and punctuation marks used correctly?

3. Are words spelled correctly?

Editing changes can be made by erasing incorrect letters or punctuation marks and inserting correct ones, just as was done with the revisions.

Use of peer editing may be the next step in the process (Harp, 1988). Students may be assigned to ongoing peer-editing groups or peer-editing partners, who consistently work together throughout the year, or they may request different peers to work as editing partners at different times. These partners may circle misspelled words and incorrect punctuation and mark places where additional punctuation is needed. One or more members of a peer-editing group may read the material carefully for mechanics.

Editing committees may also be used in the class (Harp, 1988). They are formed by checking on which children are effectively using a particular writing skill that has been taught. The teacher can choose three or four of these children to serve on the editing committee for that skill. As other children finish working with peer-editing groups or partners, they submit their manuscripts to the editing committee for the skill that is being stressed at the moment.

In any case, the final decision about changes to be made must be made by the author of the piece. He considers the suggestions from peers, double-checks such aspects as spelling and punctuation, and makes the final draft reflect this input, if it was helpful.

Figure 8.6 shows the final draft of a piece of writing done by a fifth-grade student. The students had brainstormed story ideas, and each one had chosen the type of piece he or she wished to write. Meagan's organizational web for this piece is in Figure 8.3, and a page of her rough draft is in Figure 8.4.

USING COMPUTERS TO EASE REVISION AND EDITING

If computers with **word processing software** are available for use by the children in their writing, both revision and editing are considerably eased. Not only can words be deleted without making gaps in the work and added without writing between lines and in the margins, but blocks of text can also be moved around to improve organization, without the necessity of rewriting the content completely. Removing the drudgery of recopying makes a remarkable difference in students' attitudes. The students tend to view revision with less distaste, and they enjoy seeing the professional look of their pieces when they are printed. Some children find that proofreading their work is easier when it is printed from the computer than when it is written in their own handwriting. If a spelling checker is available, it can highlight words that *may* be misspelled, and the students then have some additional guidance as to which words should be looked up in the dictionary or checked in some other way. The students need to be aware that the checker is not infallible, and they need to know that it is important to check each questionable word personally. Some teachers find that students pay more attention to words marked by a spelling checker on a computer than they do to words marked by the teacher. Most spelling checkers offer suggestions for correct spellings. Sometimes these spellings actually are for different words that are spelled somewhat like the word in question. Each suggestion should be checked for appropriateness before it is used. Merely accepting the spelling checker's suggestion may result in nonsense. Therefore, critical thinking is needed to use a spelling checker successfully.

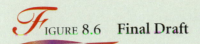

FIGURE 8.6   **Final Draft**

The Whitewater Rafting Trip

Michael had been driving for maybe 2 hrs. one Friday morning in North Carolina. Asking for directions to the Pidgeon River. He is 30 years old, tall, slim, and handsome. Meagan is 10 years old, tanned, with medium long dark brown hair. She had become bored because she had played with every toy and read every book she had packed for the trip. She kept asking Michael "Are we there yet?"

After awhile, they passed the place were they were going to go whitewater rafting on Sunday. They continued on until they came to their hotel. In their room, they found that they had a great view of the mountains and the city. They unpacked and before going to sleep put a room service sign on their door. At 8:30 the next morning room service knocked on the door, and as soon as he came in, there was a wonderful aroma of hot creamy scrambled eggs, cold o.j., warm toast and other things that smelled delicious.

That afternoon they decided to go swimming. It was an Olympic size pool. That night they went out to dinner at a fancy restaurant. They ordered fried shrimp, steak, soups and breadsticks. They were stuffed when they left the restaurant. They went back to the hotel and watched some tv before going to sleep.

On Sunday morning, it was time to go whitewater rafting. When we arrived we were told to go to the Assembly Room. That's where they give you the instructions like what to do if you fall out of the boat. "If you fall out of the boat, you need to lift your feet up and not touch the bottom because your foot could get stuck and you could drown."

They got their gear and loaded up the bus to go to the river. Meagan was kind of nervous but she got over it. There were 8 people on the boat including the guide. They pushed the boat out and were off! They went down the rapids one by one. On the middle of the class 4 rapid, Meagan fell out. Michael yelled for her to remember to float on the top. Before she was about to come to the next rapid, Michael pulled her back into the boat. She was a little terrified but she got over it. When they finished, they both said they had had a great time.

They went back home Sunday evening and arrived home safely. Meagan went back to school telling her friends all about her trip.

THE END

Source: Meagan Morris-Wasley, Fifth Grade, Pleasant Hill School, Pleasant Hill, TN. Used with permission.

Elementary students can develop illustrated stories with programs such as Storybook Weaver Deluxe and EasyBook Deluxe. These programs have word processors combined with graphics to help writers express themselves (Sullivan & Sharp, 2000).

Stage Five: Publishing and Sharing

The final step of the writing process, when the writing is not strictly personal, is **publishing** and sharing. This step can take many forms. The product may be shared orally by the author, may be bound into a single book by the author, or may be bound into a collection of stories by either the author or various class members. These books may be placed in a classroom library or in the school library, equipped with checkout cards, and checked out like other library books. The writing may be published in a class or school magazine, newspaper, or newsletter. The product may be displayed on the bulletin board for others to read. Regardless of how products are shared, the sharing helps to build children's self-esteem. Knowing that others find something that they have written interesting helps to build the children's confidence in themselves as writers and motivates them to continue writing.

One of the books developed by ESL students being tutored by Lance Jasitt (see Classroom Vignette 8.2.) is shown in Figure 8.7 (see pages 326–327).

One sixth-grade teacher asked her students to write a story with a moral to read to a Comprehensive Development Class (CDC) in the school. The students took the books through the entire writing process, illustrating them during the final polishing. Figure 8.8 (see pages 328–329) is an example of one of these books, showing the result of writing an assigned type of story for a specific audience.

AUTHOR'S CHAIR

One form of sharing is referred to as **Author's Chair**. When a child has completed a book or story, he sits in the Author's Chair with the other children gathered around to listen to the author read the story. When the reading has been completed, first the listeners make comments that indicate their understanding of the material and then ask the author any questions that they have (Graves & Hansen, 1983). They may ask such questions as "Where did you get your idea?" and "Is this a true story?"

WEBPAGE PUBLICATION

In recent years, webpage publication has become a popular way to publish all kinds of student work—results of research papers, creative writing, and other projects.

Author's Chair is a good way to allow students to share their writing with others.

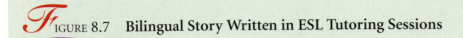

FIGURE 8.7   **Bilingual Story Written in ESL Tutoring Sessions**

The Boat Titanic

(El Barco Titanic)

by

Moyses, Jayron, and Mr. Jasitt

1

2

The people on the boat are happy,
but the boat is broken and is going down.

La gente en el barco está feliz,
pero el barco está roto y empezaba a irse abajo.

3

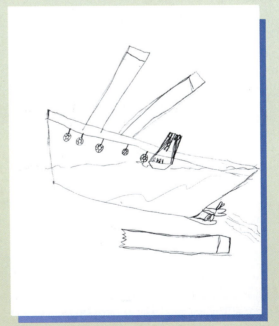

4

The people are scared,
and the boat is beginning to sink.

La gente estaba asustada,
y el barco empezo a hundirse.

5

6

And the people begin to pray to God,
as the furniture falls into the cold water.

Y la gente empezo a rezar a Dios,
mientras las trastes se venian abajo al agua fria.

7

The people were very worried,
and the people began to run quickly.
But the door was locked,
and it would not let the people go through.

La gente estaba muy preocupada,
y la gente empezo a correr hacia arriba.
Pero la puerta estaba cerrada,
y no dejaba pasar a la gente.

8

Source: Lance Jasitt, Tennessee Technological University, Cookeville, TN. Used with permission.

$\mathcal{F}$IGURE 8.8   **Book Written to Share with Comprehensive Development Class**

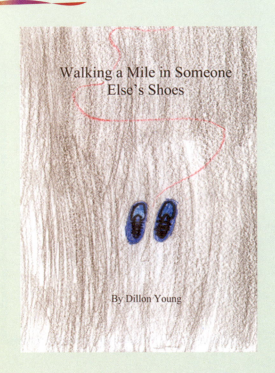

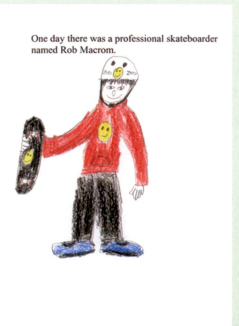

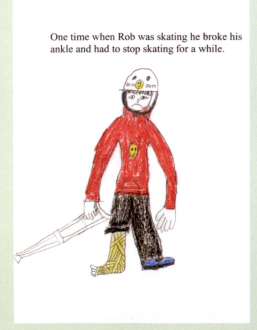

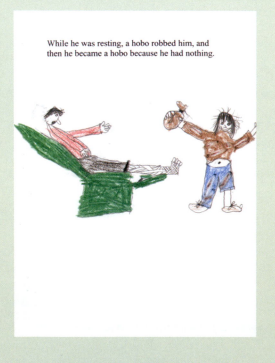

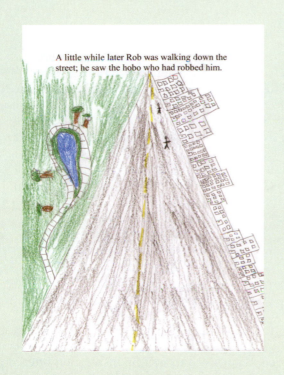

A little while later Rob was walking down the street; he saw the hobo who had robbed him.

The hobo said that he was sorry, and that he only stole the money for food. Rob instantly forgave the hobo.

After the hobo gave him his money back, Rob felt sorry for the hobo because he had been in his shoes (or so to speak) so he gave him some money.

The lesson of the story is to forgive people less fortunate than you.

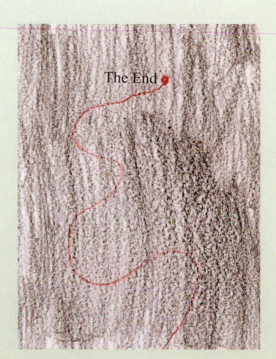

The End

Source: Dillon Young, Sixth Grade, East Middle School, Tullahoma, TN. Used with permission.

This avenue gives the students a worldwide audience, which is a powerful motivator for careful work and proofreading. Word processing programs, such as Microsoft Word, have output options for publishing on the Web (Roe, 2000).

IMPORTANCE OF VOLUNTARY SHARING

Graves (1994) points out that not all students want to share their work with others. "One of the potential weaknesses of the writing process approach, especially where children share their work with each other and with the entire class, is the force of 'group think.' . . . Group think tends to encourage children to select certain acceptable topics and ways of expression. Thus, the child who explores new ground for him or herself may be ignored when sharing with the large group" (p. 123). Graves believes that it is sometimes good for teachers to call these children's efforts to the attention of other class members, but it is not always good. It can be detrimental to do so with children who are self-conscious about their writing. It is best to ask the child if it is okay to share the writing with the others.

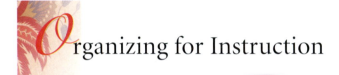

Organizing for Instruction

TEACHERS WHO use the process approach to writing instruction often organize their writing instruction into a writing workshop format. The basic format for a writing workshop includes a minilesson, a status-of-the-class report, writing time, and group sharing time (Ross, 1996). The minilesson at the beginning of a workshop may be instruction on a single skill for which your students have an immediate need or a skill that is mandated in your school's curriculum guide. The status-of-the-class report is a record of what each student in your class is doing on a particular day. As students report their planned activities for the day, you can record them with a brief code. Ross (1996) suggests DJ for dialogue journal, TS for topic search, D1 for first draft (and so on for subsequent drafts), RV for revision, ED for editing, PC for peer conference, TC for teacher conference, and PB for publishing. Any code that you can easily remember is acceptable. During actual workshop writing time, students are doing various types of writing, reading material to assist them with their writing, reflecting on what they have written, having conferences with you or with peers, and sometimes observing you as you model writing. You need to incorporate all facets of the writing process in this time period. The sharing time may consist of two or three students reading what they have written to the class, or it may consist of all students telling what they have been working on in one or two sentences each. Those who share may receive oral feedback, as described earlier in this chapter, or written feedback from their peers.

Wagner, Nott, and Agnew (2001) developed the following plan for a first-grade journal-writing workshop, based on the work of Graves (1983) and Calkins (1994). It is shown in Figure 8.9. Topics for the minilessons that are mentioned range from "how to praise a writer's work" to "using commas in a series" to "using time sequence to organize" (Wagner, Nott, & Agnew, 2001, p. 122).

$\mathcal{F}$IGURE 8.9   **Daily Schedule for First-Grade Journal-Writing Workshop**

Typical time allotted	Activity	What the teacher does	What the children do
5–15 minutes	Minilesson	I give direct instruction about workshop procedures, writing strategies and skills, and writer's craft. I sometimes use my own writing to demonstrate specific points.	Children interact with me during direct instruction, modeling, discussion, and practice of the specific element that I present.
5 minutes	Group rehearsal for writing	I lead the class in brainstorming possible topics for writing and I add the ideas to the class topics list. The written list helps jog children's thinking as they plan their writing. It simultaneously provides spelling for some difficult words.	Children offer ideas for topics that class members might choose to write about, sometimes adding a few details that might be included in the writing.
10 minutes	Individual rehearsal for writing	I model rehearsal by drawing about my own selected topic for a minute or two, and then I circulate among the children. I ask questions or make comments to help children extend or clarify their drawings and their thinking as they plan their writing.	Each child draws an illustration about the new or ongoing topic he or she has selected to write about. Children may talk with peers or with me about their topics or drawings.
15–45 minutes	Individual writing and informal peer discussion about writing	I write for a few minutes and then circulate among children to answer questions and give support.	Children write about their new or ongoing topics. Some children may do some revision of previous writing. They may talk to one another about their writing, as needed.
5–15 minutes	Sharing of writing by one-fifth of the students	I invite one-fifth of the children to share their writing each day, according to my predetermined schedule. About once a week, I also share a piece of my writing. I often model how to make specific positive comments about a child's writing, how to ask questions to clarify or extend the child's ideas, and how to make specific suggestions. I make brief notes about each child's writing to use later during teacher-child writing conferences.	Children who are scheduled to share that day bring what they want to share. All class members listen to each child read his or her writing, and then the class members offer positive comments, ask questions, and make specific suggestions to the author.

(Note: The sharing time is followed by individual teacher conferences with the children who shared their writing. These conferences begin after the class has settled into independent activities related to thematic study.)

Source: Adapted from Lyn Wagner, Jennifer Grogan Nott, & Ann T. Agnew, The Nuts and Bolts of Teaching First-Grade Writing Through a Journal Workshop, *The Reading Teacher,* 55 (October 2001), 121. Used with permission.

General Approaches to Writing Instruction

THERE ARE some approaches that are useful with all kinds of writing instruction. A process approach to writing instruction can be used with reports as well as creative writing, for example, and writing workshop can be used to organize your instruction.

Sustained Spontaneous Writing

Sustained Spontaneous Writing (SSW) is related to Sustained Silent Reading (SSR), described in Chapter 2 (Bromley, 1985). A short period of time is set aside for the children to write without interruptions. The time may vary from 5 minutes to 15 or 20 minutes and may be spent writing in journals, writing fiction, writing letters to others, or writing about some area of the curriculum. The students should be given some choice in topic unless they request direction, in which case the teacher may suggest that they write about the science experiment that was just done, a video that they saw in social studies, the most interesting thing that happened all day, the students' plans for the weekend, or some other fairly open-ended topic. When suggestions are given, they should be varied from day to day, so that children are encouraged to explore writing in different areas of the curriculum, in different forms, and on different topics unrelated to school. The writing is not graded, but children may share what they have written with the teacher and/or classmates if they choose to do so. The teacher should use the period to model the writing behavior expected of the students.

Use of Computers

Technology

Use of word processing can make writing of any kind easier for a student to handle. Teachers who have tried using word processing programs to enhance their writing instruction have often found that the children write more and revise more thoroughly when they can make revisions without the effort-intensive activity of recopying. Students who previously paid attention only to spelling, punctuation, and minor sentence structure problems when writing with pencil and paper begin to revise the organization of their pieces when they have the freedom to add, delete, and move material around without having to recopy anything. Many students find that they are prouder of their writing when it is done on the computer because it looks neater and is easier to read, and teachers also find that it is easier to read for the purpose of conferring about the writing being done, because handwriting obstacles are removed.

In experimentation with the use of the computer for implementing the language experience approach in first- and fourth-grade classes, Betty Roe had some encouraging results. The students dictated stories, and the instructor entered them into the computer. Ease of revision of the stories on the computer, as compared to stories written on the chalkboard or a chart, was over-

Reflections

What are the advantages of using word processing in the writing program? What are some possible disadvantages?

whelmingly obvious. The versions written on the board became smudgy-looking from erasures, crowded from insertions, and gappy from deletions. They had to be recopied for further use with the children. The computer versions looked perfect and did not have to be reworked. The printed copy could be provided to each child for later reading instruction. Some current word processing programs are usable by primary-level students, although word processing is more common in higher grades.

Examine the variety of word processing programs that are available for the equipment that is in your school and choose a program that is easy to use and easy to teach to the children. The features of the programs vary significantly, and it is wise to try several before choosing one for classroom purposes.

In addition to word processing programs, there are some pre- and postwriting programs to help students plan and revise writing. Prewriting programs supply activities to help students generate topics and organize ideas before writing. Postwriting programs usually provide help in revising and proofreading written products. Sometimes they ask the writer to analyze organizational aspects of the material, and sometimes they run text analyses and point out possible difficulties in spelling, style, usage, or mechanics.

Classroom Assessment for Writing Proficiency

Assessment of writing in a process writing approach is continuous. Much of the assessment is self-assessment by the students as they develop their written pieces. During the prewriting phase, they assess various topics for writing, forms of writing to use, audiences for which to write, and so on. During the drafting phase, they often assess whether they have enough information on the topic or not and make decisions about doing further research. They also assess the clarity of their ideas, and they may discuss the ideas with a peer or the teacher if they are unsure of the clarity. Peers or teachers may offer either oral or written questions or suggestions about the work. During the revision phase, the students take into account all teacher and peer comments and suggestions gleaned from peer and teacher conferences and evaluate the need to make changes based on this input. Written rubrics or checklists may be used to help in this process. During the editing phase, the students self-evaluate the writing in terms of writing conventions, spelling, grammar, and punctuation. They may also get input from editing partners or committees. During the publishing or sharing phase, there may be further evaluation from the audience, and at this point the final product may be formally graded, using a rubric.

You assess writing progress during writing conferences and also evaluate the end product to discover areas of writing in which the students need further instruction. Observation, checklists, and rubrics are the most common tools used. More on assessment and use of checklists and rubrics is found in Chapter 13.

Summary

Written communication is an extremely important curricular area and one in which many students have failed to gain proficiency. Instruction in written composition needs to be improved. The instructional focuses should be as follows: an emphasis on communication, purposeful assignments, stimuli for writing, provision of time for writing, encouragement of risk-taking in writing, provision of successful writing experiences, exposure of students to good literature, and teacher modeling of writing behavior.

There are five stages of the writing process with which you must be concerned: prewriting, writing a draft, revising, editing, and publishing and sharing. These stages are overlapping and recursive. During the prewriting stage, a topic is selected and delimited, the audience is clarified, and a decision is made about the general approach to the topic. During the drafting stage, the composition is put on paper and organized, and writing conferences are held. During the revision process, organization and clarity of presentation are considered. In the editing stage, proofreading for mechanics is done. Peer editing may be utilized. Word processing the piece can make revision easier. Publishing and sharing may take many forms, both oral and written. Writing workshop is a way to organize for writing instruction.

Some techniques are helpful for all types of writing. A process approach can be used with either creative or functional writing activities. Sustained Spontaneous Writing can be used as a device to encourage either creative or functional writing.

Discussion Questions

1. To develop proficiency in writing coherent material, would you put more emphasis on the mechanical aspects of writing (conventions of written language) or the organization of material? Why would you make this choice?

2. Describe some purposeful writing assignments that you could use in a classroom for a grade level of your choice.

3. Why do you think little writing is taking place in some classrooms? What are some ways you can alleviate the problems with having students write significant amounts each day?

4. What place do you believe literature has in the writing curriculum? How can you incorporate it into your writing instruction?

5. What aspects of the writing process would you model for the students before asking them to write a story or report? What other strategies or techniques would you model in the course of your writing instruction?

6. What advantages, or possibly disadvantages, do you see to the use of computers for writing instruction?

7. How can you make assignments that focus on audiences other than just the teacher?

8. What are some ways you can stimulate students to write in class?

9. Should you ask students to polish all of the writing that they do in class? Why, or why not?

10. Describe a variety of ways that you could have students share their writing.

Suggested Activities

1. Plan a lesson in which you model some aspect of the writing process for a grade level of your choice. Role-play this lesson with your classmates or teach it in an actual school setting.

2. Observe a writing lesson in a classroom of your choice. Note the degree to which each stage of the writing process is being emphasized. Share your reactions with your classmates.

3. Make a list of purposeful writing assignments that you might use at a grade level of your choice.

4. Lead a brainstorming session about a topic of interest involving either your classmates or elementary-level students. Expand the brainstormed ideas into a semantic web.

5. Role-play a teacher-student conference about the following beginning of a draft: We went on vacation. I had fun swimming there. The water was clear and warm.

6. Try out several different word processing programs designed for use with children. Evaluate the ease of use by the students for writing and revision.

7. Make a semantic web of how you spend your free time. Choose one branch of the web and write a paragraph based on it.

8. Plan a poetry-writing lesson for a form of poetry of your choice. Role-play this lesson with a group of your peers or teach it in an actual school setting. Evaluate its effectiveness.

9. Make a list of good purposes that students might have for letter writing in the classroom. Explain how each situation is meaningful to the students.

10. Collect samples of students' writings to share with your classmates and to analyze, based on the information in this chapter.

11. Find out what word processing programs are available for the computers in your public school or university setting. Make a chart of the features offered by each one. Evaluate the usefulness of each one for a grade level of your choice.

References

ALLINGTON, R. (1975). Sustained approaches to reading and writing. *Language Arts, 52,* 813–815.

ARNBERG, A. (1999). A study of memoir. *Primary Voices K–6, 8,* 13–19.

BLOEM, P. L. (2004). Correspondence journals: Talk that matters. *The Reading Teacher, 58,* 54–62.

BROMLEY, K. (1985). SSW: Sustained spontaneous writing. *Childhood Education, 62*(1), 23–29.

CALKINS, L. M. (1994). *The art of teaching writing* (new ed.). Portsmouth, NH: Heinemann.

CHURCH, S. M. (1985). Blossoming in the writing community. *Language Arts, 62,* 175–179.

GASKINS, I. W. (1982). A writing program for poor readers and writers and the rest of the class, too. *Language Arts, 59,* 854–861.

GOODMAN, K., & GOODMAN, Y. (1983). Reading and writing relationships: Pragmatic functions. *Language Arts, 60,* 590–599.

GRAVES, D. H. (1983). *Writing: Teachers and children at work.* Exeter, NH: Heinemann.

GRAVES, D. H. (1994). *A fresh look at writing.* Portsmouth, NH: Heinemann.

GRAVES, D., & HANSEN, J. (1983). The author's chair. *Language Arts, 60,* 176–183.

GREAT SOURCE EDUCATION GROUP. (1997). *Write on track language series sampler.* Wilmington, MA: Great Source Education Group.

HARP, B. (1988). When the principal asks: "Why aren't you using peer editing?" *The Reading Teacher, 41,* 828–829.

LONG, R., & BULGARELLA, L. (1985). Social interaction and the writing process. *Language Arts, 62,* 166–172.

NICKEL, J. (2001). When writing conferences don't work: Students' retreat from teacher agenda. *Language Arts, 79,* 136–147.

PIAZZA, C. L., & TOMLINSON, C. M. (1985). A concert of writers. *Language Arts, 62,* 150–158.

ROE, B. D. (2000). Using technology for content area literacy. In S. B. Wepner, W. J. Valmont, & R. Thurlow (Eds.), *Linking literacy and technology: A guide for K–8 classrooms* (pp. 133–158). Newark, DE: International Reading Association.

ROSS, E. P. (1996). *The workshop approach: A framework for literacy.* Norwood, MA: Christopher-Gordon.

RUSSELL, C. (1983). Putting research into practice: Conferencing with young writers. *Language Arts, 60,* 333–340.

SLUYS, K. V. (2003). Writing and identity construction: A young author's life in transition. *Language Arts, 80,* 176–184.

SMITH, F. (1983). Reading like a writer. *Language Arts, 60,* 558–567.

SULLIVAN, J. E., & SHARP, J. (2000). Using technology for writing development. In S. B. Wepner, W. J. Valmont, & R. Thurlow (Eds.), *Linking literacy and technology: A guide for K–8 classrooms* (pp. 106–132). Newark, DE: International Reading Association.

TEMPLE, C., ET AL. (1988). *The beginnings of writing* (2nd ed.). Boston: Allyn & Bacon.

WAGNER, L., NOTT, J. G., & AGNEW, A. T. (2001). The nuts and bolts of teaching first-grade writing through a journal workshop. *The Reading Teacher, 55,* 120–125.

YOUNG, D. (2004). Content area journal entry. East Middle School. Tullahoma, TN.

Books for Children and Adolescents Cited in This Chapter

LORD, B. B. (1984). *In the year of the boar and Jackie Robinson.* New York: HarperTrophy.

MARTIN, B., JR. (1983). *Brown bear, brown bear, what do you see?* New York: Holt.

NAYLOR, P. R. (1991). *Shiloh.* New York: Atheneum.

PAULSEN, G. (1987). *Hatchet.* New York: Viking Penguin.

PECK, R. (2000). *A year down yonder.* New York: Dial.

ROBINSON, B. (1972). *The best Christmas pageant ever.* New York: Avon.

SCIESZKA, J. (1992). *The true story of the 3 little pigs.* New York: Viking.

SPINELLI, J. (1997). *Maniac Magee.* New York: HarperCollins.

VIORST, J. (1972). *Alexander and the terrible, horrible, no good, very bad day.* New York: Atheneum.

VOIGT, C. (1982). *Dicey's song.* New York: Atheneum.

Chapter

9

TYPES OF WRITING

LEARNER OBJECTIVES

At the conclusion of this chapter

YOU SHOULD BE ABLE TO

1. Discuss the types of writing that students need to learn to use.

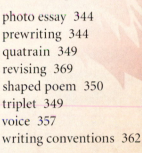

2. Implement some techniques that are of value in writing instruction.

3. Identify the following terms that are defined or explained in this chapter:

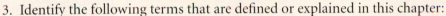

audience 359	free verse 349	photo essay 344
business letter 359	friendly letter 356	prewriting 344
cinquain 348	functional writing 354	quatrain 349
couplet 349	haiku 348	revising 369
creative writing 366	keypal project 359	shaped poem 350
dialogue journal 353	learning log 355	triplet 349
drafting 369	limericks 350	voice 357
editing 369	mechanics 362	writing conventions 362

NCTE/IRA Standards addressed in this chapter

STANDARD 4. Students adjust their use of spoken, written, and visual language (e.g., conventions, style, vocabulary) to communicate effectively with a variety of audiences and for different purposes.

STANDARD 5. Students employ a wide range of strategies as they write and use different writing process elements appropriately to communicate with different audiences for a variety of purposes.

STANDARD 6. Students apply knowledge of language structure, language conventions (e.g., spelling and punctuation), media techniques, figurative language, and genre to create, critique, and discuss print and non-print texts.

STANDARD 7. Students conduct research on issues and interests by generating ideas and questions, and by posing problems. They gather, evaluate, and synthesize data from a variety of sources (e.g., print and non-print texts, artifacts, people) to communicate their discoveries in ways that suit their purpose and audience.

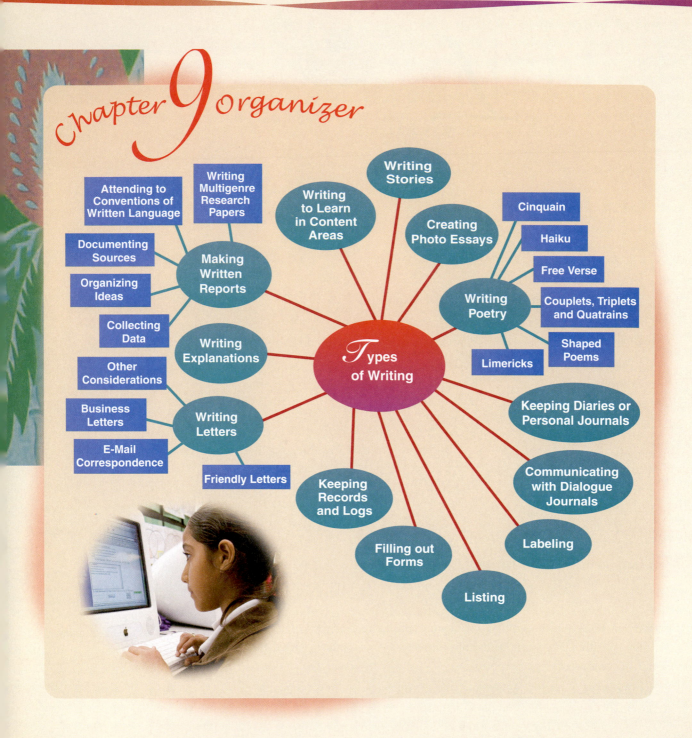

Chapter 9 Organizer

Types of Writing

- **Making Written Reports**
  - Attending to Conventions of Written Language
  - Writing Multigenre Research Papers
  - Documenting Sources
  - Organizing Ideas
  - Collecting Data

- **Writing Explanations**

- **Writing Letters**
  - Other Considerations
  - Business Letters
  - E-Mail Correspondence
  - Friendly Letters

- **Writing to Learn in Content Areas**

- **Writing Stories**

- **Creating Photo Essays**

- **Writing Poetry**
  - Cinquain
  - Haiku
  - Free Verse
  - Couplets, Triplets and Quatrains
  - Shaped Poems
  - Limericks

- **Keeping Diaries or Personal Journals**

- **Communicating with Dialogue Journals**

- **Labeling**

- **Listing**

- **Filling out Forms**

- **Keeping Records and Logs**

*M*RS. VANDEVER wants to teach her sixth-grade students about letter writing. She decides that friendly letters are easier to write than business letters, so she starts with a lesson about friendly letters. She makes charts containing examples of several friendly letters that she might have written to others or that she might have received. One is from a friend, telling about her excitement over buying a new car. One is from her sister, telling about the illness of her niece. Another is to her niece, urging her to get well and come to visit. Each letter is written in correct form, but not all of the greetings and closings are the same.

First, the class discusses many different reasons for writing friendly letters and many different people to whom they might wish to write friendly letters. They are given opportunities to tell about people who sometimes send letters to them and to whom they sometimes write letters. They are encouraged to discuss their pleasure when they receive mail and to mention people who would be pleased to hear from them. They talk about different content in the letters they have received from different people. Then Mrs. Vandever leads the students to discover that each sample letter has the same parts. Referring to the sample letters, she writes the names of these parts on the board: Heading, Greeting, Body, Closing, and Signature. She discusses with the class what each part is designed to accomplish.

Mrs. Vandever emphasizes the way that people make friendly letters personal. The class discusses the different greetings and closings on Mrs. Vandever's letters and on letters that they have received in the past. Then she says, "Now I want each one of you to think of someone to whom you would like to write a friendly letter. It could be a relative or a friend who lives in another town. It could be someone who is sick at home or in the hospital. Remember that Joey (a classmate) is still recovering from his automobile accident. You could write to him about the unit we are working on in class or about a book that you have read recently and enjoyed. What else could you write about that has happened either at home or at school?"

The students make several suggestions. Mrs. Vandever writes each suggestion on the board. Finally, she says, "Write someone a friendly letter, using the parts that we have just discussed. Be sure to include things that person would like to know. We will also learn how to address an envelope, so that you can send your letters."

Bob raises his hand. "How long should it be?" he asks.

"Write enough to tell the person what you want them to know," replies Mrs. Vandever. "Some letters will be longer than others because you will have more things to say. Joey has missed a lot of special activities. If you write to him, you can have a long letter, if you want to tell him several things. You may choose to focus on only one activity, though. It's your decision."

What's happening here?

Mrs. Vandever recognizes a real need that her students have. She plans instruction to meet the need. She stresses the practicality of the skill by showing examples to which her students can relate. She also links the lesson to their personal needs and prior experiences. The motivation for completing the assignment is the idea of communicating with someone to whom the students want to send information or ideas. The children actually send the letters to people who might respond and who certainly will appreciate hearing from them. Therefore, the task is one for which a purpose is evident. Mrs. Vandever's students' letters have authentic audiences.

In many classrooms, very little writing is done. Duplicated sheets that require a letter or a single-word response are frequently used, whereas constructed written responses to questions or problem situations and written reports and themes are not often found.

In real life, people write in many different forms. Sometimes when teachers think of writing instruction, they think primarily of writing stories, but students need to learn in the classroom how to write all kinds of discourse that they will need to function in society. This chapter addresses many types of writing that are needed in the language arts curriculum.

There are many types of writing that need to receive instructional attention. They include writing stories; creating photo essays; writing poetry; writing in diaries, personal journals, or dialogue journals; labeling, listing, filling out forms; keeping records and logs; writing letters; making written reports; writing explanations; and using various other forms of writing to learn in class.

Writing Stories

TO WRITE good stories, children need to know how good stories are constructed. A good story has a plot, or plan of action. The plot consists of a beginning that sets the stage, a middle that develops a conflict, a climax, and a fitting ending (Norton, 2003). Discussing these characteristics of stories that the children have read or listened to makes the children more aware of the need to develop a plot for the stories that they write. Children are surprisingly analytical when discussing books that they have read. "It just stopped," one sixth-grader complained of a passage that he had been asked to read. "The ending was not satisfying."

Good stories have true-to-life characters. Children need to see how authors of good literature develop characterization through description of the characters' appearances, their actions, their words, and their thoughts, as well as of the reactions of other characters to them. Stereotyped characters are less interesting than characters who project individual personalities. Children can recognize stereotypes after they have been introduced to the concept, and practice in identifying stereotypes in literature helps eliminate them in the children's own writing.

Some children do not understand that, when they write fiction, the stories are not all "fake," but are based on things that people experience. You may want to encourage them to make their stories reality-based, or grounded in their own experiences. Because fiction needs to be believable, you may want to encourage them to do research to make their fiction pieces sound realistic.

A process writing approach results in a higher level of composition than does merely providing motivation and asking children to write independently. Using a process approach takes more time than simply providing a stimulus for writing, but it is worthwhile.

Consider letting children coauthor stories, if the children show an interest in doing so, after seeing that many of their favorite books have more than one author. Collaboration results in pooling of knowledge about the subject and about writing forms and conventions and therefore helps children learn more at times than they would learn by working independently.

Creating Photo Essays

Technology

PHOTO ESSAYS are a special type of writing. They may tell stories, but they may not. They can be about anything, including content area studies.

Photo essays are a set of related photographs with an accompanying written account. This writing form requires choosing a topic, planning pictures, picture taking, and writing the account. You can ask students to choose topics of interest, decide on scenes that express ideas about the topics, and photograph each scene. Illustrating the scenes with pencil and paper often helps students. They may need help in staging the scenes and taking the photographs. After the pictures are taken and processed, the children must write titles, captions for each of the pictures, and narratives to connect the photographs. The availability of digital photography can make creating photo essays easier.

Sinatra and colleagues (1990) have used photo essays and semantic maps to build background knowledge of culturally diverse students and help them organize writing. Students worked in pairs to brainstorm possible topics, take photos, arrange the photos on storyboards, and write compositions on the topics represented. The technique was effective.

Figure 9.1 is a photo essay written by an English language learner (ELL) being tutored by Lance Jasitt.

Writing Poetry

CHILDREN ARE not likely to be excited about writing poetry just because you come in one day and say, "Today I want each of you to write a poem about winter." Many students have a certain amount of animosity toward poetry. Most children, however, enjoy poetry if it is presented to them properly. The **prewriting** phase of poetry writing is often neglected, but it is vitally important. See Chapter 2 for a discussion of the presentation of poetry to children and children's reactions to poetry.

Entice students into the world of poetry and poetry writing by giving them the opportunity to hear appropriate poems by good poets read by a person who genuinely loves poetry and who reads it well. An oral introduction is important because poetry is often written more for the ear than for the eye, although there are a few primarily visual poetry forms. Then give students the opportunity to read poetry for themselves. Prominently display books containing good poetry for children. Such selections as *Where the Sidewalk Ends* and *The Light in the Attic* by Shel Silverstein and *A*

*F*IGURE 9.1   **Photo Essay by an English Language Learner**

Photo Essay by Anareli Cruz

Estes materiales se necesitan para hacer artesanía mexicana. Con estos trabajamos la joyería.

These materials are needed to make Mexican crafts. With these we work on jewelry.

1.

Aquí estamos trabajando con shakira. El trabajo es un poco cansado.

Here we are working with beads. The work is a little tiring.

2.

Estoy terminando el final de este collar. Se necesita tener paciencia.

I am finishing the end of this necklace. You need to have patience.

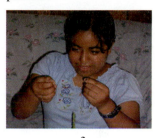

3.

Así se está ensartan las shakiras. Aquí estoy haciendo la figura.

This is how beads are connected. Here I am making a pattern.

4.

Aquí están las pulseras y collares terminadas.

Here are the finished bracelets and necklaces.

5.

Mi hermana ganó una cinta azul por una pulsera en la fería.

My sister won a blue ribbon for a bracelet at the fair.

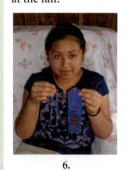

6.

Estos son todos los collares que hicimos. Ya están listo para vender.

These are all of the necklaces that we made. They are ready to sell.

7.

Source: Anareli Cruz, Jere Whitson Elementary School, Cookeville, TN. Used with permission.

Pizza the Size of the Sun by Jack Prelutsky are good sources of poems that children readily read. Also encourage students when they show an interest in producing poetry.

Like other forms of writing, poetry writing should be preceded by experiences on which the writing will be based. You can provide direct experiences or vicarious ones like those mentioned in the section in Chapter 8 on providing stimuli for writing. Encourage your students to talk about their experiences, listen to others talk, and

FIGURE 9.2 **Origins Poem Used for a Model**

Origins

I am from houses that didn't have to be locked,
    from hot summer nights, sitting outside in the warm breeze
    with lightning bugs dotting the darkness
    and crickets calling to each other.
I am from the limbs of the black cherry tree--
    from forbidden heights that were irresistible.
I am from long walks carrying laundry to the laundromat
    and carrying it back wet to hang on a line in the backyard.
I am from waxing floors on my hands and knees and polishing them
    with cloths on my feet as I skated across the floor,
    with the clean, fresh smell of the wax and the warm feeling
    of my mother working beside me, singing.
I am from long walks with my grandmother across town
    to visit friends.
I am from Saturday at the movies with a newsreel, a cartoon,
    a serial, a double feature, and previews of coming attractions,
    munching on buttered popcorn and drinking a fountain Coke,
    both purchased for a dime.
I am from cornbread, white beans, baked potatoes,
    and fried apricot pies.
I am from sitting in the heat hall at Granny's house,
    smelling the yeast rolls rise.
I am from curling up in an overstuffed chair and reading a book,
    ignoring the world.
I am from swinging across the creek on a fraying rope,
    fearful of falling in and being discovered by my mother
    doing something I had been forbidden to do.
I am from singing along as my mother played the piano by ear
    and playing duets with her, always getting the easy part.
I am from vacations in Florida,
    started in the middle of the night,
    with no stops along the way without protest.
I am from sitting up all night on Christmas Eve,
    after opening presents at three different houses
    and returning home to find that Santa had already come.
I am from bottle rockets and Roman candles and sparklers
    that lit up the sky, but never lasted long enough.
I am from lying on my stomach,
    staring into the fire in the fireplace,
    while the grownups talked companionably behind me.
I am from warmth, and security, and love.

BETTY D. ROE

Source: Betty D. Roe, Tennessee Technological University, Cookeville, TN, Copyright ©1995. Used with permission.

experiment with ways of expressing their ideas. Marshall and Newman (1997, p. 15) point out "that poetry is as much a way of seeing as writing, and that the poet's vision comes from seeing what is essential in the world around them." They encourage teachers to help students to look at things as artists do and really see them.

Roberts (2002) suggests infusing technology into the prewriting stage of poetry writing. She states, "Technological applications that use brainstorming software, databases and spreadsheet applications, presentation software, CD-ROM software, and the Internet show the variety of technological paths one may wander in the prewriting process" (pp. 678-679).

Roberts (2002) also suggests the use of a CD called *In My Own Voice,* which contains contemporary poetry by people of color and interviews with the poets. This CD helps the students to realize that poetry is often about everyday things.

Take a look at *New Kids on the Net* (Burgstahler & Utterback, 2000) for Internet sites and activities to use with your poetry instruction. A favorite site of ours is http://teacher.scholastic.com/writewit/poetry/index.htm.

Literature is one of the best ways to introduce poetry writing. Betty Roe attended a workshop by George Ella Lyons, who read a poem from Jo Carson's *Stories I Ain't Told Nobody Yet* about when you are considered to be from a place. After reading Carson's poem, Lyons asked the workshop attendees to write poems about where they were from, somewhat modeled on Carson's poem. Betty ended up writing an origins poem in a style similar to that of Carson's poem. Her poem is found in Figure 9.2. Betty went back and used the technique with a group of graduate students who were in-service teachers. These students were surprised and pleased by the products that they produced in class, but they were delighted when they tried the technique with their own elementary school students and got wonderful results. The lack of required rhyme or meter and the emphasis on images seemed to free the students to write. This technique is particularly effective for older students.

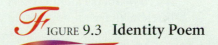

$\mathcal{F}$IGURE 9.3   **Identity Poem**

Dillon

Child of Scott and Cynthia Young
Grandson of Robert & Phyllis Young
Grandson of James & Virgie Roe
Friend to many
Who is friendly, kind, and caring
Lover of extremes, soccer, and food
Who enjoys wake-boarding
Who needs sports
Who fears failure
Who hates stinging animals
Who believes in God
Resident of Tullahoma

Young

Source: Dillon Young, Fifth Grade, Robert E. Lee Elementary School, Tullahoma, TN. Used with permission.

When Dillon Young was a fifth-grader, he was asked by his teacher to write a poem that could be classified as an identity poem. He was given beginning prompts for each line (first two words) and completed the poem about himself that is found in Figure 9.3.

Different styles of poetry may be introduced separately. For each style, you may first read examples. Then you may discuss the characteristics of the particular type, using a poem that has been read for an example. Next it may be helpful to have the children write one or more group poems of that type. After the children see how good the class products are, encourage individual productions. It is most effective if you write while the children write and share what you have written before inviting the children to share. The children should not be forced to share, but if the atmosphere of the classroom is one of trust, many of them will choose to do so. Some may ask for reactions from the group in order to revise the drafts of their poems that they have just finished. Such sharing may be conducted like peer conferences. Positive comments should always precede suggestions for improvement, and questions that show interest and indicate points of uncertainty are also preferable to negative statements. Poems that the children feel are polished can be shared orally, displayed on a bulletin board, published in a personal book, or published in a class book.

Cinquain

A good poetry form for early writing instruction is the cinquain. **Cinquains** are unrhymed five-line poems that are very easy to write. Children pick up the form quickly. The requirements for a cinquain are as follows:

Line 1: One word (the title)

Line 2: Two words (describing the title)

Line 3: Three words (expressing action)

Line 4: Four words (expressing a feeling)

Line 5: One word (referring to or repeating the title)

A good source for cinquains to read to children prior to their writing these poems is Lee Bennett Hopkins's *City Talk*. The following are examples of cinquains written by elementary school students.

Camping

Neat tents

Hiking, eating, playing

It was good fun.

Trip

Source: Toby Ray Gaddis, Second Grade, Farrar Elementary School, Tullahoma, TN. Used with permission.

Swimming

Muscle exercise

Diving, lapping, competing

It's fun and dangerous.

Meets

Source: Kristy Allison Gaddis, Sixth Grade, West Middle School, Tullahoma, TN. Used with permission.

Haiku

Haiku is another popular poetry form. It is a highly structured unrhymed form of Japanese poetry. It consists of three lines containing a total of seventeen syllables. The arrangement of syllables is as follows.

Line 1: Five syllables

Line 2: Seven syllables

Line 3: Five syllables

Haiku usually contains a reference to nature in addition to mention of the time of day, season, or setting. The following is an example of haiku.

The hummingbird swarms

around the azalea bush

gath'ring food and drink.

Source: Jennifer Oglesby, Eighth Grade, Martin Junior High School, Crossville, TN. Used with permission.

Free Verse

Free verse is a form of unrhymed poetry that has no set number of lines and no set rhythmical pattern. Free verse emphasizes the expression of the thought without having to adjust it to meet artificial restrictions. The following are examples of free verse.

Snowy white trees	The morning mist
Tall and towering	Bright shining dew
Watching over us	The clear new world
With a great deal of pride.	Innocent and free.

Source: Lee Ann Hamby, Seventh Grade, South Cumberland Elementary School, Crossville, TN. Used with permission.

Couplets, Triplets, and Quatrains

The simplest form of rhymed verse is the couplet. A **couplet** consists of two rhymed lines. Young children can be introduced to writing couplets by trying to supply last lines to go with first lines that you supply. Later the children can supply both lines themselves. A **triplet** consists of three rhyming lines. A **quatrain** is a four-line rhymed poem. It may have various rhyme schemes, such as *abab, aabb,* and *abcb.* An example of a poem written in multiple couplets follows.

A Bottle on the Shore

One night a bottle came ashore.

I lifted it and began to pour.

Then its contents made me feel grand.

For its contents was golden sand.

The sand made me very rich.

So I threw the bottle in a ditch.

The next day a gift came for me.

In my yard was a bottle tree.

In the bottles were a great treasure.

That gave me lots and lots of pleasure.

Inside the bottle was a mold,
Which makes me look beautiful till I'm old.

Soon people gave lots of money.
Then my future looked real sunny.

But don't believe the story I told.
For there's no such thing as a beauty mold.

Source: Jessamyn Bradley, Fifth Grade, Sycamore Intermediate School, Pleasant View, TN. Used with permission.

An example of a rhymed poem that was written in response to a traumatic event in our country follows.

9-11-01

You can knock down our Towers,

And kill three thousand people in just one hour.

You can make us scream,

At your little scheme.

You can make us give blood,

And make us clean up the mud.

You can make a firefighter a hero,

And make the towers go to Ground Zero.

You can make people die,

But the flag will still fly!

We have tons of people on our side,

Bin Laden you can run but you can't hide!

O, please I pardon,

But we will catch you Osama bin Laden!

Source: Kelsey Brooke Atkinson, Fifth Grade, Glenn Martin Elementary School, Crossville, TN. Used with permission.

Shaped Poems

Sometimes the shape of the poem is a part of the poem's message. Figure 9.4 is an example of two **shaped poems**.

Limericks

Limericks have five lines. The first, second, and fifth lines rhyme, and the third and fourth lines rhyme, producing a rhyme scheme of *aabba*. Limericks are generally humorous, and children enjoy them immensely. The following is an example of a limerick.

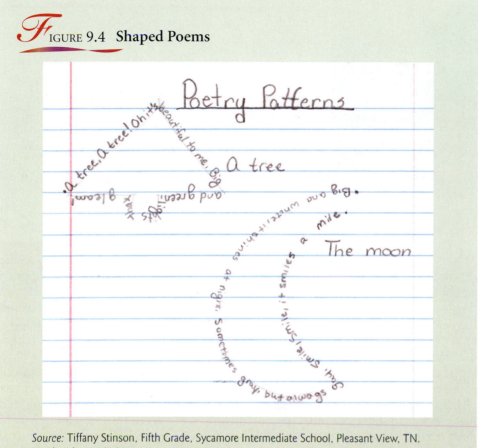

𝓕IGURE 9.4 **Shaped Poems**

Source: Tiffany Stinson, Fifth Grade, Sycamore Intermediate School, Pleasant View, TN. Used with permission.

There once was an athlete named Jerry.

He was so good it was scary,

When he got the ball,

His opponent would fall,

Because his legs were so hairy.

Source: Sean Stephens, Seventh Grade, South Cumberland Elementary School, Crossville, TN. Used with permission.

Reflections

What role does modeling by the teacher play in writing? Could it sometimes be inhibiting? How could the teacher avoid that?

𝓚eeping Diaries or Personal Journals

DIARIES OR personal journals are records of events, feelings, or ideas that the writer has each day. They serve as memory devices, ways of letting off steam, or ways of

Diaries or personal journals are records for the students, not intended to be graded.

relieving tension. They may be kept in bound journals or blank books, spiral-bound notebooks, or loose-leaf binders. They are never intended to be graded. You should not read them at all unless the children invite you to do so. If they are done in loose-leaf binders, children can take out pages to share with you without exposing the entire journals to scrutiny. Each page should have the date at the top and the student's name, if he or she wants you to read it. That way pages can be slipped into a folder for you to read and respond to and then be replaced in their chronological order when they are returned. Do not respond directly on the journal pages unless the child indicates such a preference. Put your response on a separate sheet of paper. The responses are not for the purpose of correcting the writing but for reacting to the content. If a child tells of the death of his grandfather, you might respond, "I know you are sad about this, but I can tell that you have many good memories of your grandfather. My grandfather died many years ago. It made me sad too, but I still remember the good times we had together." Although you never mention errors in the way the child expressed himself, your response should model good sentence structure, correct spelling, and accurate punctuation. If the child misspelled *grandfather,* he now sees the correct spelling and has a chance to study it in order to spell the word correctly next time. Children learn most of their speech indirectly in this same way at home with their parents. Journal responses teach without appearing to do so. You have shown through the sympathetic response in the journal that you understood what the child had to say, that it was perceived as important, and that you are a person with similar feelings. This makes the child more likely to want to share more writing with you in the future.

The children practice writing skills and can also experiment with writing without any pressure of evaluation. The writing is important to them, and, therefore, they expend effort to make it serve their purposes.

As an introduction to personal journal or diary writing, the class can do a group classroom diary by group dictation of each day's events. These diaries can then be used as the basis for a weekly or monthly letter to parents about what has been going on in class. The children will see that recording the events in the diary acts as a memory helper.

Time must be provided for journal writing. During this time you should write also, at times sharing your writing with the class and at times keeping it private, just as the students do. You may wish to model different types of journal entries during the sharing times—sometimes relating happenings, sometimes expressing feelings, and sometimes including fanciful material.

Jennifer Magnusson, a fifth-grade teacher, has her students write daily in personal journals. They may write about topics of their own choice, but she also provides some prompts for students who cannot think of their own topics. Figure 9.5 is an example from Stacie Moerdyk's personal journal, when responding to a teacher's prompt.

FIGURE 9.5   **Personal Journal Entry**

> 10-7-02
>
> Journal
> "Just Say No", means alot to me because
> it teaches kids to just say no to
> drugs and alcholhol and other dangerous
> things that people will offer you in the
> future. "Just Say No" is a good way of
> teaching children to say no.
> And that is what "Just Say No"
> is to me.

Source: Stacie Moerdyk, Fifth Grade, Pleasant Hill School, Pleasant Hill, TN. Used with permission.

Communicating with Dialogue Journals

DIALOGUE JOURNALS, in which the student writes entries and you respond in writing in the same journal, are meant to be two-way communication between you and the student, rather than being personal and private. Students can share incidents,

Applications for English Language Learners and Struggling Learners

Dialogue journals are particularly good for use with ELLs and struggling learners because they provide a risk-free environment. You, as the teacher, never correct their spelling, punctuation, or usage, but you respond to their meaning and model correct usage in your response. This nonjudgmental modeling takes place in an authentic communication event, providing students with motivation to write clearly and with self-esteem because their writing is taken seriously and given thoughtful responses.

Labeling objects in the room can help young children learn sight words, while performing a needed task.

express concerns, ask questions, and generally talk to you on paper. Once again, these are not to be graded for mechanical accuracy, but responded to in terms of content. Notebooks that have a vertical line dividing the pages are good to use for these journals. The child can write on the left side of the paper and you can respond on the right side, by making comments and asking questions. You may entice a student to write more by asking for elaboration or by expressing interest in something the child has written. You provide a writing model with your responses in the journal.

Labeling

FROM THE earliest elementary grades, children encounter the need for labeling. They may need to label their boxes of supplies, their desks, their lockers, and other personal possessions. If they are making displays of various materials, labels may be necessary. Art may be labeled as to subject matter and child artist. Posters of different types may also require labels.

To facilitate early labeling, such as that of their personal possessions, you may write the names needed on a sheet of paper or on the board and let the children copy the words. Later the children should be encouraged to use such reference materials as picture dictionaries to make needed labels.

Listing

LISTING IS a **functional writing** skill that children see adults using frequently. They see their parents making grocery lists and lists of chores. They see their teachers making lists of assignments or groups. You may want to encourage children to list things that they plan to do that they do not want to forget, supplies that they need to bring to school for particular projects, people that they would like to work with at centers, and many other things. The children practice writing skills while making the lists and also practice reading skills when they refer to the lists later.

illing Out Forms

OUR SOCIETY is richly endowed with forms that need to be completed. Children must complete many forms as part of their school lives and others as a part of activities at home. Application blanks, registration slips, subscription blanks, order blanks, headings on standardized tests, and library cards call for form-completion skills.

Generally, forms specify that they should be filled out in manuscript writing or typed. If the forms are not filled out both accurately and neatly, the children may not accomplish their purposes. This can serve as a strong motivational force to practice their best thinking and writing skills. Emphasize the importance of filling out forms correctly and provide correct models for forms that the children must complete at the times when such forms are needed. Sample forms can be completed by the class as a practice activity before the real form is used. This gives the children a chance to correct mistakes before using forms that are sometimes hard to change once they have been filled out. It gives you a chance to explain the meanings of certain entries that children are confused about, such as the heading "Class," which could mean the subject of the class or the grade level of the class.

Keeping Records and Logs

CHILDREN HAVE many in-class opportunities to keep records. They may keep a class log in which they, individually or as a group (through use of a secretary), keep a daily record of progress through a unit of work. They may keep running accounts of experiments in progress or of daily changes in the weather. Individual students may record their daily or weekly progress in one or more subject areas, such as arithmetic.

Franks (2001) had her middle school language arts students observe the weather each day and sketch cloud formations. After that, they wrote about the experience in response to their choice of five writing prompts she provided. These prompts addressed their observations, questions that they had, reflections and personal memories, associations that they made, or forecasts. This process improved their retention of science facts.

Students in Pennsylvania are taking part in an oral history project. Each student chooses a person as a subject, interviews the person, and researches his or her history and interests. Findings are presented to their classmates on a "triptych"—a three-part presentation board on which the student places a memoir written or told by the person, photos, and artifacts related to the subject. Sometimes news articles about the person and other things that convey the essence of the person to readers are included (Dickson, Heyler, Reilly, Romano, & DiLullo, 2002).

Learning logs, written accounts of thoughts, questions, and information learned in content area classes, are valuable learning devices. Children can use them to summarize what they have learned from a class period or from their reading, to record questions that they have about content, to make connections among ideas that have been presented, and to speculate about applications of the information. You may specify the questions to be answered in the logs, such as "What did you learn from Chapter 6?" and "What questions do you still have about the material that you read?" You should read these logs, note misconceptions and missing information, write some responses in the logs, and use the information gained to plan subsequent lessons. Respond to the logs, but do not grade them, to encourage free responses in the logs.

In keeping records, accuracy is vitally important. Also, generally not all information pertaining to a subject can be recorded. Therefore, the students must learn to choose the most important details and record them briefly but clearly. In making progress reports, daily entries should be dated.

If there are classroom clubs, some students will need to write minutes of the meetings. These students will be motivated to learn record-keeping skills because they are interested in club activities and because they hold the prestigious position of secretary in the clubs. If officers of clubs change frequently and if there are several clubs appropriate for students with different interests, many children can learn these important skills in a highly functional setting.

You should work with students to set standards for record keeping and help them analyze their records in view of the stated standards. Students must be helped to see that records are written to be understood by people other than the writers and that clarity of expression is therefore highly important. Children may exchange records for the purpose of proofreading and detecting omissions of necessary details.

 # *W*riting Letters

PERHAPS THE most common experience with functional writing that children have is letter writing. Letter writing should be taught to the children when they can see a real need for the writing. Many such occasions are available. Letter-writing activities are more positively received if the letters are going to be mailed. Some examples of letters that can be mailed are ones to sick classmates, invitations to class functions, requests for material to be used in a class project, requests for help from parents, requests for permission to go on field trips, and letters ordering magazine subscriptions. Vos (2002/2003) had good results letting students who had genuine purposes for writing to authors do just that in writing workshop. They took their letters through the stages of the writing process and were excited about the prospect of getting replies. To avoid undue disappointment, they need to understand that not all authors have time to reply and that the letters they get may be form letters, but the rewards of response are worth the perils of disappointment.

To encourage interest in letter writing, you may make use of Mark Teague's *Dear Mrs. LaRue*, Sesyle Joslin's *Dear Dragon*, or Janet and Allan Ahlberg's *The Jolly Postman or Other People's Letters*. The humor in these books adds some spice to discussions of proper form.

Friendly Letters

Friendly letters are characterized by informality; for example, they may use contractions. They should be newsy, containing information that has been carefully selected to interest the reader. They should express the writer's personality. The students should write friendly letters as if they are talking to the intended recipients. It may even help to address the recipients by name at times.

Students need to be aware of the characteristics of a friendly letter (heading, greeting, body, closing, and signature) and the proper punctuation to be used in different parts. You may find it helpful to devise a large poster to illustrate the correct form for a friendly letter. The five main parts could be labeled on the poster. Attention to punctuation could be encouraged by the use of a contrasting color for punctuation marks. You might suggest that each child copy the correct form, so that he could carry it home for use in personal correspondence. An example of one correct form for a friendly letter is in Figure 9.6.

Figure 9.7 shows a sample of a friendly letter written by a girl in first grade and one by the same girl written in fifth grade. Jasmin's first-grade letter was written to Betty Roe in response to a series of storytelling and language-activity sessions that she conducted in Jasmin's classroom. The teacher did not dictate anything that the students should write in their letters to Betty. The children wrote from their own feelings and in their own **voices**. Jasmin's letter shows her reaction to the entire storytelling program.

*F*IGURE 9.6   **Form for Friendly Letter**

(HEADING)   Your Street Address
City, State Zip Code
Date

Dear _____,   (GREETING)

_____
_____
_____
_____
(BODY)
_____
_____
_____
_____

(CLOSING)   **Your friend,**
Your Name
(SIGNATURE)

Jasmin

Dear Dr Roe. I thank you for telling us all the stories you have told us. And the plays you let us do. Thank you very much.

Source: Jasmin Adams, First Grade, Crossville Elementary School, Crossville, TN. Used with permission.

Rt. 9 box 71X
Crossville, TN. 38555
September 29, 1988

Dear Therese,
How have you been? Sorry I haven't written you in a long time. I haven't had enough time to write because I have been reading *The Best Christmas Pageant Ever* by Barbara Robinson.
I like the part of the book when all the kids set fire to a barn just to get donuts. Or when one of the kids went to the bathroom at church and started smoking and the people who worked there called the fire department because they thought the church was on fire but it wasn't, it was her smoking. I'm not going to tell you any more because it will spoil the book for you.
Write back when you have read it. If you have read any good books let me know so I can read them to

Your friend,
Jasmin

Source: Jasmin Adams, Fifth Grade, Crossville Elementary School, Crossville, TN. Used with permission.

358

E-mailing keypals motivates students to write with a specific audience in mind.

It is neat and carefully written, but it lacks standard form, other than the use of "Dear" in the salutation. As a fifth-grader, Jasmin showed much growth in her knowledge of letter-writing form over her first-grade performance. Her fifth-grade letter contains all of the five main parts of a friendly letter.

You may want to pair your class with another class as pen pals to provide authentic letter-writing experiences. Lemkuhl (2002) paired her inner-city second-grade class in Ohio with a class of Arizona first-graders in a bilingual program for this purpose. The letters that were exchanged turned into a cross-curricular learning experience, as the students shared information related to social studies, science, and math classes, while they were applying language, spelling, and writing skills.

E-mail Correspondence

Classes can also be paired to correspond through e-mail. In Kentucky, students correspond with students in other schools about books they are reading as a part of the Kentucky Telecommunications Writing Project (Bell, Cambron, Rey-Barreau, & Paeth, 1995; Holland, 1996). Finding out about this project prompted Betty Roe to set up a **keypal project** between her university methods students and classes of public school students. In it, methods students and their matched partners read the same literature selections and conversed about these selections through e-mail exchanges. The project was a great success in the view of the public school students and their teachers, as well as the university students and their teachers. In a seven-year period, several faculty members participated. Methods of implementation have varied from semester to semester, and different grade levels were involved over the course of the project. Roe and Smith (1997) believe that this model is helpful from the standpoint of motivation for writing, providing an authentic **audience** for writing, and providing writing models for the public school students. Other educators have reported good results with similar projects (McDermott & Setoguchi, 1999; McKeon, 1999; Niday & Campbell, 2000; Sullivan, 1998). Middle school students with special needs have also been paired with college students for e-mail exchanges (Stivers, 1996).

Business Letters

Business letters are characterized by brevity. Only the essential facts are included in such letters. Business letters have six main parts (heading, inside address, greeting, body, closing, and signature). You could make a large poster similar to the one for friendly letters to illustrate the form and punctuation of a business letter. An example of one correct form for a business letter is in Figure 9.8.

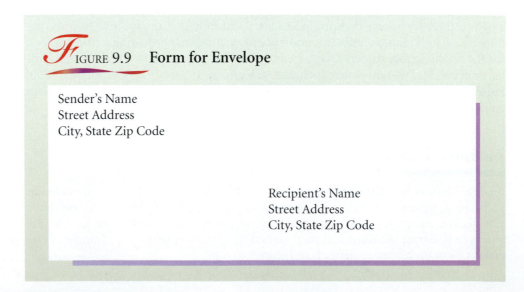

$\mathcal{F}$IGURE 9.8 **Form for Business Letter**

(HEADING)

Your Street Address
City, State Zip Code
Date

Recipient's Name
Street Address   (INSIDE ADDRESS)
City, State Zip Code

To Whom It May Concern: (GREETING)

_____
_____
_____
_____
_____ (BODY)
_____
_____

(CLOSING)   Sincerely,
                   Your Name
(SIGNATURE)

$\mathcal{F}$IGURE 9.9 **Form for Envelope**

Sender's Name
Street Address
City, State Zip Code

                        Recipient's Name
                        Street Address
                        City, State Zip Code

Other Considerations

In all letters, courtesy is important. Encourage students to proofread their letters in an effort to detect discourteous statements, so that these statements can be eliminated from the final drafts of the letters.

Attention to proper form for addressing envelopes is also important. A poster may be developed to illustrate this form. An example of one correct form for addressing an envelope is in Figure 9.9.

riting Explanations

CHILDREN OFTEN need to write explanations of how to do certain things, how various things work, or why events occur at particular times. To write such explanations, they must be aware of the need for accuracy of information, clarity of expression, and use of effective language. They need to be able to recognize causes and effects and to see relationships among ideas and facts.

Children at times need to write explanations of events that have occurred in the classroom (for example, experiments, demonstrations, explanations of the ways to solve math problems or difficulties in solving these problems). These explanations may include definitions of terms and details and sequences of events.

aking Written Reports

TEACHERS OFTEN ask students to share their research findings with others through written reports. Writing reports involves many related skills.

Collecting Data

The first step in report writing is collection of data through reading, observing, experimenting, or interviewing. These data need to be recorded in a meaningful fashion, so that students can use them with accuracy in their written reports.

NOTE TAKING

Note-taking skills can be taught in a functional setting when students are preparing written reports. Students need to be taught to include key words and phrases in their notes, include enough context to make the notes understandable after a period of time has elapsed, include bibliographical references with each note, copy direct quotations exactly, and indicate carefully which notes are direct quotations and which are reworded.

Notes can be taken in outline form, in sentence or paragraph form, or in graphic form (for example, feature matrixes, webs, or time lines). Outline form can be taught in a useful context by asking the students to fill out partial outlines of chapters in their subject-matter textbooks. Gradually, the information that is given can be decreased until the students are making out the entire outline without aid. Feature matrixes, webs, and time lines may also be taught through initial use of partially filled out devices. (Chapter 12 has more information about note taking.)

SUMMARIZING

Summarizing skills are needed if notes are taken in paragraph form. Once again, you may use subject-matter textbooks to teach summarizing. You may start by reading a sentence, identifying the key words in the sentence, and explaining why those words were chosen. Then you may ask the students to pick out the key words in other sentences. Next, you may model picking out the key sentence in a paragraph and then ask the children to pick out the key sentences in other paragraphs. Finally, you may model the process of finding the key idea or ideas in an entire selection and then ask the children to try this process. In each case, teacher modeling comes first, followed by student practice under your supervision and then by independent practice by the students. If this practice is done with their textbooks, the children are using meaningful material that they really need to understand.

Organizing Ideas

After the data have been collected, the students need to organize the ideas for the reports. Completed feature matrixes, webs, outlines, or time lines can provide the organization for writing. Information from them can then be used to write paragraphs about the material. The teacher should first model the writing of a paragraph from the organizational device to be used. Then the students write paragraphs and share their writing. One branch of a web, one row of a feature matrix, or one section of an outline could serve as the basis for each paragraph.

Documenting Sources

The inclusion of a bibliography with the report is helpful, both to the reporter and the reader. The reporter may use the bibliography to point out books that substantiate the statements he has made. The reader may use the bibliography to locate more information on the subject than is included in the report.

For students in the early grades, the bibliography need include only the title of the book and the author. Students in higher grades should include author, title, publisher, place of publication, copyright date, and, where applicable, page numbers. Examples of these two forms are as follows.

1. Lower grades
   From Slave Ship to Freedom Road by Julius Lester

2. Upper grades
   Lester, Julius. *From Slave Ship to Freedom Road.* New York: Puffin Books, 1998.

Attending to Conventions of Written Language

In writing the report, attention must be given to **writing conventions**, or **mechanics**, since the report is intended to communicate information to others. The student should proofread the report to detect errors in spelling, capitalization, punctuation, and grammar. The final copy should be written legibly and should have a neat appearance. Attention to such details as using proper spacing between words and leaving appropriate margins helps to produce an attractive report that is usable by others. Chapter 10 has suggestions for working on use of writing conventions.

Writing Multigenre Research Papers

Traditional research papers are often viewed as formulaic exercises that lack interest and originality. Some teachers have experimented with other approaches to research writing that are more motivational and relevant to students. Some have changed the mode of presentation of information. A promising new approach that Moulton (1999) uses for high school students is the multigenre research paper, developed by Romano (1995). Scaled down slightly, this approach to reports can appeal to middle school students, who frequently are already using a variety of genres that computers have made more accessible because of the font choices and formatting available on word processing programs. Newspaper articles, obituaries, ads, and editorials; birth, marriage, and death certificates; wedding invitations; advertising posters; diaries and journals; plays; different types of poems; letters; receipts; recipes; greeting cards; book covers; letters; and other genres can be formatted to look like the real thing. Pictures can be imported into the material and captioned. Students can use their creativity and take advantage of their own special strengths. Allen (2001) documents the use of such research papers in grades 4 through 6.

Technology

With multigenre papers, students research a person, event, or other topic and reveal the information in a number of creative forms, such as the genres mentioned above. There is a bibliography at the end, but the nature of the body of the paper does not allow for internal citations. Moulton (1999) suggests the use of endnotes about each genre in terms of the source of the information and the reason behind the use of that genre.

Grierson, Anson, and Baird (2002, p. 52), spurred by the adoption of a state core curriculum that requires understanding of "functional, informational, and literary texts from different periods, cultures and genres," as specified by the Utah State Office of Education in 1999, decided to experiment with the use of multigenre papers for this purpose in sixth-grade classes. After modeling by the classroom teachers, the students were asked to produce a multigenre paper about chosen ancestors. For students who could not find out enough about their ancestors to produce papers, the option was to choose from famous historical figures. In the research for family members' histories, students were encouraged to use such primary sources as genealogy charts, journals, tombstones, and interviews with relatives. They filled out Rationale Cards for recording why they chose each genre and the sources of their information for that genre. Genres used included birth certificates, letters, obituaries, and telegrams.

Moulton (1999) asked high school students to use eight different genres. We suggest that four or five different pieces in three or four different genres may be more appropriate for middle school students. Just as is true with traditional research papers, the students should be expected to use multiple sources and integrate the information from different sources into a paper that conveys the important information about the subject.

Meagan Jasitt has produced a multigenre book report on the book *The Midwife's Apprentice*. It is shown in Figure 9.10. Meagan's endnotes were on a single page at the end of her paper, but they have been integrated into Figure 9.10 for the clarity of this example.

$\mathscr{F}$IGURE 9.10 **Multigenre Book Report**

The Knight. My poem is about the dream of
a girl in the Middle Ages for her handsome knight.

▼

He's my knight in
shining armor,
I can't explain our love,
He's more precious to me than anything,
I thank God above.

Tomorrow is our wedding,
And our honeymoon is too,
We'll ride off on his horse,
After I say, "I Do".

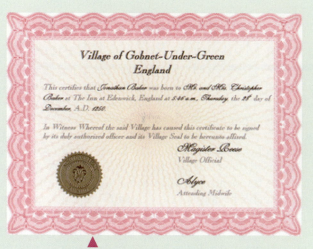

▲

Birth Certificate. Adapted from Chapter 16, "The Baby"
by Karen Cushman, *The Midwife's Apprentice.* New
York: Harper Trophy, 1995, pp. 104–111. This birth
certificate is based on my mother's birth certificate.

St. Swithin's Day Fair. Adapted from
Chapter 5, "The Merchant" by Karen
Cushman, *The Midwife's Apprentice.*
New York: Harper Trophy, 1995,
pp. 25–32. The information for this
poster came from Chapter 5. I took it
and put together a poster that looks
like one that we would see today for
a county fair in Tennessee.

►

HELP WANTED – MIDWIFE'S APPRENTICE

An English village midwife is looking for a midwife's apprentice. She must
be a fast learner and a churchgoer. She should have a cheerful personality.
Cleanliness is desired. We will train in midwifery skills including the use of
wooly nightshade, snail jelly, nettle juice, and other medicines. Experience
in collecting leeches, spider webs, and jasper stones is preferred. She must
be able to tend an herb garden, make soap, and brew cider.

There is no pay, but benefits include a straw bed in the stable,
two meals per day, and the use of a horse.

Please apply in person to Jane the Midwife,
Village of Gobnet-Under-Green, England.

▲

Help Wanted—Midwife's Apprentice. Adapted from Chapter
3, "The Midwife" by Karen Cushman, *The Midwife's
Apprentice.* New York: Harper Trophy, 1995, pp. 11–16. This
advertisement shows how difficult the life of a midwife's
apprentice could be. It gives an idea about how superstitious
and backward doctors and nurses were in the Middle Ages.

Reprinted by permission of Meagan and Lance Jasitt.

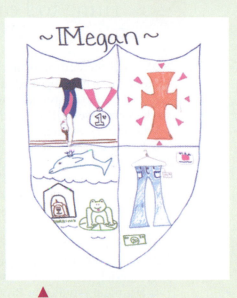

Coat of Arms. This is my personal coat of arms. One of my favorite activities is gymnastics.

Midwife's Apprentice Delivers Twins

By Meagan Jasitt
Medieval Press Writer

Alyce, the apprentice for Jane the Midwife, delivered twin calves. It was Tuesday night, June 15, 1250. Alyce was on the way home from collecting apples when she met Will Russett along the Old North Road. Tansy the cow fell into a gravel pit and Will could not get her out. Alyce realized that Tansy was about to have her baby calf and helped Will with the delivery.

To their surprise Tansy had twins. After the calves were carried out of the pit by Alyce and Will, Tansy followed them. Will said, "Tansy couldn't have done it without Alyce."

The mother and the baby calves are doing fine. The only problem was that Alyce left her fruit baskets on the road and they were taken during the night. If anyone finds the baskets, please return them to Jane the Midwife in the village of Gobnet-Under-Green.

Midwife's Apprentice Delivers Twins. Adapted from Chapter 8, "The Twins" by Karen Cushman, *The Midwife's Apprentice.* New York: Harper Trophy, 1995, pp. 48–53. Alyce's life as a midwife's apprentice was so miserable that I decided to give her credit for helping Will Russett deliver twin calves. I just took the facts from Chapter 8 and wrote a modern day newspaper article.

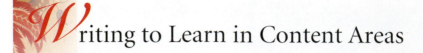Writing to Learn in Content Areas

SOME OF the writing forms discussed previously are suitable for learning content material. Learning logs and other types of record keeping, written explanations, written reports, and occasionally business letters all have a place in content area instruction, as does **creative writing** that involves basing writing on factual material. Minilesson 9.1 illustrates a writing-to-learn project.

Use of semantic webbing (see Chapter 3) before writing about a content topic can be extremely helpful. The words needed to form the web may come from personal experiences, books, videos, or other sources. Each part of the web can be used to form the basis for a paragraph or a section of writing.

Researchers have found that summary writing after reading social studies material enhances comprehension and recall (Doctorow, Wittrock, & Marks, 1978; Taylor & Berkowitz, 1980). Bromley (1985) found that both précis writing and outlining helped fifth-graders learn from content texts. A précis is a paraphrased summary of the material, condensed to about one-third of the original length. The effects of the two techniques studied by Bromley were not significantly different, so either approach

Minilesson 9.1

Writing-to-Learn Project for Social Studies

After study of the Underground Railroad, ask students to plan, research, and write a diary of either an imaginary slave being conducted to freedom or an imaginary conductor. The students must begin the diary entries of the slave from the day before he or she runs away and continue them until he or she reaches safety. The students must begin the diary entries of the conductor on the day before some runaway slaves join him or her and continue them until the conductor passes the slaves on to someone else. The students should tell how the slaves are located, how they are treated, how they travel, and how they are hidden. The feelings of the diary writer should be included, as well as an account of things that are done. If possible, contact with a real person from history should be included.

These diaries may be taken through the process writing procedure so that the final drafts are in a form suitable for sharing with a broad audience.

What are the students learning?

The students are learning to take the point of view of another person to write about events that the other person experienced. They are learning to include vivid details in written accounts of events and to consider feelings of characters as well as their experiences.

appears to be valuable. Minilesson 9.2 shows the use of summary writing after reading science material.

Of course, in content area classrooms, some writing takes place to test learning. Teachers should offer students instruction on how to answer essay questions. Organization of answers should be stressed, and commonly used terms such as *compare, contrast,* and *trace the development of* should be thoroughly explained.

Some commercial writing programs help teachers address nonfiction writing instruction. One program, *Write Time for Kids* (Teacher Created Materials, 2004), is a research-based nonfiction program that has students read nonfiction text as a springboard for writing instruction. Narrative, expository, and persuasive passages, as well as passages that contain visual presentation elements such as maps and charts, are included in separate kits for each grade level, K–8. Articles are drawn from *Time for Kids* magazine. The program is geared to the Content Standards: A Compendium of Standards and Benchmarks for K-12 Education (Mid-continent Research for Education and Learning). It has been correlated to many states' standards and to the Traits of Good Writing framework, as well as to several reading programs. Student cards are attractive and contain stimuli for reader response and writing activities. There is an extremely informative Teacher Resource Notebook and an extensive Lesson Plan Book for the teacher. A process writing approach and self-evaluation based on six traits of good writing—voice, word choice, organization, conventions, sentence fluency, and ideas—are encouraged. Many assessment rubrics are included in the resource materials. Both teachers in self-contained classrooms and content teachers in departmental settings who are not accustomed to using writing extensively in content areas should be able to implement this program.

Minilesson 9.2

Cooperative Writing in Science

Jennifer Magnusson reads a picture book entitled *Trapdoor Spiders* to her class, section by section. After she reads a section of the book—for example, one called "Shapes"—she asks the students to summarize on a transparency the information that they acquired from the reading, so that everyone can see what is written and can contribute. One student is the scribe for the class, taking dictation, as the others provide information. After the material is summarized on the transparencies, another student becomes the scribe, and the students cooperatively edit their work. Finally, they all write the edited material in their notebooks for future reference. Figure 9.11 shows their first draft, complete with editing marks (which are in a contrasting marker on the transparencies), and a typed copy of the entire edited piece.

Technology

What are the students learning?

The students are learning to listen to informational material for important details, cooperatively summarize material learned from informational books, cooperatively edit material, and use class-produced material as supplementary study resources.

$\mathcal{F}$IGURE 9.11 **Cooperative Writing**

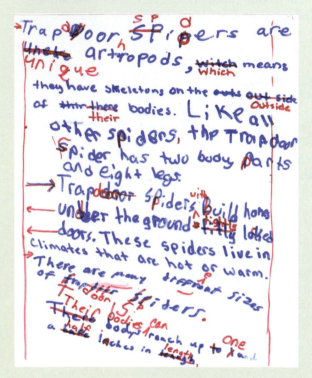

Trapdoor Spiders are unique arthropods, which means they have skeletons on the outside of their bodies. Like all other spiders, the Trapdoor Spider has two body parts and eight legs.

Trapdoor Spiders build homes under the ground with tightly locked doors. These spiders live in climates that are hot or warm.

There are many different sizes of Trapdoor Spiders. Their bodies can reach up to one and a half inches in length, and their legs are twice as long as their bodies! Trapdoor Spiders have different colors, although their colors are close to being the same. These colors are tan, brown, or red. Some of these spiders, such as the Red African Trapdoor Spider, also have a dark stripe along the bottom of their abdomen.

How do Trapdoor Spiders defend themselves? When enemies are near, this arachnid darts into it's burrow and slams the door! Once inside, it will tightly hold the door.

These examples, along with many others, are the reason Trapdoor Spiders are unique. More information about all arachnids can be found in the library.

Source: Jennifer Magnusson's Fifth-Grade Class, Pleasant Hill School, Pleasant Hill, TN. Used with permission.

Raphael, Kirschner, and Englert (1988) have developed the Expository Writing Program (EWP) to help students learn about writing expository text. Students are taught different text structures, such as comparison/contrast, problem/solution, and explanation, and they are shown that these different structures answer different types of questions and use particular key words and phrases. The EWP includes a series of "think sheets" designed to stimulate students' use of planning, information gathering, **drafting**, **editing**, and **revising** strategies. Students initially learn to use expository structures in writing by writing about things based on personal experiences, such as explanations of how to make things. Later they learn to apply such writing strategies to report writing, in which they must gather information from expository texts. Raphael and colleagues (1988, p. 794) believe that "the EWP is effective because students learn the strategies used by authors of informational text, apply the strategies in their own writing, and through participation in the writing process learn to read critically and monitor the clarity of the text they are reading whether or not they themselves are the authors."

Reflections

Do you think that it is possible to teach functional writing entirely through activities that have real meaning and purpose for the students? Why, or why not?

Classroom Assessment for Writing Proficiency

Some types of writing, such as diaries or personal journals, may not be assessed for form, but may be self-assessed for clarity. Reading their own written material after a period of time has elapsed should convince students of the need to include sufficient details in their writing. Writing to learn in the content areas may be assessed by considering the effectiveness of the writing in achieving the targeted learning objective.

When a process writing approach is used with the various types of writing, assessment by the student and the teacher is ongoing, as described in Chapter 8, with each step of the process involving at least self-assessment. Rubrics may be developed to assess any form of writing. Students and teachers may cooperatively develop such rubrics. Various assessment techniques, including use of rubrics, are discussed in more detail in Chapter 13.

SUMMARY

Children's writing often takes the form of stories, photo essays, poems, diaries or personal journals, dialogue journals, labeling, listing, filling out forms, keeping records and logs, writing letters, writing explanations, making written reports, or a variety of types of writing to learn in content areas. Each form needs special instructional attention.

To prepare written reports, students must collect data, summarize, organize ideas, and document sources. They must observe writing conventions so that they will communicate ideas clearly. Multigenre research papers involve writing in a variety of genres. These papers are often seen as more relevant and motivational for the students.

Discussion Questions

1. What are writing-to-learn activities that you find particularly useful in a content area of your choice?

2. What types of poetry would you introduce to students first? Why?

3. How do the processes of writing stories and writing reports differ?

4. What are some values of diaries or personal journals?

Suggested Activities

1. Construct a photo essay that could serve as a model for children to follow.

2. Compile a bibliography of model poems for each type of poetry discussed in this chapter.

3. Participate in a dialogue journal about a piece of literature or a chapter in a content area textbook with your teacher or with a classmate. Write an evaluation of this technique for improving writing instruction.

4. Compile a list of people to whom students could write friendly letters for authentic purposes.

5. Compile a list of people or businesses to whom students could write business letters for authentic purposes.

References

ALLEN, C. (2001). *The multigenre research paper: Voice, passion, and discovery in grades 4–6.* Portsmouth, NH: Heinemann.

BELL, N., CAMBRON, D., REY-BARREAU, K., & PAETH, B. (1995). Online literature groups. Handout at the National Council of Teachers of English Convention, San Diego.

BROMLEY, K. D. (1985). Précis writing and outlining enhance content learning. *Language Arts, 62,* 406–411.

BURGSTAHLER, S., & UTTERBACK, L. (2000). *New kids on the net: Internet activities in elementary language arts.* Boston: Allyn & Bacon.

DICKSON, D. S., HEYLER, D., REILLY, L. G., ROMANO, S. & DiLULLO, B. (2002). The oral history project. Handout at the 47th Annual Convention of the International Reading Association, San Francisco.

DOCTOROW, M., WHITTROCK, M. C., & MARKS, C. (1978). Generative processes in reading comprehension. *Journal of Educational Psychology, 70,* 109–118.

Franks, L. (2001). Charcoal clouds and weather writing: Inviting science to a middle school language arts classroom. *Language Arts, 78,* 319–324.

Grierson, S. T., Anson, A., & Baird, J. (2002). Exploring the past through multigenre writing. *Language Arts, 80,* 51–59.

Holland, H. (1996). Way past word processing. *Electronic Learning, 15,* 22–26.

Lemkuhl, M. (2002). Pen-pal letters: The cross-curricular experience. *The Reading Teacher, 55,* 720–722.

Marshall, S., & Newman, D. (1997). A poet's vision. *Voices from the Middle, 4,* 7–15.

McDermott, J. C., & Setoguchi, S. (1999). Collaborations that create real-world literacy experiences. *Journal of Adolescent & Adult Literacy, 42,* 396–397.

McKeon, C. A. (1999). The nature of children's e-mail in one classroom. *The Reading Teacher, 52,* 698–706.

Moulton, M. R. (1999). The multigenre papers: Increasing interest, motivation, and functionality in research. *Journal of Adolescent & Adult Literacy 42,* 528–539.

Niday, D., & Campbell, M. (2000). You've got mail: "Near-peer" relationships in the middle. *Voices from the Middle, 7,* 55–61.

Norton, D. E. (2003). *Through the eyes of a child,* 6th ed. Upper Saddle River, NJ: Merrill/Prentice Hall.

Raphael, T. E., Kirschner, B. W., & Englert, C. E. (1988). Expository writing program: Making connections between reading and writing. *The Reading Teacher, 41,* 790–795.

Roberts, S. K. (2002). Taking a technological path to poetry prewriting. *The Reading Teacher, 55,* 678–687.

Roe, B. D., & Smith, S. H. (1997). University/public schools keypals project: A collaborative effort for electronic literature conversations. In *Rethinking teaching and learning through technology* (pp. 361–374). Proceedings of the Mid-South Instructional Technology Conference. Murfreesboro, TN: Mid-South Technology Conference.

Romano, T. (1995). *Writing with passion: Life stories, multiple genres.* Portsmouth, NH: Boynton/Cook.

Sinatra, R., Beaudry, J., Stahl-Gemake, J., & Guastello, E. F. (1990). Combining visual literacy, text understanding, and writing for culturally diverse students. *Journal of Reading, 33,* 612–614.

Stivers, J. (1996). The writing partners project. *Phi Delta Kappan, 77,* 694–695.

Sullivan, J. (1998). The electronic journal: Combining literacy and technology. *The Reading Teacher, 52,* 90–92.

Taylor, B., & Berkowitz, S. (1980). Facilitating children's comprehension of content material. In *29th yearbook of the National Reading Conference* (pp. 64–68). Washington, DC: National Reading Conference.

Teacher Created Materials. (2004). Research-based curriculum: *Write Time for Kids.* Westminister, CA: Teacher Created Materials.

Utah State Office of Education. (1999). *Core curriculum.* Retrieved November 13, 2004, from http://www.usoe.k12.ut.us

Vos, M. (2002/2003). Author to author: Extending literacy through letters. *The Reading Teacher, 56,* 340–342.

Books for Children and Adolescents Cited in This Chapter

Ahlberg, J., & Ahlberg, A. (1986). *The jolly postman or other people's letters.* Boston: Little, Brown.

Carson, J. (1989). *Stories I ain't told nobody yet.* New York: Watts.

Gerholdt, J. E. (1996). *Trapdoor spiders.* Minneapolis: Abdo Consulting Group.

Hopkins, L. B. (1970). *City talk.* New York: Knopf.

Joslin, S. (1962). *Dear dragon . . . and other useful forms for young ladies and gentlemen engaged in everyday correspondence.* New York: Harcourt Brace & World.

Prelutsky, J. (1996). *A pizza the size of the sun.* New York: Greenwillow.

Silverstein, S. (1981). *A light in the attic.* New York: Harper & Row.

Silverstein, S. (1974). *Where the sidewalk ends.* New York: Harper & Row.

Teague, M. (2002). *Dear Mrs. LaRue.* New York: Scholastic.

THE TOOLS OF LANGUAGE

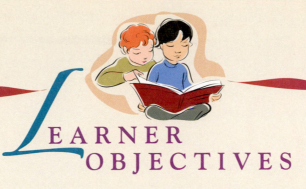

LEARNER OBJECTIVES

At the conclusion of this chapter

YOU SHOULD BE ABLE TO

1. Understand the importance of correct spelling and some difficulties associated with it.

2. Describe the developmental stages of spelling in children.

3. Choose appropriate spelling words for instruction.

4. Implement some strategies for spelling instruction.

5. Explain the basic components of a spelling program.

6. Know some definitions of grammar and how it develops.

7. Describe some ways to teach grammar in context.

8. Appreciate the importance of conventions in written language.

9. Appreciate the value of legible handwriting.

10. Identify the following terms that are defined or explained in this chapter:

NCTE/IRA Standards addressed in this chapter

STANDARD 6. Students apply knowledge of language structure, language conventions (e.g., spelling and punctuation), media techniques, figurative language, and genre to create, critique, and discuss print and non-print texts.

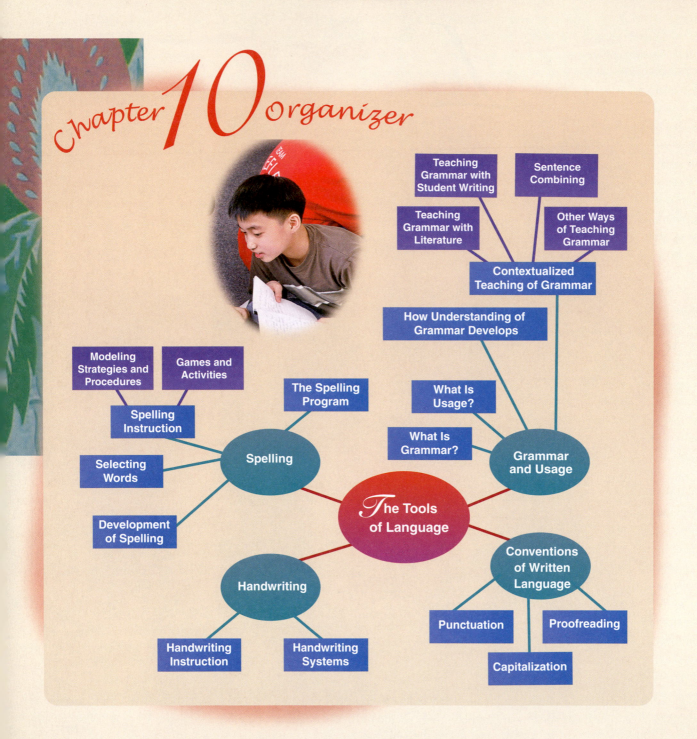

Chapter 10 Organizer

The Tools of Language

Spelling
- Modeling Strategies and Procedures
- Games and Activities
- Spelling Instruction
- The Spelling Program
- Selecting Words
- Development of Spelling

Grammar and Usage
- How Understanding of Grammar Develops
- What Is Usage?
- What Is Grammar?
- Contextualized Teaching of Grammar
  - Teaching Grammar with Student Writing
  - Sentence Combining
  - Teaching Grammar with Literature
  - Other Ways of Teaching Grammar

Handwriting
- Handwriting Instruction
- Handwriting Systems

Conventions of Written Language
- Punctuation
- Proofreading
- Capitalization

MARK, A fourth-grader, is deeply involved in writing his story. He thinks it is the best story that he has ever written. He wants to say that the hero is disappointed about missing a special event, but he can't think of how to spell *disappointed*. Finally, he writes *disupointed* and circles the word, continuing with his story. Later he will look the word up in the dictionary or get help from his teacher. He knows that she wants him to get his ideas down in his first draft and to worry about polishing the spelling only when he revises his piece for inclusion in the class book.

What's happening here?

Mark is aware of the importance of using exact words in his story and knows that spelling doesn't matter on an early draft. By circling the word, he can return to it later and find the exact spelling for the word he wants to use. His teacher has always told him that it is important to get his ideas down first and proofread to make corrections later.

Teachers need to address some skills that enhance the effectiveness of oral and written communication. Spelling, handwriting, capitalization, and punctuation apply only to written communication, but concerns about grammar and usage relate to both oral and written products.

We consider spelling first by looking at reasons for spelling difficulties, ways that spelling develops, how to select words, strategies for instruction, and the place of spelling in the curriculum. Teachers face many questions when teaching spelling: Is invented spelling a good thing? Should I use a spelling textbook? How could I individualize spelling according to students' developmental levels? What strategies should I use? When should I expect words to be spelled correctly?

Next, we consider grammar and usage—types of grammar, development of grammatical understanding, and instructional techniques for teaching grammar. Conventions of written language, such as capitalization and punctuation, and handwriting are other tools of written language that require attention.

Spelling

FEW PEOPLE would deny the need for students to develop spelling skills. Correct spelling in written work is important for accurate communication between the writer and the reader. It is also a way that people project an image of themselves to others. Misspelled words on job applications may give negative impressions to prospective employers, and carelessly spelled words may cause embarrassment for the writer. In a survey, Chandler and the Mapleton Teacher-Research Group (2000) found that parents considered spelling a high priority in the school curriculum.

Many educators point out that spelling is an integral part of literacy. Early on, children develop concepts about the sound-symbol relationships used in spelling through experiences with books and through opportunities to play with spoken language by repeating rhyming words and making up jingles. Gentry and Gillet (1993) recommend integrating spelling with all subjects, but believe that children should also spend time specifically on spelling. To develop as spellers, children need to read and write daily in an environment rich in language. Turbill (2000) regards spelling as a language process that is controlled by the same subsystems as reading and writing: the semantic, syntactic, and graphophonic systems. She also believes that spelling is learned primarily through reading, which provides demonstrations of spellings, and that proofreading enables students to learn about spelling because it involves careful reading, attention to spelling patterns, and scrutiny of written words. Reading and writing for real purposes are important conditions for learning to spell (Chandler & the Mapleton Teacher-Research Group, 2000), and children need many opportunities to write for many purposes and in different genres to become good spellers (Snowball & Bolton, 1999).

Because of the many irregularities and inconsistencies in the English language, spelling can be difficult for the student "hoo duznt no enuf wurdz two spel rite." Many words have come to us from other languages and have kept the spellings associated with their languages of origin. Also, pronunciations have changed over time so that words often do not have a one-to-one correspondence between letters and sounds. Letters of the alphabet may stand for several different sounds. The letter *a* has a different sound in *cape, can, car, soda,* and *father,* for example. Although vowel letters represent more

Classroom Vignette 10.1

Janey Bassett notices that some of her fourth-graders are having difficulty spelling words in the stories they are writing. She is concerned about how to improve their spelling and has tried different approaches. Other teachers are experiencing similar problems, so Janey decides to talk with her students. She begins by asking them what they find difficult when they try to spell, and here are some of their answers.

Sometimes you can't sound out words and get the letters right.

It's hard to know how to spell homophones, like *pear* and *pair*.

You don't always know when words have silent letters, like *know*, *write*, and *island*.

When there are two vowels together and you don't know which goes first, like *ie* and *eo*.

When letters sound like something else, like /ph/ sounds like /f/.

Sometimes the same name is spelled different ways, like *Rachael* and *Rachel*.

If I write it the wrong way, I remember it wrong.

It's hard to remember to put in every letter in a long word.

If I say it wrong, I spell it wrong.

Another time, Janey asks her students what helps them spell words correctly and get these responses.

Some rules help, like "*i* before *e*."

Sound it out.

Think of word parts, like *geo* for *earth* when spelling *geography*.

Try to think of word patterns, like *-ight*.

Write it down, look at it, cover it up, and remember how you wrote it.

Think if it looks right.

What's happening here?

Janey is learning about the problems her students have with spelling, as well as some of their solutions. Through these questioning sessions, she can consider ways to help them become better spellers. The students are realizing that their peers experience similar problems, and that they can help each other by sharing their strategies. Because of the time devoted to this discussion and the thoughtful comments made, the students may also become more fully aware of the importance of spelling.

---

different sounds than consonant letters, consonant letters can also represent different sounds, as /s/ in *save, measure,* and *his.* Some letters in certain positions may make no sound at all, as in *lamb* and *calm.* Cunningham & Allington (1999) point out that many words that appear with high frequency in early reading, such as *of, they,* and *what,* are not spelled in regular, predictable ways, thus creating confusion for young readers and writers. Despite the irregularities, however, knowledge of sound-symbol associations is helpful for spellers. Classroom Vignette 10.1 shows some ideas a class shares about spelling words.

Students should realize that the primary purpose of spelling is enabling others to read their writing (Snowball & Bolton, 1999). Spelling is not an end in itself, but it is an important part of written communication. Good spellers care about their writing and realize that accurate spelling is a necessary component of effective writing.

Development of Spelling

In Chapter 4 we looked at early stages of spelling when children attempt to match letter sounds with letters, based on their understanding of the alphabetic principle. They use

Applications

for English Language Learners

If some of your students are nonnative English speakers, find out what you can about their languages in order to become aware of similarities and differences that may cause confusion as they learn the English alphabet. If their first language is not alphabetic, you may need to give them more assistance in learning the English alphabet and the sounds the letters represent. Also, some children may use characters from other languages in their invented spelling (for example, Chinese), especially if they live in neighborhoods where they see these characters on signs. Be sure to value their writing until they are gradually able to make the transition to using standard English letters (Snowball & Bolton, 1999).

invented spelling when they write, a practice many researchers consider useful for helping children understand phonemic principles (Gentry, 2000; Sipe, 2001; Snow, Burns, & Griffin, 1998). Learning to spell is a developmental process, much like learning to speak, and invented spelling sets the foundation for spelling proficiency (Gentry & Gillet, 1993).

Gentry (1981, 1982, 2000) has identified five **developmental stages of spelling.** Veronica, age five, could only string letters together randomly a short time ago, but now proudly writes "I LV U" (I love you). She has moved from the precommunicative to the semiphonetic stage. Based on Gentry's work, Figure 10.1 shows the five stages and gives a brief description of the characteristics of each stage, along with a sample of the children's writing at each level. The children were asked to write "The dog can't jump high." Notice how the spelling begins simply with a series of letters and progresses through stages until it is standard.

Spellers move from one stage to the next gradually, and a child may show signs of more than one stage in his spelling at any particular time. You should offer students many opportunities for frequent and purposeful writing to foster growth in spell-

Applications

for English Language Learners

Speech synthesizer software can support the spelling development of ELL writers. A basic word processing program and an external speech synthesis unit let children listen to a word they tried to spell on the screen, listen to the whole text that they typed on the screen, or not use speech synthesis at all (Snow, Burns, & Griffin, 1998).

IGURE 10.1   **Stages of Spelling Development**

The Precommunicative Stage

The speller uses letter forms to represent a message.

The speller shows no awareness of letter-sound correspondence.

The speller may mix numbers, uppercase letters, and lowercase letters.

The Semiphonetic Stage

The speller shows an awareness that letters have sounds that represent sounds in words.

An entire word may be represented by one, two, or three letters.

A letter may represent a word, such as *r* for *are* or *u* for *you*.

The Phonetic Stage

The speller represents all of the sound features of the words.

Letters are based strictly on sounds, without regard for acceptable English conventions.

The past tense is represented.

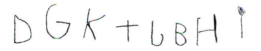

The Transitional Stage

The speller conforms to the basic conventions of English spelling (e.g., a vowel in each syllable, inflectional endings spelled correctly).

The child becomes a visual speller and may include all appropriate letters but may reverse some.

The Correct Stage (Conventional Stage)

The speller understands the basic rules of spelling.

The child accumulates a large number of learned words.

The speller can spell prefixes, suffixes, and contractions; distinguish homonyms; and use silent consonants and double consonants appropriately.

ing. If you are a primary-grade teacher, you should de-emphasize spelling correctness and memorization, adjusting expectations to the child's stage of development. Students need to develop spelling consciousness naturally as they write and receive feedback from you, and they should be encouraged to proofread and edit their own work (Gentry, 1982).

Selecting Words

You can choose spelling words in a variety of ways. Spelling textbooks can be useful in providing readily available word lists that are constructed from research on word frequencies and usefulness for particular grade levels. Some texts focus on spelling generalizations and include words that illustrate the generalizations being stressed, and some may introduce related words that have common patterns or meaning bases. Instead of using lists only from these texts, however, you may prefer to supplement them or simply create your own lists based on your firsthand knowledge of words needed by the students in their current writing activities. Figure 10.2 shows some ways to select words.

How would you choose words to use in a spelling instructional program? Would you use a spelling textbook? Would every child study the same word list? What alternatives might you choose?

Children are more likely to accept responsibility for correct spelling if they can make some choices. Each student might make a personal list of words frequently used but often misspelled. One teacher assigns five words from a standard spelling list and five words from a theme or subject being studied, and then asks each student to choose five personal words. Children may want to record their personal words in a book organized alphabetically so that they can refer to these words easily (Snowball & Bolton, 1999).

Spelling Instruction

Learning to spell is a complex process, and research has not identified a single best method for teaching spelling. Teachers may choose from many approaches, and good spellers use a variety of strategies (Rogers, 1999). Proficient spellers are more likely to observe patterns than rules (Gentry & Gillet, 1993; Johnston, 2000/2001), and they often compare spellings, visualize words, and form generalizations when they attempt to spell words in their writing. Gentry and Gillet (1993) give some suggestions for instruction, based on children's developmental stages (see Figure 10.3).

Instead of having students memorize spelling generalizations (deductive teaching), have them figure useful ones out for themselves from examples (inductive teaching). For example, list words with the same pattern, such as *make-making, ride-riding,* and *hope-hoping.* Ask the children to discover the rule for adding *-ing* to these words.

MODELING STRATEGIES AND PROCEDURES

Snowball & Bolton (1999) stress the importance of modeling spelling strategies by demonstrating ways

F IGURE 10.2   Selection of Spelling Words

Word lists: Lists of words organized by frequency of use, common misspellings, sound or letter patterns, and origins (Gentry & Gillet, 1993)

Patterns: Letters or sequences of letters, as in the following (Gentry & Gillet, 1993):

Word families: Words that differ in beginning sound but have the same ending letter(s) and sound (called rimes or phonograms), such as the *-at* family: *fat, sat, mat, cat, rat, that, scat*

Visual patterns: Words with the same visual pattern but sometimes different sounds, as with *-ough* in *cough, tough, thought, through,* and *though*

Letter patterns: Ways to spell a long or short vowel sound, such as the long *a* sound in *eight, break, make,* and *paint*

Common prefixes and suffixes: Words beginning with *un-, re-,* or *dis-* or ending with *-tion* or *-ment*

Latin or Greek bases: Latin base *medica* in *medicine* or *medic,* or Greek base *-scope* in *telescope* and *microscope*

Semantic, or meaning, patterns: Verb forms with *walk* in *walking, walks,* and *walked* and noun forms with plurals by adding *-s* in *dogs* and *cats*

Spelling demons: Words that are especially tricky or difficult, such as *because, February,* and *muscle*

Spelling generalizations: Letter combinations that usually hold true, such as *i* before *e* except after *c*

Theme words: Commonly used words within a theme study, such as *Conestoga wagon* for a unit on transportation (may be needed only temporarily)

Personal words: Words chosen by students because of special interests or needs, such as *dinosaur, soccer,* or names of classmates

Misspellings: Words taken from frequently misspelled words in children's writing, such as *said, family, friend,* and *clothes*

Words from an integrated language arts basal reader: Words listed in the basal reader selection that are recommended for spelling words

Content area words: Words frequently used in social studies, math, or science, such as *revolution, multiplicand,* and *osmosis*

Review words: Words that have been taught but continue to be misspelled

FIGURE 10.3   Instruction Based on Developmental Stages

1. *Precommunicative and semiphonetic stages:* Develop *concept of word,* through big-book sharing and language experience chart writing; *letter-sound correspondence* by sorting picture cards into groups with the same beginning sound and listening for words with the same or different beginning and ending sounds; *phonemic segmentation* through clapping for syllables; and *willingness to invent spellings while writing* through daily journal writing. (See Chapter 4 for more ideas on how to teach these skills.)

2. *Semiphonetic and phonetic stages:* Teach *rhyming words and word families* with familiar nursery rhymes and by building word families; *letter-sound relationships* by hunting for objects in the room and searching through magazines for words that begin with a particular consonant; *visual memory* with Making Words activities (explained later in this chapter), finger tracing, and a word wall (see Chapter 4).

3. *Transitional and correct stages:* Develop awareness of *structural patterns* (prefixes, suffixes, root words) by searching for words with certain structural features and by separating big words into parts to identify their structure and meaning; *derivational patterns* by finding words with the same base (for example, *receive, receipt, reception*) and engaging students in word sorts (explained later in this chapter).

Source: Based on Gentry & Gillet, 1993.

Writing

to figure out how to spell words, preferably in the context of actual writing (see Figure 10.4). You can model strategies during *modeled writing,* when you do the actual writing; *shared writing,* when you and your children create the content together, but you do the writing while they offer suggestions about spelling and punctuation; or *interactive*

Applications **for Students with Special Needs**

Many students with learning disabilities can find misspelled words from their journal entries or other writing and are able to use the Have-a-Go sheet effectively (see Figure 10.6). Routman (1991) reports that a child with special needs was able to find and circle words that looked wrong and then work them out with the help of his tutor, a spelling dictionary, and other resources.

FIGURE 10.4 Modeling Spelling Strategies

Remembering how to spell irregular, high-frequency words (*some, been, goes*)

Figuring out the spellings of words using onset and rime analogies (*play-please, set-pet*)

Listening for sounds in words (*splash, flag, united*)

Thinking about the appearance of the word (*elephant, monkey*)

Building compound words (*air-plane, mail-box*)

Using generalizations for adding prefixes and suffixes (*re-cycle, content-ment*)

Applying knowledge of derivatives (*astro-* for *astronaut, astronomy*)

Using homophones (*beat, beet; their, there, they're*)

Using apostrophes (*can't, won't, captain's*)

Source: From Snowball & Bolton, 1999, pp. 9-10.

writing, when both you and the students write the words. Similar opportunities for modeling spelling strategies occur when children dictate stories as they share during Morning News and when they engage in the language experience approach.

You can also model study procedures and give students time to practice. For each word missed on a pretest or during self-selected writing, the student can follow the steps shown in Figure 10.5: look, say, look again, cover, write, and check (Snowball & Bolton, 1999; Wing Jan, 1991). If the word is written correctly at the end of the procedure, the student may write it one or two more times to set it in memory. If the word is missed, the student may begin the procedure again. You may vary this procedure to accommodate different types of learners. Auditory learners may need to focus more on pronunciation of the word and its parts; visual learners may need to examine the appearance of the word more systematically; and kinesthetic learners may benefit more from writing the word.

Another procedure that you can model is **Have-a-Go**, which uses sheets of paper with four col-

FIGURE 10.5 Study Procedure for Spelling

1. **Look** carefully at the word for basic word recognition.

2. **Say** the word slowly, listening for the sounds you can hear.

3. **Look again** for details (such as prefixes, suffixes, root words, parts of a compound word, tricky parts, and shape). Underline the tricky part and recite the letters.

4. **Cover** the word and visualize it in your mind.

5. **Write** the word from memory.

6. **Check** the spelling of the word against the original copy.

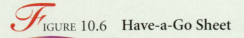

$\mathcal{F}$IGURE 10.6   **Have-a-Go Sheet**

Copy Word	First Attempt	Second Attempt	Correct Spelling
peeple	pieple	poeple	people
belive	beleeve	beleive	believe

umns as shown in Figure 10.6 (Routman, 1991; Snowball & Bolton, 1999). When a word does not look right, the student can try to spell it more than one way until it appears to be correct. Students may choose words from their daily writing that they think may be spelled incorrectly and "have a go" at standard spellings. You can confer with them to guide their thinking and confirm or help them with the correct spelling.

Teaching Tip

Have resources available for children to check their spelling independently. They might include dictionaries, rhyming dictionaries, thesauri, spell checkers, spelling games, and hand-held spelling "calculators."

Technology

GAMES AND ACTIVITIES

Children can learn by playing games, and spelling games can be beneficial learning activities. Many games and activities provide motivation for working with words and help children improve their spelling. Both commercial games and computer games that focus on spelling are also available. You can provide spelling activities in which students find other words with the same root word, the same vowel sound, the same meaning, and so on. These activities may include using the words in sentences and stories also, thereby focusing on their use in context with appropriate meanings.

Word sorts are activities that let children sort words into categories according to certain features, such as double letters, words with the same sound, long words, words with the same spelling pattern, words that end the same, and so on (Snowball & Bolton, 1999). Children may work alone, in pairs, or in small groups. Word sorting lets children examine words for similarities and differences, then construct understandings about spelling patterns as they place words into categories (Fresch, 2000). Minilesson 10.1, adapted from ideas in Henderson (1985), is a word sorting activity that can help children focus on long *e* patterns in words.

Children look for spelling or word family patterns in their word cards as they sort and arrange them.

Word Sort Lesson for Long *e* Spellings

Make a list of words on the board that includes words from the students' reading vocabularies. In this list, include words with common long *e* spelling patterns. For example:

green	sea	see
eat	me	tree
she	team	we

Discuss the vowel sound that is heard in all of the words and the different ways that the vowel sound is spelled. Have the children sort the words into three spelling patterns and list them on their papers. Then let the children come to the board and list the words on the board according to their patterns.

Have the children search for additional words that fit into each of the three lists. They may look in their basal readers, library books, and magazines and newspapers. They may even look at signs and product labels. You may create a short story that contains words that fit a particular pattern so that they have something readily accessible to search for the words. For example, you might make up a paragraph such as the following.

> Joe's dream of fishing with his very own tackle was about to come true. He hurried to get dressed. His pants had a hole in the left knee and a rip in the seat, but that would be okay for fishing. He couldn't squeeze his feet into the boots his aunt had given him. Impatient to start fishing, he finally left the house barefooted, hurrying toward the creek. He waded in eagerly and started upstream. What a treat!

Let the children add the words that they have found to the appropriate lists on their papers and on the board. Remind the children that they must think about which letter combination is the correct one to use when they write words with the long *e* sound.

What are the students learning?

The students are learning to look carefully at the spellings of words in various texts to find words that fit one of the three patterns identified for the long *e* sound. They become aware that different combinations of letters can make the same sound, and they learn to apply this knowledge when they spell words in their writing. They may also realize that other sounds can be made from different letter combinations.

Another activity to make children aware of spelling patterns is **Making Words**, which is part of the Four Block program (Cunningham & Allington, 1999). Give the children selected letters that they can use to make words. Start with the letters that make a "secret" word, and ask children to form words from these letters as you direct

Teaching Tip

Make wall charts of words with different spelling patterns from activities you do with your class. Leave room for students to add new words that fit these patterns. These charts become resources for helping students spell words correctly in their writing.

them, beginning with short words and moving into longer words. You have a pocket chart with the letters in it, and each child has a holder with the same letters arranged in random order. Choose one child to make the words in the pocket chart. Minilesson 10.2 is a partial lesson for Making Words, with the secret word *planet*. For a complete lesson on making words, see Cunningham and Allington (1999, pp. 151-158).

Research has found some methods for teaching spelling to be generally ineffective. Assigning words to be memorized has not been successful (Fresch, 2000; Gentry & Gillet, 1993), and spelling generalizations have many exceptions, so few are worth teaching (Gentry & Gillet, 1993). Rymer and Williams (2000) reported that prepackaged spelling programs failed to impact young children's writing, mainly because the

Minilesson 10.2

Making Words

The children have their letters and are ready to begin making words. The teacher gives the following directions.

Take two letters and make *an.*

Add a letter and make the three-letter word *tan.* Some of you have a good tan from the summer. Everybody say *tan.*

Change one letter and make *ten.* You have ten fingers. Say *ten.*

Take away the *t* and put *p* in front to make *pen.* I write with a pen. Say *pen.*

Now take away the *p* and put back the *t* to make *ten* again. Change the letters around to make *net.* You can catch a butterfly in a net. Say *net.*

Take away the *n* and put *p* in its place. Now we have the word *pet.* Some of you have a pet dog or cat. Say *pet.*

Take away these letters and start again with *an.* Add *t* to the end of *an* to make the word *ant.* Jamie saw an ant on the playground. Say *ant.*

Take away the *t* and put *pl* in front of *an* and you have a four-letter word: *plan.* Maybe you plan to do something special tomorrow. Say *plan.*

Add *t* to the end of *plan* and we have a five-letter word: *plant.* You may plant a garden. All of you say *plant.* Stretch out the word so you can hear each sound.

Take away the *p* and the *t* and put *e* on the end of the word. Now you have the word *lane.* Clay lives on Beechwood Lane. Say *lane.*

children already knew how to spell many of the words and they rarely used these words in their journals.

The Spelling Program

Because reading and writing occur in most curricular areas, every teacher needs to teach spelling (Snowball & Bolton, 1999). Teachers in different subjects can teach high-frequency words related to their areas, along with useful strategies for learning how to spell them. Knowing derivations of words helps students spell many words; for example, the word *divide* in math is the base word for *division* and *dividend*.

One way to teach spelling is through a **workshop approach** (Gentry & Gillet, 1993), based on the pattern and goals of reading and writing workshops. (Explicit procedures for these workshops are given in Chapters 7 and 8.) Essential aspects of the spelling workshop include organizing time, space, and materials; establishing student ownership; responding to students; and providing developmentally appropriate spelling

We can add *p* to the front of *lane* and have *plane*. I flew in a plane to see my sister. Say *plane.*

Has anyone found the secret word yet? I'll come around and check to see.

The lesson continues with sorting the words into patterns, as follows.

an	ten	net	lane	ant
tan	pen	pet	plane	plant
plan				

Other rhyming word activities and manipulations with letters occur later in the lesson.

What are the students learning?

By creating words according to the teacher's directions, the children are discovering spelling patterns that they will be able to apply to new words they are likely to encounter in their reading and writing. When saying the words, they hear the sounds that the letters make. As they listen to the teacher give each word in a sentence, they understand the words in meaningful contexts. Further experimentation with moving letters around and adding rhyming words reinforces the patterns demonstrated in this lesson.

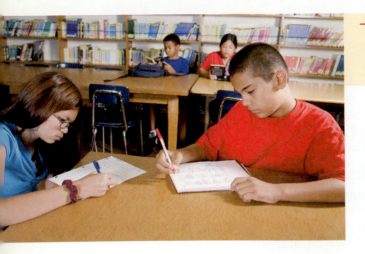

Two students are checking each other's papers for spelling errors by circling words they think may be mispelled.

instruction as needed, perhaps in the form of minilessons. There should be a period of about 15 minutes a day for specific, intentional study of words so that students can work on the spelling and use of selected words. Students establish ownership by choosing words to study from their own writing, and the teacher provides positive feedback to develop positive attitudes toward spelling. Developmentally appropriate instruction and activities, as suggested previously, are important for helping students become independent spellers. In the workshop approach, spelling is learned in the context of reading, writing, and studying words by comparing, contrasting, and associating them.

Many teachers follow a traditional approach with a spelling textbook that usually goes from Monday to Friday with a pretest on Monday, practice activities Tuesday and Wednesday, a trial test on Thursday, and the spelling test on Friday. If this approach is used, having students correct their own papers on the trial test appears to be beneficial in learning the words for the final test. Many researchers, however, advocate a more individualized approach that enables students to study the words they often misspell and need to use in their daily writing. Sometimes teachers combine words from research-based lists with student-selected words. Some believe that spelling instruction should be embedded within a workshop approach to give children authentic purposes for learning to spell, whereas others claim that direct spelling instruction is a major component of the language arts program (Fresch, 2000).

Teachers have discovered other effective organizational patterns as well. Wright (2000) introduced spelling meetings to her fourth-graders. The class held weekly meetings, during which each student shared three interesting words. The purpose was to encourage students to become curious about spelling patterns, spelling strategies, and the sounds of words in order to apply effective spelling practices to their writing. Students liked sharing their strategies and learned more about spelling as a result. Similarly, Gentry and Gillet (1993) suggest using cooperative learning techniques by encouraging student collaboration in setting goals, building teams, and measuring progress in spell-

Teaching Tip

Have a challenge word or activity each week to arouse students' interest in spelling. Examples: Find a word with three double letters (*Mississippi*), homophone triplets (*so, sew, sow*), words beginning with the Greek prefix *tele-* (*telescope*), words with five syllables (*multiplication*), and homographs (*wind-wind*).

ing. Also believing in the value of student collaboration, Buschman (2003) created a Share and Compare program that resembles "buddy reading." Younger and older children are paired so that older children mentor the younger ones during guided writing activities.

Many educators are concerned about having children move from invented spelling to conventional spelling. This shift occurs gradually, for even adults sometimes must use invented spelling when they are uncertain of standard spelling. When children reach the transitional stage, they are ready for formal spelling instruction (Gentry & Gillet, 1993). You should encourage students to work toward correct spelling in their writing, and children should be expected to spell words accurately when they have been taught the words, when the correct spellings are readily accessible to them, and when they write for publication.

Parents should be involved in the spelling program. They need to understand the use of invented spelling, as well as the goals and procedures of your spelling program. They can be a great asset in helping children learn to be good spellers by coaching them at home.

Spelling assessment, discussed more fully in Chapter 13, is an important issue. Traditionally, spelling is measured by weekly spelling tests, but often students who make perfect scores on tests fail to spell words from spelling lists correctly in their daily writing (Hughes & Searle, 2000). The true test of spelling achievement is the student's ability to transfer knowledge of spelling patterns and strategies to written work.

Reflections

How did you learn to spell? What helped you most? Did you interact with other students as you learned to spell? What kind of spelling program would you like to have?

Grammar and Usage

GRAMMAR IS important for both spoken and written communication. It is the teacher's responsibility to demonstrate standard forms of English and help students adjust their use of language to meet the purpose, audience, and situation (Wing Jan, 1991).

Appendix A, the Grammar Handbook, contains rules with examples for grammar, punctuation, and capitalization and identifies potential problems in usage. In the remainder of this chapter, references are made to Appendix A. For example, if you read (see II.C.1.a.), you should refer to Appendix A and find the relevant rule by looking under II., C., 1., a.). Knowing the rules and how to apply them should support your instruction and help you model Standard English in both spoken and written form.

What Is Grammar?

Grammar is "conformity to certain structural aspects of speech and writing that we judge acceptable" (Williams, 1995, p. 99). Three types of grammar have been studied in U.S. schools: traditional, structural, and transformational.

Traditional grammar has rules that are taught as prescriptions for use. It includes definitions of the eight parts of speech—nouns, verbs, pronouns, adjectives, adverbs, prepositions, conjunctions, and interjections (see I.A.)—and their combinations into phrases, clauses, and sentences. The primary focus is on syntax (word order) in sentences, phrases, and clauses (see I.B., C., D.)

Structural grammar is a descriptive model, as opposed to the prescriptive model of traditional grammar, that considers the ways in which ordinary people use language (Hagemann, 2003). Structural grammar focuses on the concepts that words can serve different functions (such as *strike,* which can be used as a noun or a verb) and that sentences can have different patterns (such as *noun-verb* or *noun-verb-noun*) (see I.D.).

Transformational grammar is "a theory of grammar that contains a set of rules for producing all possible grammatical—and no ungrammatical—sentences in a language" (Harris & Hodges, 1995, p. 260). Like structural grammar, it is descriptive and shows how sentences can be changed, or transformed, into different, related sentences.

What Is Usage?

Grammar and usage differ in that **usage** is "the way in which the native language or dialect of a speech community is actually used by its members" (Harris & Hodges, 1995, p. 267). In other words, people do not always adhere strictly to the rules of grammar in ordinary conversation. The contrast is like that between proper etiquette (grammar) and actual behavior (usage). **Standard English** generally follows grammatical rules and is the way most educational texts, media, and government publications are written (Harris & Hodges, 1995). It is the language modeled and taught in the classroom, which should be used for job interviews, formal occasions, and so forth. Home language is the language of the playground and family activities. Although home lan-

JUMPSTART © Reprinted by permission of United Feature Syndicate, Inc.

guage is acceptable for most occasions, students need to know Standard English as an alternative for those situations that call for it. Minilesson 10.3 shows an occasion in which Standard English is important.

People are often judged by the language they use. Even in informal occasions, it is important to use the correct word, as shown in the *Jump Start* comic on page 390. Here the speaker uses *good* when he actually means *well*. The listener pretends not to understand in order to shame the speaker, who isn't using Standard English (see I.A.4b., 5.).

How Understanding of Grammar Develops

Children rapidly develop an understanding of the basic structures of language (Snow, Burns, & Griffin, 1998). Soon after they are able to comprehend simple sentences, they begin to combine words into meaningful syntactic relationships. During the preschool period, children's sentences grow in length and complexity so that by the time they enter school, most children can produce and understand many grammatical forms. Routman (1991) believes that children do not have to be able to define and label parts

Minilesson 10.3

Usage Versus Standard English

The teacher has written a script that shows the responses a person who does not use Standard English makes during a job interview. In the dialogue, the interviewee says such things as "Him and me seen this ad you had. He don't know nothing about machinery, but I done a lot of work on machines last year. I've went to a class for mechanics, too."

The teacher gives the students printed copies of the script to work with in small groups. First, the students read the script and decide on the answer to the teacher's query: "Do you think this person will get the job? Why, or why not?" The children discuss the question in their small groups, and then the teacher leads a whole-group discussion of the question, emphasizing the reasons that the children give.

Then the students return to their small groups and rewrite the language to fit the situation. Finally, each group chooses two children to role-play the scene with their revision. After all groups have performed, there may be comparisons of word choices and general evaluation of the use of school language.

What are the students learning?

When they examine the language of the interviewee, they are discovering a number of deviations from Standard English in his speech. They begin to realize that using Standard English in certain situations is necessary in order to be accepted. Although home language is not wrong, it may not be the language that is acceptable for certain professional and social situations.

of speech in elementary school in order to use them correctly. Instead, they should internalize the structure of language through support from others and immersion in authentic experiences with language. Hagemann (2003) points out that parents do not need to explain parts of speech to their children or lecture them on rules. Most children discover the underlying rules that control their language for themselves.

Contextualized Teaching of Grammar

Although much grammar is learned intuitively, students do benefit from some kinds of instruction. Teachers are often perplexed, however, when students fail to apply the rules they have been taught. Research shows that there is little connection between knowledge of grammar and application of it in speech and writing (Cooper, 1997; Hagemann, 2003; Tchudi & Tchudi, 1999; Weaver, 1996). In fact, too much emphasis on awareness of syntax and traditional grammar exercises may cause students to read and write language in parts rather than consider entire passages (Barnitz, 1998). Grammar lessons are rarely relevant to students who are creating their own sentences during authentic writing activities.

Writing

How, then, should grammar be taught? Many authorities support **contextualized teaching**, that is, teaching grammar in the context of real reading and writing. Grammar, form, spelling, and handwriting can be taught both directly and indirectly within the writing workshop (see Chapter 8) in ways that make sense to the students without providing them with isolated skill instruction (Bromley, 1999). Students need to learn to use constructions such as appositives (see II.D.6.b.) and participial phrases (see I.B.1.d.) in their writing, but these can be taught with minilessons, conferences, and hands-on guidance (Weaver, McNally, & Moerman, 2003). They can learn grammatical constructions and names for parts of speech incidentally as they read and write (Hagemann, 2003; Weaver, 1996). As the teacher, you can use appropriate terminology, such as *noun, verb, clause,* and *phrase,* as you discuss students' writing until they become familiar with grammatical terms from hearing them repeatedly.

Reflections

How did you learn to use Standard English in your speech and writing? Did textbooks help? Did your teachers teach grammar in context?

Applications

for English Language Learners

Hagemann (2003) recommends making use of the language skills that ELLs already possess in order to support their English language learning. They should be able to transfer some knowledge of reading and writing in their home language to English. Also, you should focus more on content than grammar and remain tolerant of grammatical errors because most of them will eventually disappear.

Teaching Grammar with Literature

Use of children's literature and students' own writing is the most effective way to help students understand and appreciate the use of grammar (Hagemann, 2003). Literature provides a model for writing effective sentences and paragraphs (Weaver, McNally, & Moerman, 2003). Students improve their reading and writing abilities as they encounter a diverse range of syntax in the various styles, dialects, and genres found in literature (Barnitz, 1998) written by a wide range of authors. You should talk with your students about how the different authors have constructed their sentences.

Sentences are classified in two ways. The classification by form or structure includes simple (one independent clause), compound (two independent clauses), complex (one independent and one or more dependent clauses), and compound complex (two independent clauses and at least one dependent clause) (see I.D.3.). Independent clauses can stand alone, but dependent, or subordinate, clauses must be connected to an independent clause. Figure 10.7 shows the four structural classifications of sentences.

The classification by function includes declarative (telling), interrogative (asking), exclamatory (showing emotion), and imperative (commanding) sentences (see I.D.2.). Students need to learn to use these different forms appropriately in their writing. Minilesson 10.4 shows how literature can make students aware of these four sentence types.

You can use both fiction and nonfiction to help students discover various syntactic structures and sentence patterns. Ruth Heller created a beautifully illustrated series of books that draw students' attention to parts of speech. These books are listed at the end of this chapter. Reading and listening to stories, participating in Readers Theatre and choral readings, and writing stories according to patterns modeled in lit-

 IGURE 10.7   **Structural Classification of Sentences**

Simple sentence: One main clause

Mike went to school.

Compound sentence: Two main clauses connected with a conjunction (*and*)

Mike went to school, and he learned about the Civil War.

Complex sentence: One dependent or subordinate clause and one main clause

When he got home, he studied hard.

Compound-complex sentence: Two main clauses and one dependent or subordinate clause

He took a test over the Civil War, and he was glad that he had studied hard.

Minilesson 10.4

Types of Sentences

Mrs. Fernandez: I've been reading you *Sadako* by Eleanor Coerr. Today I wrote four sentences from this book on the board. Let's look at them together and see if we can tell how they are different from each other.

> Sadako was always looking for good-luck signs.
>
> "Mother, can we please hurry with breakfast?"
>
> "I can hardly wait for the carnival!"
>
> "Close your eyes," she said.

SONJA: Some of them have quotations and some of them don't.

CARLOS: They end with different kinds of punctuation marks.

MRS. FERNANDEZ: You are both right, but let's consider Carlos's answer. What we have here are different types of sentences. Can anyone tell me what they are?

ELENA: The first one just tells something and ends with a period, and the next one asks a question and ends with a question mark.

MRS. FERNANDEZ: We call the first sentence that tells something a statement or a *declarative* sentence, and this one tells us something about Sadako's upbeat personality. The second one is a question or an *interrogative* sentence. Sadako is asking her mother to hurry so that she can go to the Peace Park. What about the other two?

Writing

erature enhance students' syntactic skills (Barnitz, 1998). Weaver (1996) believes that imitating sentence patterns in writing is useful. Many songs, poems, and books contain predictable patterns that guide children toward composing pieces with similar patterns. Figure 10.8 shows examples of books with patterns. As children encounter

Applications
for English Language Learners and Students with Special Needs

Ask ELLs to use English the best way they can. Social interaction, reading, and writing to share ideas support the acquisition of functional English more than studying rules of grammar (Weaver, 1996). Buddy reading and collaborative writing help both ELLs and struggling readers develop their use of language when they are paired with proficient English speakers (Snow, Burns, & Griffin, 1998).

JOSH:	The next one is exciting and ends with an exclamation point.
MRS. FERNANDEZ:	We call that an *exclamatory* sentence—easy to remember because of the exclamation point. Here Sadako is excited, and this mark shows her excitement.
CELIA:	I know the last one. It's when you tell somebody to do something.
MRS. FERNANDEZ:	Right, and that's what we call a command or *imperative* sentence. In this sentence, Chizuko wants to surprise Sadako with paper and scissors to make paper cranes. This story has other examples of these kinds of sentences. Think about the types of sentences you use in your writing. Are you using different kinds?

What are the students learning?

Writing

The students are becoming aware that authors use a variety of types of sentences in their stories. They are introduced to four types and reminded how they were used in the story. Some children will remember the terms, but knowing the terminology is not as important as being able to use the different types of sentences in their writing.

FIGURE 10.8   **Books with Patterns**

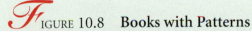

Brett, Jan. *The Mitten: A Ukranian Folktale*

Carle, Eric. *The Very Quiet Cricket* (and other books by Eric Carle)

Hutchins, Pat. *Rosie's Walk*

Joose, Barbara. *Mama, Do You Love Me?*

Martin, Bill, Jr. *Brown Bear, Brown Bear, What Do You See?*

Salley, Coleen. *Epossumondas*

Viorst, Judith. *Alexander and the Terrible, Horrible, No Good, Very Bad Day*

Yolen, Jane, & Teague, Mark. *How Do Dinosaurs Say Good Night?*

ways that language is used in literature, they learn a great deal about grammar in a meaningful way.

TEACHING GRAMMAR WITH STUDENT WRITING

Students' own writing provides opportunities for teaching grammar. You can observe your students carefully and focus on those concepts and terms that students need for sentence expansion, revision, and editing (Weaver, 1996). Minilessons provide brief, direct explanations of something that is likely to benefit students. One way to teach a minilesson is to model a procedure step by step so that students can understand how to use the procedure themselves. You may also select a sample of student work (with permission), project it so that all can see, and point out ways to improve it, or you may help a student with a particular skill on an individual basis during a conference. Figure 10.9 gives some typical difficulties that can be addressed effectively during minilessons and conferences (Hagemann, 2003; Weaver, 1996).

To avoid embarrassing students in your class, use writing samples from students you had in previous years or from students in another class. Never use an identifiable piece without first getting the student's permission.

SENTENCE COMBINING

Consistent with transformational grammar, **sentence combining** enables students to manipulate sentences and experiment with different combinations. Students actually create their own sentences, as opposed to traditional grammar exercises when students analyze and label existing sentences (Hagemann, 2003). Sentence combining develops an awareness of sentence structure as students transform sentences by rearranging, combining, elaborating, substituting, adding, and deleting (Barnitz, 1998). Students can learn sentence combining during minilessons (see Minilesson 10.5) or conferences centered around their own writing.

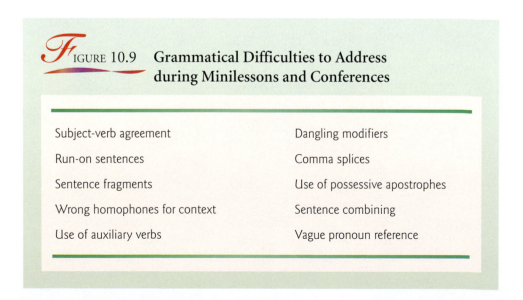

$\mathcal{F}$IGURE 10.9 **Grammatical Difficulties to Address during Minilessons and Conferences**

Subject-verb agreement	Dangling modifiers
Run-on sentences	Comma splices
Sentence fragments	Use of possessive apostrophes
Wrong homophones for context	Sentence combining
Use of auxiliary verbs	Vague pronoun reference

Minilesson 10.5

Writing

Sentence Combining

Show the students a paragraph that contains short, choppy sentences, such as:

> Joe saw a bird. It was hurt. He was sorry for the bird. He took it home. He wanted to help it get well.

TEACHER: How could we make the first two sentences into one sentence?

KAYLA: We could say, "Joe saw a bird that was hurt."

TONY: I know, "Joe saw an injured bird."

TEACHER: That's the idea. Either one of those works. There may be other ways, too. (Teacher writes one of these sentences on the board.) Now look at the next two sentences. How could we combine them?

SABRA: We could say, "Because he was sorry for the bird, he took it home."

TEACHER: Good answer. Can you think of a way to combine the last sentence with the one Sabra gave us?

JESSE: "Because he was sorry for the bird, he took it home to help it get well."

TEACHER: (Teacher writes this sentence on the board.) Very good. You may be able to think of other ways that work also. Now let's read the first paragraph with its five sentences and then the new paragraph you've dictated. What do you notice?

SELENA: The second one sounds better. It's not so short and choppy.

TEACHER: Today, I'd like you to look through your writing folders to see if there are places where you could combine sentences to improve your writing. Make sure your writing is clear and that it flows well. You may use connectives, leave out words, move words around, and change words to make your writing clear.

What are the students learning?

Through the example shown, the children are learning that combining sentences can improve the flow and clarity of written work. They are learning to look back at their writing to see how they might combine sentences to improve them, and they are becoming more aware of the need to avoid short, choppy sentences in future work.

OTHER WAYS OF TEACHING GRAMMAR

Although use of literature and student writing appears to be the most effective way to teach grammar, teachers have found other ways to help children learn concepts and terminology about grammar. Some of these ideas follow.

■ *Sentence expansion*: Start with a kernel sentence, such as *people sing*. Point out that we know very little from this sentence and that it would be helpful to expand it. Ask students to brainstorm ways to add descriptive words, phrases, and clauses to give us a clearer picture of how, where, and why these people are singing. Minilesson 10.6 is a lesson on sentence expansion.

■ *Computer grammar checkers*: Grammar programs help with proofreading and also teach a little grammar, mechanics, and spelling. Some programs flag something in the writing and offer brief, practical lessons about

Technology

Writing

Minilesson 10.6

Sentence Expansion

MR. GRAY: I've noticed that sometimes your writing doesn't help me visualize what is happening. I can't see in my mind what you are trying to tell me. When many authors write, they use words that help the reader get a clear picture of what they are saying. Today we're going to try something that should help you make your writing more interesting.

I'm going to give you a kernel sentence, just a noun and a verb, and we'll see how we can make this sentence grow by adding words, phrases, and perhaps clauses. When we're finished, we should be able to visualize the scene more clearly.

We'll start with *fish swim*. That doesn't tell us very much, does it? How can we add to this kernel sentence to help a reader understand what's really happening? I'll write *fish swim* on the board and then you can tell me what words I should add.

KATHY: Put *the big* in front.

MR. GRAY: That's the idea. What else can we say?

TOWANNA: You can say *under the water* after *swim*.

MR. GRAY: Okay. What would we call *under the water*?

ROBIN: A phrase?

MR. GRAY: Yes, but what kind of phrase?

ROBIN: Prepositional?

MR. GRAY: Yes, because it starts with a preposition. What else?

TAMARA: How about adding *while the children watch*?

MR. GRAY: Excellent! And what is the term for this group of words?

TAMARA: I'm not sure.

JEFF: Is it a clause?

comma placement, use of homophones, and grammatical constructions (Tchudi & Tchudi, 1999).

- *Sentence collecting:* As children read, ask them to collect sentences that interest them because of their meaning, function, or structure. Display them and encourage the class to discuss them (Barnitz, 1998).

MR. GRAY: You're absolutely right. Our sentence is growing nicely. What else?

LANCE: We could say *quickly* after *swim.*

MR. GRAY: That works. Who knows what part of speech *quickly* is?

RAY: I think it's an adverb because it ends in *-ly.*

MR. GRAY: You're right. It is an adverb. Can anyone think of an adjective?

RONNY: I know! The big fish swim quickly under the *muddy* water.

MR. GRAY: That's right. *Muddy* is an adjective that describes the water. Does anyone else have an idea?

TAMARA: Let's make the fish *striped.* That would be another adjective.

MR. GRAY: I'll put *striped* right after *big.* We could add other words, phrases, and clauses, but we might end up with a really long run-on sentence. Let's read what we have now.

MR. GRAY
AND CLASS: *The big striped fish swim quickly under the muddy water while the children watch.*

MR. GRAY: Now close your eyes and think about that sentence. Can you visualize the scene? You have lots of clues to help you.

What are the students learning?

They are reinforcing their understanding of what makes a kernel sentence and discovering ways to add modifiers to expand it. They are using correct terms for parts of speech and grammatical structures, and they are learning appropriate placements for modifiers. They are learning that there are many ways to add to sentences to make their writing more descriptive.

- *Sentence reduction:* Using a sample run-on sentence from student writing or a complex sentence from literature, ask students to reduce it to its core elements, or separate it into two or more sentences. Each sentence needs a subject and verb.
- *Enactments:* Hands-on, concrete actions sometimes produce results. Give children word cards and ask them to arrange themselves into sentences, or give them letters that can change two words into one by removing letters and adding an apostrophe (such as *did not* into *didn't*).

Conventions of Written Language

A **CONVENTION** is an accepted practice in the act of writing. Conventions include use of punctuation and capitalization, indentations for new paragraphs, spacing between words, left-to-right and top-to-bottom directionality, and standardized spellings (Atwell, 1998). Conventions are like signposts that guide the reader toward understanding the written material. They are useful tools for enabling the writer to communicate effectively with the reader. Children begin noticing conventions in trade books and gradually acquire a sense of their usefulness (Graves, 1994). We have already covered spelling in this chapter, so now we consider punctuation and capitalization.

Punctuation

Punctuation helps the writer turn speech into print. Conversely, it helps the reader turn print into speech. It represents the intonation patterns in oral language, although it does this imperfectly. Periods, question marks, and exclamation marks designate the ends of sentences and signal pauses in the flow of words (see II.A., B., C.). Colons and semicolons (see II.H., I.) represent pauses between independent clauses that could be separate sentences in some cases; commas may also serve this function. Commas as internal punctuation in sentences separate items in a series and set off appositives, relative clauses, and quotations (see II.D.). In these cases, they represent vocal pauses that are generally of shorter duration than those signaled by end punctuation marks. Dashes and semicolons (see II.I., K.) at times serve functions similar to those served by commas.

Other uses of periods that must be taught include use after abbreviations and after initials (see II.A.2.). Additional uses of commas include use in dates (see II.D.6.d.), after greetings and closings in letters (see II.D.4.), and in numbers of four or more digits (see II.D.5). The colon is also used after the salutation in a business letter, to set off a list of items, and in writing times (for example, 6:40 P.M.).

Other punctuation marks that should be taught are apostrophes (see II.E.) and quotation marks (see II.F., G.). Apostrophes are used in both contractions and possessives. Quotation marks are used to begin and end direct quotations and to set off titles of poems, stories, and articles.

Minilesson 10.7

Teaching Commas in a Series with Literature

MR. GOMEZ: One of the books we read during our theme study on oceans was Debra Frasier's *Out of the Ocean*. You liked this book, and several of you have written your own stories about the ocean. Do you remember that the author found many treasures on the beach? What were some of those?

CHILDREN: A board, smooth broken glass, coconuts, sea turtle shells

MR. GOMEZ: Yes, all those things and many more. I want to show you a page that tells some treasures. Listen as I read it.

"Walking this beach, I've found pelican feathers, a wooden shoe, floating glass balls, skate egg pouches, plastic boats, . . ." (unpaged)

How do you think the author kept all these words from running together? Look carefully at the page before you answer.

ROBERTO: I can see. There is a comma between each thing.

MR. GOMEZ: That's right. Writers use commas to separate things so that readers can make sense of the writing. This is called *commas in a series*. Try to remember to use commas when you write several items in a series so the reader won't be confused.

What are the students learning?

By reminding the children of how the author uses commas in a series in a favorite book, the teacher is calling attention to a skill the children need to use in their own writing. They begin to realize the importance of separating items with commas so that the reader will not be confused.

As with grammar, children learn about punctuation and capitalization from trade books and their own writing. As you read big books to them during shared reading, ask them what they notice about the marks on the pages or point out conventions that they need to know. Minilesson 10.7 shows how a teacher used Debra Frasier's *Out of the Ocean* to model the use of commas in a series.

In Minilesson 10.8, the teacher impresses on the children the value of using commas to clarify meanings. The failure to use and observe commas during reading can affect comprehension. The teacher has placed the following words on the board: *ice cream, coffee cake,* and *cheese.*

Children also learn to use punctuation when you model standard conventions during language experience lessons and other forms of shared writing. Minilessons, such as Minilessons 10.7 and 10.8 offer opportunities for you to focus on certain conven-

Writing

Teaching Commas in a Series with Writing

MRS. FRANCK: Today I want to show you how important it is to use commas in a series correctly. We'll see what can happen if we don't use them the way we need to. Lee, would you please go to the board and read us the shopping list.

LEE: Ice cream, coffee cake, and cheese.

MRS. FRANCK: How many items are there?

LEE: Three.

MRS. FRANCK: Put another comma in this series so that you have four items and read us the list.

LEE: (puts a comma between *coffee* and *cake*) Now it's four things: ice cream, coffee, cake, and cheese.

MRS. FRANCK: That comma makes a big difference, doesn't it? Can someone come to the board and fix the series so that there are five things? Stephanie, how about you?

STEPHANIE: I'll put a comma between ice and cream. That makes five things.

MRS. FRANCK: Now read us the list with five items.

STEPHANIE: Ice, cream, coffee, cake, and cheese.

MRS. FRANCK: That's a lot different from what the list said originally. Can you see what a difference commas can make? I hope you'll remember that in your writing.

What are the students learning?

The students are discovering that commas really do matter and that they can change the meanings of words and sentences. Instead of thinking that putting commas in the right places is just for getting test answers correct, students find that commas serve a real purpose.

tions that the children need to know for their writing. Hagemann (2003, p. 135) believes children can increase their "sense of punctuation" with lots of practice in writing.

Capitalization

Young children often mix capital letters with lowercase letters indiscriminately, and later they tend to overuse capital letters. As with punctuation, they can learn standard use of capitalization by observing its use in trade books, paying close attention during

FIGURE 10.10 Items That Should Be Capitalized

The word *I*

Names of people (Mary Brown)

The first word of a sentence (He laughed.)

Names of days of the week (Monday)

Names of months of the year (January)

Names of holidays (Thanksgiving)

Names of towns, states, countries (Rochester, New York, United States)

Names of streets (Main Street)

Titles of people (Mr., Mrs., Dr.)

The first word in the greeting of a letter (Dear Joe)

The first word in the closing of a letter (Your friend)

The first word and other important words in a title (*Treasure Island*, "Home on the Range")

Proper adjectives (Chinese restaurant)

Brand names (Keebler crackers)

minilessons and teacher modeling, and practicing appropriate use of capital letters in their own writing. Figure 10.10 is a list of items that students should learn to capitalize (see also III).

Unfortunately, the widespread use of e-mail and chat rooms by older students exposes them to many communications that are devoid of punctuation and capitalization. Teachers must work to overcome these outside influences on their students' use of writing conventions.

Proofreading

During the editing stage of the writing process, students **proofread** their work to look for nonstandard or

Two students are engaged in a peer conference as they proofread each other's work before publishing their pieces.

$\mathcal{F}$IGURE 10.11 **Proofreading Symbols**

Symbol	Meaning	Example
∧	insert	Sally went to the store.
∼	reverse	I beli(e)ve it.
≡	capitalize	we went home.
⌐	delete	Look at that ~~that~~ horse!
⬭	check spelling	It's a (suprise).
⊙	add period	Come home.
∧	add comma	Joe, Mike, and I played.
⫫	indent	⫫ Once upon a time

unconventional usage. (See Chapter 8 for the editing stage.) Proofreading begins with the author examining the piece critically, looking for any deviations from standard conventions. If the student is uncertain about the spelling of a word, the student should circle it and check it later. The student should be familiar with other widely recognized marks that indicate changes that need to be made. (See Figure 10.11 for proofreading symbols.)

After the student has proofread the piece, other students may examine it for possible nonstandard usage. Finally, the teacher should have a conference with the student about any other changes that need to be made before publishing the piece.

Editing, or correcting errors, is a complex procedure, one that is used over a lifetime. It is primarily the responsibility of the writer, but peers and the teacher help the writer by suggesting additional improvements. Some ways to teach proofreading (looking for errors) and editing (correcting errors) follow (Hagemann, 2003).

- *Modeling*: Project an unedited writing sample on a screen and read it to the class. Ask: What is good about this piece? Do you see anything that needs to be changed?

  As the students identify any errors and suggest changes, make the corrections with a colored marker and explain why each correction is needed. You may also list the kinds of corrections made and find additional errors that need attention. Students should then proofread their own writing and refer to the list for types of errors to consider.

- *Individual editing conferences*: Meet briefly with a student to help with editing a nearly completed piece of writing. Instead of marking each error, look for recurrent errors (such as use of commas) and advise the student to look for these throughout the paper. You may work with the student on a few of these errors, explaining the reasons for making changes, until the student understands what to do.

- *Peer proofreading*: Students can work together in pairs or small groups as they edit each other's papers. Another person can often spot errors that

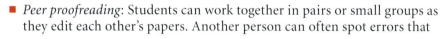

Teaching Tip

Some teachers say, "Ask three; then ask me." This means that students should ask three peers to go over their work before asking the teacher. Let each reviewer use a different colored pen or pencil to mark changes so that the teacher knows how often the piece has been edited.

Applications for English Language Learners

For all students, skills are best taught in the context of the writing process. ELLs, however, may need more direct instruction for developing Standard English skills. Individual teacher-student conferences can help these students focus on the specific skills they need (Hagemann, 2003).

the writer missed, and the pairs collaborate on moving the papers toward final copy. If you make all the corrections, the students are not learning to identify and correct their own errors and are likely to repeat their errors in later writing (Routman, 1991). Atwell (1998) role-plays successful and not-so-successful peer editing conferences with her students to make them aware of what to do and what not to do. Figure 10.12 is a proofreading checklist for students to use in editing their own work and that of their peers.

- *Minilessons*: Brief, 10-minute lessons can focus on needs that students have shown in their writing. For instance, if students seem confused about the use of quotation marks, you can model correct usage on a projected sample. Together, you and your students derive rules from editing the sample and post them on a chart for quick referral. The students can then apply what they learned to their writing.
- *Computers*: Word processing makes editing much easier and faster. Instead of laboriously recopying drafts, students can quickly make changes in their papers. The computer also offers such aids as a spell checker, thesaurus, and grammar checker, although the writer still needs to examine the piece for items that the computer may have missed. Students with poor handwriting or students with

Reflections

Can you remember when a teacher made red marks all over a paper you had tried hard to write well? How did it make you feel? How can you avoid discouraging students who have poor use of conventions but good ideas?

*F*IGURE 10.12 **Proofreading Checklist**

I will look for

- Capital letters at the beginnings of sentences, in proper names and names of places, and in important words in titles.

- End punctuation for each complete sentence.

- Quotation marks around what people say.

- Correct spelling of words.

- Appropriate use of commas, semicolons, and colons.

- Indentation of paragraphs.

- Clear, legible handwriting.

A student is word processing a piece of writing that is to be placed in a booklet for other students to read.

learning disabilities who may have difficulty writing appreciate the convenience of word processing (Routman, 1991).

Be selective when responding to errors in students' writing. Rather than marking every error, look for patterns that individual students make. Research fails to show that marking all errors makes a significant difference in the quality of writing, and students become discouraged when they see their papers full of red marks. Extensive corrections focus on errors instead of ideas (Hagemann, 2003). To avoid frustration, Routman (1991) suggests spelling a few remaining misspelled words "for free" after students have done their best proofreading.

Handwriting

STUDENTS NEED to learn to write neatly and legibly in order to exchange handwritten messages and fill out forms. Although word processing is becoming widespread, children still need to learn how to form letters correctly because computers are not always available or appropriate for the task.

Handwriting Instruction

Preparation for writing begins in the early years with manipulative tasks, art activities, and use of different types of tools or utensils. Children can develop the basic strokes of handwriting through such activities as finger painting and making patterns in sand. They can form letters with clay or pipe cleaners, position their bodies in the forms of circles, and trace over raised letters.

The classroom environment should contribute to learning handwriting skills. Lighting should be adequate, but there should be no glare on work areas. The children should be seated comfortably at seats appropriate for their size so that they can use the correct writing posture. An alphabet strip of the handwriting system being taught should be available for reference, either at each child's work place or displayed where all children can see it easily. They should be able to study the letters carefully, trace them with their fingers, and copy them. Even older children should be able to refer to an alphabet strip, which is often placed above the board. At no time should handwriting be used as punishment, because nothing causes handwriting skills to deteriorate as effectively as having students copy sentences a certain number of times.

When practicing handwriting, the student should sit erectly but comfortably, leaning forward slightly with hips touching the back of the seat and both feet on the floor. The forearms should rest on the desk at a 45-degree angle to the body, with the elbows just off the desk for easy arm movement. The paper should be parallel with the edge of the desk or at a slight slant for manuscript writing, but it should be slanted for cursive writing (slanted to the left for right-handers and to the right for left-handers). The writer should hold the writing instrument lightly between the thumb and middle finger, about one inch above the point, and let the index finger rest on top of the instrument. The other hand should hold the paper in place and move it slightly as the writing progresses across and down the page.

Students should be aware of the following factors that affect legibility.

- *Letter formation*: Basic strokes for manuscript and cursive letters, including connecting strokes for cursive writing
- *Alignment*: All letters resting evenly on the baseline
- *Spacing*: Consistent spacing between letters, words, and sentences
- *Slant*: Vertical letters in manuscript; consistent slant to the letters in cursive writing
- *Size*: Uniform letter size
- *Line quality*: The evenness, thickness, and smoothness of the pen or pencil stroke

You should model good handwriting and also provide direct instruction with supervised practice so that students can learn to write clearly and legibly. When planning instruction, you should keep in mind the objectives of a good handwriting program, which are to help students

- Develop neat and legible handwriting for purposes of communication.
- Acquire facility in both manuscript and cursive writing so that writers can use either style.

Reflections

What practices do teachers sometimes follow that may prevent students from doing their best handwriting? How could these be avoided? What can teachers do to encourage good handwriting?

Teaching Tip

Help left-handed children write comfortably by following these suggestions. (1) Have students slant their papers to the right. (2) Teach them to use pushing strokes instead of pulling strokes. (3) Seat left-handers in slightly lower desks so that they can see what they have written. (4) Have students place the paper to the left side of the desk. (5) Have them grip the writing instrument about one and a half inches from the point (farther away than for right-handers).

- Gain speed and proficiency in writing.
- See the value of good handwriting.

Teachers have used a variety of methods to teach handwriting, including copying, tracing, and demonstration along with verbal instruction. Instruction usually follows this sequence:

- Readiness activities in kindergarten and beginning first grade
- Manuscript printing in kindergarten, first, and second grades
- Cursive writing at the end of second grade or beginning of third grade

These time periods should be flexible and should depend primarily on the readiness levels of the students.

Most teachers rightly value content above handwriting, but writing must be legible in order for others to read the text. Some students tend to be careless in their writing, may be in a hurry to finish, or may think that handwriting doesn't count. By helping

Classroom Vignette 10.2

The students were turning in their social studies assignments to Mr. Burris, their teacher, and he noticed that much of their handwriting was practically illegible.

MR. BURRIS: Why is it that so many of you can do nice writing, but you write poorly on your social studies papers? I can hardly read some of them.

JOSHUA: This is social studies. What difference does it make how we write?

KAYLA: It takes longer to write neatly. I want to get finished.

JEREMY: Handwriting doesn't count as part of our grade, does it?

After school, Mr. Burris expresses his concern to Mrs. Greer, who admits she has a similar problem.

MRS. GREER: They don't think they have to write neatly and legibly, so I came up with some ideas to make them realize that their handwriting is important.

MR. BURRIS: How did you do that?

MRS. GREER: I began stressing handwriting in everything they did, other than rough drafts, notes, or things they didn't consider worth saving. I gave them purposes for writing that made them

want to write well. I asked them to write books for their families and classmates to read, and I had them display their final reports from our theme studies. Sometimes I gave them special purposes for writing in the classroom—putting directions on the board, writing captions for artwork, or constructing bulletin boards.

MR. BURRIS: I see what you mean. If they write for an audience, they see a reason to write legibly. My students have been working in groups on projects, and they could probably put together some interesting reports. Maybe I'll have them do that and then display their reports for others to read.

MRS. GREER: You might even ask our media specialist about placing them in the library. The students really get excited when they see others reading their work.

What's happening here?

The students see no reason to be careful with their writing, so they write carelessly. Providing purposes for good handwriting and letting students know that audiences will be reading some of their writing increases their interest in writing legibly throughout the day.

Minilesson 10.9

Introduction to Cursive Writing

You have been writing the daily news story in cursive for two weeks and feel that the students are ready to begin learning to write in cursive. You ask them how cursive writing differs from printing.

JEREMY: The letters in a word are all strung together.

ISAAC: It looks like they're slanty.

KAYLA: The round letters aren't as round.

Tell the children that they are correct and that you are going to show them how they can begin making cursive letters by connecting printed letters. Print the word *cone* on the board. Then show them how to use connecting strokes to form this word in cursive. (See Figure 10.13.)

Ask the children to print the word *cone* at their seats and then use connecting strokes to make the cursive form. Follow the same procedure with the words *hat, lend,* and *mill.*

What are the students learning?

By modeling cursive writing, you are familiarizing students with the formation of words in cursive. They are becoming aware of the differences between manuscript and cursive writing, can recognize certain features of cursive, and have opportunities to practice with letters that connect easily. They are easing into cursive writing with supervised instruction.

---

students understand why handwriting is important, you can encourage students to write legibly. Classroom Vignette 10.2 shows how to provide authentic purposes for good handwriting.

Many children are eager to learn to write in cursive because that is how most adults write. Making the transition from manuscript to cursive requires a great many new skills, however, and should not be treated lightly. Children should be able to print reasonably well and have a desire to write in cursive. They also need to be able to read cursive writing. You can prepare them for doing this by writing assignments or directions in cursive and reading them aloud from charts or the board as children observe. Children need to use fine-muscle control for new movements as they write connected letters with a slant. Practice in making connected loops and upswings helps prepare them for these new demands, but you should avoid too much preparation before moving into teaching actual letter formations. Minilesson 10.9 shows one way to introduce children to cursive writing.

Some students have difficulty learning to write in cursive. Figure 10.14 gives some remedial strategies for students like these.

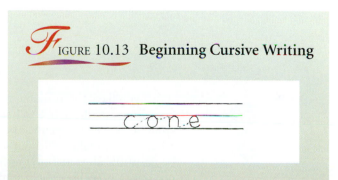

*F*IGURE 10.13 **Beginning Cursive Writing**

 IGURE 10.14 **Remedial Strategies for Problems in Cursive Writing**

Problem	Remedial Strategy
Poor letter formation	Demonstrate correct formation; provide model for student to copy; let student compare own letter form with sample and note discrepancies; have student write letter in air with arm.
Too light or heavy lines	Check writing instrument for fineness and hardness; check student's grip on instrument and amount of pressure being applied.
Nonparallel slant	Check the position of the paper and child's posture.
Too little spacing between letters	Let student practice spacing by placing a small oval between letters.
Poor spacing between words	Show that the beginning stroke in the second word starts just below the ending stroke of the previous word.
Too small or large letter size	Check position of arm on desk for movement of forearm. Too much movement may cause large letters; too little movement may cause small letters.
Inadequate speed	Check body position and grip on writing instrument. A tight grip produces slow, tense writing.
Too-short connecting strokes	Encourage student to "swing" between letters.
Careless writing	Provide purposes for good handwriting so that the student will want to write well.
Generally illegible writing	Show examples of legible and illegible writing. Ask student which communicates better and why legible writing is important.

If you have the available hardware, you may also offer students instruction in keyboarding, an alternative to handwriting needed for word processing. Although most students write with pens or pencils, many are learning keyboarding skills when computers are available. Without some training in using the keyboard, however, work can be painfully slow and inefficient (Jongsma, 2001). *Type to Learn, Jr.* is one of several programs available to help students learn to use the computer efficiently. It promotes proper posture and correct placement of hands on the keyboard, and it helps students use left-hand or right-hand keys to locate letters and numbers. Students also learn to use the space bar, the shift keys, the keys for common punctuation marks, and the return or enter key. Students can practice keyboarding skills and then apply their skills to school activities.

Handwriting Systems

Several commercial handwriting systems exist, with many showing only slight variations in letter forms and others advocating more innovative letter styles. The aim of most systems is to present letter forms and instructional strategies that will prompt fluent writing and legibility. Two handwriting systems are widely used. The Zaner-Bloser program uses traditional letter formations (see Figure 10.15), and the D'Nealian program attempts to modify letter formations to ease the transition from manuscript to cursive (see Figure 10.16).

Handwriting is an individual matter, a means of personal expression. It is unlikely that any two individuals write exactly the same way. Handwriting systems vary, and even within a system individuals develop their own idiosyncrasies. The goal of handwriting instruction is not for everyone to follow a model to perfection, but to

FIGURE 10.15 **Zaner-Bloser Handwriting System**

FIGURE 10.16 **D'Nealian Alphabet**

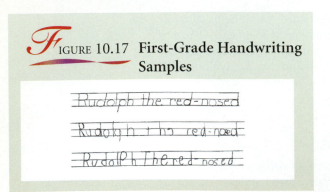

$\mathcal{F}$IGURE 10.17   **First-Grade Handwriting Samples**

develop an easy, fluent style within the limits of legibility. Observation, informal checklists, or commercial handwriting evaluation scales' overlays are useful for evaluating handwriting. Children can also assess their own writing by comparing their work with correct models. Figure 10.17 shows samples of first-grade printing, which teachers can help children evaluate by looking for spacing between words, appropriate use of lower- and uppercase letters, and correctly formed letters.

Classroom Assessment for Using Language Tools

It is common practice in many classrooms to give weekly spelling tests from spelling books, but you may prefer to assign more meaningful and relevant words for students to learn. You can use workbook pages and informal tests to assess students' knowledge of the conventions of language. The most authentic assessment, however, is evaluation of a student's writing to see if the writer is able to apply knowledge of spelling, grammar, and the conventions of written language in legible form.

$\mathcal{S}$ummary

Correct spelling is important for communicating effectively in writing, but standard spelling is difficult because of the many irregularities in the English language. As children learn to spell, they move through a series of five steps, beginning with random placement of letters and progressing to accuracy. Teachers may either adhere to a spelling textbook or select words for spelling instruction from word lists, words that follow patterns, theme words, or other options.

Modeling strategies and procedures for spelling can be very helpful, especially in the context of actual writing. Have-a-Go, word sorts, and Making Words are useful activities for learning to spell, but research has found memorizing assigned words to be generally ineffective for long-term results. Spelling can be taught through a workshop approach, a traditional approach with a spelling book, or spelling meetings.

Grammar is defined in three ways: traditional grammar with rules taught as prescriptions for use; structural grammar with consideration for the ways people actually use language; and transformational grammar, which has rules for sentence generation and changes, or transformations, into related sentences. Research shows little connection between knowing the rules of grammar and their application to speech and writing, so it appears that students learn how to apply knowledge of grammar better when they learn it by using it. They learn to use grammar by observing ways that authors use it in literature, through minilessons that occur during writing workshops, by engaging in sentence combining activities, and in a variety of other ways.

Conventions are accepted practices in writing and include spelling, punctuation, capitalization, spacing, and directionality. Students need to understand the importance of using conventions in their writing. As with the other tools of language, they learn conventions through literature and their own writing.

Proofreading, which occurs during the editing stage of the writing process, enables students to examine their written work for conventional usage. They can learn to proofread from teacher modeling, individual editing conferences, peer proofreading, minilessons, and computer aids. Legible handwriting is also important, and students learn its value when they have authentic purposes for using it.

Discussion Questions

1. What do you consider to be the most desirable features of a spelling program? How can you teach spelling most effectively? Would all children learn the same words?

2. Turbill (2000) believes that children must develop a spelling conscience, or an awareness of why spelling is important, before they commit themselves to being careful, accurate spellers. How could you develop this conscience?

3. What role does proofreading play in spelling? How is proofreading connected to developing a spelling conscience?

4. How would you manage a spelling program in which children were choosing different words to learn, according to their individual needs and developmental stages? Is this a good idea? Why, or why not? How would you assess their progress?

5. Parents are very interested in their children's spelling progress. How would you justify invented spelling? How would you suggest parents help their children become better spellers?

6. Are minilessons adequate for teaching grammar and the conventions of written language? Do some children need more extensive instruction? What other options are there for teaching in context?

7. If the school system required you to use a grammar textbook, what would you do? How might you use it selectively or integrate it with writing activities? What other options might you have?

8. What kind of teaching in grammar, spelling, and use of conventions do most of the references support? What are the main features of this type of instruction? Do you agree with these views?

Suggested Activities

1. List several words that you would not spell correctly if you sounded them out. Try to determine the reason for the lack of sound-symbol regularity. Decide if there are other clues (possibly morphemes in the words) that could help with the spelling of these words.

2. Get a large sheet of poster board and twenty-four library card pockets.

Place the pockets so that there are six rows down and four across each row. On each pocket, put a letter of the alphabet from A to W, and put XYZ on the last pocket. In each pocket, place a 3" x 5" card with a list of high-frequency words that begin with the letter on the pocket. (Example: For A, you might list *about, after, around, almost*.) Children can use this pocket chart as a spelling reference.

3. Locate incorrectly spelled words in the newspaper. Make a learning activity from these misspelled words that will help students see how incorrect spelling interferes with communication.

4. Compare two student copies of different spelling textbooks for the same grade. Look for the amount of overlap in the lists of words. Decide on what basis words were chosen for each book. Look at the teachers' manuals to see how to use the books.

5. Obtain some samples of writing from a kindergartner or first-grader. Determine the developmental stage exhibited by each piece of writing, based on Gentry's stages.

6. Brainstorm some challenge words or activities, similar to those given as a Teaching Tip in the section about the spelling program.

7. Find the book *C D B!* by William Steig. Ask children to read the book and see if they can spell the words that the letters represent. Help them if they are having difficulty. (The answers are in the back of the book.)

8. Examine the teacher's manual of a language arts textbook to discover how grammar is presented. Decide if you would want to use this approach in your classroom.

9. Look at a child's piece of writing. Consider the content, spelling, and use of Standard English. How would you evaluate the child's work? How much weight would you give to the content, and how much to the use of grammar and spelling?

10. Find several books from children's literature that have patterns that students could use as models for their writing. Make a list of the books and identify the patterns.

References

ATWELL, N. (1998). *In the middle* (2nd ed.). Portsmouth, NH: Boynton/Cook.

BARNITZ, J. (1998). Revising grammar instruction for authentic composing and comprehending. *The Reading Teacher, 51,* 608–610.

BROMLEY, K. (1999). Key components of sound writing instruction. In L. B. Gambrell, L. M. Morrow, S. B. Neuman, & M. Pressley (Eds.), *Best practices in literacy instruction.* New York: Guilford.

BUSCHMAN, L. (2003). Buddies aren't just for reading, they're for spelling too! *The Reading Teacher, 56,* 747–752.

CHANDLER, K., & MAPLETON TEACHER-RESEARCH GROUP. (2000). Squaring up to spelling: A teacher-research group surveys parents. *Language Arts, 77,* 224–231.

COOPER, J. D. (1997). *Literacy: Helping children construct meaning* (3rd ed.). Boston: Houghton Mifflin.

CUNNINGHAM, P., & ALLINGTON, R. (1999). *Classrooms that work* (2nd ed.). New York: Longman.

FRESCH, M. J. (2000). What we learned from Josh: Sorting out word sorting. *Language Arts, 77,* 232–240.

GENTRY, J. R. (1981). Learning to spell developmentally. *The Reading Teacher, 34,* 378–381.

GENTRY, J. R. (1982). An analysis of developmental spelling in GNYS AT WRK. *The Reading Teacher, 36,* 192–200.

GENTRY, J. R. (2000). A retrospective on invented spelling and a look forward. *Language Arts, 54,* 318–332.

GENTRY, J. R., & GILLET, J. W. (1993). *Teaching kids to spell.* Portsmouth, NH: Heinemann.

GRAVES, D. (1994). *A fresh look at writing.* Portsmouth, NH: Heinemann.

HAGEMANN, J. (Ed.). (2003). *Teaching grammar.* Boston: Allyn & Bacon.

HARRIS, T., & HODGES, R. (Eds.). (1995). *The literacy dictionary.* Newark, DE: International Reading Association.

HENDERSON, E. (1985). *Teaching spelling.* Boston: Houghton Mifflin.

HUGHES, M., & SEARLE, D. (2000). Spelling and "the second 'r'." *Language Arts, 77,* 203–208.

JOHNSTON, F. (2000/2001). Spelling exceptions: Problems or possibilities? *The Reading Teacher, 54,* 372–378.

JONGSMA, K. (2001). Using CD-ROMS to support the development of literary processes. *The Reading Teacher, 54,* 592–595.

ROGERS, L. (1999). Spelling cheerleading. *The Reading Teacher, 53,* 110–111.

ROUTMAN, R. (1991). *Invitations.* Portsmouth, NH: Heinemann.

RYMER, R., & WILLIAMS, C. (2000). "Wasn't that a spelling word?": Spelling instruction and young children's writing. *Language Arts, 77,* 241–249.

SIPE, L. (2001). Invention, convention, and intervention: Invented spelling and the teacher's role. *The Reading Teacher, 55,* 264–273.

SNOW, C., BURNS, M. S., & GRIFFIN, P. (Eds.). (1998). *Preventing reading difficulties in young children.* Washington, DC: National Academy Press.

SNOWBALL, D., & BOLTON, F. (1999). *Spelling K–8.* York, ME: Stenhouse.

TCHUDI, S., & TCHUDI, S. (1999). *The English language arts handbook* (2nd ed.). Portsmouth, NH: Boynton/Cook.

TURBILL, J. (2000). Developing a spelling conscience. *Language Arts, 77,* 209–217.

TYPE TO LEARN, JR. (1999). Pleasantville, NY: Sunburst.

WEAVER, C. (1996). *Teaching grammar in context.* Portsmouth, NH: Boynton/Cook..

WEAVER, C., MCNALLY, C., & MOERMAN, S. (2003). To grammar or not to grammar: That is *not* the question. In J. Hagemann (Ed.), *Teaching grammar* (pp. 48–64). Boston: Allyn & Bacon.

WILLIAMS, J. (1995). Grammar and grammatical. In T. Harris & R. Hodges (Eds.), *The literacy dictionary* (pp. 99–100). Newark, DE: International Reading Association.

WING JAN, L. (1991). *Spelling and grammar.* Sydney, Australia: Ashton Scholastic.

WRIGHT, K. (2000). Weekly spelling meetings: Improving spelling instruction through classroom-based inquiry. *Language Arts, 77,* 218–223.

Books for Children and Adolescents Cited in This Chapter

BRETT, J. (1989). *The mitten: A Ukrainian folktale.* New York: Putnam.

CARLE, E. (1990). *The very quiet cricket.* New York: Philomel.

COERR, E. (1993). *Sadako.* New York: Putnam.

FRASIER, D. (1998). *Out of the ocean.* San Diego: Harcourt Brace.

HELLER, R. (1987). *A cache of jewels and other collective nouns.* New York: Scholastic.

HELLER, R. (1988). *Kites sail high: A book about verbs.* New York: Scholastic.

HELLER, R. (1989). *Many luscious lollipops: A book about adjectives.* New York: Scholastic.

HELLER, R. (1990). *Merry-go-round: A book about nouns.* New York: Scholastic.

HELLER, R. (1997). *Mine, all mine: A book about pronouns.* New York: Scholastic.

HELLER, R. (1991). *Up, up and away: A book about adverbs.* New York: Scholastic.

HUTCHINS, P. (1968). *Rosie's walk.* New York: Macmillan.

JOOSE, B. (1991). *Mama, do you love me?* New York: Scholastic.

MARTIN, B., JR. (1982). *Brown bear, brown bear, what do you see?* Toronto: Holt, Rinehart & Winston.

SALLEY, C. (2002). *Epossumondas.* San Diego: Harcourt.

STEIG, W. (2000). *C D B!* New York: Simon & Schuster.

VIORST, J. (1972). *Alexander and the terrible, horrible, no good, very bad day.* New York: Macmillan.

YOLEN, J., & TEAGUE, M. (2000). *How do dinosaurs say good night?* New York: Blue Sky.

VISUAL AND MEDIA LITERACY

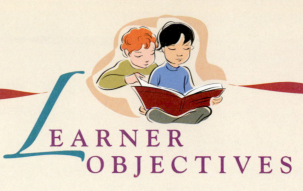

LEARNER OBJECTIVES

At the conclusion of this chapter

YOU SHOULD BE ABLE TO

1. Define and explain visual literacy, media literacy, and digital literacy.

2. Discuss the use of viewing skills.

3. Describe methods of visually representing information.

4. Identify the following additional terms that are defined or explained in this chapter:

chat room 439
diagrams 430
digital literacy 422
e-mail 439
emoticons 439
graphs 432
HTML 444

hypermedia 438
hypertext 438
Internet 437
maps 431
media literacy 422
multimedia
   presentations 442

Seeing-Thinking
   Activities 428
simulation programs 435
tables 431
technological literacy 422
visual literacy 422

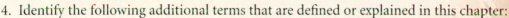

NCTE/IRA Standards addressed in this chapter

STANDARD 1. Students read a wide range of print and non-print texts to build an understanding of texts, of themselves, and of the cultures of the United States and the world; to acquire new information; to respond to the needs and demands of society and the workplace; and for personal fulfillment. Among these texts are fiction and nonfiction, classic and contemporary works.

STANDARD 3. Students apply a wide range of strategies to comprehend, interpret, evaluate, and appreciate texts. They draw on their prior experience, their interactions with other readers and writers, their knowledge of word meaning and of other texts, their word identification strategies, and their understanding of textual features (e.g., sound-letter correspondence, sentence structure, context, graphics).

STANDARD 4. Students adjust their use of spoken, written, and visual language (e.g., conventions, style, vocabulary) to communicate effectively with a variety of audiences and for different purposes.

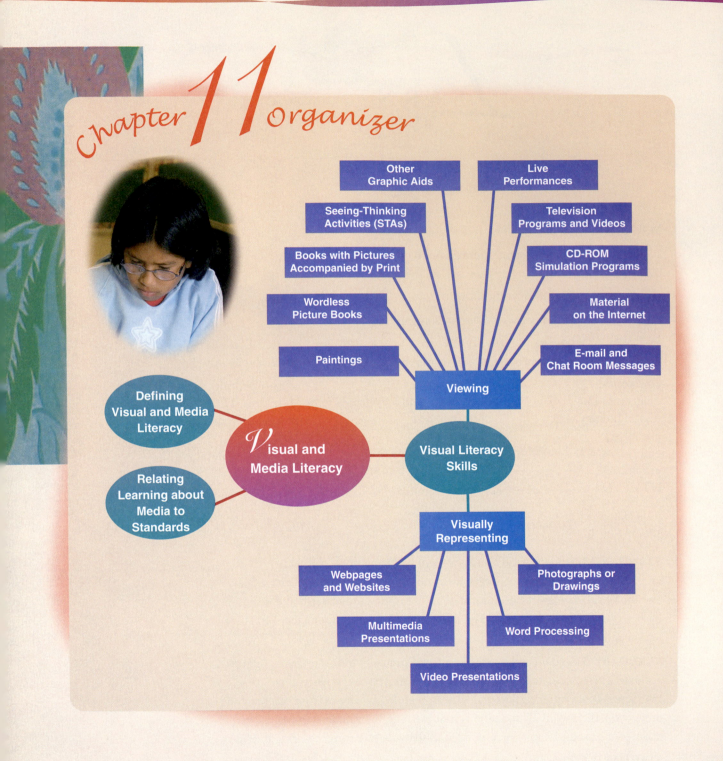

Chapter 11 Organizer

Visual and Media Literacy

- Defining Visual and Media Literacy
- Relating Learning about Media to Standards

Viewing
- Other Graphic Aids
- Live Performances
- Seeing-Thinking Activities (STAs)
- Television Programs and Videos
- Books with Pictures Accompanied by Print
- CD-ROM Simulation Programs
- Wordless Picture Books
- Material on the Internet
- Paintings
- E-mail and Chat Room Messages

Visual Literacy Skills

Visually Representing
- Webpages and Websites
- Photographs or Drawings
- Multimedia Presentations
- Word Processing
- Video Presentations

STANDARD 6. Students apply knowledge of language structure, language conventions (e.g., spelling and punctuation), media techniques, figurative language, and genre to create, critique, and discuss print and non-print texts.

STANDARD 7. Students conduct research on issues and interests by generating ideas and questions, and by posing problems. They gather, evaluate, and synthesize data from a variety of sources (e.g., print and non-print texts, artifacts, people) to communicate their discoveries in ways that suit their purpose and audience.

STANDARD 8. Students use a variety of technological and information resources (e.g., libraries, databases, computer networks, video) to gather and synthesize information and to create and communicate knowledge.

STANDARD 12. Students use spoken, written, and visual language to accomplish their own purposes (e.g., for learning, enjoyment, persuasion, and the exchange of information).

*B*ARBARA VAUGHN, a seventh-grade literacy teacher in a rural school, teamed with Betty Roe, a university professor of reading and language arts methods classes, to help Barbara's students become familiar with good literature and become more proficient in literacy skills, using technology as a tool. In the process, Barbara had to familiarize the students with some of the technological tools that they were about to use.

Barbara and Betty paired their students for one-on-one e-mail exchanges about literature selections (referred to briefly in Chapter 8). Many students needed explicit instructions about the use of e-mail as a medium of communication.

Betty's students read the same literature selections that their partners were reading, on the same time schedule. As each segment was read, the partners exchanged e-mail about it. Betty's students modeled such writing skills as correct format for friendly letters, syntactic structures, spelling, and punctuation as they offered their insights about the books that they were reading. The first book that the participants read was Katherine Paterson's *Bridge to Terabithia*.

When the participants finished reading the book, both groups, seventh-graders and university students, watched a movie of the book and corresponded with one another, comparing and contrasting the movie and the book, discussing how and why they are different, and explaining which one they liked better. The seventh-graders were unanimous in liking the book better, and they were critical of the differences that they saw in the book and the movie.

The university students helped the seventh-graders see that the time constraints placed on the movie made including all of the book's action impossible. There was agreement between the university students and the seventh-graders that two characters were collapsed into one in the movie for that reason, and they felt it hurt the story a little, but was reasonable. The seventh-graders were more critical of the fact that every mention of church and religion was left out of the movie; and, although they acknowledged that the movie fit the time slot better with these deletions, they were not sure that these were the best parts to remove. They were particularly annoyed that the children got into Terabithia over a log in the movie, when they used a rope to swing over in the book. In their opinions, it took some of the realism out of the situation that the book created. They also said that the ending was changed "for no reason at all," and their university partners were generally in agreement with this sentiment.

The enthusiasm and critical analysis that came from using the e-mail exchanges were not the only benefits of the program. Some of the seventh-grade students began to write more, stay on task better, and respond more deeply to the reading. Whereas this response was not universal, Barbara was extremely pleased with the improvements that she observed in her students' work.

Barbara also familiarized her students with the workings of the mPower multimedia presentation software. This program allowed them to combine print, graphics, still and moving images, sound effects, and speech into a presentation about the book. The class discussed the scenes in the book and broke up into groups to design scenes for an mPower presentation to share with their university partners. They took the scenes that they felt were most vital (including the one where Leslie went to church with Jess's family) and wrote a bit of text to go with either a still picture or an animated graphic. They staged the still pictures themselves and took the pictures with a digital camera. Then they merged the pictures with their text. Finally, they chose a sound track to go behind their presentation.

The presentation could be viewed on the computer, but the teacher also copied it onto a video and sent it to campus for the university students to view. The university students, who were also learning to do mPower presentations in another methods course, were impressed with the attention to design details, such as fading scenes in and out, animating certain parts, and so on.

What's happening here?

Writing

The learning experience went far beyond a literature discussion and involved critical thinking, reading, writing, listening (in their group work), speaking (in their group work), viewing, and visually representing. The students had individuals who served as audiences for their writing, providing motivation to do well. Their partners offered models for writing, and many seventh-graders showed signs of using the modeled techniques in their own writing. Some personalized their letters with comments outside the range of the assignment, but, in general, they remained task oriented and showed signs of having read and comprehended the book and having viewed and analyzed the movie. The mPower product was impressively done, and many students became avid e-mailers with their partners after the project ended, providing additional writing engagement.

Today students are inundated with visual images, both in print sources and in media. As Flood and Lapp (1997/1998) point out, these images include a range of forms from drama, movies, and television to video games; the language arts of listening, speaking, reading, and writing are embedded in many of these forms. Like reading print materials, reading still pictures and reading video images entail attention to facts, relationships, inferences, and critical analysis. Different media also present students with new location, navigation, and organizational patterns that require different approaches to comprehension and production. There are also increased challenges to critical analysis when use of the Internet exposes students to material that is posted without regard to accuracy or clarity.

Both the interpretation of these images and media messages and the construction of similar images are needed skills in the classroom and the outside world. You must find ways to help students deal with these means of conveying information.

Media are used as information sources when studying content area topics. Various media are useful for learning about almost any content area theme. They also provide vehicles for presenting information to classmates in the form of culminating projects and reports.

Defining Visual and Media Literacy

GIORGIS AND her colleagues (1999) have said that **visual literacy** is being able to interpret the meaning of visual images. Valmont (2003) and Heinich and colleagues (1999) add to this definition being able to construct effective visuals in order to convey ideas to others. Photographs, line drawings, diagrams and charts, maps, and graphs appear in both textbooks and trade books, as well as in magazines and newspapers, and these days all of these images may be downloaded from electronic media. Images that must be interpreted and constructed are not always the static images just described. Because of the increasing importance of television, videos, CDs, DVDs, computer programs, the Internet, and cellular phones with video capabilities, people also have to interpret and construct animations, live action dramatizations, and real-life video scenes. Visual literacy in all of these aspects is becoming more and more important in school and in many everyday life activities.

Technological literacy, according to the U.S. Department of Education (1997), is being able to use technology, including computers, to enhance learning, performance, and productivity. To achieve technological literacy, students must acquire **media literacy**, which involves questioning and analyzing material that you read and view (Scharrer, 2002/2003)—tasks that require comprehending the materials—and creating messages in varied mass communications media (Valmont, 2003). Scharrer (2002/2003, p. 355) points out that media literacy involves considering "how media messages are created, marketed, and distributed" as well as how they affect attitudes and behavior. **Digital literacy**, a subset of media literacy, is the ability to interpret

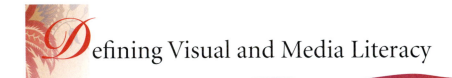
Reflections
How are visual literacy and technological literacy interrelated?

and evaluate material in formats delivered by the computer (Pool, 1997) and to construct images, sounds, movements, animations and other nonverbal components to electronic messages (Valmont, 2003).

isual Literacy Skills

AN EARLY opportunity to work on visual literacy skills is analyzing the pictures in picture books. Some picture books have no words at all. Others have pictures that add information to the information offered in the words. Still others have pictures that depict in a visual form what the words are communicating.

Viewing

Viewing is a language arts skill that, until recently, was largely ignored. Students often were given books and asked to read chapters or sections without being given any instruction or encouragement to "read" the pictures, diagrams, tables, maps, and graphs. Such graphic aids are generally included in books to do one of two things—convey information that is not offered by the print or to illustrate scenes or concepts that are in the printed text. As is true with reading, students need to view material to acquire details, make inferences, evaluate material, and go beyond the material with creative responses.

With instruction, students can learn to view these aids in a way that will provide them with helpful information about the material being read. Without instruction, the students probably will just skip the visual aids and fail to get all of the available information from the material. The stories in picture books are almost always incomplete without the pictures, which may be paintings, line drawings, photographs, or other forms of representation. The drawings may range from cartoon style to highly realistic depictions. Susan Jeffers's illustrations in Charles Perrault and Amy Ehrlich's *Cinderella* are pen-and-ink drawings with dyes to color them. Loreen Leedy's illustrations for

Applications for English Language Learners

Use of wordless picture books is especially helpful in working with ELLs. They can analyze the pictures either in English or in their first language as they work on visual literacy skills. In this way, as long as there is a person present to translate their first language contributions, they can offer as much to the learning process as a native English speaker does.

her book *Measuring Penny* are done with acrylic on watercolor paper. Max Ginsburg's art in Robert San Souci's *Kate Shelley: Bound for Legend* was done as an oil painting that was color-separated and reproduced in full color. Paul Fleischman's *Townsend's Warbler* is not a picture book, but a nonfiction book that uses photographs liberally to enhance the text. Artists choose styles of illustration that fit the mood, culture, or purpose of the book. In Doreen Cronin's *Click, Clack, Moo: Cows That Type,* Betsy Lewin uses a cartoon style for a humorous book. Cartoon illustrations often have nonverbal clues to meaning, as is also true of comic strips such as the *Family Circus* comic strip shown below. Each of the books mentioned in this section has visual features that enhance the text that accompanies it.

In the *Family Circus* cartoon, lines are used to show PJ's movement on the tricycle; the flight of Jeffy's plane; the movement of the light fixture; the mother's movement to avoid the plane; the trajectory of Billy's ball; the wagging of the dogs' tails; the sounds of the video game, the telephone, the push toy, and the dog; the running of the dog; the falling of the rain; and the spinning feeling in the mother's head. Examining cartoons for such clues and others seems like a game to many students, and they readily participate.

Viewers use information from text and knowledge of verbal, visual, and audio messages to comprehend material that is viewed. Information gained through one medium often enhances understanding in others (Watts Pailliotet, Semali, Rodenberg, Giles, & Macaul, 2000).

© Bill Keane, Inc. Reprinted with special permission of King Features Syndicate.

Viewing skills are important in the study of all subjects because textbooks and trade books in each area are filled with images. These skills are important in another way in mathematics, a field of study in which patterns and geometric shapes are particularly important. Students who perceive patterns readily have an advantage in learning many mathematics concepts. This was brought to the attention of Betty Roe when she was playing with her five-year-old nephew, Dryden. Dryden had been learning letters and numbers in school, so Betty drew the following on a piece of paper and asked him how many *f*s there were:

f h t l f

g a f r o

f l i n f

Dryden replied, "There are five of them. I didn't even count them. You know how I knew? They are in those places like the dots on the dice that are five."

Dryden's perception of the pattern and the analysis of the pattern showed development of an extremely useful visual literacy skill.

Critical viewing, or viewing for the purpose of evaluation, has recently become a prominent concern. Students are spending more and more time with media such as television, computers, video games, videos, and radio. Roberts, Foehr, Rideout, and Brodie (1999) and Scharrer (2002/2003) say students spend an average of six-and-a-half hours each day this way, and Comstock and Scharrer (1999) indicate that an average of three-and-a-half hours of this time is spent watching television. Students need help in analyzing all types of visual media.

Watts Pailliotet and her colleagues (2000) recommend "deep viewing" for visual analysis. With this procedure, students view a television commercial, website, newspaper or magazine advertisement, or other material multiple times. While they are viewing and after they finish, the students write down their reactions, being specific about the elements of the material that caused each reaction. This process helps them to see how the producers of the material affect the viewers' reactions. They learn to recognize bias and misrepresentations and to challenge the authority of the presentations. When doing deep viewing, students look for the action, the objects represented and their characteristics, the actors and their words and inflections, the actors' movements, the symbols used, the cultural targets for the presentation, and the quality of the presentation. They think about purposes of the material and motivation for its presentation. Students can work in groups, with a recorder writing down group responses. They also think about the effects that the material has on them personally.

Teaching Tip

When choosing commercials or advertisements for students to analyze visually, include ones that attempt to appeal to and persuade children who are the same age as the ones in your class. In this situation, students are able to bring more of their background experience to the analysis.

PAINTINGS

Ehrenworth (2003) displays works of art for middle school students to view and then models analysis of the artworks through think-alouds. In this way, she shows them how to observe detail and to form interpretations of the art. At times, she provides background information about the painter and the subjects of the paintings that offer context for the interpretations. Students make notes on color, form, and composition as they view the works. Then they respond to the paintings in writing, sometimes through poetry or journal entries and sometimes through other forms of writing. In their writing, students describe what they see in the paintings or what the paintings make them feel.

Piro (2002) used paintings with middle school students to enrich a thematic unit on ancient Greek and Roman mythology. Peter Bruegel's *Landscape with the Fall of Icarus* was shown to illustrate how paintings served as visual stories to illiterate people in earlier days. Piro shared the myth orally along with a reproduction of the painting. He and his students made a graphic organizer of the story elements. Then students visually analyzed the painting and told what they saw in it. The uses of size, color, and light in the painting to produce certain effects were discussed. Next the students wrote a sequel to the myth on which the painting was based.

WORDLESS PICTURE BOOKS

Wordless picture books, such as Emily Arnold McCully's *First Snow,* discussed in Figure 11.1, offer students the chance to interpret the meaning of the book strictly

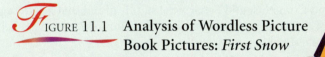

FIGURE 11.1   Analysis of Wordless Picture Book Pictures: *First Snow*

The main warm-looking item on most of the pages is the truck, which is red, a "warm" color. The protagonist mouse's hat and scarf are in a warm pink tone. At the end of the book, the large soup pot is red. The blues and greens that predominate in the illustrations are "cool" colors that set the mood for the cold weather depicted.

Dots of various kinds suggest motion, falling snow, and footprints leading from mouse to truck, for example. The artist uses a painting technique that uses lines and shading to give an illusion of the texture of the disturbed snow, the tree bark, and the needles and branches of the tree.

The two-page spreads and the angles of the lines suggest upward and downward movement as the mice move up and down the hill. The relative size of the truck and the mice at the bottom of the hill give an idea of how high the hill is from the protagonist's perspective.

The multiple depictions of the protagonist going up and down the hill on two adjacent pages suggest that after defeating the hill once, the mouse liked it enough to do it again and again. The final picture with the one droopy mouse, identified by the pink scarf, shows how tired the mouse was from going up and down the hill so many times.

A child who can recognize the depiction of cold and the directions of the movement, follow the story line, and infer the protagonist's feelings has a good grasp of picture interpretation, an aspect of visual literacy.

Applications for English Language Learners and Students with Special Needs

Hibbing and Rankin-Erickson (2003) found that picture books helped ELLs and struggling readers in the middle school understand content. The pictures helped the students build needed background knowledge and understand the emotions of characters in books about World War II and the Holocaust, for example. These pictures also provided memory aids for details for these students.

from the pictures, illustrating how use of dots, lines, shadings, color, texture, direction, and scale help to interpret pictures. A series of dots can suggest direction and motion (Valmont, 2003). Lines serve many purposes, from leading the eye in a particular direction to outlining shapes and indicating textures, strength, balance, or moods. Shadings help viewers to see depth and textures. Layering techniques with watercolors, pastels, or oil paints can also depict texture. Colors can indicate warmth or lack thereof. Warm colors are red, orange, and yellow. Cool colors are blue, green, and purple. The warm colors also often indicate excitement, whereas the cool colors indicate calmness. Size of objects can establish perspective. Page composition and design, which include placement of text, use of borders, and choice of fonts, produce the overall impression (Giorgis et al., 1999; Valmont, 2003).

BOOKS WITH PICTURES ACCOMPANIED BY PRINT

After examining wordless picture books, books with pictures accompanied by print can be examined. Picture storybooks must have words and art that work together to create meaning for the reader. Sometimes the art simply reinforces or complements the words, but sometimes it extends the information offered in the words. For example, Brian Pinkney's scratchboard illustrations bring the music alive through spiraling, wavy, and swirling lines in Andrea Davis Pinkney's *Duke Ellington: The Piano Prince and His Orchestra* (Giorgis et al., 1999).

Textbooks have illustrations that often carry much important information to clarify the material in the printed text or to supplement and extend it. Asking students to examine the illustrations in a chapter for significant details adds to the learning that takes place about a topic, since the ability to visualize what the text is describing is an important skill that is not easily acquired by some students. In addition to photographs, line drawings, and paintings, textbooks have diagrams and charts, maps, and graphs to be interpreted for pertinent information.

Pictures in books help English language learners understand content that is being studied.

Applications for English Language Learners and Students with Special Needs

Anstey (2002) considers postmodern picture books to have characteristics helpful in teaching new literacies. Authors and illustrators of such books use a number of techniques to produce multiple meanings for readers to discover or construct. Designs and layouts are unusual; illustrative styles are mixed; plots, characters, and settings are presented in nontraditional ways; the narrative voice may vary; and readers may have to use outside information to help them decide on meanings. David Macaulay's *Black and White* and Jon Scieszka and Lane Smith's *The Stinky Cheese Man and Other Fairly Stupid Tales* are examples of postmodern picture books that teachers may wish to explore.

Cortese (2003/2004) suggests using Question-Answer Relationship (QAR) strategies with pictures to work on comprehension skills and making students aware of various sources of information available for answering questions. (QARs are discussed in more detail in Chapter 7.) Teaching students to use information in topic-related pictures improves their ability to understand the accompanying text. Interpreting written language is generally a harder task than interpreting pictorial images because the written word is more abstract.

Pictures that should be analyzed for information also appear in electronic reference books, such as dictionaries and encyclopedias, as well as other electronic references.

Seeing-Thinking Activities (STAs)

Valmont (1976; 2003) suggests the use of **Seeing-Thinking Activities (STAs)** to increase students' visual literacy skills, while also working on prediction skills. STAs are like DR-TAs (discussed in Chapter 7) and DL-TAs (discussed in Chapter 5) in that they involve making predictions from available information, collecting additional information, and revising predictions, when necessary. They are unlike these other techniques in that they use visual, nonverbal clues as the basis for their predictions, whereas DR-TAs use primarily print with limited visual information and DL-TAs use oral language. Valmont (1976; 2003) describes four types of STAs—simple, single-frame, alternative-

Applications for English Language Learners and Students with Special Needs

Use of pictorial images to teach QARs is especially helpful for ELLs and struggling learners. Such activities reduce the cognitive linguistic load on the students so that they can focus on the comprehension task (Cortese, 2003/2004).

ending, and multiple-frame—any of which can be projected on a screen for viewing by the entire class.

Simple STAs reveal parts of objects little by little. After viewing the first part of a line drawing of an object, perhaps a circle with four curves outside, the students would be asked to predict what the drawing will be in its completed form. See Figure 11.2 for an example of the stages of drawing at which the students would make predictions, followed by the finished drawing.

Single-frame STAs offer a detailed picture of a situation, perhaps a family spreading out a lunch on a picnic table with a dark cloud in the sky. The students would first be asked what was happening in the picture. Then they would be asked what happened just before this. They might be asked to draw a picture that shows what happened. In either case, the students should discuss their verbal responses or their pictures and decide if they make sense. Finally, they would be asked what might happen after the scene in the picture. Again, they might be asked to draw a picture of something that might happen next. The verbal or drawn responses should be discussed again.

Alternate-ending STAs have two frames that show sequential action; for example, the first frame might have a person setting a ball of yarn with a loose end on a table, with the loose strand dangling over the side of the table. In the next frame, a cat might be shown looking at the dangling strand. The students can discuss and predict how they think the story will turn out. Then they can be shown pictures of possible alternate endings to the story. Valmont (2003) uses three. Possible endings might be the cat jumping up on the table with the yarn and knocking off the lamp, the cat pulling the ball of yarn off onto the floor, and the cat batting the loose strand of yarn with its paw. The students can discuss these endings and compare their predictions with these endings. They can discuss if each of these endings is possible and also if each of their own predicted endings makes as much sense as the ones shown. This is a great way to encourage creative thinking on the part of the students.

Multiple-frame STAs show a story in a number of frames, perhaps six to eight. The students are shown the frames one at a time and asked what is happening and what might happen next. After the students make predictions based on each frame, the next frame is shown, predictions are confirmed or corrected, and the procedure continues. There should be group discussion before the last frame is shown, with the group members citing reasons that they think the story will end a certain way. Discussion of the last frame should include whether or not the students' predicted end-

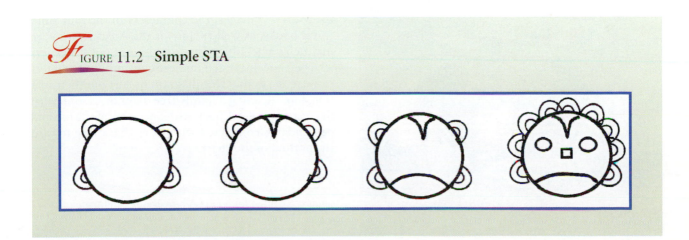

$\mathcal{F}$IGURE 11.2 **Simple STA**

Applications for English Language Learners and Students with Special Needs

Initally use fewer frames in the multiple-frame STAs for ELLs and struggling learners. Simplifying the task at first makes success more likely for them, and they are more likely to acquire the needed skill. Later more frames can be used.

ings were as reasonable as the actual ending. Wordless picture books can be used as ready-made multiple-frame STAs. Paula Winter's *The Bear & the Fly* is a good book to use in this way. You can also draw or photograph a series of scenes to make your own multiple-frame STAs.

OTHER GRAPHIC AIDS

Diagrams are often found in content area textbooks and other nonfiction books, but they also occasionally appear in fiction. Students need to have the different types of diagrams that they will encounter explained, and they need practice interpreting and producing diagrams of various types.

In E. L. Konigsburg's *From the Mixed-up Files of Mrs. Basil E. Frankweiler*, there is a floor plan of the Metropolitan Museum of Art that helps readers picture the children's movements around the building. Reading floor plans requires attention to the keys to symbols used and to spacial relationships.

In *Math Curse* by Jon Scieszka and Lane Smith, there is a Venn diagram of the books that Scieszka and Smith have done separately and together. Reading Venn diagrams allows students to perceive comparisons and contrasts quickly, as they realize that the overlapping areas are designated for likenesses and the areas that do not overlap are designated for the unique characteristics of each of the things being compared.

In Madeleine L'Engle's *Many Waters,* one of her time-travel books, there is a family tree diagram for the Murry-O'Keefes, the characters in the four time-travel books, as well as one for the Austins, who are main characters in another series of books. Readers who become interested in these continuing characters can use the family tree diagram to sort out their relationships. Reading a family tree diagram is somewhat like reading a flow chart, with ancestors at the top and descendants connected with lines that move toward the bottom of the chart.

Diagrams are often found in both textbooks and trade books.

In *The Human Body* by Gallimard Jeunesse and Sylvaine Perols, there are many types of illustrations, including cut-away diagrams of the human body that show the different body systems—respiratory, circulatory, digestive, nervous, muscular, skeletal—as well as cut-away cross-sections of the skin and some other parts. Aleksander Jedrosz's *You and Your Body: Eyes* includes cut-away and cross-section diagrams of the eye and the brain. In Fiona MacDonald's *Houses: Habitats & Home Life*, there are cut-away and cross-section diagrams of dwellings, and in David Macaulay's *Building Big*, the many types of diagrams include cut-away looks at bridge construction, tunnels, dams, domes, and skyscrapers. Students need help in understanding what they are actually looking at in such diagrams. You may use manipulatives, such as models of the human body, to show how the diagrams picture what is beneath the outside covering of the thing being examined. A field trip to a museum sometimes affords a chance to see a structure in various stages of construction. Displaying a diagram of a cross-section of an apple and then cutting an apple in two for comparison helps to show how cut-away diagrams picture the inside of an object. Gail Gibbons's *Apples* shows a good cross-section of an apple, as does Charles Micucci's *The Life and Times of the Apple*.

Students have to realize that diagrams are extremely abstract, because they simplify what they are displaying, to focus on the part that they want the viewer to notice. In many cases, three-dimensional figures are represented in two-dimensional form, and parts of the item other than the parts of interest are not pictured at all. Discussion of many diagrams of different types is necessary if students are to comprehend the diagrams in their classroom materials.

Tables offer a great amount of information in a very compact manner. Students need to be provided with a procedure for reading tables to help them be successful. They should check the title to find out the overall focus of the table. Then they should examine row and column headings to find out how the material is organized. Finally, they should learn to enter the table by locating the intersection of a specific row with a specific column. The teacher should model this process and then give students practice reading tables found in classroom materials. The end papers of *Math Curse* display tables of measures and the multiplication table. These make good materials to use in teaching the reading of tables.

Maps are graphic aids that are found in both content area textbooks and works of nonfiction and fiction. They help students to see the political, topographical, and other features of an area, as well as allowing them to check paths and distances for journeys described in their reading and see reasons for some of the problems that arose on such journeys. Students can track how areas have changed in land features, political units, population, and other features over time by using maps. They can also use maps to help them understand the effects of resources or scarcity thereof on population distribution and land disputes.

Map reading must be carefully taught. Students must learn to check the title of the map for the area under consideration, the direc-

Maps appear in both textbooks and trade books.

tional indicator for the orientation of the map, the scale to determine distances, and the legend to locate map features. They should also be encouraged to see how the area being studied fits into a larger area of which it is a part, for example, where Texas is located in relation to the rest of the United States or how Massachusetts is located in relation to the other northeastern states. They should be encouraged to draw conclusions as to why certain areas were settled when they were settled, and relate the map features to population density and movements. Teachers need to explain each of these features and processes and then model map reading and drawing conclusions for the students. Then students need to practice reading maps in their classroom materials.

James Giblin's *George Washington: A Picture Book Biography* contains a map of the United States in 1797, the year that Washington retired as president. The map allows students to track where Washington was born, where the fighting in the Revolutionary War started, where Washington and his men fought after crossing the Delaware River, where they spent the winter of 1777-1778, where the British surrendered in 1781, and where Washington died in 1799. Joseph Bruchac's *Native American Stories* contains a map of the United States that shows where the Native North American tribes lived around 1600, except for the Seminole Indians (dating from 1775) and Tuscarora Indians (who moved from the Southeast further north beginning about 1711). Students can locate the areas in which the stories in the book originated, using this map. Studying the stories of the various people can help students realize that Native Americans were not all alike, with the same cultures and beliefs. Will Hobbs's *Beardance*, *The Big Wander*, and *Ghost Canoe*, among others, have maps of the areas in which the adventures take place. In each case, an inset map shows a broader area than the large map, so that the students can place the location in relation to states with which they are familiar. All of the maps have directional indicators and show features such as bodies of water. The map in *Beardance* shows the locations of the many mountains in the region. The one in *Ghost Canoe* has a scale of miles. These maps help the reader comprehend the action of the stories.

Graphs are found most often in content area textbooks and nonfiction books. There are picture graphs, bar graphs, line graphs, and pie graphs. Each one has special qualities that students need to learn in order to benefit from their inclusion in the class's reading.

Picture graphs allow comparisons of amounts with pictures. They generally have a legend that tells the numerical value of each picture, unless the value is one. Sometimes only a portion of a picture is needed, requiring students to estimate the fraction of the picture that is shown and use their mathematics skills to decide how many of something a partial picture indicates. Charles Micucci's *The Life and Times of the Apple* and Jerry Pallotta's *The Hershey's Kisses Addition Book* both have examples of picture graphs. Apple production is shown on two graphs in *The Life and Times of the Apple*, and addition facts and their answers are graphed in *The Hershey's Kisses Addition Book*.

Bar graphs compare amounts with either vertical or horizontal bars plotted on vertical and horizontal axes. One axis indicates the amount being represented (often with a unit of measure, such as millions or pounds, indicated). The other axis shows the items or time periods being compared. Students have to learn to check the title of a graph to see what it compares and then determine

Reflections

What reading material for elementary and middle school students, other than the ones suggested in this section, do you know that have graphic aids in them that the students need to be able to interpret?

what the vertical and horizontal axes represent. For example, in *Math Curse* there is a vertical bar graph for which the vertical axis is the number of students who have birthdays in each month that is designated on the horizontal axis. In *Measuring Penny* by Loreen Leedy, there is a bar graph that compares Penny's walking times in minutes in different temperatures.

Viewing live performances with good comprehension generally requires instruction.

Line graphs show changes in amounts over time. They are often found in social studies and science textbooks, but are sometimes also found in other nonfiction books. Using classroom textbooks to work with line graphs is a good idea. As is true with bar graphs, the students need to read the title, check to see what the vertical and horizontal axes represent, and look to see if a particular unit of measure is indicated.

Circle graphs, or pie graphs, show the proportions of particular amounts in relationship to the whole. For example, they may show how much time in the school day is spent on each content area subject, lunch, recess, and other activities. These graphs are also often found in science and social studies textbooks. Math textbooks generally address circle graphs when the topic of study is fractions or percentages.

Live Performances

When viewing live performances, students need to learn about factors that add to comprehension. Lighting and music can help to set the mood of the play. Lighting also directs the audience's focus to specific areas of the stage. Costumes help the students to decide the approximate time in which the play takes place or, sometimes, whether the play is realistic or a fantasy. Costumes also help them to identify the social classes or occupations of the characters. The set gives clues to the location of the action and helps to set the mood. Characters' facial expressions and gestures, their posture, and their ways of moving add information that helps viewers interpret the meaning of the

Teaching Tip

If there is a community theater in your area, plan a field trip to an age-appropriate play. Before you go, discuss the visual elements of the performance that the students should watch for in the production. Afterward, discuss the mood of the play, the setting, and the characters. Be sure to talk about the effects that were created by lighting and sound, as well as the visual impressions of the set construction and the makeup and costumes.

Some theaters have educational information available that helps students be more effective viewers. They may have material that discusses technical aspects of performances or background information on particular plays.

performance. For example, a character who frowns, slumps, and shuffles when he walks may be judged to be unhappy, unwell, or worried. Makeup conveys the age of the characters and clues to their personalities. A scar across a character's dirty-looking cheek conveys the idea that he is an unsavory character or has been in a fight. Vocal expression, use of particular speech registers, and use of specific vocabulary terms further help viewers to pinpoint the types of characters that are being represented.

TELEVISION PROGRAMS AND VIDEOS

Viewing television shows and videos requires attention to the same factors that must be considered in live performances, but has added demands. Very rapid changes of images on a screen add to a sense of action and excitement. Irregular changes of camera angles give a feeling of out-of-control action.

Ends of scenes may at times be signaled by commercials on television, but not on videos. They are often signaled in both media by the scenes going out of focus and being replaced by other scenes that are shown coming into focus (Valmont, 2003). Scene transitions also can be made in other ways, and students can discuss techniques that they have seen or that they see when you show a video in class. They learn that changes of scene can involve changes of location and/or changes of time. Passage of time may be indicated by these scene changes or by print on the screen that indicates dates.

Mood is set in television shows and videos with music and lighting and also with types of camera shots. Suspense is built in a murder mystery when you see a person's gloved hands holding a gun or knife and then see just the person's feet and hear the sound of the footsteps as the murderer approaches the victim. Close-ups of people's hands are used to show their nervous tapping of fingers or twisting of hands together. Close-ups of faces show expressions of surprise, fear, or cunning. The camera directs attention to details that are important for absorbing the impact of a conversation or for following a development in the plot.

Loud music often alerts viewers that something important is about to happen. Ominous music makes viewers expect to see a crime committed. Tranquil music usually indicates a calm, pleasant scene.

Commercials on television use louder sound than is used in the programs, in many cases, to grab the viewers' attention. Commercials use a variety of propaganda techniques to persuade viewers to buy products or services. Lessons on these techniques and discussions of techniques used in various commercials that are viewed in class are beneficial to students. Common techniques used are bandwagon (encouraging people to join the crowd), transfer (relating product to respected person or symbol), testimonial (endorsement by a celebrity or a person "like the viewers themselves"), card stacking (telling only one side of a story or issue), and glittering generalities (empty statements). Political advertisements that are designed to persuade people to vote for candidates often use all of these plus name-calling and plain folks talk (pretending to be "one of the common people").

Williams (2003) believes that teachers need to connect experiences and skills developed from viewing television programs to print literacy. Students need to see how different media are related to one another. As early as kindergarten, children are able to recognize television programs that are designed for them to watch and those that are designed for adults. This ability is much more sophisticated by the time students reach adolescence. Elementary school students can distinguish between the commercials that are targeted for males and females. This sense of audience can be applied to the children's writing endeavors (Williams, 2003).

Students also know how to recognize the genres of television programs (for example, sitcom, documentary, or drama) and can describe characteristics of different genres. This understanding of the concept of genres also helps students in their writing endeavors (Williams, 2003).

There are many television programs that, although designed for viewing, promote literacy skills. *Reading Rainbow* is a PBS program that is designed for five-year-old to eight-year-old viewers. On the show, a featured book is read; there is a segment of real-life information related to the content of the book; children review related books; and other things related to the target book's theme may be included.

Wood and Duke (1997) found that *Reading Rainbow* provides many literacy experiences for viewers. It exposes them to quality literature selections, as well as a great deal of environmental print related to the themes of the episodes. It models the use and enjoyment of literacy skills, and it encourages the children to read related books. Each episode activates and builds background for understanding the book that is presented, develops vocabulary by introducing new words, relates the content of the shared book to the viewers' lives, and provides ways of summarizing ideas that have been covered. Different genres are included in the selections that are presented. Both written registers (book reading) and oral registers (conversations between the host and others) of communication are displayed on the program. The program also encourages both efferent (information getting) and aesthetic (emotional) responses to the books. Minilesson 11.1 on page 436 shows one way to use *Reading Rainbow* in the classrooom.

Another television program, *Between the Lions*, has been put to effective use in kindergarten and first-grade classrooms by St. Clair and Schwetz (2003). They use a View-Read-Do approach. The class first views an episode of the program, which features a family of lion puppets in a library setting. The teachers often follow the viewing by reading a book related to the content of the episode, which includes a story, a key word, or related word play with word families, word parts, or word meanings. They also may do related art activities.

St. Clair and Schwetz (2003) found that they have to be active viewers of the program along with their students. They pause the videotapes to discuss facets of the program. When the program encourages verbal responses from the viewers, the teachers and students read or sing along, as appropriate.

Music is used liberally in *Between the Lions* for such purposes as singing out vowel sounds and singing about word families. The teachers sometimes accompany the songs with letters set up on a magnetic board that the children can see. Some of the songs have print on the screen (providing practice with directionality and return sweeps in reading). Animations are used to model blending of word parts.

Movies can also be used to develop background for content area unit studies. Students who are unfamiliar with the Holocaust, for example, can read Jane Yolen's *The Devil's Arithmetic* and other novels about the Holocaust, as well as textbook discussions of this aspect of World War II, after they have viewed videos of historical documentaries and movies about the Holocaust. Hibbing and Rankin-Erickson (2003) prepared middle school students to read about the Holocaust in this manner and found that the use of the videos increased the students' learning of the content considerably.

CD-ROM SIMULATION PROGRAMS

Interactive CD-ROM **simulation programs** (programs that simulate real-life events) are often interdisciplinary, blending reading, writing, health, science, history, geography, and math, for example, as is true in *The Oregon Trail II* (MECC) program (Bigelow,

Reading Rainbow Lesson Plan

Show an episode of *Reading Rainbow* on tape in class and pause to have the students respond orally to the background-building segment. Ask them what they saw and heard that they already had known and what was new to them. Make a semantic web of the information about the topic of the segment on the dry-erase board as they offer their information. Let the students copy the web in their reading notebooks, either writing the words that you have on the board or drawing pictures that represent the words.

Play the part of the tape that includes the reading of the book. Stop the tape and let the students discuss any additional information about the topic that they obtained from the book. Have them tell whether they got this information from the illustrations that were shown or from the words. Have them add the new information to their webs.

Play the part of the tape that has the reviews of additional books. Stop the tape and let the children discuss each book that is reviewed. If the students have read the book themselves or had it read to them, let them add to the review. Ask the children if they would want to read each book, based on the review.

Finally, let the children tell you about any related books that they know personally. Ask for a critique of each book, so that others in the class will know enough about it to decide if they are interested in the book.

What are the students learning?

They are learning how to use background information that they see on television, CDs, DVDs, or videotapes to help them expand their vocabularies and to help them understand things that are read to them. They are also learning to examine pictures carefully and to combine information gained from the pictures with the text. They are learning how to think critically about a story and how to explain their thinking to their classmates.

1997). They offer students an opportunity to make critical reading and thinking decisions and see the consequences of their decisions. They are asked to act as if they are a particular character in an event and make decisions that that person would be expected to make.

Bigelow (1997) acknowledges that *The Oregon Trail II* program with its accompanying trail guide provides much information about geography along the trail, ailments confronted by the travelers, treatments that were used, equipment and supplies, and other factors. However, he sees this simulation and many others as "sexist, racist, culturally insensitive, and contemptuous of the earth" (Bigelow, 1997, p. 85), because they put the players in the decision-making position of white males, who necessarily would have different motivations and responsibilities than those of females or blacks. He also faults the program for not having the students treat the Native Americans that they encounter in a culturally sensitive way, not pointing out the impact the settlers had on these people and the land that they crossed, and not letting the students have the option to act as anyone other than a white male of that time may have acted to reach a goal. It seems that Bigelow thinks that a single simulation program should be able to encompass every concern of every segment of the population and take on modern attitudes toward ecological and cultural issues that were not in place during the time period being studied.

Any simulation, by its very nature, is a simplified version of reality. We believe that Bigelow (1997) is correct that teachers need to be aware of the particular perspective that the program allows users to take and that teachers should make students aware of this perspective. They can then use the simulation to acquire the material that is in the program to be learned, while not believing that everyone had the same outlook or reactions to events that the protagonist of this game takes. Then they can use other resources—CDs, Internet sites, books, videos, and so on—to help them see how the journeys of the pioneers along the trail affected travelers other than white males and affected the people who were already living on the land. They might even write a series of stories or plays depicting the story of the journey on the trail from the viewpoint of a female or an African American, or depicting the reactions of a group of Native Americans whose land was being crossed by this wave of pioneers.

No single CD-ROM simulation covers all aspects of any situation, but by knowingly taking the perspective of a particular individual and making decisions to help that individual be successful at a task, students learn a great deal about critical reading. They learn to collect data and come to informed conclusions. When they make mistakes, they see the consequences of such mistakes. Even if the game ignores some mistakes that they may have been able to make in real life, it can produce a positive effect on their decision-making abilities.

Educational simulations are not meant to be used without teacher guidance. Teachers need to know the philosophies and perspectives of the simulations being used in class, and they need to make the students aware of them. Then teachers need to expand the learning about the topic of concern by using other source material and activities.

Reflections

What other simulation programs have you used? Do they cause you concerns similar to those that Bigelow had about *Oregon Trail*? If so, what can you do to make the use of these simulation programs profitable for the students?

MATERIAL ON THE INTERNET

Webpages on the **Internet** demand viewing that may include all of the factors mentioned previously. They may have illustrations, diagrams, tables, maps, and graphs. They may have animated graphics or actual movie clips. They may have music and other sounds. There may be spoken material or all written text.

In addition to the demands of the other media involved, viewing material on the Internet presents some unique problems. First, there is finding information on the desired topic. To accomplish this, students need to understand how to type a known URL (Universal Resource Locator, or Internet address) into the correct place on a web browser, such as Microsoft Internet Explorer or Netscape Navigator. They may obtain URLs from their teachers, other students who have visited particular sites, or from books or magazines. You may think today's students will have this skill at least by the time they reach the intermediate grades. Not all students, however, have this background of experience in their home environment, and you must provide instruction in use of web browsers if students are expected to use them to access information.

Sefton-Green (2001) found that students from low-income backgrounds who came to an out-of-school program on web design in the United Kingdom had to be taught basic skills of using a browser before they could approach web design. Betty Roe has found that many students in elementary schools in rural areas of the United States have little opportunity to access information on the Internet either at home or at school because of limited financial resources. Some of Roe's colleagues have reported similar situations in urban areas in which they work. Therefore, wherever students are, there are probably some who have limited experience with the Internet, even if they have used computers for computer-assisted instruction and games that are not Internet connected. Students cannot be expected to teach themselves to use this complex tool (Sefton-Green, 2001).

A webpage students reach by entering a URL may have a number of links (highlighted words or icons) that will take them to additional information on the topic. Reading a webpage includes recognizing links and knowing to click on the links to move to the additional information. Students also need to know how to navigate back to the original page with the back button. If they follow several links on succeeding pages, this return to their starting place may be difficult at first.

The reader of webpages chooses the links to follow and the order in which to follow them. This type of reading is very different from reading a book from front to back and each page from top to bottom. Text and various media that allow random access to their parts are referred to as **hypertext** and **hypermedia**. CDs and DVDs share this random access feature with the Internet.

If a reader decides to return to a previous webpage and repeat the same sequence of reading again later, he may find that the same links are not available because the sites are constantly changing. Some are relocated to different areas or are removed, and others are added (Schmar-Dobler, 2003).

There is a massive amount of material posted on the Internet, but not all of it is reliable. Anyone may develop and post a webpage and include anything that she decides to include. Webpages may contain inadvertent errors of fact, intentional efforts to mislead, poorly organized material that leads to inappropriate conclusions, outdated information, and so on.

When students reach websites using URLs or links from other webpages, they need to critically analyze the material on the sites to see if it is applicable to their topics, timely, and produced by reliable sources. They may want to note some of the material and check it in other sources, perhaps even in print media.

If students do not have initial URLs to locate, they may go to a search engine, such as Yahooligans or Ask Jeeves for Kids, and use keyword searches to find appropriate sites to visit. This involves knowing how to decide on terms that are likely to lead to the best sites for their purposes. Students need much practice in determining words to use for searches. They benefit from practice in generating related words and synonyms for their topics, so that their searches are more complete and focused (Sutherland-Smith, 2002). They also need to learn how to do advanced searches that allow them to narrow their searches. Otherwise they may get thousands of "hits" for the general terms that they enter, and it is not feasible for them to check all of the possibilities. Additionally, the first "hits" may not be the most appropriate.

Owens, Hester, and Teale (2002) suggest previewing and bookmarking sites where students can safely search

Reflections

What precautions would you take when having students use a search engine, in order to ensure that the students do not end up at inappropriate sites?

for information. This approach seems to be especially appropriate for primary-grade students. It allows them to visit and evaluate suitable sites without the danger of accidentally arriving at inappropriate sites. Martin (2003) successfully used this approach with third-graders who were learning about one-room schoolhouses like the one depicted in the picture book *My Great Aunt Arizona* by Gloria Houston.

E-MAIL AND CHAT ROOM MESSAGES

Reading **e-mail** (electronic mail) and **chat room** messages (electronic conversations in print in special areas on the Internet) may seem to be not that much different from reading from the printed page. The reality, however, is that many e-mail and chat room exchanges are written much more informally than other print messages. They often involve little or no punctuation or capitalization, and they may make liberal use of unusual abbreviations (*LOL* for *laughing out loud*, *IMHO* for *in my humble opinion*, and *BTW* for *by the way*) and **emoticons** to show feelings (☺, ☹). Students who have not had access to computers at home are faced with learning this new way of communicating when they become involved in e-mail exchanges at school.

Visually Representing

There are many ways to represent ideas visually. Such presentations can be done through photographs or drawings, formatting of information on a page with a word processing program, video presentations, multimedia presentations, or webpages.

PHOTOGRAPHS OR DRAWINGS

Use of photographs or drawings is the most common way of visually representing ideas in the classroom. Students may choose a topic and photograph the essential elements of the topic, and then either tell about the photographs orally or write captions or explanations to go with the pictures. Careful framing of the items being photographed helps the viewers comprehend the purpose. Overall composition of the photographs needs to emphasize important elements.

Drawings can be used the same way that photographs are used, but drawings are more versatile. Actual objects do not have to be in the students' possession for them to represent the objects in drawings. They may draw from memory or from pictures or videos that they have available. Color, line quality, and composition help to convey the desired meaning in the drawings.

Morrison, Bryan, and Chilcoat (2002) suggest another way of using drawings with middle school students. They recommend having

Photographs or drawings are the most common ways of visually representing ideas in the classroom.

students create comic books at the end of a unit of study, as a way of visually representing material that they have learned in a form that is of high interest to most middle school students.

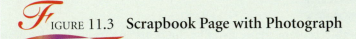

WORD PROCESSING

Students often word process reports and creative writing that they do. Current word processing programs allow them to do creative things with formatting that make their papers more attractive and convey their message more completely. They may use boldface or italic print, or they may underline, highlight, or use a different colored font to emphasize particular words, sentences, or phrases. They may enlarge or boldface the font to make headings stand out or use numbered or bulleted lists to call attention to their points. Different fonts may be used to emphasize different parts of the paper: For example, in a multigenre paper, the student may use the Times New Roman font for one type of document (perhaps a newspaper article) and the Lucida Handwriting font for a diary entry. Lead your students to be judicious in the use of

𝓕IGURE 11.3 **Scrapbook Page with Photograph**

Our Family Heirloom Quilt

This quilt was pieced and quilted by my mom's mom's mom (my Great~great~grandmother) shortly after the Civil War in the late 1800's. It is called a Bow~tie quilt because of the pattern of the pieces. It was made from scraps of old clothes. My great grandmother had the quilt until she moved in with my Gramma. Then my Gramma got the quilt. She gave it to my mom in the 1980's. Mom has it hanging on our dining room wall.

Source: Dillon Young, Sixth Grade, East Middle School, Tullahoma, TN. Used with permission.

different colors, fonts, and typographical clues so that the information is transmitted without the page becoming too "busy."

Current programs also make possible importing clip art, photographs, and the output of drawing programs into word processed documents. Some students take advantage of this feature to decorate pages and add important information; others simply draw or paste illustrations onto the word processed pages. Unfortunately, without guidance, they may tend toward decoration rather than presentation of information in the illustrations that they use. Show them how the visual materials must illuminate the texts and help to carry the messages they wish to convey. Figures 11.3 and 11.4 show pages that sixth-grader Dillon Young included in his scrapbook project for school. Notice that Dillon chose different fonts for different pages but was wise enough not to mix many fonts on a single page. Also notice that both his photograph and his clip art were chosen to enhance the information on the page, not just to decorate it. In Figure 11.3, especially, the picture clarifies the meaning of the Bow-tie quilt pattern.

Figure 8.1 in the chapter on writing shows how second-grader Amanda Wyatt added a drawing to her word processed page, and the book examples in Figures 8.7 and 8.8 also use hand-drawn pictures on word processed pages. In both books, a larger font is used for the title than for the running text. Figure 9.3 shows how a fifth-grader uses formatting of a poem with centering and two font sizes to enhance the poem.

VIDEO PRESENTATIONS

Students may videotape reports that they have presented, especially ones that involve visual aids and demonstrations; documentaries of topics of study, such as area pollution;

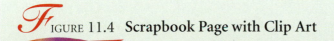

𝓕IGURE 11.4 **Scrapbook Page with Clip Art**

> MODEL CARS
>
> I am very interested in my Granddad's model cars and here is some information about them. He started his collection at age 40 because he didn't have enough money until then. His oldest model is a Rolls Royce Silver Ghost. His most unique model is a Golden Tucker because only three or four of the real car were made.

Source: Dillon Young. Sixth Grade, East Middle School, Tullahoma, TN. Used with permission.

plays that they have written and produced; and Readers Theatre performances that they have developed and presented.

In all of the video situations mentioned above, students must plan and write an appropriate script that can either be read or spoken in the video; must choose needed properties; must practice the oral reading or speaking to use appropriate expression; and must choose camera angles, places where close-ups are needed, and appropriate lighting. After a taping takes place, the product can be viewed and retaped, or it can be edited by splicing in needed material and adding captions and background sounds and music.

Students may start their planning for a video with a storyboard to plot the sequence of the presentation. Many students have their own camcorders to use in producing video presentations, but most schools have at least some camcorders available to be checked out for such projects. Most classrooms are equipped with video recorders or players to play the videos that are produced, or the teachers have access to video recorders or players for checkout. Some schools even have digital video camcorders. The resulting video can be loaded onto computer hard drives and edited (Adams & Hamm, 2000).

MULTIMEDIA PRESENTATIONS

Multimedia presentations require students to develop some combination of text, graphics, sound, video clips, and animations. Among the many tools that are available to help students do this are mPower (Multimedia Design) and PowerPoint (Microsoft). Students design slides that incorporate a number of features:

- Text (requiring decisions about style, color, and size of font, as well as layout on the page)
- Pictures (imported clip art, imported files that have been produced by a drawing program such as Corel Draw, or imported pictures taken with a digital camera)

Applications

for Students with Special Needs

Goetze and Walker (2004) had at-risk intermediate-grade students respond to narrative picture books with thought-provoking themes by constructing Hyperstudio slides with pictures that they drew and sentences explaining the main ideas or main characters. They used their slides to retell the stories and explain the themes in the books they had read. They also used Inspiration software to create visual maps with the books they had read on lines connected to a center circle in which they indicated central themes that they could see running through all of the books. They were able to use both words and graphics to represent the interconnections among the books. Goetze and Walker (2004, p. 780) found that "these at-risk readers were able to tie their responses to the books together, creating intertextual understanding" through use of technology.

Classroom Vignette 11.1

Barbara Vaughn, a seventh-grade literacy teacher in a rural school, and a coworker, Nickey Franklin, who teaches seventh-grade social studies, have their students use technology to learn literacy and social studies content. In the process, they have to familiarize the students with some of the technological tools that they are about to use.

First, Barbara familiarizes the students with the workings of the mPower multimedia presentation software. This program allows them to combine print, graphics, still and moving images, sound effects, and speech in their class presentations.

The students then search print sources in the library and the Internet for information about the fifty U.S. states. Each student has an assigned state. The students have to include certain information in each presentation: the state's motto, tree, flower, bird, flag, map, song, length, width, number of counties, number of square miles, and other items. Students can use scanned-in freehand drawings or clip art for the illustrations, and they can incorporate music. All of the presentations are viewed by the classmates of the presenters. The presentations are evaluated on the effectiveness of the presentation of the information, as well as the completeness and accuracy of the information included.

What's happening here?

The students are learning social studies content from their searches of resource material, some located on the Internet. They are also learning how to design slides that clearly represent the information so that their classmates can learn from their presentations. They are learning how to integrate text, graphics, and sound, as well as how to provide reasonable transitions between slides.

- Sound (recorded by the students or imported from prerecorded sound files)
- Video clips (recorded on digital video recorders or imported from prerecorded files)
- Animations (imported from available files)

Other decisions that must be made are how to make transitions between slides; how to incorporate the images, sounds, and text into a coherent whole; and how to determine the appropriate sequence for the material. The classroom vignette at the beginning of this chapter tells how Barbara Vaughn's students used the mPower program in a language arts application. Classroom Vignette 11.1 tells how she teamed with a social studies teacher to have students use such presentations to learn about that content (Roe, 2000).

Even first-graders can make simple multimedia presentations with computers. First-grade teachers used Kid Pix to allow students who had been gradually introduced to reading and writing on a computer to publish their own books. The children developed their stories off the computer in a writing workshop. Then they entered the stories and illustrations on the computer. The teachers printed the books, added covers, and bound the books with spiral bindings (Eisenwine & Hunt, 2000).

WEBPAGES AND WEBSITES

Many schools and classrooms have their own webpages. Students can be the designers of a classroom webpage that meets a particular educational need. Often the need is to display student work, including creative writing, content area reports, and special interest projects, often related to thematic units.

Students have to make many design decisions in order to produce webpages. They have to decide on a name for the page; the page background, color, and pattern, if any; the fonts; graphic elements such as photographs, scanned-in drawings, and clip art; animations; sounds; video clips; and other features (Valmont, 2003). Background patterns should not be busy or intrusive. Backgrounds with a textured look generally are not hard to read, but backgrounds that have pictures, lines, or words can make distinguishing the actual foreground message difficult.

Designers should limit the number of font variations to no more than four (Heinich et al., 1999; Ko & Rossen, 2001). Generally they should pick one readable font and use the same font when italics and boldface type are used for emphasis and when larger or smaller sizes are chosen.

The webpage title should inform the reader of the focus of the page. It should be in a large font and be easily located. The remainder of the material on the page should be organized logically.

Pages need to have some white (or background colored) space. Pages should not be cluttered with too many graphics, especially "busy" animations. Text should not be packed in too tightly. Lines of text should be short enough that users do not have to scroll to read them (Ko & Rossen, 2001).

There should be a strong contrast between the background color and the text on the page—very dark text on a light background or very light text on a dark background (Ko & Rossen, 2001). Readers should not have to strain to distinguish the print.

If a multipage site is being developed, navigation buttons should make it easy to move from page to page within the site and to return to the home page. Links to pages outside the site can also be used, but the links should have an obvious and useful connection to the content of the page.

You should not allow students to put personal information on the page for safety concerns. Students may sign work with first names only. In this way, parents and friends will know who is being credited, but strangers will not.

There are a number of software packages that help in the development and editing of webpages. Netscape Composer (a component of Netscape Navigator 3.0 Gold and Netscape Communicator), Microsoft FrontPage, and Claris Homepage facilitate page design because they don't require learning **HTML** (HyperText Markup Language), which is the specific code for structuring files so that they can be interpreted by a web browser (Lockard & Abrams, 2001). Another approach is to use an HTML converter feature that many word processing programs have. For example, Microsoft Word allows a user to save a Word file as HTML. It automatically converts the file into a webpage without the need for the user to know HTML code. Even though it is possible to develop webpages completely without the direct use of HTML, sometimes knowing the code is helpful when difficulties arise with the page. Middle school students often enjoy the challenge of learning this new language and become adept at it. Those who do can become resources for the rest of the students.

Students may import clip art and text from other sources into their webpages, but they should not make use of copyrighted material without permission. You

Reflections

How is each of the language arts involved in webpage design?

must impress on the students the importance of not copying material directly from other sources, but putting the material into their own words and synthesizing material from a number of different sources into a coherent document.

Students can search for Internet sites that include lists of criteria for website evaluation, print the criteria from several sites, and develop their own list to use in evaluating their sites. This is a good research and critical reading task for them.

If you are hesitant to have students' work placed on the Internet, you can still allow them to design HTML pages on the classroom computer without posting them to the Internet. Web browsers will treat these pages just like normal websites. Therefore, pages can be shared within the classroom without accessing the Internet and can be copied onto disks for sharing with other classes. Classroom Vignette 11.2 demonstrates how students incorporate language arts skills through web design.

Relating Learning about Media to Standards

WATTS PAILLIOTET and her colleagues (2000) designed media learning activities to mesh with their teaching goals. They found that their instruction incorporated standards from the Wisconsin English/language arts (Fortier, Grady, Karbon, & Last, 1998), visual arts (Nikolay, Grady, & Stefonek, 1997), and technology literacy model academic standards (Fortier, Potter, Grady, Lohr, & Klein, 1998). Figure 11.5 shows the relationships that they found.

Classroom Vignette 11.2

Basden (2001) describes a middle school web design course that incorporates authentic tasks for the students as they learn about design. The students make use of computers with web authoring software, digital cameras, and school blueprints to plan, create, and publish on the Internet an electronic tour of their school. They complete the work in small, cooperative groups. The students see a purpose for the skills that they are learning and feel pride in the project.

What's happening here?

The students are learning the technological skills associated with using computers and digital cameras. They also are improving language skills as they work in their groups, listening, discussing, reading blueprints, and writing.

FIGURE 11.5 Integration of Standards Influencing Intermedial Curriculum

English language arts

Reading–Discern how written texts and accompanying illustrations connect and convey meaning. Read, interpret, and critically analyze.

Writing–Write clear and pertinent responses to verbal or visual material that communicate, explain, and interpret the reading or viewing experience to a specific audience.

Language–Choose words purposefully and evaluate their use in communications designed to inform, explain, and persuade. Make informed judgments.

Media and technology–Compare effect of symbols and images in various media tools.

Research and inquiry–Conduct research/inquiry on self-selected/ assigned topics, issues, or problems and share findings in an appropriate form.

Visual arts

Visual design and production–Know about artists and designers in students' community. Explore elements and principles of quality design. Know how the design of art changes its meaning.

Visual communication and expression– Communicate complex ideas by producing design art forms, such as graphic design, product design, architecture, landscape, and media arts, such as film photography and multimedia.

Visual media and technology– Understand the production techniques on viewers' perceptions.

Making connections– Use a variety of words, numbers, sounds, images, and objects to communicate.

Analyze and critically respond to viewing and visual design.

Use words, images, symbols, and sounds to design, revise, and communicate intermedial links.

Conduct research/inquiry focused on issues and problems using print, nonprint, and electronic sources and present applying software tools to organize and create.

Understand, apply, and evaluate elements/principles of quality design to communicate ideas using a variety of words, numbers, sounds, and images to communicate to others.

Information and technology

Media and technology–Use a graphic program to create or modify detail to an image. Use computer productivity software to organize and create. Use media and technology to create and present. Evaluate the use of media and technology in production or presentation.

Information and inquiry–Access, evaluate, and apply information from a variety of print, nonprint, and electronic sources related to issues and problems.

Source: Figure from Pailliotet, Ann Watts, Semali, Ladislaus, Rodenberg, Rita K., Giles, Jackie K., & Macaul, Sherry L. (2000, October). Intermediality: Bridge to critical media literacy. *The Reading Teacher, 54* (2), 208-219. Reprinted with permission of the International Reading Association.

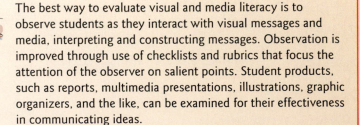

Classroom Assessment for Visual and Media Literacy

The best way to evaluate visual and media literacy is to observe students as they interact with visual messages and media, interpreting and constructing messages. Observation is improved through use of checklists and rubrics that focus the attention of the observer on salient points. Student products, such as reports, multimedia presentations, illustrations, graphic organizers, and the like, can be examined for their effectiveness in communicating ideas.

Summary

Visual literacy is being able to interpret the meaning of visual images and to construct effective visuals in order to convey ideas to others. Media literacy involves understanding and critically analyzing material that you read and view and creating messages in varied mass communications media. Media literacy is important to technological literacy in general. Digital literacy is a subset of media literacy that involves interpreting and evaluating material in formats delivered by the computer.

Visual literacy skills include viewing and visually representing. Viewing is a skill that has long been ignored in school, but it is an important skill that can be taught. Visually representing has recently become more prominent as the technological media have become more available for use by students.

Students can learn to view pictures, other graphic aids, live performances, television programs and videos, and material on the Internet with understanding. They can learn to visually represent information with photographs or drawings, video presentations, multimedia presentations, and webpages.

Learning about viewing, visually representing, and media involves teachers in instruction related to numerous standards in literacy, English language arts, and visual arts.

Discussion Questions

1. Why have visual literacy skills not received much attention in the classroom in years past? Are you seeing examples of these skills receiving attention in current classrooms? If so, what are some reasons for the change?

2. Why is media literacy important for today's students? How can you help them to attain a higher level of media literacy?

3. What aspects of viewing are likely to be most difficult for you to teach? Why?

4. What language and thinking skills are emphasized most when Seeing-Thinking Activities are used? Which types of STAs appear to be most appropriate for the primary grades? Which types appear to be most appropriate for intermediate grades? What students in middle school might benefit most from them? Why?

5. What language activities lend themselves to video presentations? What skills are involved in producing video presentations?

6. What are some ways that webpages can be developed? What language skills are involved in the production of webpages?

Suggested Activities

1. Plan a wordless picture book activity to do with a group of primary students or older ELLs. Explain why you chose the book you did for the particular group and how you presented the activity.

2. Choose one type of STA and develop an activity to use in a classroom. Explain why you chose that particular type of STA, and evaluate the effectiveness after you use it in the classroom.

3. Make a list of books for children and adolescents that include graphic aids that need to be read carefully in order to comprehend the material fully. Make a plan for helping students better understand these graphic aids.

4. Do a video presentation to share information that you have gathered for a thematic unit. Discuss with your classmates the skills that you used to develop the presentation.

5. Design a webpage to accompany a thematic unit that you have developed. Have classmates use a rubric that your class has located or developed to evaluate your webpage.

References

ADAMS, D., & HAMM, M. (2000). *Media and literacy.* Springfield, IL: Charles C. Thomas.

ANSTEY, M. (2002). "It's not all black and white": Postmodern picture books and new literacies. *Journal of Adolescent & Adult Literacy, 45,* 444–457.

BASDEN, J. C. (2001). Authentic tasks as the basis for multimedia design curriculum. *T.H.E Journal, 29,* 16–21.

BIGELOW, B. (1997). On the road to cultural bias: A critique of *The Oregon Trail* CD-ROM. *Language Arts, 74,* 84–93.

COMSTOCK, G., & SCHARRER, E. (1999). *Television: What's on, who's watching, and what it means.* San Diego: Academic Press.

CORTESE, E. E. (2003/2004). The application of Question-Answer Relationship strategies to pictures. *The Reading Teacher, 57,* 374–380.

EHRENWORTH, M. (2003). Literacy and the aesthetic experience: Engaging children with the visual arts in the teaching of writing. *Language Arts, 81,* 43–51.

EISENWINE, M. J., & HUNT, D. A. (2000). Using a computer in literacy groups with emergent readers. *The Reading Teacher, 53,* 456–458.

FLOOD, J., & LAPP, D. (1997/1998). Visual literacy: Broadening conceptualizations of literacy: The visual and communicative arts. *The Reading Teacher, 51,* 342–344.

FORTIER, J. D., GRADY, S. M., KARBON, J. C., & LAST, E. L. (1998). *Wisconsin's model academic standards for English language arts.* Madison: Wisconsin Department of Public Instruction.

FORTIER, J. D., POTTER, C. J., GRADY, S. M., LOHR, N., & KLEIN, N. (1998). *Wisconsin's model academic standards for information & technology literacy.* Madison: Wisconsin Department of Public Instruction.

GIORGIS, C., JOHNSON, N. J., BONOMO, A., COLBERT, C., CONNER, A., KAUFFMAN, G., & KULESZA, D. (1999). Visual literacy. *The Reading Teacher, 53,* 146–153.

GOETZE, S., & WALKER, B. J. (2004). At-risk readers can construct complex meanings: Technology can help. *The Reading Teacher, 57,* 778–780.

HEINICH, R., MOLENDA, M., RUSSELL, J. D., & SMALDINO, S. E. (1999). *Instructional media and technologies for learning.* Upper Saddle River, NJ: Merrill/Prentice Hall.

HIBBING, A. N., & RANKIN-ERICKSON, J. L. (2003). A picture is worth a thousand words: Using visual images to improve comprehension for middle school struggling readers. *The Reading Teacher, 56,* 758–770.

KO, S., & ROSSEN, S. (2001). *Teaching online: A practical guide.* Boston: Houghton Mifflin.

LOCKARD, J., & ABRAMS, P. D. (2001). *Computers for twenty-first century educators.* New York: Longman.

MARTIN, L. M. (2003). Web reading: Linking text and technology. *The Reading Teacher, 56,* 735–737.

MORRISON, T. G., BRYAN, G., & CHILCOAT, G. W. (2002). Using student-generated comic books in the classroom. *Journal of Adolescent & Adult Literacy, 45,* 758–767.

NIKOLAY, P., GRADY, S. M., & STEFONEK, T. (1997). *Wisconsin's model standards for the visual arts.* Madison: Wisconsin Department of Public Instruction.

OWENS, F. O., HESTER, J. L., & TEALE, W. H. (2002). Where do you want to go today? Inquiry-based learning and technology integration. *The Reading Teacher, 55,* 616–625.

PIRO, J. M. (2002). The picture of reading: Deriving meaning in literacy through image. *The Reading Teacher, 56,* 126–134.

POOL, C. R. (1997). A new digital literacy: A conversation with Paul Gilster. *Educational Leadership, 55,* 6–11.

ROBERTS, D. R., FOEHR, U. G., RIDEOUT, V. J., & BRODIE, M. (1999, November). *Kids and media at the new millennium.* Menlo Park, CA: Kaiser Family Foundation Report.

ROE, B. D. (2000). Using technology for content area literacy. In S. B. Wepner, W. J. Valmont, & R. Thurlow (Eds.), *Linking literacy and technology: A guide for K-8 classrooms* (pp. 133–158). Newark, DE: International Reading Association.

SCHARRER, E. (2002/2003). Making a case for media literacy in the curriculum: Outcomes and assessment. *Journal of Adolescent & Adult Literacy, 48,* 354–358.

SCHMAR-DOBLER, E. (2003). Reading on the Internet: The link between literacy and technology. *Journal of Adolescent & Adult Literacy, 47,* 80–85.

SEFTON-GREEN, J. (2001). Computers, creativity, and the curriculum: The challenge for schools, literacy, and learning. *Journal of Adolescent & Adult Literacy, 44,* 726–728.

ST. CLAIR, J., & SCHWETZ, L. R. (2003). *Between the Lions* as a classroom tool. *The Reading Teacher, 56,* 656–659.

SUTHERLAND-SMITH, W. (2002). Weaving the literacy web: Changes in reading for page to screen. *The Reading Teacher, 55,* 662–669.

U.S. DEPARTMENT OF EDUCATION. (1997). President Clinton's call to action for American Education in the 21st Century: Technological literacy. Retrieved from http://www.ed.gov/updates/PresEDPlan/part 11.html

VALMONT, W. J. (1976). *See-listen-think.* New York: McCormick-Mathers.

VALMONT, W. J. (2003). *Technology for literacy teaching and learning.* Boston: Houghton Mifflin.

WATTS PAILLIOTET, A. W., SEMALI, L., RODENBERG, R., GILES, J. K., & MACAUL, S. L. (2000). Intermediality: Bridge to critical media literacy. *The Reading Teacher, 54,* 208–219.

WILLIAMS, B. T. (2003). What they see is what we get: Television and middle school writers. *Journal of Adolescent & Adult Literacy, 46,* 546–554.

WOOD, J. M., & DUKE, N. K. (1997). Inside "Reading Rainbow": A spectrum of strategies for promoting literacy. *Language Arts, 74,* 95–106.

Books for Children and Adolescents Cited in This Chapter

BRUCHAC, J. (1991). *Native American stories.* Golden, CO: Fulcrum.

CRONIN, D. (2000). *Click, clack, moo: Cows that type.* New York: Simon & Schuster.

FLEISCHMAN, P. (1992). *Townsend's warbler.* New York: HarperCollins.

GIBBONS, G. (2000). *Apples.* New York: Scholastic.

GIBLIN, J. C. (1992). *George Washington: A picture book biography.* New York: Scholastic.

HOBBS, W. (1993). *Beardance.* New York: Avon.

HOBBS, W. (1992). *The big wander.* New York: Avon.

HOBBS, W. (1997). *Ghost canoe.* New York: Avon.

HOUSTON, G. (1997). *My Great Aunt Arizona.* New York: HarperTrophy.

JEDROSZ, A. (1992). *You and your body: Eyes.* Mahwah, NJ: Troll.

JEUNESSE, G., & PEROLS, S. (1996). *The human body.* New York: Scholastic.

KONIGSBURG, E. L. (1967). *From the mixed-up files of Mrs. Basil E. Frankweiler.* New York: Simon & Schuster.

LEEDY, L. (1997). *Measuring Penny.* New York: Scholastic.

L'ENGLE, M. (1986). *Many waters.* New York: Dell.

MACAULAY, D. (1990). *Black and white.* Boston: Houghton Mifflin.

MACAULAY, D. (2000). *Building big.* Boston: Houghton Mifflin.

MACDONALD, F. (1994). *Houses: Habitats & home life.* New York: Franklin Watts.

McCULLY, E. A. (1985). *First snow.* New York: HarperTrophy.

MICUCCI, C. (1992). *The life and times of the apple.* New York: Scholastic.

PALLOTTA, J. (2001). *The Hershey's Kisses addition book.* New York: Scholastic.

PATERSON, K. (1978). *Bridge to Terabithia.* New York: Crowell.

PERRAULT, C., & EHRLICH, A. (1985). *Cinderella.* New York: Dial.

PINKNEY, A. D. (1998). *Duke Ellington: The piano prince and his orchestra.* New York: Hyperion.

SAN SOUCI, R. D. (1995). *Kate Shelley: Bound for legend.* New York: Dial.

SCIESZKA, J. (1992). *The stinky cheese man and other fairly stupid tales.* New York: Viking.

SCIESZKA, J., & SMITH, L. (1995). *Math curse.* New York: Viking.

WINTER, P. (1976). *The bear & the fly.* New York: Crown.

YOLEN, J. (1990). *The devil's arithmetic.* New York: Viking Penguin.

LITERACY IN THE CONTENT AREAS

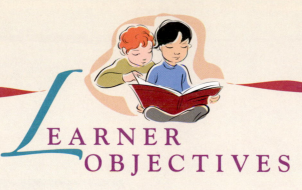

LEARNER OBJECTIVES

At the conclusion of this chapter

YOU SHOULD BE ABLE TO

1. Use some specific instructional approaches and materials for reading and writing in the content areas.

2. State some specific strategies and guidelines for instruction in science, social studies, and mathematics.

3. Understand how to help learners develop effective study strategies and procedures.

4. Discuss the nature of inquiry in the learning process.

5. Describe ways to encourage readers and writers to research topics effectively.

6. Describe the wide range of materials available for study and research.

7. Identify the following terms that are defined or explained in this chapter:

anticipation guides 473	inquiry 483	study guides 476
content area 454	K-W-L 474	text structure 455
data chart 489	SQ3R 476	thematic unit 463
graphic organizers 477		

NCTE/IRA Standards addressed in this chapter

STANDARD 7. Students conduct research on issues and interests by generating ideas and questions, and by posing problems. They gather, evaluate, and synthesize data from a variety of sources (for example, print and non-print texts, artifacts, people) to communicate their discoveries in ways that suit their purpose and audience.

STANDARD 10. Students whose first language is not English make use of their first language to develop competency in the English language arts and to develop understanding of content across the curriculum.

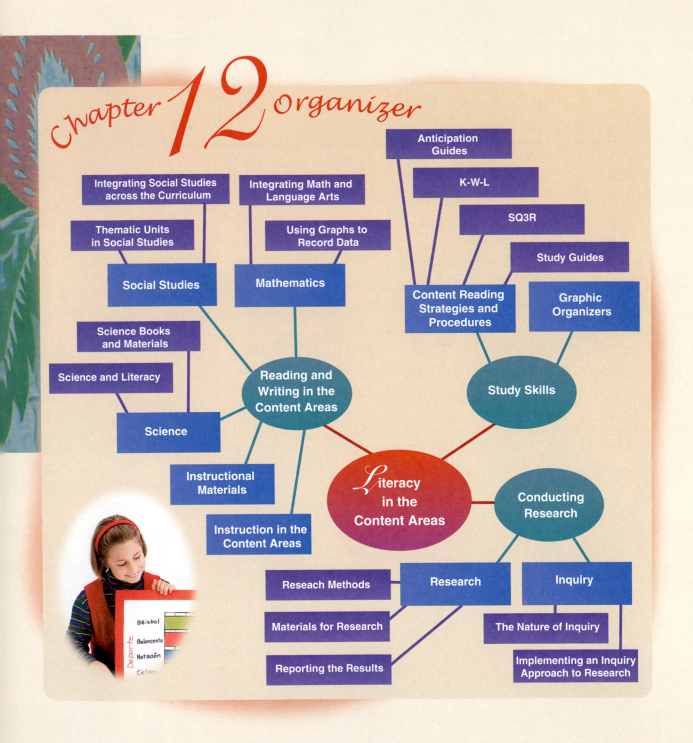

Chapter 12 Organizer

Anticipation Guides

K-W-L

SQ3R

Study Guides

Integrating Social Studies across the Curriculum

Integrating Math and Language Arts

Thematic Units in Social Studies

Using Graphs to Record Data

Content Reading Strategies and Procedures

Graphic Organizers

Social Studies

Mathematics

Science Books and Materials

Science and Literacy

Reading and Writing in the Content Areas

Study Skills

Science

Instructional Materials

Literacy in the Content Areas

Conducting Research

Instruction in the Content Areas

Reseach Methods

Research

Inquiry

Materials for Research

The Nature of Inquiry

Reporting the Results

Implementing an Inquiry Approach to Research

Deporte

Béisbol

Baloncesto

Natación

Ciclism

MR. STULTZ is going to give his fifth-graders a test over a unit they have been studying on the Southwest. They have spent two weeks viewing videotapes, reading books, and doing projects on this topic. He has advised them to review the chapter in their textbook carefully because it will help them recall what they have been learning. The class consists of many types of learners, and we look in on two of them as they prepare for the test. Each student is thinking to himself about the upcoming test.

LARRY: We've got a test in social studies tomorrow so I'd better study. Mom'll get me if I fail this one. The book is too hard for me—I can't read all of the words. Oh well, I'd better get started. I'll read the chapter all the way through two times—that should be enough studying.

LARRY (LATER): I almost went to sleep, but I read each page two times. I don't know whether I know the chapter or not, but that's all I'm going to do.

BOB: Another test in social studies! How hard will I need to study so that I will do well on the test tomorrow? I've already read the chapter, and we've been working on it in class for almost two weeks now. I already know it pretty well, but I'll reread it to make sure I understand everything.

The chapter begins with life on reservations. That should be easy to remember because we acted it out in class, so I can skim over it. What are the names of the different tribes? I have trouble remembering them. Maybe it will help if I write them down.

What is the main idea here? I can't figure it out. Oh, I see. The heading is "Regional Cooperation," so it must be talking about how the states work together on saving the grazing lands. What does the word *petrified* mean here? When I'm petrified, I'm scared, but I don't think that's what the book means. Maybe I can figure out the meaning from the rest of the words in the sentence—it must mean "turned into stone." Why do I have so much trouble understanding this part about mining? Maybe I'll read it again and then try to put it in my own words. Why is this part so confusing? I can skim ahead and see if it's explained more later. If not, I guess I'll just have to slow down and reread until I get it.

BOB (LATER): I've gone over the whole chapter. I think I understand it pretty well. I'll look at the names of the tribes again before I take the test.

What's happening here?

Larry and Bob approach the task of studying for a test entirely differently. Larry has no grasp of what he knows and what he needs to know. His reading of the chapter two times has little purpose, and when he finishes he has no idea if he knows the material. On the other hand, Bob is aware of what he already knows and what he needs to learn. He approaches the task purposefully and constantly monitors or checks his understanding. He uses a variety of strategies to help himself learn the material. When he finishes studying, he knows what he has learned and is aware of the need to review difficult material before the test. The process of knowing what you know and don't know, checking your understanding, and evaluating your performance is called *metacognition* (explained in Chapter 7).

A **content area** is an organized body of knowledge, a subject, or a discipline. Math, science, and social studies are examples of content areas. Reading in the content areas places many demands on students who are accustomed to reading basal reader stories or fiction trade books. Concepts are often presented in rapid succession, and various types of vocabulary, such as specialized words (*photosynthesis* and *multiplicand*), multiple-meaning words (*revolution* and *root*), and abbreviations (*oz.* and *cm*), can create problems. Students may not know how to read the graphic aids, use organizational cues, or report on what they have learned. They may lack the study skills needed for deriving meaning from the text and remembering it for tests. In this chapter, we look at some of these potential difficulties and ways to overcome them.

We also consider ways to encourage students to investigate topics of interest, organize material, and share their findings. Most students are naturally curious and eager to learn about the world around them. Even in the primary grades, children are capable of conducting simple research to satisfy their curiosity. Teacher guidance and an abundant supply of nonfiction trade books, as well as reference materials, support students' efforts to learn, and thematic units provide a framework for enabling them to investigate topics in depth. (See Chapter 14 for information on thematic units.)

Reading and Writing in the Content Areas

Writing

AT ONE time, educators believed reading and writing should be taught directly as discrete subjects and that textbooks should be used as a single source for studying material in different content areas. Now, many believe that reading and writing are essential for learning across the curriculum so that children see purposes for applying their literacy skills. Educators also find that many resource materials in addition to textbooks are useful in helping students discover new information and ways to share it.

Instruction in the Content Areas

Because content area literacy requires different skills from those used with fiction, teachers need to consider how to approach instruction. Researchers have studied the effectiveness of various instructional strategies, and some of their findings follow. Figure 12.1 summarizes Eanes's paradigm for promoting content area literacy (1997, pp. 15-28), and Figure 12.2 provides general guidelines for instruction in the content areas (Bromley, 2000; Cooper, 1997; Guillaume, 1998; Ruddell, 2002).

Understanding **text structures**, such as comparison and contrast or cause and effect, is an important skill for learning subject matter, but many students fail to recognize such relationships without direct instruction (Cunningham & Allington, 1999; Pearson & Fielding, 1994; Ruddell, 2002). Figure 12.3 is an example of frames for expository material that teachers can use to provide practice in identifying text structures.

Once emphasized for upper-grade students, content area reading is now a focus in the primary grades as well (Guillaume, 1998). Primary-level materials build a foundation for reading more sophisticated texts, and the questions they raise offer motivation and purposes for further investigation. Most of the guidelines given for content area literacy apply at the primary level, but you may need to modify your approach somewhat. For example, you need to read aloud from books that are too advanced for young children to read independently and encourage discussion of complex concepts in those texts. (Classroom Vignette 5.1 in chapter 5 gives an example of this.) You should also provide more concrete, hands-on experiences, such as science experiments and map making, to help children develop understandings of concepts and vocabulary.

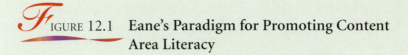

Eane's Paradigm for Promoting Content Area Literacy

I. Flexible scheduling and multiage grouping: Flexible scheduling adjusts for differences in rates of learning and provides flexible blocks of time for students to work with teams of teachers on interdisciplinary projects. Multiage grouping allows students to progress to higher grade levels at individual rates.

2. Motivation for quality learning: Motivation, encouragement, positive reinforcement, and quality learning are stressed so that students recognize the value of what they are learning and move toward achieving personal goals.

3. Synergy through cooperative learning and cross-age learning: The combined efforts and talents of students working together result in greater performance than students working alone. They become members of a classroom community and learn to work as teams, solve problems cooperatively, and stimulate creativity in each other.

4. More student responsibility for learning: The new paradigm for content area literacy stresses the learning process, critical thinking, and self-evaluation. Students learn how to use literacy for discovering and mastering content and how to design rubrics for evaluating their work.

5. Active learning and authentic assessment: A shift from passive to active learning means that students become decision makers who conduct meaningful research and apply literacy skills to content information to answer questions and solve problems. Students construct portfolios of work samples.

6. Textbook alternatives and supplements: Instead of relying heavily on textbooks, manuals, worksheets, and workbooks, teachers use textbooks only as guides. They also include trade books, text sets, and other materials and tools appropriate for ongoing projects in the content areas.

7. Teacher as facilitator and consultant: Teachers become members of a classroom learning community, providing leadership through modeling but also working as partners with students. They collaborate with other teachers in designing and implementing projects that integrate instruction in content areas.

8. Meeting the special needs of every student: Through a policy of inclusion, all students work together in the same classroom setting, but instruction is tailored to each student's unique learning strengths and challenges.

Instructional Materials

Textbooks are useful for teaching in the content areas, particularly for providing a knowledge base for information that students need to know. Before using the text-

FIGURE 12.2   Guidelines for Instruction in the Content Areas

- Set authentic purposes and goals for learning in language arts and content areas.

- Activate students' prior knowledge and help them to see the relevance of what they are learning to their own lives.

- Provide modeling and guided practice for students so that they learn how to find and use resources.

- Allow students to make choices and decisions about their learning whenever possible.

- Establish different kinds of class organization: individual, pairs, small-group, and whole-class.

- Encourage student interaction. Children learn from each other.

- Collect a variety of resources and encourage students to contribute their own.

- Provide different ways for students to learn, including listening, speaking, reading, writing, viewing, and visually representing.

- Involve colleagues or resource people from the community who have specialized knowledge.

- Construct relationships between old and new knowledge. Help students see the connections.

- Integrate study skills instruction with textbook use.

- Use thematic units for cross-curricular integration of content areas and language arts.

- Encourage students to apply strategic reading skills such as predicting, monitoring, constructing meaning, and summarizing. (See Chapter 7 for more on this.)

- Include informational books during read-aloud times and for student self-selection.

- Consider the standards for planning, instruction, and assessment.

book, however, teachers may wish to involve students in a variety of activities related to the topic being studied. Meaningful experiences provide motivation and familiarize students with the material they will encounter in their textbooks, which may be too difficult for many students to read without preliminary activities. Many textbooks are complex, dated, and developed for a national audience that may be unlike the stu-

FIGURE 12.3   **Frames for Expository Text Structure**

Comparison and Contrast

Ponds and lakes are similar.
Both ponds and lakes are _____.
They both have _____.
They are different because _____.

Description

Birds are very interesting creatures.
They have _____, _____, and _____.
Some birds _____.
Other birds _____.
Birds are _____ and _____.

Sequence

To plant a garden, you must do several things.
First, you _____.
Then you _____.
Next you _____.
Finally, you _____.

Cause and Effect

Sometimes it rains.
Spring rains cause _____.
Very heavy rains can cause _____.
When it rains, I have to _____.

Problem and Solution

Bears live in forests.
They can be a problem when they _____.
One way to solve this problem is _____.
Another way to solve the problem is _____.

dents. Also, they may lack the organization and style that young readers need to construct meaning and may cover too many topics without going into depth on any of them (Cooper, 1997).

Trade books are a valuable supplement to textbooks. Nonfiction picture books offer in-depth coverage of specific topics with outstanding illustrations that enhance

Applications

for English Language Learners

The concepts and vocabulary found in most textbooks are particularly difficult for ELLs. Cooperative learning, discussion of the text in small groups, and entries in journals or learning logs that reflect students' thinking are useful strategies for helping ELLs comprehend the text. The learning logs may consist of a mixture of the student's first language and English until English proficiency is attained (Strickland, Ganske, & Monroe, 2002).

the text. Historical fiction provides insights into the thoughts and feelings of people who lived during particular time periods, and biographies give details of prominent figures in such areas as political leadership, the arts, inventions, and so forth. Children's magazines offer articles and pictures on topics of high interest to young readers. Chapter 2 provides additional information on these types of resources.

Bromley (2000) suggests ways that teachers can plan for content area instruction by using computers and the Internet. You can use CD-ROM or DVD-ROM encyclopedias and the Internet to access and download information, including historical documents or data from museums or observatories. Websites also contain actual lessons, projects, and units that teachers can adapt for their own purposes. You may arrange electronic key pal exchanges with classes in different geographic regions so that students can learn about other cultures and lifestyles, and your classes may take electronic field trips to places around the world to extend their learning.

Not only does content area reading differ from story reading in generic ways, each content area offers its own set of challenges and guidelines. The following discussions focus on literacy in science, social studies, and mathematics.

Reflections

Recall the time when you were first required to read textbooks. What were some problems you had? What might have made your assignments easier? How might you help students read their textbooks with increased understanding?

Technology

Science

Science is more than a collection of facts; it is way of dealing with experience, usually through investigation, and it crosses subject matter boundaries (Pappas, Keifer, & Levstik, 1999). Children need to understand science

Students are looking at a computer screen to find information to use for their unit.

so that they can use it in their daily lives, satisfy their natural curiosity, explore their environments, and appreciate scientific phenomena. Instead of emphasizing right answers, science relies on asking questions, taking risks, remaining open to new ideas, and gathering and interpreting data. The changing emphasis from knowledge transmission to inquiry invites children to participate in genuine scientific activity (Ebbers, 2002).

As an integral part of science, health uses many of the same types of methods, procedures, and materials. Particularly with the threat of obesity to even the young, students need to understand the roles of nutrition, exercise, and care of the body in order to become healthy adults.

SCIENCE AND LITERACY

Activities that encourage students' talking, reading, and writing about science support both inquiry-based science instruction and literacy (El-Hindi, 2003). Literacy requires knowledge of specialized vocabulary, close attention to detail, awareness of sequence, and careful adherence to following directions when conducting experiments. Opportunities for talking arise as students ask questions, discuss their observations, share their findings, and reason out loud. Talking about what is happening during observations of scientific occurrences allows children to express their theories about phenomena and communicate with others about their interpretations. While reading science books aloud, you can stop and engage children in thoughtful discussion by reflecting on the text or asking questions that cause students to wonder. When a classroom is well supplied with relevant text materials, students can select such books for reading during SSR time, or they can gather in literature circles to read about a particular topic.

Writing about science can occur in a variety of ways, beginning with simple recording of data, such as temperature variations or plant growth under differing circumstances. First-graders can learn to make graphs to help them sort, organize, categorize, and count objects and concepts; complete observation charts for later discussion; and make webs that help them plan future investigations (Fisher, 1995). Walpole (1998/1999) suggests that students can create graphic organizers to highlight relationships between headings and subheadings, or they can study the graphic design of a science text and write an additional page using the same format. Students may keep science journals that include observations and drawings, descriptions of classroom experiments or demonstrations, and current events related to science and scientific terms (Popp, 1996).

The students in Jill Ramsey's fourth-grade science class kept journals for recording their activities. They wrote definitions of scientific terms and illustrated them (see Figure 12.4), made graphic organizers to represent scientific processes, took notes from videotapes, and demonstrated their understanding of the ecosystem with drawings (see Figure 12.5). Using bags full of mixed beans, small groups of students created charts that compared the characteristics of the different beans. They created hypotheses for experiments they were performing (see Figure 12.6), observed what was happening, and then recorded their findings. Mrs. Ramsey used extensively Joanna Cole's Magic School Bus series as a resource for teaching scientific concepts.

Every week, fifth-grade teacher Julie Bauermeister assigns three children to collaborate on planning and gathering scientific information for conducting an experiment. They have to read for information, find appropriate equipment, conduct the experiment, write up the results, and explain to their classmates what happened. In these lessons, the children are demonstrating literacy skills along with scientific inquiry.

*F*IGURE 12.4   **Definitions for Scientific Terms**

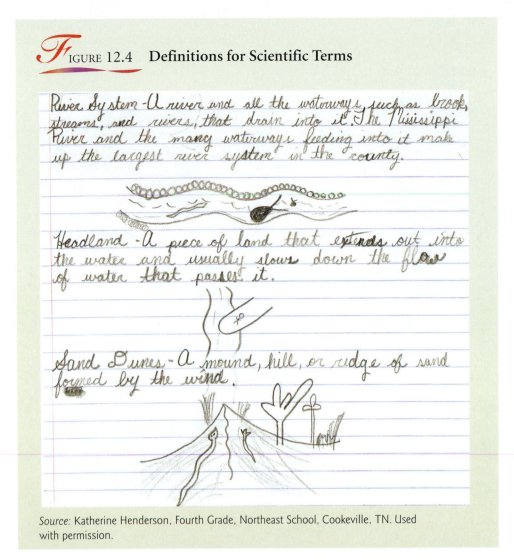

Source: Katherine Henderson, Fourth Grade, Northeast School, Cookeville, TN. Used with permission.

SCIENCE BOOKS AND MATERIALS

A variety of reading materials on science find their way into elementary classrooms (Ebbers, 2002; Guillaume, 1998; Rice, 2002). Richly illustrated textbooks compete with trade books, and other resources include field guides that organize and classify information, reference materials that report on current scientific understandings, and how-to books that illustrate particular procedures in science. Eric Carle's science-related books and Joanna Cole's Magic School Bus series fascinate young readers, and Richard Platt's *Stephen Biesty's Incredible Cross-Sections* and David Macaulay's *The Way Things Work* intrigue older students interested in architecture and machines. National Geographic has published series of health-related books for preK-3 with titles such as *I Like Being Outdoors, Keeping Clean,* and *Staying Healthy* and for grades 3 through 8 with such titles as: *Fighting Disease, Making Healthy Choices,* and *Keeping Fit.* Although trade books should be part of the science curriculum, Rice (2002) advises teachers to

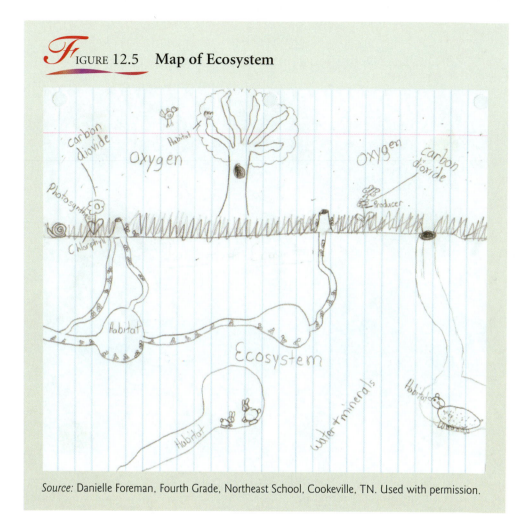

$\mathcal{F}$IGURE 12.5 **Map of Ecosystem**

Source: Danielle Foreman, Fourth Grade, Northeast School, Cookeville, TN. Used with permission.

When selecting science books and materials, check copyright dates to see how current they are, the credentials of the authors for evaluating their expertise, and the publisher for its reputation for comprehensiveness and accuracy.

select them carefully because some may contain errors of omission, incomplete statements, inaccuracies, or outdated information.

Social Studies

Social studies deals with the ways that people live together and is often the core of an integrated curriculum (Pappas, Kiefer, & Levstik, 1999). It considers powerful and often controversial themes related to human behavior in a diverse society, and it includes history, geography, and sociology. The arts (music, drama, and visual arts) often enhance social studies, particularly during theme studies. Biographies and informational books help children understand the struggles and achievements of individuals and their impact on history (Norton, 2003). As children investigate prominent individuals and social issues, they learn to

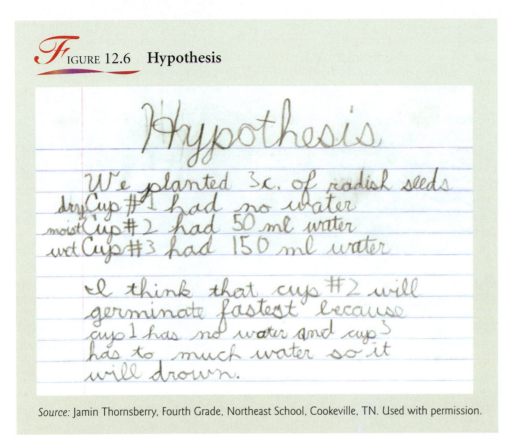

*F*IGURE 12.6   **Hypothesis**

> Hypothesis
>
> We planted 3c. of radish seeds
> dryCup #1 had no water
> moistCup #2 had 50 ml water
> wet Cup #3 had 150 ml water
>
> I think that cup #2 will
> germinate fastest because
> cup1 has no water and cup3
> has to much water so it
> will drown.

Source: Jamin Thornsberry, Fourth Grade, Northeast School, Cookeville, TN. Used with permission.

look at such relationships as cause and effect, problem and solution, and comparison and contrast.

THEMATIC UNITS IN SOCIAL STUDIES

A **thematic unit** is a study organized around a central topic or theme that lasts anywhere from a few days to several weeks, depending on the depth of the theme and the interest of the students. The interdisciplinary nature of social studies is ideal for thematic units that cross curricular boundaries and connect with the language arts. Overviews of three thematic units are given here. (Chapter 14 contains additional information on thematic units.)

THEMATIC UNIT: WESTWARD HO! The purpose of this unit was to develop first-graders' awareness of the differences among people and help them value the diversity of nationalities, customs, and ethnic groups (Fisher, 1995). The class began by discussing their roots, sharing information about their ancestors and how they immigrated to this country, and comparing stories. Children discussed information with family members, listened to stories, and looked at books. They also completed questionnaires and surveys with their families and collected artifacts, such as dolls, jewelry, and old family photographs, which became part of a museum display or props for the homestead they created. Throughout the unit, the teacher read aloud stories, biographies, and other informational books about the theme, including Donald Hall's *Ox-cart Man* and Joanne

Henry's *Log Cabin in the Woods: A True Story about a Pioneer Boy.* The culmination was a Visitor's Day that featured the museum, the homestead, and a group presentation. Children presented guests with printed programs, and all of them announced a part or recited a line from two texts they had written. They also introduced themselves, spoke about the countries of their ancestors, recited a poem, and sang five songs.

THEMATIC UNIT: TEXAS REVOLUTION Linking literature with social studies, two fourth-grade classes investigated the Texas Revolution. Historical fiction, biography, and information texts were the bases for study of a historical period that focused on such universal themes as human rights, ethics, courage, and sacrifice (Roser & Keehn, 2002). Phase 1 of the six-week unit began with each teacher reading a biography aloud; in Phase 2, students met as members of book clubs; and in Phase 3, they gathered as a class to raise questions and address uncertainties. Further experiences included field excursions, consultation with authorities, use of print and electronic sources, and examination of artifacts. Along with extensive reading, students corresponded with pen pals, constructed data charts, and compared information from various sources. Two of the many books used were Margaret Cousins's *The Boy in the Alamo* and Jean Fritz's *Make Way for Sam Houston.*

Writing

THEMATIC UNIT: MIGRATIONS With the intent of helping fifth-graders consider the interpretive nature of historical reporting, a teacher began reading aloud from Russell Freedman's *Immigrant Kids* and sharing the accompanying photographs (Pappas, Kiefer, & Levstik, 1999). He gathered other materials dealing with immigration, located copies of slave narratives from the state historical society, and found collections of pictures of Manhattan's ethnic neighborhoods. Students found reference materials and textbook information that they used to analyze various interpretations. Visual images, such as photographs, paintings, and drawings, played an important role in helping students understand situations. Soon they were developing their own criteria for evaluating historical fiction and informational books, and they then began writing their own books based on new knowledge and the criteria they had developed. In this critical analysis, students had learned to compare and contrast interpretations and look for errors or bias in reporting.

Reflections

Social studies involves many language processes and artistic expressions. From the overview of thematic units given here, what ways did students use language arts to develop their understanding of social studies, including the arts? Can you think of other possibilities for integrating language arts?

INTEGRATING SOCIAL STUDIES ACROSS THE CURRICULUM

As with science, social studies involves learners in talking, reading, writing, and inquiry. Students talk as they interview, discuss, ask questions, share information, debate, and give reports. Reading occurs as they peruse reference materials, trade books, textbooks, and all sorts of relevant print materials, and writing takes place when students make graphs, charts, timelines, and written reports in various forms. Often, they learn and report through the arts as well. Folksongs and crafts offer insights into time periods, and music, drama, and artistic displays are viable forms of reporting. The Internet is also useful as a source of information, and students can present their findings through Microsoft PowerPoint presentations. One sixth-grade teacher printed a news story from the Internet and used it as the focus for studying current events in social studies.

Technology

Applications *for English Language Learners*

Although all students enrich their understanding through the arts, ELLs find them particularly beneficial. With drama, they can acquire concepts through such activities as pantomime (no need to speak English), puppetry (talking as puppets may be easier than speaking as themselves), creative dramatics with multicultural literature that is familiar to them, and dramatic play centers, such as a covered wagon or country store. The rhythms and melodies of music help them remember special words and phrases and sense the flow of language. The visual arts enable them to comprehend meaning through illustrations rather than text and also offer ELLs a way to respond through art rather than words. For these children, a picture may indeed be worth a thousand words.

Another used situations from the Future Problem Solving Program (annual) as stepping stones to such real-world, contemporary problems as homelessness, violence, and prejudice. With heads together and voices competing to be recognized, groups of sixth-graders excitedly identified underlying problems, gathered information, brainstormed possibilities, evaluated solutions, and arrived at the solution they felt was best.

The social studies textbook provides a useful framework for covering material mandated by the curriculum, but lively, meaningful instruction should precede its use. Children need to be familiar with specialized vocabulary and have an understanding of the subject before reading an often challenging textbook. Difficult concepts may be presented in rapid succession without full explanations; relationships (for example, cause-effect) may be elusive; and graphics, such as diagrams and tables, may be hard to interpret. Rich experiences through simulations (for example, acting out a day in pioneer life), field trips, hands-on activities, role-playing, graphic organizers, resource people, interviews, videotapes, and stories from a particular region, time period, or culture help students acquire meaningful concepts about social studies. Figure 12.7 is a list of multicultural trade books, many from different historical periods, that can help children gain insights into various lifestyles.

Teaching Tip

When selecting books for your classroom library, include multicultural books that represent the ethnicity of your students. In this way, you help children from different ethnic backgrounds build their self-esteem.

Technology

Mathematics

Mathematics is the science of patterns and relationships. Rather than just emphasizing correct answers, the current view is that the math curriculum should help children understand how and when to use mathematical techniques, become aware of why they

FIGURE 12.7   Multicultural Books for Social Studies

Title and Author	Content	Culture
Talking Walls M. B. Knight	Walls around the world from ancient to modern times are significant.	Many cultures
Nory Ryan's Story P. R. Giff	Nory Ryan tries to survive during the great potato famine in Ireland.	Irish
Behind the Mountains E. Danticat	While living in Haiti, Celiane anxiously awaits Papa's call to come to New York.	Haitian
Crispin: The Cross of Lead Avi	Crispin, pursued by enemies, encounters many adventures in medieval England.	English
The Whispering Cloth P. D. Shea	A girl living in a Thai refugee camp in the mid-1970s finds her story.	Thai
Through My Eyes R. Bridges	Ruby Bridges tells her story of integration in New Orleans in 1960.	African American
Sadako E. Coerr	Sadako, living in Hiroshima, fights leukemia by folding paper cranes.	Japanese
Family Pictures C. L. Garza	Garza describes her experiences while growing up in a Texas Hispanic town.	Mexican American
The Lotus Seed S. Garland	A girl who has to flee saves a lotus seed that reminds her of her brave emperor.	Vietnamese
Dinner at Aunt Connie's House F. Ringgold	Portraits of twelve inspirational women speak about their courageous lives.	African American
Grandfather's Journey A. Say	A Japanese American man has feelings for both California and Japan.	Japanese American
Pink and Say P. Polacco	Two boys, one black and the other white, meet during the Civil War.	African American
Coolies Yin	Chinese brothers come to the United States to help build a railroad.	Chinese American

(continued)

$\mathcal{F}$IGURE 12.7   **Multicultural Books for Social Studies,** *Continued*

Title and Author	Content	Culture
From Sea to Shining Sea A. Cohn	Over 140 folk songs, poems, and stories tell the history of America.	English
A Single Shard L. Park	A young boy carries his master's pottery through many hazards in medieval times.	Korean
Number the Stars L. Lowry	Brave Annemarie helps save her friend during the Nazi occupation of Denmark.	Danish
Catherine, Called Birdy K. Cushman	In the year 1290, a young girl defies traditions by seeking adventure.	English
My Place N. Wheatley, D. Rawlins	Through the decades, many changes occur in the environment of Sydney.	Australian
Shabanu: Daughter of the Wind S. F. Staples	A young girl lives in the desert with her family of nomadic camel herders.	Pakistani
... And Now Miguel J. Krumgold	Of Spanish heritage, Miguel Chavez is the son of a proud sheep-raising family.	Hispanic
Sing Down the Moon S. O'Dell	In the mid-1800s, the Navaho were forced to march 300 miles to relocate.	Native American
The Talking Earth J. C. George	A Seminole girl from a reservation travels through a swamp.	Native American
Dogsong G. Paulsen	A boy travels 1,400 miles by dogsled across ice to discover old Eskimo ways.	Eskimo
Letters from Rifka K. Hesse	Through letters, Rifka tells how she and her Jewish family flee Russia in 1919.	Russian
A Girl Named Disaster N. Farmer	A girl travels by river from Mozambique to Zimbabwe, guided by family spirits.	African
Dragonwings L. Yep	A boy helps his father build and fly an airplane in 1903 in San Francisco.	Chinese American

work, and know how they are developed. Research supports an integrated language perspective for helping children learn math (Pappas, Kiefer, & Levstik, 1999).

INTEGRATING MATH AND LANGUAGE ARTS

Integrated language arts classes promote active problem solving and a spirit of inquiry that provide opportunities for children to talk, read, and write with others about mathematical issues and problems. Communication is a key to deeper understanding of math, and talking through a problem, listening to ways others solve problems, and writing about the steps taken in solving a problem help students organize their thinking (Silbey, 2003). Students are required to explain their thinking and support their answers in writing in many classrooms and on some state assessments, but before they can write about their solutions, they must be able to talk with others about their strategies and explain why they make sense (Silbey, 2003).

Instead of directing all classroom interactions, you should encourage students to grapple with problems independently first, find strategies and solutions that make sense, and evaluate results. As is true for other content areas, children learn mathematics best when it is embedded within meaningful activities with problems that arise from real needs and purposes.

Counting, graphing, telling time, basic computations, classification, patterns, money, and measurement are mathematical concepts that young children need to learn in manipulative, concrete ways. A good foundation in the early grades enables students to deal with more complex, expanded concepts later. Children should appreciate the need for accuracy and attention to detail for each of these concepts and learn to use correct vocabulary in their labeling and discussions. Counting and number books, including Frank Mazzola's *Counting Is for the Birds,* Denise Fleming's *Count!,* and Pam Ryan and Jerry Pallotta's *The Crayon Counting Book,* help children develop basic concepts. Fisher (1995) offers classroom-based suggestions for integrating literacy with math concepts with first-graders (see Figure 12.8).

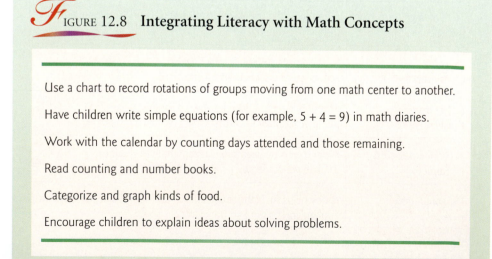

***F*IGURE 12.8   Integrating Literacy with Math Concepts**

Use a chart to record rotations of groups moving from one math center to another.

Have children write simple equations (for example, $5 + 4 = 9$) in math diaries.

Work with the calendar by counting days attended and those remaining.

Read counting and number books.

Categorize and graph kinds of food.

Encourage children to explain ideas about solving problems.

Many situations can become story problems, which children can represent through manipulation of objects, construction of numerical equations, or word stories. Ann Burns involves her first-graders in such stories and allows them to solve problems according to their developmental levels. Minilesson 12.1 shows how she introduces a story problem, provides children with manipulatives, and lets them solve the problem in different ways.

Writing

In Bonnie Kurimay's fifth-grade class, students begin and end their math lesson with writing (Welbes, 2003). The students copy a word problem into their journals, write step-by-step strategies for solving the problem, and share answers by writing them on a chalkboard. Students discover that there are different ways to solve the same problem. At the end of class, they write a summary of what they learned that day. This team teaching approach to math also involves the reading and writing teachers.

Students can find many occasions to apply their knowledge of mathematical concepts during thematic units. In one city, the Grand Prix is about to occur, and the entire population is both excited and concerned. Picking up on the local enthusiasm, a sixth-grade teacher uses the race as the topic of a thematic unit. Minilesson 12.2 shows the result.

Minilesson 12.1

Solving Story Problems

Ann Burns creates a story problem and writes it on a chart for the class to read together during circle time. The story is about a hungry monster who likes to eat wheels. The monster finds two skates with six wheels on each skate and a wagon with four wheels. Ann asks her first-graders to figure out how many wheels the hungry monster eats for his breakfast. Children work on the floor in pairs, with one partner responsible for getting and returning the manipulatives. They move small objects that represent wheels to solve the problem and then show their answers by drawing pictures of wheels, writing numerals to represent wheels, writing word and number statements (6 wheels + 6 wheels + 4 wheels = 16 wheels), or responding in narrative form to the chart story. When they are finished, the children return to the circle, share their processes and answers when called on, and observe that there are many ways to go about solving problems. Not all of the answers are correct, but Ms. Burns praises children's efforts and shows appreciation for their work.

What are the students learning?

The children are learning to manipulate concrete objects to find solutions to math problems. They are learning to communicate their ideas and speculations with their partners, and they are finding that there are different ways to solve problems and show their work. Instead of thinking of mathematics as isolated calculations, they realize that it is used to solve problems.

Minilesson 12.2

Automobile Race

With the media's extensive coverage of the coming Grand Prix race, students quickly become engrossed in the unit by delving into print materials, writing articles for the school newspaper, speculating about the race's impact on the city and the nearby park, considering safety aspects, and collecting artifacts. Mathematical implications are extensive, and during this lesson the teacher encourages students to create and solve their own math problems that deal with such issues as

- Noise levels in decibels.
- Braking time needed at different speeds.
- Total distance traveled per car and for all cars.
- Sales of merchandise versus cost of booth space.
- Cost of extra security guards and police officers.
- Number of laps and average lap time (including pit stops).
- Provision of food and drink (for example, how many hamburgers would people consume?).
- Time needed for setting up and taking down barricades, stands, booths, and so forth.
- Cost and amount of fuel.
- Analysis of safety records from previous races.
- Required daily attendance to break even with anticipated costs.

Deeply committed to their investigation, students collect data, make graphs and charts, report their findings, and share information.

What are the students learning?

Students are discovering the effects of a major event on their city. The unit involves many mathematical calculations and estimations, and it crosses the curriculum into science (effects of fumes emitted from engines, wear and tear on tires) and social studies (high noise levels likely to disturb elderly residents and birds in the nearby park). They learn that many issues must be considered when planning a major event and that mathematics plays an important role in determining its potential success.

USING GRAPHS TO RECORD DATA

One of the most effective ways to record data, graphs may take the form of line graphs that show changes in amounts, bar graphs that use bars to compare quantities, or circle graphs that show relationships of parts to the whole (Burns, Roe, & Ross, 1999). Students need to understand how to read graphs by looking at the title and the information along the side and bottom of the graph. Constructing their own graphs from meaningful data helps students learn how to interpret and use data from graphs in texts. For example, Figure 12.9 shows how a teacher helped children convert their preferences for certain fast-food restaurants into a bar graph. In some classes, students use

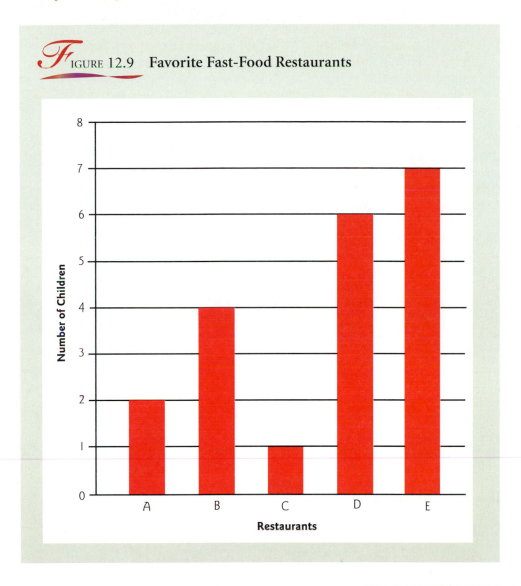

$\mathcal{F}$IGURE 12.9   **Favorite Fast-Food Restaurants**

line graphs to keep ongoing records of their spelling test scores or their reading rates after repeated readings. Older students may use circle or pie graphs to show the proportions of students attending different schools within the local district or to represent percentages of funding for state government expenditures. Chapter 11 contains additional information about graphs.

Students are studying a graph that they have constructed and plan to use in their class presentation at the conclusion of a unit.

The use of graphs can be expanded and enhanced through the use of computer spreadsheet programs (Goldberg, 2003). Children can learn about computer-based graphing by counting and sorting candies or cereals by color, size, or shape. By entering data on a spreadsheet and using the information to make graphs, students can compare sets of data, manipulate the results, and gain deeper insight into how graphs work.

McDonald (1999) helps first-graders connect graphs with literature by asking them to make predictions about how stories will end. She reads books aloud until she reaches the climax and then asks her class to discuss possible outcomes. She records their predictions on bar graphs or circle graphs before finishing the story. She selects books with strong climaxes and many possible outcomes, including John Steptoe's *Mufaro's Beautiful Daughters,* Janet Perlman's *The Emperor Penguin's New Clothes,* Jerry Pinkney's *Rikki Tikki Tavi,* and Lydia Bailey's *Mei Ming and the Dragon's Daughter.* Children expand their reading strategies by making predictions, and they enhance their mathematical knowledge by connecting graphical data to their experiences.

Study Skills

SOME STUDY skills relate to any content area, while others apply only to specific areas. For any subject, students must understand the organization of the text and the chapters within the text so that they can make good use of such devices as tables of contents, indexes, glossaries, headings, and chapter summaries. They should learn study techniques to help them remember what they read, and they need to learn to read various types of graphic aids, including the pictures, graphs, diagrams, and charts that appear in many textbooks.

Content Reading Strategies and Procedures

In the classroom vignette at the beginning of the chapter, Bob shows that he is able to apply a variety of strategies to his textbook reading. He recalls knowledge from previous class experiences, uses context to figure out word meanings, looks at the text organization, adjusts his rate according to the difficulty of the material, and uses other strategies to get meaning. Good readers continually question themselves to make sure they are comprehending text material, but not all students know and use these study techniques. You can teach students to apply effective reading strategies through explicit instruction and modeling, and then by providing time for them to practice using the strategies with your guidance. Using such strategies not only helps them learn and understand the material, but also enables them to be successful on tests. Chapter 7 provides additional information on strategic reading.

Educators have devised numerous procedures for helping students understand content area material. Instruction in these procedures is most effective when it uses actual text material that students are studying in class and is not presented as isolated practice (Roe, Smith, & Burns, 2005). We consider four of the most useful procedures here: anticipation guides, K-W-L, SQ3R, and study guides.

ANTICIPATION GUIDES

Anticipation guides prepare students to read by making them aware of their prior knowledge and opinions about a topic or issue, and by reinforcing their understanding or by correcting misconceptions. Before reading a selection, students check whether they agree or disagree with statements about the topic. As they read, they consider the information in the text in light of their preconceptions, and they return to the guide to see if they want to change any answers when they finish reading. After students complete this activity, you should ask them if they need to change any answers and what new information caused them to make changes. Figure 12.10 is an anticipation guide for Patricia Polacco's partial autobiography *Thank You, Mr. Falker*, the story of a girl who had difficulty learning to read. You can construct anticipation guides from fiction or nonfiction materials by identifying key concepts or ideas and then writing statements for students to consider.

*F*IGURE 12.10   **Anticipation Guide for *Thank You, Mr. Falker***

Directions: Put a check beside each statement. Check under *Agree* if you agree with the statement. Check under *Disagree* if you disagree with the statement.

Agree	Disagree	Statement
_____	_____	Children who can't read are stupid.
_____	_____	Changing schools makes you a better student.
_____	_____	Everybody likes to read.
_____	_____	Everybody sees letters and numbers the same way.
_____	_____	There are many ways to teach children to read.
_____	_____	Teasing is fun.
_____	_____	If you can't read by third grade, you'll never be able to read.

A variation of the anticipation guide is the anticipation/reaction guide. In this guide, students indicate their beliefs by writing *yes, no,* or *sometimes* in *Before* and *After* columns, as shown in Figure 12.11, which is based on Jerald Halpern's *A Look at Spiders.*

K-W-L

K-W-L, a procedure introduced by Ogle (1986), consists of three parts: "What I *K*now," "What I *W*ant to Know," and "What I *L*earned." You lead the class in brainstorming what the students already know about a topic and record their responses on a chart under the heading "What I Know." Next, students generate questions about the topic that stem from genuine curiosity, which you list under "What I Want to Know." Students locate answers to their questions through reading, watching videos, searching the Internet, interviewing experts, or in some other way. When they have gathered information, you record their findings under "What I Learned." In Cynthia Burton's third grade, children made individual K-W-Ls for their unit on penguins (see Figure 12.12).

Teaching Tip

When asking children to fold papers lengthwise, tell them to make a hotdog fold. When you want them to fold their papers the other way, ask them to make a hamburger fold. If you want them to fold their papers diagonally, ask them to use a taco fold.

FIGURE 12.11 Anticipation/Reaction Guide

Directions: Read each statement. Write *yes, no,* or *sometimes* under *Before* to show what you think is true before reading the book. Read the book and then read the statements again. Write *yes, no,* or *sometimes* under *After* to show what you think after you have read the book. See if any of your ideas have changed.

Before   *After*

_____ _____ 1. A spider can be bigger than an adult's hand.

_____ _____ 2. Spiders are insects.

_____ _____ 3. Few spiders are harmful to people.

_____ _____ 4. All spiders make webs.

_____ _____ 5. Male spiders are bigger than female spiders.

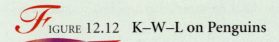

𝓕IGURE 12.12 K–W–L on Penguins

What I Know	What I want to know	What I Learned
Penguins eat fish. They Like swimming. There's Lots of snow. Where do peguins Live. They Live in the southploe.	Do penguins fly? Do They eat? Do They hatch in a egg?	Penguins Don't fly Now I know That Baby Chicks hatch in eggs

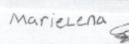

Marielena

Source: Marielena Juan, Jere Whitson School, Cookeville, TN. Used with permission.

Each child folded a sheet of paper lengthwise, cut the front fold into three sections, and labeled each section. Under each flap, the child wrote what he knew, wanted to know, and learned. Some children illustrated their papers on the back.

K-W-L offers many advantages as an instructional procedure. It activates prior knowledge during the first stage, sets purposes that grow from the students' desire to know during the second stage, and motivates learners to uncover information during the third phase. Some teachers add other headings, including *H* for "*How* to Find Out," which causes students to consider how they will locate the information, and *S* for "*Still* Want to Know" when questions remain unanswered or new information causes additional questions to arise. Sampson (2002) found that sometimes students were incorrect during the initial brainstorming or that information from their research was contradictory, so she modified K-W-L from "What We *Know*" to "What We *Think* We Know." Students then had to identify at least two current sources that agreed before placing a check in the new "Confirmed" column.

SQ3R

The third procedure, **SQ3R** (Robinson, 1961) is primarily for middle-grade students who must read textbooks and learn the material. It is a systematic approach for helping students develop effective study habits by providing a framework for previewing the text, setting purposes, reading actively, recalling information, and assessing learning. Each letter in SQ3R stands for a process:

- *Survey:* Skim through the chapter, looking at the title, objectives, introduction, headings, graphic aids, and summary.
- *Question:* Turn headings into questions that establish purposes for reading. Example: The question for the heading of this section on page 472 might be: What are some content reading strategies and procedures?
- *Read:* Read to find answers to the questions and any other important information.
- *Recite:* Say answers to questions.
- *Review:* Assess and reflect on knowledge gained. Refer back to the text for clarification or to find answers that you cannot recall.

Students do not automatically understand how to implement these processes, so it is important for you to give detailed instructions and model the procedures by thinking aloud (Eanes, 1997). Then guide students through each step, checking to make sure they understand what they are to do and why it is helpful, until you feel reasonably sure they can use SQ3R independently.

STUDY GUIDES

Intended to help students better understand and remember what they read, **study guides** are prepared by the teacher and distributed to students. They guide students through a reading assignment, focusing attention on the main points and providing structure (Irvin, 1998). Study guides consist of questions and activities related to the text, and students interact with these prompts as they read. They should be easy to read and simple to follow, focusing only on key ideas. They may include specific page and paragraph references to help students locate answers. Figure 12.13 shows possible prompts for a piece about the Pilgrim's voyage on the *Mayflower*.

A variation of the study guide is the three-level guide, with each level representing a level of comprehension: literal, inferential, and evaluative (Herber, 1978). This guide encourages readers to examine the text in different ways. For the piece about the *Mayflower* voyage, the questions might be the following.

Literal: How many people came over on the *Mayflower*?

Inferential: What problems that the passengers encountered on the ship were caused by being at sea for such a long period of time?

Evaluative: The Pilgrims landed in December. Was it wise to arrive in winter? Would it have been easier for them if they had landed in spring or summer? Why, or why not?

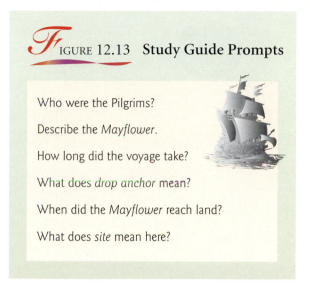

FIGURE 12.13   Study Guide Prompts

Who were the Pilgrims?

Describe the *Mayflower*.

How long did the voyage take?

What does *drop anchor* mean?

When did the *Mayflower* reach land?

What does *site* mean here?

Graphic Organizers

Students need to know how to gather, sort, and organize information, but this is not an easy task. With so much information readily available, how do they learn to select what is important and decide how to organize it logically? Harvey (1998) points out that traditional, formal outlining is giving way to less structured forms of organization. She suggests making lists and indenting some items in the list to show that they are less important than the key ideas. She also recommends using graphic organizers to show the relationships between main ideas and details, instead of the numerals and letters that characterize formal outlining. In many cases, informal webs are easily converted later into formal outlines, if they are required. Students need to become familiar with a wide range of organizational strategies, take time to explore them, and choose those that work best for their own learning styles.

Graphic organizers are visual representations of knowledge that facilitate reading, writing, and reasoning in all subjects (Bromley, Irwin-De Vitis, & Modlo, 1995). They are particularly helpful for visual learners (Eanes, 1997) and are wonderfully adaptable

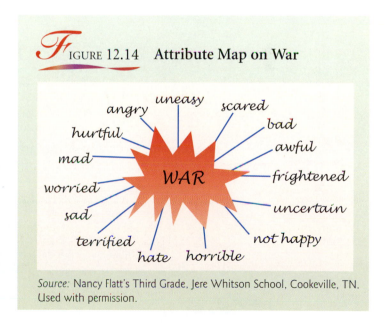

FIGURE 12.14   Attribute Map on War

angry uneasy scared
hurtful   bad
mad   awful
worried   **WAR**   frightened
sad   uncertain
terrified   not happy
       hate horrible

Source: Nancy Flatt's Third Grade, Jere Whitson School, Cookeville, TN. Used with permission.

Writing

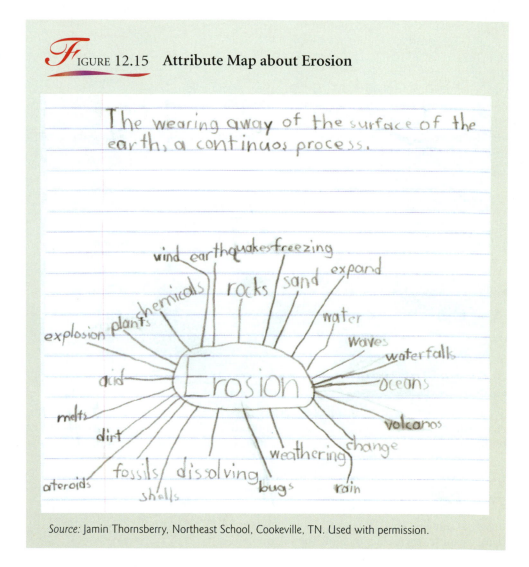

F IGURE 12.15 **Attribute Map about Erosion**

The wearing away of the surface of the earth, a continuos process.

wind earthquakes freezing
expand
chemicals rocks sand
plants water
explosion
Erosion waves
acid waterfalls
oceans
melts
volcanos
dirt change
weathering
fossils dissolving
asteroids bugs rain
shells

Source: Jamin Thornsberry, Northeast School, Cookeville, TN. Used with permission.

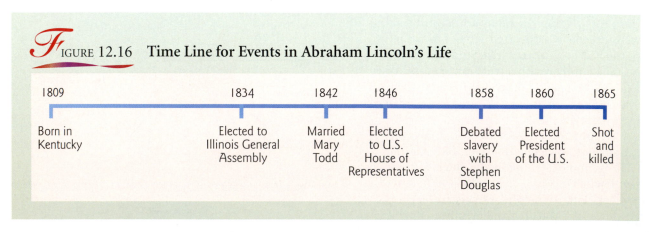

F IGURE 12.16 **Time Line for Events in Abraham Lincoln's Life**

1809	1834	1842	1846	1858	1860	1865
Born in Kentucky	Elected to Illinois General Assembly	Married Mary Todd	Elected to U.S. House of Representatives	Debated slavery with Stephen Douglas	Elected President of the U.S.	Shot and killed

to different situations and purposes. You can construct them with contributions from students, or students can construct their own to show their understanding of relationships. After creating their own graphic displays, students are likely to interpret charts and diagrams more easily when they encounter them in texts. You can use a graphic organizer before introducing a topic or unit and modify it as the unit progresses, or you can use one to summarize material in an orderly manner at the conclusion of a unit. You may have noticed that each chapter in this text opens with a graphic organizer that shows the key concepts addressed within the chapter. Some widely used graphic organizers are the following.

- *Attribute map:* Display of characteristics, thoughts, or ideas related to a central topic. Nancy Flatt created an attribute map when she asked her third-graders to express their feelings about war (see Figure 12.14 on page 477). In another class, a fourth-grader made his own attribute map that shows concepts and materials related to erosion (see Figure 12.15).
- *Time line:* A line extending from the beginning of a period of time to the end of the period with intervening events placed at intervals. See Figure 12.16 about major events in Abraham Lincoln's life for an example of a time line.
- *Venn diagram:* Two or more overlapping circles to compare and contrast concepts or information. Figure 12.17 shows a Venn diagram that compares

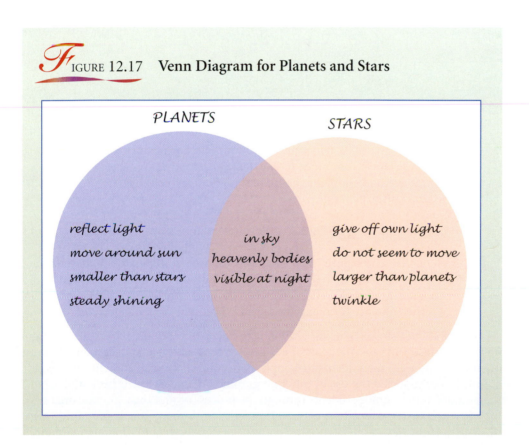

$\mathcal{F}$IGURE 12.17   **Venn Diagram for Planets and Stars**

PLANETS   STARS

reflect light

move around sun

smaller than stars

steady shining

in sky
heavenly bodies
visible at night

give off own light

do not seem to move

larger than planets

twinkle

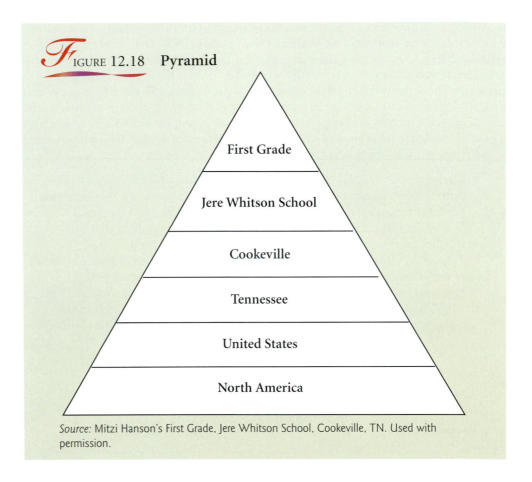

𝓕IGURE 12.18   **Pyramid**

First Grade

Jere Whitson School

Cookeville

Tennessee

United States

North America

Source: Mitzi Hanson's First Grade, Jere Whitson School, Cookeville, TN. Used with permission.

stars and planets. The center part is common to both, whereas the parts beneath the labels are unique to one or the other.

■ *Pyramid:* A progression of expanding sizes or areas, as in Figure 12.18 created by Mitzi Hanson's first-graders.

■ *Semantic map:* An organization of information or ideas related to a central topic in a graphic form. Figure 12.19 shows relationships between main ideas and details on a semantic map of tornadoes created by Linda Lee's third-graders. (See also Figure 7.9 in Chapter 7 for a semantic map of polar bears.)

■ *Flow chart:* A visual representation of a sequence of events or operations. For an assignment to make a flow chart of a familiar procedure, Julie Harris shows the sequence for making chicken broccoli bake (see Figure 12.20).

Fisher (2001) suggests using graphic organizer notebooks, which are custom-designed to use with specific texts. They are collections of teacher-developed blank organizers and webs for students to complete after they have read content material for a unit. Fisher modeled the use of different graphic organizers with think-alouds and then guided fourth-grade students through the process of making a graphic organizer for a science lesson. After discussion and practice with many forms of graphic organizers, students understood structural patterns better, learned to separate main ideas and details, were able to discover relationships, and could eventually create their own graphic organizers.

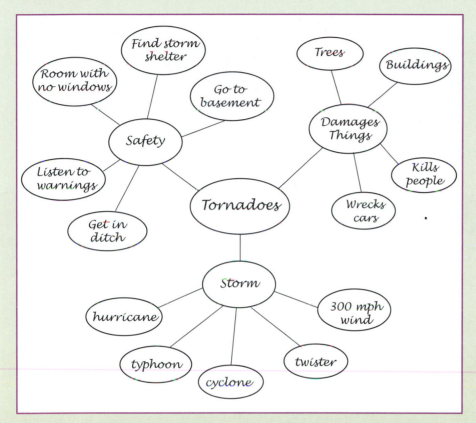

$\mathcal{F}$IGURE 12.19   **Semantic Map of Tornadoes**

Source: Linda Lee's Third Grade, Jere Whitson School, Cookeville, TN. Used with permission.

Applications *for English Language Learners and Students with Special Needs*

Graphic organizers are particularly helpful for students who have difficulty reading lengthy expository material. In a review of research on graphic organizers, Fisher (2001) found that their use caused dramatic improvement for students with learning disabilities and that they had a positive effect on student achievement in science. They also help ELLs, who find it easier to examine webs with few words than to read detailed text when trying to learn new concepts.

Writing

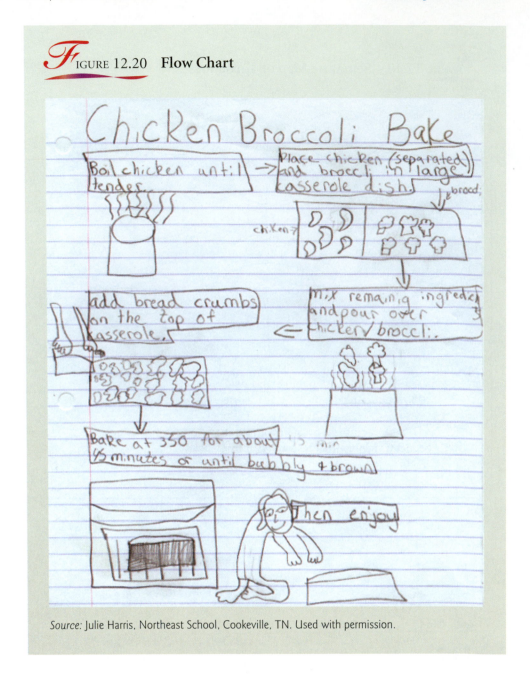

$\mathcal{F}$IGURE 12.20 **Flow Chart**

Source: Julie Harris, Northeast School, Cookeville, TN. Used with permission.

Writing

$\mathcal{C}$onducting Research

TRUE RESEARCH is more than collecting information and writing reports; it evolves from an inquiring mind with a desire to know more. In this section, we look at the process of inquiry, types of materials and tools to use in collecting data, and a variety of ways to share findings.

Inquiry

One approach to research occurs when students pursue their natural sense of curiosity. They want to investigate what interests them. The following discussion centers on the nature of inquiry and how to implement inquiry-based research.

THE NATURE OF INQUIRY

Inquiry begins with a sense of wonder (Harvey, 1998; Harvey, 2002; Routman, 2000). It involves raising questions and seeking answers, thinking about and interpreting information, and understanding ideas and concepts well enough to draw conclusions. Inquiry should be at the center of the curriculum as much as possible because students are far more likely to become enthusiastic researchers through an inquiry approach than through studying textbooks. They should be able to choose a topic of high interest and investigate it with open-ended activities until they become experts on that topic (Routman, 2000). Even young children can do research. Through an Explorers Club, kindergartners express their interests during class discussions, generate a list of possible topics, choose their favorites, join groups with similar interests, and obtain information through books, videos, resource people, and field trips (Seifert, 1999).

Integration of the language arts and connections across the curriculum occur naturally as students delve into their research (Routman, 2000; Schmidt, Gillen, Zollo, & Stone, 2002). They acquire and manipulate information by engaging in listening, speaking, reading, writing, viewing, and visually representing, and their investigations spill over into such areas as science, health, art, music, and social studies. Children generate questions, record observational data, share thoughts and information, explore literature, listen to experts, watch videos, and give reports. Although such integration is desirable in many cases, inquiry must be genuine, worthwhile, and authentic. When integration is forced or contrived simply to include a wide variety of language skills or subjects, it serves no purpose (Shanahan, 2000).

IMPLEMENTING AN INQUIRY APPROACH TO RESEARCH

With so much emphasis on curricular mandates, standards, and accountability through standardized testing, you must give careful consideration to how you implement inquiry learning. On occasion you may assign specific topics, expect students to use multiple resources, and ask them to present information in certain ways so that the students may encounter a variety of processes and subjects. National and state standards that present essential skills and content can provide guides for instruction (Routman, 2000). Pataray-Ching and Roberson (2002) point out that an inquiry perspective should be woven through the curriculum rather than being added to it. They also advise that whole-class inquiries can meet the demands of the required curriculum while allowing students to explore individual inquiries.

A comfortable, stimulating classroom environment supports inquiry learning. Area rugs, plentiful resources, computer access, and secluded places to work, often set off by shelves or partitions, promote independent study in a relaxed atmosphere. Charts that remind students of research procedures, list inquiry-based questions, or

Applications for English Language Learners and Students with Special Needs

Mansukhani (2002) started an Explorers Club in which second language learners acquire information through inquiry, a method that seems particularly effective for students who come from around the world with varying levels of English proficiency. Students improve their English as they become immersed in challenging and meaningful content. Inquiry learning also works for students with special needs in literacy learning by involving them in critical thinking, questioning, and problem solving while providing practice in using language arts (Schmidt, Gillen, Zollo, & Stone, 2002).

suggest ways of reporting findings are also helpful. Figure 12.21 gives some typical inquiry questions (Routman, 2000, pp. 476–477, 495).

Even hallways offer opportunities for students to work quietly alone or in pairs during their investigation and to display their work. One school where students were studying different environments converted its hallways into different habitats by creating a rain forest, a desert, and an arctic landscape.

To guide students in selecting appropriate topics, begin with topics that you wonder about yourself, explaining why you wonder and how you plan to find out more information. You might wonder aloud as you read to them or as you discuss an event or situation that caused you to want to know more. As you model for them, you may awaken their sense of wonder. Most students are curious to know more about topics that are already familiar and interesting to them (Harvey, 1998).

For students to become effective researchers when pursuing compelling topics, you need to teach explicitly the steps of the research process, model ways to use them, provide time for practice, support students' efforts through conferences, and gradually turn over the responsibility for learning to the students (Harvey, 1998; Routman, 2000). In their approach to guiding students to become inquiry-based researchers, Pappas, Kiefer, and Levstik (1999) recommend a three-step procedure that leads to reflective, disciplined inquiry.

1. The first part consists of an investigation based on a question or set of questions that has power for the student or group of students. Once the question is determined, students observe, infer, classify, and hypothesize to analyze data and suggest possible solutions.

FIGURE 12.21 Typical Inquiry Questions

- What are the big ideas and essential questions?
- What do we already know?
- How can we find the information we need?
- How has our thinking changed?
- What did we find that is significant?
- Why is it this way?
- Could it be otherwise?
- What do we still need to know?

2. The second part refers to the need for students to understand the goals and procedures related to their fields of investigation in order to make sense of the information they have acquired.

3. The third part consists of reflection or debriefing, a time for thinking and discussing. During this period, students consider the processes they used, their application to similar problems, and ways to put their conclusions to use.

Reflections

If you were to choose a topic for inquiry, what would it be? Were you ever given opportunities to research topics that interested you? How would selecting your own topic motivate you to conduct more intensive research than a teacher-assigned topic would?

Research

Students need a great deal of instruction before undertaking a research project. They need to know where and how to locate information, how to take notes and organize information, and how to present their findings. Much instruction occurs through modeling the procedures, demonstrating the use of materials, and brainstorming effective ways to present information to an audience. With the help of the media specialist, you can have relevant materials readily available and prepare students for conducting research. You may have to help students identify subtopics within the main topics so that they can organize information, possibly by using semantic maps to classify information and see connections. You may also have to help them narrow a topic that is too broad (for example, from "fish" to "swordfish"). There are many ways to teach beginning research, and Minilesson 12.3 shows one teacher's approach.

RESEARCH METHODS

You need to teach and have students practice the components of the research process before they engage in a large-scale project. You may need to teach them to use the Dewey Decimal System, find reference materials, access nonfiction materials with the card catalog or computer, and use the Internet. You may even need to point out the organization of textbooks so that they know how to use the table of contents, index, glossary, and other features to quickly locate information, as demonstrated in Minilesson 12.3. Setting deadlines helps students complete their investigations in a timely manner.

Students must know how to take notes, either on note cards or in a notebook. They need to decide what information best suits their purposes and jot down main ideas in their own words, giving the source with the page number. Notes may be in the form of lists,

The teacher confers with the media specialist in order to select books for a thematic unit.

Minilesson 12.3

Locating Information in Texts

Mrs. Stone is introducing a theme study on Australia. She has shown a video and read portions of some books on Australia, and students are enthusiastic about knowing more. Mrs. Stone asks them to create a semantic map based on what they already know, and the class eagerly contributes words for the map. Together, she and the students organize the words into six major categories: animals, aborigines, Outback, Great Barrier Reef, big cities, and rain forests.

Taking three sheets of chart paper, Mrs. Stone cuts each in half lengthwise and tapes the six panels to the board. At the top of each panel she writes one of the six topics. She then places the students in groups and gives them scissors, markers, glue, and blank sheets of paper.

MRS. STONE: With our librarian's help, I've gathered together many books about Australia. I'm going to appoint a captain for each group. After I show you what to do, the captains will each select three books from the table in the back of the room and bring them back to the group. Then I want all of you to look through the books and find information related to our six topics. When you find something, write it across the top of one of the sheets of paper. Then cut the strip of paper with writing on it and glue it under the right heading.

Let me show you how it works. I'm going to look in the index in the back of this book for rain forests. Here it is—page 46. I find that the Daintree rain forest is in the northeastern part of Australia. I'll write this information in my own words at the top of a sheet of paper. Now I'll cut off the strip with the writing on it and glue it under Rain Forests. Each of you can find information on any of these six topics, write it down, and put it under the correct heading. We'll see if we can fill up these charts. Does anyone have a question?

PEGGY: Do we have to use our own words, or can we copy it from the book?

MRS. STONE: Try to put it in your own words. You may have to read a whole paragraph to get the information, and that would be too long to copy.

GREG: Suppose we can't find anything.

MRS. STONE: Where might you look to find what you need?

SONJA: I know. You used the index. We could look there first to see if there is something on one of these topics.

MRS. STONE: That's right. Do you remember how to find it and how it is arranged?

MAGGIE: It's in alphabetical order, and it's in the back of the book.

MRS. STONE: Could you look anywhere else?

SABRINA: How about the table of contents?

MRS. STONE: That could help you, too. Where will you find it?

ANNE: In the front of the book, but it's by chapters, not in alphabetical order.

TED: Could we find something in the glossary?

MRS. STONE: What might you find there?

CLAYTON: Maybe the definitions for rain forest or the Great Barrier Reef. And it's in alphabetical order like a dictionary.

MRS. STONE: Good thinking! Remember that these books are all different, so some may have glossaries and indexes and some may not. You might want to see how your book is organized before you use it. What other aids might the author give you?

STEVE: Maybe maps, or captions under pictures.

MRS. STONE: Yes, that's the right idea. See what you can discover about each book.

VICTORIA: If somebody already wrote something and I find the same thing, can I write it too?

MRS. STONE: What do you think about that, class?

TORRIE: No. I don't think we should put the same thing up twice.

CASSIE: Can we borrow books from other groups?

MRS. STONE: If another group wants to trade books with you, that's fine. Any other questions? (pause) All right, then, let's get started.

The captains get the books, and the students begin looking through them to find information on the six topics. Some are easier to find and have longer lists than others, but the students find some information for each topic. Each group then chooses one of the six topics to develop into a presentation for the rest of the class.

What are the students learning?

By making the semantic map from what they already know, they are using key vocabulary (rain forest, Outback) and learning to organize ideas into categories. They are becoming familiar with the organization and features of a variety of informational books as they search through them. Learning is authentic; that is, they have real purposes, not just worksheets, for using indexes and other aids for locating information. In most cases, they are paraphrasing, or learning to put information into their own words. By modeling what is expected, the teacher has helped the class understand what to do. This lesson is particularly effective for kinesthetic learners, who need to move and be active as they learn.

continued

Minilesson 12.3

Locating Information in Texts (*continued*)

After they have completed this task, each group can choose a topic, find additional information on it, and plan a way to present it to the class at a later time. Presentations may be displays, reports, maps, PowerPoint slides, or any other medium that the group chooses. Freedom to choose the best way to present their information promotes creativity and a sense of ownership among group members.

Teaching Tip

When facilitating students' research activities, confer with them often to see what help they need and to assess progress. Provide time for whole-class discussions to allow students to report progress, discuss problems that may arise, and share ideas.

abbreviated text, or some form of graphic organizer—whatever works well enough for the student to recall the information when it is needed. Note taking is not an easy skill, and you may need to model the procedure, thinking aloud about how to condense information and why you include some material and leave out other material.

Make sure students can find and correctly record bibliographic information. Young children may only be able to write the title and the author, but older researchers should also include the publisher and date and place of publication. Point out

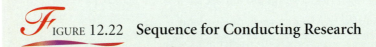

*F*IGURE 12.22 **Sequence for Conducting Research**

Selection of a topic: Consider curriculum mandates, standards, and student interests as you begin. Create a K-W-L chart, semantic map, or other graphic organizer.

Sources of information: Include reference materials, nonfiction books, magazines, resource people, and the Internet. Use the classroom, school library, public library, and community resources.

Gathering information: Find materials, identify knowledgeable individuals, explore the Internet, and locate other resources specifically related to the topic.

Taking notes: Make sure students keep well documented notes from materials and personal interviews.

Organizing material: Have students collect all information and organize it by topics and subtopics.

Presenting results: Although results are often presented as written reports, permit students to choose other options.

that they need this information in case they want to verify their work later. Figure 12.22 shows a typical sequence for conducting research, which can be used for individual, partner, group, or whole-class projects.

One framework for helping students record and organize information is a **data chart**, shown in Figure 12.23. Notice that the data chart begins with what the student already knows (always a good place to start) and provides spaces for entering data from three references. If no information is available from a reference about a topic, the cell is left blank. You can model the use of a data chart by posting the grid on a large sheet of paper and showing students how to complete it. Year-six students in a Melbourne, Australia, classroom were investigating relationships among earth and other heavenly bodies in our solar system, and each student chose a topic to research independently, using an enlarged version of the data chart (approximately 11" by 17"). Jake chose Mars for his topic, and his theme was "to see how Mars compares with Earth." He chose the

$\mathcal{F}$IGURE 12.23   **Data Chart**

DATA CHART

TOPIC:	THEME:			
Subtopics:				
What I Know				
Reference Title: Author: Pages:				
Reference Title: Author: Pages:				
Reference Title: Author: Pages:				

following as subtopics: Location, Surface Features, Weather, Satellites, and Size. At the time one of the authors (Ross) was observing, Jake had completed his data chart and was working on a detailed poster to present his findings to the rest of the class.

Three classrooms illustrate ways that teachers have taught students to use research. Wanting to move her students toward becoming self-regulated learners, Drummond (Perry & Drummond, 2002) helped her second- and third-graders gather information from multiple sources, organize it into a semantic map, write multiple drafts, edit, and publish final reports. These children decided for themselves about what to work on and where, when, and with whom to work, depending on their needs, interests, and available support. Buerger (2002) used a Fact, Question, and Response chart to help her fourth- and fifth-graders gather information from a cover story in *National Geographic for Kids*. The Fact column was for recording important information; the Question column listed questions raised by students as they read; and the Response column allowed them to comment on their reading. In a fifth-grade class, students discovered points of interest for research, learned how published authors wrote about the subject, read widely to build a knowledge base, focused on topics of personal interest, and decided how to organize research data. Some students used writer's notebooks, and others used various organizational frameworks, including data charts and graphics for problem-solution or cause-effect structures (Broaddus & Ivey, 2002).

MATERIALS FOR RESEARCH

Once a topic or question for investigation is assigned or selected, students should consider both primary and secondary source materials to obtain information. Primary research includes personal interviews, letters, surveys, and original documents, whereas secondary research is information based on a primary source, such as videotapes, CD-ROMs, text sets (explained in Chapter 2), encyclopedias, nonfiction trade books, magazines (see Figure 2.10), and the Internet (Harvey, 1998). Many publishers feature nonfiction materials, including National Geographic (1-800-368-2728), which publishes over four hundred nonfiction readers in social studies and science for pre-kindergarten through grade 8; *Time for Kids* (1-800-777-8600), a news magazine with current events and nonfiction; and Teacher Created Materials (1-800-662-4321), which covers reading and writing in science and social studies (also available in Spanish). School libraries, computer labs, and even classrooms equipped with encyclopedias or trade books are good places to begin the investigation, which may eventually extend into the community and the public library, or even beyond. In addition to the materials already mentioned, Figure 12.24 lists free or low-cost, readily available materials that support research.

In addition to materials, students may need a variety of tools to support their research, such as cameras, tape recorders, computers, microscopes, magnifying glasses, and cages for animals. Young researchers should also carry clipboards, recorders, or other notetaking equipment with them and keep notebooks, sets of index cards, or computer files to record information.

REPORTING THE RESULTS

Although many investigations result in written reports, students may choose alternatives, such as making posters, presenting dramas, exhibiting artifacts, or sharing information through musical interpretations. Students vary in their preferred learning styles, with some being linguistically oriented but others finding that their strengths lie in art, music, drama, or some other area. Whenever possible, allow students to choose their preferred method of reporting the results of their research to enable them to use their

$\mathcal{F}$IGURE 12.24   **Materials for Research**

Newspapers provide current information on a wide variety of topics. Many newspapers have Newspaper-in-Education programs that offer newspapers at a discount and give suggestions for using the newspaper in the classroom.

Almanacs publish facts and figures about a particular year. Almanacs are available free or for a low price and provide current information on many topics.

Travel brochures are available for learning about different geographic regions. Students can get them free from travel agents, airlines, and tourist bureaus, or they can send to different countries for brochures and catalogs.

Health information on exercise, nutrition, physical fitness, and effects of drugs is readily available at no charge from departments of health or clinics.

Maps, globes, and atlases are indispensable for researching many topics. City or community maps are usually available free or at low cost from banks or the Chamber of Commerce.

Environmental materials are often available through the Department of Forestry or the Department of Environment and Conservation. These agencies sometimes even supply young trees for students to plant.

Telephone books are useful for contacting sources and getting information. Recently expired phone books are available free from the telephone company and contain information about time zones, government agencies, and additional resources.

Catalogs supply a wide variety of information on almost any subject. They are available at stores, from the Internet, and by calling toll-free numbers.

strengths and their creativity. In any case, students probably need to include some sort of written caption, explanation, directions, or program with their presentation.

If students decide to report their findings in written reports, they should follow the steps outlined in Chapter 8: topic search, drafts, revision, editing, and publishing. Publication can take many forms, such as the following.

Writing

- Stapling the report between two sheets of construction paper
- Fastening the pages with a spiral binding in a more durable cover (perhaps laminated tagboard)
- Sewing the report with dental floss and placing it between two wallpaper-covered matting boards that are bound with tape
- Constructing a flip booklet consisting of three layered sheets of typing paper (preferably of different colors) folded at three-, four-, and five-inch distances from the top and stapled at the top along a common fold (Routman, 1991). The student writes information under each labeled

Reflections

Can you recall a time when you were proud of a final project? What had you done? What made you proud? How did you share your project?

flap. Figure 12.25 shows Baltazer Pascual's flip book entitled *Polar Animals* and what he wrote and illustrated under the flap labeled *Puffling*. Figure 12.26 shows some alternatives to traditional research reports.

When projects are completed, they should be shared. One second-grade class decided the books that they had made about patriotism should go to dentists' offices so that other children could read them while waiting for their appointments. Some reports remain in the classroom for parents and other children to see, whereas others

𝓕IGURE 12.25   **Flip Booklet on Polar Animals**

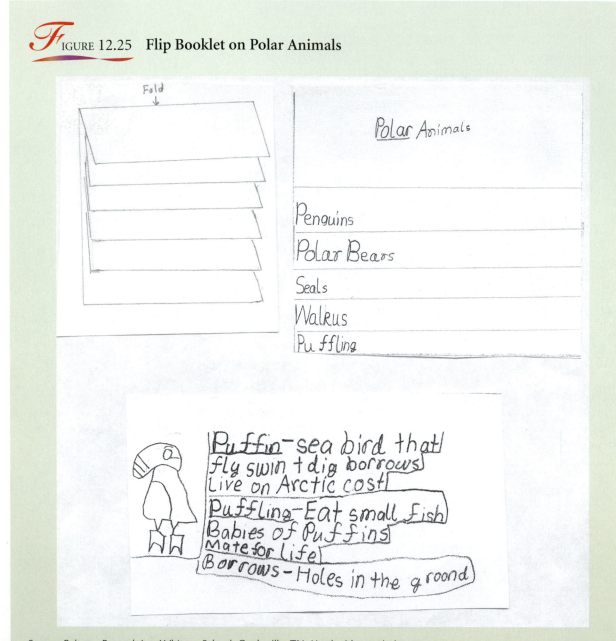

Source: Baltazar Pascual, Jere Whitson School, Cookeville, TN. Used with permission.

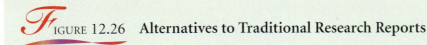

FIGURE 12.26   Alternatives to Traditional Research Reports

Literary Forms

Writing journal and diary entries from particular time periods.

Writing and formatting newspapers from historical or recent events.

Creating time lines to show the sequence of events.

Creating graphic organizers to show relationships (for example, a flow chart to illustrate a process).

Composing annotated, illustrated ABC books with each letter of the alphabet representing something related to the topic. For example, a group of students studying Native Americans identified each letter with a tribe, a cultural artifact, or significant feature.

Art

Making murals, posters, displays, dioramas, models, and illustrated books.

Assembling scrapbooks with photographs, newspaper clippings, and artwork.

Using artifacts for a museum display (described earlier in this chapter). One third-grade class, assisted by the shop teacher, concluded a unit on transportation by constructing models of a train, an airplane, a ship, and a space shuttle.

Oral Presentations

Simulating historical events or scientific processes.

Enacting Readers Theatre scripts, either from published copies or from those written by students.

Debating or engaging in panel discussions.

Role-playing interactions among prominent individuals.

Music and Dance

Composing lyrics and melodies for ballads that represent events in history.

Playing instruments and singing songs.

Dancing folk dances and interpreting situations through modern dance. Some classes use music and dance from other countries as part of their culminating activity.

Playing tapes or CDs of music to set the mood.

Technology

Creating PowerPoint presentations.

Making videotaped presentations.

Using computer graphics for illustrations.

Taping interviews or oral histories.

Broadcasting information on a school radio station.

Posting results on a webpage.

---

go to the library for a wider viewing audience. Parents and other caregivers are sometimes invited to see displays or view performances of music, dance, or drama. Sharing the results is an important part of the process, especially for the students.

Classroom Assessment for Content Area Literacy

You may make your own tests over the material covered to assess student learning and use rubrics to evaluate activities. Consider oral presentations, written reports, entries in learning logs or notebooks, portfolios, and participation in projects for giving grades.

Summary

Content areas are the subjects students learn in school. Literacy in the content areas places new demands on students who may be familiar only with fiction books and basal readers. Students need to see authentic purposes for reading and writing in the content areas so that they realize the value of what they are learning. Textbooks often pose challenges for students, but teachers can also use trade books and the Internet as resource materials.

Each content area differs in the demands it places on readers and writers. Science encourages students to explore, investigate, and collect and analyze data. Students must pay close attention to detail and learn specialized vocabulary. Science journals enable them to record data and activities. Social studies, consisting of history, geography, and sociology, can readily become the core of an integrated curriculum. The arts enhance themes in social studies by offering opportunities for students to create and appreciate the visual arts and to perform music and drama. Textbooks are often difficult for students to read, and a wide variety of multicultural trade books are available for supplementing them. Mathematics deals with problem solving and inquiry. Students need to talk about problem-solving strategies and write explanations to clarify their understanding of math concepts. They learn through solving story problems, investigating real-life experiences, and graphing data.

Students need to know how to apply study strategies and procedures in content area reading. They need to understand the organization and features of their textbooks for learning and retaining information. Four study procedures—anticipation guides, K-W-L, SQ3R, and study guides—can also be helpful. Students can interpret and organize information in graphic forms as graphic organizers, which include attribute maps, time lines, Venn diagrams, pyramids, semantic maps, and flow charts.

Ideally, research begins with inquiry, or a sense of wonder. Students raise questions, seek answers, reflect on their findings, and interpret information. Research is a way to integrate the language arts and the content areas. Teachers need to teach the steps in the research process and model them. The procedure consists of selecting the topic, considering information sources, gathering information, taking notes, organizing material, and presenting results. Data charts help students record and organize information. Many resource materials are available: videos, CD-ROMs, DVD-ROMs, text sets, reference materials, trade books, magazines, the Internet, and free and inexpensive materials such as telephone books and catalogs. Students can report in a variety of ways, including literary reports, artistic representations, music and dance, oral reports, and technology.

Technology

Discussion Questions

1. How can you respond to students' genuine interest in researching a topic that is not part of the mandated curriculum?

2. How does changing from knowledge transmission to inquiry change the role of the teacher? How does this affect the learner?

3. How could you teach U.S. history without a textbook?

4. Figure 12.21 gives a list of typical inquiry questions. What other "big questions" can you add to this list?

5. Look at Figure 12.2 that gives guidelines for teaching in the content areas. As a class, choose the three to five guidelines that you consider most important. Explain your reasons for selecting these.

6. This chapter focuses on four study procedures: anticipation guides, K-W-L, SQ3R, and study guides. What are some other strategies that you have found to be helpful, and how do they work?

7. Why is it important for students to be able to interpret and construct graphic organizers? What kinds might they find outside of school, and where will they find them?

8. Consider the paradigm for content area literacy in Figure 12.1. Working in pairs or small groups, select one of the eight items listed and expand on it in terms of your knowledge and experience. Be prepared to share your ideas with the whole class.

Suggested Activities

1. Look at the classroom vignette at the beginning of the chapter and identify the specific strategies Bob uses when he studies for the test. (You should find at least eleven.)

2. Find a textbook, preferably social studies or science, and make an expository frame. Give the bibliographic information for the textbook and identify the text structure you are using for the frame.

3. Brainstorm at least twenty resources you would like to have in your classroom for inquiry-based learning.

4. Investigate local community or city resources that might provide you with personnel or free and inexpensive materials to support research studies.

5. Several ideas for recording science information in journals are given. Brainstorm other types of science activities that students could record.

6. Make up a story problem for math and ask a child to explain how to solve it.

7. What kinds of math activities might evolve from a circus that is coming to town?

8. Design a classroom setting that would enable students to investigate chosen topics. What resources would you have, and where would you place them?

9. Look at the list of multicultural books for social studies in Figure 12.7. Add five more books to the list, giving statements about the content and their origins.

References

BROADDUS, K., & IVEY, G. (2002). Surprising the writer: Discovering details through research and reading. *Language Arts, 80,* 23–30.

BROMLEY, K. (2000). Integrating language arts with the content areas. In K. D. Wood & T. S. Dickinson (Eds.), *Promoting literacy in grades 4–9* (pp. 220–232). Boston: Allyn & Bacon.

BROMLEY, K., IRWIN-DE VITIS, L., & MODLO, M. (1995). *Graphic organizers.* New York: Scholastic.

BUERGER, M. (2002). Integrating nonfiction reading strategies. *Nonfiction Literacy, 1*(1), 12–13.

BURNS, P., ROE, B., & ROSS, E. (1999). *Teaching reading in today's elementary schools* (7th ed.). Boston: Houghton Mifflin.

COOPER, J. D. (1997). *Literacy: Helping children construct meaning* (3rd ed.). Boston: Houghton Mifflin.

CUNNINGHAM, P., & ALLINGTON, R. (1999). *Classrooms that work* (2nd ed.). New York: Longman.

EANES, R. (1997). *Content area literacy.* Albany, NY: Delmar.

EBBERS, M. (2002). Science text sets: Using various genres to promote literacy and inquiry. *Language Arts, 80,* 40–50.

EL-HINDI, A. (2003). Integrating literacy and science in the classroom: From ecomysteries to Readers Theatre. *The Reading Teacher, 56,* 536–538.

FISHER, A. (2001). Implementing graphic organizer notebooks: The art and science of teaching content. *The Reading Teacher, 55,* 116–120.

FISHER, B. (1995). *Thinking and learning together.* Portsmouth, NH: Heinemann.

FUTURE PROBLEM SOLVING PROGRAM (annual). 2028 Regency Road, Lexington, KY.

GOLDBERG, L. (2003). Easy, colorful graphs. *Instructor, 112*(7), 16–17.

GUILLAUME, A. (1998). Learning with text in the primary grades. *The Reading Teacher, 51,* 476–486.

HARVEY, S. (1998). *Nonfiction matters.* York, ME: Stenhouse.

HARVEY, S. (2002). Nonfiction inquiry: Using real reading and writing to explore the world. *Language Arts, 80,* 12–22.

HERBER, H. (1978). *Teaching reading in content areas* (2nd ed.). Englewood Cliffs, NJ: Prentice Hall.

IRVIN, J. (1998). *Reading and the middle school student* (2nd ed.). Boston: Allyn & Bacon.

MANSUKHANI, P. (2002). The Explorers Club: The sky is no limit for learning. *Language Arts, 80,* 31–39.

McDONALD, J. (1999). Graphs and prediction: Helping children connect mathematics and literature. *The Reading Teacher, 53,* 25–29.

NORTON, D. (2003). *Through the eyes of a child* (6th ed.). Upper Saddle River, NJ: Merrill/Prentice Hall.

OGLE, D. (1986). K-W-L: A teaching model that develops active reading of expository text. *The Reading Teacher, 39,* 564–570.

PAPPAS, C., KIEFER, B., & LEVSTIK, L. (1999). *An integrated language perspective in the elementary school* (3rd ed.). New York: Longman.

PATARAY-CHING, J., & ROBERSON, M. (2002). Misconceptions about a curriculum-as-inquiry framework. *Language Arts, 79,* 498–505.

PEARSON, P. D., & FIELDING, L. (1994). Comprehension instruction. In R. Barr, J. L. Kamil, P. Mosenthal, & P. D. Pearson. (Eds.), *Handbook of reading research* (vol. 2, pp. 815–860). New York: Longman.

PERRY, N., & DRUMMOND, L. (2002). Helping young students become self-regulated researchers and writers. *The Reading Teacher, 56,* 298–310.

POPP, M. (1996). *Teaching language and literature in elementary classrooms.* Mahwah, NJ: Erlbaum.

RICE, D. (2002). Using trade books in teaching elementary science: Facts and fallacies. *The Reading Teacher, 55,* 552–565.

ROBINSON, F. P. (1961). *Effective study* (rev. ed.). New York: Harper & Row.

ROE, B. D., SMITH, S. H., & BURNS, P. C. (2005). *Teaching reading in today's elementary schools* (9th ed.). Boston: Houghton Mifflin.

ROSER, N. L., & KEEHN, S. (2002). Fostering thought, talk, and inquiry: Linking literature and social studies. *The Reading Teacher, 55,* 416–426.

ROUTMAN, R. (1991). *Invitations.* Portsmouth, NH: Heinemann.

ROUTMAN, R. (2000). *Conversations.* Portsmouth, NH: Heinemann.

RUDDELL, R. (2002). *Teaching children to read and write.* Boston: Allyn & Bacon.

SAMPSON, M. B. (2002). Confirming a K-W-L: Considering the source. *The Reading Teacher, 55,* 528–529.

SCHMIDT, P. R., GILLEN, S., ZOLLO, T. C., & STONE, R. (2002). Literacy learning and scientific inquiry: Children respond. *The Reading Teacher, 55,* 534–548.

SEIFERT, P. (1999). Inquiry in the kindergarten. In J. W. Lindfors & J. S. Townsend (Eds.), *Language arts: Learning through dialogue* (pp. 103–118). Urbana, IL: National Council of Teachers of English.

SHANAHAN, T. (2000). Reading-writing relationships, thematic units, inquiry learning . . . In pursuit of effective integrated literacy instruction. In N. Padak, T. Rasinsky, J. Peck, B. W. Church, G. Fawcett, J. Hendershot, et al. (Eds.), *Distinguished educators on reading* (pp. 305–316). Newark, DE: International Reading Association.

SILBEY, R. (2003). Math out loud! *Instructor, 112*(7), 24–26.

STRICKLAND, D., GANSKE, K., & MONROE, J. (2002). *Supporting struggling readers and writers.* Portland,

ME: Stenhouse; Newark, DE: International Reading Association.

WALPOLE, S. (1998/1999). Changing texts, changing thinking: Comprehension demands of new science textbooks. *The Reading Teacher, 52,* 358–369.

WELBES, J. (2003). One way for kids to learn their math: Write about it. *Pioneer Press.* http://www.twincities.com/mld/pioneerpress/living/education/7104283.htm

Books for Children and Adolescents Cited in This Chapter

AVI. (2002). *Crispin: The cross of lead.* New York: Hyperion.

BAILEY, L. (1990). *Mei Ming and the dragon's daughter.* New York: Scholastic.

BRIDGES, R. (1999). *Through my eyes.* New York: Scholastic.

COERR, E. (1993). *Sadako.* New York: Putnam.

COHN, A. (1993). *From sea to shining sea.* New York: Scholastic.

COUSINS, M. (1983). *The boy in the Alamo.* San Antonio: Corona.

CUSHMAN, K. (1994). *Catherine, called Birdy.* New York: Clarion.

DANTICAT, E. (2003). *Behind the mountains.* New York: Scholastic.

FARMER, N. (1996). *A girl named Disaster.* Danbury, CT: Orchard.

FLEMING, D. (1992). *Count!* New York: Scholastic.

FREEDMAN, R. (1980). *Immigrant kids.* New York: Dutton.

FRITZ, J. (1986). *Make way for Sam Houston.* New York: Putnam.

GARLAND, S. (1993). *The lotus seed.* San Diego: Harcourt Brace Jovanovich.

GARZA, C. L. (1990). *Family pictures.* San Francisco: Children's Book Press.

GEORGE, J. C. (1983). *The talking earth.* New York: Harper & Row.

GIFF, P. R. (2000). *Nory Ryan's song.* New York: Delacorte.

HALL, D. (1979). *Ox-cart man.* New York: Viking.

HALPERN, J. (1998). *A look at spiders.* Austin, TX: Steck-Vaughn.

HENRY, J. (1988). *Log cabin in the woods: A true story about a pioneer boy.* New York: Macmillan.

HESSE, K. (1992). *Letters from Rifka.* New York: Holt.

KNIGHT, M. B. (1992). *Talking walls.* Gardiner, ME: Tilbury House.

KRUMGOLD, J. (1953). *. . . And now Miguel.* New York: Crowell.

LOWRY, L. (1989). *Number the stars.* Boston: Houghton Mifflin.

MACAULAY, D. (1988). *The way things work.* Boston: Houghton Mifflin.

MAZZOLA, F., JR. (1997). *Counting is for the birds.* Watertown, MA: Charlesbridge.

O'DELL, S. (1970). *Sing down the moon.* Boston: Houghton Mifflin.

PARK, L. (2001). *A single shard.* New York: Clarion.

PAULSEN, G. (1988). *Dogsong.* New York: Bradbury.

PERLMAN, J. (1995). *The emperor penguin's new clothes.* New York: Viking.

PINKNEY, J. (1997). *Rikki Tikki Tavi.* New York: Morrow.

PLATT, R. (1992). *Stephen Biesty's incredible cross-sections.* New York: Knopf.

POLACCO, P. (1994). *Pink and Say.* New York: Philomel.

POLACCO, P. (1998). *Thank you, Mr. Falker.* New York: Philomel.

RINGGOLD, F. (1993). *Dinner at Aunt Connie's house.* New York: Hyperion.

RYAN, P. M., & PALLOTTA, J. (1996). *The crayon counting book.* Watertown, MA: Charlesbridge.

SAY, A. (1993). *Grandfather's journey.* Boston: Houghton Mifflin.

SHEA, P. D. (1995). *The whispering cloth.* Honesdale, PA: Boyds Mills.

STAPLES, S. F. (1989). *Shabanu: Daughter of the wind.* New York: Knopf.

STEPTOE, J. (1987). *Mufaro's beautiful daughters.* New York: Lothrop, Lee & Shepard.

WHEATLEY, N., & RAWLINS, D. (1988). *My place.* North Blackburn, Victoria, Australia: HarperCollins.

YEP, L. (1975). *Dragonwings.* New York: Harper & Row.

YIN. (2001). *Coolies.* New York: Philomel.

chapter 13

ASSESSMENT AND INTERVENTION

LEARNER OBJECTIVES

At the conclusion of this chapter

YOU SHOULD BE ABLE TO

1. Understand some features of assessment and how it is linked to instruction.

2. Describe a variety of ways to assess students in the classroom.

3. Describe some types of assessment appropriate for the different language arts.

4. Name some features of formal assessment.

5. Appreciate the need for providing interventions for struggling students.

6. Discuss how to report student progress.

7. Identify the following terms that are defined or explained in this chapter:

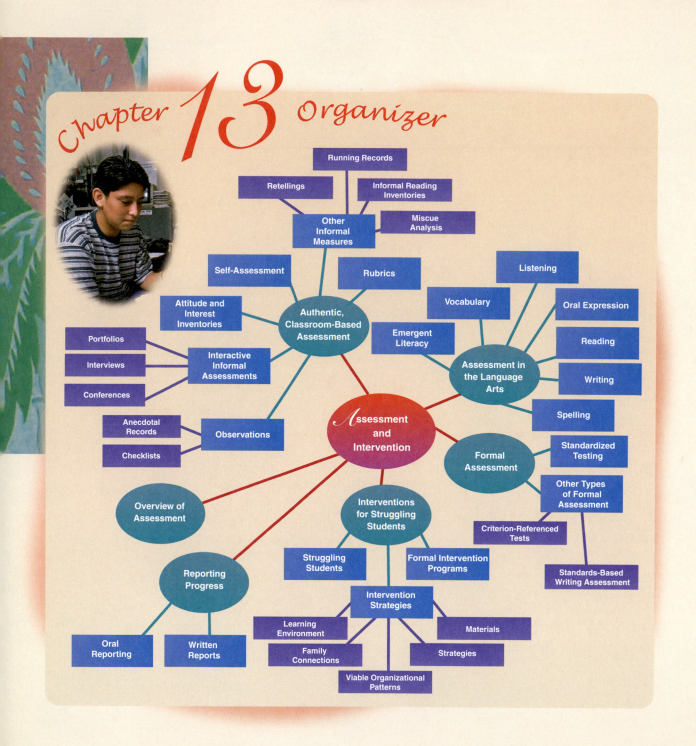

*T*WO TEACHERS are holding a discussion about how to arrive at grades for the report cards that must be distributed later in the week.

JENNIFER: My students have really done well this grading period, but it's still hard for me to know how to put grades on their report cards. Although it would take more time, I almost wish we had narrative reports in order to avoid giving letter grades.

HUGH: It used to be easier when we simply gave tests and averaged the grades. There was no doubt about report card grades then, but those grades didn't tell the whole story.

JENNIFER: That was so unfair! Some students freeze when they see a test and don't do their best, but they show what they can do through projects and other activities.

HUGH: You're right, of course. Pedro hardly knows any English, so he wouldn't do well on a written test, but he's a bright kid and is learning fast. I want to give him credit for that.

JENNIFER: Language is the hardest for me to grade because there are so many considerations. I look through their portfolios to see what progress they've made, consider their journal writing, and sit in on their literature circles. Somehow I pull all of that together, analyze it, and reach a ballpark estimate.

HUGH: I've kept records of conferences we held during writing workshop, and the kids and I developed a writing rubric that will help. Have you tried self-assessment?

JENNIFER: Yes, and it's definitely part of their grades. The students are getting better at understanding their own strengths—and at recognizing some areas that need improvement. I taught a couple of minilessons on how to assess yourself, but I still needed to meet with a few students individually who don't seem to understand. Some don't realize they need to do better, and others aren't aware of how well they are doing.

HUGH: I feel that we actually communicate better with parents during conferences. My students usually sit in on the conferences and are proud to show their portfolios. I believe their parents understand what their children can do better from conferences than report card grades.

What's happening here?

The teachers are expressing their desire to give report card grades that reflect what their students actually know and can do. They are considering a variety of assessments other than tests that can be used in language arts to determine grades, and they realize that a parent-student-teacher conference, supported with a portfolio, is an effective way to communicate information.

Assessment plays an essential role in the educational process. Over the past decades, it has changed dramatically, moving from testing highly structured, quantifiable skills with mastery tests to a more authentic, classroom-based perspective. Today the pendulum appears to be swinging back to more skill-based assessment as teachers follow standards-based curricula and prepare their students to take standardized tests. The federal government is demanding more standardized testing so that schools can be held accountable for student achievement. Teachers, however, have retained many desirable alternative assessments, such as observations, rubrics, portfolios, and conferences. These types of assessment can give you insights into how your students learn and can help guide instruction.

By observing attitudes, behaviors, and performance, you consider your students' strengths and needs as you develop the curriculum. You can plan interventions for those who are struggling in order to help them succeed, and you can prepare students for taking standardized tests that they may find difficult and unfamiliar. You need to use a variety of tools to measure student progress since no single form of assessment tells the whole story. This chapter discusses a variety of classroom-based assessments, information about formal tests, types of interventions that are likely to help struggling learners, and ways to report student progress.

*O*verview of Assessment

COLLECTING INFORMATION about student strengths and weaknesses is known as **assessment.** A difficult and complex procedure, assessment serves two major purposes: to guide instruction and to satisfy requirements for accountability. **Authentic assessment** occurs in the context of meaningful, real-world tasks and helps teachers understand the needs of their students. **Formal assessment**, on the other hand, usually consists of standardized tests that report student achievement for accountability purposes. Both are necessary, but authentic assessment is more useful for classroom teachers. Some writers use the term *assessment* to refer also to evaluations or judgments that are made after data have been gathered (Harris & Hodges, 1995). In this chapter, we use *assessment* to mean both the gathering of data and its analysis. **Evaluation** is defined as a judgment of performance (Harris & Hodges, 1995); it is a summation used on completion of instruction for assigning grades or determining grade placement (Cobb, 2003/2004).

For assessment to be useful to the classroom teacher, it must be linked to instruction (Cobb, 2003/2004; Fountas & Pinnell, 1996; Serafini, 2000/2001; Valencia, 2000). Teachers who carefully observe and assess their students' progress, needs, and difficulties are able to plan instruction accordingly. Their informal assessments provide information that helps them make informed decisions and guide their teaching. Figure 13.1 shows interactions between assessment and instruction.

To further illustrate the relationship between instruction and assessment, consider this example. Mr. Elsahwy notices that his students are confused about when to use *its* or *it's* (observes a need), so he teaches a minilesson on the difference between the two (gives instruction). He provides opportunities for students to apply their understanding as they write in their journals and during class activities (students practicing skills or strategies). He observes their use of the words (assessment) and then decides to either (1) reteach the lesson in a different way to the whole class, (2) provide corrective instruction for a few students who still don't understand, or (3) move on.

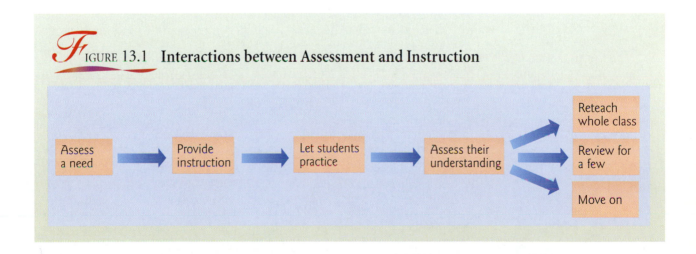

*F*IGURE 13.1   **Interactions between Assessment and Instruction**

Researchers have identified some general principles or guidelines for authentic, or classroom-based, assessment (Ruddell, 2002; Salinger, 1998; Searfoss, Readence, & Mallette, 2001; Tierney, 1998). They appear in Figure 13.2.

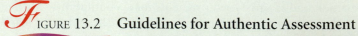

Figure 13.2   Guidelines for Authentic Assessment

■ *Make assessment continuous:* Assessment is more than giving tests and averaging scores to get a grade. Opportunities for assessment occur daily as you observe students' behaviors, check samples of their work, involve them in discussions, and confer with them. Assessment should continue over a period of time in a variety of circumstances.

■ *Use a variety of assessment tools and strategies:* A single test is inadequate for determining what students know. The measures given later in this chapter, such as rubrics, running records, and checklists, provide valuable information.

■ *Encourage student participation:* Let students share the responsibility for assessing their work so that they grow in their understanding of their strengths and needs. They can complete self-assessment checklists, help construct rubrics, and decide what to include in their portfolios. Let assessment be a collaborative endeavor.

■ *Record observations:* Although you think you will remember what you observed, you may not recall exactly what a student did or when he did it. It is not necessary to record everything (That would be impossible!), but you may want to document evidence that reveals a student's growth over time or that helps determine the grades you give.

■ *Keep a file folder on each student:* Your file folders are useful for keeping track of progress and can include work samples and records of informal assessments.

■ *Make assessment as close as possible to the task being assessed:* To provide information about what students know and can do, assess them while they are engaged in an activity. If you want to know how well they write, observe them as they write instead of giving a test on isolated writing skills.

■ *Provide a supportive environment:* Make assessment a comfortable, collaborative venture where students are free to make approximations until they are able to do the task exactly right. Avoid creating stress.

■ *Focus assessment on instructional goals:* Align your assessments with instructional goals and curriculum mandates so that students know what is expected of them. Help them to understand the reasons for your assessments and see their purposes. Make sure that what you are assessing is worth doing.

■ *Look for strengths, not just weaknesses:* Although you need to recognize needs, identify strengths. Then base your instruction on students' strengths. Look first at what they *can* do.

Applications *for English Language Learners and Students with Special Needs*

Be sensitive to the special needs of diverse learners. You may want to team with their special teachers in collecting data and assessing progress and needs. A student who has great difficulty writing may dictate to a teacher instead of writing, and an ELL student may convey knowledge in her native language to an interpreter or by drawing or graphing responses. Allow ELLs to use bilingual dictionaries when answering test questions, and shorten portions of some tests whenever possible. Some students may need to answer orally to show their knowledge, and some simply need more time to complete tasks.

Authentic, Classroom-Based Assessment

GOOD TEACHERS have always observed their students closely and found ways to assess their progress. In this section, we consider some types of assessment for you to use in your classroom. They are divided into six categories: observations of student work with notes, checklists, and anecdotal records; conferences, interviews, and portfolios; attitude and interest inventories; self-assessments; retellings, running records, informal reading inventories, and miscue analysis; and rubrics that can be used with a number of activities.

Observations

One of the most useful forms of assessment is **observation**, which you can use daily in a variety of ways. Notice what your students are doing—or not doing—when they are supposed to be engaged in learning tasks. You may see that Darryl is eagerly beginning a first draft of a new story, that Dakota has chosen a book that may be too difficult for her, that Ricardo isn't paying attention, and that Kaitlyn looks puzzled. Although none of these observations may appear to be significant, over time they may form patterns that you need to address. Some guidelines for observing appear in Figure 13.3.

Teaching Tip

In a busy classroom, it is hard to find time to write down observations. Try this: Jot a comment on a sticky note, temporarily attach it to a clipboard, and later place it inside the student's file. A series of dated notes provides a record of what each child is doing.

*F*IGURE 13.3 **Guidelines for Observations**

- *Record observations whenever possible:* Write the name of the student, the date, and the behavior you observed.

- *Collect data that indicate growth:* Look for breakthroughs in learning, ability to construct meaning, application of background knowledge, and effective oral expression.

- *Look for patterns of behavior that may affect learning:* Notice a student's preferred learning style, ability to work in groups, level of concentration, and similar attributes.

- *Observe throughout the year:* A few occasional observations are insufficient for providing information. Find a systematic way to record observations during the school year.

- *Include all students in your observations:* Some students are attention seekers, whereas others quietly work on task. Observe *all* of the students.

CHECKLISTS

Checklists provide a structured way of recording observations and are useful for any subject at any grade level. They should show what students know and can do when engaged in authentic literacy tasks. Simply glancing over the list enables you to see a student's present status and if he is making progress. A checklist should include those items that are critical for your purpose and should not include too many criteria. Students can contribute to the checklist by adding items that reflect their personal goals. Checklists need a primary focus with related criteria, as well as a rating scale.

Appropriate topics for checklists include those listed in Figure 13.4.

The rating scale may be from one (low achievement) to ten (high achievement), or simply + for *doing well*, 0 for *adequate*, or − for *needing improvement*. The checklist should be completed on a regular basis, such as for the duration of a project or for each grading period. You can file checklists along with other records of student achievement to use as one source for reporting progress.

The teacher is carefully observing her students as they work. She fills out a checklist for one of the students.

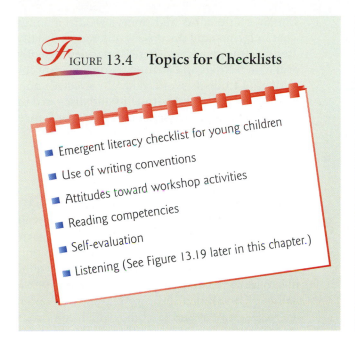

FIGURE 13.4 **Topics for Checklists**

- Emergent literacy checklist for young children
- Use of writing conventions
- Attitudes toward workshop activities
- Reading competencies
- Self-evaluation
- Listening (See Figure 13.19 later in this chapter.)

FIGURE 13.5 **Questions for Anecdotal Records**

- What is this student able to do?
- How does this student read, write, work in groups, contribute to projects, or participate in other tasks that may guide instruction?
- What does the student's attitude indicate about her growth or progress?
- What does this student know, and what questions does she have about class work?
- What help does this student need?

ANECDOTAL RECORDS

Longer than a quick note during an observation or a mark on a checklist, **anecdotal records** are informal observations about how students are responding to instruction, what they are learning, and particular behaviors or actions that might help teachers gain insights (Winograd & Arrington, 1999). You should take anecdotal records while students are actually working, and you should focus on such questions as those in Figure 13.5.

Anecdotal records can be time-consuming to write, so they should be as simple as possible. You may want to use a form with the child's name, the date, and the topic (such as fluency or literature response).

Interactive Informal Assessments

Talking with students often reveals important information about their comprehension, attitudes, interests, and concerns that you may not otherwise realize. While

Teaching Tip

One way to record and organize anecdotal records is to write them on 3″ x 5″ or 4″ x 6″ cards and place them in a file box that has dividers with children's names on them in alphabetical order. You could also record entries in a loose-leaf notebook so that you can remove full sheets of paper and place them in student folders, add more paper as needed, and easily reorganize for new students or students who withdraw.

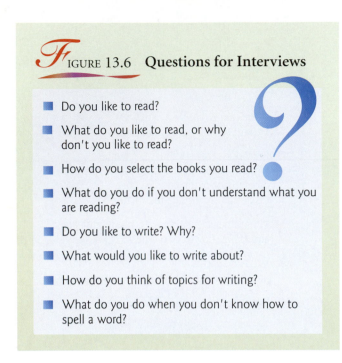

$\mathcal{F}$IGURE 13.6 **Questions for Interviews**

- Do you like to read?
- What do you like to read, or why don't you like to read?
- How do you select the books you read?
- What do you do if you don't understand what you are reading?
- Do you like to write? Why?
- What would you like to write about?
- How do you think of topics for writing?
- What do you do when you don't know how to spell a word?

similar, conferences and interviews differ somewhat in format and purpose. Conferences usually are academic in nature, whereas interviews usually deal with feelings and attitudes. Portfolios are collections of students' work, generally selected cooperatively by you and the students and discussed in order to make valid assessments of performance and progress.

CONFERENCES

A **conference** is a discussion between you and a student about student work. It can provide you with information about what the student is learning, areas where the student needs help, how you can help the student, and what the student would like to learn next (Winograd & Arrington, 1999). Salinger (1998) identifies two reasons for conferences, assessment and teaching, which can occur during the same conference, if necessary. You and your student are likely to be focusing on a piece of writing or a reading selection at a conference. During the discussion, you can informally assess the student's knowledge, and at the same time take advantage of teachable moments to clarify or extend understanding.

You may hold conferences during reading and writing workshops, but you may need them at other times as well. They may be scheduled so that students can prepare for them and bring their work, or they may be spontaneous when you or a student senses a need. Sometimes a small-group conference is appropriate if students have similar concerns about their work. Conferences may last only a few minutes, and notes taken during conferences should be added to students' files. For students to share their thoughts openly and honestly, hold conferences in a secure, comfortable manner (Winograd & Arrington, 1999).

INTERVIEWS

Interviews are usually structured around predetermined questions that can reveal information about what students are thinking and how they are learning. Questions may center around attitudes and behaviors, such as those found in Figure 13.6 (Salinger, 1998). Conferences and interviews can create a close bond between you and a student and bring to both of you a better appreciation of the other.

PORTFOLIOS

A **portfolio** is a carefully selected, organized collection of a student's work accumulated over a period of time. Portfolios appear in a variety of forms and serve many purposes (Winograd & Arrington, 1999). They are essentially a display of what children are learning and have learned (Searfoss, Readence, & Mallett, 2001), and, for

A student and a teacher are looking through a portfolio that contains examples of the student's work.

many, portfolios are a way of assessing student growth (Atwell, 1998; Graves, 1994; Ruddell, 2002). Courtney and Abodeeb (1999) claim that viewing them as collections and reflections of a learner's work is their unifying image. Although portfolios require time and effort, they have a number of advantages (see Figure 13.7).

Selection of items for inclusion in portfolios is usually a collaboration between you and the student. You may guide student selection, particularly at first, until criteria for selection are determined. These might include representation of the student's best work, consistency with the learner's goals, and relevance to the curriculum. Some portfolios may focus on a single reading or writing task and show the student's development over time (Searfoss, Readence, & Mallett, 2001), whereas others may include a wide variety of artifacts. Instead of including only the best piece of writing, some portfolios include drafts leading up to the final draft to show the writer's process for developing the piece. When selecting items to include, the student should justify in writing why the selection was made (Graves, 1994). Telling why the piece was selected causes the student to reflect on its significance and see how it indicates

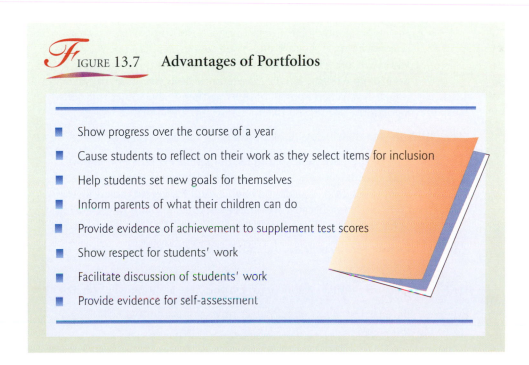

FIGURE 13.7   Advantages of Portfolios

- Show progress over the course of a year
- Cause students to reflect on their work as they select items for inclusion
- Help students set new goals for themselves
- Inform parents of what their children can do
- Provide evidence of achievement to supplement test scores
- Show respect for students' work
- Facilitate discussion of students' work
- Provide evidence for self-assessment

growth, originality, a breakthrough, or something else. Figure 13.8 is a form that students could use for this purpose.

Implementing portfolios should be a gradual process or it could seem overwhelming. Parents and students both need to understand what you are attempting, and you might begin by simply saving some of the students' pieces and placing them in folders. You may want to start by focusing on a single topic or skill, such as writing. During minilessons similar to Minilesson 13.1, you could introduce your class to the basic concept and tell them to start thinking about what they would like to include. You might begin your own portfolio, share it with the class, and explain why you selected each artifact. As you begin turning more of the responsibility over to the students, you might schedule individual conferences to work with students on their selections and organization. A table of contents helps locate materials easily. They should know that you, their peers, and their parents are likely to see their portfolios, so they should try to make them neat, well organized, attractive, and representative of their best work.

Portfolios can take many forms. A three-ring binder is useful because you can remove or insert pages as needed, and you can use dividers to set off different sections. Accordian-pleated folders work well because they expand, and simple folders with closed ends can also be used. One teacher used covered pizza boxes, and another used cereal boxes. You may want to try several types of containers until you find what

Minilesson 13.1

Introduction to Portfolios

TEACHER: Today I'd like to share something with you that I've been doing. In this folder, I have a few things I've been working on, things that I've selected because they are important to me. Here is a poem I wrote while we were writing our poems together, and this is a picture I drew to go with the poem. I wrote some thoughts about my favorite books, too. When I put all of this together, I have something called a portfolio. Would you like to make your own portfolios?

The children nod their heads, look puzzled, or raise their hands.

TEACHER: I know you have some questions, but let me explain a little more. Each of you would have your own portfolio, and you could select what to put in it. You should have a good reason for including each piece, however, because we don't want the portfolios to get too big. What would you like to include?

MICKEY: I wrote a really neat story about an avalanche. Could I put that in my portfolio?

TEACHER: Of course—that's a good idea. Do you have a reason why you like it?

MICKEY: Because I used lots of neat descriptive words and told how dangerous it was.

$\mathcal{F}$IGURE 13.8   **Reasons for Portfolio Inclusions**

Name _____   Date _____

Name of piece selected _____

I selected this piece because _____

_____

_____

TEACHER: Good. Put your reason in your portfolio along with the story. Does anyone else have an idea?

BETSY: I made a time line for the research I was doing on the Civil War. I worked really hard on it, and I like the way it turned out.

TEACHER: That's fine. I want all of you to be thinking of something you want to include and be able to tell why it's important to you. You may each select a folder and decorate the cover. Think about what you want to put in it, and we'll talk more about this tomorrow.

What are the students learning?

When they are asked to include their work in portfolios, the students learn that their work is valued. Selecting artifacts causes them to reflect on what they have done well and motivates them to produce good-quality work that is worth adding to their portfolios. When they realize that their portfolios may be viewed by others, they may want to organize and illustrate them. Their self-esteem improves as they become aware of their progress through the year.

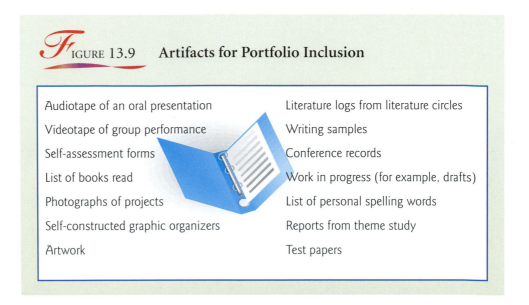

FIGURE 13.9   Artifacts for Portfolio Inclusion

Audiotape of an oral presentation   Literature logs from literature circles

Videotape of group performance   Writing samples

Self-assessment forms   Conference records

List of books read   Work in progress (for example, drafts)

Photographs of projects   List of personal spelling words

Self-constructed graphic organizers   Reports from theme study

Artwork   Test papers

works best for your class. Figure 13.9 shows some artifacts students can include in their portfolios.

Ruddell (2002) discusses two types of portfolio evaluation—formative and summative. A formative evaluation, or assessment, occurs during conferences when you discuss the child's ongoing work, perhaps by comparing a piece of writing that is in development to an earlier piece to see what progress has been made. Summative, or overall, portfolio evaluation occurs at periodic intervals throughout the school year to determine progress toward instructional goals. Summative evaluation often coincides with preparation for report cards or parent conferences.

Attitude and Interest Inventories

Knowing how a student feels about literacy and what topics are of interest helps you know how to approach reading and writing tasks and select materials that are likely to motivate students. By carefully observing students and talking with them informally, you can gain some knowledge about attitudes and interests, but an **inventory** or survey can provide specific information that is helpful for making decisions about

Applications **for English Language Learners**

Alternative assessments often work well for ELLs. Classroom Vignette 13.1 shows how a doctoral student uses an interest and attitude survey with two Spanish-speaking boys.

Classroom Vignette 13.1

Lance Jasitt is tutoring two Guatemalan brothers, ages eight and ten, who have recently arrived in the United States. The boys cannot read or write in either English or Spanish, the language spoken at home. Despite their lack of knowledge of English, they find themselves immersed in an English-speaking community and enrolled in a school where most of their peers and all of the teaching staff are English-only speakers.

Over the course of six months, Lance uses a variety of informal assessment tools to plan instruction to help the boys develop basic literacy skills. He begins by developing and administering the Informal Literacy Stance and Interest Assessment for Elementary-Level English and Spanish Students. (See Figure 13.10 for the first portion of this assessment. The remainder gives additional choices of topics for reading and writing.) Each boy completes this simple survey, dictated in Spanish, by circling the appropriate and generally understood smiley-face response. The results provide Lance with insights for the selection

of quality literature to support his instruction, and the assessment provides each student with one of his first successful test-taking experiences.

Once complete, the survey reveals that even though the boys show a strong interest in books and writing, they are aware that they are behind in literacy skills. This assessment indicates that although they enjoy looking at books, they may not have had the benefits of living in a print-rich environment and being read to by adults. The boys are clearly at risk for reading failure, but the inventory also indicates that they are eager to learn.

What's happening here?

A caring tutor with some knowledge of Spanish begins working with the boys by giving them a "test" that they are able to complete successfully, thus raising their self-esteem. He learns about their feelings toward reading and writing, as well as their interests, so he can personalize their tutoring program. As a result, both boys begin making progress toward acquiring literacy skills.

methods and materials. In Classroom Vignette 13.1, the teacher uses such an inventory with his students.

Self-Assessment

An important aspect of assessment is student **self-assessment,** the process of having students judge their own knowledge and abilities. They are thus more able to become

Teaching Tip

Give students 3" × 5" or 4" × 6" cards and ask them to evaluate themselves at the end of a lesson or a project. On one side, they write "What I learned," and on the other side, "What I still need to know." They become more aware of what they have learned and also give you direction for future lessons.

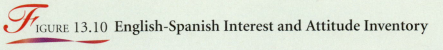

FIGURE 13.10 English-Spanish Interest and Attitude Inventory

Informal Literacy Stance and Interest Assessment for Elementary-Level English and Spanish Students			
When someone reads a book to you, how do you feel? ¿Cuando alguien te lee un cuento, cómo te sientes?		🙁	🙂
Do you read well? ¿Tú lees bien?		🙁	🙂
Do you read at home? ¿Tú lees en casa?		🙁	🙂
Do you like to read: ¿Te gustas leer:	books? libros?	🙁	🙂
	magazines? revistas?	🙁	🙂
	newspapers? periódicos?	🙁	🙂
Are you a good writer? ¿Tú escribes bien?		🙁	🙂
Do you write at home? ¿Tú escribes en casa?		🙁	🙂
Do you like to read and write about: ¿Te gusta leer y escribir acerca de:	your country? tu país?	🙁	🙂
	your family? tu familia?	🙁	🙂
	your friends? tus amigos?	🙁	🙂

Source: Lance Jasitt, Tennessee Technological University, Cookeville, TN (2003). Used with permission.

F IGURE 13.11 **Procedure for Self-Assessment**

1. Identify the activity to be assessed, explain to the students the purpose for judging their own work, and decide together which criteria to use.

2. Let the students brainstorm appropriate criteria. Encourage them to be specific.

3. From their list of ideas, let the class select those to include with consideration for learning outcomes, grade level, past experience, and what is manageable.

4. Discuss how the criteria will be measured, such as with a rating scale or simply the presence or absence of a criterion.

5. Select two or three students to develop a form to use.

aware of what they know, how they are doing, and how they learn best (van Kraayenoord, 2003). Students are empowered as learners when they help set their own criteria and use them to assess their work (Fryar, 2003). In her classroom, Fryar (2003) teaches her students how to assess themselves by involving them in the steps shown in Figure 13.11.

You need to provide training before students can judge their work effectively. They may have little insight into reading and writing processes at first. For example, they may evaluate their reading in terms of how many books they read and base their writing assessment on how many pages they write or the quality of their handwriting. You can guide students by modeling ways to critique your own writing during a minilesson, analyzing techniques authors use in trade books, and letting students assess their work during individual or small-group conferences.

A simple way to self-assess is to use the sample format in Figure 13.12, which emphasizes what children know and can do. Too often children learn about their inadequacies and mistakes from red-marked papers, but a form such as this builds a sense of self-worth, along with developing powers of self-reflection. Janet Ross, a literacy leader, uses the shape of a hand as a guide for having students evaluate their writing in the lower grades. The children look at each finger to check their pieces before they finish (see Figure 13.13).

Van Kraayenoord (2003) sees two major advantages to self-assessment: Students develop a sense of ownership and a sense of responsibility. Ownership develops as students participate in the assessment, thinking about the quality of their

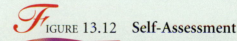

F IGURE 13.12 **Self-Assessment**

What Heather knows about using capital letters:

1. I know to begin each sentence with a capital letter.

2. I know people's names begin with capital letters.

3. Names of cities and states begin with capitals.

4. Put important words in titles in capital letters.

5. When *I* is by itself, make *I* a capital letter.

6. I can use capital letters right most of the time.

FIGURE 13.13 Self-Evaluation Form for Writing

Do my sentences . . .

Have an end mark?

Have space between words?

Look right? (Spelling/Punctuation)

Make sense?

Begin with a capital letter?

Five Finger Check for Writing

Source: Janet Ross. Jere Whitson School, Cookeville, TN. Used with permission.

Reflections

Reflect on your attitudes and performance in the course you are taking. How would you assess yourself? What successes have you achieved, and how could you have done better?

work and reflecting on what they know and can do. They become aware of their strengths and areas in which they could improve. Responsibility means that students have control of and authority over their own learning. They are involved in setting goals and making choices and decisions. Instead of passively receiving a grade from you, they have a say in evaluating their progress. Self-assessments should be part of students' grades if they are to be taken seriously.

Other Informal Measures

Many teachers use retellings, running records, informal reading inventories, and miscue analysis to gather informal assessment data. These measures are discussed in this section.

RETELLINGS

Retellings assess a student's comprehension of a story. The student either listens to a story or reads it, and then you ask the student to retell the story in sequence (Fountas & Pinnell, 1996). You may tape and analyze the retelling according to the criteria in Figure 13.14.

Students attempt to retell the story on their own, but you may offer prompts to remind them of portions they omitted. You may ask, "What happened after Jake broke the chair?" or "Do you remember what happened when the train blew its whistle?" Students can also write their retellings, but they are not likely to recall as much information as when they tell the stories orally (Glazer, 1998). Salinger (1998) suggests folding paper into thirds and asking young children to draw something about the beginning, middle, and end of the story. If able, they would also write a sentence about the story. For older students, completing a story framework that focuses on story elements (see Figure 2.2 in Chapter 2) and constructing story maps or webs (see Figure 8.2 in Chapter 8) are two additional options for retellings.

FIGURE 13.14 Criteria for Evaluating Retellings

- Accurate reporting of events
- Understanding of the main idea of the story
- Use of words and phrases directly from the text
- Inclusion of characters and setting
- Use of details
- Connections to personal knowledge

RUNNING RECORDS

A **running record** is a means for documenting a child's reading of a text in order to find the level of difficulty and analyze reading behaviors. It provides quantitative information (scores that determine whether the material is too difficult, too easy, or at the child's instructional level), as well as qualitative information derived from analyzing reading behaviors. You need to consider the child's ability to apply strategies and use semantic (meaning), syntactic (structure), and graphophonic (visual information) cues (see Chapter 7 for more on these cues). Each incorrect attempt or self-correction provides information about how the child is thinking during the reading process. You can use this information to help you identify a reader's strengths and weaknesses and plan appropriate instruction (Fountas & Pinnell, 1996).

The procedure requires training and practice, but with experience you can take running records quickly and easily. As the child reads, you and the child look at the same book, while you observe closely and mark behaviors in code on a sheet of paper. For each correct response, make a check mark. Other marks are used to indicate substitutions, words that are told to the student, omissions, insertions, repetitions, and self-corrections. By following a simple formula, you can determine the rate of accuracy (Fountas & Pinnell, 1996). Running records can be used with other tools to assess progress.

As a child reads, the teacher is taking a running record by placing check marks on a paper that represent what the child has read.

Janet Ross, literacy leader at an elementary school, took the running record shown in Figure 13.15. The student's score was 91 percent, which placed him at his instructional level. Janet observed that he was able to chunk known components to decode words. He also self-corrected four of his seven miscues (indicated by *sc*) for an acceptable one-to-two ratio, thus indicating he was monitoring his reading to obtain meaning.

INFORMAL READING INVENTORIES

An **informal reading inventory** (IRI) is a series of graded passages, increasing in difficulty, used to determine a child's reading level for both word identification and

FIGURE 13.15   Running Record

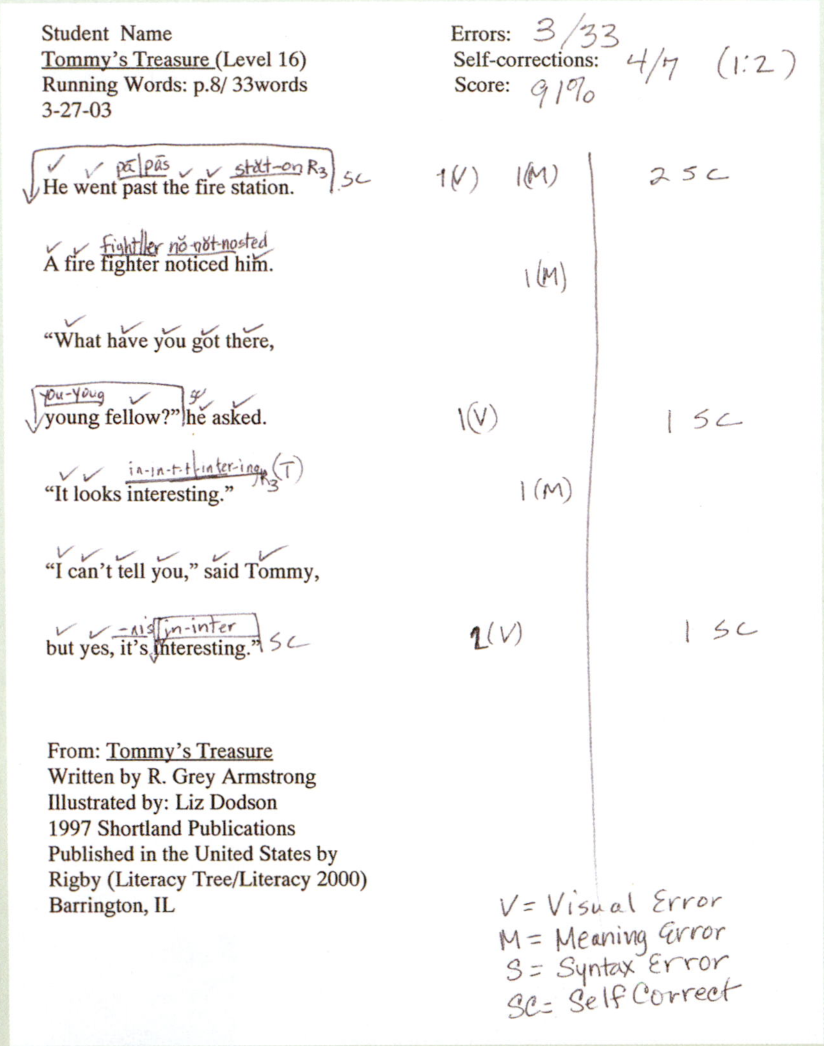

Taken from *Tommy's Treasure* by R. G. Armstrong. (1997). Published by Shortland Publications.

Applications for English Language Learners

Running records are helpful with ELLs because they provide insight into the way they learn to speak and read (Afflerbach, 1999). These students often rely heavily on only one or two cueing systems. Running records show that, as their oral language improves, they are able to transfer their knowledge to reading and use all cueing systems simultaneously.

comprehension. It enables you to observe strengths and weaknesses, as well as gain insights about individual readers. The primary purpose for using IRIs is to diagnose difficulties and provide appropriate instruction directed toward the skills children lack. Although once constructed by classroom teachers, commercial IRIs are now readily available. They often include assessment of oral reading accuracy, grade-level word lists, comprehension questions, and rubrics for retelling (Paris & Carpenter, 2003).

An IRI yields four levels of reading performance, which are based on accuracy in both word recognition and comprehension (Roe, Smith, & Burns, 2005). Figure 13.16 gives the levels used and their criteria.

Ideally, children should be reading at their instructional level when you are with them to provide guidance and support. When they choose to read books during their free time, they should be reading at their independent level. If they are having great difficulty and are frustrated, the material is too advanced. The capacity, or potential, level is the highest level at which the reader can comprehend 75 percent of the material. You find this level by reading aloud to the child after the frustration level has been reached.

Commercially prepared IRIs give detailed instructions for their use. They are given individually and are coded, similar to running records, to indicate types of responses that do not match the text. The grade levels indicated are estimates, and the IRI should be used in conjunction with other assessment tools. Although the percentages are significant in determining levels, so are your observations of the student engaged in

FIGURE 13.16 Levels for an Informal Reading Inventory

- Independent reading level (99-100% word recognition; 90% or higher comprehension)
- Instructional level (95% word recognition; 75% comprehension)
- Frustration level (below 90% word recognition; below 50% comprehension)
- Capacity (listening) level (75% comprehension)

Applications *for Students with Special Needs*

To code the miscues of deaf students, videotape them because of the speed and subtleties in signing their reading. You may need to view the tape several times to code everything. Expand miscue analysis so that it includes a "probe" segment, as well as the reading and retelling. This consists of asking open-ended questions to find the strategies the deaf reader is using to understand the text (Chaleff & Ritter, 2001).

reading the text and answering questions. IRIs such as the *Burns/Roe Informal Reading Inventory* (Burns & Roe, 2002) have an extensive qualitative analysis in addition to the quantitative analysis.

MISCUE ANALYSIS

A **miscue** is any deviation from the text that occurs when a child is reading (an error), and **miscue analysis** is a way of looking at miscues to determine the reader's strengths and weaknesses. Instead of simply being considered a mistake, a miscue informs you about a child's reading development (Chaleff & Ritter, 2001). You have opportunities to observe the miscues that students make during the oral reading that occurs with running records and informal reading inventories. By analyzing miscues, you can learn much about the student's use of reading strategies. The most important consideration is whether or not the miscue disrupts the meaning (Goodman, 1997).

For example, students are reading the text that says:

Jason was injured when he fell.

The first student reads:

Jason was *injuiced* when he fell.

The second student reads:

Jason was *hurt* when he fell.

An analysis of these two miscues reveals that the first student is relying heavily on visual, or graphophonic, information without regard for meaning, unless he self-corrects when he realizes it doesn't make sense. The second student uses a synonym for the word as he reads for meaning (semantics) with little regard for visual information. From these examples, you can see that the first child needs to construct meaning as he reads, and the second child should pay closer attention to the appearance of the word. By analyzing miscues over time, you discover patterns that you can use to plan individualized reading instruction.

Rubrics

A **rubric** is a form that enables the user to rate the quality of student performance according to a predetermined set of criteria and standards. The criteria refer to what

Applications **for English Language Learners and Students with Special Needs**

Designing rubrics appears to be very helpful for children from other language backgrounds due to the repetition and the different ways concepts are presented. Children of all abilities seem to respond well to the repeated practice of developing the criteria after modeling by the classroom teacher (Skillings & Ferrell, 2000). You should distribute rubrics or checklists to struggling students before they work on assignments so that they will know what criteria are being emphasized (Ganske, Monroe, & Strickland, 2003).

is being measured, such as the content or organization of a piece of writing, and standards refer to the level of proficiency. Although there is no set rule, rubrics usually have three-to-six point scales, with the highest number representing the best work. Figure 13.17 is an example of a rubric for assessing oral expression.

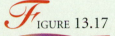

FIGURE 13.17   Rubric for Assessing Oral Expression

Criteria	Standards		
	3	**2**	**1**
Voice	Uses fluid speech and inflection. Has adequate volume.	Uses some inflection. Inconsistent volume.	Uses a monotone voice with inadequate volume.
Eye Contact	Uses direct eye contact with audience throughout.	Has some eye contact with audience.	Has no eye contact with audience.
Body Language	Uses fluid movements with appropriate descriptive gestures.	Has some descriptive gestures with some awkward movements.	Has no supportive movements but some distracting moves.
Introduction	Captures audience's attention and sets the mood.	Uses brief introductory remark.	Begins without clear introduction of topic.
Content	Gives interesting, well-focused, and well-organized content.	Has interesting but not clearly focused content.	Gives confusing, poorly organized information.

You can construct rubrics yourself to assess student work, but students may work with you to create rubrics. Skillings and Ferrell (2000) involved second- and third-graders in constructing rubrics by modeling the thinking that goes into developing criteria and then inviting the students to create a class rubric. The children looked at work samples to determine criteria for each level and came up with several criteria that matched their ideas for "Very best level," "Okay level," and "Not so good level." Through this type of collaboration, they are able to understand what is expected of them and know how to earn good grades.

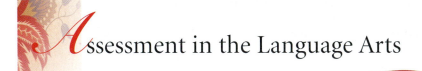

Assessment in the Language Arts

MOST OF these informal classroom assessment tools can be used for any of the language arts, but some types are more useful than others for specific areas. We consider each area and appropriate ways to assess it.

Emergent Literacy

Children vary considerably in their readiness for literacy, so it is wise to assess their knowledge of concepts about print, phonemic awareness, and the alphabetic principle to know where to begin instruction. Because of their short attention spans and limited ability to do pencil and paper tasks, most young children are not good test takers. Therefore, you may need to rely on such informal assessment techniques as observation ("kidwatching"), interviews and conferences, story retellings, and anecdotal records for much of your information.

Because of the recent emphasis on phonemic awareness for beginning readers, some tests have been developed to assess this skill (Good & Kaminski, 2002; Yopp, 1999). Such tests indicate children's levels of phonemic awareness and thus provide you with valuable information for addressing students' needs. Other commercially prepared tests are also available to evaluate a child's book handling and awareness of concepts about print (Clay, 1979).

Vocabulary

Vocabulary knowledge can be assessed both formally and informally. The best indication of vocabulary knowledge is the child's ability to understand and use words effectively. Understanding and using vocabulary differ according to each language art. For example, mature readers understand more words in the context of reading than they are able to use correctly when they speak. The opposite is true of beginning readers. Figure 13.18 shows some ways to observe vocabulary in the different language arts.

FIGURE 13.18 Procedures for Observing Use of Vocabulary

- *Listening*: observing the appropriateness of responses when selected words are spoken to the child in conversation or other activities

- *Speaking*: listening for correct use of selected words in conversation or other oral language activities

- *Reading*: observing oral and written responses to the reading of material containing selected words for appropriateness of response

- *Writing*: analyzing written products for correct use of selected words

- *Viewing and visually representing*: observing the ability to interpret and apply specialized vocabulary as needed

Listening

To check student performance in listening, you can use daily observation to discover a student's attention span, reactions to oral presentations, ability to follow oral directions, apparent interest in class discussions, and ability to make remarks that are pertinent to the topic being discussed. You may record observations on a checklist, such as the one in Figure 13.19 on page 524.

Oral Expression

You may use two methods for assessing speaking skills. The first is an observational approach, in which you simply listen carefully to the students' speech and assess it informally. The second is a structured approach, in which assessment is based on students' performances on specific speech tasks, as in the case of the score cards used to measure 4-H demonstrations and the rubric given in Figure 13.17 earlier in this chapter.

In an effort to guide teachers' observations of children's language and literacy skills, Dickinson and his colleagues (2003) developed an instrument based on standards for listening and speaking. Teacher Rating of Oral Language and Literacy (TROLL) is a rating scale similar to a rubric that addresses critical speaking and listening skills. It includes such topics as starting a conversation, communicating personal experiences, asking questions, pretending, using varied vocabulary, and recognizing and producing rhymes.

$\mathcal{F}$IGURE 13.19   **Checklist for Effective Listening**

Listening Checklist

Student's Name _____

Rating Scale: 5 = Always; 4 = Usually; 3 = Sometimes; 2 = Rarely; 1 = Never

Characteristic	Date	Date	Date	Date
Pays attention to oral presentations.				
Enjoys listening to stories and poems.				
Listens without interrupting.				
Participates in discussions.				
Follows oral directions accurately.				
Seems to think while listening.				

Reading

You can use a variety of informal assessments for reading. You may use running records with guided reading, observations recorded on checklists or as anecdotal records, and informal reading inventories. Logs from literature circles, retellings, and interviews or conferences about what students are reading are other possibilities for assessment.

The critical test of fluency is to be able to decode and comprehend a text at the same time (Guthrie, 2002). You can assess fluency by asking a student to read a passage aloud and then tell everything she can remember about it. If the student omits details, you can prompt recall with specific questions. As the student reads orally, you should record word recognition errors, reading rate, comprehension, and an estimate of oral reading expression.

The Elementary Reading Attitude Survey (ERAS) measures children's attitudes toward reading by having them mark one of four poses of the comic strip character *Garfield,* which show him looking very happy to very upset. It can be given to an entire class in a short time (McKenna & Kear, 1999).

Writing

Both you and the student should evaluate written work. You should ask for areas in which additional instruction is needed, and each student should look for evidence of growth and improvement. The student-teacher conferences and peer conferences held during writing workshops are forms of ongoing assessment, and rubrics are widely used to assess writing skills according to specific criteria.

Salinger (1998) suggests that teachers assess writing by periodically asking all students to write about the same topic and analyze these samples for style, tone, writing conventions, and awareness of audience. Students can also select writing samples for analysis during conferences. Self-selected samples are particularly valuable when students attach explanatory notes.

Because of the link between motivation and literacy learning, you should assess students' attitudes toward writing (Kear, Coffman, McKenna, & Ambrosio, 2000). Children's attitudes toward writing appear to decline as they advance in school. Kear and his colleagues (2002) have developed the Writing Attitude Survey (WAS) for the purpose of enabling teachers to use survey results for planning instruction.

Writing

Spelling

Many teachers use traditional weekly spelling tests. From these, students can note the words they miss each week and chart their progress in an attempt to improve. Children may do quite well on these tests and still misspell the same words in written work, however. You should impress on your students that spelling is important for communication and it should be correct when publishing or sharing writing with others. A spelling grade should consider accuracy of spelling on finished pieces, as well as spelling test scores. If students list their misspelled words in spelling logs, along with the correct spellings, you can look for patterns in spelling errors and provide corrective instruction.

Fresch and Wheaton (2002) developed a Spelling Knowledge Inventory (SKI) that teachers can use to assess students' knowledge of the following word features: print and symbol awareness, print and sound awareness, print and sound connections, and self-reliance. It provides structure, but teachers can customize it for their own classrooms.

Formal Assessment

SERAFINI (2000/2001) contrasts assessment as inquiry with assessment as measurement. We have been looking at assessment as inquiry, in which you, as a teacher, inquire about learners and how they learn. You observe, record information, talk with students, interpret their responses, look through their portfolios, invite student participation in the assessment process, and reflect on the knowledge you have gained to plan instruction. Now we look briefly at assessment as measurement, which deals with tests that are intended to measure objectively what a student knows. Assessment as inquiry, or authentic, classroom-based assessment, is useful for the classroom teacher on a daily basis, whereas assessment as measurement serves the need for accountability to various government agencies and the public in general.

Standardized Testing

State-mandated achievement testing has increased rapidly in the last twenty years (Hoffman, Assaf, & Paris, 2001), and the federal No Child Left Behind Act requires annual testing for all children in grades 3 through 8. As a teacher, you probably will be involved in administering standardized tests at least once during the year.

A **standardized test** is a test prepared by experts and administered, scored, and interpreted according to certain criteria. Before publication, these tests are given to large groups of students at different grade levels across the country to establish statistical norms or standards. These norms represent the average achievement of students at specific ages and grade levels, and they are used as the basis for comparing students across the nation. For this reason, standardized tests are sometimes referred to as *norm-referenced tests*. They usually include many multiple-choice items, and subtests may cover vocabulary, word attack skills, comprehension, and occasionally listening skills. Clear directions are given for administering them, and they can be machine scored.

Standardized tests are often considered "high stakes" because they can be the basis for making decisions about promotion and placement of students into special classes. When a single test score is used to make such decisions, the score can have many consequences for the child, the parents, and the teacher (Guthrie, 2002). The International Reading Association is concerned that testing is becoming a way of controlling instruction instead of a means for collecting information to guide instruction (*High-Stakes*

Classroom Vignette 13.2

A few teachers have gathered after school to talk about the upcoming standardized test they will soon be giving.

MS. HASELTON: I dread giving these tests. I've been preparing my children for taking them since January. We start each language arts class with workbooks that show children how to take the tests. They don't like doing this, but maybe they will score better.

MR. FRANK: I haven't been doing that. It takes too much instructional time. I just hope they'll do okay when they see the tests. No use in worrying.

MS. RAMIREZ: I'm taking no chances. Since the first day of school, I've had my children in workbooks practicing to take the tests. They count for so much, and I want them to get good scores. I don't want to feel that it's my fault if they don't do well.

MS. RUSSELL: I do a little of both, I guess. I don't want them to be surprised by the format of the test, so I give them sample test materials for practice a week or two in advance. The rest of the time, I simply do the best teaching I can and hope they will learn what they need to know.

What's happening here?

The teachers are sharing their views on preparing their students to take standardized tests, and they show that there are many ways to approach the issue. Spending a lot of time on sample tests and workbook pages steals valuable instructional time, but students probably need some practice in using the format before they encounter the actual tests.

Assessments in Reading, 1999). Because of the importance attached to standardized tests, you must decide how you will prepare your classes for taking these tests, which often take most of a week to administer. Classroom Vignette 13.2 shows some teachers' thoughts on test preparation.

A certain amount of test preparation is helpful (Guthrie, 2002). Certainly, the children need to be familiar with the test format, especially if it is completely new to them. They should not have to spend valuable time during the actual test trying to figure out what they are supposed to do. In their review of research regarding instruction for test taking, Armbruster and Osborn (2002) caution against spending too much time teaching test-taking strategies. Although some test preparation activities are helpful, they should be part of ongoing instruction in reading and writing. Extensive instruction in test-taking strategies has limited effectiveness for improving test scores.

Different test formats often call for different study procedures. Some guidelines for test taking, whether formal or informal, appear in Figure 13.20.

Two teachers, Meg Johnson and Agua Caliente, found a way to teach test taking to their second-graders that was compatible with their teaching practices in a

Reflections

How do you feel about taking standardized tests? What can you do to relieve stress? When you were a child, did any teacher prepare you for taking such tests? If so, how?

FIGURE 13.20   Guidelines for Test Taking

- Pay close attention to directions and follow them exactly.
- Understand the test format (for example, practice filling in bubbles on formal tests).
- Skip over difficult or confusing questions and answer questions that you know and can answer quickly.
- On essay tests, answer what is being asked (for example, compare, contrast, explain, or describe).
- Learn important terms and their definitions for objective tests.
- For true-false questions, look carefully for such words as *not*, *never*, and *always*, which are likely to affect your answer.
- Be aware of time limitations and move through the test at a reasonable pace.
- Unless there is a penalty for guessing, answer each question the best you can.
- When you finish, check your answers and return to the more difficult questions.

Applications

for Students with Special Needs

Although struggling readers need to be taught at their instructional levels, they also need to learn how to cope with the grade-level texts that they will encounter in testing situations. Test preparation should be integrated with everyday learning, and practice should relate to topics they are studying. For example, they should learn to use a scoring rubric to self-assess and revise their answers to open-ended questions related to topics they are studying (Ganske, Monroe, & Strickland, 2003).

student-centered, literature-based classroom (Worthy & Hoffman, 2000). They developed materials and minilessons, and students worked together to read and discuss the test as a genre of literature. They analyzed the tests and developed strategies for succeeding, such as looking for tricks and traps, finding the answer on the page, and discovering that finding a good title is the same as finding the main idea. Instead of the nervousness and apprehension that many young test takers feel, these second-graders actually enjoyed taking the test.

Other Types of Formal Assessment

In addition to norm-referenced, standardized tests, educators have developed a number of other ways to formally assess student progress. Some of those are given here.

CRITERION-REFERENCED TESTS

A **criterion-referenced test** measures a learner's ability to master knowledge and skills at a particular level of performance. Students take these tests so that you can see if they have mastered a specific performance objective, such as knowing where to place the accent above the stressed syllable in two-syllable words. You present the information or skill, and the student takes a test over it. If the student attains a satisfactory level of mastery (perhaps 80–100 percent), you present more information or another skill, and so the cycle repeats itself. Although they are not norm-referenced, these tests have predetermined criteria for meeting performance standards. Examples of criterion-referenced tests include those in reading management systems and end-of-unit tests in basal readers (Ruddell, 2002). They flourished in the 1970s and 1980s and have recently been revived (Pearson, 2003).

Writing

STANDARDS-BASED WRITING ASSESSMENT

Many states have implemented standards-based writing assessments. Not convinced that multiple-choice tests fully measure writing skill, researchers designed tests in which students have to write essays in response to prompts. Tests are given annually at selected grade levels, and rubrics are often used to assess student progress. For example, Tennessee gives these tests at grades 5, 8, and 11 and uses a six-point rubric for identifying different levels of writing proficiency.

Kern and her colleagues (2003), working in Rhode Island with grades K-12, have developed guiding principles and lesson plans for preparing students to take statewide writing tests. Their principles and plans are based on six of the twelve NCTE/IRA language arts standards (one, two, three, five, eleven, and twelve), which are addressed in the first chapter of this text. Lesson plans deal primarily with literature, writing, and personal experiences, and the guiding principles are as follows.

- All students have something important to communicate.
- Students need to participate actively in writing and be fully engaged in constructing meaning.
- Students need variety in topics and styles, along with direct instruction.
- Literature provides clear models to follow and authentic purposes for writing.
- The teacher should write along with the students.

Interventions for Struggling Students

THE RESULTS of some of our assessments will no doubt show that some students are not performing as well as we would like. With increased attention turning to students who are struggling with reading and writing, it seems appropriate to mention briefly some ways teachers help these students. Many of the suggestions given earlier in this book are appropriate for all students, but those who struggle may need special modifications.

Struggling Students

Many school-age children, including some from all social classes, have significant difficulty learning to read (Snow, Burns, & Griffin, 1998). Reasons for these difficulties include

- A history of preschool language impairment.
- Limited English proficiency.
- Parents who had difficulty learning to read.
- Attention deficit hyperactivity disorder (ADHD) (inability to focus attention).
- Little motivation to read (Strickland, Ganske, & Monroe, 2002).

Intervention Strategies

Interventions are ways that teachers provide additional support for struggling students to keep them from failing. You can help these students in a variety of ways, such as those suggested here.

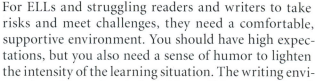

Learning is a social process, and working in small groups is one way to help struggling learners build confidence and achieve success.

LEARNING ENVIRONMENT

For ELLs and struggling readers and writers to take risks and meet challenges, they need a comfortable, supportive environment. You should have high expectations, but you also need a sense of humor to lighten the intensity of the learning situation. The writing environment should be safe, so that students know that their writing will be accepted and valued. They need to participate in tasks and work with materials that enable them to succeed (Ganske, Monroe, & Strickland, 2003).

FAMILY CONNECTIONS

As discussed in Chapter 4, early literacy develops with family members, and family support continues to play an important role in literacy learning. Contact parents early in the school year to introduce yourself, send home information in clear and simple language, and make videotaped explanations of what you want them to know about their children's literacy learning. If parents speak little or no English, community members who are fluent in both English and children's home languages may be willing to translate information about helping their children. Some teachers use family message journals in which children write something about their school day and a parent responds. Reading backpacks sent home with children contain books to share, along with easy activities to do as a family (Ganske, Monroe, & Strickland, 2003). Parents can also provide support by helping students read and complete their homework assignments (Hettinger & Knapp, 2001).

VIABLE ORGANIZATIONAL PATTERNS

All children should feel part of the classroom learning community and have some way to contribute. Even underachievers can participate in book discussions and share insights. Doing so increases their sense of self-worth (Hettinger & Knapp, 2001). Learning is a social process, and students who discuss their ideas with others construct and internalize understandings through their talk (Walker, 2003).

Working in small groups with students who have similar needs is an effective and efficient way to provide extra support. Grouping needs to be flexible, however, so that students can experience working with those whose literacy development is similar, as well as with those whose abilities differ (Strickland, Ganske, & Monroe, 2002). Literature circles enable struggling readers to share in discussions of books that may be too difficult to read, but are within their interest and comprehension levels (Ganske, Monroe, & Strickland, 2003). Guided reading groups provide guidance for readers in small group settings (Fountas & Pinnell, 1996). Hettinger and Knapp (2001) believe that partner reading with more competent readers is effective for struggling students, and Walker (2003) found that working with students in pairs promotes social interactions and enables each individual to demonstrate personal strengths.

STRATEGIES

Some instructional procedures are particularly effective with struggling students. Scaffolding, providing extra help to enable a child to move to a higher level of performance, is essential for these children (Hettinger & Knapp, 2001; Strickland, Ganske, & Monroe, 2002; Walker, 2003) (see Chapter 4). Assigning multilevel tasks, those requiring varying levels of skill, allows students of different abilities to attempt assignments with some expectation of success (Strickland, Ganske, & Monroe, 2002). Struggling writers need multiple demonstrations in different contexts to understand writing strategies, and readers need explicit demonstrations of how good readers think as they read in order to understand what they should be doing. Many opportunities for guided practice should follow demonstrations (Ganske, Monroe, & Strickland, 2003).

Because students draw from their own experiences and use their own words, the language experience approach is useful for both ELLs and those who are struggling (see Chapter 7). They also benefit from the modeling of graphic organizers and think-alouds, as well as from the open-ended discussions that go along with read-alouds (Ganske, Monroe, & Strickland, 2003). Readers who struggle find graphic organizers reduce the reading load and help them grasp concepts through graphic designs. In their work with struggling readers, Hoover and Fabian (2000) found that their students benefited from highly structured programs that present regular spelling patterns and decodable text written in patterns. They reinforce phonics instruction with games and "review and double back" to earlier lessons (p. 475).

MATERIALS

Students struggling with literacy need to read easy, predictable, patterned texts to be successful and move toward fluency, but they also benefit from reading more difficult text if it matches their interests and background experiences (Ganske, Monroe, & Strickland, 2003). Children should be allowed to select books from a wide variety of levels and topics (Vogt & Nagano, 2003). Materials on ethnic history and literature that reflect students' backgrounds often result in more motivated students with higher self-esteem and greater expectations (Hoover & Fabian, 2000). Comic books, books from the Magic School Bus series, Eyewitness books with their detailed illustrations, and high-interest, low-vocabulary books can also tempt the struggling reader (Hettinger & Knapp, 2001).

Computers are useful for both readers and writers. Motivated students who avoid books may work hard to "surf the Web" for information, or they may play complex role-playing or strategic games. Some computer programs pronounce words that students do not recognize when they point and click on them. Writers find computers convenient for checking spelling and editing drafts of their texts (Hettinger & Knapp, 2001).

Formal Intervention Programs

Evidence indicates that patterns of school failure start early and continue throughout a child's schooling. Children become discouraged when they fail at reading, so they read less, thus getting less practice in reading than good readers, and consequently have lower achievement. In an attempt to correct this situation, educators have devel-

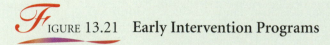

*F*IGURE 13.21   **Early Intervention Programs**

Name of Program	Features of Program
Reading Recovery	First-graders. One-on-one tutoring from highly trained teachers. Lessons involve reading books, word analysis and comprehension strategies, writing and reading child's own sentences.
Early Reading Intervention (ERI)	First- and second-graders. Tutoring in small groups. Children read individually. Lessons include word analysis strategies during the reading of storybooks.
Book Buddies	Early grades. One-on-one tutorials from community volunteers. Lessons consist of repeated readings of familiar text, phonics, writing for sounds, and reading a new book.
First Steps	Early grades. Tutoring program. Lessons include rereading a leveled book, word study with letter and word sorts, a writing activity, and reading a new story.
Success for All	Grades 1 through 6. Comprehensive, school-restructuring program. Uses cooperative learning strategies. Lessons include phonics, direct instruction of comprehension strategies, and listening skills.
Kamehameha Early Education Program (KEEP)	Kindergarten through grade 6. Program includes writers' and readers' workshops, word-reading and spelling strategies, portfolio assessment, voluntary reading, and benchmarks for success.

oped formal intervention programs. Six of these, along with their characteristics, are identified in Figure 13.21 (Strickland, 2002).

Reporting Progress

AT SOME point, most teachers need to sort through their assessments of individual children, summarize the results, and arrive at grades for the report period. Analyzing authentic assessments makes grading more difficult than just averaging test scores, but it also gives a better picture of what each child can do. Parents want to be informed and are often able to help their children at home if they understand their learning needs. Communication between school and home is important; it should occur on a regular basis and in an effective manner. In this section, reporting is divided into oral and written reporting.

Oral Reporting

The first opportunity for you and the students' parents to meet is often at a school-sponsored Open House near the beginning of the year. Typically, after a brief meeting of the parent-teacher organization, parents visit their children's classrooms. Here, you have opportunities to explain your philosophy of teaching, your policies and goals, homework expectations, and the kinds of activities children will be doing. This is an excellent time to invite parents to participate and volunteer, to find out if any of them can offer special talents, and to tell them how they may contact you. If time permits, parents may want to talk to you about their children individually. Earlier in the day, the children should have put samples of their best work at their places so that parents can see what they have been doing.

Parent-teacher conferences are scheduled meetings between you and the parents for the purpose of communicating information about their children. Sometimes children are also invited to participate; after all, they are the real experts on what is happening. A conference is an opportunity to share what you know about a child's progress and to understand more about the child's perceptions and home background. Some schools set aside times for conferences two or three times a year, but you can call or e-mail a parent to schedule a conference if you see a need. Some guidelines for holding conferences are listed in Figure 13.22 on page 534.

Written Reports

The school system generally determines what kind of report to use and how often to send it home. Traditional report cards inform parents about their child's performance

𝓕IGURE 13.22 **Guidelines for Parent Conferences**

1. Consider inviting the child to join you during the conference to explain his or her work.

2. Select a pleasant, comfortable place for the conference where you can look at the student's work together.

3. Always begin with something positive about the child's performance or behavior.

4. If you haven't done so before, explain your goals and policies.

5. Have available the child's work samples, preferably in a portfolio, and records you have kept (perhaps anecdotal records or notes from literature circles).

6. Review the materials in relation to your goals. Invite comments.

7. Listen to the parents' (and child's) concerns.

8. Share any concerns you have.

9. Offer constructive suggestions for ways to work together for the child's benefit.

10. Leave on a pleasant note, with the understanding that you want the child to succeed.

in school in terms of letter or percentage grades. Information is incomplete because little or nothing is said about the child's interests, attitudes, or effort. Report cards sometimes provide limited space for teacher comments, but clear, informative narrative reports, although time-consuming, enable you to describe a child's progress. Some report cards use a continuum, showing little or no competence at one end and full competence at the other end. You place a mark at some point on the continuum line to show the child's level of proficiency for each criterion.

You can also send home newsletters, notes, and announcements. Sometimes the school distributes brochures about policies, announcements of upcoming events, and other information, and the librarian may issue lists of recommended books for recreational reading. At the end of the school year, you may provide a list of ideas for activities that can extend learning over the summer. One effective three-way communication is shown in Figure 13.23 on page 535. The student shares a favorite piece of work with a parent or caregiver, who then responds to the piece on the form provided; the student returns the form to you, so that you can also respond.

Figure 13.23   Sample Communication Form between School and Home

Date _____

Dear _____

Today I am bringing my best work to show you. It is _____

It is my best work so far because _____

_____

Please write a comment about my work.

_____

_____

Signature _____

Teacher's comments _____

_____

Teacher's signature _____

_____

Summary

Assessment is collecting information about student performance that may be analyzed to determine strengths and weaknesses. It serves two purposes: to guide instruction and to provide accountability. Evaluation is a periodic summation of student progress. Authentic, or classroom-based, assessment occurs as you observe students while they are working in order to plan appropriate instruction. You can record observations with brief notes, checklists, and anecdotal records, and you can learn more about students through conferences, interviews, and analysis of portfolio artifacts that represent student work. Self-assessments reveal students' perceptions of themselves. Rubrics guide assessment of student work by providing criteria and standards for judgment. Other informal measures include retellings, running records, informal reading inventories, and miscue analysis.

Writing

Different language arts can be measured through one or more of these assessment tools, but some types are more appropriate than others for each area. For example, rubrics are particularly useful for assessing writing, and running records and informal reading inventories are used for reading. Formal assessments consist of norm-referenced, standardized tests that are generally given annually. Other types of formal assessments include criterion-referenced tests and standards-based writing assessment.

For a variety of reasons, many students have difficulty learning. These struggling students need interventions to avoid failure. You can intervene by providing a safe classroom environment, connecting with families, arranging flexible groupings, and using appropriate strategies and materials. Formal intervention programs are also available. You need to find effective ways to report student progress, either orally or in written reports.

Discussion Questions

1. How are assessment and instruction related? How useful are standardized test results to classroom teachers?

2. Prioritize the types of informal assessments that are presented in this chapter. Which ones are most useful for guiding instruction?

3. In Classroom Vignette 13.2 teachers compare their ideas about test preparation. What are your thoughts? Do you agree with any of these teachers? Why?

4. How can you get students to self-assess objectively? What can you do if they consistently misrepresent themselves by inflating or deflating their abilities?

5. What is high-stakes testing? How can it be integrated with instructional objectives in a typical classroom? What are some problems associated with high-stakes testing?

6. What kind of report card is best for informing parents? Consider the practicalities of reporting and the ability of parents to interpret what is on the report card?

7. Although this chapter includes a number of types of assessment, it does not include all types. Can you think of others that teachers might use?

Suggested Activities

1. With a partner or as a member of a small group, pick one of the guidelines for authentic assessment (see Figure 13.2). Discuss why it is important and share your ideas with the class.

2. Make a checklist for one of the following: fluency, emergent writing, oral expression, or a topic of your choice. What rating scale will you use? If possible, use it with children.

3. Create your own portfolio. What will you include, how will you organize it, and for what purposes will you use it?

4. Find out what your district or state policies are on standardized testing. What test is given? How often is it given? What types of questions does it include?

5. Does your state have a writing assessment? If so, find out what it consists of and how the results are used.

6. Talk to a teacher or observe a class you are teaching to identify a struggling student. What problems does the student have, and what interventions are planned?

7. As a class, examine report cards from different schools. How useful are they for parents?

8. Obtain a practice copy of a standardized test that is given in your school system. How clear are the directions? What types of questions are asked? How much time is required? What kind of scoring is available?

9. Construct a rubric, either with or without input from children, and use it for assessing report writing, oral retellings, or a topic of your choice.

eferences

AFFLERBACH, P. (1999). Teachers' choices in classroom assessment. In S. Barrentine (Ed.), *Reading assessment: Principles and practices for elementary teachers* (pp. 68–72). Newark, DE: International Reading Association.

ARMBRUSTER, B., & OSBORN, J. (2002). *Reading instruction and assessment.* Boston: Allyn & Bacon.

ATWELL, N. (1998). *In the middle* (2nd ed.). Portsmouth, NH: Boynton/Cook.

BURNS, P. C., & ROE, B. D. (2002). *Burns/Roe Informal Reading Inventory* (6th ed.), Boston: Houghton Mifflin.

CHALEFF, C. D., & RITTER, M. H. (2001). The use of miscue analysis with deaf readers. *The Reading Teacher, 55,* 190–200.

CLAY, M. (1979). *The early detection of reading difficulties* (3rd ed.). Portsmouth, NH: Heinemann.

COBB, C. (2003/2004). Effective instruction begins with purposeful assessments. *The Reading Teacher, 57,* 386–388.

COURTNEY, A., & ABODEEB, T. (1999). Diagnostic-reflective portfolios. *The Reading Teacher, 52,* 708–714.

DICKINSON, D., McCABE, A., & SPRAGUE, K. (2003). Teacher Rating of Oral Language and Literacy (TROLL): Individualizing early literacy instruction with a standards-based rating tool. *The Reading Teacher, 56,* 554–564.

FOUNTAS, I., & PINNELL, G. S. (1996). *Guided reading.* Portsmouth, NH: Heinemann.

FRESCH, M. J., & WHEATON, A. (2002). *Teaching and assessing spelling.* New York: Scholastic.

FRYAR, R. (2003). Students assess their own reporting and presentation skills. In H. Fehring (Ed.), *Literacy assessment* (pp. 36–39). Newark, DE: International Reading Association.

GANSKE, K., MONROE, J., & STRICKLAND, D. (2003). Questions teachers ask about struggling readers and writers. *The Reading Teacher, 57,* 118–128.

GLAZER, S. M. (1998). *Assessment is instruction.* Norwood, MA: Christopher-Gordon.

GOOD, R. H., & KAMINSKI, R. A. (Eds.). (2002). *Dynamic indicators of basic early literacy skills* (6th ed.). Eugene, OR: Institute for the Development of Educational Achievement.

GOODMAN, Y. (1997). Reading diagnosis—qualitative or quantitative? *The Reading Teacher, 50,* 534–538.

GRAVES, D. (1994). *A fresh look at writing.* Portsmouth, NH: Heinemann.

GUTHRIE, J. (2002). Preparing students for high-stakes test taking in reading. In A. Farstrup & S. J. Samuels (Eds.), *What research has to say about reading instruction* (3rd ed., pp. 370–391). Newark, DE: International Reading Association.

HARRIS, T., & HODGES, R. (Eds.). (1995). *The literacy dictionary.* Newark, DE: International Reading Association.

HETTINGER, H. R., & KNAPP, N. F. (2001). Lessons from J. P.: Supporting underachieving readers in the elementary classroom. *The Reading Teacher, 55,* 26–29.

High-stakes assessments in reading: A position statement of the International Reading Association. (1999). Newark, DE: International Reading Association.

HOFFMAN, J., ASSAF, L. C., & PARIS, S. (2001). High-stakes testing in reading: Today in Texas, tomorrow? *The Reading Teacher, 54,* 482–492.

HOOVER, M. R., & FABIAN, E. M. (2000). A successful program for struggling readers. *The Reading Teacher, 53,* 474–476.

KEAR, D., COFFMAN, G., McKENNA, M., & AMBROSIO, A. (2000). Measuring attitude toward writing: A new tool for teachers. *The Reading Teacher, 54,* 10–23.

KERN, D., ANDRE, W., SCHILKE, R., BARTON J., & McGUIRE, M. C. (2003). Less *is* more: Preparing students for state writing assessments. *The Reading Teacher, 56,* 816–826.

McKENNA, M., & KEAR, D. (1999). Measuring attitude toward reading: A new tool for teachers. In S. Barrentine (Ed.), *Reading assessment: Principles and practices for elementary teachers* (pp. 199–214). Newark, DE: International Reading Association.

PARIS, S., & CARPENTER, R. (2003). FAQs about IRIs. *The Reading Teacher, 56,* 578–580.

PEARSON, P. D. (2003). Looking backward: A brief history of reading comprehension assessment. 48th Annual Convention, Orlando, International Reading Association.

ROE, B. D., SMITH, S. H., & BURNS, P. C. (2005). *Teaching reading in today's elementary schools* (9th ed.). Boston: Houghton Mifflin.

RUDDELL, R. (2002). *Teaching children to read and write* (3rd ed.). Boston: Allyn & Bacon.

SALINGER, T. (1998). How do we assess young children's literacy learning? In S. Neuman & K. Roskos (Eds.), *Children achieving: Best practices in early literacy* (pp. 223–249). Newark, DE: International Reading Association.

SEARFOSS, L., READENCE, J., & MALLETTE, M. (2001). *Helping children learn to read: Creating a classroom literacy environment* (4th ed.). Boston: Allyn & Bacon.

SERAFINI, F. (2000/2001). Three paradigms of assessment: Measurement, procedure, and inquiry. *The Reading Teacher, 54,* 384–393.

SKILLINGS, M. J., & FERRELL, R. (2000). Student-generated rubrics: Bringing students into the assessment process. *The Reading Teacher, 53,* 452–455.

SNOW, C., BURNS, M. S., & GRIFFIN, P. (Eds.). (1998). *Preventing reading difficulties in young children.* Washington, DC: National Academy Press.

STRICKLAND, D. (2002). The importance of early intervention. In A. Farstrup & S. J. Samuels (Eds.), *What research has to say about reading instruction* (3rd ed., pp. 69–86). Newark, DE: International Reading Association.

STRICKLAND, D., GANSKE, K., & MONROE, J. (2002). *Supporting struggling readers and writers.* Portland, ME: Stenhouse; Newark, DE: International Reading Association.

TIERNEY, R. (1998). Literacy assessment reform: Shifting beliefs, principled possibilities and emerging practices. *The Reading Teacher, 51,* 374–390.

VALENCIA, S. (2000) In R. Tierney, D. Moore, S. Valencia, & P. Johnston, How will literacy be assessed in the next millennium? *Reading Research Quarterly, 35,* 244–250.

VAN KRAAYENOORD, C. (2003). Toward self-assessment of literacy learning. In H. Fehring (Ed.), *Literacy assessment* (pp. 44–54). Newark, DE: International Reading Association.

VOGT, M., & NAGANO, M. (2003). Turn it on with Light Bulb Reading! Sound-switching strategies for struggling readers. *The Reading Teacher, 57,* 214–221.

WALKER, B. (2003). Instruction for struggling readers contains multiple features. *The Reading Teacher, 57,* 206–207.

WINOGRAD, P., & ARRINGTON, H. J. (1999). Best practices in literacy assessment. In L. Gambell, L. M. Morrow, S. Neuman, & M. Pressley (Eds.), *Best practices in literacy instruction* (pp. 210–241). New York: Guilford.

WORTHY, J., & HOFFMAN, J. (2000). The press to test. *The Reading Teacher, 53,* 596–598.

YOPP, H. (1999). A test for assessing phonemic awareness in young children. In S. Barrentine (Ed.), *Reading assessment: Principles and practices for elementary teachers* (pp. 166–176). Newark, DE: International Reading Association.

THEMATIC UNITS

LEARNER OBJECTIVES

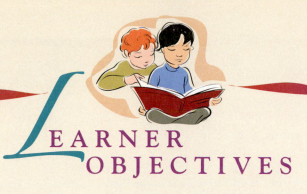

At the conclusion of this chapter

YOU SHOULD BE ABLE TO

1. Explain the value of teaching with thematic units.

2. Develop a thematic unit.

3. Use a variety of formats for thematic units to meet the needs of your students.

4. Plan for flexibility and for responding to student interest.

5. Identify the following terms that are defined or explained in this chapter:

integrated curriculum 546   thematic unit 545   topical unit 545

NCTE/IRA Standards addressed in this chapter

STANDARD 1. Students read a wide range of print and non-print texts to build an understanding of texts, of themselves, and of the cultures in the United States and the world; to acquire new information; to respond to the needs and demands of society and the workplace; and for personal fulfillment. Among these texts are fiction and nonfiction, classic and contemporary works.

STANDARD 2. Students read a wide range of literature from many periods in many genres to build an understanding of the many dimensions (e.g., philosophical, ethical, aesthetic) of human experience.

STANDARD 7. Students conduct research on issues and interests by generating ideas and questions, and by posing problems. They gather, evaluate, and synthesize data from a variety of sources (e.g., print and non-print texts, artifacts, people) to communicate their discoveries in ways that suit their purpose and audience.

STANDARD 8. Students use a variety of technological and information resources (e.g., libraries, databases, computer networks, video) to gather and synthesize information and to create and communicate knowledge.

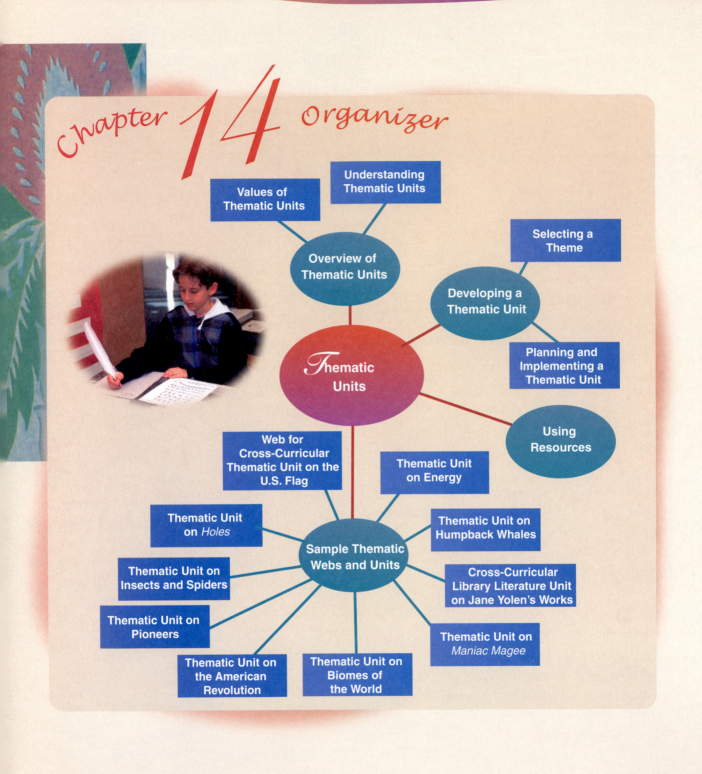

Chapter 14 *Organizer*

Values of Thematic Units

Understanding Thematic Units

Overview of Thematic Units

Selecting a Theme

Developing a Thematic Unit

Thematic Units

Planning and Implementing a Thematic Unit

Using Resources

Web for Cross-Curricular Thematic Unit on the U.S. Flag

Thematic Unit on Energy

Thematic Unit on Humpback Whales

Sample Thematic Webs and Units

Cross-Curricular Library Literature Unit on Jane Yolen's Works

Thematic Unit on *Holes*

Thematic Unit on Insects and Spiders

Thematic Unit on Pioneers

Thematic Unit on the American Revolution

Thematic Unit on Biomes of the World

Thematic Unit on *Maniac Magee*

*M*S. JUDD chooses Lynne Cherry's *A River Ran Wild* as the focus of her thematic unit on the environment. The book tells the story of an idyllic American Indian settlement along the banks of the Nash-a-way River, the occupation of the land by English settlers, the Industrial Revolution that caused the river to become polluted, and the subsequent cleansing of the river. She is aware that this book covers historical periods in the development of our country, as well as environmental issues, so she finds it to be a good blend of social studies and science. After reading the book to the class, she leads a discussion about the issues involved and relates the contaminated river to the pollution of a nearby creek. The students become excited about the issues, and Ms. Judd begins recording their ideas in the form of a semantic map. As students categorize and label the ideas on the map, five subtopics become obvious (see Figure 14.1). Ms. Judd then asks the students to sign up for their first and second choices of subtopics to investigate. She forms groups from their preferences, and the students eagerly begin their work.

What's happening here?

The book provides a stimulus for creating interest in the environment. By relating the polluted river to the local creek, Ms. Judd helps the students see the relevance of the story to their own environment. Through the discussion, they become actively involved in the issues and want to know more. The semantic map enables Ms. Judd to assess the students' present knowledge, and it provides an organizational framework for the unit with related items already identified in each category. After the lively discussion and creation of the web, most students are ready to choose a subject for further investigation. By giving students choices, Ms. Judd allows them to pursue individual inquiries within the required curriculum.

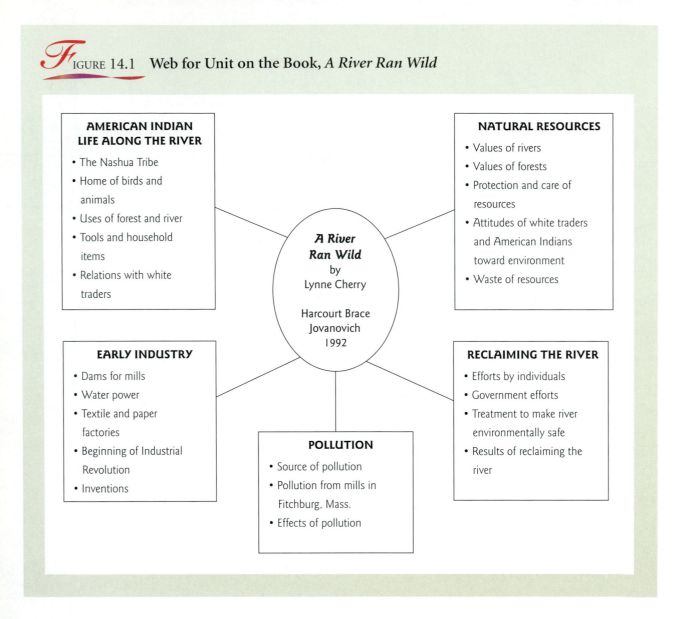

$\mathcal{F}$IGURE 14.1 **Web for Unit on the Book, *A River Ran Wild***

AMERICAN INDIAN LIFE ALONG THE RIVER
- The Nashua Tribe
- Home of birds and animals
- Uses of forest and river
- Tools and household items
- Relations with white traders

NATURAL RESOURCES
- Values of rivers
- Values of forests
- Protection and care of resources
- Attitudes of white traders and American Indians toward environment
- Waste of resources

A River Ran Wild
by
Lynne Cherry

Harcourt Brace
Jovanovich
1992

EARLY INDUSTRY
- Dams for mills
- Water power
- Textile and paper factories
- Beginning of Industrial Revolution
- Inventions

RECLAIMING THE RIVER
- Efforts by individuals
- Government efforts
- Treatment to make river environmentally safe
- Results of reclaiming the river

POLLUTION
- Source of pollution
- Pollution from mills in Fitchburg, Mass.
- Effects of pollution

Thematic units provide you with organizational plans for teaching a single topic or theme in depth. Instead of being limited to textbook coverage, students have opportunities to plunge into subjects that cross curricular boundaries and to discover new ways of learning. They use all sorts of resource materials—print and nonprint texts, the computer, and the community—to seek answers to their inquiries, and they present their findings in unique ways. Thematic units open an entirely new way of learning to students who have been bound by traditional lecture and textbook instruction.

In this chapter, we present an explanation of thematic units and contrast them with topical units and integrated curriculum. The benefits of thematic units are presented, and plans for selecting appropriate themes, developing and implementing them, and evaluating student progress are given. The second part of this chapter includes sample thematic units on a variety of topics that are suitable for different grade levels and curriculum designs.

Overview of Thematic Units

THEMATIC UNITS are frameworks for organizing content and learning experiences around topics or themes that cross curricular boundaries (Cooper, 1997; Shanahan, 2000). They provide a way for integrating language arts and relevant content areas, and they can be constructed in a variety of ways around many types of concepts or ideas. They may arise from students' inquiry, although the grade-level curriculum may determine the subject to some extent. They begin with a topic, which is expanded into a theme or purpose worthy of investigation. As students immerse themselves in the topic through reading and discussion, subtopics emerge. The classroom vignette at the beginning of the chapter shows how a book can be the hub of a thematic unit.

Understanding Thematic Units

Because thematic units can be constructed in a variety of ways around many topics, they offer students opportunities to explore areas of interest in depth. Instead of viewing subjects narrowly, they become aware of connections among the disciplines. Students investigate various aspects of the theme, seek answers, and often discover solutions to authentic problems. Kettel and Douglas (2003, p. 48) state, "Single theme multiple text instruction helps students understand the theme from a variety of perspectives." Because some students have trouble responding to multiple texts, the use of picture books, rather than chapter books, can be helpful when multiple-text units are first introduced. Kettel and Douglas (2003) also encourage the use of other print materials, such as textbooks, magazines, newspapers, and the Internet. Reading such materials and having discussions and reflective writing based on the materials, comparing the information in different sources, and responding to open-ended questions about the theme all enhance understanding.

Since they generally cross curricular areas during a large portion of the school day, thematic units differ from topical units (Sawyer & Sawyer, 1993). **Topical units** usually cover a topic within a single subject, such as focusing on measurement in mathematics class. Although thematic units typically spill over into different subject areas, they seldom connect naturally with every subject. Teachers should use the unit in only those areas where there are logical connections and avoid forcing contrived connections. Subjects that do not fit into the theme can be taught in a more traditional manner.

Thematic units provide more than factual information related to curricular objectives; they help students acquire meaning, develop attitudes, and direct their own learning. They enable students to develop an understanding of their social and physical worlds as they interact with others.

In his discussion of **integrated curriculum**, Beane (1997) points out that it differs from thematic units in that curriculum boundaries are blurred or disappear entirely as students become involved. An integrated curriculum is centered around personal and social issues that are collaboratively planned and implemented by teachers and students, without regard for content areas. Examples of topics include "Living in the Future," "Conflict," "Change," and "Who Am I?" Even though thematic units recognize different content areas and connections among them, many also stress issues of personal and social significance that are the essence of an integrated curriculum. Figure 14.2 shows the four major aspects of curriculum integration, according to Beane (1997).

Values of Thematic Units

Educators see many advantages for using thematic units as students become active participants in the authentic, meaningful experiences these units offer. The following list identifies some of the benefits of thematic units.

- *Social collaboration:* Students work with each other and the teacher on selecting, planning, and implementing thematic units. They learn to communicate effectively, accept differences of opinion, and create joint projects.

*F*IGURE 14.2   **Aspects of Integrated Curriculum**

Aspect	Explanation
Integration of experiences	People's experiences create their perceptions, beliefs, values, and ideas about themselves and their world. Reflections from these experiences help them deal with problems, issues, and situations as they arise.
Social integration	A major purpose for schools is to provide common or shared educational experiences for young people of diverse backgrounds and characteristics in order to create classroom communities.
Integration of knowledge	Individuals use whatever knowledge is appropriate for addressing a situation or problem intelligently without regard for content area designations.
Integration as a curriculum design	The curriculum is based on issues and problems of social and personal significance in the real world. Projects and activities involve application of knowledge for authentic purposes.

- *Meaningful learning:* Thematic units that deal with issues of personal and social significance are more meaningful to students than isolated practice of skills.
- *Learning skills:* Skills learned in the context of purposeful activities help students see their application to actual situations and recognize their usefulness
- *Cultural diversity:* Social interactions enable students from different backgrounds to appreciate each other's characteristics as they collaborate on projects. Electronic collaboration on the Internet often helps to achieve the goal of cultural diversity.
- *In-depth investigation:* Students have time and opportunity to pursue subjects of interest through research, experimentation, and discovery.
- *Choice:* Thematic units offer students choices instead of whole-class assignments. Students may usually choose projects that interest them, ways to conduct investigations, students with whom to work, and the formats for their final reports or projects.
- *Language development:* Students use all forms of language purposefully as they investigate their themes. Language is integrated with content areas in authentic ways.
- *Connections:* Instead of isolating subjects artificially, thematic units enable students to become aware of natural connections across the curriculum. Students realize that they need to cross curricular boundaries to solve problems and define issues.
- *Brain compatibility:* Recent research indicates that the brain processes information more effectively through patterns and connections than through fragmentation. The more that knowledge is unified, the better the brain functions (Beane, 1997).

Developing a Thematic Unit

MUCH CAREFUL thought and planning goes into developing a thematic unit. Selecting the topic, developing relevant activities and projects, locating resources, and evaluating student learning are major considerations. Thematic units may last only a few days or extend as long as ten weeks, depending partly on the students' level of interest and partly on the breadth and depth of the topic.

Selecting a Theme

When selecting a theme, consider many factors, including the students' developmental levels, their areas of expressed interests, curriculum requirements, and compatibility with standards. Establish learning goals and your rationale—the reason this theme is important for students to understand. Also consider the significance or worthiness of the theme in terms of social or personal growth. Although themes about teddy bears

Teaching Tip

If you are required to follow a curriculum guide, you may be able to combine the students' interests with broad topics from the guide. For example, if you are expected to teach about transportation, allow individual students to make choices for the focuses of independent activities within this topic, such as submarines, jet planes, hybrid electric cars, tractor-trailer rigs, or hot air balloons.

and clowns may be fun, they contribute little to the advancement of knowledge or thought.

From observing your students, you should be aware of what they are able to do, the extent of their prior knowledge, and their interests. Choose a theme that is within their grasp but also challenges them to go beyond their present levels. Consider their interests, and, when possible, let them help select the theme so that they feel a sense of ownership. Your school may expect you to follow the curriculum guide and meet certain standards, so you may be somewhat limited in your choices.

Each class can select its own theme, but in many cases the same themes are found at a particular grade level because teachers are using the same curriculum. Elinor Ross met with a team planning a unit that involved all of the third-grade teachers in a school, including the media specialist and the physical education teacher. Together, they were planning the next thematic unit and considering how each of them could contribute. They developed an overall plan but realized that each class might go in a different direction, depending on the students' inquiries and responses. In another school, all of the children from kindergarten through grade 6 were investigating the theme of peace, but each class was pursuing the theme in a different way. One sixth-grade class focused on inner peace, which led to a study of health issues that cause stress.

Planning and Implementing a Thematic Unit

After selecting the theme, you may want to assess students' prior knowledge by using a semantic map or the K-W-L procedure (see Chapters 7 and 12). Once you know their levels of understanding, you can begin to plan the unit. With your students, identify some big questions to stimulate exploration and discovery. Pose some real-world problems that have no easy solutions. Let inquiry be a driving force as you plan your unit.

As you work with students in planning and developing the unit, consider the questions in Figure 14.3. Involve students in each step of the thematic unit, from helping to select the theme to developing and implementing it. You may want to ask them to brainstorm possible activities and then add ideas of your own to provide a well-rounded unit (Brazee & Capelluti, 1995). Consider which activities will be initiating, ongoing, culminating, or evaluative. Initiating activities should spark interest and motivate students to become involved. Ongoing activities may evolve as you move through the unit, and the culminating activity (or activities) should pull together learning experiences and result in some form of creative presentation, such as a project, play, exhibit, or demonstration. Evaluation occurs as you observe student participation, read journals or other documents, peruse

Reflections

What are some of your big questions? How would you go about finding resources to answer them? What areas of the curriculum would you find useful, or would you need to go beyond the curriculum to seek answers?

$\mathcal{F}$IGURE 14.3   **Questions to Consider in Planning and Developing a Unit**

1. How will I establish appropriate learning goals with my students?

2. How can I involve students in the planning?

3. What big questions should I be asking them?

4. How can our theme mesh with the curriculum for this grade?

5. How compatible is our theme with the standards?

6. What literature is appropriate to use with this theme?

7. What information is available on the Internet?

8. How can I accommodate students of diverse backgrounds?

9. How will I be sure that each student is working up to capacity level?

10. Am I providing authentic, meaningful activities and projects?

11. Where will I find the resources I need?

12. Can I find materials that are suitable for different ability levels?

13. How can I involve the community? Can we help them, or can they help us?

14. Will other teachers and the support staff be able to work with us?

15. How can this unit cross into different curricular areas?

16. How well does this theme relate to students' needs, concerns, and interests?

17. How will I evaluate what the students have learned?

Applications for English Language Learners and Students with Special Needs

Many features of thematic units are particularly appropriate for ELLs and students with special needs. ELLs who have opportunities to activate prior knowledge and engage in hands-on activities before they are asked to respond orally show the greatest gains in both language and content acquisition (Hoyt, 2002). These students also hear more language and have more language directed to them when they are in small groups, so their output of language is increased and they have opportunities to clarify meanings. Because of the variety of levels and types of resources, students with special needs have a better chance to achieve during thematic units than when teachers simply lecture from the textbook. The variety of resources, from tape recordings to large-print trade books, enables most students to experience success.

students' portfolios, and observe their final projects. Students at times may work individually, with partners, in groups, or as a whole class. Although you should have in mind an overall plan for the thematic unit, the plan needs to be flexible enough to respond to students' interests and input as the unit progresses.

Using Resources

RESOURCES MUST include more than textbooks and encyclopedias, although both provide valuable information. Ask your students to brainstorm where to search for answers to the big questions. They may have some excellent ideas and know of resources that you can't even imagine. They may have artifacts to share, relatives with expertise, or experiences that bring depth and meaning to the theme. Your media specialist may be able to provide your class with videotapes, different genres of literature, photographs, puppets, and displays to enhance your unit. From teaming with other teachers, you may discover other resources that can be shared.

Your community can also be a great resource, with students both learning from the community and giving back to it. The historical society, the Chamber of Commerce, and banks may have maps, historical documents, information about places and events, and promotional brochures. Visits to nursing homes cheer patients but also enable students to view a different side of life. Resource people, such as firefighters, police officers, and computer specialists, can visit schools to provide information and demonstrations. People from different parts of the world give new insights into cultural differences. With your class, think about what resources are available in your community to support your theme. In the classroom vignette on environment at the beginning of the chapter, children became interested in how to reclaim their own creek and contacted city officials.

Classroom Assessment for Thematic Units

You may use rubrics or rating scales to evaluate student performance during thematic units. You may construct and administer tests over the content or require research papers from older students. In many cases, however, you will evaluate performance by observing student participation and response, by examining portfolios and other written work, and by judging the quality of the final product.

$\mathcal{S}$UMMARY

Thematic units are frameworks for in-depth study of topics that cross the curriculum but still recognize subject area boundaries. They differ in these ways from topical units that are limited to a single subject area for a brief part of the day and from integrated curriculum that deals with major concepts and disregards curricular boundaries. Thematic units have many advantages, including social collaboration, connections among subjects, and brain compatibility.

Selecting a theme is critical, for it must be developmentally appropriate, fit into curriculum and standards guidelines, be worthy of extended investigation, and appeal to students. Planning should involve the students from the onset of the unit, and an opening K-W-L or semantic map activity helps you assess students' existing knowledge about the theme focus. Although activities and projects are roughly planned, you must respond to student interest and be flexible enough to change direction if so indicated. Evaluation is ongoing and generally occurs as you observe student participation, examine written work, and evaluate major projects.

Several examples of organizational webs for thematic units and complete units that teachers can use as starting points or models for developing their own units appear at the end of this chapter. These cover different grade levels and offer a variety of formats.

Discussion Questions

1. If your media center has limited holdings, how can you find the resources you need to develop your thematic unit? What other options do you have?

2. If you have ELLs, how will you make sure that they participate in group work and not rely on native English speakers to speak for them?

3. Should students be allowed to use the Internet to locate information? Does your school have a rule about student use? Is undesirable material blocked from access?

4. How does an integrated curriculum differ from a thematic unit? Could a thematic unit ever be the same as an integrated curriculum? If so, how?

5. If you are in a departmentalized situation, how can you develop a thematic unit? How can you involve other teachers and get their cooperation?

Suggested Activities

1. Consider the class you are teaching or the grade you would prefer to teach. If you are currently teaching, what is the range of achievement levels within that class? How do you know, or how can you find out? List the kinds of resources that are available for these levels.

2. Choose a topic that interests you. Develop five "big questions" that might motivate students to seek answers.

3. Select the thematic unit format that you like best in this chapter. Why do you prefer it? What are its special features? Would you add anything to it? If so, what?

4. Given the theme of environment, how many different directions might it take? List the topics that could naturally develop from this theme. Would the grade level make a difference in how the theme might develop? If so, in what ways?

5. Create your own design for a thematic unit. Think of what is most important to you and how you would proceed.

References

BEANE, J. (1997). *Curriculum integration: Designing the core of democratic education.* New York: Teachers College Press.

BRAZEE, E., & CAPELLUTI, J. (1995). *Dissolving boundaries: Toward an integrative curriculum.* Columbus, OH: National Middle School Association.

COOPER, J. D. (1997). *Literacy: Helping children construct meaning* (3rd ed.). Boston: Houghton Mifflin.

HOYT, L. (2002). *Make it real: Strategies for success with informational texts.* Portsmouth, NH: Heinemann.

KETTEL, R. P., & DOUGLAS, N. L. (2003). Comprehending

multiple texts: A theme approach incorporating the best of children's literature. *Voices from the Middle, 11,* 43–49.

Sawyer, W., & Sawyer, J. (1993). *Integrated language arts for emerging literacy.* Albany, NY: Delmar.

Shanahan, T. (2000). Reading-writing relationships, thematic units, inquiry learning . . . In pursuit of effective integrated literacy instruction. In N. Padak, T. Rasinsky, J. Peck, B. W. Church, G. Fawcett, J. Hendershot, et al., (Eds.), *Distinguished educators on reading* (pp. 305–316). Newark, DE: International Reading Association.

Sample Thematic Webs and Units

The sample thematic webs and units in this section address different grade levels and a variety of themes. They are here as models for teachers to use, but ideally each teacher will develop unique units for each particular group of students. There is not one correct way to plan and implement units, and these units show different approaches and degrees of documentation that teachers have taken.

SAMPLE *1*

Web for Cross-Curricular Thematic Unit on the U.S. Flag

Sample 1 is an organizational web of activities to use in a unit on the flag. The unit is designed for fourth grade. The activities for the unit reach across curricular areas. For a teacher who is working from her own web, the degree of detail here may be sufficient to guide classroom activities.

SAMPLE *2*

Thematic Unit on Energy

Sample 2 is an example of a theme study on energy that extends across a number of subject areas and involves a wide variety of resources. This thematic unit is a broad overview that focuses on major ideas and concepts. Detailed lists of resources and activities will develop as the unit progresses. This unit is most appropriate for grades 4–8.

SAMPLE *3*

Thematic Unit on Humpback Whales

Sample 3 is a thematic unit about humpback whales, appropriate for grades 2–5. This unit provides detailed activities and resources, including fiction and nonfiction literature, audio and video recordings, photographs, computer software, and virtual field trips. It also suggests both teacher-directed and student-directed activities.

SAMPLE *4*

Cross-Curricular Library Literature Unit on Jane Yolen's Works

Sample 4 is a cross-curricular library literature unit that can be adapted for use with students in grades 2–8. The unit focuses on the works of Jane Yolen, and the activities are categorized under different genres of literature and different subjects in the curriculum.

SAMPLE 5

Thematic Unit on *Maniac Magee*

Sample 5 is a thematic unit that uses the novel *Maniac Magee* to focus instruction across the curriculum for grades 5–8. Both fiction and nonfiction resource books are used in this unit.

SAMPLE 6

Thematic Unit on Biomes of the World

Sample 6 is a thematic unit for the area of science that has biomes of the world as its focus. It is appropriate for grades 6–8. It features active learning and a mixture of concrete and vicarious learning activities.

SAMPLE 7

Thematic Unit on the American Revolution

Sample 7 is a thematic unit for the area of social studies that focuses on the American Revolution. It is appropriate for the middle grades, especially grades 4 and 5. This unit incorporates a variety of literature selections, as well as a video on the topic.

SAMPLE 8

Thematic Unit on Pioneers

Sample 8 is a thematic unit on pioneers. The unit is appropriate for grades 4–8 in its current form, but it could easily be adjusted for use in higher or lower grades. The unit spans a number of curricular areas, and it makes use of resource books, artifacts, websites, and a videotape. There are varied activities to engage the students who learn in different ways.

SAMPLE 9

Thematic Unit on Insects and Spiders

Sample 9 is a thematic unit on insects and spiders. It is designed for pre-kindergarten through third grade. The unit includes both teacher-directed and student-directed activities, and these activities engage the children's senses. Resources are drawn from both informational books and works of fiction, as well as videos, computer software, photographs, audiotapes, and virtual field trips on the Internet.

SAMPLE 10

Thematic Unit on *Holes*

Sample 10 is for a thematic unit based on the book *Holes*. It is organized around students choosing related questions to answer. It is appropriate for grades 7 and 8.

Web for Cross-Curricular Thematic Unit on the U.S. Flag

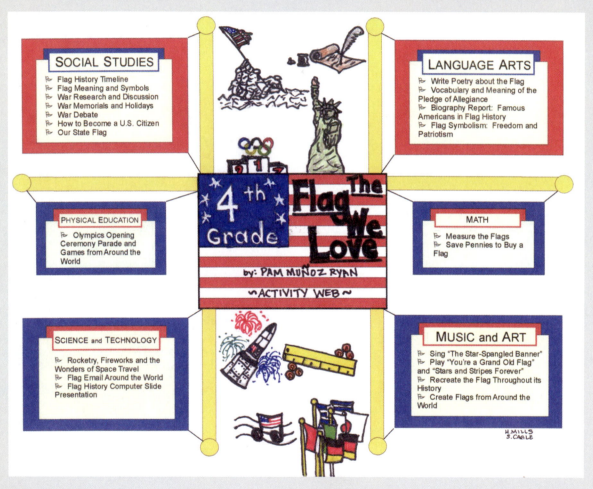

Source: Holly Mills and Sabrina Cagle, Graduate Students, Tennessee Technological University, Cookeville, TN. Used with permission.

Thematic Unit on Energy

Topic

Energy

Theme

To become aware of some sources and effects of various types of energy

Big Questions

What alternatives are there to traditional energy sources? How do they work?

How do we get energy that we can use? Can we store it to use later? How can we conserve it?

What kinds of energy are found in our solar system? Find examples.

Trace the use of energy from early civilizations to the present. What might the future hold in terms of energy resources and production?

Overview of Content

Science concepts: energy sources (wind, sun, water, fossil fuels, nuclear energy, geothermal energy)

Social issues: pollution, radiation, conservation, recycling, depletion of resources

Mathematical calculations: relative cost and efficiency of energy sources; units for measuring energy

Health: effects of using various types of energy on humans (radiation, clean air, acid rain, asphyxiation)

Processes

Surveying home and school for energy conservation opportunities

Interviewing resource people and writing reports

Using textbooks, reference materials, the Internet, and other media

Participating in oral presentations (debates, panel discussions, reports)

Conducting experiments on energy efficiency

Discovering and suggesting solutions for local energy problems

Keeping records of observations on energy consumption with charts, graphs, and diagrams

Making illustrated books on energy

Building models related to energy sources and utilization

Writing government representatives about energy concerns

Resources

Trade books: fiction (*Letting Swift River Go* by Jane Yolen), biography (*Benjamin Franklin: The New American* by Milton Meltzer), and science books (*The Way Things Work* by David Macaulay)

Reference materials (encyclopedias, textbooks, almanacs, atlases)

Resource people (power distributors, conservation officials)

Writing materials (notebooks, binders, graph paper, index cards)

Computers (Internet, word processing, e-mail correspondence)

Local newspapers

Government pamphlets and publications

Evaluation

Written project reports

Oral presentations

Tests over concepts

Completion of projects or experiments

Thematic Unit on Humpback Whales

Theme

The humpback whale, an endangered species, is a large mammal with many interesting features.

Grade levels

2–5

Duration

Approximately two weeks, depending on extent of student interest

Learner Objectives

The learner will

1. Develop an appreciation for humpback whales.

2. Gain understanding of environmental threats to humpback whales.

3. Acquire knowledge about characteristics and lives of humpback whales.

4. Compare and contrast whales with fish.

5. Understand how whales communicate with each other.

Activities

Initiating Activity

Read *Humphrey, the Lost Whale: A True Story* by Wendy Tokuda, and/or show the video with the same name. This is the story of Humphrey, the humpback whale, who was stranded in the Sacramento River near San Franscisco in 1985 and how he was rescued. He was also stranded in San Francisco Bay in 1990. Arouse curiosity about whales by asking

■ How would a whale get stranded?

■ How could a whale be rescued?

■ What do you think happens to Humphrey after he is rescued?

■ Can you find on a map where Humphrey was stranded?

Tell the students that they will be learning much more about humpback whales.

Teacher-Directed Activities

1. Investigate Adopt-a-Whale programs. Ask students how to raise money to adopt a whale. An adopter gets photos of the whale, the whale's biography, an adoption certificate, an audio CD of unique humpback whale calls, and a one-year subscription to the newsletter *Flukeprints*. (Information is available at http://www.whalecenter.org/adopt.htm.)

2. Play a recording of a whale song. Ask students to guess what they are hearing. Lead a discussion of how whales communicate through their songs. Let the students imitate some whale songs. (See audio resources for websites that give whale sounds.)

3. Have students contribute ideas for making a Venn diagram to compare a fish and a whale. Point out similarities and differences concerning how they swim, how they breathe, how their young are born, and the kind of skin they have. Also, make a Venn diagram to compare the flukes (horizontal parts of the tail) of a whale with the tail fins of a fish.

4. Encourage students to investigate why the humpback whale is an endangered species and what can be done to save it. They may contact Greenpeace (http://whales.greenpeace.org), the International Wildlife Coalition (http://www.iwc.org), the Center for Coastal Studies (http://www.coastalstudies.org), and the Marine Conservation Biology Institute (http://www.mcbi.org) for information. Discuss the issues involved in commercial whaling and saving the whale.

5. Ask students to find the size of a typical humpback whale.

6. Let students choose three to five of the following activities. To avoid having all students choose the same activities, make a sign-up sheet with a limited number of students for each activity. Provide time for them to share what they have done and learned.

Student-Directed Activities

Sign up for the activities you prefer. Use reference materials, Internet sites, and other resources to get the information you need. You may work individually, with a partner, or in a small group. Complete each activity that you choose and put your work in your portfolio.

1. Make a chart comparing humpback whales with other whales in terms of size, weight, places where found, and special characteristics. How does the humpback whale compare to a school bus or an eighteen-wheeler?

2. Humpback whales make the most famous sounds, which are sung only by the males (Simon, 1989). To make sounds using bottles of water, pour water in increments of 1/8 cup into eight identical bottles. Blow across the tops of the bottles and notice how the pitch varies. Try to make a tune.

3. What happens when a whale "blows"? How do whales use their blowholes to breathe? How do you breathe? How do fish breathe? Some whales can hold their breath for over an hour. Get someone to time how long you can hold your breath.

4. Learn about the history of whaling. What is a harpoon? How is it used? After a whale is killed, how is it brought on board a ship? What happens to the whale on a ship? Make a flow chart, a time line, or another type of graphic organizer showing the process of harpooning and processing a whale.

5. Whales are covered with fatty tissue called blubber beneath their skin. How does blubber help the whale? Find out why whales were hunted for their blubber and how it was used. Make a list of other products that come from whales.

6. A newly born humpback whale is 12 to 14 feet long. Ask your parents how long you were when you were born. If you are working individually, use this length. If you are working with

a partner or in a group, compute the average birth length. Make a drawing on newsprint comparing your birth length or average length with that of the humpback whale. Also, mark the size of an average fully grown person (just under 6 feet) on your drawing.

7. Get a map of the world and cut out tiny shapes representing whales. Put the map on a bulletin board and place a whale shape wherever whales are found. You may want to label the kind of whale that is found in each location.

8. The International Whaling Commission banned all commercial whaling, beginning in 1985. Why did they do this? Is the ban being enforced all over the world? Find out at http://www.iwcoffice.org and share your findings with the class.

9. Some whales migrate. Why do they migrate, and where do they go? Trace their routes on a map.

10. Keep a portfolio of your investigations and activities about whales. Organize it, make a table of contents, illustrate parts of it, and make it available for others to see.

11. Write a journal entry as one of the following: a child on a whale-watching expedition, a whale enjoying its typical daily activities, or a person on a whaling vessel on a day when a whale is harpooned.

12. Debate the positive and negative aspects of commercial whaling. Study the issues and be prepared to support your views and respond to members of the other team.

13. Read three books about whales. You may use those listed as resources or find other books about whales. Discuss the books with a group of other students or write reviews of them.

14. Dramatize the story of Humphrey. Someone plays the part of Humphrey, and others are concerned spectators and rescuers.

15. Make a mural of a *pod* (group or school) of whales in the sea. Find out what sea plants and creatures are likely to be present in the background.

16. Create a diorama of a scene featuring a humpback whale. Use clay to mold the whale and suspend it from the top of the box. Create other sea creatures and plants to put in your diorama.

17. Dramatize people on a commercial fishing boat as they harpoon a whale, haul it on board, and process it.

18. Study the movements of whales. They *breach*, or jump almost clear out of the water, and then crash down. They swim with up-and-down pushes of their *flukes* (tail fins), and they use their paddle-like flippers for turning and balancing. They dive to great depths to search for food. They sleep by resting near the surface. Act out these movements in the gymnasium or on the playground.

Culminating Activity

Make a class semantic map with students contributing what they have learned about whales. From the topic "Humpback Whales," let students choose their preferred subtopics, and divide them into groups according to the preferences. Give each group a reasonable amount of time to develop a project related to their subtopic. Depending on their developmental levels, students might choose to draw pictures or murals, make scrapbooks, create an annotated bibliography, give a dramatic presentation, write and illustrate a story from a whale's point of view, debate the issue of whale hunting, or create a Microsoft PowerPoint presentation.

Cross-Curricular Connections

Language arts: nonfiction and fiction books, written and oral reports, portfolios, dramatizations, new vocabulary, websites, audio- and videotapes, journal entries, debates, reference materials

Science: living things and the environment, breathing through blowholes, comparison of mammals and fish, features of whales, sound-making in water

Mathematics: problem solving, comparisons of sizes and weights, averages, statistics, distances of migration, amounts of food and water intake

Social studies: history and processes of the whaling industry, issue of saving a species versus serving an industry

Geography: locations of whales, migratory paths, water temperatures in different locations

Visual arts: making murals, scrapbooks, dioramas, illustrations, clay models, and other representations of humpback whales

Music: listening to and imitating whale songs, creating tunes with bottles containing varying amounts of water

Physical education: moving as whales: breaching, swimming, diving, and resting

Evaluation

Evaluation can occur in a variety of ways, including the following.

1. Observation of completeness, accuracy, and presentation of culminating activity

2. Observation of class participation during activities

3. Observation of thoroughness, neatness, and organization of portfolio

4. Teacher-made test over facts about whales and/or understanding of their endangered status

5. Student-teacher conferences for discussions that reveal understanding and appreciation of whales

6. Self-evaluation of effort and knowledge acquired

Resources and Materials

Nonfiction Books

Gibbons, G. (1991). *Whales.* New York: Holiday House. Presents different kinds of whales. Cassette also available.

Lauber, P. (1991). *Great whales: The gentle giants.* New York: Holt. Tells the characteristics of different kinds of whales and why some are endangered.

McMillan, B. (1992). *Going on a whale watch.* New York: Scholastic. Describes the experiences of two children on a whale watching expedition who see different kinds of whales.

Patent, D. (1989). *Humpback whales.* New York: Holiday House. Discusses the habitat, physical features, and behavior of humpback whales.

Simon, S. (1989). *Whales.* New York: Scholastic. Presents the habits, physical characteristics, and environment of different types of whales.

Smyth, K. (1986). *Crystal: The story of a real baby whale.* Camden, ME: Down East Books. Depicts the first year of Crystal, a humpback whale.

Tokuda, W. (1986). *Humphrey, the lost whale: A true story.* Torrance, CA: Heian. Tells the true story of a trapped whale and efforts to rescue him.

Fiction Books

Allen, J. (1993). *Whale.* Cambridge, MA: Candlewick Press. A mother whale and her baby try to outswim a spreading oil slick.

Day, E. (1989). *John Tabor's ride.* New York: Knopf. John Tabor, on his first whaling voyage, meets a strange old man who takes him on a journey.

Sheldon, D. (1991). *The whale's song.* New York: Dial. After hearing her grandmother's tales about whales, Lilly hopes to see the whales and hear their songs.

Starbuck, D. (1986). *Manny's whale.* Parsippany, NJ: Dillon. With his uncle, Manny helps rescue a beached whale.

Weller, F. (1991). *I wonder if I'll see a whale.* New York: Philomel. A child watches the activities of a humpback whale while on a whale-watching boat.

Videotapes and Videodiscs

Encounters with whales of the St. Lawrence. (1996). Montreal, Quebec, Canada: Animavision. Film on video. 52 minutes.

The magnificent whales. (1988). Smithsonian. VHS.

To save a whale. (1989). The Blue Frontier Series. Bennett Marine Video. 30 minutes. VHS.

Computer Software and CD-ROMs

"Whale," *Mammals: A multimedia encyclopedia.* (1990). National Geographic. CD-ROM.

"Whale," *The New Grolier multimedia encyclopedia on CD-ROM.* (2002). Grolier.

"Whale," *Microsoft Encarta multimedia encyclopedia.* (2001). Microsoft Corp.

Whale Video Company: Series of fourteen videos of North Atlantic humpbacks. http://whalevideo.com/index2.htm

Photographs

Photos of humpbacks in Silver Banks by Kaz Zirkle. http://www.naturalextremes.com

Photos of humpbacks by Jim Nahmens. http://www.natures-spirit.com

Photos of humpbacks by Cynthia D'Vincent. http://www.intersea.org/photo.html

Audiotapes

Whale sounds, cries, howls, whistles, and songs. http://dkd.net/whales/wsounds.html. Gives whales' cries, howls, songs, and whistles; also sounds of a humpback whale feeding.

Ocean Mammal Institute: Listen to whale songs. http://www.oceanmammalinst.com/songs.html. Contains songs of the humpback whale.

Field Trips

Whale-watching trips all over the world available at Whale Watching Web.
http://www.physics.helsinki.fi/whale

Virtual whale watching. http://www.whalewatch.ca

Sources

Thematic unit: Humpback whales. (April, 1994). Library Links, *2*(2). Baton Rouge, LA: Louisiana Energy and Environmental Resource and Information Center.

Adcock, A., & McCormick, K. *Collaborative thematic unit: Whales.* http://www.libsci.sc.edu/miller/whales.htm

Various Internet sites.

Cross-Curricular Library Literature Unit on Jane Yolen's Works

By Holly Mills

Fairy Tales, Folktales, and Legends

Dove Isabeau

The Emperor and the Kite
  Research the origin of this folktale.

The Girl in the Golden Bower

The Girl Who Loved the Wind

The Moon Ribbon and Other Tales

Rainbow Rider
  Explore alternate theories for the creation of our world and human beings, other than creationism and evolution. Share findings with the class.

The Seeing Stick
  Read a biography of Louis Braille or Helen Keller and write a brief report about that person.

Sky Dogs
  Locate other tales of Native American folklore that attempt to explain the existence of some beings.

Language Arts Rhyme Time

All in the Woodland Early: An ABC Book

A Sip of Aesop

Beneath the Ghost Moon

How Do Dinosaurs Say Good Night?

The Ballad of the Pirate Queens

The Three Bears Holiday Rhyme Book
  Write a poem about your favorite animal, place, or holiday

Fantasy/Science Fiction

Twelve Impossible Things Before Breakfast

The Pit Dragon Trilogy (Dragon's Blood, Heart's Blood, A Sending of Dragons)

Sword of the Rightful King

The Faery Flag
  Submit a short fantasy or science fiction story. All submissions will be bound and kept in the library's collection.

The Young Merlin Trilogy (Passager, Hobby, Merlin)
  Read *Passager*, along with *Children of the Wolf* (also by Yolen). Visit the website www.feralchildren.com and write a brief summary of one other case of feral children.

Families

All those Secrets of the World
Grandad Bill's Song
Owl Moon

Share a favorite happy or sad family moment.

Fiction

Armageddon Summer

Girl in a Cage and *Queens' Own Fool*
  Read and compare these two family powers.

Science

Before the Storm
  Find out how thunderstorms happen and why they are more common in the summer. OR Write about the hottest summer day you can remember. Use lots of adjectives and descriptions to make us feel the heat.

Bird Watch
  Locate information about your favorite bird and write a brief "bird biography."

Honkers
  What is the normal migratory pattern of Canadian geese?

Welcome to the Green House (Ice House, River of Grass, Sea of Sand . . .)
  Research a member of the flora or fauna mentioned in the book and tell the class what you learned.

Just for Fun

Commander Toad in Space (Series)

The Giants' Farm and *The Giants Go Camping*

Hark! A Christmas Sampler

Piggins and *Piggins and the Royal Wedding*

Rounds About Rounds (Collected and Edited By Jane Yolen)
  Participate in a group performance of rounds.

History/Social Studies

The Devil's Arithmetic
  Locate a nonfiction book on the Holocaust. Compare the details of this book with those in the novel. Does the novel seem authentic?

Encounter
  You are Christopher Columbus. Write a letter to the Taino boy telling him how you feel after reading his side of the story.

Letting Swift River Go
  Research the flooding of the south by TVA. Were the details similar to this story? Why, or why not?

The Mary Celeste: An Unsolved Mystery from History
  Read the story and answer the questions relating to the theories. What is your theory?

Overview

This unit will be taught during scheduled library time for classes ranging from grades 2 to 8. The content of this unit will be adapted for each grade level with which it is used, choosing only age-appropriate material from the possibilities that follow. Because this unit will be taught in a library, an author study is appropriate. However, many of the activities, though centered on research or information, can be used by classroom teachers in connection with content area studies. Students will be studying the author Jane Yolen, who has published more than 130 books. Unlike many authors, her books have covered multiple (nearly all) genres of literature and all grade levels, making her an ideal author for a cross-curricular study.

Objectives

Note: TLW stands for "The learner will."

- TLW become familiar with the author Jane Yolen and her various works.
- TLW participate in research relating to some of Jane Yolen's material.
- TLW participate in group discussions and literature circles centered on some of Jane Yolen's material.
- TLW utilize the library resources to find information relating to Jane Yolen's works, as dictated by chosen activities.
- TLW be an active participant in discovery learning by choosing appropriate activities to complete.

Description of Activities

Fairy Tales, Folktales, and Legends

1. *The Emperor and the Kite*
   Students who choose this activity will read this folktale and then conduct library print and electronic resources research to determine its origin. Results will be handwritten in short paper form (one page).

2. *Rainbow Rider*
   Students who choose this activity will explore alternate theories for the creation of our world and human beings. Students must use library print and electronic resources to find this information, and they must look for views other than those of creationism and evolution.

3. *The Seeing Stick*
   Students who choose this activity will choose to read a biography of either Louis Braille or Helen Keller. A brief written report will be required.

4. *Sky Dogs*
   Students who choose this activity will locate other tales of Native American folklore that attempt to explain the existence of certain beings in our world. Students will orally share their findings during library time.

Families

Students choosing to participate in this activity will share happy family moments or sad family moments. Students will be encouraged to share any interesting family traditions, such as the one described in *Owl Moon*. This discussion will take place in a small group.

Fantasy/Science Fiction

1. Students may choose to submit short original fantasy or science fiction stories. All submissions will be read to the class by the authors, and with the authors' approval, submissions will be cataloged and held as part of the library's collection.

2. *Passager* and *Children of the Wolf*
   Students who choose this activity will read the books *Passager* and *Children of the Wolf,* which share a theme of feral children. Students will compare, in single paragraphs, the circumstances of the feral children in these stories. In addition, the students will access the website http://www.feralchildren.com and write a brief summary of one other case of a feral child.

Fiction

1. *Armageddon Summer*
   Students will be required to participate in a literature circle discussion of this book. Reading logs will be kept and insights will be shared during circle time.

2. *Girl in a Cage* and *Queen's Own Fool*
   Students choosing this activity will read these two novels and compare, in a short paper, the two ruling powers in the books.

History/Social Studies

1. *The Devil's Arithmetic*
   Students choosing this activity will read this book and then locate a nonfiction book about the Holocaust with which to compare it. Students will be asked if the novel seemed authentic and if the details in the books were comparable. Findings will be shared during a group discussion.

2. *Encounter*
   Students choosing this activity will take the persona of Christopher Columbus. They must write a letter to the Taino boy telling him how they feel after reading his side of the story.

3. *Letting Swift River Go*
   Students choosing this activity will research the flooding of same areas by TVA. Students must address whether any of the details with TVA were similar to the details in the story and be able to explain how and why.

4. *The Mary Celeste: An Unsolved Mystery from History*
   Students choosing this activity will read the book and answer the questions relating to the theories in the back of the book. Students will be encouraged to state their own theories or take positions for theories in the book.

Just for Fun

This arm of the unit contains more of the nonsense or silly works by Yolen. Students will not be required to participate in any activities but may wish to participate in singing rounds during the last day of the author study.

Language Arts Rhyme Time

Students choosing to read from this section and participate in this activity will write poems about their favorite animal, place, holiday, or topic of their choosing. Poems will be compiled for a poetry keepsake book to be kept in the classroom.

Science

1. *Before the Storm*
   Students choosing this activity will read this book and then find out how thunderstorms happen and why storms are more common during the summer months, or students may choose the book and write brief narratives of the hottest day they can remember. Emphasis here will be on descriptive words and creativity.

2. *Bird Watch*
   Students choosing this activity will locate information via the library's print and electronic resources on favorite birds or especially interesting birds. Findings will be written in brief (one page or less) "bird biographies" to be shared with the class.

3. *Honkers*
   Students choosing this activity will seek information regarding the normal migratory patterns of Canadian geese.

4. *Welcome to the . . .* (Series)
   Students choosing this activity will choose one of the four books from the series to read. Each student will then research one member of the flora or fauna present in the chosen book that is of interest, and they will share their findings orally with the class.

Most activities will be initiated in the library setting. Any activity requiring written work may be worked on in the library but will also be combined with language arts classroom work.

Students will sign contracts designating which books will be read and in which activities they will be participating. The librarian's emphasis will be placed on reading for enjoyment, understanding the diverse works one author can have, and appreciation of the enrichment activities offered in each section.

This study should take at least one month, but it could become a nine-week unit.

Thematic Unit on Maniac Magee

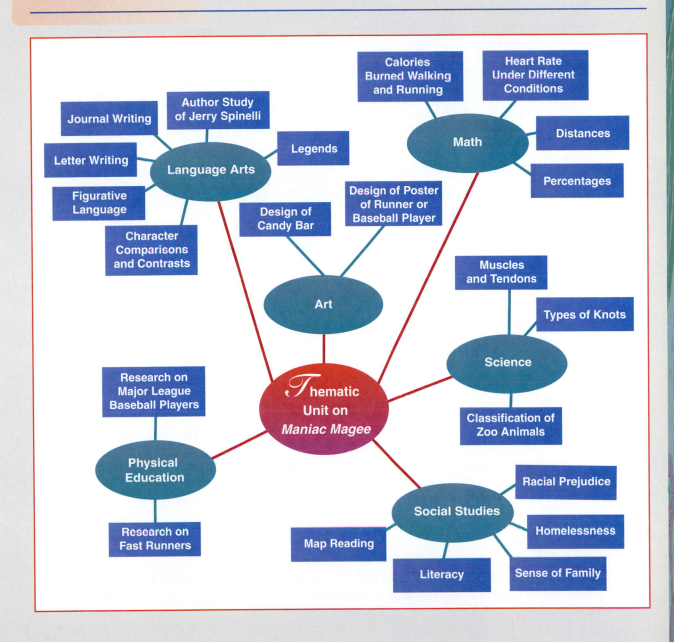

Grade levels

5–8

Goal

To use the novel *Maniac Magee* by Jerry Spinelli as a literature focus for learning across the curriculum.

Learner Objectives

Note: TLW stands for "The learner will."

TLW apply units of measurement in mathematics to real-life problems.

TLW explain the functions of the muscles and tendons in the body.

TLW tie various knots and tell the functions of different knots.

TLW be able to classify zoo animals into scientific categories.

TLW participate in discussions about prejudice, homelessness, sense of family, and literacy issues related to the book.

TLW demonstrate an ability to read maps.

TLW do research on fast runners and major league baseball players and write papers on each topic.

TLW participate in discussions on Jerry Spinelli's books and his writing style.

TLW describe the attributes of a legend.

TLW compare and contrast the Beale and McNab families and analyze Maniac Magee's character.

TLW write effective letters about real-life situations.

TLW write journal entries that record predictions about the plot of the core book and personal reactions to the content.

TLW recognize and use new vocabulary words, including figurative expressions.

Plot Summary

Jeffrey Magee, a twelve-year-old orphan, arrives in Two Mills, a town divided into the East End for black people and the West End for white people. He quickly earns the nickname of Maniac because he is different. His amazing feats become legendary. He can run faster than anyone else and win athletic events against older kids. He is also able to view black people and white people as the same.

Curriculum Connections

The organizational web shows the curriculum connections for *Maniac Magee.* Sample activities with challenging questions from various areas of the curriculum follow.

Math

(a) Find the number of calories burned per hour when people walk or run. Record your heart rate when at rest, when walking, and when running. How does it change? How does running increase heart rate and help burn calories? (b) Measure the distance around a walking track. How many feet, yards, and meters are there? What percentage of a mile is the track?

Science

(a) Find out how muscles, tendons, and ligaments enable people to run. What is the difference between voluntary and involuntary muscles? (b) Invite a Boy Scout leader to demonstrate knot tying and learn to tie and untie different kinds of knots. How are knots used for different purposes? (c) Plan a field trip to a zoo. How are zoo animals classified?

Social Studies

(a) Research the history of prejudice by reading about Rosa Parks, Martin Luther King, Jr., and others who have fought for racial equality. How did these people demonstrate courage? (b) Research issues of homelessness. How did Jeffrey deal with homelessness? Was his approach reasonable in real life? (c) Discuss illiteracy. What causes illiteracy? Are there illiterate people in your neighborhood? How could you help them become literate? What are some good books to use for helping people learn to read? (d) Locate on a map of Pennsylvania places that are mentioned in the book. Create an imaginary map of Two Mills that shows places important to the story.

Physical Education

(a) Research famous runners, including Wilma Rudolph, Jackie Joyner-Kersee, Jesse Owens, and Edwin Moses. What makes a runner fast? What are some speed records set by these runners? (b) Read about major league baseball players. What makes them great? What are their batting averages?

Language Arts

(a) Read some other books by Jerry Spinelli (see Resource Books). What do you notice about his style of writing? What makes him a popular author with students? (b) Many of Maniac's acts are legendary. What is a legend? Give some examples of Maniac's legendary acts. Read some legends or tall tales about American heroes, such as Paul Bunyan (see Resource Books). (c) Read about the McNab and Beale families. Compare them by making a Venn diagram or a T chart. (d) Do a character analysis or make a character map of Maniac. (e) Look for examples of onomatopoeia in *Maniac Magee.* (Examples: *crunch, fizz, hiss, slurp, sizzle*) (f) Look for similes in the book, and write some. (Examples: *Maniac is as speedy as . . . ; Mars Bar is as mean as . . .*) (g) Look for metaphors in the book (comparisons without the word *like* or *as*), and write some. (h) Create an illustrated dictionary with onomatopoeia, similes, metaphors, and new vocabulary words. (i) Write letters to the local paper about problems in the community, such as homelessness, prejudice, and illiteracy. What solutions might you suggest? (j) Keep a journal for writing predictions and reactions as you read. In your journal, answer these questions: How can uncontrollable events change and affect the way you feel about life? Why did Maniac want someone who would care about him and accept him for who he was?

Art (with writing, math, and physical education)

(a) Design an original candy bar wrapper. Include weight (both metric and traditional U.S.), calories, vitamins, minerals, other nutritional information, and price. Write a rationale for creating the candy bar and reasons for including the ingredients. (b) Design a poster of a famous runner or baseball player.

Assessment

Rubrics given to students in advance will enable them to understand how they will be assessed on various activities. By knowing the expectations for each activity, students are challenged to meet the highest requirements.

Resource Books

Folktales and Tall Tales

Balcziak, B. (2003). *Paul Bunyan (Tall Tales)*. Minneapolis: Compass Point.

Dorson, R. M. (1975). *Folktales from around the world*. Chicago: University of Chicago Press.

Contemporary Realistic Fiction

Fenner, C. (1998). *The king of dragons*. New York: Scholastic.

Fox, P. (1991). *Monkey Island*. New York: Orchard.

Holman, F. (1974). *Slake's limbo*. New York: Scribner.

Nonfiction

Russell, J. (1981). *Useful knots*. New York: Arco.

Biography

Adler, D. A. (1991). *A picture book of Martin Luther King, Jr.* New York: Holiday House.

Adler, D. A. (1995). *A picture book of Rosa Parks*. New York: Holiday House.

Burleigh, R. (1998). *Home run: The story of Babe Ruth*. New York: Harcourt.

Krull, K. (1996). *Wilma unlimited: How Wilma Rudolph became the world's fastest woman*. New York: Harcourt.

Other Books by Jerry Spinelli

Crash. (1996). New York: Knopf.

Fourth grade rats. (1991). New York: Scholastic.

Knots in my yo-yo string: The autobiography of a kid. (1998). New York: Knopf.

Loser. (2002). New York: HarperTrophy.

Milkweed. (2003). New York: Knopf.

Space station seventh grade. (1982). Boston: Little, Brown.

Stargirl. (2000). New York: Knopf.

There's a girl in my hammerlock. (1991). New York: Simon & Schuster.

Wringer. (1997). New York: HarperCollins.

Source: Ideas from "Maniac Magee: A Literature Study" by Rebecca Reed, Graduate Student, Tennessee Technological University, Cookeville, TN. Used with permission.

SAMPLE **6**

Thematic Unit on Biomes of the World

Unit: *Biomes of the World — a study of interactions between living things and their environment*

Resources What has already been produced in this area? What materials are available to us? Do we need to do any reading about the topic? Do we know any "experts" in the area?	— *Schlessinger Media Biome Videos: deserts, forests, marine, freshwater, ecosystems, grasslands, tundra* — *"Project Wild" — interdisciplinary environmental & conservation education program* — *Eyewitness science books, videos* — *Wesley Woods Environmental Camp (Smoky Mtns.) — will take 3 day/2 night field trip there* — *Knoxville Zoo outreach program*
Understandings What do we hope children will understand about their social or physical world by the end of this unit? What is important and relevant for these children?	— *TLW investigate biomes of the world* — *TLW investigate how living things interact with one another & with non-living elements of their environment* — *TLW understand the nature of symbiotic relationships* — *TLW examine competitive relationships w/in an ecosystem* — *TLW recognize relationships within food chains* — *TLW understand how organisms are adapted for surviving in certain environments*
What CONCEPTS may be emphasized?	— *Symbiosis, biome, food chain, mutualism, commensalism, parasitism, adaptation, conservation*
Tuning In/Preparing to Find Out How can we engage children in this topic? What media can we use? What literature can we use? How can we assess their prior knowledge? How can we involve them in negotiating the direction of the unit?	— *KWL chart (ongoing) about biomes* — *Ask, "What determines the type of plants & animals that thrive in an area?"* — *Read throughout "There's An Owl In The Shower" by Jean Craighead George* — *Schlessinger Media Biome Videos* — *"What's It Like Where You Live?" Website* — *www.brainpop.com — ecosystem short video*

Investigating   What experiences can we organize that will enable children to gather new information about the topic? How can we help to FOCUS their investigations?

Tuning In/Preparing	**Investigating**	**Sharing & Explaining**
Biome/Ecosystem Interactions Among Living Things — readings & discussion *Biome/Ecosystem Readings & Discussion, imagery (C)*	*(C - Class, G - Groups, I - Individuals)* *Students will view teacher-made symbiosis Power Point (C)* *Explore NASA Earth Observatory website; record information pertaining to assigned biome for future reference during project (G, I)*	*(thro' art/craft, drama, language, music, movement, math, etc.)* *Students may choose to create a Power Point to explain one of the 3 types of symbiosis* *Students may choose to convey information in the form of a skit, diorama, posters or report, etc.*

* data charts will be completed at each level of study

| Year Level: 6 | Duration of Unit: 3 — 5 weeks | (...../...../..... to ...../...../.....) |

Tuning In/Preparing	Investigating	Sharing & Explaining
Discuss food chains within a forest ecosystem *Discuss & view video — Animal Adaptations; read section in text pertaining to & other various sections of picture books; information books*	*(C - Class, G - Groups, I - Individuals)* *Dissect owl pellets (C, G, I); reconstruct 1 skeleton from pellet; label according to chart and classify* *Arrange for Knoxville Zoo outreach program to visit — "Animals In Action" — observe animals in action & explore adaptations for movement (C)*	*Discuss findings; how many & what types of creatures were found w/in the pellet* *— Create hypothetical adaptations for an imaginary creature* *— Describe creature's environment & means of movement & survival* *— Creative writing story about creature and habitat* *— Create 3-D creature*

Sharing & Explaining to Make Connections How can we assist children to pull it all together? What curriculum processes would help here? (Art, drama, language…?) How can we see if they are making connections?	*— Students will create a "Biome In A Box" (shoebox or larger) depicting characteristics — biotic/abiotic of assigned biome; one food chain must be represented.* *— Students will research biome, present findings to the class via posters, dioramas, skits, diagrams and the presentation of the biome in a box (in groups).*
Reflection and Action How can we empower children to act on what they have learned?	*— After attending Wesley Woods Environmental Camp, students may become "Honorary Stewards of the Earth" by pledging to do more conservation awareness activities at home.* *— Students will adopt a zoo animal at the Knoxville Zoo. The "Flat-Pak Adoption" kit for $35 includes adoption certificate, animal facts, Wild Wonders magazine & helps to pay for food for an animal at the zoo.*

Related Experiences / Student Assessment / Notes:

"Oh Deer" game from Project Wild program — allows students to see the cycle of deer populations in an ecosystem.	*Teacher and Student* *Assessments will be completed at end of group project — following a rubric for the presentation (teacher assessed) and a self-evaluation rubric for the group & individual student — all 3 are considered when calculating final grade.*

Source: Tera Witcher, Graduate Student, Tennessee Technological University, Cookeville, TN. Used with permission.

Thematic Unit on the American Revolution

Unit: *American Revolution: Causes and Effects and 1st Major Battles of the War*	

Resources
 	
What has already been produced in this area?
 	
What materials are available to us?
 	
Do we need to do any reading about the topic?
 	
Do we know any "experts" in the area?
	Books: *Yankee Doodle by Gary Chalk*
	          The Boston Tea Party by Klingel and Noyed
	          The Eve of Revolution by Barbara Burt
	          The Boston Massacre by Allison Draper
	          Revolutionary War by Scott Marquette
	          Lexington and Concord by Deborah Kent
	          Paul Revere's Ride by Lucia Raatma
	          The Declaration of Independence by Stuart Kallan
	          Revolutionary War on Wednesday by Mary Pope Osborne
	Video: *School House Rock* *Magazine: Cobblestone Magazine*
	Poetry: *Phyllis Wheatly, "The Midnight Ride of Paul Revere" by Longfellow*
	Songs: *"Yankee Doodle"* *Technology: Kid Pix CD-ROM*
	Websites: *www.historyplace.com* *www.americaslibrary.gov*

Understandings What do we hope children will understand about their social or physical world by the end of this unit? What is important and relevant for these children? What CONCEPTS may be emphasized?	*TLW list causes for the Revolutionary War.* *TLW discuss the battles of Lexington and Concord.* *TLW explain the importance of Paul Revere's Ride.* *TLW sing songs and read poetry related to the time period.* *TLW explore the Declaration of Independence.* *TLW list and discuss the effects of the war and explain how they affect our lives today: Articles of Confederation, Constitution, Bill of Rights*
Tuning In/Preparing to Find Out How can we engage children in this topic? What media can we use? What literature can we use? How can we assess their prior knowledge? How can we involve them in negotiating the direction of the unit?	*Make a semantic map together about things they think are related to the Revolutionary War.* *Ask each child to complete a K-W-L chart about the topic. Discuss with the class.* *Sing "Yankee Doodle" — discuss vocabulary in the song.* *Create a reference table with books and materials that can be used.*

Investigating   What experiences can we organize that will enable children to gather new information about the topic? How can we help to FOCUS their investigations?

Tuning In/Preparing	**Investigating**	**Sharing & Explaining**
Ask children what things they think of when they hear the words "Revolutionary War." *Discuss the things they know and make a list of things they want to find out about.* *In the song "Yankee Doodle," what does it mean by "Stuck a feather in his hat and called it macaroni?"* *Write down possible causes for the war.*	(C - Class, G - Groups, I - Individuals) C - *Read Revolutionary War on Wednesday.* C - *Read Lexington and Concord.* C/G - *Teacher will read Paul Revere's Ride to class.*	(thro' art/craft, drama, language, music, movement, math, etc.) *Respond to literature in a journal. Record feelings, questions, and ideas. Draw pictures too!* *Discuss the importance of the battles. Draw a map and label these places.* *Students will act it out.*

| Year Level: 4 – 5 | Duration of Unit: 2 weeks | (...../...../..... to ...../...../.....) |

Tuning In/Preparing	Investigating	Sharing & Explaining
Let students create a word board to collect new words throughout the unit.	(C - Class, G - Groups, I - Individuals) I - Choose an important person from the time period to research. (Use Internet sources.) G - Students will explore causes of the war. (1 cause per group) C - Read poems by Phyllis Wheatly. C - Read Declaration of Independence. G - Investigate effects of the war & impact on today. C - Watch School House Rock Video.	Write a report and create a poster to share with the class. Jigsaw the groups so members can be the expert and share with the other groups. Write and illustrate a poem about Rev. War. Make posters with the facts. Discuss its meaning. Create informational big books to share with class.

Sharing & Explaining to Make Connections	
How can we assist children to pull it all together? What curriculum processes would help here? (Art, drama, language...?) How can we see if they are making connections?	1. Make timelines of major events from the unit. (Whole class) 2. Using the timeline as a guide, write a summary about the Revolutionary War, its causes and effects. (Individual) 3. Students will write a paragraph explaining how this war has shaped our lives today.

Reflection and Action	
How can we empower children to act on what they have learned?	Write letters to American troops in Iraq. (Think about how we are standing up for our freedom.)

Related Experiences / Student Assessment / Notes:

1. Students will revise the original semantic map on an individual basis.

2. Students will complete their K-W-L charts from the beginning of the unit.

3. Using the graphic organizers from 1 & 2, students will create a slide show with 5 facts they learned. Presentations will be shared with the class.

Source: Michelle South, Graduate Student, Tennessee Technological University, Cookeville, TN. Used with permission.

Thematic Unit on Pioneers

Objectives

1. To learn about the everyday lives of pioneers

2. To learn about the homes in which pioneers lived

3. To learn about the food pioneers ate and how they prepared and preserved it

4. To learn about the modes of transportation that the pioneers used

5. To discover other interesting facts about the pioneers from reading, listening, and viewing

Materials

Resource books and media, artifacts, writing and art materials. Most of these resources are designed for grades 4–8. The books marked (P) are accessible to primary-grade children. These books also have much information that would be useful for older students, and can be especially helpful for use with struggling readers.

■ Resource books

Selections from *The American West: A historical reader* (pp. 72–96, 107–114, 138–152, 194–219). (2001). Evanston, IL: McDougal Littell.

Selections from *How America grew 1775–1914: Stories in history* (pp. 97–136) (2003). Evanston, IL: McDougal Littell.

Beatty, P. *Wait for me, watch for me, Eula Bee.* (1978). New York: Morrow.

Brenner, B. *Wagon wheels.* (1978). New York: Harper & Row.

Conrad, P. *Prairie songs.* (1983). New York: Harper & Row.

Dodd, C. H. *California trail: Voyage of discovery: The story behind the scenery.* (1996). Las Vegas: KC Publications.

Kalman, B. *Historic communities: Games from long ago.* (1995). New York: Crabtree. (P)

Kalman, B. *Life in the Old West: The wagon train.* (1999). New York: Crabtree. (P)

Kalman, B. *Pioneer life from A to Z.* (1998). New York: Crabtree. (P)

Kalman, B., & Hale, L. *Historic communities: Pioneer recipes.* (2001). New York: Crabtree. (P)

Kimball, V. T. *Stories of young pioneers in their own words.* (2000). Missoula, MN: Mountain Press.

Laurgaard, R. K. *Patty Reed's doll.* (1984). Davis, CA: Tomato Enterprises.

Moeri, L. *Save Queen of Sheba.* (1981). New York: Dutton.

Morrow, H. *On to Oregon!* (1954). New York: Morrow.

O'Brien, M. B. *Into the western winds: Pioneer boys traveling the Overland Trails.* (2003). Guilford, CT: Globe Pequot Press.

O'Brien, M. B. *Toward the setting sun: Pioneer girls traveling the Overland Trails.* (1999). Guilford, CT: Globe Pequot Press.

Steber, R. *Children's stories: Tales of the Old West.* (1989). Prineville, OR: Bonanza.

Turner, A. *Dakota dugout.* (1985). New York: Macmillan. (P)

Turner, A. *The grasshopper summer.* (1989). New York: Macmillan.

Wilder, L. I. *By the shores of Silver Lake.* (1953). New York: Harper & Row.

Wilder, L. I. *Little house in the big woods.* (1953). New York: Harper & Row.

Wilder, L. I. *Little house on the prairie.* (1953). New York: Harper & Row.

Wilder, L. I. *On the banks of Plum Creek.* (1953). New York: Harper & Row.

Wisler, G. C. *Jericho's journey.* (1993). New York: Puffin.

- Video

Forgotten journey. (2000). Produced by John Krizek, Miles Saunders, and Kit Tyler in association with the International Documentary Association and KTEH Television. Toluca Lake, CA: Forgotten Journey Productions.

- Websites

http://www.monroe.lib.in.us/childrens/frontierbib.html

http://library.thinkquest.org/6400

http://www.kidinfo.com/American_History/Pioneers.html

http://www.isu.edu/~trinmich/Oregontrail.html

- Artifacts

Tallow candles; iron kettles; earthenware jugs; tin lanterns; early textbooks; quilts; tools; period clothing

- Writing and art materials

Drawing paper; construction paper; pencils; markers; crayons; pastels; tempera paint; brushes; plain white paper; computer with printer; materials for dioramas, such as popsicle sticks, glue, yarn, scraps of cloth

- Outline maps of the United States

Introductory Procedures

Choose from these activities ones that work best for your students.

1. Read aloud a selection from *Stories of Young Pioneers in Their Own Words.*

2. With the students, create a semantic web based on words and concepts that students know about pioneers. It might resemble the following.

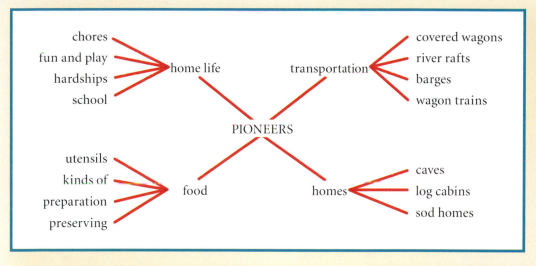

chores
fun and play
hardships
school
→ home life

covered wagons
river rafts
barges
wagon trains
← transportation

PIONEERS

utensils
kinds of
preparation
preserving
→ food

caves
log cabins
sod homes
← homes

3. Fill out the *K (Know)* and *W (Want to Learn)* sections of a K-W-L chart with the students.

4. In collaboration with the students, record objectives for the unit. These might include the following.

   a. To find out how pioneers lived their daily lives

   b. To learn how pioneers traveled and where they settled

   c. To discover how pioneers coped with hardships

   d. To find out about pioneer children: their school, work, and play

Unit Activities

Choose from these activities ones that work best for your students.

1. View the videotape *Forgotten Journey* and discuss the revelations about pioneer life in the videotape.

2. Divide the class into research groups to study such topics as education during pioneer days, home life of pioneer children, and travel conditions for pioneers. Let the students visit the media center, as well as your resource book area, to find books and materials about their topics. Help them find the material, take notes on it, organize it, and write reports on it to share with the other students.

3. Provide a map of the United States so that students can mark routes of early pioneers. Have them identify hazards for each route (for example, mountains and rivers) and compute the mileage.

4. Read aloud or let students read *Jericho's Journey*, if you have it in a class set. It tells about moving from Tennessee to Texas in 1852 so a family can make a fresh start.

5. As students read about pioneer days, have them record words and expressions that are different from those that people use today. The students should give the meaning (perhaps with an illustration) on a separate page for each expression. At the end of the unit, ask a group of students to alphabetize the expressions, eliminate duplications, write a title page, make a cover, and "publish" a dictionary of pioneer language.

6. Have each student assume the identity of a pioneer and write a fictional journal of his or her adventures.

7. Teach students folk songs and ballads sung during the pioneer period, such as "Home on the Range," "Cindy," "Sweet Betsy from Pike," and "I Ride an Old Paint." Make an audio-recording of them.

8. Teach children to do folk dances and provide tapes or records of fiddle music to accompany the dances.

9. If possible, find a resource person to help the students with such projects as soap and candle making, quilting, and making corn husk dolls.

10. Have students form literature circles to read different Little House books by Laura Ingalls Wilder. As a follow-up activity, have each group select a scene to dramatize.

11. Have students participate in literature circles for another set of books they choose from the resource list for which you have multiple copies. Let them choose a way to share information from their books with students in the other circles.

12. Let students make a time line that shows when different regions of the country were settled.

13. Have students identify problems of frontier life and decide how they would solve them. Examples include preserving food, replacing a broken wagon wheel, and building a home.

14. Let students select aspects of pioneer life and compare them with life today. After a discussion, ask the students to write summaries of the advantages of each lifestyle.

15. Have students plan a menu and prepare food for a lunch that the pioneers might have eaten. Include such foods as corn pone, molasses, squash, tea, baked beans, and dried apples. Let them make butter by shaking whipping cream in a tightly covered jar and adding salt. Then let them eat the lunch.

16. Divide the students into groups according to regions where pioneers settled. Ask the students to investigate ways that the environment affected the lives of the pioneers.

17. Have students investigate conflicts between Native Americans and pioneers over territorial rights and present a debate or panel discussion on relevant issues.

18. Let students create art projects in such forms as dioramas of typical log cabins, murals of pioneer villages, and models of covered wagons.

19. Have students role-play such situations as deciding what to take on a long journey, moving away from friends, and adapting to a new life on the frontier.

Culminating Activities

Choose from these activities ones that work best for your students.

1. Make a class newspaper that could have been written during pioneer days. Features might include the following.

   a. Dangerous criminals wanted

   b. Classified advertisements for help wanted, guides wanted, and land for sale

   c. News stories about government policies related to acquiring land and establishing communities

d. Editorials about advantages or disadvantages of moving into unsettled territories

   e. Illustrated advertisements about new products, such as medicines that supposedly heal any disease

2. Let small groups of students develop PowerPoint or mPower presentations about segments of the unit. Let them share these presentations with other classes.

3. Guide the students in planning a program for other students or parents. They may wish to distribute copies of the newspaper, display their work, sing folk songs, do folk dancing, present reports, serve refreshments (pioneer food), and dress in period costumes.

Evaluation

1. Observe students' study in progress.

2. Return to the K-W-L chart that was started at the beginning of the unit and have the students fill in the *L* (What I Learned) portion. Consider the accuracy of their answers.

3. Return to the objectives set at the beginning of the unit. With the students, decide whether the objectives have been met or further study is needed.

4. Analyze the chosen culminating activities using a rubric.

Thematic Unit on Insects and Spiders

Grade levels

PreK–3

Goal

To understand how insects and spiders can help us or harm us

Learner Objectives

1. To understand the life cycles of insects and spiders

2. To know how spiders and insects are alike and different

3. To learn the body parts of insects and spiders

4. To see connections between ant and human communities

5. To identify some insects and spiders

Challenge Questions

1. How can insects and spiders help us? How can they harm us?

2. How are spiders and insects alike? How are they different?

3. How can flies walk upside down?

4. How do fireflies (lightning bugs) flash their lights?

5. Why do mosquito bites itch?

6. How do bees fly?

7. Where do butterflies come from?

8. How do spiders spin webs?

Learning Center Resources:

With the help of the media specialist, set up a learning center about insects and spiders. Change the center so that it reflects what you are currently investigating. Include materials such as the following.

1. Magazines, including *National Geographic Kids, Ranger Rick,* and *Your Big Backyard*

2. Books (look under Resources)

3. Commercially available live insects (Insect Lore at 1-800-LIVE BUG or e-mail at customerservice @insectlore.com has many live insects available, including ant, butterfly, and ladybug kits; praying mantises; silkworms; and millipedes.)

4. Writing materials, including colored pencils, markers, notebooks, paper, and paper stapled together in booklets for writing and recording information

5. Posters, charts, and models on insects

Cross-Curricular Connections

Geography

What are the locations of specific types of insects and spiders? Where do mosquitoes breed? What climates are best for insects and spiders?

Social studies

How can insects and spiders help or harm us? For example, how much damage do locusts do? How can spider webs help us?

Math

How can we measure spider webs? How big and small are some insects and spiders? How much do they grow? How many legs do centipedes have? How long does it take for different stages of life cycles (use calendar)? How can we show information about insects and spiders on a graph?

Art

How can we represent different insects by using clay, crayons, pipe cleaners, egg cartons, and other materials?

Initiating Activities:

Bring in several clear jars with small holes in the lids, each containing an insect or nonpoisonous spider for students to observe. Place a magnifying glass nearby. Ask them to tell or write everything they can find out about the insect or spider.

Make a semantic map by getting the children to tell you what they know about insects and spiders from their observations and prior experiences. Organize their contributions into categories, as shown on the next page.

Ongoing Activities

You may choose from the following activities, modify them to suit your needs, or add other activities—especially those suggested by the children.

1. Read E. B. White's *Charlotte's Web* aloud, a chapter at a time, during the unit. Discuss each chapter and make predictions about what might happen next.

2. At the top of a chart, write "Words about Insects and Spiders." During the unit, add words and their meanings to the chart as children encounter new words.

3. Take an "observation walk" around the outside of the school and look for the following.

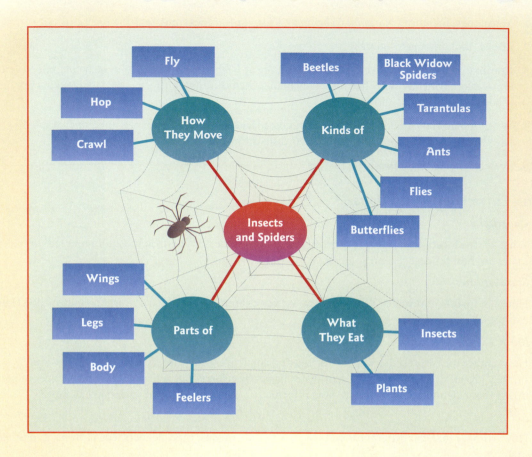

a. A spider spinning a web

b. An ant pulling something or building an anthill

c. The colors of butterflies

d. Unusual bugs and what they are doing

After returning to the classroom, ask students to discuss and then record their observations in an ongoing journal. Repeat the walk at intervals to observe, discuss, and record changes. For example, if a spider is observed spinning a web, let the children measure the diameter of the web and count the strands on each visit.

4. Divide the class into groups to study different kinds of insects and spiders. (Insect types might include bees, butterflies, ants, grasshoppers, and beetles.) Guide each group in developing a project to present to the class. (Projects might include making a diorama of a scene with plastic insects and spiders, drawing and labeling a large diagram of the insect, writing and illustrating a booklet, and dramatizing lives of or stories about insects and spiders.)

5. On the top of a poster board or chart paper, write "Kinds of Insects and Spiders." Let the children cut out or draw pictures of different kinds of insects and spiders, glue them onto the chart, and label them.

6. Help the children build a wire mesh or screened cage and put soil, twigs, and grass in it. Place a harmless spider or an insect, such as a grasshopper, in the cage so that the children can observe it. Encourage them to name their pet spider or insect and write stories about it.

7. Set up an ant colony from a kit (see Learning Center Resources) so that children can observe activities within the colony. Help them understand the roles of ants and compare them to roles of humans in communities.

8. Keep center activities going so that children have opportunities to identify different kinds of insects and spiders, trace their life cycles, and answer challenge questions.

Special Activities

1. Invite a resource person to come to class and discuss how insects and spiders can both help and harm us. The resource person might be a beekeeper, a biologist, or a representative from the Farm Bureau or Department of Agriculture.

2. Read *Fireflies for Nathan* by Shulamith Oppenheim, the story of a young boy and his love for fireflies. While visiting his grandparents, he gathers fireflies and places them in a jar. Relate the story to children's experiences with fireflies and discuss what causes luminescence.

3. Read aloud Simms Taback's *There Was an Old Lady Who Swallowed a Fly* and/or Mary Howitt's *The Spider and the Fly*. Since both story poems lend themselves to dramatization, help children act them out. Verna Aardema's *Why Mosquitoes Buzz in People's Ears* is a good legend to dramatize by letting the children play the roles of the different animals. Discuss whether these stories are real or make-believe. Have students give reasons, based on their class discoveries.

4. Let students make models of insects and spiders from clay, pipe cleaners, and other materials. The children can write labels with brief descriptions for each insect or spider. Example: Make a caterpillar from an egg carton (one row of egg cups for each child), pipe cleaners, and roly-poly eyes. Glue eyes on head, attach short antennas, punch holes in body, and thread pipe cleaners through for legs. Have class compute how many supplies are necessary to make enough caterpillars for everyone (math connection).

5. Compare spiders and insects by using a Venn diagram or other graphic organizer that shows similarities and differences between the two. With the students make a large drawing of a spider and another of an insect, showing the body parts and labeling them.

6. *Author Study of Eric Carle and his books about insects and spiders:* Most children love Eric Carle's books, which combine fact and fiction. Children can learn about Eric Carle and how he creates his books by going to http://www.eric-carle.com. They can write their own books based on the patterns they observe in Carle's texts. They can also learn to make collages from cutouts of their own tissue paper paintings in order to illustrate their books.

Text Set of Eric Carle Books for this Unit

The grouchy ladybug. (1986). New York: HarperCollins. The ladybug learns appropriate social behavior. Available in Spanish.

The honeybee and the robber. (1981). New York: Scholastic. The brave honeybee saves the day (with pop-ups and movables).

The very busy spider. (1984). New York: Philomel. The spider persists in building her web (connections to telling time, with raised printing). Available in Spanish.

The very clumsy click beetle. (1999). New York: Philomel. The beetle clicks as it learns to land on its feet (clicking sound from computer chip).

The very hungry caterpillar. (1969). New York: Philomel. The caterpillar eats his way through foods and becomes a butterfly. Available in Spanish.

The very lonely firefly. (1995). New York: Philomel. The firefly wants to belong (with tiny blinking lights from computer chip).

The very quiet cricket. (1990). New York: Philomel. The cricket seeks someone special (with cricket's song from computer chip). Available in Spanish.

Other Resources for Eric Carle

Videotape: *Eric Carle: Picture writer* (1993). Searchlight Films. Interview with Eric Carle and hands-on demonstration of tissue paper painting.

Carle, E. (1998). *You can make a collage: A very simple how-to book.* Palo Alto, CA: Klutz Press. Gives directions for making illustrations and has seventy-two full-color tissue paper paintings by Eric Carle.

Culminating Activities

Choose one or more of these activities or invent your own.

1. Let students create imaginary insects and spiders. Each child draws an insect or spider, labels its parts, names it, and describes it. The children may want to write stories about their insects or spiders. Compile their work and publish it for the class to see.

2. Have the children create a class dictionary of insects and spiders by writing and illustrating a page for each insect or spider, alphabetizing the pages, and publishing the dictionary as a class reference.

3. Help students make a grid or chart of the characteristics of various insects and spiders. Have them identify characteristics, such as senses, body parts, colors, shapes, and number of legs.

4. Allow children to present their projects to the rest of the class.

5. Return to the questions asked at the beginning of the unit to see if the students can answer them. Provide review and reteaching if necessary.

Evaluation

In preschool and kindergarten, observation is the key to assessing progress. It is also important in grades 1, 2, and 3, but in these grades you may also consider children's written work, completion of projects, work samples, tests, and presentations.

Resources

Fiction Books

Aardema, V. (1975). *Why mosquitoes buzz in people's ears.* New York: Dial. (folktale)

Cole, J. (1996). *The Magic School Bus gets ants in its pants.* New York: Scholastic. (bus to anthill where each ant is observed doing its job)

Godkin, C. (1995). *What about ladybugs?* San Francisco: Sierra Club Books for Children. (how ladybugs eat aphids)

Howe, J. (1987). *I wish I were a butterfly.* San Diego: Gulliver. (cricket who wants to be a butterfly)

Howitt, M. *The spider and the fly.* New York: Simon & Schuster. (spider inviting fly to come into its parlor)

Mead, K. (1998). *How spiders got eight legs.* Austin, TX: Steck-Vaughn. (folktale)

Oppenheim, S. (1994). *Fireflies for Nathan.* New York: Tambourine. (Nathan's love of fireflies)

Taback, S. (1997). *There was an old lady who swallowed a fly.* New York: Viking. (silly poem about lady who swallows different things)

Van Allsburg, C. (1988). *Two bad ants.* Boston: Houghton Mifflin. (two ants who desert their ant colony)

White, E. B. (1952). *Charlotte's web.* New York: Harper & Row. (chapter book about how a spider saves a pig)

Informational Books

Halpern, J. (1998). *A look at spiders.* Austin, TX: Steck-Vaughn. (facts with photographs)

Markle, S. (1996). *Creepy, crawly baby bugs.* New York: Scholastic. (amazing photographs, baby bugs)

Nyquist, K. B. (2002). *Amazing animals.* Washington, DC: National Geographic Society. (many kinds of animals, including some insects)

O'Toole, C. (1986). *Discovering ants.* New York: Bookwright. (body parts, colonies, kinds of ants, glossary)

Pallotta, J. (1986). *The icky bug alphabet book.* Watertown, MA: Charlesbridge. (pictorial alphabet book of insects)

Parker, N. W., & Wright, J. R. (1987). *Bugs.* New York: Greenwillow. (labeled drawings of insect body parts)

Sill, C. (2003). *About arachnids: A guide for children.* Atlanta: Peachtree. (facts about arachnids)

Taylor, K. (1990). *Hidden by darkness.* New York: Delacorte. (many nocturnal animals, including some nocturnal insects)

Yoshi. (1987). *Who's hiding here?* Natick, MA: Picture Book Studio. (rhyming text with camouflaged insects and animals)

Other Resources

1. "Nearly Wild Garden" for butterflies, a magic carpet 12" by 38". This is a mat with over two thousand seeds of plants to attract butterflies. Roll it out and water it. Send order to New Holland, P.O. Box 335, Rockport IL 62370.

2. Poems: "Butterfly" by John Bannister Tabb, "White Butterflies" by Algernon Charles Swinburne, "Caterpillar" by Lillian Vabada, "Spiders" by Janet Bruno," "The Caterpillar" by Christian Georgia Raced, and "Caterpillar" by Aileen Fisher

3. Nursery rhymes: "Eensy-Weensy Spider" with motions, "Little Miss Muffet"

Thematic Unit on Holes

Holes

By Louis Sachar

Dear _____,

Welcome to Camp Green Lake! While you are here, you will be expected to "dig holes" in order to enhance your reading skills.

Read over this contract. Each acceptably completed activity or answered question is worth 2 points. When you finish digging a hole (completing the activity or answering the question), color the hole beside it with a green colored pencil or highlighter. If the "hole" has been dug satisfactorily, I will initial it. If it is not initialed, you will have to keep digging until it is acceptable, or you may select another hole to dig by answering a different question.

You may stop when you have successfully earned 76 points, which means that you have successfully answered 38 questions. After you have answered 38 questions satisfactorily, you may stop "digging" when your parent signs here: _____.

Here are the conditions of your contract:

- You may dig only at Camp Green Lake (in the classroom) until you have permission to work at home.
- Write page numbers in your answers and refer to the text.
- All holes must be dug in complete sentences.
- Holes must be "dug" on your notebook paper, not the contract.
- Sloppy digging (writing) will not be acceptable.
- Your "shovel" must be a pencil or blue or black ink pen.
- Unlike Stanley and the other boys, you are not allowed to spit in the holes!
- Holes will be inspected daily so that I can monitor your progress and help you if you need it.
- All holes must be dug by the end of reading period on _Wednesday, Nov. 13_____.
- Digging is hard, but there are treasures to be found! Some holes may be very valuable to you! Small treats or privileges can be earned while you are digging at Camp Green Lake, so take pride in your work!

I hope you have a pleasant stay! Thank you in advance for your hard work and positive attitude!

Sincerely,

Mrs. Bigford

1. "If you take a bad boy and make him dig a hole every day in the hot sun, it will turn him into a good boy." Do you agree or disagree with this statement? Write a 1-2-3-2-3 paragraph that explains.

2. The protagonist in a story is the main character or hero of the story. Who is the protagonist in *Holes?*

3. The antagonist(s) can be any thing or character that works against or opposes the protagonist. Name as many antagonists as you can think of that worked against the protagonist.

4. The setting of the book is the time and place where the story happens. What is the setting of the book?

5. The climax is the element of literature where the major events in the book change course and the reader can predict how the story will turn out. What is the climax in the book *Holes?*

6. List the 5 major events of the book in chronological order.

7. Why did Stanley and his family have such bad luck? When did their fortune change?

8. Describe Stanley's character at the beginning of the book, the middle of the book, and at the end. Explain what traits changed and what traits stayed the same.

9. Stanley was wrongly accused of a crime and went willingly to the detention center. Would you have been as cooperative as Stanley? Wh,y or why not? Explain in a 1-2-3-2-3 paragraph.

10. There are several one-sentence paragraphs found throughout *Holes.* In most writing, it is unacceptable to write paragraphs like this. Why does Louis Sachar use this technique in his writing? Furthermore, why is he allowed to do this?

11. Barf Bag had been one of the boys in the group before Stanley arrived. Imagine the experiences Barf Bag could have had that made him so miserable and to have caused him to earn his nickname. In character as Barf Bag, write a letter to your parents before you go to dig your last hole.

12. Is Clyde "Sweet Feet" Livingston a real baseball player? Prove his existence or nonexistence.

13. Stanley had been tortured by a bully named Derrick Dunne. What are your opinions on bullies and how Stanley dealt with Derrick? How should bullies be dealt with in school?

14. Why do you think the boys spit in their holes once they were dug?

15. Research these, and explain whether or not they were real: yellow spotted lizards in Texas, the invention of the motor or engine before the turn of the twentieth century, botulism, the use of leeches as a cure.

16. List as many reasons as you can think of as to why *Holes* is an appropriate title for the book. Try to come up with at least 3.

17. Create explanations as to why each boy had the nickname he did.

18. Go through the book and select 10 chapters to give appropriate but mysterious chapter titles.

19. Pretend that you are Stanley after his ordeal at Camp Green Lake is over. He has become famous and is now well known. For what is he now well-known? Prepare a speech that Stanley would give to seventh graders in schools across the country. Write the speech and deliver it to your classmates. You may use props as you deliver your speech.

20. What are some examples of foreshadowing that let us know that the warden was descended from Trout Walker and his wife?

21. Complete the graphic organizers.

22. Summarize the 3 stories found in *Holes*, and explain how they all were related to each other.

23. Explain how "God's Thumb" could have been a symbol of good fortune and inspiration for Stanley during his trek across the lake.

24. Research the medicinal powers of the onion. Was there any truth to Sam's claim that the onion was a kind of cure-all for ailments?

25. In the book, what lessons do you think the author wanted the reader to understand?

26. Explain the character of Mr. Pendanski. Is he likeable throughout the book? Do you think his personality was the same throughout the book, or did it change? Write 1-2-3-2-3 paragraphs to support your opinion. Use passages and page numbers from the book.

27. "Myra's head is as empty as a flower pot." What is this kind of comparison called? Find two other examples from the book. Give page numbers as to where these can be found.

28. On page 24, Stanley had felt as though he was "holding destiny's shoes." How does this sentence foreshadow the events in the remainder of the book?

29. What passages from the book would indicate that digging holes does indeed "build character"? What passages would show that it has a negative effect on character?

30. Stanley Yelnats is a palindrome. What are 5 other examples of a palindrome?

31. On page 94, how does the author let the reader know that Zero had dug Stanley's hole while he was with the warden?

32. What are two ways that onions saved Stanley and Zero from death?

33. Describe the character of Zero.

34. Why do you think the author chose to have some of the characters be African Americans? Did this fact make the events in the book more meaningful? Why, or why not?

35. On page 99, why is the print different?

36. What is the first hint that Stanley and Zero had ancestors who knew each other?

37. On page 186, we find out that Stanley likes himself. How do you think his experiences at Camp Green Lake made him feel better about himself?

38. Zero says that he and his mother always took what they needed when he was little. He did not know that this is stealing. Should children be held responsible for their actions if their parents have not taught them differently? Why, or why not?

39. Write down your thoughts and questions about the events in the book on sticky notes. Be sure to include page numbers. Stick these onto a sheet of notebook paper.

40. Where and when do the 3 stories in *Holes* take place?

41. Why do you think Camp Green Lake went dry?

42. What is fate? What is destiny? Are they synonyms or antonyms?

590

43. On page 161, what was so humorous about the conversation concerning Mary Lou?

44. On page 233 at the end of the book, who was sitting with Hector?

45. Why do you suppose the author began to call Zero "Hector" instead of "Zero."

46. On page 209, explain how Stanley came to be "in the snow."

Words in Context

Use your book to explain the meanings of these words in context.

47. (p. 8) "He looked out the window at the **vast** emptiness."

   (p. 8) "Stanley's father was smart and had a lot of **perseverance**..."

   (p. 11) "The land was **barren** and **desolate**."

   (p. 17) "The boys glanced **wearily** at Stanley..."

   (p. 24) "...holding **destiny's** shoes..."

48. (p. 25) "The judge called Stanley's crime **despicable**."

   (p. 30) "Madame Zeroni hated to see Elya so **forlorn**"

   (p. 34) "...when the dirt was in the ground, it was **compacted**."

   (p. 35) "He couldn't afford to **dawdle**."

   (p. 39) "He **grimaced** as he..."

49. (p. 74) "...the shovels were locked up at night, **presumably**..."

   (p. 90) "It's only **toxic** while it's wet."

   (p. 91) "...Mr. Sir's pain seemed to **recede**."

   (p. 92) "His body **writhed** in agony."

   (p. 121) "Kate could see her **rummaging** through the cabin."

50. (p. 193) "His voice was dry and **raspy**..."

   (p. 197) "They climbed down into **adjacent** holes..."

   (p. 218) "He is no longer in your **jurisdiction**."

   (p. 230) "...the answers tend to be long and **tedious**."

   (p. 232) "...it **neutralizes** odor causing fungi..."

Source: Towanna Bigford, Seventh Grade Teacher, Irving College Elementary School, McMinnville, TN. Used with permission.

Appendix A

GRAMMAR HANDBOOK

WE ARE including a handbook on grammar in this language arts text. Why? It's because there are teachers who do not know how to speak or write correctly. Should you say, "She is the first person who I met," or "He did good"? If you are in doubt, you will find this appendix helpful.

English is a complex language with many rules. Standard American English refers to English as it is used by those who are socially, economically, or politically powerful in the United States. Although pronunciation and idiomatic expressions vary considerably across the country, grammatical structures remain fairly uniform (Harris & Hodges, 1995). As an educated person and as a teacher who models standard usage for others, you need to use Standard English in your speech and writing.

This appendix is a summary of information concerning widely accepted practices for using grammar, punctuation, and capitalization. You may use it both as a reference for teaching and as a reminder of proper usage for your own speaking and writing. It begins with grammar, including parts of speech, phrases, clauses, and sentences, and it concludes with information about punctuation and capitalization.

I. **Grammar**
  A. Parts of speech
    1. **Nouns**: A noun is the name of a person, place, thing, or idea.
      a. Kinds of nouns
        (1) **Proper noun**: A proper noun is capitalized and names a specific person, place, or thing. Examples: *Ashley, Mrs. Rankin, Oklahoma, Red Cross, Kingston Elementary School*
        (2) **Common noun**: A common noun is nonspecific and is not capitalized. Examples: *child, telephone, city, freedom*
        (3) **Collective noun**: A collective noun refers to a group. Examples: *group, herd, family, class, International Reading Association, Rotary Club* (Note: Collective nouns are usually singular if they are considered to be a unit. They are plural if each member of the group is considered to be a separate unit. Examples: *The group is going on tour.* [group considered as a unit] *The group of teachers are disagreeing about where to eat dinner.* [group considered as different individuals] When there is doubt about usage, the U.S. preference is the singular.)

Potential problem: Collective nouns should not be used as singular and plural in the same sentence (Lovinger, 2000).
Correct: *The group was eating when it was called upon to perform.*
Incorrect: *The group was eating when they were called upon to perform.*

Potential problem: The nouns *media* and *data* are actually plural and should be treated as such in formal language, but they are often used as singular in informal language.
Formal: *The media are covering the event.* Informal: *The media is covering the event.*
Formal: *The data are accurate.* Informal: *The data is accurate.*

        (4) **Compound noun**: A compound noun consists of two or more nouns. Examples: *birdhouse, half-hour, police officer*
        (5) **Concrete noun**: A concrete noun is something that you can see or touch. Examples: *piano, sailboat, moon, apple*
        (6) **Abstract noun**: An abstract noun generally cannot be touched. It refers to a quality or idea. Examples: *loyalty, humiliation, joy*
        (7) **Possessive noun**: A possessive noun shows ownership or other relationships. If the noun is singular, an apostrophe comes before *s*; if it is a plural noun formed by adding *s* or *es*, the apostrophe comes after the *s*. Examples: *boy's coat, children's books, girls' dresses, classes' projects*

Potential problem: Don't confuse possessive forms with plural forms.
Correct: *He earned a week's pay.* Incorrect: *He earned a weeks pay.*
Correct: *He was paid two weeks ago.* Incorrect: *He was paid two week's ago.*

        (8) **Gerund**: A gerund is a verbal ending in *-ing* that acts as a noun. Examples: *Walking is good exercise. It is hard to find time for studying.*
    2. **Pronouns**: A pronoun takes the place of a noun.

Potential problem: Make sure the referent for each pronoun is clear or use a noun instead.

Clear: *When Alex played basketball with Scott, <u>Alex</u> supplied the ball.*
Ambiguous: *When Alex played basketball with Scott, he supplied the ball.*

    a. Kinds of pronouns

        (1) **Personal pronoun**: A personal pronoun designates the speaker or writer, the person spoken or written to, or the person spoken or written about. Personal pronouns can be singular or plural and can be masculine or feminine. They can also express case, or the way the pronoun is used in a sentence. Cases are **nominative** (used as a subject), **objective** (used as an object), and **possessive** (used to show relationship or ownership).

Personal Pronouns

		Nominative (the subject)	Objective (receiver of action)	Possessive (shows ownership)
Singular	First person	I	me	my, mine
	Second person	you	you	your, yours
	Third person	he, she, it	him, her, it	his, her, hers, its
Plural	First person	we	us	our, ours
	Second person	you	you	your, yours
	Third person	they	them	their, theirs

        (2) **Possessive pronoun**: A possessive pronoun indicates ownership. (See table for possessive pronouns.)

Potential problem: A possessive pronoun must agree in number (singular or plural) with its antecedent (the noun or word group to which it refers).

Correct: *Every <u>teacher</u> should have <u>his or her</u> own computer. All <u>teachers</u> should have <u>their</u> own computers.* Incorrect: *Every teacher should have their own computer.*

        (3) **Reflexive, or intensive, pronouns**: A reflexive pronoun is formed by adding *-self* to a singular pronoun or *-selves* to a plural pronoun. Examples: *She hurt <u>herself</u>. The children went shopping by <u>themselves</u>.*

Potential problem: Do not add *-self* to *his* or *-selves* to *their.*
Correct: *He did it <u>himself</u>.* Incorrect: *He did it hisself.*
Correct: *They went by <u>themselves</u>.* Incorrect: *They went by theirselves.*

        (4) **Demonstrative pronoun**: A demonstrative pronoun points out something. There are four demonstrative pronouns: *this, that, these,* and *those.* Examples: *<u>This</u> camera is faulty, but <u>those</u> cameras seem to work all right.*

        (5) **Relative pronoun**: A relative pronoun introduces a dependent clause and relates it to the rest of the sentence. The relative pronouns are *who, whom, whose, which, that,* and *what. Who* is in the

nominative case (subject); *whom* is in the objective case (object); and *whose* is in the possessive case (ownership). Examples: *Here is the man <u>who</u> is coming for dinner. Here is the man <u>whom</u> I met yesterday. Here is the man <u>whose</u> jacket I borrowed. This is the pie <u>that</u> I like best.*

Potential problem: Be careful about using *who* and *whom*. Remember that *who* is in the nominative case (acts as a subject) and *whom* is in the objective case.
Correct: *She is the first person <u>whom</u> I met.*   Incorrect: *She is the first person who I met.*

(6) **Interrogative pronoun**: An interrogative pronoun asks a question. These pronouns are *which, who, whose, whom,* and *what.* Examples: *<u>Which</u> one do you want? <u>Whose</u> book is that? <u>Who</u> is going?*

(7) **Indefinite pronouns**: An indefinite pronoun refers to nonspecific people or things. Examples: *Does <u>anyone</u> know the answer? There is <u>nothing</u> left. <u>Everybody</u> came.*

Potential problem: Know if your indefinite pronoun takes a singular or plural verb. Examples of pronouns taking singular verbs: *each, everyone, much, everything.* Examples of those taking plural verbs: *both, many, few, several.*
Correct: *<u>Each</u> of the children <u>is</u> going.*   Incorrect: *Each of the children are going.*
Correct: *<u>Few</u> <u>are</u> going.*   Incorrect: *Few is going.*

b. Cases of pronouns
Pronouns can be in the nominative, objective, or possessive case. They are in the **nominative case** when they are the subject of a verb or a predicate nominative (subject complement). Examples: *<u>He</u> started the engine.* (subject) *She is <u>somebody</u> important.* (predicate nominative)

Any pronoun is in the **objective case** when it is used as a direct object, indirect object, or object of a preposition. Examples: *He found <u>her</u>.* (direct object) *He gave <u>her</u> the key.* (indirect object) *Give it to <u>me</u>.* (object of a preposition)

Potential problem: Selecting the wrong case often causes errors.
Correct: *<u>He and I</u> rode the motorcycle.*   Incorrect: *Him and me rode the motorcycle.*
(needs nominative case because pronouns are used as the subject)
Correct: *Show the book to Caitlin and <u>me</u>.*   Incorrect: *Show the book to Caitlin and I.*
(needs objective case because the pronoun is the object of the preposition *to*)
(Hint: When in doubt, try omitting the noun that follows the preposition and using only the pronoun to see which pronoun sounds right. Example: *Show the book to <u>me</u>,* not *Show the book to <u>I</u>.*)
Correct: *It was <u>he</u> who made the error.*   Incorrect: *It was him who made the error.*
(needs nominative case because the pronoun is the predicate nominative)
When used in the possessive case, a pronoun shows ownership. Example: *They ordered <u>their</u> dinners.*

Potential problem: The **possessive case** of a pronoun should be used before a gerund, but often is not.
Correct: *His parents approved of <u>his</u> working late.*   Incorrect: *His parents approved of him working late.*

3. **Verbs**: A verb expresses action or state of being. The principal parts of a verb are present (*drive*), past (*drove*), and past participle (*driven*).
a. Kinds of verbs

(1) **Regular verbs**: A regular verb forms its past tense or past participle by adding -*d* or -*ed* to its present form. Examples: *moved, believed, jumped, called*

(2) **Irregular verbs**: An irregular verb does not follow the regular pattern for forming the past tense and past participle. Examples: *go, went, (has or have) gone; give, gave, (has or have) given; swim, swam, (has or have) swum*

Potential problem: Irregular verbs can be confusing. Be sure to use the correct form, which depends on whether or not you are using a participle.
Correct: *She <u>has gone</u> away. She <u>went</u> away.*   Incorrect: *She has went away.*
Correct: *He <u>saw</u> it. He <u>has seen</u> it.*   Incorrect: *He seen it.*

(3) **Auxiliary verb**: An auxiliary verb, or helping verb, precedes another verb to show tense, mood, or voice. Examples: *be, am, is, are, has, have, was, were, shall, will.* Sample sentences: *She <u>has been going</u> twice a week. He <u>was listening</u> carefully.*

(4) **Transitive verb**: A transitive verb has an object. *The dog <u>caught</u> the <u>ball</u>.*

(5) **Intransitive verb**: An intransitive verb has no object. Example: *The dog <u>ran</u>.*

(6) **Linking verb**: A linking verb connects the subject to the predicate complement. It is also called a state-of-being verb. Examples: *be* (various forms), *seem, feel, become, smell, sound, taste.* Sample sentences: *Fresh baked bread <u>smells</u> good. I <u>felt</u> sick after dinner.*

b. Tenses of verbs

(1) **Present tense**: Action occurring at the present time. Example: *Aaron <u>plays</u> the guitar well.*

(2) **Past tense**: Action that occurred in the past. Example: *Aaron <u>played</u> the guitar yesterday.*

Potential problem: Even though you may not hear it clearly spoken, be sure to add -*d* or -*ed* when using the past tense.
Correct: *He <u>asked</u> to go.*   Incorrect: *He ask to go.*
Correct: *She <u>used</u> to go.*   Incorrect: *She use to go.*
Correct: *I'm <u>supposed</u> to be here now.*   Incorrect: *I'm suppose to be here now.*

(3) **Future tense**: Action that will occur in the future. Example: *Aaron <u>will play</u> the guitar tomorrow.*

(4) **Present perfect tense**: Action that occurred sometime before now. Example: *Kelsey <u>has worked</u> hard during the semester.*

(5) **Past perfect tense**: Action that occurred before a specific time in the past. Example: *Jeremy <u>had intended</u> to wash the car before his date last night.*

(6) **Future perfect tense**: Action that will occur before a specific time in the future. Example: *Zachary's work <u>will have been completed</u> before the game starts.*

c. Voices of verbs

(1) **Active voice**: The subject does the action. Example: *The pitcher <u>threw</u> the ball.*

(2) **Passive voice**: The subject receives the action. Example: *The ball <u>was thrown</u> by the pitcher.*

    d. Moods of verbs

        (1) **Indicative mood**: A verb in the indicative mood makes a statement or asks a question. Example: *The crowd <u>cheered</u>. Who <u>performed</u> at the coliseum Saturday night?*

        (2) **Imperative mood**: A verb in the imperative mood makes a command or request. Example: <u>*Turn*</u> *the light on. Please <u>help</u> me.*

        (3) **Subjunctive mood**: A verb in the subjunctive mood expresses a hypothesis, recommendation, or condition contrary to fact. It is often preceded by *if*. Example: *If I <u>were</u> rich, I could afford a new house.*

4. **Adjectives**: An adjective describes a noun or pronoun. It usually appears in front of the word it modifies and tells how many, what kind, or which one. Examples: <u>*Ninety*</u> *people attended the gala.* (*Ninety* modifies the noun *people.*) *The <u>lucky</u> few were allowed to stay up late.* (*Lucky* modifies the pronoun *few.*) *The pianist was <u>brilliant</u>.* (*Brilliant* is a predicate adjective modifying *pianist.*)

    a. **Articles**: An article is a type of adjective. The definite article is *the* and refers to a specific person or thing. The indefinite articles are *a* and *an*, which are used when the person or thing is general. *A* is used before a word beginning with a consonant, and *an* is used before a word beginning with a vowel. Examples: <u>*The*</u> *collie with white paws belongs to me. I'd like <u>an</u> apple and <u>a</u> plum.*

    b. **Comparison of adjectives**: Adjectives can be used to compare people or things. There are three degrees of comparison: **positive, comparative**, and **superlative**. Examples: *bad, worse, worst; tall, taller, tallest; beautiful, more beautiful, most beautiful.* Sample sentences: *Roger is a <u>good</u> ball player, but Ronnie is <u>better</u>. Joshua is the <u>best</u> player.*

Potential problem: Avoid using double forms of adjectives.
Correct: *Tamara is <u>prettier</u>.* Incorrect: *Tamara is more prettier.*

Potential problem: Avoid common usage problems. Use *fewer* when modifying plural words. Use *less* when modifying singular words.
Correct: *There were <u>fewer</u> guests than expected.* Incorrect: *There were less guests than expected.*
Correct: *There is <u>less</u> food than we need.* Incorrect: *There is fewer food than we need.*
Don't confuse *well* and *good. Well* is an adverb that modifies a verb, and *good* is an adjective that modifies a noun.
Correct: *Alaina did <u>well</u>.* Incorrect: *Alaina did good.*
Correct: *That is a <u>good</u> paper. That paper is <u>well</u> done.*
Incorrect: *That is a well paper.*

5. **Adverbs**: An adverb is a word that modifies a verb, an adjective, or another adverb. It tells how, when, where, or to what extent. It often ends in *-ly. Never* and *not* are negative adverbs. Sample sentences: *Pablo ran <u>quickly</u>. The days are getting <u>gradually</u> warmer. Kelsey was <u>there yesterday</u>, but she is <u>not here today</u>.*

Potential problem: Avoid using double negatives. (The word *hardly* is a negative.)
Correct: *I <u>can hardly</u> do it. I <u>can't</u> do it.* Incorrect: *I can't hardly do it.*
Correct: *He <u>doesn't have</u> any money. He <u>has no</u> money.* Incorrect: *He doesn't have no money.*

Like adjectives, adverbs have **positive, comparative**, and **superlative** degrees. Examples: *early, earlier, earliest; well, better, best*. Sample sentence: *Patti speaks <u>quietly</u>, but Haleigh speaks <u>more quietly</u>.*

Potential problem: Avoid using adjectives instead of adverbs when modifying verbs. Correct: *She sings <u>well</u>. She is a <u>good</u> singer.*   Incorrect: *She sings good.*

6. **Prepositions**: A preposition is a word that shows a relationship between a noun or pronoun and the rest of the sentence. Prepositions introduce phrases. Some common prepositions are *above, across, around, at, beside, between, for, from, in, on, to,* and *under*. Sample sentences: *He went <u>to</u> the bakery. I need the money <u>for</u> tools. Come <u>with</u> me.*

7. **Conjunctions**: A conjunction is a word that connects words or groups of words. There are three kinds of conjunctions.
   a. **Coordinate conjunction**: A coordinate conjunction connects words, phrases, or sentences that are of equal importance. Examples: *and, but, or, so, yet*. Sample sentence: *Ben <u>and</u> Jerry got some ice cream, <u>but</u> it melted before they finished it.*
   b. **Correlative conjunction**: Correlative conjunctions are used in pairs and also connect words, phrases, and clauses of equal rank. Examples: *either/or, both/and, neither/nor*. Sample sentence: *<u>Both</u> Cheryl <u>and</u> John enjoy sailing.*

Potential problem: When using *either/or* or *neither/nor*, treat the subject as singular. Correct: *<u>Either</u> Tracy <u>or</u> Jon <u>is going</u>.*   Incorrect: *Either Tracy or Jon are going.* Correct: *<u>Neither</u> the train <u>nor</u> the bus <u>goes</u> to Wilmington.* Incorrect: *Neither the train nor the bus go to Wilmington.*

   c. **Subordinate conjunctions**: A subordinate conjunction connects unequal clauses. It introduces a dependent clause. Examples: *because, if, since, until, when, after*. Sample sentence: *<u>Because</u> Stacy teaches school, she can stay home in the summer.*

8. **Interjections**: An interjection expresses strong feelings and may or may not be part of a sentence. It is often followed by an exclamation point. Examples: *Oh! Ouch! Hey! Help!* Sample sentences: *<u>Well</u>! It's about time. <u>Well</u>, it's about time!*

B. **Phrases**: A phrase is a group of two or more related words without a subject and/or predicate.
   1. Kinds of phrases
      a. **Noun phrase**: A noun phrase consists of a noun with all of its modifiers. Example: *<u>Last year's freshman class</u> was the largest.*
      b. **Verb phrase**: A verb phrase is a group of verbs that acts as a single verb. Examples: *might have been, try out, could have seen*
      c. **Prepositional phrase**: A prepositional phrase consists of a preposition with an object and any modifiers. Examples: *to the store, with great effort, from above, into the deep pool*
      d. **Verbal phrase**: A verbal phrase consists of a verbal (verb form) and related words, such as objects, complements, and modifiers. Verbal phrases are used as nouns, adjectives, or adverbs. Participles, gerunds, and infinitives are verbals. They do not take the place of verbs in sentences. There are three types of verbal phrases.

(1) **Participial phrase**: A participial phrase may be a verb phrase or may act as a modifier. Example of verb phrase: *was running*. Examples as modifiers: *The pictures <u>hanging on the walls</u> were crooked. We saw the cows <u>running through the pasture</u>.*

Potential problem: Avoid dangling participles, which modify the wrong subject.
Correct: *<u>Hanging from the ceiling</u>, <u>the streamers</u> created a pleasant effect.*
Incorrect: *Hanging from the ceiling, I saw the pretty streamers.*
The participial phrase should be placed immediately next to the word or phrase it modifies.

(2) **Gerund phrase**: A gerund phrase consists of a verb with an *-ing* ending that functions as a noun with its modifiers. Examples: *She liked <u>being in charge</u>. <u>Running away</u> didn't solve his problem.*

(3) **Infinitive phrase**: An infinitive phrase consists of the word *to* followed by a verb and sometimes its modifiers or complements. It can be used as a noun, an adjective, or an adverb. Examples: *He wanted <u>to run</u> for office.* (noun, used as direct object) *The woman <u>to impress</u> was at the front desk.* (used as an adjective modifying *woman*)

Potential problem: A split infinitive occurs when at least one word, generally an adverb, is inserted between *to* and the verb. Many grammarians object to splitting an infinitive.
Correct: *Jess wants <u>to finish</u> the assignment quickly.* Incorrect: *Jess wants to quickly finish the assignment.*

C. **Clauses**: A clause is a group of related words that has a subject and a predicate. Clauses may be independent (main) or dependent (subordinate).

1. **Independent clauses**: An independent clause could become a simple sentence that can stand alone. Example: *The cat ate the tuna fish.*

2. **Dependent clauses**: A dependent clause can be used as an adverb, an adjective, or a noun. It can never stand alone as a simple sentence and must be attached to the main clause, even though it has a subject and predicate. It *depends* on the rest of the sentence to make meaning. Examples of words and phrases that introduce dependent clauses: *because, since, once, if, whether, while, so, that, inasmuch as.* Sample sentences: *<u>Because the waves were so high</u>, no one went into the ocean.* (used as an adverb telling why) *<u>Whoever wins the race</u> gets the prize.* (used as a noun clause for the subject) *The student <u>who scores highest</u> will get an A.* (used as an adjective modifying *student*)

D. **Sentences**: A sentence consists of a subject and a predicate and expresses a complete thought.

1. Parts of a sentence: A subject and predicate are the parts of a sentence.

a. **Subject**: The subject is a noun or pronoun that performs the action, except when the sentence is in the passive voice, when it receives the action. It identifies the person, place, thing, or idea of the sentence. There are three kinds of subjects.

(1) **Simple subject**: A simple subject is only the noun or pronoun, not including its modifiers. Example: *The angry <u>man</u> in the long overcoat spoke to the crowd.*

      (2) **Complete subject**: A complete subject is the simple subject with its modifiers. Example: _The angry man in the long overcoat_ spoke to the crowd.

      (3) **Compound subject**: A compound subject consists of two or more simple subjects, often joined by _and_ or _or_. Example: _The angry man in the long overcoat and his companion_ spoke to the crowd.

  b. **Predicate**: The predicate tells the action of the sentence or the state of being. There are three kinds of predicates.

      (1) **Simple predicate**: A simple predicate is a verb or verb phrase that expresses action or state of being. Examples: _Maggie was going to the beach._ (action) _She is happy there._ (state of being)

      (2) **Complete predicate**: A complete predicate is the simple predicate with its modifiers. _Maggie went to the beach. She is happy there._

      (3) **Compound predicate**: A compound predicate is two or more verbs, usually connected by _and_ or _or_. Example: _Maggie went to the beach and stayed two weeks._

2. Types of sentences: Sentences are classified by type. There are four types of sentences.

  a. **Declarative sentence**: A declarative sentence is a statement. It tells something and ends with a period. Example: _The wind blew hard._

  b. **Interrogative sentence**: An interrogative sentence asks a question and ends with a question mark. Example: _Did the wind blow hard?_

  c. **Imperative sentence**: An imperative sentence gives a command or makes a request. The subject _you_ is often not given, but it is understood. Example: _Come inside._

  d. **Exclamatory sentence**: An exclamatory sentence expresses surprise or strong emotion and ends with an exclamation point. Example: _Get help!_

3. Forms of sentences: Sentences are classified by form. There are four forms of sentences.

  a. **Simple sentence**: A simple sentence has one subject and one predicate. Example: _The dog jumped through the hoop._

  b. **Compound sentence**: A compound sentence contains at least two independent clauses and no dependent clause. Example: _The dog jumped and the kitten pounced._

  c. **Complex sentence**: A complex sentence consists of an independent clause and one or more dependent clauses. Examples: _When the trainer signaled, the dog jumped through the hoop. She couldn't go home while it was raining. The children who were playing hard had a good time._ (Dependent clauses are underlined.)

  d. **Compound-complex sentence**: A compound-complex sentence has two or more independent clauses and one or more dependent clauses. Examples: _When the band played, the crowd watched and the people cheered. The drummers marched and the buglers played as the parade continued._ (Dependent clauses are underlined.)

Potential problem: Avoid using sentence fragments in place of sentences. Correct: _He was prying off the lid with a screwdriver._ Incorrect: _Prying off the lid with a screwdriver._ (The incorrect example is a sentence fragment. It has a verbal (_prying_) but no verb.)

Correct: *The boat was struck by lightning and soon sank into the sea.* Incorrect: *And soon sank into the sea.* (The incorrect example has no subject. Also, avoid starting sentences with *and*.)

Potential problem: A run-on sentence consists of two or more sentences run together without punctuation or conjunctions to separate them.
Correct: *The teachers met after class <u>and</u> then had their annual picnic. The teachers met after class, <u>and</u> then they had their annual picnic.*
Incorrect: *The teachers met after class then they had their annual picnic.*

Potential problem: Observe parallel construction when writing sentences. This means to use grammatically equal elements in sentences in order to make the sentences flow smoothly. Use the same style or form throughout.
Correct: *The children enjoyed playing with toys, listening to stories, and eating lunch.*
Incorrect: *The children enjoyed playing with toys, listening to stories, and ate lunch.*
Correct: *Please observe the following rules: no running in the halls, no hurting someone else, no talking when someone else is speaking, and no snacking during lessons.*
Incorrect: *Please observe the following rules: no running in the halls, don't hurt anyone, no talking when someone else is speaking, and don't snack during lessons.*

II. **Punctuation**
   A. **Periods**: The period is used to end sentences and mark abbreviations.
      1. The period is used at the end of a declarative or imperative sentence. Examples: *The team won the <u>championship.</u> Take care of <u>yourself.</u>*
      2. The period is used after initials and some abbreviations. Examples: *a.m., Dr., Mrs., etc., C. S. Lewis, St.*
   B. **Question marks**: The question mark is used at the end of a direct question.

Potential problem: Use question marks only with direct questions, not indirect questions.
Correct: *Will she <u>go?</u> He asked if she would <u>go.</u>* Incorrect: *He asked if she would go?*

   C. **Exclamation marks**: The exclamation point is used after interjections or strong commands. Examples: <u>*Wow!*</u> *Do it <u>now!</u>* (Caution: Avoid overusing exclamation points.)
   D. **Commas**: A comma usually indicates a short pause. Rules for using commas are somewhat flexible and depend on the styles of different publications. When using commas, be consistent and follow basic principles (Hodges, Horner, Webb, & Miller, 1994).
      1. **Commas with coordinating conjunctions**: Commas are usually placed before coordinating conjunctions that combine two independent (main) clauses. Example: *The student parking lot was full<u>, and</u> it was time for class to begin. I tried to find another place to park<u>, but</u> there was no other place available.* (Note: When a statement is very short, there is no need for a comma. Example: *I parked and I got to class on time.*)
      2. **Commas after introductory words, phrases, or clauses**: To make the meaning clear, writers often use commas so that the reader will know when to pause. Examples: <u>*Well*</u>*, I guess it's time to go. <u>From the top deck of the ship</u>, we could see the whales in the distance. <u>When the bell rang</u>, the students hurried to their classes.* When the introductory part is short, a comma may not be needed. Example: *In school we learn to read.*

3. **Commas in a series**: Commas are needed to separate three or more words, phrases, or clauses in a series. Examples: *When I went to the store, I bought <u>apples, oranges, and pears</u>.* (Note: A comma before *and* is preferred but not mandatory.) *I found confetti everywhere: <u>on the sidewalk, in the bushes, and even in my hair</u>.* When items in a series contain internal commas, they should be separated with semicolons. (Caution: Don't use a comma to separate only two items.) Example: *In the grocery store, we saw <u>ripe, sweet-smelling melons; large, plump mushrooms; and yellow squash</u>.*

4. **Commas in letters**: Commas follow greetings and closings in friendly letters. Examples: *Dear Sonja, Yours truly, Sincerely,*

5. **Commas in numbers**: Commas occur in numbers of four or more digits, separating numbers in groups of three starting from the right. Examples: *4,234; 19,574,650*

6. **Commas to set off selected elements**

   a. **Nonrestrictive clauses or phrases**: Nonrestrictive clauses or phrases contain nonessential information and are set off by commas. Example: *Jason<u>, who used to be my neighbor,</u> now lives in Florida.* Restrictive clauses or phrases are essential for identifying words in a sentence and are not set off by commas. Example: *The boy <u>with the red hair</u> got the coveted part in the play.*

   b. **Appositives**: An appositive renames a noun, and it may be restrictive or nonrestrictive. Nonrestrictive appositives are set off by commas, but restrictive appositives do not need commas. Example of a nonrestrictive appositive: *Tommy<u>, my cousin,</u> lives in Minneapolis.* Example of a restrictive appositive: *<u>My cousin Tommy</u> lives in Minneapolis.*

   c. **Contrasted elements**: A comma is needed to show contrasts. Examples: *Houston<u>, unlike his brother Bobby,</u> enjoyed playing football. Our teacher made us work hard<u>, but</u> we learned a lot.*

   d. **Geographical names, addresses, and items in dates**: Commas separate items as in the following examples. Geographical names: *She moved to <u>Helena, Montana,</u> from <u>Birmingham, Alabama</u>.* (Note: Use a comma after both the city and the state when the state is not the last word in the sentence.) Items in addresses: *Send the letter to Colin <u>Edwards,</u> 109 Cedar <u>St.,</u> <u>Wenonah,</u> N.J. 76387.* (Note: There is no comma before the zip code.) Items in dates: *She spoke to our class on <u>Monday, February 7, 2005</u>.* When the day of the month or the week is not given, do not use a comma. *He entered college in <u>September 2003</u>.*

   e. **Parenthetical words, phrases, and clauses**: Commas separate parenthetical expressions. Examples: *I believe, for example, however, in my opinion.* Sample sentences: *The rain will be here<u>, I think,</u> by midnight. If the front moves quickly<u>, on the other hand,</u> it may get here sooner.*

   f. **Quotation marks**: Commas are used with direct quotations to set off the speakers. Examples: *<u>She asked,</u> "Who is coming?" "Who<u>," she wondered,</u> "is coming?"*

   g. **Words or phrases set off with commas** to avoid confusion and for ease in reading. Example: *<u>In 2004,</u> 2,100 students entered Spring City College.*

E. **Apostrophes**: Apostrophes serve several functions.
 1. Apostrophes show **possession** for nouns and indefinite pronouns.
   a. **Singular nouns**: Add the apostrophe and -s. Examples: *fox's tail, dog's kennel, Bess's notebook, book's author*
   b. **Plural nouns ending in s:** Add only the apostrophe. Examples: *the Joneses' home, the bunnies' burrow, the detectives' cases, ladies' day*
   c. **Plural nouns not ending in s:** Add the apostrophe and -s. Examples: *men's clubs, women's rights, children's games*
   d. **Compounds**: Add the apostrophe and -s to only the last word for compounds or for joint ownership. Example: <u>*Stuart and Joyce's house was built in 1892.*</u>
   e. **Individual ownership**: Add the apostrophe and -s to each name to show individual ownership. Example: <u>*Tanya's and Burt's houses*</u> *were on the same street.*
 2. An apostrophe marks **omitted letters in contractions and numbers**. Examples: *can't, wouldn't, o'clock, class of '07*

Potential problem: Don't confuse possessive pronouns with contractions.
Correct: <u>*It's*</u> *a cloudy day.* Incorrect: *Its a cloudy day.*
Correct: *The cat found* <u>*its*</u> *lost kitten.* Incorrect: *The cat found it's lost kitten.*
Correct: <u>*Who's*</u> *coming to dinner?* Incorrect: *Whose coming to dinner?*
Correct: <u>*Whose*</u> *glove is that?* Incorrect: *Who's glove is that?*
Correct: <u>*You're*</u> *going to make the team.* Incorrect: *Your going to make the team.*
Correct: *It's* <u>*your*</u> *turn.* Incorrect: *It's you're turn.*
(Hint: When in doubt, think: Can I substitute *it is* for *it's*? If not, use *its*. For example, you wouldn't say, *The cat found it is lost kitten.* The same principle applies to *who's* and *whose* and to *you're* and *your*.)

 3. An apostrophe is used in forming **plurals of letters and numbers** referred to as objects. Examples: *Make a row of* <u>*m's.*</u> *Try to get all* <u>*A's*</u> *on your report card. Your* <u>*7's*</u> *look like* <u>*1's.*</u>
F. **Double quotation marks**: Double quotation marks are used in several ways.
 1. Use quotation marks to mark what is **directly spoken**. Example: <u>*"My mom made that chocolate cake,"*</u> *she said.* <u>*"My mom,"*</u> *she said,* <u>*"made that chocolate cake."*</u> Note: Do not use quotation marks for indirect quotations, as in *She said that her mom made that chocolate cake.* When using quotation marks, use exactly what is directly stated without changing any words. When quoting more than one paragraph by the same speaker, put quotation marks in front of each paragraph, but put final marks only at the end of the last paragraph spoken by that individual.
 2. Use double quotation marks for **titles** of short stories, poems, essays, songs, and other minor titles. Examples: *Robert Frost wrote* <u>*"Birches."*</u> *The class sang* <u>*"This Land Is Your Land"*</u> *to close the program.*
 3. Use double quotation marks to enclose **special words or phrases**. Examples: *He called his daughter his* <u>*"little princess."*</u> *Because Dylan got high grades, students called him* <u>*"the brain."*</u> *After returning from Australia, Jenny talked about her experiences* <u>*"Down Under."*</u>

Potential problem: Observe the correct placement of punctuation marks used with quotation marks. Place the comma, period, question mark, dash, and exclamation

point inside the quotation mark when they refer only to the quoted material. The semicolon and colon follow the quotation mark.
Correct: *"Jody is already <u>here,"</u> she said.* Incorrect: *"Jody is already here", she said.*
Correct: *Jake sang "Blowin' in the <u>Wind"</u>; the choir sang <u>"America."</u>*
Incorrect: *Jake sang "Blowin' in the Wind;" the choir sang "America".*
Place the comma, period, question mark, dash, and exclamation point outside the quotation mark when they refer to the whole sentence.
Correct: *What is a synonym for <u>"reply"</u>?* Incorrect: *What is a synonym for "reply?"*

G. **Single quotation marks**: Use single quotation marks to enclose a title or quotation within a direct quotation. Example: *Jenny said, "My favorite poem is '<u>Casey</u> at the <u>Bat'."</u> Mom says, "The first thing a toddler learns to say is '<u>no'."</u>*

H. **Colons**: Colons are used in time, for business salutations, to call attention to what follows, and for various other purposes.
   1. Use the colon between the hour and minute or the minute and second. Examples: *12:15; 7:45:30*
   2. Use the colon after the greeting in a business letter. Example: *Dear Sir:*
   3. Use the colon between titles and subtitles. Example: I checked *Indian Captive: The Story of Mary Jemison.*
   4. Use the colon in bibliographies for separating the place of publication and the publisher. Example: *Boston, MA: Allyn & Bacon.* (See other examples in the bibliography.)
   5. Use the colon to separate verses from chapters in the Bible. Example: *Mark 4:12.*
   6. Use the colon to set off a list of items or direct attention to what follows, usually a summary or explanation, a series, or a quotation. Examples: *We need to bring several things to class <u>tomorrow:</u> pencils, rulers, graph paper, and calculators. The speaker said the <u>following:</u> "Wisdom comes with experience."*

Potential problem: Avoid using a colon between a verb and its complement or direct object, after *such as,* or between a preposition and its object.
Correct: *Three people <u>volunteered:</u> Cal, Kyra, and Bo. The three volunteers were Cal, Kyra, and Bo.* Incorrect: *The three volunteers were: Cal, Kyra, and Bo.*

I. **Semicolons**: Two major purposes for the semicolon are to separate independent (main) clauses that have no coordinating conjunction and to separate items in a series when there is a comma within one or more of the items.
   1. Use a semicolon to connect two main clauses not joined by a coordinating conjunction. Example: *John heard the call for <u>help;</u> he left immediately.*
   2. Use a semicolon to separate elements that contain commas within them. Example: *The reading association wanted several hard-working, experienced <u>leaders;</u> a convenient, low-rent <u>office;</u> and an adequate supply of stationery and other materials.*
   3. Place a semicolon before a conjunctive adverb when it comes between two main clauses. Examples of conjunctive adverbs: *however, therefore, moreover, consequently, also.* Sample sentences: *I'm <u>thirsty; therefore,</u> I'll stop for a soda. Josh wants to leave <u>now; however,</u> I must pack our belongings before we go.* (Note: A comma follows the conjunctive adverb.)

Potential problem: Avoid using semicolons to connect unequal grammatical elements.

Correct: *The professor called the <u>roll;</u> he skipped my name.*
Incorrect: *The professor called the roll; skipping my name.*

  J. **Hyphens**: A hyphen separates words by syllables.
   1. When coming to the end of a line of print, use a hyphen to divide a long word according to its syllables. Examples: *mul-ti-pli-ca-tion, in-di-vid-u-al.* Note: Do not divide one-syllable words or abbreviations.
   2. Use hyphens to form compound adjectives. Examples: *an up-to-date list, first-grade class, second-hand store, two-thirds majority*

Potential problem: Some words are hyphenated only when used as adjectives.
Correct: *My brother is in a <u>sixth-grade</u> class. My brother is in <u>sixth grade</u>.*
Incorrect: *My brother is in a sixth grade class. My brother is in sixth-grade.*

   3. Use a hyphen for compound numbers that are written as words. Example: *Only <u>seventy-eight</u> people came, even though there are <u>ninety-seven</u> members.*
   4. Sometimes use a hyphen with prefixes. Examples: *high self-esteem, re-enact the events*
   5. Use a hyphen between some compound words. Examples: *mother-in-law, president-elect*
  K. **Dashes**: A dash marks an abrupt break in thought. Show a dash as two hyphens without a space on either side. Use dashes sparingly.
   1. Use a dash to show a sharp break in thought. Example: *Let's get some hamburgers at the <u>grill—oh</u> no, it's time for class!*
   2. Use a dash after an introductory series of items. Example: *Tall, dark, <u>handsome—he</u> was the man of every girl's dreams.*
   3. The dash sets off a parenthetical element for emphasis or clarity. Example: *He was prepared to move into the <u>dorm—the</u> one on Maple <u>Street—before</u> he saw the new apartments.*
  L. **Parentheses**: Parentheses are used primarily to set off supplementary material and to enclose figures or letters that confirm a written number in text.
   1. Use parentheses to set off supplementary, illustrative matter. Examples: *Kim earned good grades in her classes <u>(all but one)</u>. Dr. Eliason ordered new furniture <u>(tables, lamps, and a lounge chair)</u> for his bungalow.*
   2. Use parentheses to enclose numerals after number words in written text. Example: *The results will be available in thirty <u>(30)</u> days.*
   3. Use parentheses to enclose numbers or letters that precede items in a series within a sentence or paragraph. Example: *There are three main steps for planting a rose: <u>(1)</u> dig a deep hole, <u>(2)</u> plant the rose, <u>(3)</u> and water it.*
  M. **Brackets**: Brackets set off extraneous material.
   1. Use brackets to enclose parenthetical matter within material that is already enclosed in parentheses. Example: *Band members (those who were raising funds <u>[needed for new uniforms]</u>) canvassed the neighborhood.*
   2. Use brackets around *sic* when quoting an author directly to show what was written, even though it contains an error. Example: *Attorneys met at the capitle <u>[sic]</u> prior to the convention.*
  N. **Ellipses**: An ellipsis indicates an omission from a quoted passage. Three periods at the beginning or in the middle of a quotation indicate that mate-

rial has been omitted, and four periods at the end of a quotation show that the concluding part has been omitted. Examples: *"... the program consists of music, poetry, and drama."* *The professor concluded his ... lecture with kind remarks."* *"He kept his promise to run the marathon...."*

III. **Capitalization**

A. Capitalize the first word of a sentence, a unit written as a sentence, and a direct quotation. Examples: *He ran home. Amazing! She said, "Come here."*

B. Capitalize proper nouns.

1. Names and nicknames of people and things: *Samuel Higgins, Ford Motor Company, Vickie, Central High School*

2. Ethnic groups and their languages: *Hispanics, African Americans, Yiddish, Swahili, French*

3. Geographical names: *Cumberland River, Maine, United States, Mexico, Rocky Mountains, Yellowstone, Vancouver Island, the Outback*

4. Government agencies, companies, organizations, and institutions: *Central Intelligence Agency, General Motors, National Council of Teachers of English, Harvard, Municipal Hospital*

5. Religions, holy days, holy books, deities: *Hindu, Christmas, Koran, Jehovah, Yom Kippur, Buddha, God*

6. Historical documents, events, periods: *Bill of Rights, Civil War, Dark Ages*

7. Days of the week, months, holidays: *Wednesday, July, Labor Day* (Note: Seasons are not capitalized—spring, summer, fall, winter.)

8. Names of planets, stars, constellations: *Mercury, North Star, Big Dipper, Milky Way*

C. Capitalize acronyms and abbreviations of capitalized words. Examples: *NY, CBS, B.S., MADD* (Some acronyms are added to the dictionary as common uncapitalized words after a period of time. Example: *radar*)

D. Capitalize the pronoun *I*. Example: *He and I are brothers.*

E. Capitalize titles when they precede names or refer to a specific person, but do not capitalize them when they appear elsewhere. Examples: *President Roosevelt; General Clark; Uncle Jack; the President signed the treaty today; Mr. President, we want to express our support. When presidents are elected; he became a general; she is my aunt.*

F. Capitalize the first and last words in titles and other significant words. Do not capitalize the articles *a, an,* and *the* unless one of them is the first word in a title; coordinating conjunctions (*and, but, so*); prepositions (*to, through, for, between*); and the *to* in infinitives. Examples: *The Tale of the Missing Sock, Striving to Win the Game, Duty and Honor* (Note: Underline or italicize titles of books; place quotation marks around the titles of lesser works.)

Bibliography

Bonner, W. H. (1992). *Contemporary business English* (2nd ed.). Eden Prairie, MN: Paradigm.

Gibaldi, J. (2003). *MLA handbook for writers of research papers* (6th ed.). New York: The Modern Language Association.

Hacker, D. (2003). *A writer's reference* (5th ed.). Boston: Bedford/St. Martin's.

Harris, T. L., & Hodges, R. E. (Eds.). (1995). *The literacy dictionary.* Newark, DE: International Reading Association.

HODGES, J., HORNER, W., WEBB, S., & MILLER, R. (1998). *Harbrace college handbook* (13th ed.). Fort Worth: Harcourt Brace.

LOVINGER, P. W. (2000). *The Penguin dictionary of American usage and style.* New York: Penguin.

Target writing and grammar skills. (2003). Circle Pines, MN: American Guidance Service.

WALKER, B. (1997). *Using parts of speech.* Circle Pines, MN: American Guidance Service.

Children's Book Awards

Newbery Award Winners

Caldecott Award Winners

Coretta Scott King Book Award Winners

Newbery Award Winners

THE NEWBERY award is named after the first English publisher of children's books, John Newbery. Granted by the Children's Services Division of the American Library Association, the medal is presented annually for the best contribution to children's literature published in the United States. In addition to the Newbery winner, there are honor books that also receive awards. The awards, which began in 1922, are listed here.

2005 Medal Winner

Kira-Kira by Cynthia Kadohata (Atheneum)

Honor Books

Lizzie Bright and the Buckminster Boy by Gary D. Schmidt (Clarion)
Al Capone Does My Shirts by Gennifer Choldenko (Putnam)
The Voice that Challenged a Nation: Marian Anderson and the Struggle for Equal Rights by Russell Freedman (Clarion)

2004 Medal Winner

The Tale of Despereaux: Being the Story of a Mouse, a Princess, Some Soup, and a Spool of Thread by Kate DiCamillo (Candlewick)

Honor Books

Olive's Ocean by Kevin Henkes (Greenwillow)
An American Plague: The Truth and Terrifying Story of the Yellow Fever Epidemic of 1793 by Jim Murphy (Clarion)

2003 Medal Winner

Crispin: The Cross of Lead by Avi (Hyperion)

Honor Books

The House of the Scorpion by Nancy Farmer (Atheneum)
Pictures of Hollis Woods by Patricia Reilly Giff (Random House/Wendy Lamb Books)
Hoot by Carl Hiaasen (Knopf)
A Corner of the Universe by Ann M. Martin (Scholastic)
Surviving the Applewhites by Stephanie S. Tolan (HarperCollins)

2002 Medal Winner

A Single Shard by Linda Sue Park (Clarion)

Honor Books

Everything on a Waffle by Polly Horvath (Farrar Straus Giroux)
Carver: A Life in Poems by Marilyn Nelson (Front Street)

2001 Medal Winner

A Year Down Yonder by Richard Peck (Dial)

Honor Books

Hope Was Here by Joan Bauer (Putnam)
Because of Winn-Dixie by Kate DiCamillo (Candlewick)
Joey Pigza Loses Control by Jack Gantos (Farrar Straus Giroux)
The Wanderer by Sharon Creech (Joanna Cotler Books/HarperCollins)

2000 Medal Winner

Bud, Not Buddy by Christopher Paul Curtis (Delacorte)

Honor Books

Getting Near to Baby by Audrey Couloumbis (Putnam)
Our Only May Amelia by Jennifer L. Holm (HarperCollins)
26 Fairmount Avenue by Tomie dePaola (Putnam)

1999 Medal Winner

Holes by Louis Sachar (Frances Foster)

Honor Book

A Long Way from Chicago by Richard Peck (Dial)

1998 Medal Winner

Out of the Dust by Karen Hesse (Scholastic)

Honor Books

Ella Enchanted by Gail Carson Levine (HarperCollins)
Lily's Crossing by Patricia Reilly Giff (Delacorte)
Wringer by Jerry Spinelli (HarperCollins)

1997 Medal Winner

The View from Saturday by E. L. Konigsburg (Jean Karl/Atheneum)

Honor Books

A Girl Named Disaster by Nancy Farmer (Jackson/Orchard)
Moorchild by Eloise McGraw (McElderry/Simon & Schuster)
The Thief by Megan Whalen Turner (Greenwillow/Morrow)
Belle Prater's Boy by Ruth White (Farrar Straus Giroux)

1996 Medal Winner

The Midwife's Apprentice by Karen Cushman (Clarion)

Honor Books

What Jamie Saw by Carolyn Coman (Front Street)
The Watsons Go to Birmingham: 1963 by Christopher Paul Curtis (Delacorte)
Yolonda's Genius by Carol Fenner (McElderry/Simon & Schuster)
The Great Fire by Jim Murphy (Scholastic)

1995 Medal Winner

Walk Two Moons by Sharon Creech (HarperCollins)

Honor Books

Catherine, Called Birdy by Karen Cushman (Clarion)
The Ear, the Eye and the Arm by Nancy Farmer (Jackson/Orchard)

1994 Medal Winner

The Giver by Lois Lowry (Houghton Mifflin)

Honor Books

Crazy Lady by Jane Leslie Conly (HarperCollins)
Dragon's Gate by Laurence Yep (HarperCollins)
Eleanor Roosevelt: A Life of Discovery by Russell Freedman (Clarion)

1993 Medal Winner

Missing May by Cynthia Rylant (Jackson/Orchard)

Honor Books

What Hearts by Bruce Brooks (HarperCollins)
The Dark-thirty: Southern Tales of the Supernatural by Patricia McKissack (Knopf)
Somewhere in the Darkness by Walter Dean Myers (Scholastic)

1992 Medal Winner

Shiloh by Phyllis Reynolds Naylor (Atheneum)

Honor Books

Nothing But the Truth: A Documentary Novel by Avi (Jackson/Orchard)
The Wright Brothers: How They Invented the Airplane by Russell Freedman (Holiday House)

1991 Medal Winner

Maniac Magee by Jerry Spinelli (Little, Brown)

Honor Book

The True Confessions of Charlotte Doyle by Avi (Jackson/Orchard)

1990 Medal Winner

Number the Stars by Lois Lowry (Houghton Mifflin)

Honor Books

Afternoon of the Elves by Janet Taylor Lisle (Jackson/Orchard)
Shabanu, Daughter of the Wind by Suzanne Fisher Staples (Knopf)
The Winter Room by Gary Paulsen (Jackson/Orchard)

1989 Medal Winner

Joyful Noise: Poems for Two Voices by Paul Fleischman (Harper)

Honor Books

In the Beginning: Creation Stories from Around the World by Virginia Hamilton (Harcourt)
Scorpions by Walter Dean Myers (Harper)

1988 Medal Winner

Lincoln: A Photobiography by Russell Freedman (Clarion)

Honor Books

After the Rain by Norma Fox Mazer (Morrow)
Hatchet by Gary Paulsen (Bradbury)

1987 Medal Winner

The Whipping Boy by Sid Fleischman
(Greenwillow)

Honor Books

A Fine White Dust by Cynthia Rylant (Bradbury)
On My Honor by Marion Dane Bauer (Clarion)
Volcano: The Eruption and Healing of Mount St. Helens
by Patricia Lauber (Bradbury)

1986 Medal Winner

Sarah, Plain and Tall by Patricia MacLachlan
(Harper)

Honor Books

Commodore Perry in the Land of the Shogun by Rhoda
Blumberg (Lothrop)
Dogsong by Gary Paulsen (Bradbury)

1985 Medal Winner

The Hero and the Crown by Robin McKinley
(Greenwillow)

Honor Books

Like Jake and Me by Mavis Jukes (Knopf)
The Moves Make the Man by Bruce Brooks (Harper)
One-Eyed Cat by Paula Fox (Bradbury)

1984 Medal Winner

Dear Mr. Henshaw by Beverly Cleary (Morrow)

Honor Books

The Sign of the Beaver by Elizabeth George Speare
(Houghton Mifflin)
A Solitary Blue by Cynthia Voigt (Atheneum)
Sugaring Time by Kathryn Lasky (Macmillan)
The Wish Giver: Three Tales of Coven Tree by Bill
Brittain (Harper)

1983 Medal Winner

Dicey's Song by Cynthia Voigt (Atheneum)

Honor Books

The Blue Sword by Robin McKinley (Greenwillow)

Doctor DeSoto by William Steig (Farrar Straus Giroux)
Graven Images by Paul Fleischman (Harper)
Homesick: My Own Story by Jean Fritz (Putnam)
Sweet Whispers, Brother Rush by Virginia Hamilton
(Philomel)

1982 Medal Winner

*A Visit to William Blake's Inn: Poems for Innocent and
Experienced Travelers* by Nancy Willard (Harcourt)

Honor Books

Ramona Quimby, Age 8 by Beverly Cleary (Morrow)
*Upon the Head of the Goat: A Childhood in Hungary
1939–1944* by Aranka Siegal (Farrar Straus Giroux)

1981 Medal Winner

Jacob Have I Loved by Katherine Paterson (Crowell)

Honor Books

The Fledgling by Jane Langton (Harper)
A Ring of Endless Light by Madeleine L'Engle (Farrar
Straus Giroux)

1980 Medal Winner

*A Gathering of Days: A New England Girl's Journal, 1830–
1832* by Joan W. Blos (Scribner)

Honor Book

The Road from Home: The Story of an Armenian Girl by
David Kherdian (Greenwillow)

1979 Medal Winner

The Westing Game by Ellen Raskin (Dutton)

Honor Book

The Great Gilly Hopkins by Katherine Paterson (Crowell)

1978 Medal Winner

Bridge to Terabithia by Katherine Paterson (Crowell)

Honor Books

Ramona and Her Father by Beverly Cleary (Morrow)
Anpao: An American Indian Odyssey by Jamake
Highwater (Lippincott)

1977 Medal Winner

Roll of Thunder, Hear My Cry by Mildred D. Taylor
(Dial)

Honor Books

Abel's Island by William Steig (Farrar Straus Giroux)
A String in the Harp by Nancy Bond (Atheneum)

1976 Medal Winner

The Grey King by Susan Cooper (McElderry/Atheneum)

Honor Books

The Hundred Penny Box by Sharon Bell Mathis (Viking)
Dragonwings by Laurence Yep (Harper)

1975 Medal Winner

M. C. Higgins, the Great by Virginia Hamilton (Macmillan)

Honor Books

Figgs and Phantoms by Ellen Raskin (Dutton)
My Brother Sam Is Dead by James Lincoln Collier & Christopher Collier (Four Winds)
The Perilous Gard by Elizabeth Marie Pope (Houghton Mifflin)
Philip Hall Likes Me, I Reckon Maybe by Bette Greene (Dial)

1974 Medal Winner

The Slave Dancer by Paula Fox (Bradbury)

Honor Book

The Dark Is Rising by Susan Cooper (McElderry/Atheneum)

1973 Medal Winner

Julie of the Wolves by Jean Craighead George (Harper)

Honor Books

Frog and Toad Together by Arnold Lobel (Harper)
The Upstairs Room by Johanna Reiss (Crowell)
The Witches of Worm by Zilpha Keatley Snyder (Atheneum)

1972 Medal Winner

Mrs. Frisby and the Rats of NIMH by Robert C. O'Brien (Atheneum)

Honor Books

Incident at Hawk's Hill by Allan W. Eckert (Little, Brown)
The Planet of Junior Brown by Virginia Hamilton (Macmillan)

The Tombs of Atuan by Ursula K. LeGuin (Atheneum)
Annie and the Old One by Miska Miles (Little, Brown)
The Headless Cupid by Zilpha Keatley Snyder (Atheneum)

1971 Medal Winner

Summer of the Swans by Betsy Byars (Viking)

Honor Books

Knee Knock Rise by Natalie Babbitt (Farrar Straus Giroux)
Enchantress from the Stars by Sylvia Louise Engdahl (Atheneum)
Sing Down the Moon by Scott O'Dell (Houghton Mifflin)

1970 Medal Winner

Sounder by William H. Armstrong (Harper)

Honor Books

Our Eddie by Sulamith Ish-Kishor (Pantheon)
The Many Ways of Seeing: An Introduction to the Pleasures of Art by Janet Gaylord Moore (World)
Journey Outside by Mary Q. Steele (Viking)

1969 Medal Winner

The High King by Lloyd Alexander (Holt)

Honor Books

To Be a Slave by Julius Lester (Dial)
When Shlemiel Went to Warsaw and Other Stories by Isaac Bashevis Singer (Farrar Straus Giroux)

1968 Medal Winner

From the Mixed-Up Files of Mrs. Basil E. Frankweiler by E. L. Konigsburg (Atheneum)

Honor Books

Jennifer, Hecate, Macbeth, William McKinley, and Me, Elizabeth by E. L. Konigsburg (Atheneum)
The Black Pearl by Scott O'Dell (Houghton Mifflin)
The Fearsome Inn by Isaac Bashevis Singer (Scribner)
The Egypt Game by Zilpha Keatley Snyder (Atheneum)

1967 Medal Winner

Up a Road Slowly by Irene Hunt (Follett)

Honor Books

The King's Fifth by Scott O'Dell (Houghton Mifflin)

Zlateh the Goat and Other Stories by Isaac Bashevis Singer (Harper)
The Jazz Man by Mary Hays Weik (Atheneum)

1966 Medal Winner

I, Juan de Pareja by Elizabeth Borton de Trevino (Farrar Straus Giroux)

Honor Books

The Black Cauldron by Lloyd Alexander (Holt)
The Animal Family by Randall Jarrell (Pantheon)
The Noonday Friends by Mary Stolz (Harper)

1965 Medal Winner

Shadow of a Bull by Maia Wojciechowska (Atheneum)

Honor Book

Across Five Aprils by Irene Hunt (Follett)

1964 Medal Winner

It's Like This, Cat by Emily Neville (Harper)

Honor Books

Rascal: A Memoir of a Better Era by Sterling North (Dutton)
The Loner by Ester Wier (McKay)

1963 Medal Winner

A Wrinkle in Time by Madeleine L'Engle (Farrar Straus Giroux)

Honor Books

Thistle and Thyme: Tales and Legends from Scotland by Sorche Nic Leodhas, pseud. (Leclaire Alger) (Holt)
Men of Athens by Olivia Coolidge (Houghton Mifflin)

1962 Medal Winner

The Bronze Bow by Elizabeth George Speare (Houghton Mifflin)

Honor Books

Frontier Living by Edwin Tunis (World)
The Golden Goblet by Eloise Jarvis McGraw (Coward)
Belling the Tiger by Mary Stolz (Harper)

1961 Medal Winner

Island of the Blue Dolphins by Scott O'Dell (Houghton Mifflin)

Honor Books

America Moves Forward: A History for Peter by Gerald W. Johnson (Morrow)
Old Ramon by Jack Schaefer (Houghton Mifflin)
The Cricket in Times Square by George Selden, pseud. (George Thompson) (Farrar Straus Giroux)

1960 Medal Winner

Onion John by Joseph Krumgold (Crowell)

Honor Books

My Side of the Mountain by Jean Craighead George (Dutton)
America Is Born: A History for Peter by Gerald W. Johnson (Morrow)
The Gammage Cup by Carol Kendall (Harcourt)

1959 Medal Winner

The Witch of Blackbird Pond by Elizabeth George Speare (Houghton Mifflin)

Honor Books

The Family Under the Bridge by Natalie Savage Carlson (Harper)
Along Came a Dog by Meindert De Jong (Harper)
Chucaro: Wild Pony of the Pampa by Francis Kalnay (Harcourt)
The Perilous Road by William O. Steele (Harcourt)

1958 Medal Winner

Rifles for Watie by Harold Keith (Crowell)

Honor Books

The Horsecatcher by Mari Sandoz (Westminster)
Gone-Away Lake by Elizabeth Enright (Harcourt)
The Great Wheel by Robert Lawson (Viking)
Tom Paine, Freedom's Apostle by Leo Gurko (Crowell)

1957 Medal Winner

Miracles on Maple Hill by Virginia Sorenson (Harcourt)

Honor Books

Old Yeller by Fred Gipson (Harper)
The House of Sixty Fathers by Meindert De Jong (Harper)
Mr. Justice Holmes by Clara Ingram Judson (Follett)
The Corn Grows Ripe by Dorothy Rhoads (Viking)
Black Fox of Lorne by Marguerite de Angeli (Doubleday)

1956 Medal Winner

Carry On, Mr. Bowditch by Jean Lee Latham (Houghton Mifflin)

Honor Books

The Secret River by Marjorie Kinnan Rawlings (Scribner)
The Golden Name Day by Jennie Lindquist (Harper)
Men, Microscopes, and Living Things by Katherine Shippen (Viking)

1955 Medal Winner

The Wheel on the School by Meindert De Jong (Harper)

Honor Books

Courage of Sarah Noble by Alice Dalgliesh (Scribner)
Banner in the Sky by James Ullman (Lippincott)

1954 Medal Winner

. . . And Now Miguel by Joseph Krumgold (Crowell)

Honor Books

All Alone by Claire Huchet Bishop (Viking)
Shadrach by Meindert De Jong (Harper)
Hurry Home, Candy by Meindert De Jong (Harper)
Theodore Roosevelt, Fighting Patriot by Clara Ingram Judson (Follett)
Magic Maize by Mary & Conrad Buff (Houghton Mifflin)

1953 Medal Winner

Secret of the Andes by Ann Nolan Clark (Viking)

Honor Books

Charlotte's Web by E. B. White (Harper)
Moccasin Trail by Eloise Jarvis McGraw (Coward)
Red Sails to Capri by Ann Weil (Viking)
The Bears on Hemlock Mountain by Alice Dalgliesh (Scribner)
Birthdays of Freedom, Vol. 1 by Genevieve Foster (Scribner)

1952 Medal Winner

Ginger Pye by Eleanor Estes (Harcourt)

Honor Books

Americans Before Columbus by Elizabeth Baity (Viking)
Minn of the Mississippi by Holling C. Holling (Houghton Mifflin)

The Defender by Nicholas Kalashnikoff (Scribner)
The Light at Tern Rock by Julia Sauer (Viking)
The Apple and the Arrow by Mary & Conrad Buff (Houghton Mifflin)

1951 Medal Winner

Amos Fortune, Free Man by Elizabeth Yates (Dutton)

Honor Books

Better Known as Johnny Appleseed by Mabel Leigh Hunt (Lippincott)
Gandhi, Fighter Without a Sword by Jeanette Eaton (Morrow)
Abraham Lincoln, Friend of the People by Clara Ingram Judson (Follett)
The Story of Appleby Capple by Anne Parrish (Harper)

1950 Medal Winner

The Door in the Wall by Marguerite de Angeli (Doubleday)

Honor Books

Tree of Freedom by Rebecca Caudill (Viking)
The Blue Cat of Castle Town by Catherine Coblentz (Longmans)
Kildee House by Rutherford Montgomery (Doubleday)
George Washington by Genevieve Foster (Scribner)
Song of the Pines: A Story of Norwegian Lumbering in Wisconsin by Walter & Marion Havighurst (Winston)

1949 Medal Winner

King of the Wind by Marguerite Henry (Rand McNally)

Honor Books

Seabird by Holling C. Holling (Houghton Mifflin)
Daughter of the Mountain by Louise Rankin (Viking)
My Father's Dragon by Ruth S. Gannett (Random House)
Story of the Negro by Arna Bontemps (Knopf)

1948 Medal Winner

The Twenty-One Balloons by William Pène du Bois (Viking)

Honor Books

Pancakes-Paris by Claire Huchet Bishop (Viking)
Li Lun, Lad of Courage by Carolyn Treffinger (Abingdon)

The Quaint and Curious Quest of Johnny Longfoot by Catherine Besterman (Bobbs-Merrill)
The Cow-Tail Switch, and Other West African Stories by Harold Courlander (Holt)
Misty of Chincoteague by Marguerite Henry (Rand McNally)

1947 Medal Winner

Miss Hickory by Carolyn Sherwin Bailey (Viking)

Honor Books

Wonderful Year by Nancy Barnes (Messner)
Big Tree by Mary & Conrad Buff (Viking)
The Heavenly Tenants by William Maxwell (Harper)
The Avion My Uncle Flew by Cyrus Fisher, pseud. (Darwin L. Teilhet) (Appleton)
The Hidden Treasure of Glaston by Eleanor Jewett (Viking)

1946 Medal Winner

Strawberry Girl by Lois Lenski (Lippincott)

Honor Books

Justin Morgan Had a Horse by Marguerite Henry (Rand McNally)
The Moved-Outers by Florence Crannell Means (Houghton Mifflin)
Bhimsa, the Dancing Bear by Christine Weston (Scribner)
New Found World by Katherine Shippen (Viking)

1945 Medal Winner

Rabbit Hill by Robert Lawson (Viking)

Honor Books

The Hundred Dresses by Eleanor Estes (Harcourt)
The Silver Pencil by Alice Dalgliesh (Scribner)
Abraham Lincoln's World by Genevieve Foster (Scribner)
Lone Journey: The Life of Roger Williams by Jeanette Eaton (Harcourt)

1944 Medal Winner

Johnny Tremain by Esther Forbes (Houghton Mifflin)

Honor Books

These Happy Golden Years by Laura Ingalls Wilder (Harper)
Fog Magic by Julia Sauer (Viking)
Rufus M. by Eleanor Estes (Harcourt)
Mountain Born by Elizabeth Yates (Coward)

1943 Medal Winner

Adam of the Road by Elizabeth Janet Gray (Viking)

Honor Books

The Middle Moffat by Eleanor Estes (Harcourt)
Have You Seen Tom Thumb? by Mabel Leigh Hunt (Lippincott)

1942 Medal Winner

The Matchlock Gun by Walter Edmonds (Dodd)

Honor Books

Little Town on the Prairie by Laura Ingalls Wilder (Harper)
George Washington's World by Genevieve Foster (Scribner)
Indian Captive: The Story of Mary Jemison by Lois Lenski (Lippincott)
Down Ryton Water by Eva Roe Gaggin (Viking)

1941 Medal Winner

Call It Courage by Armstrong Sperry (Macmillan)

Honor Books

Blue Willow by Doris Gates (Viking)
Young Mac of Fort Vancouver by Mary Jane Carr (Crowell)
The Long Winter by Laura Ingalls Wilder (Harper)
Nansen by Anna Gertrude Hall (Viking)

1940 Medal Winner

Daniel Boone by James Daugherty (Viking)

Honor Books

The Singing Tree by Kate Seredy (Viking)
Runner of the Mountain Tops: The Life of Louis Agassiz by Mabel Robinson (Random House)
By the Shores of Silver Lake by Laura Ingalls Wilder (Harper)
Boy with a Pack by Stephen W. Meader (Harcourt)

1939 Medal Winner

Thimble Summer by Elizabeth Enright (Rinehart)

Honor Books

Nino by Valenti Angelo (Viking)
Mr. Popper's Penguins by Richard & Florence Atwater (Little, Brown)
Hello the Boat! by Phyllis Crawford (Holt)

Leader by Destiny: George Washington, Man and Patriot by Jeanette Eaton (Harcourt)
Penn by Elizabeth Janet Gray (Viking)

1938 Medal Winner

The White Stag by Kate Seredy (Viking)

Honor Books

Pecos Bill by James Cloyd Bowman (Little, Brown)
Bright Island by Mabel Robinson (Random House)
On the Banks of Plum Creek by Laura Ingalls Wilder (Harper)

1937 Medal Winner

Roller Skates by Ruth Sawyer (Viking)

Honor Books

Phoebe Fairchild: Her Book by Lois Lenski (Stokes)
Whistler's Van by Idwal Jones (Viking)
The Golden Basket by Ludwig Bemelmans (Viking)
Winterbound by Margery Bianco (Viking)
The Codfish Musket by Agnes Hewes (Doubleday)
Audubon by Constance Rourke (Harcourt)

1936 Medal Winner

Caddie Woodlawn by Carol Ryrie Brink (Macmillan)

Honor Books

Honk, the Moose by Phil Stong (Dodd)
The Good Master by Kate Seredy (Viking)
Young Walter Scott by Elizabeth Janet Gray (Viking)
All Sail Set: A Romance of the Flying Cloud by Armstrong Sperry (Winston)

1935 Medal Winner

Dobry by Monica Shannon (Viking)

Honor Books

Pageant of Chinese History by Elizabeth Seeger (Longmans)
Davy Crockett by Constance Rourke (Harcourt)
Day on Skates: The Story of a Dutch Picnic by Hilda Von Stockum (Harper)

1934 Medal Winner

Invincible Louisa: The Story of the Author of Little Women by Cornelia Meigs (Little, Brown)

Honor Books

The Forgotten Daughter by Caroline Snedeker (Doubleday)
Swords of Steel by Elsie Singmaster (Houghton Mifflin)
ABC Bunny by Wanda Gág (Coward)
Winged Girl of Knossos by Erik Berry, pseud. (Allena Best) (Appleton)
New Land by Sarah Schmidt (McBride)
Big Tree of Bunlahy: Stories of My Own Countryside by Padraic Colum (Macmillan)
Glory of the Seas by Agnes Hewes (Knopf)
Apprentice of Florence by Ann Kyle (Houghton Mifflin)

1933 Medal Winner

Young Fu of the Upper Yangtze by Elizabeth Lewis (Winston)

Honor Books

Swift Rivers by Cornelia Meigs (Little, Brown)
The Railroad to Freedom: A Story of the Civil War by Hildegarde Swift (Harcourt)
Children of the Soil: A Story of Scandinavia by Nora Burglon (Doubleday)

1932 Medal Winner

Waterless Mountain by Laura Adams Armer (Longmans)

Honor Books

The Fairy Circus by Dorothy P. Lathrop (Macmillan)
Calico Bush by Rachel Field (Macmillan)
Boy of the South Seas by Eunice Tietjens (Coward-McCann)
Out of the Flame by Eloise Lownsbery (Longmans)
Jane's Island by Marjorie Allee (Houghton Mifflin)
Truce of the Wolf and Other Tales of Old Italy by Mary Gould Davis (Harcourt)

1931 Medal Winner

The Cat Who Went to Heaven by Elizabeth Coatsworth (Macmillan)

Honor Books

Floating Island by Anne Parrish (Harper)
The Dark Star of Itza: The Story of a Pagan Princess by Alida Malkus (Harcourt)
Queer Person by Ralph Hubbard (Doubleday)
Mountains Are Free by Julia Davis Adams (Dutton)
Spice and the Devil's Cave by Agnes Hewes (Knopf)

Meggy MacIntosh by Elizabeth Janet Gray (Doubleday)
Garram the Hunter: A Boy of the Hill Tribes by Herbert Best (Doubleday)
Ood-Le-Uk the Wanderer by Alice Lide & Margaret Johansen (Little, Brown)

1930 Medal Winner

Hitty, Her First Hundred Years by Rachel Field (Macmillan)

Honor Books

A Daughter of the Seine: The Life of Madame Roland by Jeanette Eaton (Harper)
Pran of Albania by Elizabeth Miller (Doubleday)
Jumping-Off Place by Marion Hurd McNeely (Longmans)
The Tangle-Coated Horse and Other Tales by Ella Young (Longmans)
Vaino by Julia Davis Adams (Dutton)
Little Blacknose by Hildegarde Swift (Harcourt)

1929 Medal Winner

The Trumpeter of Krakow by Eric P. Kelly (Macmillan)

Honor Books

Pigtail of Ah Lee Ben Loo by John Bennett (Longmans)
Millions of Cats by Wanda Gág (Coward)
The Boy Who Was by Grace Hallock (Dutton)
Clearing Weather by Cornelia Meigs (Little, Brown)
Runaway Papoose by Grace Moon (Doubleday)
Tod of the Fens by Elinor Whitney (Macmillan)

1928 Medal Winner

Gay Neck, the Story of a Pigeon by Dhan Gopal Mukerji (Dutton)

Honor Books

The Wonder Smith and His Son by Ella Young (Longmans)
Downright Dencey by Caroline Snedeker (Doubleday)

1927 Medal Winner

Smoky, the Cowhorse by Will James (Scribner)

Honor Books

[None recorded]

1926 Medal Winner

Shen of the Sea by Arthur Bowie Chrisman (Dutton)

Honor Book

The Voyagers: Being Legends and Romances of Atlantic Discovery by Padraic Colum (Macmillan)

1925 Medal Winner

Tales from Silver Lands by Charles Finger (Doubleday)

Honor Books

Nicholas: A Manhattan Christmas Story by Annie Carroll Moore (Putnam)
The Dream Coach by Anne Parrish (Macmillan)

1924 Medal Winner

The Dark Frigate by Charles Hawes (Little, Brown)

Honor Books

[None recorded]

1923 Medal Winner

The Voyages of Doctor Dolittle by Hugh Lofting (Lippincott)

Honor Books

[None recorded]

1922 Medal Winner

The Story of Mankind by Hendrik Willem van Loon (Liveright)

Honor Books

The Great Quest by Charles Hawes (Little, Brown)
Cedric the Forester by Bernard Marshall (Appleton)
The Old Tobacco Shop: A True Account of What Befell a Little Boy in Search of Adventure by William Bowen (Macmillan)
The Golden Fleece and the Heroes Who Lived Before Achilles by Padraic Colum (Macmillan)
The Windy Hill by Cornelia Meigs (Macmillan)

Caldecott Award Winners

NAMED IN honor of Randolph Caldecott, who was a British illustrator of children's books, the Caldecott award is given to the illustrator of the best picture book for children published in the United States. Awards are granted annually by the Children's Services Division of the American Library Association. In addition to the Caldecott award, one or more honor books are presented with awards. Caldecott award and honor books are listed here.

2005 Medal Winner

Kitten's First Full Moon by Kevin Henkes (Greenwillow)

Honor Books

The Red Book by Barbara Lehman (Houghton Mifflin)
Coming on Home Soon, illustrated by E. B. Lewis, written by Jacqueline Woodson (Putnam)
Knuffle Bunny: A Cautionary Tale by Mo Willems (Hyperion)

2004 Medal Winner

The Man Who Walked Between the Towers by Mordicai Gerstein (Roaring Brook Press/Millbrook Press)

Honor Books

Ella Sarah Gets Dressed by Margaret Chodos-Irvine (Harcourt)
What Do You Do with a Tail Like This? by Steve Jenkins and Robin Page (Houghton Mifflin)
Don't Let the Pigeon Drive the Bus by Mo Willems (Hyperion)

2003 Medal Winner

My Friend Rabbit by Eric Rohmann (Roaring Brook Press/Millbrook Press)

Honor Books

The Spider and the Fly, illustrated by Tony DiTerlizzi, written by Mary Howitt (Simon & Schuster)
Hondo and Fabian by Peter McCarty (Holt)
Noah's Ark by Jerry Pinkney (SeaStar)

2002 Medal Winner

The Three Pigs by David Wiesner (Clarion)

Honor Books

The Dinosaurs of Waterhouse Hawkins, illustrated by Brian Selznick, written by Barbara Kerley (Scholastic)
Martin's Big Words: The Life of Dr. Martin Luther King, Jr., illustrated by Bryan Collier, written by Doreen Rappaport (Jump at the Sun/Hyperion)
The Stray Dog by Marc Simont (HarperCollins)

2001 Medal Winner

So You Want to Be President? illustrated by David Small, written by Judith St. George (Philomel)

Honor Books

Casey at the Bat, illustrated by Christopher Bing, written by Ernest Thayer (Handprint)
Click, Clack, Moo: Cows that Type, illustrated by Betsy Lewin, written by Doreen Cronin (Simon & Schuster)
Olivia by Ian Falconer (Atheneum)

2000 Medal Winner

Joseph Had a Little Overcoat by Simms Taback (Viking)

Honor Books

A Child's Calendar, illustrated by Trina Schart Hyman, written by John Updike (Holiday House)
Sector 7 by David Wiesner (Clarion)
When Sophie Gets Angry—Really, Really Angry . . . by Molly Bang (Scholastic)
The Ugly Duckling, illustrated by Jerry Pinkney, written by Hans Christian Andersen, adapted by Jerry Pinkney (Morrow)

1999 Medal Winner

Snowflake Bentley, illustrated by Mary Azarian, written by Jacqueline Briggs Martin (Houghton Mifflin)

Honor Books

Duke Ellington: The Piano Prince and the Orchestra, illustrated by Brian Pinkney, written by Andrea Davis Pinkney (Hyperion)
No, David! by David Shannon (Scholastic)
Snow by Uri Shulevitz (Farrar Straus Giroux)
Tibet Through the Red Box by Peter Sis (Frances Foster)

1998 Medal Winner

Rapunzel by Paul O. Zelinsky (Dutton)

Honor Books

The Gardener, illustrated by David Small, written by Sarah Stewart (Farrar Straus Giroux)
Harlem, illustrated by Christopher Myers, written by Walter Dean Myers (Scholastic)
There Was an Old Lady Who Swallowed a Fly by Simms Taback (Viking)

1997 Medal Winner

Golem by David Wisniewski (Clarion)

Honor Books

Hush! A Thai Lullaby, illustrated by Holly Meade, written by Minfong Ho (Melanie Kroupa/Orchard)
The Graphic Alphabet by David Pelletier (Orchard)
The Paperboy by Dav Pilkey (Jackson/Orchard)
Starry Messenger by Peter Sís (Foster/Farrar Straus Giroux)

1996 Medal Winner

Officer Buckle and Gloria by Peggy Rathmann (Putnam)

Honor Books

Alphabet City by Stephen T. Johnson (Viking)
Zin! Zin! Zin! a Violin, illustrated by Marjorie Priceman, written by Lloyd Moss (Simon & Schuster)
The Faithful Friend, illustrated by Brian Pinkney, written by Robert D. San Souci (Simon & Schuster)
Tops & Bottoms, adapted and illustrated by Janet Stevens (Harcourt)

1995 Medal Winner

Smoky Night, illustrated by David Diaz, written by Eve Bunting (Harcourt)

Honor Books

John Henry, illustrated by Jerry Pinkney, written by Julius Lester (Dial)

Swamp Angel, illustrated by Paul O. Zelinsky, written by Anne Issacs (Dutton)
Time Flies by Eric Rohmann (Crown)

1994 Medal Winner

Grandfather's Journey by Allen Say, edited by Walter Lorraine (Houghton Mifflin)

Honor Books

Peppe the Lamplighter, illustrated by Ted Lewin, written by Elisa Bartone (Lothrop)
In the Small, Small Pond by Denise Fleming (Holt)
Raven: A Trickster Tale from the Pacific Northwest by Gerald McDermott (Harcourt)
Owen by Kevin Henkes (Greenwillow)
Yo! Yes? illustrated by Chris Raschka, edited by Richard Jackson (Orchard)

1993 Medal Winner

Mirette on the High Wire by Emily Arnold McCully (Putnam)

Honor Books

The Stinky Cheese Man and Other Fairly Stupid Tales, illustrated by Lane Smith, written by Jon Scieszka (Viking)
Seven Blind Mice by Ed Young (Philomel)
Working Cotton, illustrated by Carole Byard, written by Sherley Anne Williams (Harcourt)

1992 Medal Winner

Tuesday by David Wiesner (Clarion)

Honor Book

Tar Beach by Faith Ringgold (Crown)

1991 Medal Winner

Black and White by David Macaulay (Houghton Mifflin)

Honor Books

Puss in Boots, illustrated by Fred Marcellino, written by Charles Perrault, translated by Malcolm Arthur (Di Capua/Farrar Straus Giroux)
"More More More," Said the Baby: Three Love Stories by Vera B. Williams (Greenwillow)

1990 Medal Winner

Lon Po Po: A Red-Riding Hood Story from China by Ed Young (Philomel)

Honor Books

Bill Peet: An Autobiography by Bill Peet (Houghton Mifflin)

Color Zoo by Lois Ehlert (Lippincott)

The Talking Eggs: A Folktale from the American South, illustrated by Jerry Pinkney, written by Robert D. San Souci (Dial)

Hershel and the Hanukkah Goblins, illustrated by Trina Schart Hyman, written by Eric Kimmel (Holiday House)

1989 Medal Winner

Song and Dance Man, illustrated by Stephen Gammell, written by Karen Ackerman (Knopf)

Honor Books

The Boy of the Three-Year Nap, illustrated by Allen Say, written by Diane Snyder (Houghton Mifflin)

Free Fall by David Wiesner (Lothrop)

Goldilocks and the Three Bears by James Marshall (Dial)

Mirandy and Brother Wind, illustrated by Jerry Pinkney, written by Patricia C. McKissack (Knopf)

1988 Medal Winner

Owl Moon, illustrated by John Schoenherr, written by Jane Yolen (Philomel)

Honor Book

Mufaro's Beautiful Daughters: An African Tale by John Steptoe (Lothrop)

1987 Medal Winner

Hey, Al, illustrated by Richard Egielski, written by Arthur Yorinks (Farrar Straus Giroux)

Honor Books

The Village of Round and Square Houses by Ann Grifalconi (Little, Brown)

Alphabatics by Suse MacDonald (Bradbury)

Rumpelstiltskin by Paul O. Zelinsky (Dutton)

1986 Medal Winner

The Polar Express by Chris Van Allsburg (Houghton Mifflin)

Honor Books

The Relatives Came, illustrated by Stephen Gammell, written by Cynthia Rylant (Bradbury)

King Bidgood's in the Bathtub, illustrated by Don Wood, written by Audrey Wood (Harcourt)

1985 Medal Winner

Saint George and the Dragon, illustrated by Trina Schart Hyman, retold by Margaret Hodges (Little, Brown)

Honor Books

Hansel and Gretel, illustrated by Paul O. Zelinsky, retold by Rika Lesser (Dodd)

Have You Seen My Duckling? by Nancy Tafuri (Greenwillow)

The Story of Jumping Mouse: A Native American Legend, retold and illustrated by John Steptoe (Lothrop)

1984 Medal Winner

The Glorious Flight: Across the Channel with Louis Bleriot by Alice & Martin Provensen (Viking)

Honor Books

Little Red Riding Hood, retold and illustrated by Trina Schart Hyman (Holiday House)

Ten, Nine, Eight by Molly Bang (Greenwillow)

1983 Medal Winner

Shadow, translated and illustrated by Marcia Brown, original text in French by Blaise Cendrars (Scribner)

Honor Books

A Chair for My Mother by Vera B. Williams (Greenwillow)

When I Was Young in the Mountains, illustrated by Diane Goode, written by Cynthia Rylant (Dutton)

1982 Medal Winner

Jumanji by Chris Van Allsburg (Houghton Mifflin)

Honor Books

Where the Buffaloes Begin, illustrated by Stephen Gammell, written by Olaf Baker (Warne)

On Market Street, illustrated by Anita Lobel, written by Arnold Lobel (Greenwillow)

Outside Over There by Maurice Sendak (Harper)

A Visit to William Blake's Inn: Poems for Innocent and Experienced Travelers, illustrated by Alice & Martin Provensen, written by Nancy Willard (Harcourt)

1981 Medal Winner

Fables by Arnold Lobel (Harper)

Honor Books

The Bremen-Town Musicians, retold and illustrated by Ilse Plume (Doubleday)

The Grey Lady and the Strawberry Snatcher by Molly Bang (Four Winds)
Mice Twice by Joseph Low (McElderry/Atheneum)
Truck by Donald Crews (Greenwillow)

1980 Medal Winner

Ox-Cart Man, illustrated by Barbara Cooney, written by Donald Hall (Viking)

Honor Books

Ben's Trumpet by Rachel Isadora (Greenwillow)
The Garden of Abdul Gasazi by Chris Van Allsburg (Houghton Mifflin)
The Treasure by Uri Shulevitz (Farrar Straus Giroux)

1979 Medal Winner

The Girl Who Loved Wild Horses by Paul Goble (Bradbury)

Honor Books

Freight Train by Donald Crews (Greenwillow)
The Way to Start a Day, illustrated by Peter Parnall, written by Byrd Baylor (Scribner)

1978 Medal Winner

Noah's Ark by Peter Spier (Doubleday)

Honor Books

Castle by David Macaulay (Houghton Mifflin)
It Could Always Be Worse, retold and illustrated by Margot Zemach (Farrar Straus Giroux)

1977 Medal Winner

Ashanti to Zulu: African Traditions, illustrated by Leo & Diane Dillon, written by Margaret Musgrove (Dial)

Honor Books

The Amazing Bone by William Steig (Farrar Straus Giroux)
The Contest, retold and illustrated by Nonny Hogrogian (Greenwillow)
Fish for Supper by M. B. Goffstein (Dial)
The Golem: A Jewish Legend by Beverly Brodsky McDermott (Lippincott)
Hawk, I'm Your Brother, illustrated by Peter Parnall, written by Byrd Baylor (Scribner)

1976 Medal Winner

Why Mosquitoes Buzz in People's Ears, illustrated by Leo & Diane Dillon, retold by Verna Aardema (Dial)

Honor Books

The Desert Is Theirs, illustrated by Peter Parnall, written by Byrd Baylor (Scribner)
Strega Nona by Tomie de Paola (Prentice Hall)

1975 Medal Winner

Arrow to the Sun by Gerald McDermott (Viking)

Honor Book

Jambo Means Hello: A Swahili Alphabet Book, illustrated by Tom Feelings, written by Muriel Feelings (Dial)

1974 Medal Winner

Duffy and the Devil, illustrated by Margot Zemach, retold by Harve Zemach (Farrar Straus Giroux)

Honor Books

Three Jovial Huntsmen by Susan Jeffers (Bradbury)
Cathedral by David Macaulay (Houghton Mifflin)

1973 Medal Winner

The Funny Little Woman, illustrated by Blair Lent, retold by Arlene Mosel (Dutton)

Honor Books

Anansi the Spider: A Tale from the Ashanti, adapted and illustrated by Gerald McDermott (Holt)
Hosie's Alphabet, illustrated by Leonard Baskin, written by Hosea, Tobias & Lisa Baskin (Viking)
Snow White and the Seven Dwarfs, illustrated by Nancy Ekholm Burkert, translated by Randall Jarrell, retold from the Brothers Grimm (Farrar Straus Giroux)
When Clay Sings, illustrated by Tom Bahti, written by Byrd Baylor (Scribner)

1972 Medal Winner

One Fine Day, retold and illustrated by Nonny Hogrogian (Macmillan)

Honor Books

Hildilid's Night, illustrated by Arnold Lobel, written by Cheli Durán Ryan (Macmillan)
If All the Seas Were One Sea by Janina Domanska (Macmillan)
Moja Means One: Swahili Counting Book, illustrated by Tom Feelings, written by Muriel Feelings (Dial)

1971 Medal Winner

A Story, A Story, retold and illustrated by Gail E. Haley (Atheneum)

Honor Books

The Angry Moon, illustrated by Blair Lent, retold by William Sleator (Atlantic)

Frog and Toad Are Friends by Arnold Lobel (Harper)

In the Night Kitchen by Maurice Sendak (Harper)

1970 Medal Winner

Sylvester and the Magic Pebble by William Steig (Windmill)

Honor Books

Goggles! by Ezra Jack Keats (Macmillan)

Alexander and the Wind-Up Mouse by Leo Lionni (Pantheon)

Pop Corn and Ma Goodness, illustrated by Robert Andrew Parker, written by Edna Mitchell Preston (Viking)

Thy Friend, Obadiah by Brinton Turkle (Viking)

The Judge: An Untrue Tale, illustrated by Margot Zemach, written by Harve Zemach (Farrar Straus Giroux)

1969 Medal Winner

The Fool of the World and the Flying Ship, illustrated by Uri Shulevitz, retold by Arthur Ransome (Farrar Straus Giroux)

Honor Book

Why the Sun and the Moon Live in the Sky, illustrated by Blair Lent, written by Elphinstone Dayrell (Houghton Mifflin)

1968 Medal Winner

Drummer Hoff, illustrated by Ed Emberley, adapted by Barbara Emberley (Prentice Hall)

Honor Books

Frederick by Leo Lionni (Pantheon)

Seashore Story by Taro Yashima (Viking)

The Emperor and the Kite, illustrated by Ed Young, written by Jane Yolen (World)

1967 Medal Winner

Sam, Bangs & Moonshine by Evaline Ness (Holt)

Honor Book

One Wide River to Cross, illustrated by Ed Emberley, adapted by Barbara Emberley (Prentice Hall)

1966 Medal Winner

Always Room for One More, illustrated by Nonny Hogrogian, written by Sorche Nic Leodhas, pseud. [Leclaire Alger] (Holt)

Honor Books

Hide and Seek Fog, illustrated by Roger Duvoisin, written by Alvin Tresselt (Lothrop)

Just Me by Marie Hall Ets (Viking)

Tom Tit Tot, retold and illustrated by Evaline Ness (Scribner)

1965 Medal Winner

May I Bring a Friend? illustrated by Beni Montresor, written by Beatrice Schenk de Regniers (Atheneum)

Honor Books

Rain Makes Applesauce, illustrated by Marvin Bileck, written by Julian Scheer (Holiday House)

The Wave, illustrated by Blair Lent, written by Margaret Hodges (Houghton Mifflin)

A Pocketful of Cricket, illustrated by Evaline Ness, written by Rebecca Caudill (Holt)

1964 Medal Winner

Where the Wild Things Are by Maurice Sendak (Harper)

Honor Books

Swimmy by Leo Lionni (Pantheon)

All in the Morning Early, illustrated by Evaline Ness, written by Sorche Nic Leodhas, pseud. [Leclaire Alger] (Holt)

Mother Goose and Nursery Rhymes, illustrated by Philip Reed (Atheneum)

1963 Medal Winner

The Snowy Day by Ezra Jack Keats (Viking)

Honor Books

The Sun Is a Golden Earring, illustrated by Bernarda Bryson, written by Natalia M. Belting (Holt)

Mr. Rabbit and the Lovely Present, illustrated by Maurice Sendak, written by Charlotte Zolotow (Harper)

1962 Medal Winner

Once a Mouse, retold and illustrated by Marcia Brown (Scribner)

Honor Books

Fox Went Out on a Chilly Night: An Old Song by Peter Spier (Doubleday)

Little Bear's Visit, illustrated by Maurice Sendak, written by Else H. Minarik (Harper)

The Day We Saw the Sun Come Up, illustrated by Adrienne Adams, written by Alice E. Goudey (Scribner)

1961 Medal Winner

Baboushka and the Three Kings, illustrated by Nicolas Sidjakov, written by Ruth Robbins (Parnassus)

Honor Book

Inch by Inch by Leo Lionni (Obolensky)

1960 Medal Winner

Nine Days to Christmas, illustrated by Marie Hall Ets, written by Marie Hall Ets and Aurora Labastida (Viking)

Honor Books

Houses from the Sea, illustrated by Adrienne Adams, written by Alice E. Goudey (Scribner)

The Moon Jumpers, illustrated by Maurice Sendak, written by Janice May Udry (Harper)

1959 Medal Winner

Chanticleer and the Fox, illustrated by Barbara Cooney, adapted from Chaucer's *Canterbury Tales* by Barbara Cooney (Crowell)

Honor Books

The House that Jack Built: La Maison Que Jacques A Batie by Antonio Frasconi (Harcourt)

What Do You Say, Dear? illustrated by Maurice Sendak, written by Sesyle Joslin (W. R. Scott)

Umbrella by Taro Yashima (Viking)

1958 Medal Winner

Time of Wonder by Robert McCloskey (Viking)

Honor Books

Fly High, Fly Low by Don Freeman (Viking)

Anatole and the Cat, illustrated by Paul Galdone, written by Eve Titus (McGraw-Hill)

1957 Medal Winner

A Tree Is Nice, illustrated by Marc Simont, written by Janice Udry (Harper)

Honor Books

Mr. Penny's Race Horse by Marie Hall Ets (Viking)

1 Is One by Tasha Tudor (Walck)

Anatole, illustrated by Paul Galdone, written by Eve Titus (McGraw-Hill)

Gillespie and the Guards, illustrated by James Daugherty, written by Benjamin Elkin (Viking)

Lion by William Pène du Bois (Viking)

1956 Medal Winner

Frog Went A-Courtin', illustrated by Feodor Rojankovsky, retold by John Langstaff (Harcourt)

Honor Books

Play with Me by Marie Hall Ets (Viking)

Crow Boy by Taro Yashima (Viking)

1955 Medal Winner

Cinderella, or the Little Glass Slipper, illustrated by Marcia Brown, translated from Charles Perrault by Marcia Brown (Scribner)

Honor Books

Book of Nursery and Mother Goose Rhymes, illustrated by Marguerite de Angeli (Doubleday)

Wheel on the Chimney, illustrated by Tibor Gergely, written by Margaret Wise Brown (Lippincott)

The Thanksgiving Story, illustrated by Helen Sewell, written by Alice Dalgliesh (Scribner)

1954 Medal Winner

Madeline's Rescue by Ludwig Bemelmans (Viking)

Honor Books

Journey Cake, Ho! illustrated by Robert McCloskey, written by Ruth Sawyer (Viking)

When Will the World Be Mine? illustrated by Jean Charlot, written by Miriam Schlein (W. R. Scott)

The Steadfast Tin Soldier, illustrated by Marcia Brown, written by Hans Christian Andersen, translated by M. R. James (Scribner)

A Very Special House, illustrated by Maurice Sendak, written by Ruth Krauss (Harper)

Green Eyes by A. Birnbaum (Capitol)

1953 Medal Winner

The Biggest Bear by Lynd Ward (Houghton Mifflin)

Honor Books

Puss in Boots, illustrated by Marcia Brown, translated from Charles Perrault by Marcia Brown (Scribner)
One Morning in Maine by Robert McCloskey (Viking)
Ape in a Cape: An Alphabet of Odd Animals by Fritz Eichenberg (Harcourt)
The Storm Book, illustrated by Margaret Bloy Graham, written by Charlotte Zolotow (Harper)
Five Little Monkeys by Juliet Kepes (Houghton Mifflin)

1952 Medal Winner

Finders Keepers, illustrated by Nicolas, pseud. [Nicholas Mordvinoff], written by Will, pseud. [William Lipkind] (Harcourt)

Honor Books

Mr. T. W. Anthony Woo by Marie Hall Ets (Viking)
Skipper John's Cook by Marcia Brown (Scribner)
All Falling Down, illustrated by Margaret Bloy Graham, written by Gene Zion (Harper)
Bear Party by William Pène du Bois (Viking)
Feather Mountain by Elizabeth Olds (Houghton Mifflin)

1951 Medal Winner

The Egg Tree by Katherine Milhous (Scribner)

Honor Books

Dick Whittington and His Cat by Marcia Brown (Scribner)
The Two Reds, illustrated by Nicolas, pseud. [Nicholas Mordvinoff], written by Will, pseud. [William Lipkind] (Harcourt)
If I Ran the Zoo by Dr. Seuss, pseud. [Theodor Seuss Geisel] (Random House)
The Most Wonderful Doll in the World, illustrated by Helen Stone, written by Phyllis McGinley (Lippincott)
T-Bone, the Baby Sitter by Clare Turlay Newberry (Harper)

1950 Medal Winner

Song of the Swallows by Leo Politi (Scribner)

Honor Books

America's Ethan Allen, illustrated by Lynd Ward, written by Stewart Holbrook (Houghton Mifflin)
The Wild Birthday Cake, illustrated by Hildegard Woodward, written by Lavinia R. Davis (Doubleday)
The Happy Day, illustrated by Marc Simont, written by Ruth Krauss (Harper)
Bartholomew and the Oobleck by Dr. Seuss, pseud. [Theodor Seuss Geisel] (Random House)
Henry Fisherman by Marcia Brown (Scribner)

1949 Medal Winner

The Big Snow by Berta & Elmer Hader (Macmillan)

Honor Books

Blueberries for Sal by Robert McCloskey (Viking)
All Around the Town, illustrated by Helen Stone, written by Phyllis McGinley (Lippincott)
Juanita by Leo Politi (Scribner)
Fish in the Air by Kurt Wiese (Viking)

1948 Medal Winner

White Snow, Bright Snow, illustrated by Roger Duvoisin, written by Alvin Tresselt (Lothrop)

Honor Books

Stone Soup by Marcia Brown (Scribner)
McElligot's Pool by Dr. Seuss, pseud. [Theodor Seuss Geisel] (Random House)
Bambino the Clown by Georges Schreiber (Viking)
Roger and the Fox, illustrated by Hildegard Woodward, written by Lavinia R. Davis (Doubleday)
Song of Robin Hood, illustrated by Virginia Lee Burton, edited by Anne Malcolmson (Houghton Mifflin)

1947 Medal Winner

The Little Island, illustrated by Leonard Weisgard, written by Golden MacDonald, pseud. [Margaret Wise Brown] (Doubleday)

Honor Books

Rain Drop Splash, illustrated by Leonard Weisgard, written by Alvin Tresselt (Lothrop)
Boats on the River, illustrated by Jay Hyde Barnum, written by Marjorie Flack (Viking)
Timothy Turtle, illustrated by Tony Palazzo, written by Al Graham (Welch)
Pedro, the Angel of Olvera Street by Leo Politi (Scribner)
Sing in Praise: A Collection of the Best Loved Hymns, illustrated by Marjorie Torrey, selected by Opal Wheeler (Dutton)

1946 Medal Winner

The Rooster Crows by Maude & Miska Petersham (Macmillan)

Honor Books

Little Lost Lamb, illustrated by Leonard Weisgard, written by Golden MacDonald, pseud. [Margaret Wise Brown] (Doubleday)
Sing Mother Goose, illustrated by Marjorie Torrey, music by Opal Wheeler (Dutton)
My Mother Is the Most Beautiful Woman in the World, illustrated by Ruth Gannett, written by Becky Reyher (Lothrop)
You Can Write Chinese by Kurt Wiese (Viking)

1945 Medal Winner

Prayer for a Child, illustrated by Elizabeth Orton Jones, written by Rachel Field (Macmillan)

Honor Books

Mother Goose, illustrated by Tasha Tudor (Oxford University Press)
In the Forest by Marie Hall Ets (Viking)
Yonie Wondernose by Marguerite de Angeli (Doubleday)
The Christmas Anna Angel, illustrated by Kate Seredy, written by Ruth Sawyer (Viking)

1944 Medal Winner

Many Moons, illustrated by Louis Slobodkin, written by James Thurber (Harcourt)

Honor Books

Small Rain: Verses from the Bible, illustrated by Elizabeth Orton Jones, selected by Jessie Orton Jones (Viking)
Pierre Pidgeon, illustrated by Arnold E. Bare, written by Lee Kingman (Houghton Mifflin)
The Mighty Hunter by Berta & Elmer Hader (Macmillan)
A Child's Good Night Book, illustrated by Jean Charlot, written by Margaret Wise Brown (W. R. Scott)
Good-Luck Horse, illustrated by Plato Chan, written by Chih-Yi Chan (Whittlesey)

1943 Medal Winner

The Little House by Virginia Lee Burton (Houghton Mifflin)

Honor Books

Dash and Dart by Mary & Conrad Buff (Viking)
Marshmallow by Clare Turlay Newberry (Harper)

1942 Medal Winner

Make Way for Ducklings by Robert McCloskey (Viking)

Honor Books

An American ABC by Maud & Miska Petersham (Macmillan)
In My Mother's House, illustrated by Velino Herrera, written by Ann Nolan Clark (Viking)
Paddle-to-the-Sea by Holling C. Holling (Houghton Mifflin)
Nothing at All by Wanda Gág (Coward)

1941 Medal Winner

They Were Strong and Good by Robert Lawson (Viking)

Honor Book

April's Kittens by Clare Turlay Newberry (Harper)

1940 Medal Winner

Abraham Lincoln by Ingri & Edgar Parin d'Aulaire (Doubleday)

Honor Books

Cock-a-Doodle Doo by Berta & Elmer Hader (Macmillan)
Madeline by Ludwig Bemelmans (Viking)
The Ageless Story by Lauren Ford (Dodd)

1939 Medal Winner

Mei Li by Thomas Handforth (Doubleday)

Honor Books

Andy and the Lion by James Daugherty (Viking)
Barkis by Clare Turlay Newberry (Harper)
The Forest Pool by Laura Adams Armer (Longmans)
Snow White and the Seven Dwarfs by Wanda Gág (Coward)
Wee Gillis, illustrated by Robert Lawson, written by Munro Leaf (Viking)

1938 Medal Winner

Animals of the Bible, A Picture Book, illustrated by Dorothy P. Lathrop, selected by Helen Dean Fish (Lippincott)

Honor Books

Four and Twenty Blackbirds, illustrated by Robert Lawson, compiled by Helen Dean Fish (Stokes)
Seven Simeons: A Russian Tale, retold and illustrated by Boris Artzybasheff (Viking)

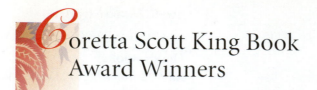

Coretta Scott King Book Award Winners

THE CORETTA Scott King Book Awards are presented annually to an African American author and an African American illustrator of outstanding books for children and young adults.

2005

Author Award
Toni Morrison, *Remember: The Journey to School Integration* (Houghton Mifflin)

Award for Illustration
Kadir Nelson, *Ellington Was Not a Street* (Simon & Schuster)

2004

Author Award
Angela Johnson, *The First Part Last* (Simon & Schuster)

Award for Illustration
Ashley Bryan, *Beautiful Blackbird* (Atheneum)

Coretta Scott King/John Steptoe New Author Talent Award
Hope Anita Smith, *The Way a Door Closes* (Holt)

Steptoe New Illustrator Talent Award
Elbrite Brown, *My Family Plays Music* (Holiday House)

2003

Author Award
Nikki Grimes, *Bronx Masquerade* (Dial)

Award for Illustration
E. B. Lewis, *Talkin' About Bessie: The Story of Aviator Elizabeth Coleman* (Orchard)

Coretta Scott King/John Steptoe New Author Talent Award
Janet McDonald, *Chill Wind* (Foster/Farrar Straus Giroux)

Steptoe New Illustrator Talent Award
Randy DuBurke, *The Moon Ring* (Chronicle)

2002

Author Award
Mildred D. Taylor, *The Land* (Fogelman)

Award for Illustration
Jerry Pinkney, *Goin' Someplace Special* (Atheneum)

Coretta Scott King/John Steptoe New Author Talent Award
Jerome Lagarrigue, *Freedom Summer* (Atheneum)

2001

Author Award
Jacqueline Woodson, *Miracle's Boys* (Putnam)

Award for Illustration
Bryan Collier, *Uptown* (Holt)

2000

Author Award
Christopher Paul Curtis, *Bud, Not Buddy* (Delacorte)

Award for Illustration
Brian Pinkney, *In the Time of the Drums* (Jump at the Sun/Hyperion)

1999

Author Award
Angela Johnson, *Heaven* (Simon & Schuster)

Award for Illustration

Michele Wood, *I See the Rhythm* (Children's Book Press)

1998

Author Award

Sharon M. Draper, *Forged by Fire* (Atheneum)

Award for Illustration

Javaka Steptoe, *In Daddy's Arms I Am Tall: African Americans Celebrating Fathers* (Lee & Low)

1997

Author Award

Walter Dean Myers, *Slam!* (Scholastic)

Award for Illustration

Jerry Pinkney, *Minty: A Story of Young Harriet Tubman* (Dial)

1996

Author Award

Virginia Hamilton, *Her Stories: African American Folk Tales, Fairy Tales, and True Tales* (Blue Sky)

Award for Illustration

Tom Feelings, *The Middle Passage: White Ships Black Cargo* (Dial)

1995

Author Award

Patricia C. & Frederick L. McKissack, *Christmas in the Big House, Christmas in the Quarters* (Scholastic)

Award for Illustration

James Ransome, *The Creation* (Holiday House)

1994

Author Award

Angela Johnson, *Toning the Sweep* (Orchard)

Award for Illustration

Tom Feelings, *Soul Looks Back in Wonder* (Dial)

1993

Author Award

Patricia A. McKissack, *The Dark-thirty: Southern Tales of the Supernatural* (Knopf)

Award for Illustration

Kathleen Atkins Wilson, *The Origin of Life on Earth: An African Creation Myth* (Sights Productions)

1992

Author Award

Walter Dean Myers, *Now Is Your Time: The African American Struggle for Freedom* (HarperCollins)

Award for Illustration

Faith Ringgold, *Tar Beach* (Crown)

1991

Author Award

Mildred D. Taylor, *The Road to Memphis* (Dial)

Award for Illustration

Leo & Diane Dillon, *Aida* (Harcourt Brace Jovanovich)

1990

Author Award

Patricia C. & Frederick L. McKissack, *A Long Hard Journey: The Story of the Pullman Porter* (Walker)

Award for Illustration

Jan Spivey Gilchrist, *Nathaniel Talking* (Black Butterfly)

1989

Author Award

Walter Dean Myers, *Fallen Angels* (Scholastic)

Award for Illustration

Jerry Pinkney, *Mirandy and Brother Wind* (Knopf)

1988

Author Award

Mildred Taylor, *The Friendship* (Dial)

Award for Illustration

John Steptoe, *Mufaro's Beautiful Daughters: An African Tale* (Lothrop, Lee & Shepard)

1987

Author Award

Mildred Pitts Walter, *Justin and the Best Biscuits in the World* (Lothrop, Lee & Shepard)

Award for Illustration

Jerry Pinkney, *Half a Moon and One Whole Star* (Macmillan)

1986

Author Award

Virginia Hamilton, *The People Could Fly: American Black Folktales* (Knopf)

Award for Illustration

Jerry Pinkney, *The Patchwork Quilt* (Dial)

1985

Author Award

Walter Dean Myers, *Motown and Didi* (Viking Kestral)

Award for Illustration

None given

1984

Special Citation

Coretta Scott King, *The Words of Martin Luther King, Jr.* (Newmarket)

Author Award

Lucille Clifton, *Everett Anderson's Goodbye* (Holt, Rinehart & Winston)

Award for Illustration

Pat Cummings, *My Mama Needs Me* (Lothrop, Lee & Shepard)

1983

Author Award

Virginia Hamilton, *Sweet Whispers, Brother Rush* (Philomel)

Award for Illustration

Peter Mugabane, *Black Child* (Knopf)

1982

Author Award

Mildred Taylor, *Let the Circle Be Unbroken* (Dial)

Award for Illustration

John Steptoe, *Mother Crocodile* (Delacorte)

1981

Author Award

Sidney Poitier, *The Measure of a Man: A Spiritual Autobiography* (Harper)

Award for Illustration

Ashley Bryan, *Beat the Story Drum, Pum-Pum* (Atheneum)

1980

Author Award

Walter Dean Myers, *The Young Landlords* (Viking)

Award for Illustration

Carole Byard, *Cornrows* (Coward, McCann & Geoghegan)

1979

Author Award

Ossie Davis, *Escape to Freedom: A Play About Young Frederick Douglass* (Viking)

Award for Illustration

Tom Feelings, *Something on My Mind* (Dial)

1978

Author Award

Eloise Greenfield, *Africa Dream* (Day)

Award for Illustration

Carole Bayard, *Africa Dream* (Day)

1977

Author Award

James Haskins, *The Story of Stevie Wonder* (Lothrop, Lee & Shepard)

Award for Illustration

None given

1976

Author Award

Pearl Bailey, *Duey's Tale* (Harcourt Brace Jovanovich)

Award for Illustration

None given

1975

Author Award

Dorothy Robinson, *The Legend of Africania* (Johnson)

Award for Illustration

None given

1974

Author Award

Sharon Bell Mathis, *Ray Charles* (Crowell)

Award for Illustration

George Ford, *Ray Charles* (Crowell)

1973

Author Award

Alfred Duckett, *I Never Had It Made: The Autobiography of Jackie Robinson* (Putnam)

1972

Author Award

Elton C. Fax, *Seventeen (17) Black Artists* (Dodd, Mead)

1971

Author Award

Charlemae Rollins, *Black Troubadour: Langston Hughes* (Rand McNally)

1970

Author Award

Lillie Patterson, *Martin Luther King, Jr.: Man of Peace* (Garrard)

Subject Index

workshop approach for, 387–388

Spelling Knowledge Inventory (SKI), 525

Spiders, thematic unit on, 582–587

Spreadsheet programs, 472

SQ3R, 476

SSR (Sustained Silent Reading), 50, 261

SSW (Sustained Spontaneous Writing), 332

Standard English, 390–391
  direct instruction in, for ELLs, 405
  learning usage of, 392
  lesson on usage of, 391
  standards for language arts 8, 23-24, 29, 77, 79, 119, 165, 167, 199, 201, 237, 289, 291, 339, 341, 373, 417, 419, 451, 483
  biography study related to, 43
  inquiry learning and, 483
  media learning related to, 445–446
  oral language and, 209
  research and, 488
  selecting a theme and, 547, 548

Standardized tests, 526–529
  guidelines for taking, 527
  preparation of struggling readers for, 528

Standards
  for language arts, 23–25
  media learning related to, 445–446

Standards-based writing assessment, 528–529

STAs (Seeing-Thinking Activities), 428–429

Stories
  for ELLs, 48
  picture walks to introduce, 273
  retelling of, for authentic assessment, 517
  tape recording, 145
  writing, 343–344

Story maps, 34–35, 37

Story packs, 274

Story problems, lesson on solving, 469

Story reading. See also Reading aloud
  benefits of, 34
  in language experience approach, 266
  for listening instruction, 186
  literature and, 52–53, 112
  for oral language expression instruction, 224–225
  for vocabulary instruction, 102, 112

Storytelling
  codeswitching in, 208
  exposure to, 14
  in home language, 213
  listening for critical analysis during, 175, 177

for listening instruction, 186, 189

literature and, 52–53, 112

for oral language instruction, 224–225

by parents, 133, 185

as vocabulary teaching technique, 102

voice control in, 208

Strategic reading, teacher modeling of, 254

Stress, in speech, 207

Structural analysis
  as vocabulary teaching technique, 91–94
  word identification and, 244–245

Structural grammar, 390

Structured Listening Activity (SLA), 190, 191

Struggling students, 577
  beginning writing activities for, 305
  definition of, 430
  dialogue journals for, 353
  dramatization activities for, 102
  ELLs as. See English language learners (ELLs)
  functional English acquisition by, 394
  instructional materials for, 531–532
  interventions for. See Interventions for struggling students
  literature circles for, 276
  partner (buddy) reading for, 271
  pictorial images to teach QARs to, 428
  picture books for, 427
  prewriting activities for, 298
  reading aloud for, 83
  rubrics for, 521
  Seeing-Thinking Activities for, 305
  teaching word identification to, 248
  test preparation for, 528
  think-alouds for, 255
  writing in patterns and, 302

Student modeling, 419, 421
  of reading, 262, 263
  of writing, 309

Students with special needs
  assessment of, 505
  classroom environment for, 141
  conversations for, 58
  dramatization activities for, 102
  explicit instruction in reading for, 247
  figurative expressions and, 14, 110
  functional English acquisition by, 394
  graphic organizers for, 481

hearing aid use by, 184

hearing impaired, miscues and, 520

inquiry learning for, 484

instructional questioning for, 221

language experience approach for, 268

listening comprehension of, 182

literature circles for, 276

partner (buddy) reading for, 271

pictorial images to teach QARs to, 428

picture books for, 428

preteaching vocabulary words for, 11

read-alouds for, 83, 173

rubrics for, 521

seating close to speaker, 188

spelling instruction for, 382

talking to, 123

technology to create interconnections among books and, 442

text preparation for, 528

thematic units for, 550

"think-alouds" for, 110

vocabulary instruction for, 85

Study guides, 476–477

Study skills, 472–482
  anticipation guides and, 473–474
  graphic organizers and, 477–482
  K-W-L and, 474–476
  SQ3R and, 476
  study guides and, 476–477

Subjects of sentences, 599–600

Subjunctive mood, 597

Subordinate conjunctions, 598

Success for All, 532

Successful experiences, in writing instruction, 305–306

Suffixes, 91, 93

Summarizing
  for reading comprehension, 256, 258
  for report writing, 362

Superlative adjectives, 597

Superlative adverbs, 598

Sustained Silent Reading (SSR), 50, 261

Sustained Spontaneous Writing (SSW), 332

Synonyms, 106–107

Syntactic cues, 246, 247

Synthetic phonics, 242

T

Tables, viewing, 431

Tape recordings
  for listening instruction, 181
  quality of, 183
  of stories, making, 145

Teacher conferences, 562
  as assessment method, 502, 505, 507, 508, 522, 524, 525
  during drafting, 318–319, 320

in grammar instruction, 392, 396

group, 515

with parents. See Parent conferences

on portfolios, 510, 512

purposes of, 508

in reading instruction, 239, 278, 281

for research instruction, 484

for teaching proofreading, 404

in writing instruction, 305, 318–319, 330, 333, 404, 405, 525

Teacher modeling, 19, 123, 137, 175
  of choral reading and choral speaking, 226
  of good listening behaviors, 180–181
  of grammar, 389–390, 393, 396
  of graphic aid use, 431, 432, 435, 480, 531
  of handwriting, 407, 409
  to increase children's awareness of language, 124
  of metacognition, 249
  in oral language instruction, 207, 209, 212, 218, 225, 226, 229
  of punctuation, 401
  of reading, 56, 60
  in reading instruction, 240, 249, 251, 252, 253–254, 255, 260, 262
  of research, 484, 485, 487, 488, 489
  for rubrics, 521, 522
  of self-assessment, 515
  of spelling strategies and procedures, 380, 382–384
  of storytelling, 225
  of strategic reading, 254
  of study skills, 472, 476
  to support parent involvement, 132
  for teaching proofreading, 404
  of topic selection for writing, 311–312
  of usage, 390, 405
  of use of unfamiliar words, 97
  in writing instruction, 147, 153, 156, 295, 307, 308, 311–312, 314, 320, 321, 322, 330, 332, 351, 352, 353, 362, 363, 403, 404

Teachers
  effective, characteristics of, 240, 241
  reflections on own learning of reading and writing, 141

Teaching strategies
  for listening instruction, 189–194
  for reading comprehension, 255–260
  for struggling students, 531

Technological literacy, 422

Technology, 12, 14, 19, 20, 22,

23, 45, 51, 102, 114, 115, 128, 138, 140, 145, 170, 171, 172, 176, 181, 183, 188, 189, 194, 195, 216, 225, 230, 231, 266, 267, 274, 298, 300, 301, 312, 316, 322, 323, 325, 330, 332, 333, 334, 335, 344, 347, 359, 363, 367, 370, 384, 398, 406, 410, 459, 464, 472, 490, 494, 531, 547, 563, 564. *See also* CD-ROMs; Computers; DVDs; Electronic *entries;* E-mail; Internet; Software programs; Television; Webpages; Websites

Telephone books, for research, 491

Telephone conversations, 218, 219, 220
    courtesy in, 218, 219
    lesson on, 220

Television, 99, 171, 283
    books with tie-ins to, 171–172
    classroom interference by, 188
    commercials on, 425, 434
    game shows on, 171
    increasing importance of, 422, 425
    for listening instruction, 171, 176, 189
    listening to, 170
    viewing, 12
    visual literacy skills and, 434–435

Tempo, of speech, 207

Tense, of verbs, 596

Tests, 502, 503
    criterion-referenced, 528
    norm-referenced, 526
    spelling, tape recording, 181
    standardized, 526–529

Texas Revolution thematic unit, 464

Textbooks, 22–23, 34, 271, 362, 422, 425, 455, 456–458, 545, 557
    concept and vocabulary in, learning by ELLs, 459
    evaluating, 462
    figurative expressions in, 110, 111
    graphic aids in, 430, 431, 432, 433
    images in, 425, 427
    locating information in, lesson on, 486–488
    organization of, 485
    problems encountered in reading, 459
    in social studies, 464, 465
    spelling, 380, 388
    study skills for, 472–477

Text sets, 37, 277, 490, 585–586
    on Holocaust, 39
    on trees, 39

Text structures, 455
    identification of, 455, 458

Thematic units, 541–551, 554–591

on American Revolution, 575–576
    assessment for, 551
    on biomes of the world, 573–574
    on Cinderella, 187
    cross-curricular thematic unit on U.S. flag, web for, 556
    developing, 547–550
    for ELLs and students with special needs, 550
    on energy, 557–558
    on *Holes,* 588–591
    on humpback whales, 559–564
    on insects and spiders, 582–587
    integrated curriculum versus, 546
    on Jane Yolen's works, 565–568
    literature-based, 277–279
    on *Maniac Magee,* 569–572
    on migrations, 464
    on pioneers, 577–581
    planning and implementing, 548–550
    resources and, 550–551
    selecting themes for, 547–548
    in social studies, 463–464
    on Texas Revolution, 464
    topical units versus, 545
    values of, 546–547
    as vehicle for integrating language instruction across curriculum, 23
    Westward Ho!, 463–464

Thematic webs, 11, 460, 477, 481
    for cross-curricular thematic unit on U.S. flag, 556

Themes, identifying, lesson involving, 36

Thesauruses
    electronic, 97, 405
    junior, 97, 98
    synonyms and, 106–107
    in vocabulary teaching, 97–99

"Think-alouds," for teaching figurative expressions and allusions, 110

Think-aloud strategy, for reading comprehension, 254–255

Thinking
    language arts and, 16–17
    stimulating through discussion, 223

Think-Pair-Share, 59

Time lines, 478, 479

Titles, quotation marks for, 603

Topical units, thematic units versus, 545

Topics, for writing, selecting and delimiting, 309–310, 311–312

Trade books, 34, 44, 129, 283, 422, 454, 455, 494, 515
    in basal reader approach, 268, 269, 271
    conventions of written language in, 400, 401, 402

in Directed Reading-Thinking Activity, 259
    for ELLs, 83, 276, 306, 307, 308
    images in, 425, 430, 431
    multicultural, 465, 494
    for research, 490
    in science curriculum, 461–462, 464, 558
    selecting, 126–128
    for students with special needs, 550
    as supplement to textbooks, 458–459
    for teaching reading comprehension strategies, 251

Traditional grammar, 389–390

Traditional literature, 37, 40, 41
    Native American, 47

Transformational grammar, 390

Transitive verbs, 596

Travel brochures, for research, 491

Trees, text set on, 39

Triplets, 349

Twin texts, 42–43, 50

U

Unison recitation, 227

United States flag, web for cross-curricular thematic unit on, 556

Units, phrases as, 6

URLs (Universal Resource Locators), 437

Usage, 390–391
    language arts and, 18

V

Venn diagrams, 479–480

Verbal phrases, 598

Verb phrases, 598

Verbs, 595–597

Vertical construction, 210–211

Vicarious experiences, concept development and, 83

Video presentations, 441–442

Videos, viewing, 434–435

Viewing, 12, 423–439
    of books with pictures accompanied by print, 427–428
    of CD-ROM simulation programs, 435–437
    of chat room messages, 439
    of diagrams, 430–431
    of e-mail, 439
    of graphs, 432–433
    of Internet material, 437–439
    listening related to, 172–173
    of live performances, 433–434
    of maps, 431–432
    of paintings, 425–426
    relationships to other language arts, 15–18, 19
    Seeing-Thinking Activities for, 428–429
    of tables, 431
    of television programs and videos, 434–435

of wordless picture books, 426–427

Visual arts, for ELLs, 465

Visualization, 11, 33, 35, 42, 52, 56, 98, 177, 225, 249, 251, 427
    lesson on, 252–253
    of spellings, 380
    writing to facilitate, 398, 399

Visual literacy, 416–422
    assessment for, 446
    skills for. *See* Viewing; Visual representation
    technological literacy related to, 422

Visual representation, 12–13, 439–445
    drawings for, 439–440
    multimedia presentations for, 442–443
    photographs for, 439–440
    relationships to other language arts, 15–18, 20
    video presentations for, 441–442
    webpages and websites for, 443–445
    word processing for, 440–441

Vocabulary, 76–114
    abbreviations and, 112
    acronyms and, 112–113
    antonyms and, 107–108
    assessment of, 113, 522–523
    concept development and, 81–85
    figurative expressions and, 14, 110–112
    games for teaching of, 105–106
    homonyms and, 108
    language arts and, 18
    listening, 85–86
    logical errors in, 83
    making connections between words for ELLs, 82
    multiple-meaning words and, 80, 108–109
    preteaching for ELLs and students with special needs, 11
    reading, 86
    reteaching of words for, 88
    speaking, 86
    synonyms and, 106–107
    using new words and, 203
    words from other languages and, 113
    writing, 86–87

Vocabulary instruction, 87–106
    analogies for, 91
    categorization for, 89–90
    comic strips and cartoons for, 101
    computer applications for, 102–103
    context clues for, 94–97
    dictionary and thesaurus and, 97–99
    for difficult terms, 209
    dramatization for, 101–102
    for ELLs and students with

Name and Title Index

$\mathcal{P}$hoto Credits